THE LAW OF COMPUTER TECHNOLOGY

Raymond T. Nimmer

Professor of Law
University of Houston Law Center

WARREN, GORHAM, & LAMONT
Boston • New York

130871

Copyright © 1985 by

WARREN, GORHAM & LAMONT, INC.
210 SOUTH STREET
BOSTON, MASSACHUSETTS 02111

ISBN 0-88712-355-4

Library of Congress Catalog Card No. 85-51427

PRINTED IN THE UNITED STATES OF AMERICA

To Trish Krauthaus
for tireless and invaluable help

Preface

OUR SOCIETY IS increasingly characterized by use of computers and microprocessors. Once limited to an elite few with highly specialized training and substantial financial support, computers and related technology are now available to millions of people and businesses. This development has long-range implications for our social system and has already had a substantial impact on the practice of law.

This is a book about the law as it pertains to computers and information technology. Perhaps as recently as 1970, the book would have been premature and applicable to only a small fraction of the legal community. Legal matters pertaining to computers and information technology arose infrequently in a general practice and, as with the users of the technology, there was a core of specialists, often with technical backgrounds, who formed the bulk of the legal community concerned about computer law. This has changed. Many practitioners now regularly encounter aspects of the law pertaining to computers. This is true in a commercial practice where many sale contracts or leases involve computer equipment and software. Similarly, in criminal law, financial crimes increasingly involve the use of computers to aid in or to conceal thefts. Personal injury claims more and more often involve machinery that is augmented or controlled by microprocessor applications. Consumer protection issues must be formulated in the context of a sophisticated technology suddenly adapted to mass-market environments.

This book is not written solely for the specialist. Ultimately, all practitioners will be forced not to develop technical sophistication, but to deal with the technology in context of law. One purpose of this book is to provide a basis for the nontechnical specialist to deal with computer-related issues that will arise in most areas of practice.

Much of this book deals with areas of law that are not limited to computer and information technology. Included is a discussion of the law of contracts as applied to computer software and hardware transactions. Contract law was not developed to deal with computer-related transactions, but the technology-based transactions place new pressures on the

v

older doctrine. They require the practitioner to deal with issues that have not historically been major concerns in a commercial law practice. This book focuses on these issues and on the manner in which existing commercial law concepts have an impact on the technology contracts.

While contract and tort law encompass primarily a need to adapt existing doctrine and expertise, other subject matter in this book is either entirely new law developed within the past 10 years or is at least a legal environment that many have not previously encountered. For example, computer technology accessible beyond an expert elite creates a context in which intellectual property doctrine has widespread application. The historical premise that our legal system can and should promote technological development is tested in this new environment. Not only the industrial innovator, but also the more common retail or mercantile environment is affected.

While these issues are of vital significance, a further array of questions may ultimately have a greater effect on society and our daily lives. Categorizing these questions is in itself difficult. They are potentially ubiquitous and their long-range effects not only involve adapting existing legal concepts, but developing entirely new concepts of law, property, and civil rights. These are referred to as information age issues, but the label is only a label. There is much diverse substance encompassed within it.

Contemporary society is passing from an industrial age to an information age. The full meaning of this statement varies among those who use it, but the observation is increasingly an article of faith and an important policy-making premise. What is the meaning of the term "information age"? What is its significance for the legal system? These questions merit full consideration, but at present at least, they lack coherent, fully articulated answers. This book is not a philosophical treatise on the nature of society. Nevertheless, it is important to discuss the meaning of an information age and the immediate significance that this may have for the legal system.

The characteristics of an information age are diverse, but they all relate to two core events. The first consists of a change in both the manner in which human beings spend their time and the type of work with which they are associated. The industrial age was characterized by substantial commitment of human and physical resources to the creation of tangible items—cars, planes, buildings, and the like. This corresponded to the age of consumers and conspicuous consumption that is not likely to disappear in our lifetimes. However, increasingly less human effort will be directed to producing tangible products in the United States. The shift will involve a redirection of manufacturing to other countries and increased automation of the industrial plants that remain.

Given a reduced commitment to some activities, other work or leisure activity will replace the older benchmarks of an industrial era. While
a full definition of this shift can be left to others with more expertise in
futurism, significant social dislocation and stress can be expected. It is
already clear that the shift will, in part at least, entail an increasing focus
on services and on the production, dissemination, and analysis of information. "Information" in this sense is roughly equivalent to data: It consists of material about events, trends, and resources—the material on
which decisions and communications are based.

As the production of information becomes a major commercial
undertaking, the value of information for its own sake will increase. The
development of a new form of valuable property is already beginning to
show. If not new in an absolute sense, it is new at least in the relative
sense that the scope, accessibility, and interpretative power of information has changed in a considerable manner. The information storage, processing, and communication capabilities of contemporary computer systems are only beginning to be tapped. Already, even within the legal
profession, practitioners routinely connect with remote computer systems
that enable individual attorneys to tap a full case law library and rapidly
search for specific cases without the benefit (and cost) of the volumes of
books that would previously have been needed. Although for many the
search routines in WESTLAW and LEXIS are cumbersome and, perhaps,
unintelligible, this is a temporary result of outmoded, primitive search
software that will be changed and a lack of thorough training that will be
altered as law schools emphasize these systems. Ultimately, it is predictable that more user-friendly systems in which the profession is fully
trained will become commonplace and alter the manner of research, the
cost of maintaining an office, and perhaps even the categories in which
legal issues are customarily thought of.

The WESTLAW and LEXIS systems illustrate a form of electronic
publishing that would have been impossible 30 years ago, but that will
become increasingly common in the future. There are certain stable characteristics in such publishing. There are also unique legal issues. For
example, what is the significance of the use of telecommunications and
how should such activities be regulated, if at all? What is the role of the
First Amendment in such a publishing enterprise? Is the publisher
responsible for the accuracy of the information it provides? To what
extent can or will these systems replace traditional publishing? Are other,
analogous models available for that arena of publishing? How can the
value of the database itself (the information for its own sake) be determined and protected? If different databases are included (e.g., telephone
directory, voting list), what is the significance of the computer's ability to

reorganize, search, and analyze volumes of data in a manner qualitatively different from that possible by humans acting without computer assistance?

Information in the form of data made available electronically is one characteristic of an information age. A second characteristic is the use of electronic systems to represent traditional items of value and to conduct transactions. Again, the development is already in progress. There is a move increasingly toward a society in which wealth and power are encapsulated in electronic form, rather than in the physical possession of tangible items. Virtually all bank records are automated, as are many stock records. It is possible to conduct a retail purchase without visiting a store and without transferring cash, check, or other tangible symbols of value. Paychecks are displaced by direct deposit systems. The new transaction and representational systems use electronic impulses to signify value and to facilitate transfers.

The new systems create both opportunities and risks. The opportunities involve new forms of transactions that reduce the risks or costs present in older systems in which value transfers are physically delayed. The risks involve the ease of access and of manipulation that is present in an electronic system where little or no paper trail exists to track transfers. An additional risk concerns the possible impact on privacy of the vast volume of data that is accumulated and can be analyzed by a computer.

This book begins an exploration of the legal issues involved in these social developments. The characteristics of law in an information age are ultimately open-ended and unpredictable. As a consequence, this book is equally open-ended. Chapters can be expected to expand as the information era advances and as the demands on legal expertise and law practice increase.

RAYMOND T. NIMMER

Houston, Texas
April 1985

Acknowledgments

IN COMPILING any work of this size and scope it is obvious that the efforts of more than one individual are integral to the successful completion of the project. While I accept sole responsibility for any errors or misperceptions contained herein, it is important to recognize the contributions of three individuals among the many who have assisted me during the period in which this book was completed.

Foremost in this regard is Patricia Ann Krauthaus. Trish has spent substantial time and effort providing invaluable professional assistance in compiling and critiquing the material presented in this book. A graduate of the University of Houston Law Center, Trish left a position with the law department of a major oil company early in the project in order to serve as both a legal and an editorial assistant. In many cases, her efforts were directly responsible for the development of major themes in the book, and her ability to maintain a general grasp of the subject matter and to direct the effort has been invaluable.

In a different, but also significant manner, the completion of this book is attributable to the efforts of Mary Madden and the support of Dean Robert L. Knauss of the University of Houston Law Center. Mary spent uncounted hours in composing, correcting, and recorrecting the chapters of this book, as well as in managing my schedule in a manner that permitted the allocation of the time needed for its completion. Similarly, while Dean Knauss did not participate in the research or writing, his willingness to accept the hours and days away from normal work assignments that this book has required was an essential contribution to completing the work.

Finally, given the nature of the subject matter, I would be remiss in not recognizing that completion of this book would have been impossible in the time allocated had the manuscript not been written with the aid of a computer. For better or worse, one by-product of the computer era is an increased ability to compile, reconstruct, and publish critical thought. It is left to the reader to determine if this is a net gain or a net loss resulting from the availability of computers.

Summary of Contents

Table of Contents

2 Patent Law: Software and Systems

3 *Trade Secrets and Confidentiality*

PART B. CONFIDENTIALITY

PART C. PATENT AND COPYRIGHT

PART D. REMEDIES AND MISAPPROPRIATION

4 Research, Development, and Ownership

PART II

Transactions and Third-Party Liability

5 Technology Licensing

6 Computer Contracts: Leases and Sales Agreements

7 *Computer-Related Torts*

PART C.   COMPUTER USERS AND LIABILITY RISKS

8 International Trade Considerations

PART A.   IMPORT CONSIDERATIONS

PART B.   EXPORT CONSIDERATIONS

PART III

Information Age Issues

9 Computer Crime

11 Electronic Publishing and Data Communications

12 Computer Privacy and Data Disclosure

Glossary

algorithm

"A procedure for solving a given type of mathematical problem." Gottschalk v. Benson, 409 US 63 (1972).

"A fixed step-by-step procedure for accomplishing a given result. . . . [A] defined process . . . that leads [to] a desired output from a given input." Diamond v. Diehr, 450 US 175 (1981).

application program

"[Programs that] usually perform a specific task for the computer user, such as word processing, checkbook balancing, or playing a game." Apple Computer, Inc. v. Franklin Computer Corp., 714 F2d 1240 (3d Cir. 1983).

"[The] programs that are written to solve specific problems, to produce specific reports, to update specific files." *Encyclopedia of Computer Science and Engineering* (2d ed. 1983) (*Encyclopedia*).

assembly language

"If the source program is in assembly (i.e., symbolic) language, the process of translating it is called assembling and the result is an object program in machine language, ready to be executed." *Encyclopedia*.

compiling

"If the source program is in a high-level language like FORTRAN or COBOL, the translating process is called compiling, and may involve one or more steps [in transition into machine language for execution by the computer]." *Encyclopedia*.

CPU (central processing unit)

"[Where] most of the logical functions and calculations are performed [in the system]." Telex Corp. v. IBM Corp., 367 F. Supp. 258 (ND Okla. 1973).

"[The] integrated circuit that executes programs." Apple Computer, Inc. v. Franklin Computer Corp., 714 F2d 1240 (3d Cir. 1983).

CRT (cathode ray tube or display terminal)

"A hardware component which is connected by a cable to the CPU and is a televisionlike screen which displays information and data stored on the system or processed by the system. . . ." Christo, "The Computer as God," 2 CLR 14 (1982).

flowchart

"[Graphic] representation for the definition, analysis or solution of a problem in which symbols are used to represent operations, data flow, or equipment." *National Commission on New Technological Uses of Copyrighted Works, Final Report 21 (CONTU Report).*

hardware

"[The] tangible machinery of the computer." United States v. Seidlitz, 589 F2d 152 (4th Cir. 1978).

machine language

"[The] lowest level computer language . . . a binary language using two symbols, 0 and 1, to indicate an open or closed switch." Apple Computer, Inc. v. Franklin Computer Corp., 714 F2d 1240 (3d Cir. 1983).

"Machine language consists of a very explicit set of instruction and operation codes capable of direct execution by the hardware of the computer. . . ." *Encyclopedia.*

object code

"[The] version of a program in which the source code language is converted or translated into the machine language of the computer with which it is to be used." *CONTU Report.*

"An object program is the output of a translating program, such as an assembler or a compiler which converts a source program written in one language into another language, such as machine language, capable of being executed on a given computer." *Encyclopedia.*

"Statements in machine language...." Apple Computer, Inc. v. Franklin Computer Corp., 714 F2d 1240 (3d Cir. 1983).

operating system programs

"[Programs that] generally manage the internal functions of the computer or facilitate use of application programs." Apple Computer, Inc. v. Franklin Computer Corp., 714 F2d 1240 (3d Cir. 1983).

"[The] software (programs and data) that initiate the interaction of electronic and electromechanical components of a computer so that they constitute a useful system.... The operating system is responsible for sharing the computer equipment among users and is ... sometimes identified by functional names such as control programs, supervisor, executives or monitors...." *Encyclopedia.*

peripheral devices

"[Devices] connected with the central processing unit and which perform various special functions in the ... system. These include information storage components ... terminal devices ... memory units [and similar devices]." Telex Corp. v. IBM Corp., 510 F2d 894 (10th Cir. 1975).

program

"A set of statements or instructions to be used directly or indirectly in a computer in order to bring about a certain result." 17 USC § 101 (1980).

ROM (read only memory)

"[An] internal permanent memory device consisting of a semiconductor 'chip' which is incorporated into the circuitry of the computer.... Information stored on a ROM can only be read, not erased or rewritten." Apple Computer, Inc. v. Franklin Computer Corp., 714 F2d 1240 (3d Cir. 1983).

service bureau

"An organization that leases or sells computer time, manpower, or other computational support...." Systems Dev. Corp. v. United States, 531 F2d 529 (Ct. Cl. 1976).

"A service bureau ... performs data processing for customers for a fee." Telex Corp. v. IBM Corp., 367 F. Supp. 529 (ND Okla. 1975).

software

"[A] term ... used in the industry to describe computer programs." Parker v. Flook, 437 US 584 (1978).

Compare "Computer programs, procedures, rules, and possibly associated documentation. ..." *American National Dictionary for Information Processing.*

source code

"[A] computer program written in any of several programming languages employed by computer programmers." *CONTU Report.*

Compare "A source program is a computer program written in a language one or more steps removed from the machine language of a given computer. ... [A] source program ... must be translated by one means or another into the language of the machine before it can be executed." *Encyclopedia.*

system programs (see also operating systems)

"[Programs] that have to do with translation, loading, supervision, maintenance, control, and running of computers and computer programs. [System programming] produces the software tools which applications programmers use to develop the applications for which the computer is actually used." *Encyclopedia.*

turnkey system

"[A] system which is pre-prepared and can be virtually plugged right in and ready to function immediately." Triangle Underwriter, Inc. v. Honeywell, Inc., 604 F2d 737 (2d Cir. 1979).

PART I

Innovation and Incentives

WHILE OTHER TECHNOLOGIES have altered the character of society and the legal system, computer technology and information systems present a unique circumstance. In part, this is due to their ubiquitous potential for change. However, the computer revolution is also unique in its reliance on remarkable and remarkably rapid innovation. Microprocessors continually become more compact, faster, and more capable. Software is increasingly sophisticated. Communications systems are increasingly intelligent. New product announcements arrive on a daily basis.

There is an industry-wide emphasis on innovation, research, and new product development. Indeed, while this has been described as the information or computer age, it might equally be described as an age of innovation. The ability of businesses to remain or become commercially viable within computer and information industries often hinges on their ability to lead—or at least closely follow—technological innovation. In many industries, research and development play a significant role; in the computer and related industries, they are critically important.

An appropriate legal system for the twenty-first century is one that optimally promotes and encourages innovation, placing only those restraints mandated by clear, countervailing policies. This policy premise is already widely accepted. Nevertheless, many difficult judgments remain to be made, and there is substantial doubt about whether existing laws provide an adequate framework. The resolution of these doubts and the definition of a framework will have an impact on not only the pace of continued innovation, but also the legal restraints imposed on secondary users of the developed technology.

The primary areas of law that affect innovation are copyright, patent, and trade secret law. While their interrelationship is not always clear, each is based at least in part on an underlying premise of exclusivity. Creativity and innovation are encouraged by granting a creative individual the right to control the use or dissemination of his product. The creative product is viewed as a form of property, hence the description of this area as intellectual property law. Although it involves other factors, this approach is primarily commercial in orientation. The creative individual benefits commercially by exercising the right to exclusive personal use or by obtaining compensation for disseminating the property to authorized users.

This commercial orientation can be contrasted to what might be described as a scientific or public model for encouraging innovation. The commercial model operates on a presumed financial incentive. The scientific model is oriented more toward multiparty involvement. It presumes that innovation can best be promoted by widespread dissemination of ideas and data so that functionally diverse innovators can build upon the insights and findings of others. This process requires a right of access and use.

Our legal system does not entirely adopt either approach to the exclusion of the other. The resulting balance is handled differently under copyright, patent, and trade secret law. Three major themes reflect the contours of this balancing process. The first involves public disclosure. One approach to reconciling commercial and scientific models is to condition a grant of exclusivity on a requirement of public disclosure. Under this format, other innovators are able to discern critical features of an innovation, but are barred from certain uses most directly associated with commercial benefits. Patent law most directly reflects this compromise by expressly conditioning all rights of exclusivity on disclosure of the invention by the inventor. In contrast, trade secrecy permits enforcement of secrecy and confidentiality restraints established by the parties if relative secrecy has in fact been maintained.

A second theme concerns distinguishing the subject matter to which exclusive rights attach from that that is beyond the control of the original innovator. The balance achieved on this issue is central to reconciling the scientific and commercial models. The issue involves extending exclusive control as far as necessary to create financial incentives without crippling the potential for cumulative innovation by third parties. Consistent with this, in copyright and patent law exclusive rights can not be obtained over an idea or a natural law. The law in these areas does not protect discovery or pure insight, but only particular applications of these. The unprotected core is reserved for the scientific model of access and use by others. Of course, the line is difficult to draw in practice, especially as applied to technology in the field of computers and software.

The third theme involves the type of use exclusively vested in the original innovator. As to the scientific and commercial models, the concern is with the degree of access accorded to third parties who are potential innovators or who might otherwise build upon the original. From a scientific perspective, the chief interest lies in the ability to learn techniques and, perhaps, experimentally replicate performance. From the commercial standpoint, it is important that the exclusive right encompass those areas that are most significant commercially.

Beyond intellectual property law, innovation is also directly affected by other areas of law. In Part I, two of these are examined: antitrust and federal tax treatment of research and development. Antitrust directly affects commercial incentives by establishing boundaries of lawful competition. Tax laws shape the economic benefits in fact received as a result of research expenditures.

CHAPTER *1*

Copyright and Computer Technology

¶ 1.01 INTRODUCTION

This chapter deals with the relationship between copyright law and computer technology, most particularly the technology involved in computer software. The use of copyright as a major form of protection for an area of technology is a recent development that reflects the unique character of computer software. Historically, copyright has been concerned primarily with the expressive work of authors and artists. It was for these works that the basic tools and terminology of copyright were developed. The transposition to technology and utilitarian fields has been awkward and halting. Nevertheless, the nature of copyright protections makes them the principal source of protection for those portions of the software industry oriented to mass markets. As a result, while copyright is a poor vehicle to implement basic social policies relevant to software, it is often the only viable method.

The relationship between copyright and computer technology has been troubled from the beginning due to the conflict of two basic themes. The first emphasizes the private, proprietary nature of information and ideas, while the second emphasizes the public nature. On one hand, there is a recognized need to provide economic incentives for innovation by granting the innovator control over aspects of the use or distribution of his product. On the other hand, there is a desire to encourage dissemination and exchange of ideas. This is grounded in longstanding notions of scientific and cultural discourse where advances result from interchange among a community of scholars. In the context of commercialized scientific and technological development, the themes conflict. Evolving from the conflict will be the basic structure of the industry.

PART A. COPYRIGHTABILITY

¶ 1.02 COPYRIGHT SUBJECT MATTER

While the question of whether computer programs are copyrightable subject matter has been extensively debated,[1] it is now clear that most computer programs are within the scope of federal copyright law.[2] Section 102 of the Copyright Act (the Act) provides three basic criteria for determining whether a work qualifies as copyrightable subject matter:[3] (1) the work must be an "original [work] of authorship"; (2) it must be "fixed in [a] tangible medium of expression from which [it] can be perceived, reproduced or otherwise communicated . . ."; and (3) protection of the subject matter must not extend "copyright protection . . . to any idea, procedure, process, system, method of operation, concept, principle or discovery . . . in such work." For works within the scope of copyright, the Act provides enumerated, exclusive rights to the copyright holder to control reproduction, dissemination, and adaptation of the work.[4]

[1] Originality

The least controversial of the three criteria for copyrightability is the requirement of originality. To be copyrightable, a work must be an origi-

---

[1] See, e.g., Keplinger, "Computer Software—Its Nature and Its Protection," 30 Emory LJ 483 (1981); Nimtz, "Development of the Law of Computer Software Protection," 61 J. Pat. Off. Soc'y 3 (1979); Gemignani, "Legal Protection for Computer Software: The View From '79," 7 Rutgers J. Comp., Techn., & L. 269 (1980); Note, "Copyrighting Object Code," 4 Computer LJ 421 (1983); Note, "Copyright Protection of Computer Object Code," 96 Harv. L. Rev. 1723 (1983); Stern, "Another Look at Copyright Protection of Software," 3 Computer LJ 1 (1981); Lawlor, "A Proposal for Strong Protection of Computer Programs Under the Copyright Law," 20 Jurimetrics J. 18 (1979); Note, "Software Piracy and the Personal Computer: Is the 1980 Software Copyright Act Effective?" 4 Computer LJ 171 (1983); Nat'l Comm'n on New Technological Uses of Copyrighted Works, Final Report (1978).

[2] 17 USC § 301 (1982); see Technicon Medical Information Sys. Corp. v. Green Bay Packaging, Inc., 687 F2d 1032 (7th Cir. 1982), cert. denied, 103 S. Ct. 732 (1983); see also ¶ 3.12[2].

[3] 17 USC § 102(a) (1982).

[4] 17 USC § 106 (1982).

nal work of authorship. Originality does not require that the work be unique or of high quality, but merely of independent creation.[5]

While there is no qualitative assessment of creativity, some expression must be involved. Copyright protection has been denied to blank forms and word fragments.[6] The National Commission on New Technological Uses of Copyrighted Works (CONTU) described this exclusion as the "insufficient intellectual labor exception."[7] This exclusion has application to cases in which alleged expression is created solely or primarily by machine operations not directed by a human author and to programs involving very few, simple steps.[8]

[2] Tangible Media

To be copyrightable, the work must be fixed in a tangible medium of expression. The statute makes an express distinction between the copyrightable work and the medium in which it is fixed. One can copyright a literary work, but not a book. Similarly, copyright does not protect ephemeral authorship, but only that fixed in some form for reproduction.

The requirement that a work be fixed in a tangible medium has been historically relevant to new technologies; especially to sound recordings. A controversy arose from the early U.S. Supreme Court decision of *White-Smith Music Publishing Co. v. Apollo Co.*[9] The Court held that a piano roll was not a "copy" of a musical composition, since it was not in "a form which others can see and read." This doctrine, which required

---

[5] See Hubco Data Prods. Corp. v. Management Assistance, Inc., 219 USPQ 450 (D. Idaho 1983).

[6] See Cash Dividend Check Corp. v. Davis, 247 F2d 458 (9th Cir. 1957) (blank forms); Brown Instrument Co. v. Warner, 161 F2d 910 (DC Cir. 1947) (standardized charts); Taylor Instrument Co. v. Fawley Brost Co., 139 F2d 785 (7th Cir. 1943), cert. denied, 321 US 785 (1944) (routine data presentation). Compare Harcourt Brace and World, Inc. v. Graphic Controls Corp., 329 F. Supp. 517 (SDNY 1971) (protection given to answer sheets against literal copying because symbols designating questions or response spaces are expression where design of sheet is unique to standardized testing process).

[7] See *Nat'l Comm'n on New Technological Uses of Copyrighted Works, Final Report* 20 (1978); 1 *Nimmer on Copyright* 2-14.

[8] See Keplinger, "Computer Software—Its Nature and Its Protection," 30 Emory LJ 483, 507 (1981). Keplinger cites EH Tate v. Jiffy Enters., Inc., 16 FRD 571 (ED Pa. 1954), as denying copyright protection to a simple command or instruction statement. The pertinent standards should, as this implies, derive in part from those cases that have generally denied copyright protection to the rules of games. See Affiliated Hosp. Prods., Inc. v. Merder Game Mfg. Co., 513 F2d 1183 (2d Cir. 1975); Chamberlain v. Uris Sales Corp., 150 F2d 512 (2d Cir. 1945).

[9] 209 US 1 (1908).

direct perceivability, excluded copyright for various recordings designed for subsequent replay and, thus, left out a wide range of artistically significant activities.

The Copyright Act overrules *White-Smith* and does not require that the work be directly perceivable. It is sufficient that the work be fixed in a medium from which it can be reproduced or communicated "either directly or with the aid of a machine or other device."[10] This does not, however, necessarily alter the expectation that the mechanical system serve as a means of communication to human beings.[11]

[3] Expression vs. Ideas and Processes

The most controversial criterion for copyrightability of computer software is the Section 102 exclusion of any copyright protection for ideas, processes, discoveries, or material objects. This exclusion identifies a basic dichotomy in copyright law.[12] Copyright protection attaches only to forms of expression, not to the ideas expressed or processes described. In print or other traditional forms of communication, this distinction is relatively easy to describe. The plot of a novel is not copyrightable, but the dialogue written by an author is protected.

An idea can not be copyrighted, but copyright is not denied if a work contains an idea. Rather, copyright establishes proprietary rights in the author's expression, but does not preclude use of the idea or described process by others. Knowledge of the underlying process or idea is communicated for potential use by others.[13] The author's benefit derives from publication, not control of the process or idea. The distinction between expression and ideas or processes defines a system that encourages creative expression while safeguarding the right of others to use, adapt, and build on an idea. In the case of processes, the distinction also defines the relationship between copyright law and patent protections oriented to physical processes.

These distinctions are applied in several ways within the copyright system. One application relates to determining when reproduction of part of an original work violates the original copyright—a question of copyright infringement. The statutory mandate concerning infringement

---

[10] 17 USC § 102 (1982).

[11] See Stern, "Another Look at Copyright Protection of Software," 3 Computer LJ 1 (1981).

[12] See generally *Nimmer on Copyright* §§ 2.03, 13.03.

[13] See generally Davidson, "Protecting Computer Software: A Comprehensive Analysis," 1983 Ariz. LJ 611.

requires an interpretation that allows similarity or literal reproduction insofar as the similarity encompasses ideas, rather than expression.[14] One authority argues that this is the sole manner in which it is appropriate to implement the statutory mandate to exclude ideas and processes from copyright protection.[15]

A second application affects the copyrightability of a work. If copyright protection would necessarily result in protection of an idea or process, no copyright is available under Section 102 of the Act. One variation of this theme is the "idea-expression identity" exception to copyrightability.[16] This exception denies copyrightability if there is literal, or at least, substantial identity between the idea and the manner of expression. The underlying mandate is that copyright should not create a monopoly on an idea. This mandate requires that if there is only one or a very limited number of ways to express an idea, copyright is denied in order to preserve the free use and exchange of ideas.

The exception is a limited one whose application is controlled by varying conceptions of the author's idea as contrasted to his expression. For example, it is arguable that the idea of *Hamlet* encompasses substantial elements of plot and dialogue. The result of this argument would be an unjustified limitation of copyright protection to exclude a highly creative work. In contrast, if the theory of relativity is the idea of Einstein's book, copyright protection of the text is possible without restraining use of the theory (idea).

A variant of the idea-expression exception may arise in works that describe utilitarian objects or processes. Copyright protection does not extend to the process and does not encompass the object described. The distinction between process and description (as well as the idea-expression identity theme) was first articulated by the U.S. Supreme Court in *Baker v. Seldon.*[17] *Baker* involved a book describing a system of bookkeeping. The book included forms integral to the system. The issue was

---

[14] See generally Durham Indus., Inc. v. Tomy Corp., 630 F2d 905 (2d Cir. 1980); Stern Elec., Inc. v. Kaufman, 669 F2d 852 (2d Cir. 1982); Franklin Mint Corp. v. National Wildlife Art Exch., 575 F2d 62 (3d Cir. 1978); Sid & Marty Krofft Television v. McDonald's Corp., 562 F2d 1157, 1164–1165 (9th Cir. 1977).

[15] See *Nimmer on Copyright* 2-200.

[16] See Baker v. Seldon, 101 US 99 (1879); Mazer v. Stein, 347 US 201 (1954); Morrissey v. Procter & Gamble Co., 379 F2d 675 (1st Cir. 1967); Continental Casualty Co. v. Beardsley, 253 F2d 702 (2d Cir.), cert. denied, 358 US 816 (1958). As applied to computer programs, see Apple Computer, Inc. v. Formula Int'l, 725 F2d 521 (9th Cir. 1984); Apple Computer, Inc. v. Franklin Computer Corp., 714 F2d 1240 (3d Cir. 1983).

[17] 101 US 99 (1879).

whether the defendant's use of allegedly similar forms constituted an infringement. The Court noted

> [where the process described in a book] cannot be used without employing the methods and diagrams used to illustrate the book, or such as are similar to them, such methods and diagrams are to be considered as necessary incidents to the art, and given therewith to the public. . . . [Blank] account-books are not the subject of copyright.[18]

Baker v. Seldon has been substantially criticized but has nevertheless had a lasting and substantial impact on standards of copyrightability and infringement.

Baker has been applied to instruction sets for games or contests. Copyright does not protect a method of play (process), but may protect the manner in which that method is described. However, in a case of literal copying of contest rules, the court in *Morrissey v. Proctor & Gamble Co.*[19] concluded: "[Although more than one form of expression is possible, the subject is] very narrow [admitting of] at best only a limited number [of forms]. Copyright does not extend to the subject matter at all, and plaintiff cannot complain even if his particular expression was deliberately adopted."[20] Where the specific expression is essential to a process, the distinction between form of expression and process breaks down. It is supportable if it is realistic to postulate various forms of expression as adequate for the process. As the range of available expression narrows, copyright protection gives way to the countervailing mandate denying the author a monopoly on the underlying process or idea.[21]

A similar result obtains for architectural and other designs. In draft or blueprint form, architectural plans are copyrightable. The scope of protection is constrained by the inherent limitations of the medium and the relatively limited, structured forms available for expression.[22] The majority view is that a constructed building is not an infringement of the

---

[18] Id. at 103.

[19] 379 F2d 675 (1st Cir. 1967).

[20] Id. at 678–679.

[21] See Baker v. Seldon, 101 US 99 (1879); Mazer v. Stein, 347 US 201 (1954); Morrissey v. Procter & Gamble Co., 379 F2d 675 (1st Cir. 1967); Continental Casualty Co. v. Beardsley, 253 F2d 702 (2d Cir.), cert. denied, 358 US 816 (1958); Durham Indus., Inc. v. Tomy Corp., 630 F2d 905 (2d Cir. 1980); Stern Elec., Inc. v. Kaufman, 669 F2d 852 (2d Cir. 1982); Franklin Mint Corp. v. National Wildlife Art Exch., 575 F2d 62 (3d Cir. 1978); Sid & Marty Krofft Television v. McDonald's Corp., 562 F2d 1157, 1164–1165 (9th Cir. 1977).

[22] See Tompkins Graphics, Inc. v. Zipatone, Inc., 222 USPQ 49 (ED Pa. 1983).

architect's plans.[23] Copyright protects expression, but does not establish a proprietary interest in ideas, processes, or material objects. When the two principles collide, the copyright protection is relinquished in favor of broader interests.

Both Congress and the courts have encountered difficulty in applying copyright to useful objects such as lamps, desks, and constructed buildings.[24] Copyright does not extend to utilitarian aspects of objects, only to their expressive content and form.[25] This distinction is incorporated in the Copyright Act regarding "useful articles" under the heading of pictorial, graphic, and sculptural works.

> Such works shall include works of artistic craftsmanship insofar as their form but not their mechanical or utilitarian aspects are concerned; the design of a useful article . . . shall be [copyrightable] only if, and only to the extent that, such design incorporates [expressive] features that can be identified separately from, and are capable of existing independently of, the utilitarian aspects of the article.[26]

The utilitarian and expressive aspects of the design of useful items are often difficult to distinguish.[27] However, as elsewhere, if copyright of expression threatens to establish de facto control of ideas, processes, or material objects, proprietary rights in what arguably is expression give way.

> Although the shape of an industrial product may be aesthetically satisfying and valuable . . . unless the shape of [the] product contains some element that physically or conceptually can be identified as

---

[23] See Imperial Homes Corp. v. Lamont, 458 F2d 895. Compare WPOW, Inc. v. MRLJ Enters., 222 USPQ 502 (DDC 1984) (use of engineering drawings to construct a broadcast tower). In many cases, the technical issue of whether use of the drawings to construct a building infringes the copyright is mooted by the fact that the defendant copied the architectural or other plans in the course of the construction work. See Aitken, Hazen, Hoffman, Miller v. Empire Constr. Co., 218 USPQ 409 (D. Neb. 1982); *Nimmer on Copyright* § 2.08D.

[24] See Denicola, "Applied Art and Industrial Design: Copyright in Useful Articles," 67 Minn. L. Rev. 707 (1983).

[25] See Mazer v. Stein, 347 US 201 (1954); Fabrica, Inc. v. El Dorado Corp., 217 USPQ 698 (9th Cir. 1983); Kieselstein-Cord v. Accessories by Pearl, 632 F2d 989 (2d Cir. 1980); Gay Toys, Inc. v. Buddy L. Corp., 218 USPQ 13 (6th Cir. 1983).

[26] 17 USC § 101 (1982).

[27] Underlying the decision, of course, is a judgment about whether the particular, tangible item is in itself a useful article. See Kieselstein-Cord v. Accessories by Pearl, 632 F2d 989 (2d Cir. 1980) (belt buckle is jewelry); Gay Toys, Inc. v. Buddy L. Corp., 218 USPQ 13 (6th Cir. 1983) (toy airplane has no intrinsic utilitarian function).

separable from the utilitarian aspects of that article, the design would not be copyrighted.[28]

As these distinctions suggest, copyright law is characterized by efforts to distinguish and isolate protection of expression and authorship, rather than ideas, functional processes, or utilitarian designs. The resulting issues relate to subject matter copyrightability and to defining copyright infringement. These are not merely technical or obstructive, but go to the basic nature of the copyright system. Protection for expression and authorship is significant, but extends only insofar as it can be achieved without creating a monopoly on ideas, processes, or objects. This is especially significant for various forms of computer software where the relationship between expression and process is closer than perhaps in any other creative industry. In the following sections, these themes are examined as they apply to the copyrightability of computer software and other aspects of computer technology.

¶ 1.03 COMPUTER PROGRAMS

The copyrightability of computer programs has been discussed in legal literature since the early 1970s. However, the issue was largely academic until technological advances expanded the industry into home, small-business, and other mass markets. Previously, most programs were custom-designed and subject to limited distribution or treated as adjuncts of hardware systems with little extrinsic value. The interests of the developer were protected through trade secrecy, contract, and other measures.[29] Entry into mass markets both accentuates the value of software and places the product in an environment in which prior protections appear to be inadequate. Obvious commercial value coupled with relative ease of reproduction leads to substantial levels of unauthorized copying and distribution. In this altered context, copyright protection is the predominant and most potentially effective legal protection. Copyright litigation has increased dramatically.

---

[28] HR Rep. No. 1476, 94th Cong., 2d Sess. 55 (1976); see also S. Rep. No. 473, 94th Cong., 1st Sess. 51 (1976). "[If] an article has any utilitarian function, it can be denied copyright protection except to the extent that its artistic features can be identified separately and are capable of existing independently as a work of art." Fabrica, Inc. v. El Dorado Corp., 217 USPQ 698 (9th Cir. 1983).

[29] See MacGrady, "Protection of Computer Software: An Update and Practical Synthesis," 20 Hous. L. Rev. 1033 (1983); Gilbourne, "The Proprietary Rights Pyramid: An Integrated Approach to Copyright and Trade Secret Protection for Software," 1 Comp. Law. 1 (March 1984).

In this setting, each of the previously described criteria for copyrightability has relevance in determining whether computer programs are copyrightable. However, it is often difficult to match these criteria to pertinent policies regarding computer software protection. Software protection deals with a creative industry dramatically different from the print, video, or music media that originally dominated the copyright field. Decisions about protecting software are connected to issues about protecting machine processes and scientific or technological concepts, matters traditionally addressed under patent and trade secret laws. They involve determining the criteria for and extent of protection of a technology where that protection may significantly affect the commercial and scientific options of other parties.[30] These determinations are not common matters in copyright law.

The software environment uniquely blends idea, expression, and process in a manner that can not be compared readily to books or articles that describe systems. Computer programs not only describe a process or idea, but in appropriate form directly implement it. The traditional criteria of copyrightability are apt in other environments, but are not necessarily pertinent to the new technology. The risk is that—misdirected by the awkward fit of these concepts—the development of law in this area will inadequately balance the competing scientific and commercial interests.

[1] CONTU Report

The copyright status of computer programs was unclear under the former copyright law. In 1976, Congress enacted a revised Copyright Act to adjust copyright to emergent forms of communication and expression. Section 117 of that Act expressly disclaimed any intention to alter the status of computer program copyrights. The exclusion was not intended to deny copyright protection to computer programs, but to allow for an interim period of further study. Thus, CONTU was appointed and its report was submitted in 1978, which led to the enactment of The Computer Software Copyright Act of 1980.[31]

The CONTU majority strongly favored the application of copyright to computer programs and argued that with the exception of Section 117, the 1976 Act reflected a congressional decision to extend copyright to

---

[30] See Denicola, "Applied Art and Industrial Design: Copyright in Useful Articles," 67 Minn. L. Rev. 707 (1983); Note, "Toward a Unified Theory of Copyright for Advanced Technology," 96 Harv. L. Rev. 450 (1982).

[31] Pub. L. No. 96-517, 94 Stat. 3015 (1980).

computer programs.[32] The CONTU report cited several substantive arguments for the application of copyright to computer programs. Central to its position, however, was the view that programs constituted the product of "great intellectual labor" that merited legal protection. The argument for some form of protection is relatively clear. It was stated by the CONTU report in the following terms:

> The cost of developing computer programs is far greater than the cost of their duplication. Consequently, computer programs . . . are likely to be disseminated only if . . . the creator may recover all of its costs plus a fair profit on the first sale of the work . . . or the creator may spread its costs over multiple copies of the work with some form of protection against unlawful duplication. . . . [Some] form of protection is necessary to encourage the creation and broad distribution of computer programs in a competitive market.[33]

While this economic incentive justifies some protection for computer software, it does not necessarily support the view that copyright protection is desirable. In discussing this, CONTU limited itself to considering existing forms of intellectual property protection developed for other forms of technology. Given this scope, it can be argued that patent law imposes too high a requirement of invention as an entry barrier for protection and that trade secrecy law is inadequate for mass-market products. In contrast, copyright has only minimal preconditions for protection and is designed to protect products in a mass market. Characterizing software as a relatively "new type of writing" for which copyright protection was essential to provide incentive for development and widespread dissemination, CONTU concluded that copyright was the most appropriate alternative.

Although the CONTU report advocated copyright protection, the report was less explicit as to the scope of protection. The majority rejected suggestions that would exclude programs in machine (object code) form or programs that did not lead to creation of copyrightable material. However, it acknowledged that the author's protection should be restricted by traditional, limiting concepts in copyright law.

> Copyright . . . protects the program so long as it remains fixed in a tangible medium of expression but does not protect the electro-mechanical functioning of a machine. . . . Thus, one is always free to

---

[32] See *Nat'l Comm'n on New Technological Uses of Copyrighted Works, Final Report* 16 (1978); see also S. Rep. No. 473, 94th Cong., 1st Sess. 51 (1976).

[33] *Nat'l Comm'n on New Technological Uses of Copyrighted Works, Final Report* 11 (1978).

make a machine perform any conceivable process . . . but one is not free to take another's program.[34]

CONTU recommended and Congress adopted relatively limited changes in the 1976 Act. The Section 117 exclusionary language was deleted and replaced by language authorizing limited forms of program use. Section 101 of the Act was amended to include a definition of "computer program," although this term was not then expressly incorporated as a type of copyrightable subject matter. As previously noted, the Commission believed that copyright extension to computer programs was already inherent in the 1976 Act absent the exclusionary terms of Section 117.

Despite enactment of the CONTU recommendations, the copyrightability of computer programs remained controversial. Properly understood, the controversy relates to a limited set of issues and is primarily concerned with the applicability of copyright to certain computer programs in their object code or machine form. In most other cases, the significant issue is the scope of the copyright protection, not whether the program is copyrightable.

[2] Nature of a Program

Applying even basic copyright concepts to computer software requires understanding the multiple functions that software performs and the multiple forms in which it is found. A computer program consists of a set of instructions designed to guide the operation of a computer to achieve a desired result.[35] Both the form of the instructions and the manner in which they are recorded and used vary depending on the stage of development, the result desired, the work environment, and the mode of distribution selected by the developer. Despite this variability, programs pass through several identifiable stages that are useful in discussing copyright issues.[36]

The first stage consists of the design of the program. This stage requires the specification of an outlined or structured series of steps that

---

[34] Id. at 20.

[35] See 17 USC § 101 (1982).

[36] See *Encyclopedia of Computer Science and Engineering* 1049, 1385 (2d ed. 1983); *Nat'l Comm'n on New Technological Uses of Copyrighted Works, Final Report* (1978); Keplinger, "Computer Software—Its Nature and Its Protection," 30 Emory LJ 483, 507 (1981); Laurie, "Protection of Trade Secrets in Object Form Software: The Case for Reverse Engineering," 1 Comp. Law. 1 (July 1984); Note, "Copyrighting Object Code: Applying Old Legal Tools to New Technologies," 4 Computer LJ 421 (1983).

ultimately achieve desired computer operations. This design is often called the algorithm of the program, reflecting the mathematical and engineering origins of the programming profession. The design may be expressed in the form of a flowchart or an outline in other forms.

Subsequent to or concurrent with the development and refinement of the algorithm, the steps specified in the design are converted to more specific instructions. In many cases, these are expressed in a so-called high level programming language such as FORTRAN, BASIC, or COBOL. These "languages" consist of alphanumeric symbols and commands. The resulting instructions are commonly described as source code.[37] This code may be written on paper or entered directly into a computer through an intermediary program that permits visual or printed display and modification. The instructions can be converted by various intermediary programs into an electronic configuration that guides or controls the operation of a computer.

Unconverted source code does not directly operate a computer. It must be transformed to electromagnetic configurations that are machine readable. In most cases, this transformation is accomplished by intermediary programs described as interpreters, compilers, or assemblers.[38] The ultimate result is an electromagnetic configuration that can be symbolized in binary number form as a series of zeros and ones. This manifestation of the program is often described as object code. In object code form, the program may be stored on various media such as tapes or discs, or it may be embedded in silicon chips. In this latter form, the storage device may be described as read only memory (ROM), signifying that the content may not be altered.

Once installed in any of these forms, the purpose of a program is to generate various processing functions within the computer, leading to some form of visual or printed output. The variations are virtually limitless. In general, the operation of a program is in response to external input, either directly from a user or from another machine. In some programs, a reproduction of the original source code can be generated. Often, however, this capacity is not built into the program, and external inputs lead to a variety of other resulting products. For example, a computer game program may generate audiovisual images of space craft and

---

[37] See *Encyclopedia of Computer Science and Engineering* 1385 (2d ed. 1983); *Nat'l Comm'n on New Technological Uses of Copyrighted Works, Final Report* 21 n.109 (1978).

[38] See *Encyclopedia of Computer Science and Engineering* 1049 (2d ed. 1983); *Nat'l Comm'n on New Technological Uses of Copyrighted Works, Final Report* 21 n.109 (1978).

aliens. A word processing program may display typing instructions as well as recording, editing, and reproducing text entered by the user.

Thus, a program passes through numerous and distinct phases involving not only differences in the media on which it is recorded, but also materially different expressive forms and content. While object code results from the introduction of source code into a machine, the two are not mirror images either in function or perception. Similarly, the output (visual or printed) created by interaction of electromagnetic object code and external input is produced by the program, but not identical to it. As a result, in speaking of the copyrightability of computer programs, generalizations may be inadequate unless the form and type of program, as well as the subject matter that constitutes the allegedly protected work of authorship, are specified.[39]

Despite this diversity, computer programs have common characteristics relevant to copyrightability. Program design and coding are oriented toward utilitarian and functional objectives. In most cases, the user is not expected to perceive the program design or code, but only the product of the machine's performance under the control of the program. This performance may involve highly artistic or creative effects, but the program coding is concerned with indirectly achieving those effects in an efficient and operable manner. One consequence is that, although higher level programming languages may be likened to human languages or dialects, the choice among phrases (commands or instructions) by the author is not based on the aesthetic or emotive characteristics of the code, but on utilitarian considerations. Whether one instruction sounds better than another is irrelevant. The selection is oriented solely to whether the instruction achieves the desired computer operation and whether it functions more or less efficiently than would another instruction. These choices reflect both creative and intellectual skills of a high order, but differ materially from the choices made by a novelist, composer, or other creative artist working on traditional copyright subject matter. This close and structured association to the process within the computer itself implicates previously discussed issues concerning the appropriate range of copyright protection.

---

[39] This issue may arise with reference to whether the alleged author has adequately protected the particular form of a program that is allegedly infringed. See, e.g., Stern Elecs., Inc. v. Kaufman, 669 F2d 852 (2d Cir. 1982) (appropriate steps for visual display copyright protect object code form); GCA Corp. v. Chance, 217 USPQ 718, 720 (ND Cal. 1982) (copyright of source code protects object code); Midway Mfg. Co. v. Strohon, 564 F. Supp. 741 (ND Ill. 1983) (object code infringed although resulting visual display not an infringement).

[3] Flowcharts and Source Code

To the extent that program designs and coding are reduced to tangible and reproducible form, the resulting expression is a potentially copyrightable work. This is true whether the designs and source code are in writing or are created at a computer terminal. In either case, the result is expression capable of being understood by another human being. The fact that knowledge of computer programming or of a particular programming language is necessary to understand the work is not relevant. A book written in Latin is copyrightable even though its meaning can be understood only with knowledge of Latin.

This general proposition is subject to several significant limitations. Copyright protects the author's expression, but not his underlying idea.[40] Where the idea and expression merge, copyright protection gives way to an overriding policy favoring the free use of ideas. This merger occurs if expression is essential to the idea, and there are no more than a few methods suitable to express the idea.

As applied to source code, this exclusion denies copyrightability only to the most simplistic program routines.[41] In most other cases, the source code of a complex program involves substantial individuality in selecting variable names, command sequences, output terminology, and other aspects of the program. There are numerous forms in which a program idea can be expressed. The result of the individual choices is copyrightable expression independent of the unprotected underlying idea.

A similar analysis applies to flowcharts and other drawings of a program design. The underlying design, algorithm, or idea is not copyright-

---

[40] See supra ¶ 1.02[3]; see Baker v. Seldon, 101 US 99 (1879); Mazer v. Stein, 347 US 201 (1954); Morrissey v. Procter & Gamble Co., 379 F2d 675 (1st Cir. 1967); Continental Casualty Co. v. Beardsley, 253 F2d 702 (2d Cir.), cert. denied, 358 US 816 (1958); Durham Indus., Inc. v. Tomy Corp., 630 F2d 905 (2d Cir. 1980); Stern Elecs., Inc. v. Kaufman, 669 F2d 852 (2d Cir. 1982); Franklin Mint Corp. v. National Wildlife Art Exch., 575 F2d 62 (3d Cir. 1978); Sid & Marty Krofft Television v. McDonald's Corp., 562 F2d 1157, 1164–1165 (9th Cir. 1977).

[41] See Synercom Technology, Inc. v. University Computing Co., 462 F. Supp. 1003 (ND Tex. 1978); Keplinger, "Computer Software—Its Nature and Its Protection," 30 Emory LJ 483, 507 (1981). Keplinger cites EH Tate v. Jiffy Enters., Inc., 16 FRD 571 (ED Pa. 1954), as denying copyright protection to a simple command or instruction statement. The standards should derive from those cases that deny copyright protection to the rules of games. See Affiliated Hosp. Prods., Inc. v. Mercer Game Mfg. Co., 513 F2d 1183 (2d Cir. 1975); Chamberlain v. Uris Sales Corp., 150 F2d 512 (2d Cir. 1945). In these cases, while there may have been other means of expression of the commands, the need to convey pertinent information restricts the range of alternatives in a very spartan, limited environment.

able. A particular expression in a flowchart or other form may be copyrightable, but the relatively sparse format of a flowchart increases the probability that there is an identity between idea and expression that precludes copyright. An unembellished flowchart depicting sequential steps A, B, C, and D is not copyrightable. The fact that each step in the chart might be denoted by a circle, a square, or other geometric figure does not eliminate an identity between the idea of the sequence and its expression.[42] This is especially true since methods of drawing flowcharts are relatively standardized. Written descriptions or commentary might be copyrightable, but will not indirectly protect the underlying idea, chart, or sequence. As noted in the legislative history of Section 102 of the Act: "[The] expression adopted by the programmer is the copyrightable element in a computer program.... [The] actual processes or methods embodied in the program are not within the scope of the copyright law."[43]

In the absence of substantial case law, the distinction between idea and expression in flowcharts and source code is uncertain. As a practical matter, the distinction indicates that copyright is not a viable protection for the author of a program in these forms. Unlike a fiction writer or a music composer, a program author does not benefit from the appeal of the coding, but from the performance of the program. This results largely from the design, sequencing, or structure of the program, which are its idea content. The design can be readily discerned from the flowchart or source code. Once discerned, the ideas can be appropriated despite copyright. This is a direct result of a legal system committed to the free use of ideas. Consequently, mass-market software is seldom distributed in source code.[44] In custom-designed programs, source code may be furnished to the user, but only under restrictive agreements designed to retain trade secret protections.

[4] Machine Formats: Output

In the process from design to use, computer programs are transferred into a machine form involving electromagnetic configurations often

---

[42] See Tompkins Graphics, Inc. v. Zipatone, Inc., 222 USPQ 49 (ED Pa. 1983) (circles and squares not copyrightable).

[43] HR Rep. No. 1476, 94th Cong., 2d Sess. 54 (1976); see also S. Rep. No. 473, 94th Cong., 1st Sess. 50–51 (1976).

[44] See Gilbourne, "The Proprietary Rights Pyramid: An Integrated Approach to Copyright and Trade Secret Protection for Software," 1 Comp. Law. 1 (March 1984).

described as object code. Most of the litigation concerning copyrightability focuses on programs in this form.

In discussing the issues, it is necessary to distinguish between the medium of expression (e.g., tape, disk, ROM) and the work of authorship. The medium on which a work is recorded is not copyrightable. Thus, a tape, disk, or ROM can not be copyrighted. The pertinent questions are whether the material recorded on these media is copyrightable and whether the medium meets statutory requirements for a tangible copy.

Within this framework, two distinct copyrightable works might be associated with the program. The first is the object code itself, which consists of electromagnetic configurations that determine the operations of a computer system. In many cases at least, object code derives from source or other coded forms of the program. The second is the output of the program in audio, screen display, or printed form. In this section the focus is on the copyrightability of the output. Object code issues are discussed in the next section.

The output of a computer program varies depending on the style and purposes of the program and, perhaps, the input supplied by the user. In all cases, however, output is dependent on entry into the machine of an external stimulus. The stimulus triggers instructions embodied in electromagnetic form in the computer that cause the computer to perform certain functions. The input may range from turning on a machine or loading a program, through elaborate, interactive responses or actions. Similarly, the output may range from a single word, number, or symbol, to an elaborate, visually exciting display or print.

Output that is otherwise copyrightable does not lose this status because it is in machine form.[45] Consider a program that displays visual representations of various animals. The initial question is whether the various animal figures are potentially protectible works of authorship. Assuming originality and at least minimal creativity, the sole obstacle to an affirmative answer is that these pictorial works were not produced with brush and canvas or pen and paper, but through various electrical functions leading to the display or print. The method, however, does not alter the character of the final product: pictorial representations of animals.

Section 102(a) of the Act requires that a work be "fixed in a tangible medium" of expression. Under prior law, the copyrightability of these animal figures might have been contested under authority of the piano

---

[45] See Midway Mfg. Co. v. Arctic Int'l, Inc., 704 F2d 1009 (7th Cir. 1983); Stern Elecs., Inc. v. Kaufman, 669 F2d 852 (2d Cir. 1982); Apple Computer, Inc. v. Formula Int'l, 725 F2d 521 (9th Cir. 1984).

roll case, *White-Smith Music Publishing Co. v. Apollo,*[46] which required that a copyrighted work be directly perceivable by a human. In this program, the animal images do not exist in the computer. The medium contains mere electromagnetic configurations that will cause their creation as output. However, *White-Smith* has been expressly overruled. Under current law, a work of authorship is "fixed" and meets Section 102(a) if it is capable of being reproduced or communicated "directly or indirectly with the aid of a machine or other device."[47] The fact that the visual image is generated through computer operations is immaterial.

> [Programs, videotapes and phonorecords] are capable of communicating with humans. . . . In all three instances, the medium in which copyrighted material is stored is moved past a sensing device at a set speed, causing electric current to flow, and ultimately resulting in the movement of machine parts to print words, display pictures or create sounds.[48]

The fact that the pictorial work is generated by the object code of a program no more denies its copyrightability than does the storage format of a sound recording (phonorecord) or an audiovisual work (videotape) deny copyright to those works.

This analysis treats the object code program as part of the storage medium. It does not support the conclusion that object code is copyrightable. Neither does the analysis imply that the source code is copyrighted. In fact, the identical display (output) might be generated by numerous conceptually and expressively distinct source code programs. The analysis merely confirms that output that is otherwise copyrightable is not denied this protection simply because it was generated by a machine-resident program in a computer.

[a] Computer Forms and Spreadsheets

The example discussed in the previous section represents a relatively simple application of copyright in that the animal figures are invariant and generated in response to trivial input from the user. More complex issues of copyrightability are encountered when dealing with program outputs that depend on and interact with input supplied by the user, rather than the author of the program. When the input of the user is dis-

---

[46] 209 US 1 (1908).

[47] 17 USC § 102(a) (1982).

[48] *Nat'l Comm'n on New Technological Uses of Copyrighted Works, Final Report* 21 (1978).

tinguished, the conclusion will often be that the program's output is not copyrightable.

To illustrate, it is useful to examine one of the most popular forms of software–the so-called spreadsheet program. Under this program, the user may enter numerical and textual data in the form of a spreadsheet and the computer automatically calculates relatively complex relationships as specified by the user. The basic output of the program is a grid created by rows and columns of numbers and letters at the margin of a display screen, accompanied by limited instructions or commands at the top or bottom of the screen. Other outputs are determined by actions of the user entering data and defining relationships among units of information.

Two conclusions are appropriate. The first is that the output of the program is not copyrightable. This flows from the insufficient expressive content.[49] The computer-generated display consists of a form for recording information and is both commonplace and austere. This does not suggest that there has been inadequate creative or intellectual effort in the design of the program itself. However, here the focus is on the output, which is insubstantial. If copyrightable expression is found in the output at all, it would lie in the wording of the limited commands or instructions at the top or bottom of the otherwise blank form.

A second conclusion is equally significant. The spreadsheet program in interaction with the machine user may generate copyrightable output.[50] However, the output would be the product of the user whose specification of relationships and selection of data or text might constitute

---

[49] See supra ¶ 1.02[1]; see Cash Dividend Check Corp. v. Davis, 247 F2d 458 (9th Cir. 1957) (blank forms); Brown Instrument Co. v. Warner, 161 F2d 910 (DC Cir. 1947) (standardized charts); Taylor Instrument Co. v. Fawley Brost Co., 139 F2d 785 (7th Cir. 1943), cert. denied, 321 US 785 (1944) (routine data presentation). Compare Harcourt Brace and World, Inc. v. Graphic Controls Corp., 329 F. Supp. 517 (SDNY 1971) (protection given to answer sheets against literal copying because symbols designating questions or response spaces are expression where design of sheet is unique to standardized testing process). See also EH Tate v. Jiffy Enters., Inc., 16 FRD 571 (ED Pa. 1954); Affiliated Hosp. Prods., Inc. v. Mercer Game Mfg. Co., 513 F2d 1183 (2d Cir. 1975); Chamberlain v. Uris Sales Corp., 150 F2d 512 (2d Cir. 1945).

[50] See Rand McNally & Co. v. Fleet Management Sys., Inc., 221 USPQ 828 (ND Ill. 1983) (copyright protection given to mileage charts and other facts compiled by plaintiff). As discussed in Chapter 11, database and factual compilations receive copyright protection. Even though it is accepted that no copyright can be extended to the particular "facts" in a work, the effort and creativity in selection and compilation is protected. See Miller v. Universal Studios, Inc., 650 F2d 1365 (5th Cir. 1981); Schroeder v. William Morrow & Co., 566 F2d 3 (7th Cir. 1977); Denicola, "Copyright in Collections of Facts: A Theory for Protection of Nonfic-

authorship. It would qualify for protection if it were more than momentarily stored in the relevant medium. If copyrightable matter is generated, the result is not a copyright on a variation of the program, but on the configuration of numbers and text retrievable from the computer.

[b] Video Games: Interactive Output

The significance of an interaction between user-generated and program-generated output has been litigated in the context of video or computer games. In video games, the computer program causes the machine to display various images and sequences of action based on the user's input. Substantial creative expression is common in the images and action sequences. Since the visual effects and play represent the primary commercial value of the games and can be replicated through various source code programs, it is common to copyright the display and images themselves, rather than merely the underlying program.[51]

In discussing video game output, it is necessary to distinguish the play mode of a game and what has been described as the attract mode. The play mode is an interactive sequence in which the visual and audio manifestations are controlled in part by the actions of the user (player). In contrast, the attract mode in games used in public places consists of a sequence of images generated by the program itself in the absence of any active player. The purpose is to demonstrate the game and attract paying players.

Assuming originality of expression, the attract mode display is copyrightable. The images and sounds are created by the author of the game program. Although specific images may appear and leave the screen, the overall sequence is fixed and repetitive, analogous to a motion picture in which a series of scenes are continuously repeated. The fact that the images are created by object code is immaterial. The work of authorship can be perceived "directly or indirectly with the aid of a machine or other device."[52]

The copyrightability of the play mode is less clear. For example, in a game calling for the player to destroy enemy aircraft with guided missiles,

---

tion Literary Works," 81 Colum. L. Rev. 561 (1981); *Nimmer on Copyright* § 2.11[A].

[51] See Stern Elecs., Inc. v. Kaufman, 669 F2d 852 (2d Cir. 1982).

[52] See Midway Mfg. Co. v. Arctic Int'l, Inc., 704 F2d 1009 (7th Cir. 1983); Williams Elecs. v. Arctic Int'l, Inc., 685 F2d 870 (3d Cir. 1982); In re Certain Coin-Operated Audiovisual Games and Components Thereof, No. 337-TA-105 (Int'l Trade Comm'n 1982); No. 337-TA-87 (Int'l Trade Comm'n 1981).

the program may cause images of aircraft to move from left to right across a screen and to disappear when intersected by an image of a missile moving from bottom to top. The extent to which movement and destruction occur depends on the player's skill in launching missiles at appropriate intervals. As a result, there are numerous variations in individual episodes. At appropriate complexity, the potential variations may be infinite.

The variability of individual plays and the role of the user create two major arguments against the copyrightability of the play mode of video games. The first questions the originality of the program author's alleged work. The argument is that the specific audiovisual output in a given play of the game is determined as much or more by the player (user) than by the program author. Followed to its logical conclusion, if the specific play were stored and could be reproduced, it might be copyrighted by the player, but not by the author of the program. The second argument focuses on the variability of the displays, rather than the relative contributions of the author and player. The Act requires that a work be fixed in a tangible medium.[53] To be "fixed" the work must be embodied in a form "sufficiently permanent or stable to permit it to be perceived, reproduced, or otherwise communicated for a period of more than transitory duration."[54] Arguably, the play mode consists of numerous variations, none of which is stored for more than a transitory period or is readily capable of reproduction.

These arguments have been routinely rejected in the reported cases.[55] Authorship is attributed to the programmer based on the conclusion that specific, repetitious images created directly by the programmed machine are copyrightable. Regardless of the player's performance, various game images remain the same. If these are sufficiently expressive, copyright protection attaches despite any issues as to the play of the game.

The sequence of play is also copyrightable by the program author. Independent of the particular images, substantial elements of the play are controlled by the program. These repeat throughout, despite variations caused by the player. The Third Circuit in *Williams Electronics, Inc. v. Arctic International, Inc.*[56] most clearly expressed this rationale:

---

[53] 17 USC § 102(a) (1982).

[54] *Nimmer on Copyright* 2-214.2.

[55] See Stern Elecs., Inc. v. Kaufman, 669 F2d 852 (2d Cir. 1982); Williams Elecs. v. Arctic Int'l, Inc., 685 F2d 870 (3d Cir. 1982).

[56] 685 F2d 870 (3d Cir. 1982).

Although there is player interaction with the machine during the play mode which causes the audiovisual presentation to change in some respects from one game to the next in response to the player's varying participation, there is always a repetitive sequence of a substantial portion of the sights and sounds of the game, and many aspects of the display remain constant from game to game regardless of how the player operates the controls. [57]

This substantial repetition of sights and sounds satisfies both standards of copyright law: A work must be original and fixed in an identifiable medium.

|c| Interactive Designs

The interactive character of computer program output will create issues in other contexts as computer-aided design and analysis become increasingly common. Properly focused, the *Williams* rationale provides the appropriate structure for analysis. Unlike spreadsheet, word processing, and other programs, in a video game elements of the expressive content of an interactive output are controlled by the program and are not variable by the user. Where the author's contribution to the resultant expression is substantial and repetitive, the output of the program is copyrightable by the program author. In contrast, if the program merely provides tools to convey the user's expression, the program output is not copyrightable by the program author.

|5| Machine Formats: Object Code

Audiovisual displays and source code are copyrightable even when stored in or produced by a machine-resident computer program. This does not, however, require or establish the copyrightability of the object code separate from copyrightable output or antecedents. One view is that the object code and medium represent the tangible copy. The copyrightable "work of authorship" consists of the display, output, or precedent source code. [58] The alternative views are that either the object code is the same work as the source code or that the object code is in itself copyright-

---

[57] Id. at 874.

[58] See Stern, "Another Look at Copyright Protection of Software: Did the 1980 Act Do Anything for Object Code?" 3 Computer LJ 1 (1981); Note, "Copyright Protection of Computer Object Code," 96 Harv. L. Rev. 1723 (1983); Note, "Copyrighting Object Code: Applying Old Legal Tools to New Technologies," 4 Computer LJ 421 (1983).

able.[59] Case law generally establishes some degree of protection for object code independent of output based on these views.[60]

Object code requires difficult interpretations of traditional copyright doctrine that involve transposing concepts from an environment concerned with communication among human beings into an environment concerned with the operation of a machine. The copyright issues unavoidably relate to policy questions about the nature and degree of protection that should be available for computer processes and internal operations. In fact, many of the reported cases that focus on machine code independent of copyrightable output deal with the software that establishes and controls the internal operating environment of the machine in computer systems.

Software is a significant technological field for which legal protection is appropriate. The question is not only whether protection should be available, but in what form and under what conditions. In this regard, the overlap between copyright and patent or trade secret law is significant. Copyright differs from these more traditional technology protections in that it imposes a lesser threshold to establish the right to protection, and protection extends over a longer period. A decision to include object code under copyright independent of output is equivalent to a decision that this protection is appropriate for this technology, even though it is not appropriate for most other technologies.

The basis for such a policy decision has been obscured by debate about the link between copyright and software technology. The policy choice is based in part on the lack of existing alternatives. However, such rationale is inadequate. As is discussed in Chapter 2, even though threshold standards for patent indicate that few software products are patentable, the same is true for many other technologies. Similarly, as is described in Chapter 3, trade secret doctrine is available for software, but generally does not continue in mass-market products. Again, the same is true of most mass-market technology.

The factor that distinguishes computer software from other technologies and justifies copyright protection involves the ease with which it can be reproduced or appropriated. While other unpatented technologies may be appropriated after distribution, there is often a lag time between the distribution, discovery, and exploitation that benefits the originator. It

---

[59] See Midway v. Strohon, 564 F. Supp. 741 (ND Ill. 1983) (infringement of object code without proveable infringement of display or source code); GCA Corp. v. Chance, 217 USPQ 718, 720 (ND Cal. 1982) (copyright of source code protects object code since they are treated as one work).

[60] See Apple Computer, Inc. v. Formula Int'l, 725 F2d 521 (9th Cir. 1984); Apple Computer, Inc. v. Franklin Computer Corp., 714 F2d 1240 (3d Cir. 1983).

results from the need to identify the technology and reproduce the systems needed to manufacture it. In the case of software, however, the lag time is minimal. Unlike other technologies, software is readily subject to relatively rapid reproduction of the essence of the technology. In the absence of legal restrictions, software technology could be appropriated simply by electronic duplication. Deterring mass reproduction is a traditional application of copyright law.

A primary policy argument for applying copyright to object code lies in preventing widespread reproduction for the commercial advantage of unauthorized users. Copyright is an appropriate vehicle for protection because it is readily obtained and is applicable in a mass market. This rationale establishes that protection against literal duplication is warranted, but a broader protection might severely affect the development of competing technologies. A preferable alternative might be to enact more limited, but explicitly applicable laws.[61]

[a] Expressive Programs

Sound policy supports application of copyright law to programs in machine-resident form. If the program directly produces copyrightable output, this protection is clearly implemented in the Act.[62] A more difficult question involves copyright claimed for object code, independent of any copyright of output or source code. The question of whether copyright protection extends to object code per se has been raised in two distinct contexts. The first, discussed here, involves object code copyright where the program itself produces substantial, expressive communication. The second context, discussed in the following section, involves copyright protection for operating systems and other programs lacking substantial expressive content.

A copyright on object code separate from copyrightable output was considered by the Third Circuit in *Williams Electronics, Inc. v. Arctic International, Inc.*[63] In *Williams*, the court was faced with an alleged infringement of a copyrighted video game program. As previously noted, the court concluded that an enforceable copyright existed for video displays produced as the game was played. Although this was sufficient to

---

[61] See infra ¶ 1.05. This option has been adopted for microchip protections.

[62] See Stern Elecs., Inc. v. Kaufman, 669 F2d 852 (2d Cir. 1982); Midway Mfg. Co. v. Arctic Int'l, Inc., 704 F2d 1009 (7th Cir. 1983); Williams Elecs. v. Arctic Int'l, Inc., 685 F2d 870 (3d Cir. 1982); In re Certain Coin-Operated Audiovisual Games and Components Thereof, No. 337-TA-105 (Int'l Trade Comm'n 1982); No. 337-TA-87 (Int'l Trade Comm'n 1981); Atari, Inc. v. North Am. Phillips Consumer Elecs. Corp., 672 F2d 607 (7th Cir. 1982).

[63] 685 F2d 870 (3d Cir. 1982).

establish the infringement in *Williams*, the court also considered the independent copyright of the object code. It concluded that this form of the program was copyrightable.

The defendant's claim and the court's opinion focused on whether unauthorized reproduction of the machine version of the program represented an infringing copy. The court, in essence, concluded that protection of the machine form was necessary to protect the program in other forms. "We cannot accept ... an unlimited loophole by which infringement of a computer program is limited to copying the ... text but not to duplication of a program fixed on a silicon chip."[64]

This analysis substantially misstates the issue. Assuming the existence of copyrightable source code or output, the loophole to which the court refers does not exist. The object code and the medium on which it is stored would constitute a copy of the work, and reproduction in additional copies would be an infringement. It is not necessary to conclude that the impulses on a videotape are separately copyrightable in order to prevent reproduction of the taped material. It is sufficient that the tape is a copy of a copyrighted work.

While the result in *Williams* is justified by the audiovisual display that was a proper subject for copyright, a focus on object code independent of output or preceding coding may create unexpected results. For example, in *Midway Manufacturing Co. v. Strohon*,[65] the court was faced with an alleged infringement of an object code program in a situation in which there was no infringement of the audiovisual display. Despite dissimilarity of the output, the court held that a similarity in object code constituted copyright infringement.

[b] Operating Systems: Nonexpressive Programs

The copyrightability of machine-resident programs independent of output or source code is most significant where program output is not copyrightable and the program is not intended to have the capacity of reproducing source code. This setting arises in operating system programs. Operating system software manages the internal functions of the computer and facilitates use of applications programs by the user.[66] Applications programs, such as word processing or game programs, are oriented to the performance of particular tasks by and for the user. The significance of the distinction is that while operating system software is

---

[64] Id.

[65] 564 F. Supp. 741 (ND Ill. 1983).

[66] See *Encyclopedia of Computer Science and Engineering* 1053 (1983).

complex, it is substantially directed toward machine interaction and conveys little overt communication to the computer user.

Two related copyright problems arise. The first concerns whether the machine program contains expression intended for communication to human beings. The second concerns the connection between the program and the process that it implements. Absent expressive output, the program can be viewed as essentially equivalent to the machine process, an essentially utilitarian device to which copyright does not extend. If there is an identity between the program and the process, granting a copyright to the program would monopolize the process and would be barred under Section 102(b) of the Act.

The first problem assumes that copyright encompasses only subject matter that can be communicated to or perceived by humans. This reflects a traditional limit on this area of law and is arguably implicit in the Act. For example, Section 102(a) limits copyright to works fixed in a tangible "medium of expression" from which they can be "perceived, reproduced, or otherwise communicated." This language requires human perception or communication, [67] and it can be argued that a machine program that does not produce expressive material does not have the requisite communicative role.

This argument is materially different from that raised in the early case of *White-Smith Music Publishing.* [68] In that case the issue was whether copyright requires direct human perception—an element lacking in any medium that requires a machine translation into visual or audible expression. The Act as now revised does not require direct perception. With the computer, little or no human-perceivable expression is generated. In contrast, in videotape and phonorecords the storage media contain information that when reproduced, communicates directly to human beings. This output is copyrightable while the tape or record itself is not.

There are several responses to the argument that communication is required and not present. The least acceptable focuses on terminology in the computer industry in which it is often said that computers "read" program instructions and "communicate" data among various locations or machine units. While this language reflects the ambiguity of modern reactions to machines that seem to exercise judgment and thought, these

---

[67] See Stern, "Another Look at Copyright Protection of Software: Did the 1980 Act Do Anything for Object Code?" 3 Computer LJ 1 (1981). Compare Note, "Copyright Protection of Computer Object Code," 96 Harv. L. Rev. 1723 (1983); Note, "Copyrighting Object Code: Applying Old Legal Tools to New Technologies," 4 Computer LJ 421 (1983).

[68] White-Smith Publishing Co. v. Apollo Co., 209 US 1 (1908); see also supra ¶ 1.02[2].

terms are colloquial summaries of electromagnetic processes. (As an analogy, it might be said that a light bulb "communicates" with a local power plant.)

The more pertinent arguments focus on the ability to reverse process a program from machine form to produce a facsimile of the source code or a listing of the object code. Assuming that the technology exists, it is possible to argue that this capability meets the statutory requirement. In one view, the machine-resident program is a "copy" of the source code.[69] The alternative is that the object code is itself copyrightable.[70] Often, this latter argument leads to discussion of whether the typical representation of object code, a string of binary numbers (zeros and ones) or hexidecimal numbers, constitutes a mode of human communication. However, in machine form, object code consists of a configuration of electromagnetic fields and circuits. The binary numbers are a representation of this configuration analogous to circuit diagrams. This representation can be interpreted by trained analysts, however, the analysis is the same with object or source code reproduction. In either case, the program can produce a readable copy of an arguably copyrightable work by reverse processing.

The difficulty is not that source and object code are difficult or obscure languages, but that the programmer and manufacturer do not, in many cases, intend to communicate the code to third parties via the machine program. Treating machine code as expression on the basis of interpretability would lead ultimately to describing all tangible objects as copies of the original design. Historically, this has not been the law for products such as bridges, machines, and buildings, all of which can be "reverse compiled" to produce a facsimile of the original design or plan. "That comprehensible information can be extracted from a device, like ROM, *not intended to function as a medium for human communication*, does not make the device itself an object from which the work can be perceived or otherwise communicated."[71] The seeming anomaly is that a copyright on a work does not protect the object that is described, but this is a common result in copyright law. A tangible medium of expression must be *intended* as a mode of human communication. Copyright protects "works of authorship" fixed in a tangible "medium of expression" and does not encompass tangible or mechanical objects not intended to communicate to humans.

---

[69] See GCA Corp. v. Chance, 217 USPQ 718, 720 (ND Cal. 1982).

[70] See Midway v. Strohon, 564 F. Supp. 741 (ND Ill. 1983).

[71] Stern, "Another Look at Copyright Protection of Software: Did the 1980 Act Do Anything for Object Code?" 3 Computer LJ 1, 12 (1981) (emphasis added).

For purposes of copyright protection, a machine is not a "copy" of a blueprint. Copyright does not extend to control over the use of technical writings to create a product, but only to reproduction of the writings themselves. A similar transformation occurs when a program is compiled into machine form. The chief distinction is that many transformations of programs involve mere input into the computer and operation of separate programs for compilation. The apparent ease should not mask the transformation that occurs; a transformation from descriptive "writing" to utilitarian object.

While the arguments for treating a machine-resident program as a mode of human communication of the code are weak, this result is suggested in the legislative history of the Act. For example, in describing machine-resident programs as copies, the CONTU report emphasized that a human-readable copy of the program could be reproduced from the machine version.[72] Furthermore, no element of the statute expressly requires that the author *intend* to communicate to humans in the medium used.

Ultimately, the emphasis on communication and perception is a technical, rather than a basic issue. Without direct, expressive products, the purpose of a machine-resident program is to control a machine to accept, transmit, or reproduce information and expression supplied by another source. The program is an integral part of the machine process. Control over the ability to duplicate the program in a machine-resident form may constitute control over the ability to duplicate the machine process—the organized flow of electrical impulses symbolizing information. In this form, there is an identity between process (idea) and expression that justifies denial of copyright in order to avoid monopolization of the process, a matter left to patent law under the current statutory scheme.

The basic copyright law issue concerns the extent to which copyright protection of the expression of the program can be segregated from prohibited control over the underlying machine process. Unlike other technologies, the connection between machine-resident program and computer process is close and direct, virtually inescapable. The need to distinguish expression and processs in copyright is recognized in both the statute and the legislative history of the Act. Section 102(b) of the Act expressly provides that in no event does copyright extend to control of a process described or an idea. Similarly, the legislative history of the Act expressly notes that in a computer program the expression of the

---

[72] See *Nat'l Comm'n on New Technological Uses of Copyrighted Works, Final Report* (1978).

programmer is the "copyrightable element . . . and the actual processes or methods embodied in the program are not within the scope of copyright law." [73]

Two approaches to distinguishing process and expression in this environment merit attention here. [74] The first applies Copyright Act standards for utilitarian objects to the machine-resident program. Generally, computer programs are classified under the copyright heading of "literary works." [75] However, this does not imply that all forms or products of a computer program should be so classified. For example, video game output (display) copyrights have been obtained as audiovisual works. [76] In machine-resident form, a computer program and its storage medium can be described as a "useful article," defined in the Act as an "article having an intrinsic utilitarian function that is not merely to portray the appearance of the article or to convey information." [77] This definition is used for "pictorial, graphic and sculptural works." The Act limits the copyright in the design of such works to expressive "features that can be identified separately from, and are capable of existing independently of, the utilitarian aspect of the article." [78]

This standard would focus on distinguishing utilitarian and expressive aspects of a program. For example, a program structured to receive

---

[73] HR Rep. No. 1476, 94th Cong., 2d Sess. 54 (1976); see also S. Rep. No. 473, 94th Cong., 1st Sess. 50–51 (1976).

[74] See *Nat'l Comm'n on New Technological Uses of Copyrighted Works, Final Report* (1978). In a dissent, Commissioner Hersey argued that all programs in machine form should be uncopyrightable, since they essentially are a "machine-control element, a mechanical device." Id. at 27. In contrast, Commissioner Nimmer suggested limiting copyright protection to programs that could produce copyrightable output. Id. at 27. Both proposals were rejected by the Commission.

[75] See Apple Computer, Inc. v. Franklin Computer Corp., 714 F2d 1240 (3d Cir. 1983).

[76] See Stern Elecs., Inc. v. Kaufman, 669 F2d 852 (2d Cir. 1982).

[77] 17 USC § 101 (1982).

[78] See Mazer v. Stein, 347 US 201 (1954); Fabrica, Inc. v. El Dorado Corp., 217 USPQ 698 (9th Cir. 1983); Kieselstein-Cord v. Accessories by Pearl, 632 F2d 989 (2d Cir. 1980); Gay Toys, Inc. v. Buddy L. Corp., 218 USPQ 13 (6th Cir. 1983); see Denicola, "Applied Art and Industrial Design: Copyright in Useful Articles," 67 Minn. L. Rev. 707 (1983); see also HR Rep. No. 1476, 94th Cong., 2d Sess. 55 (1976); S. Rep. No. 473, 94th Cong., 1st Sess. 51. "[If] an article has any utilitarian function, it can be denied copyright protection except to the extent that its artistic features can be identified separately and are capable of existing independently as a work of art." Fabrica, Inc. v. El Dorado Corp., 217 USPQ 698 (9th Cir. 1983). As to whether a particular item is a useful article, see Kieselstein-Cord v. Accessories by Pearl, 632 F2d 989 (2d Cir. 1980) (belt buckle is jewelry); Gay Toys, Inc. v. Buddy L. Corp., 218 USPQ 13 (6th Cir. 1983) (toy airplane has no intrinsic utilitarian function).

and record data might be uncopyrightable, while the chosen name for a variable or operation may be protected. In an operating system, this approach would substantially limit available protection under standards that are inherently unstable and imprecise.

The preferable alternative examines the extent to which copyright protection would in fact convey a monopoly over the process created by the program. An equivalence between program (expression) and machine process exists to the extent that there is only one or a very limited number of ways to express (i.e., a program) a particular machine process at the level of object code. If a variety of methods exists, copyright protection conveys important protection, but does not monopolize the process. This approach is preferable if for no other reason than that it focuses attention on the actual issue involved, rather than superimposing artificial distinctions between utilitarian and expressive aspects of a program. The restrictions of Section 102(b) are encountered only if there is no viable alternative means of implementing the process without copying the object code of the original work.

Several federal courts have reviewed this question. They were dealing with cases where there had been literal duplication of an operating system for use in a defendant's own line of computers. The economic incentive for such action involves ensuring that the second computer is capable of operating all of the software developed and available for the first computer. Especially for microcomputers or for potential users with prior investment in software, this is an important marketing step. However, even minor differences in an operating system may preclude use of some software. Hence, literal copying occurs.

The federal courts have concluded that a machine-resident operating system is copyrightable under the Act as now revised. For example, the court in *Tandy Corp. v. Personal Micro Computers, Inc.* [79] denied a motion to dismiss an infringement action based on alleged duplication of an "input-output routine" resident in a ROM chip. The defendant relied on the argument that the work should be fixed in a tangible medium of expression. In rejecting this defense, the court noted

> [An input-output routine] *tells* the computer how to take the information which is put into the computer . . . in one computer language and *translate* that . . . into a more simplified "machine" language which the computer can *understand*. . . . The imprinting of a computer program on a silicon chip, which then allows the computer to *read* the program and act upon its instructions, falls easily within

---

[79] 524 F. Supp. 171 (ND Cal. 1981).

[the statutory requirement of perceptability with the aid of a machine].[80]

As this decision indicates, the court's personification of the computer as being able to "read," "understand," and be told information allowed it to reach its conclusion with minimal analysis.

More careful discussion occurred in appellate decisions involving microcomputer operating system programs copyrighted by Apple Computer. In *Apple Computer, Inc. v. Formula International, Inc.*[81] the defendant admittedly duplicated Apple programs in its own commercial product. In response to Apple's motion for a preliminary injunction, Formula argued that "programs . . . designed and intended . . . to control computer operations and [that] do not directly produce the visual image or 'expression' which the computer user discerns" should be excluded from copyright.

Both the district and the circuit courts expressly rejected Formula's argument that machine-resident programs should be distinguished in terms of whether or not they directly produce expression perceived by the computer user. The circuit court relied on the fact that the Act did not expressly distinguish among types of programs and that the CONTU report had considered, but rejected, two arguments analogous to that asserted by Formula. Furthermore, the court suggested that the initial expression found in the nonmachine form of the programs was sufficient. "The computer program, when written embodies expression; never has the Copyright Act required that the expression be communicated to a particular audience."[82]

The court's analysis was inadequate. The alternative positions rejected by the CONTU report had little relationship to the position urged by Formula. One alternative, urged by Commissioner Hersey, was that *all* machine-resident programs should be excluded from copyright. This would have improperly encompassed even those programs that produce audiovisual or other copyrightable outputs. In contrast, the second alternative, mentioned by Vice Chairman Melville Nimmer, was that a distinction could be drawn granting copyright to works that in conjunction with the input of a computer user create copyrightable works. This would have based protection on the subsequent use of a program. Neither the Nimmer or Hersey proposals relate to copyright of a program not intended to produce communication to a human audience.

---

[80] Id. at 173 (emphasis added).

[81] 725 F2d 521, 221 USPQ 762 (9th Cir. 1984).

[82] 221 USPQ 765 (1984).

In dealing with the core question of whether a machine-resident operating system is an expression or has merged into an idea or a process, the circuit court correctly focused on the extent to which the operating system could be written in alternative forms. Merger of process and expression occurs only if no or merely a few alternative modes of expression exist. In concluding that the idea and expression did not merge, the court noted that "Apple introduced evidence that numerous methods exist for writing the programs. . . ." In fact, the evidence reported by the district court may not support this conclusion. It suggests that the circuit court ignored what may have been the most difficult issue presented in the case.

The district court had noted that the gravamen of Apple's position was that Formula should not be allowed "to market programs which perform the same function in the exact same manner" as Apple's.[83] It concluded that many methods existed for writing the subject programs. However, one function of an operating system is to provide an environment for operation of applications programs. The court cited testimony that numerous ways exist to write Apple-compatible operating systems capable of allowing operation of 98 percent of existing applications programs for use with Apple computers.

The circuit court assumed that these operating systems would perform the same function as those that were copied and that they represented alternative means of implementing the same process. But this conclusion requires further analysis. Certainly, for applications programs within the 2 percent range, the alternative operating system does not perform the same function or process. Could a formula for a chemical operation be copyrighted based on proof that altering one term of the formula would still produce 98 percent of the represented process? Could a defendant be forced to *use* that altered composition in its chemical process in order to avoid infringing the copyright? The degree of similarity necessary to conclude that two machine-resident programs perform the same process was not discussed. If less than 100 percent similarity is acceptable, copyright may control the process. In effect, that process can not be duplicated without infringing the copyright. It is possible to argue that in order to avoid establishing an indirect monopoly on a machine process through copyright law, a third party must have the ability to implement a 100 percent compatible process without infringing the copyright.

Compatability is practically and conceptually significant. The primary purpose for Formula's use of copyrighted programs is to access a

---

[83] See Apple Computer, Inc. v. Formula Int'l, Inc., 562 F. Supp. 775, 218 USPQ 47, 52 (CD Cal. 1983).

large market defined by compatible programs used with existing, popular machines. Compatibility allows the second manufacturer to benefit from a large base of existing software. In addition, use of the original program avoids substantial developmental costs and saves time. The issue in *Formula* was whether copyright stands as a barrier to this form of competition based on concepts of infringement.[84] The court answered yes without fully examining the implications of potentially foreclosing complete compatibility with the operating system process in Apple's product.

The second appellate review was in *Apple Computer, Inc. v. Franklin Computer Corp.*[85] *Franklin* involved the same programs and similar facts as *Formula*. In *Franklin*, the district court denied a preliminary injunction against use of duplicated machine-resident programs. The Third Circuit Court of Appeals reversed and remanded for further consideration. Before a final decision at the trial court level, Apple and Franklin entered into a settlement agreement.

The Third Circuit's analysis of the copyright issues in *Franklin* is generally regarded as establishing the copyrightability of operating system programs in machine form. In fact, the decision is more limited. The court concluded that operating system programs are not per se excluded and that the critical consideration is whether more than a limited number of ways exist to express the idea of the operating system. The court stopped short of even concluding that the particular programs in *Franklin* were copyrightable. It held that insufficient information existed to conclude that copyright of the operating programs would create a monopoly on the underlying process.

The Third Circuit concluded that contrary to concerns expressed by the district court, the mere transformation of a program from source to object code in a machine does not foreclose continuing copyright protection.[86] The court emphasized that this transformation retains and implements the communicative functions of the program. The current Act clearly does not require that a work be directly perceivable by a human in order to qualify for copyright protection. The circuit court also held that embodiment of a program on a ROM chip does not foreclose copyright protection based on *Williams Electronics, Inc. v. Arctic International, Inc.*[87]

---

[84] See Davis, "IBM PC Software and Hardware Compatibility," 1 Comp. Law. 11 (July 1984); Chertok, "Compatibility: Fair Use or Derivative Work," 2 CLR 1004 (1984).

[85] 714 F2d 1240 (3d Cir. 1983), cert. dismissed, 104 S. Ct. 690 (1984).

[86] See Williams Elecs. v. Arctic Int'l, Inc., 685 F2d 870 (3d Cir. 1982).

[87] 685 F2d 870 (3d Cir. 1982).

Franklin's main argument was that operating system programs in machine form should be per se excluded from copyright because an operating system program is a process or method of operation excluded under Section 102 and the earlier U.S. Supreme Court decision in *Baker v. Seldon*.[88] The Third Circuit rejected this argument and concluded that the embodiment of a program and the use of the program do not affect its status under copyright law. The mere fact that the program controls machine operations is not decisive. Such control is the function of all machine-resident programs, but at least some programs in this form are copyrightable. Further, the court noted that nothing in the legislative history or the statutory language of the Act suggests an intention to distinguish among various types of computer programs as to copyright protection.

The circuit court also rejected the argument that there is a per se merger of idea and expression in any operating system program. Instead, the correct issue is whether "other programs can be written or created which perform the same function as an Apple operating system program." If other programs can be written, the particular operating system program represents expression, separable from the underlying process. Thus, while operating system programs are not excluded per se, a case-by-case analysis is required. Exclusion depends on the interpretation of the underlying idea and proof of the extent to which the functions of the program can be performed by other programs. The case was remanded for factual findings on this issue.

The availability of alternative means of expression is the appropriate test for a merger of expression and process. However, in defining these alternatives, it is essential that an appropriate sensitivity be retained for the ability of second parties to implement identical processes with other programs. Mere similarity may be inadequate, since such a test implicitly conveys to the original author control over the specific process covered by its program. This result is prohibited by Section 102(b).

The availability of alternative means of expression with regard to operating systems is both legally and technologically complex. The circuit court rejected Franklin's claim that only a limited number of ways existed to program the machine to operate all Apple-compatible applications software. It noted

> This claim has no pertinence to either the idea/expression dichotomy or merger. . . . The idea of one of the operating system programs is, for example, how to translate source code into object code. If other methods of expressing that idea are not foreclosed . . . then there is

---

[88] 101 US 99 (1879).

no merger. Franklin may wish to achieve total compatibility ... but that is a commercial and competitive objective which does not enter into the somewhat metaphysical issue of whether particular ideas and expressions have merged.[89]

This analysis overstates the separation of commercial and doctrinal issues. One measure of whether the process originated by Apple can be duplicated consists of an analysis of whether existing applications programs for one operating system can be operated in another. Clearly, one primary function of an operating system is to provide an environment for application software, and the inability to replicate that function may indicate an inability to replicate the underlying process.

¶ 1.04 COMPUTER-ASSISTED WORKS

The copyrightability of a work produced by interaction of a user and a programmed computer is unclear. The increasing sophistication of programming techniques such as computer-assisted design ensures that these issues will become more important in the future.

The interaction between the user and a programmed machine can be viewed as a continuum. At one end, in the creation of a novel or a short story with a word processing program in a computer, the program contribution to the creative content of the final product is passive. The computer is a recording or transcription device. The final work is copyrightable by the user. In contrast, a computer programmed to generate detailed graphics with minimal input by the user (e.g., "select image number one") produces copyrightable material; but involves no creative input by the user. The author of the program has the appropriate claim to copyright of the images.

Between these extremes are various circumstances of substantially greater interaction between the user and the programmed machine. One illustration, previously discussed, involves the output of video games.[90] The program controls part of the display and the player controls another part. Nevertheless, copyrightability of the program aspects is satisfied by repetition of substantial sights and sounds generated by the program, not created by the user.[91]

---

[89] Apple Computer, Inc. v. Franklin Computer Corp., 714 F2d 1240 (3d Cir. 1983), cert. dismissed, 104 S. Ct. 690 (1984).

[90] See supra ¶ 1.03[4][b].

[91] See Stern Elecs., Inc. v. Kaufman, 669 F2d 852 (2d Cir. 1982); Midway Mfg. Co. v. Arctic Int'l, Inc., 704 F2d 870 1009 (7th Cir. 1983); Williams Elecs. v. Arctic Int'l, Inc., 685 F2d 870 (3d Cir. 1982).

In discussing computer-assisted works, the CONTU report focused on the argument that a work produced with a computer might be said to have been created by the computer, rather than by the user. This potential is associated with the field of artificial intelligence. In attributing authorship, a minimum standard of human creativity or originality must be met. The CONTU report indicates that this element will typically be attributable to the user.

> [Who] is the author of a work produced through the use of a computer [?] The obvious answer is that the author is the one who employs the computer. . . . Both the program and the data [in a computer] may be copyrighted works. The question has been raised whether authorship . . . of the program or database establishes . . . a claim of authorship of the final work. It appears to the Commission that authorship of the program or of the input data is entirely separate from authorship of the final work. [92]

This view is appropriate for passive forms of computer programs, but should be rejected where the program directly controls substantial aspects of the expression of the final work. In that case, authorship is properly in the programmer. [93]

The CONTU report misstates the issue. Whenever a computer and a user interact to produce a final work, substantial elements of human effort (most often creativity) contribute to the final product. The issue is one of assigning relative creative input between the user and the author of the program in the work itself. From the standpoint of the program author, the issue is whether the program directly controls substantial elements of the final product independent of creative input by the user. From the user's standpoint, the issue is whether in selection, arrangement, or composition the user has made a direct, creative impact on the final product.

In most current applications, allocation of creative contribution is relatively straightforward. For example, in many programs a user inputs numerical data, and the programmed computer converts this to statistical or tabular form. This final product differs from either the input data or the general, statistical, or tabular formats built into the program. In discussing the copyrightability of the completed table, the choice is not between the user and the machine, but between the user and the program author. What are the contributions of each to the final expression and do they display sufficient creativity to conclude that the authorship lies with

---

[92] See *Nat'l Comm'n on New Technological Uses of Copyrighted Works, Final Report* 112–113 (1978).

[93] See Stern Elecs., Inc. v. Kaufman, 669 F2d 852 (2d Cir. 1982); Williams Elecs. v. Arctic Int'l, Inc., 685 F2d 870 (3d Cir. 1982).

one or both parties? In this particular illustration, the program author contributed a means for calculation and a blank form for expression. This output is not copyrightable. In contrast, the user selected the data, the math analyses, and a particular display. The selections satisfy standards of originality and creativity.[94]

The issue is more complex where the programmed computer accepts data and outputs textual or expressive material based on criteria not selected or controlled by the user. For example, medical programs exist that, using data symbolizing expert knowledge, produce analytical and advisory text to guide a doctor's decisions.[95] The user merely enters factual data and the program selects among various displays. This sequence provides no basis for copyright for the user. In contrast, the program author enabled the system to select and reproduce text. To the extent that there is a potential for substantial repetition of this creative product, the programmer is the author.

The difficulty intensifies as the relationship between the program author and user to the final product becomes more indirect. For example, in a currently experimental program the user can input a general plot and the system generates text to express the plot. Such systems are not yet a commercial reality, but they do present significant issues in attributing creativity. The user contributes a general plot (i.e., an idea), but controls none of the specific expression. The program author may have no direct role in creating specific sentences, except by programming rules of selection that apply grammatical or other principles. The appropriate conclusion may be that neither person has contributed sufficiently to the final text to claim it as an original work of authorship.

¶ 1.05 MASKS AND CHIP TOPOLOGY

A major factor in the expansion of the role of computers has been the rapid advances in techniques for implanting circuitry on silicon chips

---

[94] See Rand McNally & Co. v. Fleet Management Sys., Inc., 221 USPQ 828 (ND Ill. 1983) (copyright protection for mileage charts and other compiled facts); Miller v. Universal Studios, Inc., 650 F2d 1365 (5th Cir. 1981); Schroeder v. William Morrow & Co., 566 F2d 3 (7th Cir. 1977); Denicola, "Copyright in Collections of Facts; A Theory for Protection of Nonfiction Literary Works," 81 Colum. L. Rev. 561 (1981); *Nimmer on Copyright* § 2.11[A].

[95] See Norris & Szabo, "Forward: Removing Some Impediments to Development of America's Third and Fourth Generation Health Care Delivery Systems," 7 Am. J. L. & Med. v (1981); Brannigan & Dayhoff, "Liability for Personal Injuries Caused by Defective Medical Computer Programs," 7 Am. J. L. & Med. 123 (1981).

and other semiconductor media. The processes and products of this aspect of the industry may be protected under patent or trade secret law, but beyond that there has been interest in encompassing circuitry design within copyright law because of the relative ease with which the designs can be duplicated. Also, patent protection is available only to novel, non-obvious subject matter and may not apply to relatively small but significant chip design changes.[96]

The copyright issues focus on two related stages of circuitry manufacture and design. In the manufacturing process, substantial effort is made to specify the microcircuitry's functions and the design or layout of the circuitry. These factors affect both speed and reliability of processing and largely determine the commercial viability of a microchip.

The first stage of concern is a depiction of the planned circuitry: the so-called mask. Functionally, a mask is analogous to an electrical circuit drawing except that it is employed directly in the manufacturing process. Photographic and chemical processes directly implant the design and circuits on the chip, although in some cases the design may be written directly onto the silicon wafer via an electron beam. The second stage at which protection is important involves the chip itself that contains the embedded circuitry generated from the design.

Traditional copyright law provides little or no protection for the mask or the embedded circuitry. While it is settled that technical drawings may be subject to copyright as "pictorial, graphic or sculptural" works,[97] copyright of these drawings does not extend to manufacturing the item itself.[98] The specific question is whether or at what point in moving from original design to a mask there is a movement from expression to the process of manufacture. It can be argued that masks are parts of a manufacturing process and are not copyrightable under standard tests. However, even if copyright covers this phase of manufacturing, the exclusion of copyright for ideas or processes reduces effective protection, since the mask is the sole manner in which the design idea can be expressed.

Similarly, the topology or imprinted circuit design was potentially noncopyrightable. A manufactured chip represents a "useful article."[99] The Act expressly limits protection to those aspects of the design of a useful article that can be described, independent of its utilitarian func-

---

[96] See ¶ 2.15.

[97] See, e.g., WPOW, Inc. v. MRLJ Enters., 222 USPQ 502 (DDC 1984); Tompkins Graphics, Inc. v. Zipatone, Inc., 222 USPQ 49 (ED Pa. 1983).

[98] See HR Rep. No. 1476, 94th Cong., 2d Sess. 105 (1976).

[99] 17 USC § 101 (1982).

tions.[100] In chip topology, however, the design is integral to the functional characteristics.

These barriers, coupled with the economic and technical significance of microchip designs, led to the enactment of protective legislation. The Semiconductor Chip Protection Act of 1984 (Chip Act) was enacted with the intention of resolving uncertainties in copyright treatment of semiconductor masks and products.[101] Significantly, while the Chip Act provides civil remedies for unauthorized duplication of mask works, it was not enacted merely to fit these works within a copyright framework. Given the uncertain connection between expression, process, idea, and object in this environment, traditional concepts of copyright law are quite clearly inappropriate. The "measure . . . does not engage in the fatal flaw of treating books and mask works similarly."[102] Rather, the Chip Act was regarded as the first new form of intellectual property law enacted in 100 years and as an explicit federal recognition of a right in industrial property independent of patent or copyright.

The Chip Act represents a unique blend of copyright, patent, and trade secret concepts designed to focus legal protection squarely on those acts of semiconductor piracy that create the greatest risk to continued technological growth in this area: unauthorized and literal duplication of chips for commercial exploitation. At the same time, a registration system and certain exceptions to the owner's exclusive rights protect the traditional right of third parties to conduct reverse engineering and technology-improvement analysis.

The core protections of the Chip Act in part resemble copyright law. Protection is made available for a "mask work fixed in a semiconductor chip product"[103] if the work was first commercially exploited in this country or is owned by a U.S. national or domiciliary or by a foreign national from a country that is a party to a treaty protecting mask works to which the United States is a signatory. The owner of a qualifying work that is not excluded by other provisions of the Chip Act receives the exclusive right for ten years to reproduce the work or license reproduction of the mask work.[104] In addition, the Chip Act encompasses rights more

---

[100] See Mazer v. Stein, 347 US 201 (1954); Fabrica, Inc. v. El Dorado Corp., 217 USPQ 698 (9th Cir. 1983); Kieselstein-Cord v. Accessories by Pearl, 632 F2d 989 (2d Cir. 1980); Gay Toys, Inc. v. Buddy L. Corp., 218 USPQ 13 (6th Cir. 1983); see Denicola, "Applied Art and Industrial Design: Copyright in Useful Articles," 67 Minn. L. Rev. 707 (1983).

[101] 17 USC §§ 900 et seq. See 13 Cong. Rec. 11,602–11,616 (October 9, 1984).

[102] 13 Cong. Rec. 11,611 (remarks of Rep. Kastenmeier).

[103] 17 USC § 902(a)(7) (1984).

[104] 17 USC § 905 (1984).

analogous to patent law in that it also grants the owner exclusive rights to import or distribute any semiconductor chip product embodying the mask work. The owner of the proprietary rights to the mask work is entitled to actual damages for any infringement of these exclusive rights or, at its option, statutory damages not to exceed $250,000.[105]

The unique blend of intellectual property concepts is best seen in other provisions of the Chip Act. Initially, unlike under the copyright system, protection of a mask work did not automatically arise or continue under federal law without action by the owner. Section 904 of the Chip Act provides that protection of the mask work does not commence until the work is registered or until it is first commercially exploited anywhere in the world. Protections prior to these affirmative steps by the owner are left to state trade secrecy law.

While the commencement of protection is triggered by either of these events, the Chip Act establishes a mandatory registration system that is more analogous to patent than copyright law. Under Section 908 of the Chip Act protection terminates unless the mask work is registered within two years of the date that it is first commercially exploited anywhere in the world.[106] The registration system does not involve mere filing of material, but consists of an application and review process in which the owner is required to submit such information as is required by the Registrar of Copyrights bearing on "preparation or identification" of the work, the existence of protection under the Chip Act, or ownership.[107] The Chip Act provides that the Registrar will register the work if it is entitled to protection under the Chip Act and also provides for judicial review of a negative decision on registration.[108] As of early 1985, regulations concerning the required information or the methods for decision-making had not been issued.

The foregoing implies that unlike copyright law, the Chip Act clearly contemplates that claims for protection will not automatically be registered and that not all mask works will be protected. The standard for determining the suitability of a work for protection under the Chip Act again reflects a mixture of copyright and patent standards. As under copyright law, the Chip Act expressly provides that in no case shall protection extend to any "idea, procedure, process . . . concept [or] principle," however explained or embodied in the work.[109] Yet, the Chip Act

---

[105] 17 USC § 911 (1984).
[106] 17 USC § 908 (1984).
[107] 17 USC § 908(c) (1984).
[108] 17 USC § 908(e)(g) (1984).
[109] 17 USC § 902 (1984).

goes beyond this exclusion and applies standards of originality and novelty that while less exacting than under patent law, are intended to require some threshold level of originality for protection. Specifically, protection is not available under the Chip Act if the work is not original or if it consists of designs that are "staple, commonplace, or familiar in the semiconductor industry."

A final area of protection covers the rights of third parties to use a product to discover underlying processes or ideas and improve on them in a subsequent product. As discussed in Chapter 3, limitations on control of nonpatented technology have historically included "reverse engineering"—the right of third parties to use and closely inspect distributed products to discover and then adopt technologies innovated by the initial party. Section 905 of the Chip Act provides that the owner's exclusive rights are not infringed if the work is reproduced "solely for the purpose of teaching, analyzing, or evaluating the concepts or techniques . . . or the circuitry, logic flow, or organization . . . used in the mask work."[110] This protects the right of discovery through reverse engineering. However, the Chip Act goes further and provides that there is no infringement if the person who does the analysis incorporates the results in a subsequent mask work that is to be distributed.[111]

One effect of the Chip Act is to place issues about protection of rights in mask works and semiconductor products in a framework not encumbered by copyright concepts that do not have direct relevance to the subject matter policy. Furthermore, the Chip Act expressly recognizes the historic right of third parties to engage in additive development of technology that has been distributed without infringing underlying intellectual property rights. In essence, the technology pirate is subject to civil liability, while the competing technology or scientific developer is free to use information and data rightfully acquired.

PART B. INFRINGEMENT

¶ 1.06 GENERAL STANDARDS

Assuming copyrightability and compliance with statutory requirements, an author may enforce certain exclusive rights in a work. These include the exclusive right to reproduce the work, to distribute copies, and to prepare derivative works.[112] Under the terms of the Act, a person

---

[110] 17 USC § 906(a) (1984).

[111] 17 USC § 906(a)(2) (1984).

[112] 17 USC § 106 (1982).

who acts in violation of these exclusive rights infringes the copyright and may be subject to civil or criminal liability.

The exclusive right to reproduce (copy) a work is the basic copyright power. It is intended to encourage both creation and dissemination of creative works by providing a mechanism for the author to secure financial benefits through licensing or otherwise charging for reproduction of his work. The clearest infringement of this right involves unauthorized, literal duplication of the original work. Literal copying is prohibited if the work is protected and copyrightable. More difficult cases arise where substantially less than all of the first work is literally copied in the second or where the similarity of the two works involves structure or feel without literal duplication of any specific images or words.

An action for infringing a copyright by unauthorized reproduction requires: (1) proof that the original is copyrighted by the plaintiff; and (2) proof that the defendant engaged in unauthorized reproduction.[113] The second point requires distinguishing between works copied from the original and works that were independently created. Copyright protection does not preclude independent creation of even identical works. Most often, copying is established indirectly from two criteria. First, it must be demonstrated that the defendant had access to the original work. In the absence of access, any similarities in the works must result from independent creation. Second, it must be shown that there is substantial similarity between the two works sufficient to support a conclusion that the defendant copied the original. A definition of substantial similarity depends on value judgments that balance the interests of the first author against a desire not to limit the creative expression of other authors.

Copyright protection extends to expression, but does not preclude reproduction or use of the ideas, concepts, or processes expressed. This premise, important to copyrightability, is also significant on questions about whether allegedly similar works infringe the original copyright. The statutory mandate is that copyright conveys no control over ideas, processes, and the like. If describing similarities in two works as infringement would create this result, the similarities should be viewed as acceptable, based on privileged similarity of ideas rather than unauthorized reproduction.[114]

---

[113] See *Nimmer on Copyright* § 13.01.

[114] See Sid & Marty Krofft Television v. McDonald's Corp., 562 F2d 1157, 1164 (9th Cir. 1977) ("There ... must be substantial similarity not only of the general ideas but of the expressions of those ideas as well."); Atari, Inc. v. North Am. Phillips Consumer Elecs. Corp., 672 F2d 607 (7th Cir.), cert. denied, 103 S. Ct. 176 (1982).

This issue can be viewed in two ways. First, as a technical matter, a determination must be made about which aspects of a work are unprotected ideas and which are protectible expression. Such judgments can be expressed in various ways, but are inherently unstable. A definition of what constitutes expression and what constitutes idea is a subjective judgment about the work and about whether protection should be granted against a specific subsequent work. This leads to different conceptions of idea and expression for different forms of copyrighted works with generally greater protection given to creative fictional works as contrasted to factual or utilitarian works.[115]

The subjective and inherently uncertain nature of the technical analysis justifies explicit recognition of a second level of analysis in infringement cases. In defining the scope of the unprotected idea, a court reaches a decision that shapes both the degree of protection for the original author and the appropriate degree of freedom preserved for subsequent authors. This trade-off can be addressed directly rather than indirectly. The first author is increasingly protected as the idea of a work is defined in broader, nonspecific terms. Given a broad definition, most of the work constitutes "expression." This result, however, limits the freedom for potential second authors. The converse is equally true.[116] Especially in cases involving developing technologies, courts must consider not only the technical issue, but also the express balance that must be drawn.

The distinction between ideas and expression is frequently litigated for works of fiction, and there is seldom a problem where the second work involves substantial duplication of the words of the first author. A greater difficulty exists if there is little or no identity in the language used, but the plot or characters are similar. The traditional approach to this problem is described as follows:

> Upon any work, and especially upon a play, a great number of patterns of increasing generality will fit equally well, as more and more of the incident is left out. The last may perhaps be no more than the most general statement of what the play is about . . . but there is a

---

[115] Compare Atari, Inc. v. North Am. Phillips Consumer Elecs. Corp., 672 F2d 607 (7th Cir.), cert. denied, 103 S. Ct. 176 (1982); Mazer v. Stein, 347 US 201 (1954); Dow Jones & Co. v. Board of Trade, 217 USPQ 901 (SDNY 1982). See Landsberg v. Scrabble Crossword Game Players, Inc., 221 USPQ 1140 (9th Cir. 1983); Sid & Marty Krofft Television v. McDonald's Corp., 562 F2d 1157, 1167–1168 (9th Cir. 1977).

[116] See, e.g., Mattel, Inc. v. Azrak-Hamway Int'l, 221 USPQ 302 (2d Cir. 1983) (similarity of dolls due to similar ideas where idea defined as "superhuman muscleman crouching in . . . a traditional fighting position"); Innovative Concepts, Inc. v. Entertainment Enters. Ltd., 221 USPQ 376 (EDNY 1983) (infringement of hockey player figures and game board's configuration of 'snow').

point in this series of abstractions where they are no longer protected since otherwise the playwright could prevent use of his ideas to which apart from their expression his property is never extended.[117]

Judgment about the nature or scope of the unprotectible idea will vary from case to case, but should be colored by the nature of the balance being drawn. One approach would define nonliteral copying as outside the purview of copyright. However, adherence to this view would substantially chill the creativity encouraged by copyright. In works of fiction, for example, there is substantial creativity in elements of character, structure, and plot. Granting copyright protection to these elements of the work does not substantially impede subsequent authors in light of the virtually infinite variations in plot and character available to the fiction writer. As a result, nonliteral similarity may support an action for infringement of fiction works.[118] The analysis in such cases considers which portions of a work are sufficiently central to justify protection against unauthorized use. Analysis will differ depending on the type of work involved and the range of alternatives available to subsequent authors.

One theme often employed to establish appropriate distinctions has been described as "scenes à faire." This consists of standard expressions that can be expected to appear in works of a particluar type. Because of their frequent, general use, they are regarded as unprotected elements of any work within which they appear.[119] This concept is typically involved in cases in which at least some of the second work replicates the first. Certain expressions or images are so common, given a similarity of structure, idea, or purpose, as to be insufficient to support an action for infringement. It is often suggested that these expressions are not copyrightable. It is also possible to observe that some literal duplication is inherent and will not, in itself, support a claim of copying.[120]

Given less than complete reproduction of the original work, the distinction between infringement and permitted use turns on the uniqueness and importance of the duplicated material to the original work and the need to permit subsequent authors to express their thoughts on the same subject. This latter issue becomes more acute when considering works with more structured expression and functional objectives than artistic

---

[117] Nichols v. Universal Pictures Co., 45 F2d 119, 121 (2d Cir. 1930).

[118] See Landsberg v. Scrabble Crossword Game Players, Inc., 221 USPQ 1140 (9th Cir. 1983).

[119] See See v. Durang, 711 F2d 141, 143 (9th Cir. 1983); Atari, Inc. v. North Am. Phillips Consumer Elecs. Corp., 672 F2d 607 (7th Cir.), cert. denied, 103 S. Ct. 176 (1982).

[120] *Nimmer on Copyright* § 13.03.

works. The goal of leaving ideas unprotected and the recognition of standard forms of expression may merge to substantially reduce protection. For example, in an architectural drawing, there is no copyright protection for the use of 90 degree angles in room corners or specific means of depicting a window or door. The expression is central to the work, but involves limited variations and standardized use. Barring subsequent use of these symbols by others would hinder, rather than promote and protect, creativity.[121]

This is not meant to suggest that no protection is given to such works. Rather, especially as the initial work is more structured, austere, and utilitarian, a point is reached where the idea and expression merge in such a way that only unauthorized, literal duplication is barred by copyright.[122] In essence, due to the nature of the work, the policy underlying copyright law draws the line of protection towards literal copying in order to ensure the free use of ideas and symbols by other authors. One authority describes this in terms of appropriating "copyrightable elements."[123] Infringement occurs only if those elements are copied and, given the nature of the work, significant similarities may occur even if there is no such appropriation.

The comparison of fictional and technical works suggests a basic distinction in copyright law. Expansive interpretation of protection for works of fiction may be justified to truly protect the author and does not substantially restrict subsequent authors. Conversely, in areas of technical, structured authorship, extension substantially beyond literal copying is not warranted to protect the author and would substantially affect subsequent authors.

In either event, the focus in substantial similarity cases is on the degree of similarity and not on whether the alleged infringer also made creative contributions.[124] In general, courts have examined similarity in terms of whether an ordinary observer would regard the two works as substantially similar in that the second work captures the unique expression or aesthetic appeal of the first.[125] Phrased solely in terms of the

---

[121] See Tompkins Graphics, Inc. v. Zipatone, Inc., 222 USPQ 49 (ED Pa. 1983).

[122] See Affiliated Hospital Prods., Inc. v. Mercer Game Mfg. Co., 513 F2d 1183, 1188 (2d Cir. 1975); Decorative Aides Corp. v. Staple Sewing Aides Corp., 497 F. Supp. 154 (SDNY 1980), aff'd, 657 F2d 262 (2d Cir. 1981). Compare Morrissey v. Procter & Gamble Co., 379 F2d 675 (1st Cir. 1967).

[123] *Nimmer on Copyright* §§ 2.18[A]–2.18[D].

[124] Id. at § 13.03[B].

[125] See Durham Indus., Inc. v. Tomy Corp., 630 F2d 905, 912 (2d Cir. 1980); Franklin Mint Corp. v. National Wildlife Art Exch., 575 F2d 62, 64 (3d

reaction of the audience to the two works, this approach has been criticized.[126] In practice, recent cases have retained the general standard, but have formulated various analytical models that differentiate between ordinary audience reaction and permissible similarities of ideas, scenes à faire, or other factors.[127] While the law may be uncertain, the basic tension is apparent. There is a need to blend nonexpert audience reaction and closer, analytical examination. If a work does not appear to an audience to be substantially similar to another, no wrongful appropriation occurred. However, even if there is apparent similarity, it is essential to determine whether the similarity is caused by duplication of unprotectible elements of the first work.[128]

¶ 1.07 AUDIOVISUAL COPIES

Audiovisual displays and other outputs generated by a computer program are copyrightable subject matter, independent of any copyright for source code and object code.[129] The copyrightability of this subject matter has been most frequently litigated in the context of commercially distributed video games. In that setting, copyright requirements that a work be original and fixed in a tangible medium of expression are met by a "substantial repetition of the sights and sounds" of the game.[130]

The earliest video game cases involved literal duplication of the entire game including all pertinent sights and sounds. More recent cases have involved modifications of the original work[131] or games that were allegedly similar to the original, but not identical. In these cases, the courts have applied standards of substantial similarity analogous to those developed in other contexts.

Cir. 1978); Atari, Inc. v. North Am. Phillips Consumer Elecs. Corp., 672 F2d 607 (7th Cir.), cert. denied, 103 S. Ct. 176 (1982); Sid & Marty Krofft Television v. McDonald's Corp., 562 F2d 1157, 1164–1165 (9th Cir. 1977).

[126] *Nimmer on Copyright* § 13.03[D].

[127] See Atari, Inc. v. North Am. Phillips Consumer Elecs. Corp., 672 F2d 607 (7th Cir.), cert. denied, 103 S. Ct. 176 (1982); Sid & Marty Krofft Television v. McDonald's Corp., 562 F2d 1157, 1164–1165 (9th Cir. 1977).

[128] See, e.g., Atari, Inc. v. Amusement World, Inc., 547 F. Supp. 222 (D. Md. 1981); Midway Mfg. v. Dirkenschneider, 543 F. Supp. 466 (D. Neb. 1981); Williams Elecs., Inc. v. Bally Mfg. Corp., 220 USPQ 1091 (ND Ill. 1983).

[129] See supra ¶ 1.03[4].

[130] See Stern Elecs., Inc. v. Kaufman, 669 F2d 852 (2d Cir. 1982); Williams Elecs. v. Arctic Int'l, Inc., 685 F2d 870 (3d Cir. 1982).

[131] See infra ¶ 1.13.

In *Atari, Inc. v. North American Phillips Consumer Electronics Corp.*,[132] Atari sought a preliminary injunction against distribution of the game "K.C. Munchkin," allegedly copied from Atari's copyrighted game "PAC-MAN." The Seventh Circuit Court of Appeals concluded that there was sufficient similarity between the two games to justify the preliminary injunction. The court characterized both games as maze-chase games in which the player moves a central character through a maze pursued by various other characters. In both games a gobbler proceeds "through the maze consuming dots and avoiding capture by the [ghost] monsters; by gobbling a power capsule, the player can reverse the roles [of the gobbler and ghosts]; and the ultimate goal is to accumulate the most points by gobbling dots and monsters."[133] Within this framework, the color, structure, and appearance of the mazes as well as the configuration of escape tunnels for the gobbler differed. There were differences in the shape and color of the characters. However, the ghost characters conveyed significant similarities, and the gobbler characters shared a distinctive V-shaped mouth.

The court concluded that sufficient similarity existed to grant the preliminary injunction based on the probable success of the infringement claim. The court applied a two-pronged test requiring: (1) a determination of whether copying occurred; and (2) a determination of whether the copying was improper. The court focused on the second issue and noted that an ordinary observer test should be applied, which must be accompanied by "dissection" of the works to exclude similarities based on unprotectible ideas and "incidents, characters or settings which are as a practical matter indispensable, or at least standard in the treatment of a given topic." Based on this approach, the court characterized PAC-MAN as a maze-chase game in which various items were scenes à faire protected only against identical reproduction, if at all. However, there was an infringement in the substantial appropriation of the PAC-MAN characters.

> The expression of the central character as a "gobbler"and the pursuit characters as "ghost monsters" distinguishes PAC-MAN from conceptually similar video games.... PAC-MAN's particular artistic interpretation of the game was designed to ... appeal to a nonviolent player personality. The game as such, however, does not dictate the use of a "gobbler" and "ghost monsters." ... North American not only adopted the same basic characters but also portrayed them in a

---

[132] 672 F2d 607 (7th Cir.), cert. denied, 103 S. Ct. 176 (1982)
[133] Id. at 611.

manner which made K.C. Munchkin appear substantially similar to PAC-MAN. [134]

Given the substantial similarity in the characters, the court rejected as immaterial various specific differences in the games, noting that the ordinary observer test focuses on overall impression, rather than minute differences. This was especially true in a video game where users are generally undiscriminating as to subtle differences in the relevant images. The infringing game copied the "total concept and feel" of the original work.

In contrast to *North American*, the district court in *Atari, Inc. v. Amusement World, Inc.*[135] concluded that there were insufficient similarities in the games of "Meteors" and "Asteroids." In *Amusement World*, both games involved a central figure portrayed as a spaceship that destroyed rocks floating past it by firing projectiles. There were differences in the design and color of the rocks. The court concluded that the defendant had obtained the idea for Meteors from the then commercially popular Asteroids game and that the similarity in the games was due to the transposition of idea, rather than expression. "[The similarities are] inevitable, given the requirements of the *idea* of a game involving *a spaceship combating space rocks* and given the technical demands of the medium of a videogame." As in *North American*, after discounting similarities based on the idea of the game, the court examined the remaining elements and concluded that the differences (e.g., color and design) were particularly significant and contradicted a finding of substantially similar expression.

The key to these results is the specificity or level of abstraction used in defining the idea of the game.[136] The court in *Amusement World* could have characterized the idea as a game involving the destruction of threatening objects by a central figure. Under this characterization, the choice of similar objects (spaceship or rocks) might be viewed as infringement. In contrast, the *North American* court could have defined the idea as a game involving ghost figures and a gobbler in a maze. Under that view, the particular characters are unprotected. These hypothetical recharacterizations would alter the outcome in both cases, since they would redefine the protectible expression in the games.

---

[134] Id. at 617–618.

[135] 547 F. Supp. 222 (D. Md. 1981).

[136] Similar analyses have been applied in all reported video game cases with a similar importance attached to the definition of the unprotected idea. See Midway Mfg. v. Dirkenschneider, 543 F. Supp. 466 (D. Neb. 1981); Williams Elecs. Inc. v. Bally Mfg. Corp., 220 USPQ 1091 (ND Ill. 1983).

These cases illustrate the elasticity of the idea-expression distinction. However, the results are neither arbitrary nor necessarily inconsistent. In seeking an appropriate level of abstraction for the idea content of a work, there is a need to balance protection of the original author's creative expression against the avoidance of a monopoly and the resulting restraint on subsequent authors. One method is to identify the commercially or artistically central elements of the first work and then to inquire what the effect of protecting these would be on subsequent works. In PAC-MAN, the particular gobbler character was central to the success of the work and had become well-known and widely recognized. To draw a level of abstraction that would not protect this character would allow a central element of the work to be appropriated. However, even with the character protected, there was a wide range available for subsequent works, involving even ghosts and gobblers, since the figures can be drawn in numerous ways. In contrast, the particular shape of the rocks in Asteroids was less significant to the success of that game than the concept of a space encounter with objects to be destroyed. However, protecting the rock images would unnecessarily restrict subsequent works on the same subject, since there are limited ways to express a rock in two-dimensional form. Protecting the concept of a space encounter itself would be even more restrictive of subsequent work.

¶ 1.08 SOURCE AND OBJECT CODE COPIES

Source code is copyrightable independent of the output generated by the program. Object or machine code may be directly copyrightable or, at least, protected as a copy of the source code or the program output.[137] As a result, most programs are protected under copyright law. Nevertheless, the degree of protection that is or should be available is substantially uncertain. Resolving this issue requires consideration of fair use and similar protections for third parties in the copyright system. Beyond these protections, however, there is the substantively difficult task of distinguishing ideas and expression in the highly structured environment of source and machine-coded programs. The result is that the scope of protection beyond that denying literal duplication of a program is unclear.

[1] Literal Duplication

The difficulty of distinguishing idea and expression in a coded program is generally immaterial where there is literal and complete duplica-

---

[137] See ¶ 1.03[5].

tion of the program code. One effect of concluding that program code is copyrightable is that the machine-resident program is protected against literal duplication. Thus, even absent copyright of the output of a program, if there are copyrightable elements in the underlying code, reproduction for commercial use is prohibited.[138] Literal duplication of a copyrighted program is an infringement unless the program itself does not represent copyrightable subject matter because of an identity between the expression and idea of the program.

Assuming copyrightable subject matter, literal duplication cases focus on what forms of copying are permitted by statutory exemptions.[139] It is also necessary to define what conduct constitutes reproduction of a program. In most cases, this latter question is not difficult, since the infringing act involves permanent, physical reproduction of a program on paper, disk, or other media for subsequent use or marketing. In such cases, it is obvious that a copy of the program code has been made.

It is potentially more difficult to determine whether input of a program into a computer represents the preparation of a copy that may infringe the underlying copyright. This is significant for reverse engineering and the copyright owner's right to restrict use of a program and is discussed in Chapters 4 and 5.[140] In general, however, the Act makes it relatively clear that the input of copyrighted material into a computer results in the preparation of a copy of that work. A copy is made whenever the work is fixed on a tangible medium from which it can be reproduced or perceived directly or with the aid of a machine. Although seemingly addressed more to the reproduction of traditional works in a computer, the Act is also applicable to computer programs. Loading a computer program from a diskette into the memory of a computer makes a new copy of the work. Of course, in most cases, the owner of the diskette has authority to make this additional copy by either statute or contract.[141]

---

[138] See generally Dow Jones & Co. v. Board of Trade, 217 USPQ 901 (SDNY 1982); Harcourt Brace and World, Inc. v. Graphic Controls Corp., 329 F. Supp. 517 (SDNY 1971) (protection of answer sheets against literal copying where symbols and design are unique to standardized testing process). Compare Morrissey v. Procter & Gamble Co., 379 F2d 675 (1st Cir. 1967) (no protection at all where very limited number of ways to express an idea as in an instruction set for a game). See also *Nimmer on Copyright* §§ 2.18[A]–2.18[D].

[139] See discussion infra at ¶ 1.11.

[140] See ¶¶ 4.06, 5.15[1].

[141] See infra ¶ 1.11[1].

[2] Substantial Similarity in Coded Programs

In the absence of literal duplication, the general standard for copyright infringement requires determining whether there is substantial similarity between the original work and the alleged copy. This is difficult in any environment, especially for coded computer programs where the issue of infringement is separate from questions concerning the program output.

When the alleged infringing copy does not duplicate the original in full, the question is whether and to what extent similarities in the works result from copied expression or from a similarity of unprotected ideas. In source or machine code form, computer programs have a number of characteristics that make this determination difficult. First, programs are written in a highly structured and limited language. Second, the available expressive options for the programmer are also restricted by the functional or utilitarian purposes of the medium. Depending on the type of program, coding may create expressive output for communication to humans or instruct a machine to perform specific functions; all programmers, in any case, try to write instructions that operate the machine most efficiently. This common goal encourages similarity in coding. While different programmers may use different methods or sequential operations, these may fall within the realm of unprotected idea, rather than expression. Assuming identical sequencing in two programs, identical idea, and identical programming language, there are limited expressive options.

These characteristics are encountered in other applications of copyright to technical or utilitarian works. The existence of limited, expressive alternatives affects the scope of copyright protection. There is clearly a need to calibrate the protection of the original expression so as not to pre-empt other applications of the technology.

> [That] a work is copyrighted says very little about the scope of its protection. . . . As a work embodies more in the way of particularized expression it . . . receives broader copyright protection. [The] "strongest" works [are those in] which fairly complex or fanciful artistic expressions predominate over relatively simplistic themes and which are almost entirely products of the author's creativity rather than concomitants of those themes.[142]

The scope of protection should be connected to the type of work involved. Some programs implement artistic and complex outputs, and

---

[142] Atari, Inc. v. North Am. Phillips Consumer Elecs. Corp., 672 F2d 607 (7th Cir.), cert. denied, 103 S. Ct. 176 (1982).

the expressive activity inherent in the coding that produces this output merits protection, even absent copyright of the output. Furthermore, that protection can often be implemented without infringing on other creative works, since the range of potential expression is broad. In contrast, a program oriented to efficient internal operation of a computer is more standardized and associated with the underlying process or idea. A high degree of similarity should be required to find infringement. Lesser standards might fail to avoid de facto monopolization of technical processes. In this programming environment, creativity lies substantially in the development of sequences and structures that are thematic in nature and potentially unprotectible. The options available for expressing a structure or sequence in a given programming language are limited and substantially dependent on stereotyped phrases or commands.

The earliest cases dealing with similarity in coded programs reflect inadequate development of the idea-expression distinction. The earliest relevant case was a district court opinion in *Synercom Technologies v. University Computing Co.*[143] *Synercom* involved a variety of issues encompassing several forms of alleged infringement; one of which was that the defendants developed and used an input format for a structural analysis program identical to the format previously copyrighted by Synercom. The Synercom format involved manual preordering of data prior to entry into the program. The forms for this prearrangement of data were contained in published manuals. Since Synercom's overall program was a commercial success, the defendant's new program was designed to accept identical input formats, accomplished with the aid of a preprocessor program that made the defendant's program compatible with Synercom inputs. The FORTRAN statements in the preprocessor program were "derived directly and precisely from the copyrighted manual card formats." Synercom argued that this constituted an infringing translation of its copyrighted work.

The court characterized the issue as whether the "sequence and ordering" admittedly copied by the defendant was a protectible expression or an unprotectible idea. It concluded that the sequencing was an unprotectible idea, analogizing it to an automobile manufacturer's selection of an figure-H format for manual transmissions. "The pattern . . . may be expressed in several different ways. . . . But the copyright protects copying of the particular expressions, and does not prohibit another manufacturer from marketing a car using the same pattern."[144]

---

[143] 462 F. Supp. 1003 (ND Tex. 1978).

[144] Id. at 1013.

The court's alternative holding is also important. It concluded that if sequencing consists of expression, the formats are uncopyrightable, since there is then an identity between idea and expression.

> Here if order and sequence is the expression, the skilled effort is not separable, for the form, arrangement and combination is itself the intellectual conception involved. It would follow that only to the extent the expressions involve stylistic creativity *above and* beyond the base expression of sequence and arrangement should they be protected. . . . The "idea or principle" behind the forms . . . and the "method or system" involved in them, would be no more or less than the formats.[145]

In *Synercom* the particular input format was not the only method available for inputting data into a structural analysis program. In fact, many other formats were on the market. The defendants elected to seek complete compatibility with the Synercom format that was a market leader. Had they been denied the right to do so, their market entry would have been substantially impeded by being forced to persuade users to alter existing modes of data entry. The court's decision in part reflects a judgment that this market effect was not justifiable, even though Synercom had invested substantial sums in developing its format. As a result, the court's conception of the idea underlying the specific format was extended to encompass the entire format. The relatively spartan forms used for the sequencing of data in the Synercom system were not independently protectible or infringed.

The approach in *Synercom* equates the idea of the input process with the particular features of the process in its entirety. A different conception was implicit in the district court's opinion in *Apple Computer Co. v. Formula International, Inc.*[146] and was not directly contradicted by the circuit court when it affirmed a preliminary injunction against Formula's use of duplicates of Apple's operating system programs. The purpose of Formula's conduct was to achieve compatibility with the Apple programs, permitting access to a market characterized by the availability of applications software developed for Apple computers.[147] The court rejected the contention that there was an identity between idea and expression in Apple's programs based on evidence that there were numerous methods to write programs not identical to Apple's programs that

---

[145] Id. at 1014 (emphasis added).

[146] 562 F. Supp. 775, 218 USPQ 47, 52 (CD Cal. 1983), aff'd, 725 F2d 521, 221 USPQ 762 (9th Cir. 1984); see supra ¶ 1.03[5][b].

[147] See Davis, "IBM PC Software and Hardware Compatibility," 1 Comp. Law. 11 (July 1984); Chertok, "Compatibility: Fair Use or Derivative Work," 2 CLR 1004 (1984).

would be "98 percent compatible" with Apple computers. Since *Formula* involved literal duplication, there was no discussion of the distinction between protected idea, standardized expression, and protectible expression.

As was true in the video game cases, the outcome of substantial similarity issues in coded programs depends largely on two perceptions: (1) the nature of the underlying idea involved in the program; and (2) identification of code sequences that are standard expressions in the programming profession. Little or no clear guidance exists in this environment, especially concerning idea content. The *Synercom* court extended the label "idea" to a particular ordering and sequence of data and operations. The *Formula* courts at least imply a broader definition that focuses on the generic functions of an operating system. Significantly, in both contexts, unlike in video game displays, the search is not for important aesthetic variables that are critical to the success of the original work and that extend beyond the functional attributes of the program.

In this environment, it is often difficult to even formulate a statement of what are the idea and the expression contents of the programs. The decision should and will turn even more explicitly on a balance that involves issues of commercial utility and market access with which copyright has not commonly dealt. Additionally, the definition of scope of protection affects the extent to which copyright protection is implemented without creating de facto protection of the underlying process. Only limited protection beyond that against direct, literal copying is justifiable for programs such as that involved in *Formula*. The *Synercom* result is more in accord with copyright concepts, since it avoids control over a process by indirect means.

The aforementioned cases did not involve partial similarity of coded programs. This issue was present in *Midway Manufacturing Co. v. Strohon*.[148] *Strohon* dealt with a claimed infringement of both the audiovisual display and the object code of the video game PAC-MAN. The alleged infringing work was a modification kit consisting of several ROMs to be inserted in place of the PAC-MAN ROMs.[149] The court found no audiovisual infringement, since the modifications removed the PAC-MAN characters that, in essence, represented the protected portion of the display. Nevertheless, the court concluded that the object code was copyrightable and was infringed. It noted

> Midway established . . . that 89% of the 16,000 bytes [were] identically reproduced in the corresponding CUTE-SEE ROMs. . . . 13,382

---

[148] 564 F. Supp. 741 (ND Ill. 1983).

[149] See infra ¶ 1.09[2].

contain actual sequencing instructions . . . as distinct from data that appears directly on the screen. . . . Midway's experts identified three long strings of identical locations. . . . The degree of similarity . . . is substantial. . . . [The] uncontradicted expert testimony . . . was that there is virtually an infinite number of ways to write . . . program instructions that will produce the . . . game sequencing. It is thus not at all necessary that the assembly code or object code phases of a computer program that would operate a maze chase game track the PAC-MAN program.[150]

In light of the evidence, the *Strohon* result may be reasonable, but the analysis is incomplete. The court assumed that all of the coding of the program was protectible as long as other maze game programs can be written. To the extent that this conclusion is attributable to analysis, it is based on an implicit assumption that the unprotected idea of the coded program is very general, and thus, the entire coding as well as the particular sequencing of instructions represents expression of that idea. An alternative view is that the sequence of instructions is, in itself, an unprotectible idea. Under this view, similarity in coding is not objectionable if it is necessary to implement the underlying idea.

Beyond this, no analysis or evidence was directed to the unprotected elements of the visual form of the game: the extent of similarity of assembly code inherent in any chase game program or to what extent variations in coding involve the design of the maze or the ability of characters to move around it. Furthermore, the court made no effort to identify what coding, if any, might be standard and unprotectible in this environment. For example, the three identical sequences of machine code might be a significant similarity or might merely reflect that both program authors elected to use a conventional means of integrating steps in a program.

The first step in any analysis of coded program infringement must specify what aspects of the program constitute unprotected ideas. Similarity of program coding must be tested independently of similarity of idea.[151] The second author is entitled to use the same idea and is prohibited only from reproducing expression.

---

[150] Midway Mfg. Co. v. Strohon, 564 F. Supp. 752–753 (ND Ill. 1983).

[151] See Sid & Marty Krofft Television v. McDonald's Corp., 562 F2d 1157, 1164 (9th Cir. 1977) ("There . . . must be substantial similarity not only of the general ideas but of the expressions of those ideas as well."); Atari, Inc. v. North Am. Phillips Consumer Elecs. Corp., 672 F2d 607 (7th Cir.), cert. denied, 103 S. Ct. 176 (1982); Atari, Inc. v. Amusement World, Inc., 547 F. Supp. 222 (D. Md. 1981); Midway Mfg. v. Dirkenschneider, 543 F. Supp. 466 (D. Neb. 1981); Williams Elecs., Inc. v. Bally Mfg. Corp., 220 USPQ 1091 (ND Ill. 1983); see supra discussion at ¶ 1.06.

The second step requires identifying those portions of the original or the second program coding that consist of standard coding expression for the particular type of program. Such common terms are especially significant aspects of the computer programming profession, and even in totally independent works one must anticipate significant use of similar terms. Thus, one author can not base an infringement claim on a second author's using routine commands such as GOTO or LOOP.

An infringement exists only if similarity in coding is distinct from standard phraseology or the pursuance of identical ideas. In general, to the extent that artistic expression in the programs such as text or visual images produced is not at issue, only the most proximate copying and virtually complete similarity of coding should be actionable. To go beyond that would risk imposing severe restraints on growth of program design and development.

¶ 1.09 DERIVATIVE WORKS

Section 106(2) of the Act provides that a copyright owner has the exclusive right to "prepare derivative works" from the copyrighted original. Control over derivative works is a separable element of copyright. It is seldom litigated as an independent right in traditional works such as novels. Issues about derivative works are commonly subsumed within the more general issue of direct infringement by reproduction of the copyrighted work.

Under current copyright law, a derivative work qualifies for separate copyright insofar as new material and expression are included.[152] The provision giving control over such works does not, however, extend the control of the copyright owner to secondary works that merely in colloquial terms derive from the original. Protection for derivative works must be viewed in conjunction with Section 102(b) of the Act, which expressly precludes any copyright control over ideas and limits copyright protection to an author's expression.[153] A derivative work must incorporate a sufficient amount of the expression of the original work to be considered an infringing copy. As one court noted, a subsequent computer program is a derivative work only to "the extent that the [second program] incorporates some or all of [the original] copyrighted programs."[154] In the absence of substantial expressive similarity, the second work is not deriv-

---

[152] 17 USC § 103(b) (1982); *Nimmer on Copyright* ch. 3.

[153] *Nimmer on Copyright* § 3.04.

[154] See Freedman v. Select Information Sys., 221 USPQ 848, 850 (ND Cal. 1983).

ative in a copyright sense, but is at most an extrapolation of the ideas of the original. In contrast, if there is substantial similarity, the fact that the second author has added independent expression does not insulate the derivative work from infringing the original work.

Because litigated infringement commonly involves the preparation or distribution of copies, violation of the right to prepare derivatives is generally subsumed in questions about whether an infringing copy, display, or performance has been made. The right to prepare derivative computer software works may have independent significance, however, because lawful users of a copyrighted program may seek to modify or enhance the program without subsequently intending to distribute copies of the enhanced or modified version. Where this occurs without making additional copies of the work, the right to make and use these adapted or modified versions of the original program will depend largely on the scope accorded to the derivative work right.

[1] User Modifications

Modifications or adaptations of lawfully possessed copies of a computer program may be made in various manners and with different motivations. In one common form, the user of the copy makes relatively minor modifications to facilitate use in a particular computer or system. In the contemporary microcomputer environment, the proliferation of hardware systems and mass-marketed programs leads to incompatible products that need adjustment for use in the owner's computer. In many cases, the capacity to make such modifications is built into the program itself and is either explicitly authorized or subsumed as part of the program. In addition, Section 117 of the Act gives the owner of a copy[155] the right to make such adaptations as are necessary to use the program in a particular computer as long as the adaptations are not further reproduced, except for archival purposes, or distributed without authorization from the copyright owner.

In many cases, user modifications extend beyond necessary adaptations to a particular computer. For example, the user may add or delete functions in a program to enhance its utility in his own applications. Modifications may also be made to increase the speed of performance or to interface the particular program with another program available to the user. When programs are modified, copied, and sold, infringement issues arise that are identical to those previously discussed. Issues about derivative works arise only where the modification is designed and used solely

---

[155] 17 USC § 117 (1982).

to increase the utility of the program in the authorized user's own applications.

Modifications in this latter form affect the copyright owner's economic interests only where the modifications reduce or eliminate the user's incentive to purchase additional programs from the author. This circumstance has been raised in several reported decisions involving speed-up or modification of computer-based video games. For commercial video games used in arcades, the user of the program is typically licensed to possess copies and display the program for a fee to the public. However, the popularity of video games, even after an initial period of success, subsides as players adapt to the play of the game. The purpose of modifying the game program in such cases is to enhance or alter the difficulty of the game, often by speeding up the movement of characters. The intent is to increase revenues to the licensee and extend the commercially useful life of the game copy.

The leading case on user modification in this commercial environment is *Midway Manufacturing Co. v. Arctic International, Inc.* [156] In this case, the licensed user had inserted a speed-up kit that increased the number and speed of movements of characters in the original game. The kit consisted of ROM chips to be inserted in place of some of the original chips containing the game program. The case did not involve unauthorized reproduction of the game, since possession and use of the original game was authorized and the kits merely modified existing copies. Nevertheless, the Seventh Circuit Court of Appeals concluded that an infringing derivative work was created. [157]

The court recognized that the Act does not clearly indicate that an authorized licensee is barred from modifying his own copy of a work. However, the court concluded that the economics of the context required this result, since the speed-up modification substantially increased revenues. In the absence of user modifications, the copyright holder would be able to control the distribution of modified versions of the program in order to gain a profit. This same rationale tended to rebut any argument that the right to make modifications was implicit in the license agreement. In the absence of express contract provisions, the copyright holder was "entitled to monopolize" the preparation of derivative works even for personal use by authorized licensees. [158]

---

[156] 704 F2d 1009 (7th Cir. 1983).

[157] Compare Midway Mfg. Co. v. Strohon, 564 F. Supp. 741 (ND Ill. 1983) (modifications sufficiently altered output to avoid infringement, but modification kit itself violated object code copyright).

[158] Midway Mfg. Co. v. Arctic Int'l, Inc., 704 F2d 1009, 1013 (7th Cir. 1983).

The argument against this result is based primarily on an analogy to prior law dealing with the rights of the owner of a copy after the first authorized sale. The general thrust is that the copyright owner can not exercise control over the use of the work by the owner of a copy[159] except over reproduction or public performance. Significantly, while this doctrine is recognized in Sections 119 and 117 of the Act as to owners of copies, these sections expressly exclude similar rights for lessees and licensees. In form, at least, the defendant in *Arctic* was not the owner of the copy.

As previously indicated, Section 117 of the Act grants owners of copies a right to adapt the program. While Section 117 refers to modifications "essential" to use in a computer, this language was adopted from recommendations in the CONTU report that suggested broader applicability:

> [A] right to make those changes necessary to enable the use for which it was both sold and purchased should be provided. The conversion of a program from one higher-level language to another to facilitate use would fall within this right, as would the right to add features to the program that were not present at the time of rightful possession. These rights . . . could only be exercised so long as they did not harm the interests of the copyright proprietor.[160]

While CONTU refers to authorized modifications of relatively broad scope, even where the user owns a copy of the program, the right to modify and enhance that program exists only insofar as it does not harm the interests of the copyright proprietor. This supports the result in the video game case. In the particular circumstance of commercial video speed-up kits, the interests of the author and the game operator are equally significant and financial in form. By controlling the right to modify the game, the copyright owner has access to a significant secondary market that would be lost if the owner of a copy could directly access it.

The result should be different if the copy owner's modifications are oriented to personal use unrelated to public display or distribution. While Section 117 limits even these modifications to essential adaptations, the CONTU commentary suggests that "essential" must be interpreted in light of the interests involved. Some latitude in making enhancements is permitted on a private basis as long as the copyright owner's interest is

---

[159] *Nimmer on Copyright* 2-146. Compare S&H Computer Sys. v. SAS Inst., Inc., 568 F. Supp. 416 (MD Tenn. 1983) (district court enforces license restriction concerning use of a program).

[160] *Nat'l Comm'n on New Technological Uses of Copyrighted Works, Final Report* 14 (1978).

not substantially affected. The private user modifications are analogous to underlining pages of a book or otherwise annotating a copyrighted work to enhance its usefulness. If the copyright proprietor can control these modifications, it effectively controls use of the program, a right that is not conveyed in the Act.[161]

User modifications for noncommercial use are most often a protected act, rather than an infringment. If the user owns the copy, the modifications are authorized under Section 117 unless they infringe on a clear, commercial interest of the author. Even if the user does not own the copy, such personal adaptations may be fair use or are implicitly authorized in the license agreement.

[2] Modification Kits and Programs

Modifications in existing programs may be made by a user through application of his own expertise or facilities. Often, however, the modifications are made with the aid of commercially distributed kits developed and distributed by a third party. These kits may provide a means to circumvent program limitations on copying or, more broadly, may provide a direct means to enhance program performance. The distribution of these kits often raises questions of contributory infringement—that is, under what circumstances the third party is indirectly responsible for infringement committed by another person through use of the marketed product. This issue is discussed in a later section.[162]

The third-party product may include a direct infringement of the copyrighted work, in which case no question of derivative works or contributory infringement need be considered. Although designed to aid an authorized user in extending the performance of a program or circumventing program limitations on copying or other use, reproduction and distribution of the enhancement product itself represents an infringement of copyright.

This apparently was the conclusion of the court in *Midway Manufacturing Co. v. Strohon*.[163] As previously discussed, *Strohon* involved a speed-up and modification kit for a particular video game. The kit involved several ROMs to be inserted in place of some of the originals. The replacements closely tracked the program format of the original. The

---

[161] See ¶¶ 5.16, 5.17; see also *Nimmer on Copyright* 2-146. Compare S&H Computer Sys. v. SAS Inst., Inc., 568 F. Supp. 416 (MD Tenn. 1983) (license restriction concerning use).

[162] See infra ¶ 1.10.

[163] 564 F. Supp. 741 (ND Ill. 1983).

court found an infringing substantial similarity in the machine code of the original work and the enhancement kit.

Hubco Data Products Corp. v. Management Assistance, Inc.[164] reached a similar result regarding a program designed to permit enhancement of an operating system program. In *Hubco*, Management Assistance, Inc. distributed operating systems for its microcomputers. The systems had various levels of performance related to the price charged for the license. In fact, however, the different performance levels were artificially created by built-in limiting features in the distributed copies of the program. The defendant developed a manual system by which the coded program could be printed and the program restraints identified and removed, thereby enhancing system performance. It also developed and was about to distribute a computer program that performed the same functions within the machine.

The case could have been approached in terms of a wrongful creation of a derivative work. Instead, the district court concluded that in both manual and computerized forms, the enhancement process infringed the copyrighted operating system by producing a direct copy in the process of identifying and removing the program restrictions. This conclusion was most obvious with reference to the manual process by which a printed copy of the program code was produced. The court also concluded, however, that the computer version involved an unauthorized copy: "The . . . software package essentially contains a copy of the higher-level operating code which the computer owner desires. The placement of that software in a . . . computer [constitutes an unauthorized copy]."[165]

¶ 1.10 CONTRIBUTORY INFRINGEMENT

There has developed, especially in the microcomputer industry, a relatively substantial secondary market for products that enable a user to copy or modify existing programs. These enhancement and copying programs may involve direct infringement of the underlying copyright. Even if they do not directly infringe the original copyright, they may result in indirect liability for infringing acts committed by users of the products under the copyright law doctrine of contributory infringement.

Questions of contributory infringement arise only if the secondary product is not a direct infringement. In the absence of direct infringe-

---

[164] 219 USPQ 450 (D. Idaho 1983); see also Grogan, "Decompilation and Disassembly: Undoing Software Protection," 1 Comp. Law. 1 (February 1984).

[165] Hubco Data Prods. Corp. v. Management Assistance, Inc., 219 USPQ 450, 456 (D. Idaho 1983).

ment, the pertinent question is under what circumstances the distributor of the secondary product is responsible for the infringing actions of third parties over whom it has no direct control.

The law relating to contributory infringement was recently redefined by the U.S. Supreme Court in *Sony Corp. of America v. Universal City Studios, Inc.*[166] *Sony* is a landmark case dealing with the copyright implications of the manufacture and distribution of video cassette recorder (VCR) systems. The proprietors of motion picture and television copyrights alleged that a substantial use of VCR systems by consumers infringed their copyrights and that under the doctrine of contributory infringement, the manufacturers of the VCR systems were responsible for that widespread infringement. In a five-to-four decision, the Court rejected this argument.

In rejecting the contributory infringement claim, the Court established relatively stringent standards to establish liability for the actions of third parties based on their use of a marketed product. Lower court decisions had emphasized that liability existed if the most conspicuous, intended use of the marketed product involved a copyright infringement. In contrast, the Court held that "[The] sale of copying equipment, like the sale of other articles of commerce, does not constitute contributory infringement if the product is widely used for legitimate, unobjectionable purposes. Indeed, it need merely be capable of substantial noninfringing uses."[167] In the particular application of this doctrine to VCR equipment distribution, the Court concluded that substantial noninfringing uses existed, including the protected fair use duplication for personal use in the form of shifting the time when the program could be viewed at home.

The *Sony* decision emphasizes that liability for contributory infringement can not be found merely because one application of the defendant's product allows copyright infringement or, indeed, that some or many users of the product use it in that way. Instead, the balance between the copyright proprietor and the third-party manufacturer is struck at a level that is substantially more protective of the third party. Copyright infringement claims extend to the third party only if there is no substantial, noninfringing use for the product.

The pertinent inquiry in computer-related cases involves the range of uses of a particular product and the extent to which it is capable of substantial use in a noninfringing manner. Thus, distribution of partly incomplete memory chips that can be completed solely by addition of a

---

[166] 104 S. Ct. 774 (1984).

[167] Id. at 789.

particular copyrighted work constitutes contributory infringement.[168] However, distribution of program additions and patches that may be used in an infringing manner is not contributory infringement if they are also capable of noninfringing uses.[169] The distinctions focus on the extent to which the value of the second product is conditioned solely on the infringing use of the first.[170]

Within this framework, the extreme cases can be readily identified. For example, a compiler or assembler program has general utility and is marketed based on its utility for designers of software. The author of the program is not exposed to liability if the program is in fact extensively used to infringe other copyrighted programs. In contrast, kits for the modification of a single copyrighted program expose the producer to liability if two conditions are met. First, the result of the use of the kit on the particular program must be found to constitute an infringement. Manifestly, liability for contributory infringement can not occur in the absence of an underlying infringing act. Second, the kit must have no substantial noninfringing use. For both conditions, the ultimate scope of contributory infringement will depend partly on the court's view of the scope of permissible copying or modification of copyrighted programs by persons lawfully in possession of a copy of the program.

¶ 1.11 STATUTORY EXCEPTIONS

The Act grants the author of a work exclusive rights to reproduce and distribute copies of the original work as well as to prepare derivative works from it. These rights, however, are not absolute. Various sections of the Act recognize particular exceptions to the control of the copyright owner. The primary exceptions applicable to computer programs include the copyright doctrine of fair use and a cluster of rights granted by statute to the owner of a copy of the work.

[1] Section 117: Owners of Copies

Section 117 of the Act was enacted with specific reference to computer programs. It grants the owner of a copy of a computer program limited rights to copy and adapt a program notwithstanding the otherwise exclusive rights of the author. The purpose of Section 117 is to create

---

[168] See In re Certain Personal Computers and Components Thereof, No. 337-TA-140 (Int'l Trade Comm'n 1984).

[169] See Midway Mfg. Co. v. Strohon, 564 F. Supp. 741 (ND Ill. 1983).

[170] See Midway Mfg. Co. v. Arctic Int'l, Inc., 704 F2d 1009 (7th Cir. 1983).

rights parallel to those granted to owners of copies of other types of copy-righted material and to provide statutory validation of various rights that would ordinarily be central to any transaction involving the sale of a copy of a computer program. The intent is to balance the rights of the author and the interests of one who has lawfully acquired ownership of a copy and desires to use the program.

Section 117 applies to the "owner of a copy" of a computer program. It is inapplicable to persons in possession of a copy unlawfully. Similarly, Section 117 is not applicable to a person who is in possession of a copy under a true lease or other arrangement in which another person retains title to the copy.[171] The pertinent issue here is whether the user owns the copy and not whether the transaction involved a sale of the copyright, in the same way that the purchaser of a book owns that particular copy, but does not thereby obtain control of the copyright.

There is tension between ownership of the program copy and the fact that various aspects of copyright protection may or may not be separately licensed to the user. While there are no reported decisions closely examining ownership under Section 117, cases in other contexts suggest that ownership will be determined based on the actual character, rather than the label of the transaction by which the user obtained possession.[172] Merely labeling a transaction as a lease or license is not dispositive. If a transaction involves a single payment with an indefinite period of a right to possession, it is a sale. Similarly, course of dealing and trade usage are relevant in characterizing a transaction, since they establish the actual expectations and intentions of the parties. The pertinent issue is whether, as in a lease, the user may be required to return the copy to the vendor after expiration of a particular period. If not, possession is in the form of ownership.

Under Section 117, an owner has express rights to prepare copies of the program in two contexts. First, the owner is entitled to prepare a copy of the program if this is an essential step in the utilization of the program in a computer. Second, the owner may prepare a copy for archival purposes as long as this copy is destroyed in the event that possession ceases to be rightful. Copies made under these provisions may be transferred without permission of the copyright owner only if the transfer conveys all rights of the copy owner in the program.

The owner's right to make a copy relates in part to the conception that a copy is made whenever a work is input into a computer.[173] Regarding a

---

[171] See Midway Mfg. Co. v. Arctic Int'l, Inc., 704 F2d 1009 (7th Cir. 1983); Hubco Data Prods. Corp. v. Management Assistance, Inc., 219 USPQ 450 (D. Idaho 1983).

[172] See *Nimmer on Copyright* § 8.12B.

[173] *Nat'l Comm'n on New Technological Uses of Copyrighted Works, Final Report* 31.

program, therefore, the right to make a copy is inherent in the right to use the program. It is an essential attribute of ownership. Unlike a book that can be read without making a copy, a program delivered on machine media can be used or read only through preparation of a copy.

The right to prepare an archival copy reflects general practice among computer users of making back-up copies to prevent loss of relatively volatile electronic media. On the face of the statute, the archival copy right is absolute and not conditioned on the existence of a perceived threat to the program copy. One court, however, has indicated that this right is nevertheless available only if the purpose of protecting against loss of the original is present. In *Atari, Inc. v. JS&A Group, Inc.,*[174] a district court held that a device designed to permit copying of computer games distributed in ROM chips resulted in contributory infringement of the underlying game copyrights. In reaching this result, the court concluded that the Section 117 right to prepare an archival copy did not apply to programs distributed in ROM, and thus, there was no substantial noninfringing use for the copy.

The court's analysis of the Section 117 issue is at best questionable. It cited the CONTU report to the effect that the right to make a copy was designed to protect against loss due to mechanical or electrical failure. Based on this, the court held that the right to make a copy exists only where a risk of loss based on electrical or mechanical failure exists and is not available where the only risk of loss is that inherent in possession of a copy of any copyrighted work.

> Computer programs are stored in a wide variety of media. Not all of these are subject to the same risks. . . . For example, the. . . . program can be printed on paper. . . . That piece of paper could be burned or shredded, yet it could not be destroyed by mechanical or electrical failure. The medium of storage must, therefore, determine whether the archival exception applies. Where and only where a medium may be destroyed by mechanical or electrical failure, the archival exception protects the others . . . by granting them the right to make back-up copies.[175]

This analysis enacts a distinction that is not even alluded to in the statute.

Section 117 also grants the owner a right to prepare an adaptation of the program to the extent that such adaptation is essential to the use of the program. The adaptation may not be transferred to another without permission of the copyright owner. It must be destroyed when the copy owner's possession of the program ceases to be lawful, as for example when the original copy is sold. The purpose of creating this ownership

---

[174] 597 F. Supp. 5 (ND Ill. 1983).
[175] Id. at 14.

right relates in part to the proliferation of computer systems and formats characteristic of the microcomputer industry. As a result, it is often necessary to adapt programs to run on particular computers. Similarly, with increasing computer literacy, individual users of programs are increasingly able to and interested in adapting the program copy to more closely meet their personal needs.

As discussed earlier, there is uncertainty about the right of a user of a program to make adjustments in the program for personal use.[176] Section 117 applies only to owners of copies and does not grant rights to lessees or others in lawful possession.[177] Even for an owner of a copy, however, the right to make an adaptation is limited to that necessary as an "essential step" in the use of the program in a computer.[178]

While there is no case law interpreting this phrase "essential step," the better view is that it includes adjustments that optimize personal use of the program. The focus should be on adaptations essential for the owner's intended, optimal use, rather than on a notion of absolute necessity limited to modifications essential to load and operate the program in a particular machine. This is especially true if the adaptations relate to personal or private use and do not eliminate a market that would otherwise be available to the copyright author. The CONTU report, in describing this exception, refers to the right of the owner to modify the program by adding features, translating it into another language, and taking various other steps that are clearly not essential in absolute terms. The analogy to traditional copyright works involves a reference to annotating, underlining, or otherwise adjusting a book to more fully meet intended use. The right to prepare adaptations does not, however, include a right to distribute them or, even, necessarily a right to make copies of the adaptation beyond that intended for use in the owner's machine.

[2] First Sales

The rights of an owner of a copy are also affected by Section 109 of the Act, the so-called first sale doctrine. While the copyright owner generally has the exclusive right to distribute or display copies of his work, Section 109 eliminates this exclusivity with reference to the owner of a

---

[176] See supra ¶ 1.09[1].

[177] The intent to exclude nonowners is apparent from the history of Section 117. As initially drafted, the section would have been applicable to any person in rightful possession of a program copy. See *Nat'l Comm'n on New Technological Uses of Copyrighted Works, Final Report* (1978). This was modified in Congress to the present language expressly referring to "owners."

[178] See *Nat'l Comm'n on New Technological Uses of Copyrighted Works, Final Report* 13–14 (1978).

copy.[179] Specifically, the owner of a copy may distribute the copy without permission and has a right to display it "at the place where the copy is located." These rights after the first sale do not encompass making reproductions of the owned copy.

Regarding copies of computer programs, the first sale doctrine is limited by Section 117 in two ways. First, Section 117 adaptations may not be transferred without permission of the copyright owner. Second, Section 117 copies may be transferred without permission only as part of a transfer of all rights in the underlying program. The obvious purpose of these restrictions is to avoid statutory, authorized piracy.

[3] Fair Use

Regardless of the type of copyrighted material involved, the rights of the copyright proprietor are subject to the doctrine of fair use. Fair use is an essentially equitable doctrine. It was originated by the courts and, more recently, has been expressly recognized in Section 107 of the Act.[180] Under Section 107, notwithstanding the otherwise exclusive rights of the copyright owner, the fair use of a copyrighted work is not an infringement of copyright. Fair use redefines or exempts behavior such as reproduction, adaptation, and the like that would otherwise infringe an underlying copyright. Unlike other exceptions to copyright control, fair use is not contingent on ownership of the copy. Regarding computer programs, the doctrine may be relevant to both the ability of subsequent authors to use portions of an original program and the ability of a lawful user to make modifications in a program.

The doctrine of fair use has been described as "the most troublesome in the whole law of copyright."[181] In part, this results from the fact that the doctrine mediates between the rights of the author and the rights of subsequent users in an environment where the author's otherwise absolute rights are attenuated or arguably inappropriate. It provides a forum to balance individual, group, and other interests that are especially pertinent for technical works. In addition, the troublesome nature of fair use derives from the fact that underlying limits and criteria for application of the doctrine are uncertain and difficult to apply. Although this may be endemic to any equitable concept, this doctrine creates much uncertainty and frequent dispute.

---

[179] 17 USC § 109 (1982). See generally *Nimmer on Copyright* § 8.12.

[180] See HR Rep. 1476, 94th Cong., 2d Sess. 65–66 (1976).

[181] Dellar v. Samuel Goldwyn, Inc., 104 F2d 661, 662 (2d Cir. 1939); see *Nimmer on Copyright* § 13.05.

Although recognizing the equitable and flexible nature of this exemption, Section 107 provides a nonexclusive list of factors to be considered in determining whether a particular use is an exempted fair use of a copyrighted work. These factors include: (1) the purpose and character of the use including whether the use is for commercial or nonprofit purposes; (2) the nature of the copyrighted work; (3) the amount or proportion of the original work that is used; and (4) the effect of the use on the "potential market for or value of the copyrighted work."[182]

The statute does not specify the relative importance of these or any other factors in a fair use case. In practice, there is substantial uncertainty about what factors are primary and how the listed and other factors are interrelated. A leading treatise on copyright law suggests that the primary issue concerns the effect on the potential market for the original work and whether the alleged fair use and the original work have a similar function.[183] These issues emphasize the impact on the author of the original work. A fair use is not present if it substantially injures the interests of that author, since such injury is directly contrary to the purposes of the copyright law.

Another view emphasizes that fair use is largely restricted to productive uses that do not substantially affect the market available for the original author.[184] This view identifies the other half of the balance involved. It focuses on what the user does with the copyrighted work and attempts to identify conduct that provides a social benefit. A productive use includes use of the original to create another work, including a criticism or review. The general social gain consists of an increase of knowledge or art. In essence, fair use serves as a conduit through which underlying interests in preserving an unencumbered interaction among a community of scholars and artists are preserved.

Despite differing emphasis, these viewpoints are not inconsistent. Fair use decisions balance broad interests that involve both the nature of the use and the impact on the author's economic and other rights. A convergence of productive use and minimal impact on the original author creates a clear case for application of fair use concepts.

The law relating to fair use in a technology setting was recently restated by the U.S. Supreme Court in *Sony Corp. v. Universal City Studios, Inc.*[185] As previously discussed, *Sony* involved alleged contributory infringement of motion picture and television copyrights through distri-

---

[182] 17 USC § 107 (1982).

[183] See *Nimmer on Copyright* § 13.03[b].

[184] See Sony Corp. v. Universal City Studios, Inc., 104 S. Ct. 774 (1984) (dissenting opinion).

[185] Id.

bution of video cassette recorder (VCR) systems. The Court held that there was no contributory infringement, since the VCR units had a substantial, noninfringing use in the form of permitting consumers to make copies for purposes of shifting the time that they could view the copyrighted works. This time-shifting use was a fair use.

The majority rejected the argument that fair use turned on whether the use was a productive one. Instead, it emphasized that the copying was for nonprofit, private purposes. For such noncommercial use, there is no infringement unless there is proof of a particular harm or, if the practice became widespread, an adverse effect on the market for the copyrighted work.[186] In contrast, the Court noted, harm is presumed if the use is a commercial use. Given this structure, the Court concluded that it had not been demonstrated that private time-shifting adversely affected the copyright owner by reducing the market for the works. In fact, such use benefitted society by making it possible for a greater number of people to view the works.

The application of the fair use doctrine to computer programs will necessarily depend on the nature of the secondary use. One clear application involves adaptations and copies by lawful users of a program. Absent effective contract restraints,[187] even if not authorized under Section 117, modifications and copies made for noncommercial, private use should be considered to be fair use. Adaptations to improve the performance of a program or copies to safeguard against loss harm the original author's interests only if they are marketed or directly infringe on a viable commercial market that the author might otherwise access. If the changes are idiosyncratic to the particular user, no viable market exists that can be said to have been affected by the modifications. Conversely, modifications for commercial use and resale are not a fair use.[188]

PART C.   NOTICE, DEPOSIT, AND REMEDIES

¶ 1.12 COPYRIGHT NOTICE

Although under the current Act a copyright in a work of authorship attaches automatically in most cases, effective enforcement and retention of copyright claims require affixation of appropriate copyright notice when the work is initially published. Under current law, a special savings provision for cases involving an inadvertent omission of notice permits

---

[186] Id. at 793.

[187] See ¶¶ 5.15, 5.16.

[188] See Midway Mfg. Co. v. Arctic Int'l, Inc., 704 F2d 1009 (7th Cir. 1983).

the author to act within five years after publication if this act is coupled with registration and reasonable efforts to place notice on previously distributed copies.[189] The purpose of the notice requirement is to make other people aware of the claimed copyright. The notice must contain the copyright symbol (or a specified surrogate), the owner's name, and the year of first publication. In general, an unexcused failure to affix a required notice on a published work forfeits copyright and effectively places the work in the public domain.[190]

For purposes of the Act, publication of the work requires "public distribution."[191] As a result, in cases of limited, restricted distribution, no notice may be required to retain the copyright in the unpublished work. Furthermore, even if a work has been published, notice requirements are excused if the distribution includes "a relatively small number" of copies.[192]

In computer-related works, a primary issue involving copyright notice has involved questions concerning the placement of the notice on copies distributed in machine-readable form. The statute requires that the notice be affixed to the copy of a work in a "manner and location as to give reasonable notice of the claim of copyright."[193] Pursuant to this provision, the Registrar of Copyrights is empowered to specify regulations as to method and placement of notice. Although compliance with the regulations is conclusive as to the adequacy of notice, noncomplying notice may be sufficient if it in fact provides reasonable notice.[194]

For machine-readable copies, the current regulations provide for four alternatives:

1. Notice embodied in the copy so that, on *visually perceptible printouts*, it appears either with or near the title, or at the end of the work;

---

[189] 17 USC § 405(a)(2) (1982); see Data Cash Sys. v. JS&A Group, Inc., 628 F2d 1038 (7th Cir. 1980) (distribution of stickers to distributors as a reasonable effort); Innovative Concepts and Entertainment, Inc. v. Entertainment Enters., Ltd., 576 F. Supp. 457 (EDNY 1983) (mistake of law is not an intentional omission of notice).

[190] See *Nimmer on Copyright* § 7.14[A][1].

[191] 17 USC § 401(a), 402 (1982); see Hubco Data Prods. Corp. v. Management Assistants, Inc., 219 USPQ 450 (D. Idaho 1982) (limited distribution without notice not general publication); Data Gen. Corp. v. Digital Computer Controls, 357 A2d 105 (Del. Ch. 1975) (limited distribution of manuals does not divest copyright).

[192] *Nimmer on Copyright* 7-87.

[193] 17 USC § 401(c) (1982).

[194] 46 Fed. Reg. 58,308 (1981).

2. Notice displayed at the user's terminal at sign on; [195]

3. Notice continuously on terminal display; [196] or

4. A gummed or other label securely affixed to the copy or to the permanent container of the copy. [197]

¶ 1.13 DEPOSIT AND REGISTRATION

In addition to notice requirements, the Act contains provisions for the registration and deposit of copyrighted works. These provisions blend mandatory and permissive actions that have presented problems in the context of computer programs and other works containing proprietary information.

For works published after the effective date of the current Act in 1978, registration of these works with the Copyright Office is not required as a condition to obtaining or retaining a valid copyright. [198] While technically there is a permissive attitude toward registration, various provisions of the Act make registration effectively mandatory before action can be taken to enforce the copyright. For example, registration is an element of the right to cure a faulty or omitted notice within five years of publication. [199] Also, under Section 411a, no action for infringement can be undertaken unless the work has been registered. For this purpose, registration can occur shortly before filing an infringement action and need not precede the infringing act. However, under Section 412, with the exception of registrations occurring within three months of publication, if the infringement occurs prior to registration, the copyright owner is not entitled to statutory damages or to attorney fees in a successful action. [200]

A registration certificate issued by the Copyright Office serves as prima facie proof of the validity of the copyright and the accuracy of other matters stated therein if registration occurs within five years of publication. [201] As this implies, registration entails examination by the Copyright Office. Unlike under the patent system, the examination is relatively limited and is confined to matters concerning the validity of the copyright

---

[195] See Midway Mfg. Co. v. Dirkenschneider, 543 F. Supp. 466 (D. Neb. 1981).

[196] See Videotronics, Inc. v. Bend Elecs., 28 BNA PTCJ 125 (D. Nev. 1984) (randomly flashed notices on screen are inadequate).

[197] 37 CFR § 201.20g.

[198] See *Nimmer on Copyright* 7-111.

[199] 17 USC § 405 (1982).

[200] 17 USC § 412 (1982).

[201] 17 USC § 410(c) (1982).

notice and the status of the work as original authorship. The prima facie effect of the certificate is rebuttable. Furthermore, in appropriate cases, registration may be issued pursuant to the rule of doubt reflecting an inability to determine if the material constitutes original authorship. The effect of registration under this concept is to eliminate prima facie validity.

The registration process requires deposit of copies of the work.[202] In addition, the Act also imposes a deposit requirement related to securing copies of all published works for the Library of Congress.[203] With reference to both deposit requirements, two copies of the "best edition" of the work are required, but this may be reduced by regulation.[204] With reference to examination-registration deposits, the Copyright Office is empowered to permit "deposit of identifying material instead of copies" in appropriate cases.[205]

With reference especially to computer programs, deposit requirements have presented a difficult dilemma. The concept of the deposit-registration system is to permit examination by the Copyright Office and to create a public record of the published work. This creates a conflict with software authors' desires to retain secrecy concerning the idea or structural content of a program. Deposit in human-perceivable form of the code of a program might vitiate that secrecy. This concern reflects an underlying tension between copyright principles and program protection. The copyright system is generally oriented to encouraging publication and dissemination of expressed ideas. In contrast, in the contemporary software industry, substantial value is contingent on nondisclosure of ideas or algorithms leading to particular programs.

At present, while Copyright Office regulations generally require the deposit of source code, they provide several forms of potentially effective relief for secrecy interests. The first involves the basic deposit and registration requirements that provide:

> where an unpublished literary work is fixed or a published literary work is published only in the form of machine readable copies . . . the deposit shall consist of: (A) For . . . computer programs, one copy of identifying portions of the program, reproduced in a form visually perceptible without the aid of a machine. . . . [consisting of] either the first and last 25 pages or equivalent . . . of the program.[206]

---

[202] 17 USC § 408 (1982).

[203] 17 USC § 407 (1982).

[204] 17 USC §§ 407(c), 408(c) (1982).

[205] 17 USC § 408(c)(1) (1982).

[206] 37 CFR § 202.19(c)(vii).

This form of deposit applies only if the program is published *only* in machine-readable form. Furthermore, currently, the object code of a program is acceptable only pursuant to the "rule of doubt" that, as previously noted, eliminates the outcome of registration's establishment of prima facie validity. Nevertheless, depending on the interpretation of "pages," the deposit regulation at least avoids requiring deposit of the entire program in source code form.

A second form of reconciliation of the competing interests involved entails the willingness of the Copyright Office to permit use of the "special relief" provisions of its regulations in cases where the program contains trade secrets.[207] These provisions require a request by the copyright owner justifying the need for relief from deposit requirements. Presumably, in the case of programs, this would relate to disclosure of trade secrets inherent in the program. The special relief provisions allow acceptance of an actual copy (e.g., a disk or a chip) or acceptance of "incomplete copies" other than those "normally comprising the best edition."[208] Current policy focuses on the latter alternative with options such as: "(1) Filing the first 25 and last 25 pages of source code *with trade secret information blocked out* . . . ; (2) the first 10 and last 10 pages of source code with nothing omitted; or (3) the first 25 and last 25 pages of *object code* plus any 10 consecutive pages of source code."

¶ 1.14 REMEDIES

In general, remedies for copyright infringement of computer works have not involved issues unique to a computer context. Since the applicable remedies are extensively discussed in other publications,[209] they will only be summarized briefly here. The applicable remedies for copyright infringement can be broadly differentiated into two categories—monetary recovery and action against the infringing works themselves. The two categories are not mutually exclusive.

With reference to monetary recoveries, the Act provides for an election between two compensatory systems. The election may be made by the copyright owner at any time prior to judgment. The first method of measuring damages provides for recovery of actual damages *and* the defendant's profits from the infringement.[210] Significantly, the actual damage and profit recovery are not stated as alternatives and may both

---

[207] 37 CFR §§ 202.19(e), 202.20(d).

[208] 37 CFR § 202.20(d).

[209] See *Nimmer on Copyright.*

[210] 17 USC § 504(b) (1982).

be recovered. However, this concept is limited by the principle that double recovery is not allowed. As a result, where the computation of actual damage overlaps with the defendant's profits, cumulation will not be allowed as to the overlapping elements.[211] Actual loss to the copyright owner is commonly measured in terms of the reduced market value of his work plus ancillary costs due to the infringement.[212]

In lieu of actual damage-profit recovery, the copyright owner may elect statutory damages.[213] This election is available if there has been a timely registration of the copyrighted work. The statute provides for minimum damages of $250 and a maximum recovery of $10,000 unless the infringement is willful, in which case the maximum is raised to $50,000. Within this range, specification of actual recovery is discretionary. The limits apply for "all infringements involved in the action, with respect to any one work."[214]

The Act also provides for various remedies against the infringing products in addition to damages. Initially, at any time while the case is pending, the Act provides for impounding all copies made or used in violation of the copyright and all articles "by means of which such copies . . . may be reproduced."[215] No statutory standards are specified for prejudgment impoundment. However, standards analogous to those associated with preliminary injunctions are generally assumed to apply.[216] Following judgment, the court may impose a permanent injunction against further acts of infringement and may order destruction of all infringing copies.[217]

---

[211] See *Nimmer on Copyright* 14-4.
[212] Id. at § 14.6.
[213] 17 USC § 504 (1982).
[214] 17 USC § 504(c) (1982.
[215] 17 USC § 503(a) (1982).
[216] See *Nimmer on Copyright* 14-57.
[217] 17 USC §§ 502(a), 503(b) (1982).

CHAPTER *2*

Patent Law:
Software and Systems

PART D.　INFRINGEMENT

¶ 2.01　INTRODUCTION

A major issue in copyright law as applied to computer software involves the distinction between the expressive and the utilitarian or process-oriented aspects of a copyrightable work. Although this distinction arises partly from the historical roots of copyright, it is more importantly based on the assumption that proprietary rights in utilitarian objects and processes are within the area of patent law, rather than copyright law.

The federal patent system is conceptually analogous to the copyright system in that it provides economic incentives for creative work by granting an inventor control over the product of his inventive effort. Beyond that general similarity however, the systems diverge dramatically. Patent law is expressly addressed to protecting creative achievement for utilitarian objects and processes. Unlike copyright, it imposes substantial threshold requirements of inventiveness as a precondition for statutory protection. These requirements significantly curtail protection for rapidly developing, but incremental technology, and are one explanation for the extensive efforts to bring elements of computer technology within the scope of copyright law.

Nevertheless, patent law is pertinent to various aspects of computer technology, primarily developments in manufacturing and hardware technology and computer applications in industrial systems such as robotics and process control. Within these areas, patent law protections are substantially more robust and pertinent to industrial concerns than are any potential applications of copyright law.

PART A.   CLAIMS AND SCOPE

¶ 2.02 PATENT SYSTEM OVERVIEW

Section 101 of the Patent Act provides "Whoever invents or discovers any new and useful process, machine, manufacture, or composition of matter, or any new and useful improvement thereof, may obtain a patent therefore, subject to the conditions and requirements of this title."[1] As this language implies, the patent system is directed toward innovations for utilitarian objects or processes. Patent law provides the inventor with exclusive rights to use, make, sell, and otherwise enjoy his invention for a period of 17 years after the patent is issued.[2] As with copyright, patent rights are established exclusively through federal statute. The chief means of enforcing these rights is an action for infringement with attendant rights to damages and, in appropriate cases, to injunctive relief.[3] Unlike copyright protection, patent rights are not restricted to preventing appropriation of the invention in the form of direct copying. Rather, the exclusive rights of the patent holder extend to prevent actions on the part of independent developers of the same process or object.[4]

Granting exclusive rights to exploit a patented device or process promotes creativity. The incentive, however, to an even greater extent than in the area of copyright, is tied to a clear public policy that promotes disclosure and public availability of innovative techniques and inventions. A patent does not arise automatically, but must be affirmatively claimed. The claim is pursued through an application and review process that both defines the scope and terms of the right and creates public documentation of the methods or designs of the inventor. The public record then stimulates and provides information for further innovation by other parties. Thus, while the system establishes restrictive, exclusive rights for the inventor, it is also designed to continue and promote the flow of scientific and technological data and development, thereby perpetuating an additive process of innovation among a community of scholars.

Claiming a patent involves preparing and submitting substantial documentation of the invention to the U.S. Patent and Trademark Office, where the claim is reviewed. A significant number of applications are rejected on substantive grounds or on criteria aimed at preservation of the public disclosure elements of the system. Of the patents issued, a

---

[1] 35 USC § 101 (1982).

[2] 35 USC § 105 (1982).

[3] See 2 Rosenberg, *Patent Law Fundamentals*.

[4] 35 USC § 271 (1982).

majority that are tested in subsequent litigation are held to be invalid by the courts.

A distinguishing characteristic of patent law is the requirement of significant innovation as a precondition to receiving a patent. This requirement results in substantial numbers of patent claims being rejected or, once granted, being held invalid. Although Section 101 of the Patent Act speaks of "new and useful" products, a functional deviation from existing technology is inadequate, in itself, to qualify for a patent. Even more clearly, patent law does not reward mere originality, but only useful inventiveness of a high order. Included among the elements of required innovation are statutory requirements that the patent claim recite novel[5] and useful products or processes that are not obvious to other persons skilled in the relevant art.[6]

Over the years of administration of the patent law system, these standards have developed substantial judicial gloss that has not always provided consistent guidance. The most controversial requirement relates to the obviousness of the claimed patent. As discussed later in connection with computer-related inventions,[7] this standard attempts to identify an elusive criterion that restricts patent protection to developments involving more than mere incremental advances. The premise is that the inventor must have uncovered or designed a process or object that breaks from preexisting, known applications in an unexpected manner. While it is not necessary to establish a flash of insight or innovation in terms of suddenness of development, it is essential to establish more than an incremental or modest advance.

The strict requirements required to obtain a patent are connected to the scope of protection afforded after a patent is issued. Patent rights are not restricted to preclude only copying or appropriation, but may be enforced against independent developers. Patent protection is deemed appropriate only for a relatively limited range of innovations, however, because of a desire not to stifle innovative activity by unnecessarily granting protection based on what might become a first-to-file system.

¶ 2.03 CLAIMS

The art of patent claim drafting and prosecution is, in itself, an important legal specialty involving advanced technical skill. Some major

---

[5] 35 USC § 102 (1982); see infra ¶ 2.12.

[6] 35 USC § 103 (1982); see infra ¶ 2.15.

[7] See infra ¶ 2.15.

themes of that process are discussed in the following sections and are essential to understanding the material in the remainder of this chapter.

[1] Defined Scope

Since a patent does not arise solely from the act of invention, the terms and scope of any patent are defined by the terms of the claim on which the patent is issued. Due to the importance of the claim, various specialized drafting styles have been developed.[8]

A patent claim must be written in technical language that is general enough to establish a broad claim, but which will also be sufficiently particular to establish that the claim is unique. While more general claims tend to expand the scope of protection if a patent is issued, they also increase the likelihood that the claimed process or device will be viewed as obvious to persons skilled in the art or as anticipated by prior patents or technical developments.[9] In contrast, every technical specification included in the claim limits the scope of the patent if one is granted.[10] There is a greater likelihood of obtaining a valid patent with a specifically written claim, but also of permitting development of similar, competing technology that avoids infringement.

These issues relate solely to the technical detail in a claim. The scope of the patent is not affected by restrictive reference to the industry or area of commerce for which the invention is intended. Area or field limitations are generally viewed as informational, rather than substantively limiting.[11]

Beyond specifying the scope of the claims, a patent application also must contain a recitation and discussion of preexisting technology, described in the field as "prior art." This is a basis for determining whether the claimed invention meets statutory criteria of novelty and whether it would have been obvious to people skilled in the area. This discussion also places the invention in an appropriate context, increasing the efficacy of public disclosure.

One significant issue in claim practice is selecting the category under which the invention is claimed. Section 101 of the Patent Act speaks of patents available for processes, machines, manufactures (products), or compositions of matter. In addition, patents are available for decorative designs and organic plants. Often, a particular invention can be catego-

---

[8] See Rosenberg, *Patent Law Fundamentals* § 14.05–14.06.

[9] Id. at § 14.09.

[10] Id. at 2-9.

[11] See Parker v. Flook, 437 US 584 (1978).

rized as several of these and, within any category, described to emphasize various elements. For example, an adding machine might be described as an apparatus to record and tabulate numbers or as a process for adding and subtracting. However, the claim defines the scope of protection and these two formulations claim two very different patents. For example, a patent on a process for manufacturing a given product is not infringed by duplication of the product through other processes not encompassed within the patent claim. In contrast, a patent on the product (a manufacture) precludes unauthorized duplication of the product by whatever means or method, even if the duplication occurred without knowledge that the original existed.[12]

The different approaches may not only have substantially different consequences as to what is claimed, but also as to whether a valid patent can be issued. Such variations have had significant consequences for computer-related inventions.[13]

[2] Disclosure and Secrecy

There is an inherent conflict in the patent system between the basic patent objectives of full disclosure and strong commercial interests in maintaining the secrecy of valuable systems and processes. At one level, this tension can be readily resolved. Patent protection is neither the only, nor a required form of protection for innovations in the useful arts. As discussed in Chapter 3, secrecy restraints may be enforceable. Many commercially significant innovations are protected under trade secrecy rather than patents.[14]

Beyond this, if patent protection is sought, there is an incentive to draft patent claims in a manner that retains secrecy and reveals the least possible information about the invention, while nevertheless complying with statutory requirements concerning disclosure. It is inconsistent to retain trade secrecy and patent protection for the same subject matter. However, the two forms of protection may coexist for different components of an overall process even though the components are related. For example, it is possible to patent a product and at the same time retain secrecy concerning steps in its manufacture.[15] Section 112(1) of the Patent Act and supporting regulations establish the basic criteria for disclo-

---

[12] See Rosenberg, *Patent Law Fundamentals* 6-5.

[13] See Hollander, "The Protection of Computer Software," J. Mar. Intell. Prop. Rev. 111 (1982).

[14] See Milgrim, *Trade Secrets* § 8.02[1].

[15] See Milgrim, *Trade Secrets* § 8.02[4]; see also Modern Controls, Inc. v. Andreadakis, 578 F2d 1264, 1269 (8th Cir. 1978).

sure. In essence, these require that the invention be described with sufficient precision to distinguish it from other inventions and enough detail to permit one skilled in the art to make the invention and use it. In addition, the specifications for the patent must disclose the best mode of practicing the invention contemplated by the claimant.[16] The adequacy of a disclosure is an issue in the examination process and may be an issue in subsequent litigation. In the context of computer-related inventions, the form of disclosure varies according to the type of invention.

The application of these standards of disclosure to computer programs has been frequently litigated and is controversial. Two distinct situations of fact arise. In the first there may be relatively substantial disclosure about the program, but the question is whether that disclosure meets the standards of Section 112. The cases considering this situation have generally involved a dispute over whether the entire program must be disclosed, or whether a disclosure in the form of a detailed flowchart may be adequate, even if the flowchart is in the form of a verbal description of applicable steps.[17] The adequacy of such a flowchart depends on the detail that it provides and the extent to which a relatively skilled programmer can readily convert the description into a functioning program.[18] The court in *In re Sherwood*[19] summarized the rationale for permitting such disclosure as follows

> [Writing] a computer program may be a task requiring the more sublime of the inventive faculty or it may require only the droning use of clerical skill. The difference between the two extremes lies in the creation of mathematical methodology to bridge the gap between the information one starts with ... and the information that is desired. ... If these bridge-gapping tools are disclosed, there would be no cogent reason to require disclosure of the menial tools known to all who practice this art.[20]

Under this approach, the pertinent inquiry is whether and with what degree of difficulty the flowchart description can be converted into a

---

[16] 35 USC § 112 (1982); see White Consol. Indus. v. Vega Servo-Control, 218 USPQ 961 (Fed. Cir. 1983); Noyce v. Kelly, 416 F2d 1391 (CCPA), cert. denied, 400 US 818 (1969).

[17] See In re Butler, 217 USPQ 290 (PTO Bd. App. 1982) (flowchart disclosure adequate); In re Phillips, 608 F2d 879 (CCPA 1979) (flowchart adequate even though considerable time required to convert it to a program).

[18] See In re Brown, 477 F2d 946 (CCPA 1973) (the fact that program professionals could create the required program does not excuse complete failure to specify under Section 112).

[19] 613 F2d 809 (CCPA 1980), cert. denied, 450 US 994 (1980).

[20] Id. at 816–817.

functioning program. If mere coding can make this conversion, the disclosure is adequate. Furthermore, a second party can be required to engage in some experimentation to implement the program. However, a requirement of substantial time, experimentation, and creativity to implement the program is not consistent with the public disclosure objectives of the patent system. [21]

The second situation of fact is conceptually more difficult. It arises where the disclosure refrains from describing either the coded program or the structure of the program, but refers to it mainly by type or name. In many cases, this is attempted where the program is a trade secret of the patent claimant and the claimant desires to retain the confidential, proprietary nature of the program. The standard generally applied in such cases recognizes the right to maintain some element of secrecy, but only where the ability of another to replicate or use the invention is not prejudiced. [22] The program must be disclosed unless known, equivalent substitutes are available or are attainable without undue experiment. Of course, if these standards are met, the value of the trade secret is minimal at best.

A recent application of these standards to a computer-based invention occurred in *White Consolidated Industries, Inc. v. Vega Servo-Control, Inc.* [23] In *White*, the validity of a patent was challenged in the context of an infringement action. The invention—a machine tool system controlled by a computer—required a language translator program capable of converting another program from programming language to machine language in a single pass. In the invention, a proprietary program (SPLIT) was used. In the patent claim, this program was simply referred to by name, without a detailed disclosure. The court held that the patent was invalid because an insufficient enabling disclosure had been made—that is, the disclosure would not enable replication or use of the invention by another.

Central to the result reached by the court was that SPLIT was a relatively unique program at the time of the patent application and that it would take one and one-half to two years of work to obtain an equivalent. The court noted

Though the language translator by itself is not the claimed invention, it is an integral part of the disclosure necessary to enable those

---

[21] See White Consol. Indus. v. Vega Servo-Control, 218 USPQ 961 (Fed. Cir. 1983); In re Brandstadter, 484 F2d 1395 (CCPA 1973).

[22] Milgrim, *Trade Secrets* § 8.02[4].

[23] 218 USPQ 961 (Fed. Cir. 1983).

skilled in the art to ... use [it]. Were [the inventor] to maintain SPLIT as a trade secret, it could ... theoretically extend its ... rights ... by controlling SPLIT, a result inconsistent with the objectives of the patent system.[24]

In order to uphold the patent system disclosure requirements, trade secrecy is inconsistent when applied to an element of an invention integral to implementing the subject matter of the claim. If the secret program or process is integral to the invention and unique, it must be disclosed adequately to allow replication by one skilled in the art.

PART B.   SUBJECT MATTER ISSUES

¶ 2.04   PATENT SUBJECT MATTER

Patent protection is available only if the patent claim involves subject matter included within the scope of the Patent Act. Section 101 of the Patent Act lists several major categories of invention including processes, machines, manufactures, and compositions of matter.[25] These categories have substantial significance both for the indexing and review system employed by the Patent Office and for the formulation of particular claims. For the purposes of this book, the categories can be divided into two general areas: "One embraces physical objects or instrumentalities and thus comprehends all machines, manufactures, and compositions of matter; the other embraces all physical operations and thus comprehends all processes."[26]

Subject to requirements of novelty, obviousness, and the like, physical objects are clearly within the subject matter of patent law. In contrast, while processes have long been expressly within patent law,[27] the scope of their inclusion and the availability of patent protection for various aspects of processes have been the subjects of ongoing dispute. This dispute is particularly relevant to the patentability of computer applications and spills over to affect the patentability of computer-based inventions, whether phrased as a claim to a process or to a tangible object.[28]

---

[24] Id. at 963.

[25] 35 USC § 101 (1982).

[26] See Rosenberg, *Patent Law Fundamentals* 6-5.

[27] See, e.g., Cochrane v. Deener, 94 US 780 (1877).

[28] See In re Abele, 684 F2d 902 (CCPA 1982).

[1] Natural Laws

A process may be patentable due to a "novel sequence of procedures, new combinations of materials or ingredients, or new manipulative steps leading to a useful result."[29] Regardless of the character of the claimed process, however, the physical transformations, sequences, and results are subject to natural laws that may have been previously known or may have been discovered as part of the creation of the process itself.

An underlying premise of patent law is that while the particular process may be patentable, the underlying natural law is not. This distinction is analogous, but not identical, to the idea-expression distinction in copyright law. In patent law, the distinction requires close analysis of the claim and of the extent to which the claimed patent preempts or controls the use of the underlying natural law.

The leading cases distinguishing natural laws and resulting applications are U.S. Supreme Court decisions dealing with the invention of the telegraph and the telephone. In the telegraph case, Morse was allowed a patent for the use of electromagnetism to produce telegraphic signals, but was denied a patent for use of electromagnetism "however developed" to print at distances.[30] The scope of the latter claim was too broad and preemptive of a natural process, potentially barring dissimilar, but significant applications of electromagnetism. Similarly, in *The Telephone Cases*[31] a patent was granted for the use of electric current to transmit sounds.

> [The claim is not] for the use of a current of electricity in its natural state as it comes from the battery, but for putting a continuous current, in a closed circuit, into a certain specified condition, suited to the transmission of vocal and other sounds, and using it in that condition for that purpose. [No claim is made] for the use of electricity distinct from the particular processes with which it is connected in this patent.[32]

The discovery of a natural law does not convey a right to its exclusive use separate from the particular invention it inspired. However, the issue does not consist of simply identifying a natural law and defining it to be unpatentable. Morse did not in fact claim all uses of electromagnetism. Rather, the question is more accurately understood in terms of the extent of claimed preemption of the natural law. The distinction between

---

[29] See Rosenberg, *Patent Law Fundamentals* § 6.01[1].
[30] See O'Reilly v. Morse, 56 US (15 How.) 62 (1853).
[31] 126 US 1 (1887).
[32] Id. at 534–535.

natural law and patentable process provides incentives for creativity, but maintains a free area for development and intellectual discourse. Natural laws are the subject matter on which science and technology are built. Preemptive claims to the use of these laws in general terms would inhibit, rather than promote, development of science and technology. Patent will not extend to an abstract idea, but unlike copyright, patent protection does attach to creative ideas to the extent that the ideas are reduced to operational form in a useful object or process ("reduced to practice").

[2] Mental Steps and Business Methods

The scope of patent law has historically been limited by judicially developed exclusions of protection for "mental steps" and "methods of doing business."[33] A patentable process need not involve purely mechanical or chemical steps, but may involve substantial elements of human involvement.[34] However, at some level of generality, a patent claim might purport to preempt the process of human thought.

A mental act or step is one which may be performed by the human mind without the need or intervention of physical instrumentality. Such acts are broadly divisible into: (1) those which merely involve the application of logic or deduction; and (2) those which involve aesthetic thoughts or other value judgments. Examples of mental acts involving simple logic include computing, measuring, determining, dividing, etc.[35]

Claims relating to such mental steps are excluded from patent protection.

The exclusion of mental steps must be read in the context of particular claims and the generality of the preemption that is sought under patent law. The exclusion does not apply simply because a claimed process might be accomplished mentally.[36] Rather, it applies where the claim purports to encompass an impermissibly broad range of such activity. For example, it is not possible to obtain a patent for the process of adding numbers. However, it is possible to patent an adding machine, one function of which is to add numbers. As with natural laws, the processes of

---

[33] See In re Meyer, 688 F2d 789, 215 USPQ 193 (CCPA 1982); Paine, Webber, Jackson & Curtis v. Merrill Lynch, Inc., 564 F. Supp. 1358, 218 USPQ 212 (D. Del. 1983).

[34] See In re Marshall, 578 F2d 301 (CCPA 1978).

[35] Rosenberg, *Patent Law Fundamentals* 6-10.

[36] See In re Prather, 415 F2d 1378 (CCPA 1968), modified on reh'g, 415 F2d 1939 (1969); Paine, Webber, Jackson & Curtis v. Merrill Lynch, Inc., 564 F. Supp. 1358, 218 USPQ 212 (D. Del. 1983).

judgment and calculation are the tools of science and technology and can not be preempted without substantially impeding creative enterprises.

¶ 2.05 COMPUTER PROGRAMS IN GENERAL

Since the development of the first computer, it has been generally accepted that computer hardware and manufacturing developments are within patent law subject matter.[37] However, from the late 1960s through the early 1980s there was substantial uncertainty as to whether inventions implemented in whole or in part through computer programs qualified for patent protection. The uncertainty involved an ongoing controversy between the Court of Customs and Patent Appeals (CCPA) and the Patent and Trademark Office (PTO) and was perpetuated by uncertain guidance in several Supreme Court decisions.[38] The general question of whether any software-related inventions are patentable was answered in 1981 by the Supreme Court in *Diamond v. Diehr*.[39] However, a review of the development of this issue is relevant to understanding the current status of the law on the more particular question of under what circumstances a patent claim involving a programmed computer recites patentable subject matter.

[1] *Benson* to *Diehr*

The first U.S. Supreme Court decision on the patentability of software-related inventions was *Gottschalk v. Benson*.[40] *Benson* had been preceded by a period of direct conflict between the CCPA and the PTO, with the Court of Customs being supportive of including programmed computers within the scope of the Patent Act and the Patent Office being generally resistant. *Benson* involved a patent claim for a method of programmed conversion of binary-coded decimal numbers into pure binary form. As described by the Court, "the claims were not limited to any particular art or technology, to any particular apparatus or machinery, or to any particular end use. They purported to cover any use of the claimed method in a general purpose digital computer of any type."[41]

---

[37] See Sperry Rand Corp. v. Bell Tel. Labs, 208 F. Supp. 598 (1962) (priority dispute relating to patent on ENIAC computer).

[38] See Rinkerman, "Computer Program Patentability," 1 CLR 20 (1982).

[39] 450 US 175 (1981).

[40] 409 US 63 (1972).

[41] Id. at 72.

Faced with a claim of this level of generality, the Court properly concluded that the process claim recited unpatentable subject matter. It noted that the binary conversion could be done mentally with the aid of a conversion table and that the claimed program merely reordered the sequence and symbolism of the conversion. More pertinently, it noted

> Phenomena of nature ... mental processes, and abstract intellectual concepts are not patentable as they are the basic tools of scientific and technological work. ... It is conceded that one may not patent an idea. But ... that would be the result if the formula for converting ... to pure binary numerals were patented in this case. The mathematical formula involved here has no substantial practical application except in connection with a digital computer ... the patent would wholly preempt the mathematical formula and ... would be a patent on the algorithm itself.[42]

As this language suggests, the Court equated the claim with a claim to a patent on the underlying mathematical formula.

The *Benson* decision was widely interpreted as questioning whether any computer program-based inventions were patentable. In part, this was due to the Court's closing reference to patents on an algorithm, a term used in differing ways in mathematics (as a formula) and in computer programming (a structured sequence to solve a problem).[43] In any event, the decision fueled the dispute between the CCPA and the PTO. During the interim between *Benson* and the next Supreme Court decision on the issue, the CCPA developed a two-step analysis focusing on its view that *Benson* merely precluded patents for preemptive computer-based implementations of mathematical formulas.[44] The analysis tested first whether the claim recited a mathematical formula and, if so, whether a patent would tend to wholly preempt use of that formula.

The second U.S. Supreme Court decision was in 1978 in *Parker v. Flook*.[45] *Flook* involved a program to calculate, based on a formula, an "alarm limit" for use in connection with a catalytic conversion process. The alarm limit determines the point at which abnormal conditions indicating inefficiency or danger exist in a chemical process. As in *Benson*, the

---

[42] Id. at 71–72.

[43] See Paine, Webber, Jackson & Curtis v. Merrill Lynch, Inc., 564 F. Supp. 1358, 218 USPQ 212 (D. Del. 1983).

[44] See In re Freeman, 573 F2d 1237 (CCPA 1978); see In re Richman, 563 F2d 1026 (CCPA 1977) (preliminary data gathering not sufficient to create Section 101 process); In re Waldbaum, 559 F2d 611 (CCPA 1977) (computer process to count the number of busy telephone lines not within Section 101 as claimed); In re Castelet, 562 F2d 1236 (CCPA 1977).

[45] 437 US 584 (1978).

Flook claim was drafted in terms of general applicability as to the use of the formula involved. The claim did not specify the variables to be measured, how they should be measured for input into the program, or the means for setting off or adjusting an alarm. The underlying catalytic conversion process was widely known and used in the industry. The claim merely provided a "formula for computing an updated alarm limit" and purported to cover "any use of the ... formula ... on any process variable involved" in the catalytic conversion of hydrocarbons.

The Supreme Court held that the claim did not recite patentable subject matter. However, although the Court's opinion noted the general, preemptive effect that a patent would have, it did not explicitly rest its decision on that ground. It described *Benson* as equating mathematical formulas with natural laws in terms of patentability. The Court then proceeded to focus on two other aspects of the case. First, it rejected *Flook's* argument that the physical act of resetting the alarm limit distinguished *Flook* from *Benson*. The Court simply noted that "conventional or obvious" post-solution activity (i.e., after a formula is solved) does not, in itself, transform the claim. Second, the Court attempted to specify and apply criteria for analysis of claims in which an element of the claimed novelty of the invention is a newly discovered natural law or mathematical formula. Referring to longstanding precedent, the Court noted that discovering a natural law or formula does not confer patentability on the discovery. Patent only extends to innovative processes applying that law or formula. "The process itself, not merely the mathematical algorithm, must be new and useful. ... Whether the algorithm was in fact known or unknown at the time ... it is treated as though it were a familiar part of the prior art."[46] Based on this premise, the Court noted that all elements of a catalytic conversion process were well-known, including the use of computers for monitoring, and concluded that the application for patent "contains no claim of patentable invention."

The *Flook* decision created substantial controversy, especially with its apparent emphasis on the novelty of the nonalgorithmic aspects of a patent claim. Traditionally, the novelty of a claimed invention is not pertinent to whether or not it involves potentially patentable subject matter. The CCPA rejected any view that *Flook* required novelty beyond the programmed formula. It insisted that the claim must be viewed as a whole and described *Flook* as merely clarifying the second part of its test for patentability. Under what was briefly known as the *Freeman-Walter* test, a court should first determine if a mathematical algorithm is involved in the claim. If it is, the claim will not recite potentially patentable processes

---

[46] Id. at 592.

if "the mathematical algorithm is merely presented and solved by the claimed invention ... and is not applied in any manner to physical elements or process steps, no amount of post-solution activity will render the claim statutory; nor is it saved by a preamble merely reciting the field of use."[47] The significance of linking the computed formula to physical steps in the claim is, of course, that the claim is thereby limited to use of the formula in that specific physical process.[48]

The position of the CCPA was generally supported by a narrow majority in the U.S. Supreme Court's most recent decision on this issue. In *Diamond v. Diehr*,[49] the Court reviewed claims for a rubber-curing process. The process included continuous temperature monitoring by a computer programmed to receive data about temperature and timing and to use this data in computing a formula to determine the optimal time to remove the rubber. The claimed process also involved automatically opening the curing press when that point was reached. The Supreme Court held that this claim was within the statutory subject matter of Section 101 of the Patent Act and expressly rejected the view that *Flook* required a determination of novelty as part of Section 101, noting that this issue is raised in other aspects of the patent process. Instead, the Court interpreted both *Flook* and *Benson* as disallowing a patent for claims seeking protection for a mathematical formula in the abstract. It focused squarely on the extent to which the claim, as drafted, sought to preclude general use of the mathematical formula involved.

> [The] respondents here do not seek to patent a mathematical formula [but] a process of curing synthetic rubber. Their process ... employs a well-known mathematical equation, but they do not seek to preempt the use of that equation. Rather, they seek only to foreclose from others the use of that equation in conjunction with all of the other steps in their claimed process.[50]

---

[47] In re Walter, 618 F2d 758, 767 (CCPA 1980).

[48] See In re Maucorps, 609 F2d 481 (CCPA 1979) (program to determine optimum times a representative should visit customer not within Section 101); In re Gelnovatch, 595 F2d 32 (CCPA 1979) (process for determining set of values in a model of a circuit is not within Section 101). Compare In re Johnson, 589 F2d 1070 (CCPA 1978) (method to remove "noise" from seismic data is in Section 101). But see In re Toma, 575 F2d 872 (CCPA 1978) (method to operate human language translator is within Section 101); In re Phillips, 608 F2d 879 (CCPA 1979) (word-processorlike program to create architecture drawing is within Section 101).

[49] 450 US 175 (1981).

[50] Id. at 187.

The Court confined its analysis to subject matter coverage under Section 101 and expressly reserved consideration of whether use of known physical steps and a computer control system satisfies statutory standards of novelty[51] and nonobviousness.[52] It concluded that a "claim drawn to subject matter otherwise statutory does not become nonstatutory simply because it uses a mathematical formula, computer program or digital computer."

[2] Post-*Diehr* Analysis

Although *Diamond v. Diehr*[53] was decided by a narrow majority, it provides a clear answer to whether computer program-related inventions are cognizable under Section 101. Computer-based inventions are patentable. However, as to any particular claim involving a programmed computer, a more specific analysis is necessary. This analysis requires differentiation among several forms of computer-related claims. The appellate decisions since *Diehr* reflect continuing uncertainty as to the conditions under which individual claims meet tests for statutory subject matter.

The post-*Diehr* cases continue to apply a two-step analysis for subject matter patentability. The first step is to determine whether the patent claim recites a mathematical algorithm or formula.[54] There remains uncertainty as to when such an algorithm is involved. In one sense, all computer programs involve mathematics, since the operations they encompass are ultimately reduced to a form commonly represented by binary or hexidecimal numbers and information processing proceeds on this basis. However, it is clear that this result is not contemplated either by the U.S. Supreme Court or by the attendant appellate decisions. The Supreme Court cases focus on the preemption of formulas in a manner analogous to cases dealing with attempted preemption of a natural law or an abstract idea. This issue does not arise simply because the lowest level of operation within a computer can be represented in the form of binary number manipulations.

The concerns of the Supreme Court about the preemptive effects of a claim do not arise simply because the program involves manipulation and computation of mathematical data. This was first recognized in *In re Bradley*,[55] a case decided before *Diehr* and affirmed by an equally

---

[51] 35 USC 102 (1982). See infra ¶ 2.12.

[52] 35 USC 103 (1982). See infra ¶ 2.15.

[53] 450 US 175 (1981).

[54] See In re Pardo, 684 F2d 912 (CCPA 1982); In re Taner, 681 F2d 787 (CCPA 1982).

[55] 600 F2d 807 (1979), aff'd, Diamond v. Bradley, 450 US 381 (1981).

divided Supreme Court without an opinion. *Bradley* involved a programmed read only memory (ROM) designed to establish a data structure to permit operations in an environment involving multiple programs. In reversing a rejection of the patent under Section 101, the CCPA noted that it is necessary to distinguish what a computer does from how it is done.

> [A] modern digital computer manipulates data, usually in binary form, by performing mathematical functions. . . . But this is only how the computer does what it does. Of importance is the significance of the data in the real world . . . what the computer is doing. It may represent the solution of the Pythagorean theorem or a complex vector equation . . . [or] the contents of a page . . . or the text of a court opinion. . . . [The latter] information is utterly devoid of mathematical significance.[56]

Bradley concluded that the invention did not involve a mathematical algorithm, since it did not involve any effort to preempt basic mathematical functions.[57]

Bradley establishes a framework, but one that has not been elaborated on or consistently applied in the cases. The analysis should reflect the concerns identified by the Supreme Court. A claim is excluded if it generally preempts mathematical formulas and abstract ideas at least insofar as they are computed or represented within a computer. Preemption will or will not arise depending on what the operation of the program represents and whether the process claim goes beyond mere recitation or computation of a formula. In *Diehr*, the computer operation represented and computed a formula for physical (chemical) reactions. In *Benson*, the formula derived from generally applicable numbers theory. In both cases, an excessive preemption of computation process could be tempered, if at all, only by other aspects of the claim. In contrast, in *Bradley*, a mathematical operation had relevance only as implementing a data structure, and the claim was not defined by the math process, but only by the data structure represented.

This approach can be contrasted to comments in other cases suggesting a view of the term "mathematical algorithm" that may not be connected to the concerns expressed by the Supreme Court. For example, in the case of *In re Abele*,[58] there was a concession that a mathematical algorithm was involved, but the court also noted that the existence of

---

[56] Id. at 813.

[57] See also In re Pardo, 684 F2d 912 (CCPA 1982); In re Taner, 681 F2d 787 (CCPA 1982).

[58] 684 F2d 902 (CCPA 1982).

such was confirmed by claimed steps of calculating values, since this indicated the presence of a mathematical operation.

The second step for determining subject matter patentability is to decide whether the claim as a whole limits the claimed preemption of the formula to a particular application. The courts have phrased this in various ways that often tend to obscure the basic inquiry. For example, in the case of *In re Walter*,[59] a pre-*Diehr* case, the court described an invention as patentable if the algorithm is "implemented in a specific manner to define structural relationships between physical elements of the claims . . . or to refine or limit [process] steps. . . ." After *Diehr*, several decisions continued to use the *Walter* formulation. In contrast, the court in the case of *In re Abele*[60] broadened the analysis in the following terms:

> *Walter* should be read as requiring no more than that the algorithm be "applied in any manner to physical elements or process steps" provided that its application is circumscribed by more than a field of use limitation or nonessential post-solution activity. [If] a claim would be "otherwise statutory," albeit inoperative . . . without the algorithm, the claim . . . presents statutory subject matter when the algorithm is included.[61]

While *Abele* may have misapplied the term "algorithm" for purposes of this issue, its analysis directs attention to the appropriate issue. If a formula is merely presented and the invention simply claims a method for its solution, a patent would preempt all use of the formula in computers and should be denied. In contrast, if the formula is connected to other limiting steps in a claim so that a method of solution is not preempted in the absence of these other steps, a Section 101 claim is valid.[62] One can patent the application of a formula in a process, but Section 101 precludes a patent on the formula itself.

¶ 2.06 PROGRAMS IMPLEMENTING NATURAL LAWS

The application of current standards to program-based inventions can best be seen by reviewing several different forms of invention that have arisen in the reported cases. Of these, the most readily susceptible to

---

[59] 618 F2d 758, 767 (CCPA 1980).

[60] 684 F2d 902 (CCPA 1982).

[61] Id. at 907.

[62] Compare situations in which the data collection is incidental or otherwise not required by the claims process or system. See Parker v. Flook, 437 US 584 (1978); In re Richman, 563 F2d 1026 (CCPA 1977) (preliminary data gathering not sufficient to create Section 101 process).

analysis are claims for programs that state and provide methods to solve equations representing laws of physical science or mathematics.

This type of program was involved in both the *Benson*[63] and the *Diehr*[64] cases. The external boundaries of the case law in cases such as these are relatively clear. A claim that simply recites the algorithm (formula) and presents a method to compute or solve it in a computer is not patentable subject matter. To grant a patent on this claim would effectively monopolize all computer-based implementations of the formula-solving method.[65] At the other extreme, there is no barrier in Section 101 to presenting and computing natural laws as part of a larger process or apparatus.[66] Often, this type of claim will entail using a computer and a programmed formula to monitor a chemical, mechanical, or other process. Where the claim recites the entire process, it states patentable subject matter. The novelty of the nonprogrammed aspects of the process is not an issue under Section 101, although it may be important for other statutory issues such as nonobviousness under Section 103 of the Patent Act.

Falling between these extremes are cases in which some limitations are built into the claim. Where this occurs, the focus is on whether there is in fact an effort to preempt general use of the natural law formula in computers or whether the formula is claimed only as applied to a particular task.[67] Mere recitation that a claim is limited to a particular industry or field will not, in itself, confer patentability.[68] Similarly, "obvious or conventional" pre- or post-solution activity associated with the statement and computation of the formula will not change its otherwise unpatentable character, since such activity does not materially limit the generally preemptive claim.

¶ 2.07 CONVERSION AND SIMULATION PROGRAMS

A second category of software invention under Section 101 includes the patentability of programs that accept data and convert it to more effective use by humans. Such programs have been litigated in the context

---

[63] Gottschalk v. Benson, 409 US 63 (1972).

[64] Diamond v. Diehr, 450 US 175 (1981).

[65] Gottschalk v. Benson, 409 US 63 (1972).

[66] Diamond v. Diehr, 450 US 175 (1981).

[67] See In re Abele, 684 F2d 902 (CCPA 1982).

[68] See Parker v. Flook, 437 US 584 (1978); In re Richman, 563 F2d 1026 (CCPA 1977).

of X-ray technology,[69] radar interpretation,[70] and seismic wave analysis.[71] A distinguishing characteristic of these program patents is that the data input to a program entails description of physical or electrical processes. As a result, the program output is enhanced in a form that facilitates human analysis. In many cases, the data translation is based on a mathematical model of the physical relationship between two physical phenomena.[72] In other cases, the formula estimates or extrapolates unavailable data based on existing information.[73]

The concern about preemption of natural or mathematical principles suggests that a distinction might be drawn between the two uses of mathematics. The extrapolation or estimation model does not state a general principle, but supplies a mathematical function based on the inventor's judgment that the resulting estimation will be useful. However, the reported cases have not drawn this distinction. Instead, the conversion and extrapolation programs are viewed as analogous and, ultimately, as presenting issues no different than those encountered in the context of natural law formulas.

A claim that merely recites the format and method for making the calculations is nonstatutory. This is true whether or not the claim is stated as a process or an apparatus.[74] In contrast, if the claim encompasses an otherwise statutory process or apparatus, it is within Section 101 even though it also includes an estimation or simulation formula implemented through a computer.

In data conversion programs, the program is often not attached to control a larger chemical or physical conversion process, but is grafted onto a system or device designed to collect and display data. As a result, the underlying patentability decision focuses on whether Section 101 encompasses software enhancements of information-gathering technology. The cases suggest that such enhancements are potentially patentable, subject to standards of novelty and obviousness.

For example, *In re Taner*[75] involved a program to simulate continuous wavefront responses based on spherical seismic wave data. The patent claim, however, did not focus solely on the program for making this

---

[69] See In re Abele, 684 F2d 902 (CCPA 1982).

[70] See Lockheed Aircraft Corp. v. United States, 553 F2d 69 (CCPA 1977).

[71] See In re Taner, 681 F2d 787 (CCPA 1982); In re Johnson, 589 F2d 1070 (CCPA 1978).

[72] See In re Taner, 681 F2d 787 (CCPA 1982).

[73] In re Abele, 684 F2d 902 (CCPA 1982).

[74] Id. at 909.

[75] 681 F2d 787 (CCPA 1982).

conversion. Rather, the method claimed included steps to impart the spherical waves into the ground and to collect the resulting data. These process steps were well-known in the industry. However, the court rejected the argument that Section 101 requires proof of physical novelty and held that the entire process claimed was potentially patentable. The court based its decision in part on the belief that the program involved a physical conversion of seismic signals into a different form.[76] This conversion does not occur, and an argument that it does is unnecessary and potentially misleading. The emphasis on physical conversion relates back to characteristics of physical and chemical processes. The program in fact manipulated information about the original exploratory waves. However, the court also discussed and emphasized the basic fact that the claim did not preempt the simulation formula itself. Rather, the claim extended to and was limited by the entire process of seismic exploration and affected the use of the simulation formula only in that context.

A more explicit illustration of the relevant distinction arose in the case of *In re Abele*.[77] *Abele* involved a program to extrapolate CAT scan data to eliminate artifacts in the eventual display. A number of patent claims were at issue, and they are illustrated by two formats. In the first, the claim was stated merely as a "method of displaying data in a field [by] calculating the difference between the local value ... and the average value of the data in a region ... and displaying the ... difference as a signed gray scale. . . ." The second format claimed the foregoing method where the data is "X-ray ... data produced ... by a computed tomography scanner."[78]

The court held that claims in the first format were "directed solely to the mathematical algorithm" and not statutory subject matter. The claim was not limited to a particular computer environment or to a particular type of data. It was in fact immaterial that the output of the calculations was in the form of gray shading on a display, rather than a number. Allowing the claim would effectively preclude any application of the extrapolation formula in any field and to any process or machine.

In contrast, the second claim format stated statutory subject matter under Section 101. The claim extended to and was limited by the production of x-ray data from a tomography scanner. The court rejected the view that in order to qualify for patent the algorithm must define structural relationships between physical elements or refine process steps. It noted simply:

---

[76] Id. at 790.

[77] 684 F2d 902 (CCPA 1982).

[78] Id. at 908.

What appellants have done is to discover an application of an algorithm to process steps which are themselves part of an overall process which is statutory. . . . We are faced simply with an improved CAT-scan process comparable to the improved process for curing synthetic rubber in *Diehr*. The improvement in either case resides in the application of a mathematical formula within the context of a process which encompasses significantly more than the algorithm alone. [79]

In both *Taner* and *Abele* the subsidiary issue was that the process encompassing the algorithm was oriented solely to collecting the data to which the formula was applied and the end result of the process was a display of the computation result. In some cases, this circumstance may be an effort to circumvent the bar against patenting a formula in the abstract. For example, this was true in *Flook* [80] where the Court rejected the argument that merely setting an alarm limit as a result of computation created a patentable claim. Both *Taner* and *Abele* avoid this indirect preemption. In each case, even absent the applied algorithm, the process or machine claim would be within Section 101 (i.e., tomography scanner, seismic exploration system). Under that circumstance, the relationship of the process to mere data collection is not fatal to patent eligibility.

¶ 2.08 INTERNAL OPERATION PROGRAMS

Most reported cases under Section 101 have focused on program-related inventions involving mathematical algorithms representing natural laws and mathematical principles. Where these have been claimed in the abstract they are not patentable. Where they are connected to a process historically cognizable under patent law, Section 101 eligibility is met.

Left unaddressed is most mass-marketed microcomputer software, which instructs a general purpose computer to perform useful functions, but does not on its surface either express mathematical formulas or connect to a broader, traditionally patentable process or item. For these programs, Section 101 patentability may be moot, since patent standards of obviousness preclude serious consideration for patent protection. Nevertheless, it is useful to discuss some competing lines of case law that bear on the issue. The first relates to internal operations.

---

[79] Id. at 909.

[80] Parker v. Flook, 437 US 584 (1978).

In re Bradley[81] involved a program designed to shape and control the internal operations of a computer, specifically a ROM resident program that could "alter or reposition" information in a computer's "system base" to permit operation in a multiprogrammed format. The CCPA concluded that this program, described as creating and manipulating data structures, did not involve a mathematical algorithm. As a result, it was eligible for a patent under Section 101. However, rather than support patentability for all such programs, the court noted "If appellants were claiming the information embodied in the firmware or the firmware itself, per se, a different case would be presented. We express no opinion on the statutory nature of such an invention."[82]

Programs designed to shape the internal operations of a computer do not present unique problems under Section 101 as long as the claim pertains to methods for organizing or sequencing data or information within a computer. This view is supported by *In re Pardo*,[83] a case decided after the Supreme Court decision in *Diamond v. Diehr. Pardo* involved a compiler program for converting source code programs into object code programs. It was described as converting a computer "from a sequential processor . . . to a processor which is not dependent on the order in which it receives program steps."[84] The Patent Office rejected the claim partly because it indirectly involved a mathematical calculation, since the programs affected by the resequencing were expressed as mathematical formulas. The court reversed, emphasizing that the claim related to managing the internal operations of the system and did not involve mathematical formulas.

> [We] are unable to find any mathematical formula, calculation, or algorithm . . . recited in the claimed steps of examining, compiling, storing and executing. . . . the present application is not "mathematical" (although it deals with the proper sequence for performing mathematics), but it does establish the rules which are to be followed by a data processor. . . . [the claim involves] a method for controlling the internal operations of a computer to govern the manner in which programs are executed.[85]

Pardo may reflect the manner in which claims are drafted. More generally, however, operating programs exemplify a context in which the

---

[81] 600 F2d 807 (1979), aff'd, Diamond v. Bradley, 450 US 381 (1981); see also In re Chatfield, 545 F2d 152 (CCPA 1976).

[82] In re Bradley, 600 F2d 807, 812 (1979).

[83] 684 F2d 912 (CCPA 1982).

[84] Id. at 913.

[85] Id. at 916.

transition from traditional patent subjects to a computer software environment is the least problematic, since machine operations are involved rather than pure manipulation of information. In any event, subject to other restraints, there is little rationale to deny patent protection per se to operating programs. No risk of scientific or mathematical preemption is entailed. Indeed, as *Bradley* and *Pardo* confirm, no mathematical algorithm is involved.

¶ 2.09 ARTIFICIAL INTELLIGENCE PROGRAMS

The field of artificial intelligence is at the forefront of contemporary technology development. In part, this field is dependent on software design and performance. Broadly defined, it encompasses software-driven systems that are capable of evaluating data and producing decisions for the human user. At least at present, most decision-making systems rely on structures and analytical formats established within a program with data based on expert knowledge.

If internal operating programs are closest to historical patent subject matter, artificial intelligence or decision-making programs are farthest. The processing steps created exemplify neither natural laws nor machine operations. Instead, they reflect the designer's conception of how a given problem might be analyzed or, at least, how useful information about the problem might be processed. The closest, if inexact, analogy is to the human thought process.

Although this area may ultimately become a context for substantial litigation, only one reported case directly addresses the patentability of artificial intelligence programs. In the case of *In re Meyer*,[86] the court considered the patentability of a program for identifying areas of malfunction in a complex system. Although apparently designed as an aid for medical diagnosis based on a variety of tests, the claim was stated in general terms. As described in the claim, the process entailed dividing a complex system into numerous "arbitrary subdivisions (elements) and associating a function and malfunction factor with each." For a particular application, a table would be compiled identifying the outcome of various tests of the system and associating substantively relevant function or malfunction values for each element of the system. The values associated with each element would be incremented in response to test results, eventually tabulating to indicate areas of probable malfunction in the system. The results of the analysis could be displayed in various forms depending on the nature of the complex system being tested.

---

[86] 688 F2d 790 (CCPA 1982).

The court concluded that this general claim did not recite statutory subject matter,[87] and that a mathematical algorithm was implicated in the step of modifying the value of factors associated with system elements based on the results of individual steps. Manifestly, the algorithm did not represent a natural law and the claim did not attempt to preempt the process of modifying values by addition or subtraction. Nevertheless, the claim was unpatentable because the algorithm represented a mental process or abstract idea and was not applied to an otherwise statutory subject matter.

> [It] must be determined whether a scientific principle, law of nature, idea, or mental process, which may be represented by a mathematical algorithm, is included. . . . Appellants' specification and arguments indicate that their invention is concerned with replacing, in part, the thinking processes of a neurologist. . . . Counsel . . . acknowledged . . . that the claims recite a mathematical algorithm, which represents a mental process. . . . Thus, the decisive question is whether that mental process is applied to physical elements or process steps in an otherwise statutory process, machine, manufacture or composition of matter. [Here, it is not].[88]

Meyer adopts a potentially significant expansion of Section 101 exclusionary doctrine, but adequately defines neither the rationale, nor the appropriate limits of the doctrine. It indicates that claims to mathematical procedures representing abstract ideas or mental processes must be linked with more traditional patent subject matter. This linkage does not apply if the mental process is not represented or claimed in mathematical terms.[89] Yet this aspect of the language of the claim does not affect the scope of any resulting patent. In any event, many computer programs involve information processing in a manner that in some form replicates a potential mental process. The essence of software technology is to develop processes to expedite processing of information.

Meyer should be limited or explained more by the character of the claim than by any general objection to information processing that in some form replicates human thought. As claimed in *Meyer*, the program was barely structured, unaccompanied by application to any specific complex system or series of tests. Furthermore, it was not even limited to

---

[87] Id. at 796.

[88] Id. at 795.

[89] See In re Pardo, 684 F2d 912 (CCPA 1982); In re Toma, 575 F2d 872 (CCPA 1978) (method to operate human language translator is within Section 101); In re Phillips, 608 F2d 879 (CCPA 1979) (word-processorlike program to create architecture drawing is within Section 101); Paine, Webber, Jackson & Curtis v. Merrill Lynch, Inc., 564 F. Supp. 1358, 218 USPQ 212 (D. Del. 1983).

use of the claimed analytical process in a computer environment. In this form, the claim attempts to preempt a wide variety of dissimilar applications. The judgment in *Meyer* was that basic structures around which complex analyses can be built represent tools of science, rather than patentable subject matter. These tools cannot be preempted in general, abstract terms.

¶ 2.10 APPLICATIONS PROGRAMS

Between decision-making programs and internal operating programs, there exists a wide variety of applications software that might fall within the boundaries of patent protection. These include various word processing, accounting, database management, and spreadsheet programs. In most cases, the patentability of such software may never be tested under Section 101, since they will fail to meet obviousness standards applicable to patent applications under Section 103 of the Patent Act.[90]

These applications programs clearly state patentable subject matter under Section 101 if the claim encompasses elements of the hardware environment in which they function. The patentability of software-hardware combinations is supported in each of the areas discussed here. Even if the structure of the program implicates a mathematical algorithm, it should remain patentable as part of a process or apparatus encompassing hardware elements. In all such cases, the hardware system represents an otherwise patentable subject matter, and the overall nature of the claim is not altered by inclusion of a software element.[91]

Claims that focus on software separate from a hardware environment present more difficult issues. The current PTO Guidelines concerning computer programs suggest that a claim drafted to a program instruction set separate from an operating environment may not be patentable. The reported cases do not contradict this suggestion.

Such a computer language listing of instructions, when not associated with a computing machine to accomplish a specific purpose, would not constitute a machine implemented process, but would constitute nonstatutory subject matter as the mere idea or abstract

---

[90] 35 USC § 103 (1982); see infra ¶ 2.15; see, e.g., Orthopedic Equip. Co. v. United States, 217 USPQ 193 (Fed. Cir. 1983).

[91] See In re Taner, 681 F2d 787 (CCPA 1982); In re Abele, 684 F2d 902 (CCPA 1982).

intellectual concept of the programmer, or as a collection of printed matter.[92]

This analysis, however, is restricted to programs claimed in a pure, pristine form without reference to apparatus, process operations, or the like. In fact, applications programs in various forms have been held to be patentable under Section 101 with only minimal specification of the physical environment in which they will operate.

The critical issue in such cases has been whether the applications program recites a mathematical algorithm and merely provides a process to solve that equation. In most cases, while the applications program may involve numerical processing, its operational functions do not raise the preemption issues noted in *Benson, Flook,* and *Diehr.*[93] For example, in the case of *In re Toma,*[94] a program to translate text from one language to another was held to state patentable subject matter. While the program followed a sequence of steps described as an algorithm in the software profession, the court held that there was no direct or indirect statement of a procedure to solve a mathematical problem. Similarly, in the case of *In re Phillips,*[95] a program described in mathematical form to produce architectural drawings was patentable since it did not merely solve arithmetic calculations. In *Paine, Webber, Jackson & Curtis v. Merrill Lynch, Inc.,*[96] the court affirmed patentability of a computer system to manage cash management accounts at a brokerage firm. While the program dealt with and processed numbers, none of the steps claimed a "mere procedure for solving mathematical problems."

Paine, Webber involved an additional claim often raised under Section 101 against business applications programs. In essence, it was argued that the claim merely involved a "method of doing business" that is historically excluded under Section 101. The court rejected this argument as mistakenly focusing on what the program produces. If no *Benson* mathematical "algorithm exists, the product of a computer program is irrelevant, the focus of the analysis should be on the operation of the program on the computer."[97] A business operation is unpatentable only if a claim

---

[92] See PTO, "Mathematical Algorithms or Computer Programs," MPEP 2110 (1983).

[93] Gottschalk v. Benson, 409 US 63 (1972); Diamond v. Diehr, 450 US 175 (1981); Parker v. Flook, 437 US 584 (1978).

[94] 575 F2d 872 (CCPA 1978).

[95] 600 F2d 879 (CCPA 1979).

[96] 564 F. Supp. 1358, 218 USPQ 212 (D. Del. 1983).

[97] Id. at 1358, 218 USPQ at 220.

seeks to encompass the business activity itself, including manual operation. In *Paine, Webber* this breadth of claim was clearly not present.

PART C.   NOVELTY, UTILITY, AND OBVIOUSNESS

¶ 2.11 ISSUES BEYOND SUBJECT MATTER

Assuming that a particular claim involves statutory subject matter under Section 101 of the Patent Act, the ability to obtain a patent for the invention is contingent on compliance with a variety of further, substantive standards. These additional standards provide significant barriers to effective patent protection. Unlike under the copyright system, proprietary rights under patent law are not conveyed merely on the basis that a claimed invention is new or original to the claimant, although these requirements are imposed. Rather, patent protection is granted only on the basis of relatively high standards of originality and invention.

Although a variety of substantive and procedural issues must be resolved to obtain a patent, this discussion will concentrate on three primary areas. These are: (1) the requirement of novelty and related considerations involving the timeliness of the claim; (2) the requirement that the claim involve a useful article or process; and (3) the requirement that the invention not be obvious to a person skilled in the relevant art.

¶ 2.12 NOVELTY

Section 102 of the Patent Act contains a number of "conditions for patentability." Included is the following language

> A person shall be entitled to a patent unless ... the invention was known or used by others in this country, or patented or described in a printed publication in this or a foreign country [or] described in a patent or an application for patent filed by another ... before the invention thereof by the applicant for patent.[98]

The doctrine established in this language has been described in terms of either novelty or anticipation. Under either label, this language establishes a core concept of the patent system. Subject to very limited exceptions[99] (e.g., used in a foreign country), the invention claimed by the

---

[98] 35 USC § 102(a)(e) (1982).

[99] See *Deller's Walker on Patents* § 59.

applicant must in fact be new and not already known, used, or available to others.

[1] Prior Invention

The statutory concept of novelty bars a grant of a patent if an identical or virtually identical process or machine is already known, used, or patented at the time of the claimed invention. In this regard, the criterion of novelty or anticipation has been described as a narrow technical defense.[100] It is a technical barrier at least in that anticipation of the invention can be found whether or not the applicant was aware of the existing prior art relevant to his claim.[101] In a sense, the inventor is conclusively presumed to have knowledge of the entire field in which he works. More accurately, the proprietary rights granted under patent law are reserved solely for the first to invent a given process or machine.

The barrier of novelty or anticipation, however, only applies if the preexisting work is virtually identical to the claimed invention. Cases in the area of mechanical devices commonly refer to "physical identity" between the two works.[102] Implicit within this requirement is the fact that the invention itself must be new, not merely an existing machine or process utilized for a new function. However, the courts have not always required virtual identity in order to conclude that a claimed invention has been anticipated in the prior art. Slight, relatively immaterial differences do not establish novelty unless they go to the heart of inventive change in the work. Similarly, identity must be viewed in light of what is actually being claimed in the allegedly second work. Generally, the broader the claim, the more likely that an apparently dissimilar work will constitute an anticipation.

One example of this latter point arose in *RCA v. Applied Digital Data System, Inc.*[103] In *Applied Digital*, the claim covered a system for decoding digital computer symbol controls and direct converting into digital video signal controls. Although the applicant noted that the system would increase efficiency in the use of standard TV displays without intermediate memory storage, the claim was broadly written to encompass any display device using raster scan line patterns. The lower court held that the claim was anticipated by a patent in the 1950s using dissimilar technology. The Federal Circuit Court of Appeals reversed. Although the patent

---

[100] See, e.g., RCA Corp. v. Applied Digital Sys., Inc., 221 USPQ 385 (Fed. Cir. 1984).

[101] See Mast-Foos v. Stover, 177 US 485 (1900).

[102] See, e.g., Scholl, Inc. v. Kresge Co., 580 F2d 244 (7th Cir. 1978).

[103] 221 USPQ 385 (Fed. Cir. 1984).

claim was broad as to the environment in which it operated, it did not claim all means for tracking the horizontal position of a beam. The digital process for this in the claim was not anticipated by the prior patent.

[2] Prior Publication

In addition to anticipation by prior use or patent, a patent claim is barred if the invention was previously described in a printed publication.[104] This barrier originates from the same assumption that underlies prior use, knowledge, or patent. It does not require that the inventor read or was even aware of the publication. However, the publication must have been publicly available and must have preceded the invention.[105] It is not sufficient if publication occurred in the interval from invention to grant of a patent.

¶ 2.13 TIMELY APPLICATION

Beyond establishing standards of novelty, Section 102 of the Patent Act and related case law establish timeliness limits related to applying for a patent. In general, these are oriented toward the objective of promoting public disclosure of inventions. The statutory aspect provides that: "A person is entitled to a patent unless . . . the invention was . . . described in a publication in this or a foreign country or in public use or on sale in this country, more than one year prior to the date of the application [or] he has abandoned his invention."[106]

The forfeiture after a one-year delay from public use or sale imposes what amounts to a statute of limitations between reducing an invention to practice and applying for a patent. It is buttressed by case law interpreting preapplication acts that amounted to suppressing the disclosure of the invention to constitute an abandonment.[107] Together, these doctrines preclude an inventor from exploiting an invention without patent-related disclosure for substantial periods during which commercial or other advantage might be obtained.

Application of these timeliness standards often involves several difficult issues in the normal context in which an invention proceeds through

---

[104] 35 USC § 102(a) (1982).

[105] See Lockheed Aircraft Corp. v. United States, 553 F2d 69, 74 (CCPA 1977).

[106] 35 USC § 102(b)(c) (1982).

[107] See, e.g., Kurt H. Volk, Inc. v. Foundation for Christian Living, 213 USPQ 756, 775 (SDNY 1982).

various prototype or experimental stages prior to completion. The one-year period to apply for a patent does not arise until the invention is described in a publication, placed in use, or held on sale. All of these events presume a completed invention that has been reduced to practice.[108] However, even after an operable model is developed, it is not uncommon to engage in a significant period of testing, experimental use, and modification. The results are often close questions of fact concerning when the invention was first put in use or on sale.

This issue arose with the patent issued for the ENIAC computer. A substantial period of classified development and limited use followed by some public demonstrations was held not to be public use until the machine was used for the purpose for which it was designed.[109] A significant factor in that case was the time at which the inventor's motivation shifted from a desire to experiment to a desire to commercially exploit his invention. It is important to recognize that the on-sale criterion in the statute refers not to the first actual sale, but to the point at which the invention is held out as available for a sale.[110]

¶ 2.14 UTILITY

Section 101 of the Patent Act extends patent coverage to "any new and useful process, machine, manufacture, or composition of matter." Based in part on this language and in part on an analogous reference in the constitutional grant, it has generally been held that patent protection extends only to useful or utilitarian inventions.

The criterion of utility is often misperceived. It does not require that an invention perform a function more effectively than preceding systems, although allegations to that effect are commonly included in patent applications. Rather, the reference has two more limited connotations. The first is that a claimed invention must be operable to perform the function assigned to it.[111] This is commonly encompassed within the concept that the claimed invention must have been reduced to practice to qualify for a

---

[108] See Preemption Devices v. Minnesota Mining & Mfg. Co., 559 F. Supp. 1250 (ED Pa. 1983) (demonstration models were not, under all the circumstances, on sale).

[109] See Sperry Rand Corp. v. Bell Tel. Labs, 208 F. Supp. 598 (1962).

[110] See Racal-Vadic, Inc. v. Universal Data Sys., 207 USPQ 902 (ND Ala. 1980).

[111] See Technitrol, Inc. v. Control Data Corp., 550 F2d 992, 997 (4th Cir. 1977), cert. denied, 434 US 882 (1978).

patent.[112] However, assuming operability, comparative commercial value is not an issue.[113]

The second connotation of utility is that the invention must be directed to a useful function. Again, usefulness is not value-laden and patent may encompass inventive means for entertainment. Nevertheless, an idea stated and claimed in the abstract independent of any useful function is not patentable.[114]

¶ 2.15 NONOBVIOUSNESS

While novelty and utility are major elements of substantive patent law, the requirement that the claimed invention not be obvious to persons skilled in the art is, in most cases, the single most significant barrier to obtaining and enforcing a valid patent. Section 103 of the Patent Act provides

> A patent may not be obtained ... if the difference between the subject matter sought to be patented and the prior art are such that the subject matter as a whole would have been obvious at the time the invention was made to a person having ordinary skill in the art to which said subject matter pertains.[115]

The requirement that the claimed invention be nonobvious applies over and above the requirement that it be novel. It seeks to distinguish between mere incremental or developmental change and a level of inventive change sufficient to justify the award of a patent.

The nature of the distinction attempted by the nonobviousness standard in itself defines a major portion of the difficulty in administering the criterion. Obviousness is an important barrier to obtaining a patent not only because it is often difficult to prove, but more basically because it is difficult to define what is being sought in the analysis. Over the years, the courts have attempted, with varying levels of success, to define the constituent elements of what made a particular invention nonobvious and therefore eligible for a patent. An early U.S. Supreme Court case suggested that the central distinction was that the invention "must reveal the

---

[112] See McDonnell Douglas Corp. v. United States, 670 F2d 156 (Ct. Cl. 1982) (inadequate computer simulation not reduction to practice).

[113] See, e.g., Studiengesellschaft Kohle v. Eastman Kodak Co., 616 F2d 1315 (5th Cir. 1980).

[114] See PTO, "Mathematical Algorithms or Computer Programs," MPEP 2110 (1983).

[115] 35 USC § 103 (1982).

flash of creative genius, not merely the skill of the calling."[116] This suggested the need for sudden insight and contradicted the normal, laborious, and meticulous development that accompanies most true inventions. The suggestion has since been directly overruled by a statute that provides that patentability shall not be denied by the manner in which the invention was made.[117] While the standard does not hinge on the method of invention, it nevertheless does require significant innovation. The difficulty lies in identifying the constituent elements in a particular case.

Ultimately, obviousness issues involve subjective judgments guided by a statutory reference point grounded in the prior art. The classic formulation of the steps of an obviousness analysis was stated by the Supreme Court in *Graham v. John Deere Co.*[118] "*Graham* suggests a tripartite test. A court must first determine the scope and content of the prior art and then examine the difference between the prior art and claims at issue. Finally, the court should ascertain the level of ordinary skill within the art."[119] This "test," which is cited in virtually every reported case on the issue, clearly references the nature of the factual inquiry. It stops short of providing explicit guidance on the decisional criteria once the facts have been accumulated. The eventual judgment based on this information is treated as a question of law, rather than fact.[120]

The statute requires that the invention not be obvious to persons skilled in the relevant art. This implies that the invention be different in form, method, or structure from what was previously in use and that the difference be such that would not have been expected or predictable based on then-current technology. Generally, it is not sufficient that an existing process or machine simply be applied in a new function. Similarly, it is not enough that existing developmental trends be taken to a predictable new level. A break from prior art in terms of method or structure is often required.[121]

Two major themes present in the cases on obviousness are relevant here. The first is what has been described as the combination patent. This label refers to the circumstance in which a patent claim is comprised entirely of elements already known in the prior art, but combined in an

---

[116] Cuno Eng'g Corp. v. Automatic Devices Corp., 314 US 84, 91 (1941).

[117] 35 USC § 103 (1982).

[118] 383 US 1, 17 (1966).

[119] Preemption Devices v. Minnesota Mining & Mfg. Co., 559 F. Supp. 1250, 1261 (ED Pa. 1983).

[120] Graham v. John Deere Co., 383 US 1, 17 (1966).

[121] See 2 Rosenberg, *Patent Law Fundamentals* 9-47.

allegedly nonobvious manner.[122] At a basic level, most if not all inventions share this characteristic, at least in part. A process or machine comprised of known parts is an nonobvious invention if the combination is clearly new and not obvious. A closer issue arises if the combination involves limited or relatively obvious changes from the prior art. In this context, a number of courts require that nonobviousness be found in the result of the combination and, often, that this involve what has been described as a "synergistic" result—a result apparently greater than or different from the otherwise expected product of the combination.[123]

While the notion of synergism is imprecise and the degree of difference from expected results difficult to define, it is a natural outgrowth of the context. Patent law requires some element over and above mere novelty in order to qualify for a grant of a patent. In a combination claim, by definition, this element can not be found in the discrete elements of the combination. As a result, it must reside either in the selection and combination itself, or in the result thereof.

A second theme of particular relevance is the manner in which the prior art is defined for purposes of assessing obviousness. Section 102 refers simply to a person with "ordinary skill in the art to which [the invention] pertains." In part, this requires assessment of ordinary skill levels once the art or field is identified. On this question, the relevant standards are reasonably well developed. The reference is not to the leading figures in the field, but to the ordinary practitioner.[124] However, unlike the true ordinary practitioner in many fields, the hypothetical person is presumed to be possessed of comprehensive knowledge of and familiarity with prior work in the field.[125]

Assessing an appropriate level of skill must be preceded by a determination of which fields of science or technology are pertinent to the claimed invention.[126] This does not focus on the particular field in which the alleged inventor was trained. Rather, the reference is more in the form of an external or objective standard. The pertinent fields for inquiry are

---

[122] See, e.g., Sarkasian v. Winn-Proof Corp., 697 F2d 1313 (9th Cir. 1983).

[123] See Sakraida v. Ag Pro, Inc., 425 US 273, reh'g denied, 426 US 955 (1976); American Seating Co. v. National Seating Co., 586 F2d 611 (6th Cir. 1978); Sarkasian v. Winn-Proof Corp., 697 F2d 1313 (9th Cir. 1983).

[124] Graham v. John Deere Co., 383 US 1, 18 (1966); Dann v. Johnston, 425 US 219 (1976); In re Laverne, 356 F2d 1003 (CCPA 1966).

[125] See, e.g., Toyota Shibaura Elec. Co. v. Zenith Radio Corp., 548 F2d 88, 94 (3d Cir. 1977).

[126] See Technographic Printed Circuits v. Bendix Corp., 140 USPQ 285 (4th Cir. 1964) (printed circuit claims obvious in light of other patents in the area).

those that deal with similar problems and elements or those to which an inventor might reasonably be expected to refer.[127]

This issue becomes especially important in contexts where the claimed invention involves incorporating technology from one field to improve systems in another, a circumstance characteristic of computer or information technology. The formal issue in such cases often turns on whether a court restricts its focus in selecting the prior art to the field receiving the new technology. If so, developments from another field are likely to be viewed as nonobvious. More basic is the policy question of to what extent patent law does or should support cross-fertilization of fields of technology. As is shown in subsequent sections, courts have reached different results on this issue.

[1] Hardware Technology

With the rapid growth of the microprocessor and peripheral industries, it is not surprising that various elements of computer architecture and manufacturing have been subject to patent protection. The reported case law dealing with these patents exemplifies the often close questions that are involved in obviousness litigation. It also suggests at least two generic patterns of relevance to hardware patents.

Since the earliest patents on computer hardware, the cases have focused on assessing the degree of change embodied in an invention claim relevant to the current status of information technology. Consistent with the general conception of invention, the focus is not on the extent of physical change, but rather on the significance and purpose of the change itself. A recurrent theme consists of prior art characterized by extensive research and development on a particular problem, followed by a patent claim employing methodology or structure that was previously disregarded or rejected in the earlier work in the field. To the extent that the claimed invention represents what amounts to a change of direction, it is more likely to be patentable even though, once disclosed, it entails what appears to be only a small change in applications.

United States Phillips Corp. v. National Micronetics, Inc.[128] is illustrative of this "changed direction" approach. *Phillips* involved a claim for a method for manufacturing recording heads through the use of capillarity. The court's analysis of the prior art revealed substantial and long-

---

[127] See Dann v. Johnston, 425 US 219 (1976); Mandel Bros. v. Wallace, 335 US 291 (1948); George J. Meyer Mfg. Co. v. San Marino Elec. Corp., 422 F2d 1285 (9th Cir. 1970); Weather Eng'g Corp. v. United States, 204 USPQ 41 (Ct. Cl. 1979).

[128] 550 F2d 716 (2d Cir. 1977).

standing efforts to design manufacturing processes to efficiently produce recording heads with smooth surfaces within extremely tight tolerances. This effort was noted as a secondary indicator of patentability in that it established a long-felt need for improvement of the manufacturing technology. More significantly, the claimant's approach to solving the tolerance-smoothness problem employed a process that differed materially from that previously used.

> Thus, the picture of the art of manufacturing . . . prior to Peloschek is one in which . . . each of the processes immediately preceding Peloschek employed variations on a method which bonded the magnetic and nonmagnetic materials through the use of heat and . . . pressure in a sandwich configuration. . . . The Peloschek patent differs significantly. . . . First, the Peloschek patent places the glass bonding material outside of the preset gap. . . . Second, it departs from the use of pressure to accomplish bonding and relies instead on the force of capillarity.[129]

The court sustained the validity of the patent claim. "In lieu of an unsuccessful refinement of an existing process, Peloschek reveals a flash of brilliance . . . however simple, by departing from the norm."[130] In the view of the majority, this change of direction was prototypical of what should be the focus of patent law protection. The "flash of brilliance" does not involve speed or suddenness of insight, but rather a successful effort to break from established precedent.[131]

Beneath the surface of the court's decision, however, lies an important assumption or decision about the scope of prior art against which the inventor's product should be compared. The dissenting opinion in *Phillips* describes the claim as "an adaptation of a physical process familiar to every embryonic schoolboy scientist."[132] The principle is that under correct conditions liquids permeate into other adjacent materials. In assessing the obviousness of the claim, the dissenters noted that the inventor should be viewed as having knowledge and familiarity with all of the pertinent art. The dissenters argued that the pertinent art included not only recorder head manufacturing, but also the variety of patents using capillarity to fill in areas in the closely related fields of electronics and magnetics.

---

[129] Id. at 721.

[130] Id. at 723.

[131] See Racal-Vadic, Inc. v. Universal Data Sys., 207 USPQ 902 (ND Ala. 1980); Preemption Devices v. Minnesota Mining & Mfg. Co., 559 F. Supp. 1250 (ED Pa. 1983); In re Markowitz, 143 USPQ 303 (PTO Bd. App. 1964).

[132] United States Phillips Corp. v. National Micronetics, Inc., 550 F2d 716, 784 (2d Cir. 1977) (dissent).

The majority opinion responded by indicating that capillarity had not previously been employed in this particular industry and that some research in other contexts indicated it was inappropriate for molten glass, the liquid actually used in this patent. This latter, technical issue is less important in this context than is the underlying doctrinal or policy conflict. The majority regarded importation of capillarity techniques into this particular industry as an inventive step. This view was implemented in part by focusing consideration of prior art on the particular industry. This same approach characterizes most cases in the hardware field. In contrast, the dissenters regarded this step as obvious and insisted on a higher standard of invention. This would be implemented by more broadly defining the scope of the prior art.

Even with a focus on prior art within a particular industrial application, patent protection requires more than an incremental expansion on existing techniques or structures. For example, several patent claims dealing with integrated circuit and silicon chip technology have been rejected as obvious developments in light of existing art. One illustration of this result is *Technographic Printed Circuits, Ltd. v. Bendix Corp.*[133] In *Technographic*, the patent claim involved an allegedly new technique for printing circuits with the use of thin metal foils. The court rejected the claim after an extensive review of various patents involving use of thin metal sheets for imprinting circuits. Similarly, in the case of *In re Ogiue*[134] a technique for using insulating substrata in silicon chips was deemed obvious in light of extensive prior development on refining insulation structures.[135]

Within the extremes of marginal improvement (unpatentable) of existing technique and clearly divergent (patentable) processes or structures lie a large number of potentially patentable changes in which obviousness is an issue. One peculiar characteristic of the law in this area is that as the level of research and implemented development on a particular topic increases, the range for patentable invention decreases or at least shifts to new contexts. Increased sophistication and diversification of prior art narrow the likelihood of nonobvious invention.

[2] Physical Augmentation by Computer

One characteristic of the development of information technology is the application of hardware and software systems to improve existing

---

[133] 140 USPQ 285 (4th Cir. 1964).

[134] 186 USPQ 227 (PTO Bd. App. 1975).

[135] See also Potter Instruments Co. v. ODEC Computer Sys., Inc., 370 F. Supp. 198, aff'd, 499 F2d 209 (1st Cir. 1974) (use of chain belt for high-speed printer is obvious).

industrial, medical, and other processes. For purposes of reviewing the patent implications of these innovations, it is useful to distinguish two broad categories. The first, discussed here, applies the technology to physical or chemical processes typically involving industrial or medical applications. The second, discussed in the next section, involves data processing applications to business functions such as inventory control and accounting.

Within the general area of physical process applications, in assessing obviousness an initial question arises concerning whether the relevant prior art encompasses only the field of the particular application or extends more broadly to encompass information processing techniques in general. This decision will dramatically affect the tenor of the ultimate decision. Arguably, one objective of patent law should be to encourage the transplantation of technologies from one field to improve processes in another. This is more readily accomplished through prior art definitions that, at least at the outset of the transplantation process, more narrowly define the pertinent art. After a technology has been transported to a new application and its benefits become known, a broader definition of prior art may be appropriate.

The reported cases generally support this flexible approach. For example, several recent cases have rejected patent claims relating to improved cardiac pacemakers as obvious where the improvement involves altered digital or analog techniques. This has occurred in the context of relatively broad definitions of pertinent art in a field where such techniques are already widely used. Illustrative is *Cardiac Pacemakers, Inc. v. Cordis Corp.*,[136] which defined the relevant art as not limited to biomedical implants, but included "the field of electrical engineering in general, and more specifically, the use of both digital and analog circuitry." In contrast, a number of reported cases limit pertinent art to the particularized application area.[137] While knowledge of information technology may not be appropriately assumed at the outset of developing their application to a new area, it is certainly appropriate to assume knowledge when use of the technology is widespread in the industry.

Assuming that prior art has been defined, the cases in this context parallel those discussed earlier in looking for significant changes in direction or function as a characteristic of a patentable claim. Generally, this

---

[136] 215 USPQ 604 (D. Minn. 1981); see also Medtronic, Inc. v. Cardiac Pacemakers, Inc., 555 F. Supp. 1214 (D. Minn 1983), modified and aff'd, 721 F2d 1563 (Fed. Cir. 1983).

[137] See Lockheed Aircraft Corp. v. United States, 553 F2d 69 (Ct. Cl. 1977) (radar art); Preemption Devices v. Minnesota Mining & Mfg. Co., 559 F. Supp. 1250 (ED Pa. 1983).

element is not found in the simple introduction of the new technology itself or the enhanced efficiency that may be claimed.[138] Rather, there is more particularized attention to changes in the concept or function of the process made possible and implemented by the technology. Illustrative of this point is *Lockheed Aircraft Corp. v. United States,*[139] which involved use of a computer to calculate target height based on direct measurement of the time differential between receipt of direct and ground-reflected radar echoes. At the time of the invention, the relationship between height and reflection time was known, but existing systems could not integrate the data. Existing research on the problem focused on a totally different approach to its resolution. The patent claim was held to be valid without inquiring whether the data analysis techniques were unique in the information processing art. A similar case is *Preemption Devices v. Minnesota Mining & Manufacturing Co.,*[140] which involved automated traffic light systems designed to respond to the presence of an emergency vehicle. In upholding the patent, the court emphasized that the system altered both the type of sensing device used and the sequence in which the light was changed to allow the vehicle to pass.

[3] Business Data Processing

In contrast to applications in physical processes, computer-based automation of business operations such as inventory control and accounting have generally not survived the requirement that they represent nonobvious inventions. Among the earliest cases on this issue was a U.S. Supreme Court decision in *Dann v. Johnston.*[141] *Dann* involved a "machine system for automatic recordkeeping of bank checks and deposits" in a format that permitted reports broken down by account category. At the time the system was developed, banks were making extensive use of automation, but no existing bank system had the processing and report capacity of the claimed invention. The Court held that the invention was obvious in light of the existing automation and an earlier patent on an analogous system for complex organizations, although not for banks.

> [Obviousness] is measured not in terms of what would be obvious to a layman, but rather . . . to one "reasonably skilled in [the applicable] art." [Such] hypothetical person would be aware of . . . the extensive

---

[138] See Digitronics Corp. v. New York Racing Ass'n, 553 F2d 740 (2d Cir. 1977).

[139] 553 F2d 69 (Ct. Cl. 1977).

[140] 559 F. Supp. 1250 (ED Pa. 1983).

[141] 425 US 219 (1976).

use of data processing systems in the banking industry and of the system [in the earlier] patent.[142]

Subsequent cases have been more explicit in defining the pertinent art and applying obviousness bars to business automation systems. For example, in *Orthopedic Equipment Co. v. United States*,[143] the court rejected a patent for a multi-station material and order handling system. The system was described as an obvious innovation based on the pertinent art of "information processing systems hardware" design. Similarly, in *Digitronics Corp. v. New York Racing Association*,[144] the court rejected a patent on an automated system to process, record, and update race track betting transactions with the following comment

> [The patent claims] do not perform functions that differ from prior art in the totalizer business; they achieve those functions through means that, while new to the totalizer business, were well-established in the wider [pertinent] data processing field . . . appellant's contribution involved simply the upgrading of a well-defined, existing . . . system by converting some components . . . from electromechanical to solid state electronic data processing.[145]

As these cases suggest, merely bringing data processing technology into a new business environment is typically insufficient inventiveness for purposes of patent protection. The electronic data processing profession or art is ubiquitous in character and its application to new fields is construed as obvious.[146]

PART D.   INFRINGEMENT

¶ 2.16 INFRINGEMENT

Unlike the Copyright Act, which defines specific exclusive rights held by the owner of a copyright, the Patent Act defines those acts of other people that constitute an infringement of a patent. Under Section 271 of the Patent Act, the primary form of infringement includes making,

---

[142] Id. at 229.

[143] 702 F2d 1005 (Fed. Cir. 1983).

[144] 553 F2d 740 (2d Cir. 1977).

[145] Id. at 745, 747; see also In re Kaslow, 217 USPQ 1089 (Fed. Cir. 1983) (computer checkout system is obvious).

[146] Paine, Webber, Jackson & Curtis v. Merrill Lynch, Inc., 564 F. Supp. 1358, 218 USPQ 212 (D. Del. 1983).

using, or selling any patented invention.[147] That same section also defines as actionable conduct the active inducement of infringement and certain conduct constituting contributory infringement. The holder of the patent is entitled to damages and, in appropriate cases, to an injunction against the infringing party.[148] Typically, damages involve lost profits, but the statute establishes a reasonable royalty as the minimum recovery and provides for treble damages where appropriate.[149]

Although by definition an action for patent infringement can not proceed until a patent has been issued, one of the primary issues involved in any infringement case concerns the validity of the underlying patent.[150] The grant of a patent confers presumptive validity, but the strength of the presumption varies depending on the nature of the Patent Office examination and the basis on which invalidity is alleged.[151]

Assuming that the underlying patent is valid and that one or more of the prohibited acts have occurred, the typical infringement case involves an analysis of the patent claim or claims and a comparison of these claims to the alleged infringing product or process. The beginning premise of this comparison is that an infringement has occurred only if all of the limiting elements of a patented claim are found in the other product.[152] However, this premise is mitigated by two offsetting facets of infringement litigation.

The first of these is that the terms of the patent claim must be interpreted before the comparison is made. In many cases, this requires careful analysis of the language used and its relative significance. It is necessary, for example, to distinguish between terms that structurally define or limit the claim and language that merely describes possible applications or other nonlimiting material. Infringement requires only that the limiting, structural elements be found in the other object or process. Thus, a patent on a machine is infringed by the production of an identical machine using methods other than those described by the claim. Furthermore, even within those structural terms, ambiguities must be resolved and distinctions made between language presenting illustrative characteristics and

---

[147] 35 USC § 271 (1982).

[148] 35 USC § 284, 285 (1982).

[149] 35 USC § 284 (1982).

[150] 35 USC § 282 (1982).

[151] See RCA Corp. v. Applied Digital Sys., Inc., 221 USPQ 385 (Fed. Cir. 1984); Medtronic, Inc. v. Cardiac Pacemakers, Inc., 721 F2d 1563 (Fed. Cir. 1983); Noyce v. Kilby, 416 F2d 1391 (CCPA), cert. denied, 400 US 818 (1969); Rajchman v. Herbert & Simpson, 136 USPQ 465 (CCPA 1963).

[152] See Teledyne McCormick Selph v. United States, 192 USPQ 55, 61 (CCPA 1976).

language describing essential requisites of the claimed invention.[153] The general thrust of interpretation of a valid patent in connection with an infringement action is to read ambiguous terms in a manner that expands the scope of the patent.

The need to establish literal identity is also modified by the judicially adopted doctrine of equivalents.[154] The thrust of an "equivalents" analysis is to ensure that the value of a patent is not undermined by minor modifications of a product or process. The doctrine is often described as finding an infringement where the claimed infringer uses substantially similar means to achieve substantially similar results in substantially the same way. [155] The scope of the doctrine is obviously flexible. It has been described by the Supreme Court in the following terms

> What constitutes equivalency must be determined against the context of the patent, the prior art, and the particular circumstances of the case. Equivalence, in the patent law, is not the prisoner of a formula and is not an absolute to be considered in a vacuum. It does not require complete identity for every purpose and in every respect. [156]

Recently, a court described the doctrine as involving the application of "wholesale realism" that substantially weakens the precedential value of decision.[157]

Although entailing potentially great flexibility, the doctrine of equivalents must be read in the context of the underlying assumption that infringement requires that all elements of a claim be found. It'establishes a latitude geared in part to the circumstances of the invention. For example, a broader extension of the doctrine has been considered appropriate where the underlying invention represents a pioneering work applying an approach totally new to a field.[158] In other contexts, limited or no expansion beyond literal claim language is justifiable. Furthermore, as an essentially equitable approach, it is limited by concepts of estoppel. In particular, the patent law notion of "file wrapper estoppel" may bar extension beyond the literal terms of the claim where the applicant had taken an inconsistent or limiting position in obtaining the original patent.[159]

---

[153] See generally 2 Rosenberg, *Patent Law Fundamentals* 17-34.

[154] See *Deller's Walker on Patents* § 546 et seq.

[155] See Zeigler v. Phillips Petroleum Co., 483 F2d 858, 868 (5th Cir.), cert. denied, 414 US 1079 (1973).

[156] Graver Tank & Mfg. Co. v. Linde Air Prods. Co., 339 US 605 (1950).

[157] Mead Digital Sys., Inc. v. AB Dick Co., 221 USPQ 1035 (6th Cir. 1983).

[158] See Lockheed Aircraft Corp. v. United States, 553 F2d 69 (Ct. Cl. 1977).

[159] See Rosenberg, *Patent Law Fundamentals* 17-40.

Overall, the basic premise is that infringement will be found despite relatively insignificant differences between the original and the infringing article or process.[160] Beyond that, infringement issues are resolved by applying a realistic assessment of the alleged infringing product or process in a manner such that the relevance of precedent is often overcome by the factual variations.[161]

---

[160] See Perkin-Elmer Corp. v. Computervision Corp., 680 F2d 669 (9th Cir. 1982); Sperry Rand Corp. v. Texas Instruments, Inc., 142 USPQ 411 (5th Cir. 1964).

[161] Mead Digital Sys., Inc. v. AB Dick Co., 221 USPQ 1035 (6th Cir. 1983).

CHAPTER *3*

Trade Secrets and Confidentiality

¶ 3.01 INTRODUCTION

This chapter examines the third major area of intellectual property law applicable to computer products—trade secret law. Unlike patent and copyright law, the law of trade secrets is primarily state law; its origins lie in common-law concepts of tort liability and confidentiality in employment and other relationships. Historically, trade secrecy has been a major form of protection for intellectual property in the computer industry. It protects processes and ideas that can not be protected by copyright law and that lack the level of inventiveness necessary for patent protection. Trade secrecy is also a primary form of protection because it protects commercial advantage by maintaining confidentiality. Unlike statutory copyright and patent systems, trade secrecy does not require or encourage disclosure.

Despite its widespread use, however, trade secret law has disadvantages in that it does not establish the exclusive rights found in copyright and patent law. Instead, it involves judicial enforcement of confidentiality restraints established by the parties. As a result, trade secret law is not well-suited for mass-market products or for circumstances where the elements of a product are apparent to users with technical skill and confidentiality restraints are difficult to establish. Nor is it well-suited to an environment where skilled employee mobility and entrepreneurship are common. These conditions are characteristic of the contemporary computer industry.

¶ 3.02 DEFINING PROTECTED INTERESTS

Initially, it is necessary to define the character of the legally protectible interest involved in trade secret law. The classic definition of a trade secret is found in the Restatement (First) of Torts.

> [A trade secret consists of] information which is used in one's business and which gives him an opportunity to obtain an advantage over competitors who do not know or use it.... A substantial element of secrecy must exist, so that, except by use of improper means, there would be difficulties in acquiring the information.... Protection is not based on a policy of rewarding or otherwise encouraging the development of secret processes or devices. The protection is merely against breach of faith and reprehensible means of learning another's secret.[1]

Trade secret law concerns advantageous information or processes used in a business. In a leading treatise, Milgrim notes that there is virtual unanimity in regarding a trade secret as a form of property.[2] This description is particularly useful when analyzing the circumstances under which the trade secret can be conveyed through a license, assignment, or sale. It is also relevant to tax issues.

For issues of enforcement or protection, however, describing a trade secret as property can create misleading inferences. One popular conception of a property interest is that the owner has an enforceable right to exclude all others from the use of the property. For traditional forms of property, this is subject to numerous exceptions; for trade secrets, the exceptions supplant the general rule. The right to exclude others is defined by the secrecy maintained and by the confidentiality imposed on persons to whom the secret is revealed. Trade secret law conveys no rights independent of these factors. It does not preclude independent discovery and subsequent use. The proprietary rights in a trade secret are linked to legal conceptions of misappropriation and breach of confidential relationships. The property interest arises and is defined by the legal system's willingness to enforce such relationships.

There is no dispute that computer hardware and software are potentially appropriate subject matter for trade secret protection. This does

---

[1] Restatement (First) of Torts § 757 comment b.

[2] Milgrim, *Trade Secrets* 1-7.

not, however, suggest a particularly close fit between trade secret law and computer law issues. Rather, it reflects the malleability of what constitutes a trade secret. The area is not defined in terms of subject matter, but in terms of utility, confidentiality, and equitable considerations. A list of items that have and have not come under trade secret protection ranges from commercial and industrial formulas to various manufactured products and machines.[3] The list, however, would be conceptually vague and internally inconsistent. In terms of subject matter, an "exact definition of a trade secret is not possible."[4]

It is most common to discuss trade secrets in terms of the factors used in determining if remedies are justified against unauthorized use of the secret by another. These are described in various ways and provide useful tools for understanding the reported case law and structuring litigation. Also, the included elements provide criteria for organizing business practices to enhance the legal and practical protection of commercially significant secrets.[5] Thus, issues of novelty, contract restrictions, and internal secrecy measures are important for industrial secrecy.

Trade secret cases, however, are generally not susceptible to highly structured interpretation, but are most often equitable and flexible issues. "Although courts sometimes list one or more elements which must be proven to establish a trade secret, it is rare to find a court which . . . correlates such elements with the determination that a matter is a trade secret."[6] As a result, while the following discussion is organized around factors tending to define a trade secret, it is important to focus on what the courts are protecting with trade secret law in general.

Trade secret law focuses on particular information, processes, or product designs that are elemental to the commercial advantage of a business. In practice, many businesses elect to maintain a commercial advantage by cloaking a particular subject matter in secrecy and imposing confidentiality restraints on people exposed to it. Trade secret law ratifies this business practice by enforcing the expectations of confidentiality that are established.

The ratification of confidentiality is subject to limiting considerations. The most obvious is that protection exists only where expectations of secrecy and confidentiality have in fact been established among the parties. Thus, for example, despite internal secrecy, independent discov-

---

[3] Id. at § 2.09.

[4] Restatement (First) of Torts § 757 comment b.

[5] See Gilbourne, et al., "A Case Study: An Integrated Proprietary Rights Program," in 1983 Computer Law Institute Proceedings.

[6] Milgrim, *Trade Secrets* § 2:96.

ery and subsequent use of previously secret information by third parties is not actionable. The limits of the proprietor's rights are established by the scope of the confidentiality restraints. Similarly, especially in light of public policies favoring disclosure and availability of ideas, pro forma or boilerplate declarations of confidentiality are insufficient if not enforced by the parties themselves.

There are also limits on the type of relationship in which confidentiality may be enforced; limits established by countervailing social policies on disclosure and use of scientifically valuable information. Even where confidentiality has been established, offsetting considerations may limit the allowable enforcement. This might occur, for example, where a restraint would effectively preclude a former employee from engaging in his profession. The concept of misappropriation is defined not only by the relationship from which information is obtained, but also by whether enforcement will, on balance, promote or retard creativity and fair competition.

PART A.   SECRECY

¶ 3.03 REASONABLY PROTECTED SECRETS

An element of any claim to trade secret protection is that the subject matter is in fact secret. In this connection, one issue that intermittently arises is whether the owner of a trade secret must establish "absolute secrecy" or whether it is sufficient to prove "relative secrecy."[7] Although the general view is that relative secrecy is sufficient,[8] the Restatement of Torts notes

> It is not requisite that only the proprietor of the business know it. He may, without losing his protection, communicate it to employees involved in its use.... Others may also know of it independently ... and are keeping it secret. Nevertheless, a substantial element of

---

[7] Milgrim, *Trade Secrets* 2-74–2-77.

[8] Milgrim notes that the language in a number of appellate decisions implies that the court would impose a requirement of absolute as contrasted to mere relative secrecy. Milgrim, *Trade Secrets* 2-75 n.11. See Julius Hyman & Co. v. Velsico Corp., 233 P2d 977, cert. denied, 342 US 870 (1951) (comment that the secret must be known only to the owner). In these cases, however, the comment is seldom matched in the decision, nor was it necessary to do so. Even given language suggesting a greater standard, concepts of relative secrecy are uniformly applied, although the courts may differ in the extent of relative notoriety sufficient to relinquish the secret.

secrecy must exist, so that, except by the use of improper means, there would be difficulty in acquiring the information.[9]

Ultimately, in a world comprised of businesses rather than individuals who perform all necessary tasks, the distinction between absolute and relative secrecy is a false issue. Except in the most sterile context, absolute secrecy is impossible to attain if it is viewed as information limited to a single person. Once knowledge is extended beyond the individual, it is inherently a relative secret.

The question of secrecy involves two distinct perspectives. The first is the extent to which the information is generally known in the trade, independent of disclosure by confidential sources affiliated with the holder of the alleged secret. This is the concept of novelty. The second perspective focuses on the owner's efforts to restrict the information to people who have agreed to confidentiality restraints. This element is secrecy. It is generally assumed that both elements must be present in order to justify protection as a trade secret.

¶ 3.04 NOVELTY

Patent law imposes high threshold requirements that an invention be novel and not obvious to ordinarily skilled people in order to qualify for protection.[10] An invention must represent a breakthrough and substantial advance on prior art. In contrast, while a trade secret must involve novel information or processes, the threshold of inventiveness required for protection is substantially lower; it is associated more with originality in the copyright sense and with elements of commercial advantage and investment.

In trade secret law, the concept of novelty is a negative proposition. The secret must not be so widely known that it constitutes general knowledge in the field. If this criterion is not met, the allegation that there is a commercial advantage from a claimed secret is rebutted. Where others in the field are also aware of the information, the proprietor's commercial advantage must arise from other factors. Furthermore, if the information is generally known, it is difficult to establish or accept that it has been communicated under expectations that it will be treated as confidential. Indeed, general notoriety in a particular field directly contradicts any such expectation.

---

[9] Restatement of Torts § 757B.

[10] See ¶¶ 2.12, 2.13.

Novelty considerations are distinct from the requirements of uniqueness found in patent law. Novelty in a trade secret case is determined by whether or not the parties might reasonably have developed enforceable expectations of confidentiality concerning the secret. This is most readily established where unique information is obtained through substantial investment of time and effort or by a leap of creativity. However, in a commercial environment such expectations may reasonably exist for less unique subject matter. Trade secret status does not establish a preemptive right against independent discovery, but merely a right to establish protectible expectations of confidentiality. There is, therefore, no policy rationale to establish barriers of novelty as a prelude for a grant of trade secret rights. Trade secret law enforces expectations and does not monitor or reward varying levels of inventiveness.

[1] Combination Secrets

In a computer environment, issues of novelty most commonly arise in the context of combination secrets where individual elements of a process are well-known, but the alleged secret lies in their particular combination for a commercial purpose.[11] This issue is frequently encountered in patent law, where under higher standards in that field a relatively unique effect is required to avoid a finding of obviousness. However, in trade secret law the sole issue is whether the combination as a whole is generally known in the field.

In computer software, the mere fact that a program consists of well-known subroutines does not render the design of the program ineligible for trade secret protection. For example, *Com-Share, Inc. v. Computer Complex, Inc.*[12] involved an alleged misappropriation of operating system software and a text editor. The court concluded that the programs were trade secrets despite the existence of analogous systems developed elsewhere.

> [The existing systems] all contain certain elements which perform similar functions and many utilize certain similar fundamental concepts and . . . a common base. Such is common in all engineering . . . but there the similarity stops. The varying systems . . . differ greatly in the steps taken to accomplish the objective. . . . The specific engineering . . . and their particular underlying technologies and design,

---

[11] See Motorola, Inc. v. Fairchild Camera & Instrument Corp., 366 F. Supp. 1173, 177 USPQ 614 (D. Ariz. 1973).

[12] 338 F. Supp. 1229 (ED Mich. 1971).

together with ... their "logic and coherence," as well as their speed, accuracy, cost and commercial feasibility ... differ greatly.[13]

Similarly, in *Cybertek Computer Products, Inc. v. Whitfield*[14] the court held that a management information program qualified as a trade secret. "[While] some of the concepts [were generally known] the entire bundle or combination of these concepts as developed and utilized" are trade secrets.[15]

As these decisions suggest, software based on new combinations of known subroutines qualifies for trade secret protection if the design of the program meaningfully deviates from generally known designs. The combination of elements may be sufficiently novel even though none of the individual components are protectible. A contrary conclusion would obviate enforcement of confidentiality in most commercial engineering and software development. This protection of software design, however, does not create a preemptive claim to the design. Subsequent developers are free to use the known subroutines and independently create analogous or identical combinations.

[2] Particularity and Equity

Not all software, circuitry, or process designs are trade secrets when developed in a business, even if they meet minimum standards of novelty. Novelty requires something more than showing that a particular combination was individually developed and not copied. The nature of that something more can not be precisely defined. It entails consideration of equitable factors.[16] The most significant involve the scope of what the plaintiff claims to be protectible and the impact that granting that claim will have on other parties. A broad, vaguely defined secret can seldom be protected without seriously injuring the rights of third parties. As a result, trade secret status is often denied to such secrets. In contrast, a particularized, narrowly defined secret will more often be protected.

In *Jostens, Inc. v. National Computer Services*,[17] the court refused to protect a computer-aided design and manufacturing system (CAD/CAM) used to manufacture student class rings. Jostens had created the system by purchasing three standard hardware items and commissioning

---

[13] Id. at 1234.

[14] 203 USPQ 1020 (Cal. Super. Ct. 1977).

[15] Id. at 1024.

[16] See Milgrim, *Trade Secrets* 2-84.

[17] 318 NW2d 691 (Minn. 1982).

another company to design software to its specifications. The system gave Jostens a competitive advantage; it was the only such system in the industry. This advantage was lost when the engineer who had helped develop the system left Jostens and, while at another company, developed an analogous system with the assistance of the original software company. When this new system was used by a Jostens competitor, Jostens sought an injunction against use of the system and damages.

The court rejected Jostens' claim on a variety of grounds, concluding that the system was not sufficiently novel for trade secret protection. The court noted that the software company used a modular programming technique and that as much as 90 percent of the allegedly misappropriated software consisted of standard, off-the-shelf routines. Furthermore, although not yet common in the jewelry industry, basic CAD/CAM technology was generally known.

> Both the scanner subsystem and the engraving subsystem as well as the hardware and operating systems software for the graphics subsystem were all standard vendor products. . . . [The] assembly of Jostens' CAD/CAM system did not require substantial research or experimentation. . . . Clearly, the CAD/CAM system as such, as the combination of three generally known subsystems, does not achieve the degree of novelty or "unknownness" needed for a trade secret.[18]

Although the court refers to the combination of known parts, the result in *Jostens* must be reviewed in light of the manner in which the claim for trade secret protection was stated. Jostens did not attempt to conceal its use of CAD/CAM techniques in manufacturing, nor did it claim that the fact of such use was the protectible secret. It did not establish which elements of the software system were unique in contrast to other applications of CAD/CAM technology. Its claim to the system as a whole amounted to an effort to preempt any use of CAD/CAM techniques in the industry *by the defendant* (a former employee). The defendant had general skills in CAD/CAM, and granting the claim in this form would have totally precluded use of these skills in any aspect of the school ring industry. Absent a contractually imposed limit, this broad restraint was not justifiable.[19]

In other cases, the secret is narrowly defined and the alleged misappropriation is clearly limited to elements of that particular application.[20]

---

[18] Id. at 699.

[19] See infra ¶ 3.10[3].

[20] See J&K Computer Sys. v. Parrish, 642 P2d 732 (Utah 1982); Electronic Data Sys. v. Kinder, 497 F2d 222 (5th Cir. 1974).

A more focused definition increases the likelihood that the program or process will be treated as novel for purposes of trade secrecy. Specificity highlights unique elements in the secret, and relief can be granted without freezing a former employee's professional career, restraining use of his general skills, or substantially restricting the subsequent business activities of a competitor. For example, in *J&K Computer Systems, Inc. v. Parrish*[21] protection was granted against a former employee's use of the structure of a particular accounts receivable program, but this did not extend to other database systems or even to development of other accounts receivable programs.

[3] Value and Investment

A decision to grant trade secret protection implies that the protected items are commercially significant to the proprietor. In concept, judgments about the value of the subject matter are separate and distinct from considerations of novelty. However, considerations of current value and investment are frequently weighed in deciding whether the secret is sufficiently novel for protection.[22]

Regardless of the manner in which they enter the analysis, value and cost are relevant in identifying subject matter for trade secret protection. Indeed, they are more reliable criteria in a commercial environment than abstract concepts of novelty. Trade secret law protects business expectations of confidentiality. These expectations ordinarily develop around subject matter that requires substantial investment or that, regardless of the cost, has substantial current value to the business.

¶ 3.05 SECRECY

Beyond questions of whether an alleged secret is common knowledge in the trade, trade secrecy depends on the extent to which the proprietor of the secret has undertaken successful efforts to maintain secrecy. A business is not entitled to protection of allegedly secret information unless it has established that protection through internal security and other procedures.

---

[21] 642 P2d 732 (Utah 1982).

[22] See Jostens, Inc. v. National Computer Sys., Inc., 318 NW2d 691, 699 (Minn. 1982); Computer Print Sys. v. Lewis, 422 A2d 148 (Pa. Super. Ct. 1980); Milgrim, *Trade Secrets* § 2.02.

[1] Internal Security Procedures

Trade secret protection requires at least reasonably effective efforts to restrict knowledge of the secret within the business and to limit dissemination of the secret to people who are subject to confidentiality restrictions. The actual effectiveness of internal security procedures is relevant. More commonly, however, the primary issues involve the degree of care exercised, both in terms of the procedures used and the extent to which they are followed.

There are varying terms used to describe the standard of care in internal security necessary to establish trade secrecy for particular subject matter. Some cases suggest an absolute approach, requiring a maximum security effort. Most often, however, the actual standard is the use of reasonable care in the circumstances.[23] The level of required attention to security is affected by the type of secret and the nature of the alleged misappropriation.

While any standard of reasonableness is inherently flexible, several patterns of internal protection are associated with successful trade secret claims in the computer industry. These include use of employee nondisclosure agreements, physical security measures, marking documents proprietary or confidential, informing employees that particular systems are secret,[24] and limiting access to people who must use the systems.[25] These security measures tend to be found in clusters or, typically, not found at all. That is, either the security system reflects a widespread effort to identify secret information and limit its dissemination, or it reflects little effort at all to do so. Therefore, while it is evident that the foregoing are components of an internal security system, the cases provide little guidance as to which of these elements are the most significant or how a partial absence of these elements affects the ability to establish trade secrecy status.

Internal security procedures can be oriented to several distinct and discernible objectives. The first is to establish physical security against unauthorized intrusion.[26] While relatively few reported trade secrecy cases involve actual thefts, safeguarding important commercial material from completely unauthorized access is the minimum requirement of a security system, and it is at least minimally necessary to establish that an alleged secret was viewed as important by the proprietor.

---

[23] Milgrim, *Trade Secrets* 2-26, 2-27.

[24] J&K Computer Sys., Inc. v. Parrish, 642 P2d 732 (Utah 1982).

[25] Milgrim, *Trade Secrets* 2-28–2-31.

[26] See Telex Corp. v. IBM, 510 F2d 894 (10th Cir. 1975); University Computing Co. v. Lykes Youngstown Co., 504 F2d 518 (5th Cir. 1974).

A second objective is to limit the number of people with access to the entire secret. The practical value of this is as obvious as is that of basic physical security. The greater the number of people with access to information, the greater the likelihood that that information will be communicated beyond the limits of the confidentiality restraints. Hence, restrictions on access contribute to establishing the claim that the secret information is regarded as valuable and confidential. Information freely or generally available within a large company is difficult to characterize as confidential, while information for which access is restricted is more readily understood as protectible.

A third objective, highly relevant in subsequent litigation, is to convey notice to employees and others that proprietary claims are asserted and that the subject matter should be treated as confidential. For former employees, internal notice enables classification between unprotected, general business knowledge and protectible trade secrets. To the extent that notice is clearly established for particular information or processes, the notice weakens the former employee's equitable position should he use the information in an unauthorized manner. Relatively specific notice places the employee in a position of explicitly appropriating information that has been identified as secret.

Notice to employees can be given at various points during their employment. Areas or topics of secrecy may be described when the employee is hired and specifically referenced in an employment contract. During the employee's tenure at the company, notice can be reinforced by a general security program including selective use of printed confidentiality notices. Finally, subjects regarded as confidential can be outlined at an employee's termination interview. In each of these, the emphasis is on real efforts to identify and communicate a need for confidentiality. Boilerplate forms or clauses, coupled with indiscriminate use of secrecy labels, may be inadequate or even counterproductive. Assuming real efforts, the absence of one of these security procedures is not necessarily fatal to the employer's position. However, especially where the alleged secret is of a general nature, the absence of all precautions may lead to the conclusion that the employee was not notified that "the obvious notions with which he was working were trade secrets."[27]

A lack of internal security and a resulting lack of notice often interact with the issue of novelty. This occurred in *Motorola, Inc. v. Fairchild Camera and Instrument Corp.*,[28] which involved an alleged misappropria-

---

[27] Dynamic Research Corp. v. Analytic Sciences Corp., 400 NE2d 1274 (Mass. App. Ct. 1980).

[28] 366 F. Supp. 1173 (D. Ariz. 1973).

tion of a process for mass producing integrated circuits. In *Motorola*, the original claim encompassed 140 elements of the manufacturing process, but was eventually narrowed to focus on six. The defendants were former employees who had signed a general contract agreeing to not disclose confidential information. This contract was not effectively implemented. In rejecting the trade secrecy claim, the court emphasized that at no time prior to, during, or at the end of their employment were the defendants notified in general or specific terms of what processes were to be treated as secret. At a termination interview, even though it was known that the employees were moving to a competitor, they were not informed of what was covered by the nondisclosure contract. "The . . . principle of undue burden and overbreadth [applies] to the contract here . . . to make it unenforceable without specific advice at some time . . . as to specific trade secrets claimed."[29] In addition, the court noted that the company permitted public tours viewing its production lines without obtaining agreements as to nondisclosure and that much of the allegedly secret process was inherent to the type of manufacturing or disclosed in a prior patent.

In *Motorola*, the court alluded to a factor that may be of increasing importance in determining the adequacy of security efforts. In contrast to Motorola's lax approach, the court noted that similar companies in the same industry routinely advised employees of specifically claimed secrets upon employment, during their tenure at the company, and at a termination interview. When the reasonableness of the employer's efforts is at issue, general practices within the same industry are relevant. To establish the necessary confidentiality for a trade secret, the owner's internal security must be at least equivalent to that generally followed in the industry.

Vigorous efforts at internal security and notice can not elevate common knowledge to the level of a protected secret.[30] However, such efforts may lean toward protection of a process even though elements of it are clearly within the public domain.[31]

[2] External Security Procedures

In practice, efforts to establish internal security often parallel efforts to limit external distribution of secret information. Breakdowns in one area are commonly accompanied by breakdowns in the other. Neverthe-

---

[29] Id. at 1185.

[30] Milgrim, *Trade Secrets*, 2-27.

[31] Compare Sperry Rand Corp. v. Pentronix, 311 F. Supp. 910, 913 (ED Pa. 1970) (even though some of the material was public domain matter, trade secrecy was established via substantial efforts to give notice as well as monitor access and use).

less, it is useful to distinguish external secrecy in order to identify two common issues encountered in computer-related trade secrecy cases. These involve publications related to the secret and distribution of a product or system from which the secret can be deduced.

Trade secrecy involves relative rather than absolute secrecy. By analogy, the loss of a secret through disclosure focuses on relative as compared to absolute disclosure. No cases address the extent to which a secret has *in fact* become generally known due to a disclosure. They focus instead on whether there was a release of material in a manner that could lead to general notoriety. Key factors are the restrictions placed on the audience receiving a disclosure and the degree of difficulty involved in learning the secret through use of the disclosed material. In general, a disclosure in which the recipient's use is restricted or where there is substantial difficulty in uncovering the secret will not per se relinquish trade secret status.

[a] Publications: Articles and Manuals

A recurrent issue in computer-related cases involves the effect of publication of technical information about a secret. The cases distinguish between unrestricted, general publication and publications in which distribution and use are restricted.

Unrestricted publication in technical papers or advertising brochures delivered to the public eliminates any claim to trade secret status for information contained in the publication.[32] Of course, the publication must contain sufficient information to in fact reveal the claimed secret.[33] Within this limitation, the rationale of the rule is obvious: General publication tends to establish that an alleged secret is common knowledge, and the fact of publication reflects on the nature of the alleged owner's efforts to maintain secrecy. Publications are especially significant in an industry where efforts to keep track of competitor's new products and processes are commonplace.[34]

While general purpose publications are common, other publications create more frequent controversy. These are the maintenance or operating manuals that are distributed with hardware and software products.

---

[32] See Jostens, Inc. v. National Computer Sys., Inc., 318 NW2d 691, 699 (Minn. 1982); Dynamic Research Corp. v. Analytic Sciences Corp., 400 NE2d 1274 (Mass. App. Ct. 1980).

[33] See Data Gen. Corp. v. Digital Computer Controls, Inc., 357 A2d 105, 110 (Del. Ch. 1975).

[34] See Motorola, Inc. v. Fairchild Camera & Instrument Corp., 366 F. Supp. 1173, 177 USPQ 614 (D. Ariz. 1973).

Manuals are commonly supplied to help the purchaser or licensee of equipment to use and maintain it. Necessarily, these publications provide substantial detail on the design and circuitry of the products. Where this is the alleged secret, it must be determined whether or not the publication was sufficient to relinquish secrecy.

A distinction must be made between unrestricted publication and confidential disclosure. Properly, the courts have analogized limited, confidential disclosure to the type of distribution that would normally occur within a business itself. The issue then becomes whether or not the tenor of the relationship and the efforts to maintain relative secrecy in the published manual are sufficient.[35] At a minimum, the confidentiality of the material and relevant limits on its use must be clearly communicated to the recipient of the manual. In *Data General Corp. v. Digital Computer Controls, Inc.*,[36] the printed material was a maintenance manual containing detailed drawings and specifications of a minicomputer. The manual was routinely supplied to purchasers of computer systems for purposes of maintenance and operation. The defendant obtained a copy of the manual and an operating version of the computer, intending to use the information to design a computer of its own manufacture. When the defendant obtained a copy, approximately 80 copies of the manual had been distributed. By the time of trial, almost 6000 were in circulation. Despite this distribution, the court concluded that the minicomputer design constituted a trade secret that had been misappropriated.

While *Data General* is often cited for the proposition that mass marketing does not impair trade secret status, the court's analysis reflects a significantly more limited proposition. The court emphasized that Data General maintained tight internal secrecy and distributed the manual to purchasers solely on a restricted basis. "[Each] logic diagram made available to Data General's customers . . . bears a legend . . . clearly stating that such drawings are not to be used for manufacture or sale of the items disclosed without written permission."[37] Both the method of distribution and notices placed on the manual notified recipients that their right to use the material was limited to maintenance operations.

> Other precautionary measures . . . designed to protect its alleged proprietary interest . . . involved use of standard forms of sales agreements . . . [that] contain a statement of the proprietary nature of the

---

[35] See Milgrim, *Trade Secrets* § 2.05[2]; see also Management Science, Inc. v. Cyborg Sys., 6 CLSR 921 (ND Ill. 1978); Digital Dev. Corp. v. International Memory Sys., 185 USPQ 136 (SD Cal. 1973).

[36] 357 A2d 105 (Del. Ch. 1975).

[37] Id. at 109.

data. . . . In fact, maintenance documentation . . . is not furnished to a buyer until he has agreed . . . to abide by the provisions of the proprietary legends.[38]

Distribution of proprietary data outside of the company does not relinquish trade secrecy if the distribution occurs in a manner that clearly establishes the proprietary limitations on use of the secret[39] and secures an explicit agreement to that effect from the recipient.

[b] Sale of a Product: Reverse Engineering

Trade secret status may be lost by public sale of a product embodying the secret.[40] In applying this premise, however, it is important to distinguish between secrets that are discoverable by inspection of the product and secrets that aided in production of the product but are not necessarily discoverable from it. Only the former are affected by general distribution.

The most readily understood application of this premise concerns originally secret design features discernible from visual inspection of the product. This might include, for example, an audiovisual display intended to enhance user interaction with a program or the structure of an ergonomically designed console or keyboard. Although the design might originally have been secret, once a product is released to the public the design has been generally published. The disclosure does not, however, extend to manufacturing processes or algorithms used to produce the visual effects.

The more difficult application of disclosure through product distribution involves alleged secrets not immediately perceivable that can be discovered by dismantling and closely examining the product. This process of closer inspection, known as reverse engineering, is commonplace in the computer industry, since the commercial benefits of maintaining compatible systems and matching a competitor's marketed products are significant. Reverse engineering surfaces in several aspects of computer-related trade secret law, but the concern here is solely with the extent to which the capability to reverse engineer a secret from a marketed product is tantamount to general publication or disclosure.

---

[38] Id. at 110, 111.

[39] See also M. Bruce & Assoc. v. Gladstone, 319 NW2d 902 (Wis. Ct. App. 1982). Compare Clark Equip. v. Harlan, 539 F. Supp. 561 (D. Kan. 1982) (distribution of microfilm to six largest customers relinquishes trade secrecy where no confidentiality agreements signed).

[40] See Milgrim, *Trade Secrets* 2-38.

The boundaries of this issue can be defined by two hypothetical secrets. In the first, the design secret consists of using plastic rather than metallic fasteners on the interior of a product. The fasteners can be viewed by simply loosening three screws and detaching a metal cover. In contrast, the second secret consists of a combination of chemicals to produce a substance that is used to construct internal circuitry. This secret can be discovered only through several thousand manhours of testing. Neither secret has been patented. The first secret differs in only marginal ways from the visually perceptible designs discussed previously. Outside of patent, copyright, or contractual restrictions, there is no barrier to disassembling a product and using the information that is obtained. A readily discernible secret loses its status as a trade secret even if discovery requires reverse engineering or disassembly.[41] In contrast, the second secret, while discernible, requires substantial effort. Distribution of this product does not constitute immediate disclosure of the secret since most, and perhaps all, people will not in fact learn the secret from the product.

Where the secret can be discovered only with substantial effort, distribution does not immediately forfeit trade secret status.[42] The degree of difficulty in reverse engineering necessary to retain secrecy in the face of mass distribution may involve close factual questions. However, secrecy should survive initial distribution unless the reverse engineering can be accomplished readily, with little time and effort, by procedures known to a significant portion of the audience to which distribution occurs. Treating distribution of a product as disclosure of the secret is equivalent to treating distribution as an unrestricted publication. This analogy is strained, however, where substantial effort and time are necessary to obtain the underlying secret. At a minimum, secrecy survives for the period necessary to reverse engineer after distribution. However, absent other restrictions, the purchaser who reverse engineers a product may use or disclose the secret even if distribution does not generally forfeit secrecy for other purposes. Reverse engineering does not violate confidentiality restraints. As a result, retained trade secrecy status affects only those who are in a confidential relationship with the proprietor. It does not inhibit discovery by purchasers.

---

[41] Id. at 2-38–2-42.

[42] See Smith v. Dravo Corp., 203 F2d 369 (7th Cir. 1953); Analogic Corp. v. Data Translation, Inc., 358 NE2d 804 (Mass. 1981); Data Gen. Corp. v. Digital Computer Controls, Inc., 357 A2d 105, 109 (Del. Ch. 1975) (production from confidential documents actionable even though could have discovered secret from machine itself without restriction).

One further point deserves comment. As previously discussed, the extent and nature of efforts to retain secrecy is an important element in trade secrecy cases. A similar factor plays a role in assessing the effect of distribution where the alleged secret is not apparent on the face of the product. Distributors desiring to retain a claim of trade secrecy enhance the force of their claim if distribution is in a form that tends to conceal or reduce access to the underlying secret. In the context of software, for example, if the secret resides in the underlying algorithm, distribution in object code, rather than source code form, is desirable since discovery of the underlying design is more difficult.[43] Similarly, copy protection systems may help if they actually reduce access to the design.[44] Of course, such steps may reduce the marketability of the resulting product.

PART B.   CONFIDENTIALITY

¶ 3.06 MISAPPROPRIATION AND PROTECTED RELATIONSHIPS

Establishing adequate efforts to maintain secrecy and the commercial value of secrets is a condition precedent to enforcing a trade secret claim. A second element is that the secret must have been misappropriated from a confidential relationship in a context where the appropriation is not protected by public policy. Trade secrecy does not establish a general, preemptive barrier to use of the secret. It only safeguards the owner against disclosure by misappropriation.

The clearest misappropriation involves actual theft or conversion of the secret or tangible embodiments of it.[45] Beyond theft, trade secret pro-

---

[43] See Davidson, "Protecting Computer Software: A Comprehensive Analysis," 1983 Ariz. St. LJ 611, 726, 727 (1983); MacGrady, "Protection of Computer Software—An Update and Practical Synthesis," 20 Hous. L. Rev. 1033, 1063 (1983). Reverse compilation may, however, involve an infringement of copyright. See Grogan, "Decompilation and Disassembly: Undoing Software Protection," 1 Comp Law. 1 (Feb. 1984); see ¶ 1.09[2].

[44] "Copy protection" refers to a variety of schemes used especially for microcomputer software to reduce the ease with which copies of diskette or other media-based software may be made. Unless these schemes also reduce access to allegedly secret code, they are immaterial to trade secret protections, the continuation of which depends solely on whether another person may identify the code or structure that forms the underlying secret. Trade secrecy does not bar or restrict copying of the program itself.

[45] See Telex Corp. v. IBM, 510 F2d 894 (10th Cir. 1975); University Computing Co. v. Lykes Youngstown, 504 F2d 518 (5th Cir. 1974).

tection is limited to confidential relationships in which a third party initially received the secret under restrictions implied by law or imposed by agreement. The following sections examine several relationships in which trade secret issues arise. In each, the proprietary rights are limited by the avoidance of excessive restraint on the other party.

¶ 3.07 END USERS: REVERSE ENGINEERING

Material embodying trade secrets is delivered to end users in many forms involving different physical and legal characteristics. These include outright sales, limited term leases of material objects, and licensed disclosure of particular information. The consequences applicable to trade secret protection vary depending on the characteristics of the transaction and the explicit understanding surrounding the delivery of the information and/or product.

[1] Purchasers

Confidentiality does not exist in a sale of a product encompassing the alleged trade secret. A basic premise of trade secret law is that the purchaser is free to disassemble and inspect the product and, most significantly, use the information thereby obtained.[46] This limitation on protection is one of the distinguishing characteristics of trade secret law as contrasted with copyright and patent law systems. The freedom of the purchaser to use information obtained by reverse engineering is based on common-law concepts of ownership and restraints on alienation and use. It is also based on the idea that by outright sale of a product the trade secret owner commits his secret to the marketplace. In cases of widespread mass-market distribution, the capability of discovery through reverse engineering might totally relinquish trade secret status.[47] Even absent that result, the fact of discovery from the product is not actionable.

---

[46] See Milgrim, *Trade Secrets* 5-87.

[47] See Milgrim, *Trade Secrets* § 2.05[2]; see also Davidson, "Protecting Computer Software—A Comprehensive Analysis," 1983 Ariz. St. LJ 611, 726, 727 (1983). Arguably, however, distribution in object code form does not readily reveal secrets in design and the like and does not therefore relinquish secrecy. See MacGrady, "Protection of Computer Software—An Update and Practical Synthesis," 20 Hous. L. Rev. 1033, 1063 (1983); Grogan, "Decompilation and Disassembly: Undoing Software Protection," 1 Comp. Law. 1, 7 (Feb. 1984). But see Clark Equip. v. Harlan, 539 F. Supp. 561 (D. Kan. 1982).

While the purchaser is generally free to reverse engineer an item, the capability to do so does not shield other forms of obtaining the underlying secret. For example, in *Data General Corp. v. Digital Computer Controls, Inc.*[48] the defendant obtained a copy of a computer through a lawful purchase, but rather than reverse engineer the secret from this machine, it used confidential documents. This constituted misappropriation of the plaintiff's trade secret. Although the ability to reverse engineer to the same end affected damage computation, it did not shield the particular form of taking the secret.[49]

[2] Lessees and Licensees

In contrast to purchasers, lessees of a product or process and licensees of information are more readily made subject to limitations on the right to reverse engineer a product or otherwise use available information. In a true lease, the original holder of the secret retains title and ultimate control of the product. Where the transaction places the lessee on notice as to proprietary or secrecy claims, a protected confidential relationship may arise. Given the tenor of the transaction, the holder of the secret is more able to establish enforceable barriers to disclosure and use. For example, in *K&G Oil Tool & Service Co. v. G&G Fishing Tool Service*[50] the defendant lessee was licensed to sublease equipment manufactured by K&G. The lease precluded the defendant from disassembling the product for purposes of remanufacture. Given the nature of the transaction and the clear surrounding indicia of intent to maintain internal design secrecy, the court enforced the contract against the lessee. Similarly, although the issue was raised in an antitrust context, the court in *Sum of Squares, Inc. v. Market Research Corp.*[51] indicated that restrictions on use of a data analysis program made available through a license-lease retained secrecy as to program design and that the lessee restraints on use were reasonable.

[3] Information and Products

In many transactions involving trade secrets, the subject matter is allegedly secret information or processes disclosed to a licensee. The prohibited activity is use or disclosure outside of the restrictive terms of the

---

[48] 357 A2d 105, 109 (Del. Ch. 1975); see also Digital Dev. Corp. v. International Memory Sys., 185 USPQ 136 (SD Cal. 1973).

[49] See Analogic Corp. v. Data Translation, Inc., 358 NE2d 804 (Mass. 1981).

[50] 314 SW2d 782 (Tex. 1958).

[51] 401 F. Supp. 53 (SDNY 1975).

transaction. Under appropriate circumstances, these restrictions may be implied from the transaction itself if the information recipient is aware of the restraints and the information is in fact otherwise a trade secret. A contrasting transaction involves the delivery of a tangible item or product where there is a risk that the recipient may disassemble the product and discover the secret. Here, distinctions are based on whether or not the original party retains ownership of the item.[52]

In computer-related marketing, many transactions involve both information disclosure and tangible product delivery. Where the two are clearly separable, the reported cases suggest that confidentiality and non-disclosure can be imposed on the information, but not on the product itself. This is one thrust of the *Data General* case discussed previously. While the court in that case implied that the buyer could have rightfully reverse engineered a minicomputer it purchased, use of technical manuals was wrongful since the seller's proprietary claims were clearly communicated and agreed to by the buyer.[53] *Data General* indicates that restricted conveyance of information is enforceable despite an ultimate ability to discover the same information from a product. The issue is whether or not confidentiality claims are clearly asserted at the outset, reasonably enforced in practice, and actually agreed to by the receiving party.[54]

Where the information and the marketed product are more closely intertwined, a difficult question arises. It occurs in software transactions where the program is transferred in tangible form on magnetic tapes or discs. If there are sufficient indicia of confidentiality and the recipient's continued use of the tapes is in fact restricted by the original party retaining a right to retake them, confidentiality restrictions should be enforceable.

This analysis does not apply in mass-market situations, since the transaction bears few indicia of confidentiality and there is no convincing analogy to a limited sale of information. Virtually any product based on a design contains information about that design that is decipherable by reverse engineering. Under these circumstances, the mass-market software is more like a product that, when purchased, can be reverse engineered notwithstanding trade secret claims to material that might be enforceable against other parties.

---

[52] Compare Data Gen. Corp. v. Digital Computer Controls, Inc., 357 A2d 105, 109 (1975) with K&G Oil Tool & Serv. Co. v. G&G Fishing Tool Serv., 314 SW2d 782 (Tex. 1958).

[53] Data Gen. Corp. v. Digital Computer Controls, Inc., 357 A2d 105 (Del. Ch. 1975).

[54] See Management Science v. Cyborg, 6 CLRS 921 (ND Ill. 1978); Clark Equip. v. Harlan, 539 F. Supp. 561 (D. Kan. 1982).

¶ 3.08 CONTRACTORS: MARKETING AND MANUFACTURING

Confidentiality sufficient to retain trade secrecy may exist by contract or by operation of law in relationships where the holder of the trade secret discloses the secret to another hired for developing, marketing, or manufacturing. This may involve employment agreements, which are discussed in a following section.[55] The focus here is on third-party independent contractors. In law, this relationship is characterized by the fact that the contractor maintains a separate legal identity with control over the details of its own work performance.

Disclosure of the secret to an independent contractor constitutes disclosure outside of the secret holder's own organization. Reconciling his disclosure with continued control over the secret involves balancing the interests of the secret holder and the contractor receiving the information. Use of contractors is a commercially effective method of exploiting the secret, and disclosure to the contractor differs only in part from disclosure to employees. However, since the contractor is an independent entity, it is important to preserve its rights to function outside of the contract relationship. The secret holder should not be able to establish substantial control of the contractor's business merely by disclosing secret information for a particular use.

If disclosure is pursuant to a manufacturing or supply contract, the circumstances of the transaction commonly establish that the secret holder does not intend to relinquish or generally distribute the secret. This is clearly true where processes, information, or designs are disclosed only insofar as necessary to enable performance of the assigned task. As a result, it is generally assumed that this contracting relationship entails obligations of confidentiality that are implied regardless of express contract limitations.[56] Necessarily, express contract restraints on use and disclosure are enforceable.

The fact that confidentiality is implied does not obviate all factual inquiries. There must be an effort to protect the secret and notify the contractor that secret information is involved. Excessive disclosure without restriction contradicts the presumed confidentiality of the relationship. The law enforces the understanding of the parties if the actual relationship entails sufficient indicia of confidentiality.

This analysis also applies where a third-party contractor is hired for purposes of marketing. Marketing arrangements, however, involve varying degrees of necessary disclosure. For example, a marketing company

---

[55] See infra ¶ 3.10.

[56] See Milgrim, *Trade Secrets* 5-56, 5-57.

distributing consumer refrigerators may have no need for information about the design of a particular cooling unit. Disclosure of such information may not be expressly or impliedly confidential. In contrast, a marketing agent for large computers may be required to deal with complex technical issues and some disclosure of secret designs may be necessary. A presumption of confidentiality is appropriate. The confidentiality of disclosures in marketing agreements is decided on a case-by-case basis.[57]

Where independent contractors are employed, agreements or implied duties of nondisclosure and use may be inadequate protection for the trade secret holder. It is difficult to establish that unauthorized use has occurred even if the contractor subsequently engages in competitive activity. Presumably, a contractor is selected because of its independent capability. During the course of the contract, this independent capability may be enhanced by accumulated experience. Following termination of the original contract, it can be anticipated that the independent contractor will use these capabilities for its own purposes.

Confidential disclosure of trade secrets to an independent contractor does not foreclose the contractor from using existing capability or subsequently developed experience in its own business, even if in direct competition with the proprietor of the trade secret. The trade secret barrier applies only to misappropriation of the particular secret. For example, in *Automated Systems, Inc. v. Service Bureau Corp.*[58] an IBM subsidiary contracted to market an auto parts inventory control system, but concluded that the system was not sufficiently marketable and terminated the relationship. Subsequently, it developed and marketed a competing system based in part on industry contacts and knowledge gained during the initial contract. The court rejected the original designer's contention that this subsequent system violated trade secrecy. "The system which defendant sold to Chevrolet was a quite different one than the [plaintiff's] system . . . which had elements not acceptable to Chevrolet. . . . The system . . . was different in its essentials. . . . Defendant was entitled, after termination of the contract, to use general information gained through its association with plaintiff."[59] In essence, information about the auto parts business was not a trade secret or otherwise confidential. Competition was not prohibited.

The difficult factual questions involved in such subsequent competition may lead a trade secret owner to seek more general protection by contractually restricting the contractor's right to compete. These clauses

---

[57] See Milgrim, *Trade Secrets* 5-69.
[58] 401 F2d 619 (10th Cir. 1968).
[59] Id. at 624, 625.

are independent of subsequent use of disclosed secrets and, of course, this is their primary advantage from the secret holder's perspective. While a noncompetition clause substantially restrains the contractor's business operations, the clause is generally enforceable if the restraint is reasonable and relates to protecting trade secret information.[60] The interests of both the contractor and the secret holder are significant and must be balanced. If the economic factors suggest relative parity of the parties, their contract should be enforced.[61] If there is a significant imbalance creating an inference that terms are imposed rather than negotiated, judicially imposed balancing is appropriate to avoid overreaching. The contractor's right to independent business operations should be compromised only as far as necessary to protect the holder's trade secrecy interests.

¶ 3.09　PRETRANSACTION DISCLOSURES

When an agreement is completed between the trade secret holder and a third party, the rights of the parties are affected by the contract and the indicia of confidentiality surrounding performance. In many cases however, a trade secret is at least partially disclosed during the negotiation stage in response to the third party's desire to obtain relevant technical information prior to committing to a contract. When disclosure is not followed by a contract, an issue arises about the extent to which confidentiality restrictions can nevertheless be imposed on the party receiving the secret information. Pretransaction disclosures are potentially confidential. The absence of an eventual contract is not decisive. Rather, the context of the disclosure is significant. Casual, unrestricted disclosures are not protected. Disclosures conditioned by an effort to restrict use are protected if the restrictions are understood and acquiesced to by the other party.

In *M. Bryce & Associates v. Gladstone,*[62] a vendor of a management information system made extensive presentations to a potential user, disclosing various aspects of its system. Documentation was marked proprietary and audiences at presentations were asked to sign nondisclosure agreements. Although not all did so, oral notification as to secrecy was sufficient to bind the others. When the potential user rejected the contract and developed its own system based on the plaintiff's documentation, a

---

[60] See Electronic Data Sys. Corp. v. Sigma Sys. Corp., 500 F2d 241 (5th Cir. 1974), cert. denied, 419 US 1070 (1975) (enforcing nondisclosure agreement against company hired to manufacture prototype).

[61] See Milgrim, *Trade Secrets* 5-57, 5-58.

[62] 319 NW2d 902 (Wis. Ct. App. 1982).

violation of trade secrecy occurred. Similarly, in *Digital Development Corp. v. International Memory Systems*[63] disclosures made while negotiating a joint manufacturing agreement concerning disk controllers could not be used to develop an independent product. Both parties had discussed and acknowledged that the material was proprietary and treated it as such.

Aspects of the negotiation setting favor protection of trade secrets whether or not there is an explicit prenegotiation contract. Typically, this setting involves parties with at least a modicum of equal bargaining leverage. Furthermore, some degree of disclosure is essential to establishing a contract. If preagreement disclosures were unprotected, the result would force decisions on contracts without full information or encourage unnaturally formal structures for negotiation. Nevertheless, it is necessary to recognize the independent concerns of the entity receiving the information. These revolve around the ability to exploit information that later becomes generally known or that is independently developed. There are few cases on this, but the concerns can be handled by a predisclosure contract.

> The disclosee ... will normally insist upon the right to use (1) data known by the disclosee prior to disclosure, (2) data which becomes generally known, ... and (3) data made available to disclosee by a third party under no legal duty ... not to disclose. Such provisions are relatively standard. ... Another provision ... excepts developments made by the disclosee subsequent to and independent of the discloser. Such a provision ... may be particularly suited to corporations which have several research programs ... which lead to independent development.[64]

The most complex issue in preagreement disclosures involves subsequent discovery by the disclosee. In the absence of an express agreement, trade secrecy does not bar independent discovery of similar or identical secrets. However, this principle is exceedingly difficult to apply since the factual information regarding independent development is within the control of the alleged misappropriator. While it might be desirable to deal with this issue in a predisclosure agreement, negotiating the terms of that agreement is at best awkward. The party who is to receive the secret is not yet able to evaluate whether or to what extent the information relates to areas already under development or planned for research. At best, a contract might preserve the independent development right, but it can not resolve factual questions. However, depending on the overall terms of the

---

[63] 185 USPQ 136 (SD Cal. 1973).

[64] Milgrim, *Trade Secrets* 5–67.

predisclosure contract, the absence of such a clause might waive the right to subsequent, independent discovery.

¶ 3.10 EMPLOYEES AND CONFIDENTIALITY

The most frequently litigated trade secret relationship involves employees who obtain access to an employer's trade secrets, but subsequently leave to join another company or to form their own company. The frequency with which this appears in appellate decisions relates to the common nature of the occurrence itself. Especially in the computer industry, job mobility is high and start-up companies comprised of former employees proliferate. Trade secrecy problems are a consequence of a rapid growth, entrepreneurial, and competitive commercial environment.

The law in this context involves a close balancing of strong and competing interests, both of which are socially recognized as vital concerns.[65] On one hand, use of employees to develop and exploit secret industrial information is essential to the development and expansion of commercial technology. The employer's interest in retaining and enforcing its secrets is an essential element of technology growth, since it provides the financial incentive for development even if the statutory monopoly of patent law is not feasible. In contrast, there are significant reasons to avoid constraints on the individual employee who seeks new employment or establishes his own business. In part, these relate to concepts of individual liberty and mobility. To the extent that trade secret barriers prevent an employee's use of information, the employee's free selection of jobs and ability to translate personal knowledge into financial gain are restricted. At some level, these restrictions may create a form of servitude in which the employee's options are reduced to remaining with a specific employer or changing to an entirely new field with resulting income and knowledge loss. Also, while trade secrecy encourages corporate technology development, protecting employee mobility encourages the acquisition and refinement of personal skills and knowledge. These, of course, are the building blocks of any scientific or technological development.

The employment relationship is regarded as presumptively confidential with regard to trade secret information.[66] The extent to which confi-

---

[65] See Motorola, Inc. v. Fairchild Camera & Instrument Corp., 366 F. Supp. 1173 (D. Ariz. 1973); Modern Controls v. Andreadakis, 578 F2d 1264 (8th Cir. 1978); Electronic Data Sys. Corp. v. Kinder, 360 F. Supp. 1044 (ND Tex.), aff'd, 497 F2d 222 (5th Cir. 1974); C-E-I-R, Inc. v. Computer Dynamics Corp., 183 A2d 374 (Md. 1962).

[66] See Modern Controls v. Andreadakis, 578 F2d 1264 (8th Cir. 1978); Electronic Data Sys. Corp. v. Kinder, 360 F. Supp. 1044 (ND Tex.), aff'd, 497 F2d 222

dentiality is enforced in a specific relationship depends in part on the status of the particular employee. In general, people with higher status and discretionary range in an organization are more likely to be held to confidentiality than are lower level employees.[67] The relationship is not absolute. It may be more accurate to observe that requisite confidentiality is directly related to whether, as a normal course, the employee's job responsibilities entail exposure to trade secret information. This is especially significant for software development in corporations other than software companies. While the programming staff plays a vital, developmental role, they are often not regarded as high status, discretionary employees. They do, however, have frequent contact with potentially secret material.

While confidentiality is implicit in most employment relationships, the enforceability of specific restraints is linked to the underlying question of whether or not a trade secret exists and was maintained by the former employer. As previously discussed,[68] to establish any trade secrecy claim there must be a reasonable effort at internal and external secrecy. Internal secrecy measures are particularly relevant to employees.[69]

Internal security can be viewed in purely practical terms as essential protection against general dissemination of secret information. This is a necessary element of a trade secret claim. One court indicated that it must be established that the "plaintiff was attempting to keep the secret and the program is still unavailable to the computer trade as a whole."[70] For employees, however, a more important effect of internal secrecy is the notice-giving function. To the extent that particular processes, documents, or other secrets are characterized by confidentiality notices, restricted dissemination, and protected use, a mutual expectation of confidentiality is established and will be enforced. Where internal procedures fail in this regard, it is likely that subsequent enforcement will be denied

---

(5th Cir. 1974); C-E-I-R, Inc. v. Computer Dynamics Corp., 183 A2d 374 (Md. 1962).

[67] See, e.g., Cybertek Computer Prod., Inc. v. Whitfield, 203 USPQ 1020 (Cal. Super. Ct. 1977); Sperry Rand Corp. v. Rothlein, 241 F. Supp. 549 (D. Conn. 1964).

[68] See supra ¶ 3.03.

[69] See J&K Computer Sys., Inc. v. Parrish, 642 P2d 732 (Utah 1982); Dynamic Research Corp. v. Analytic Sciences Corp., 400 NE2d 1274 (Mass. App. Ct. 1980).

[70] J&K Computer Sys., Inc. v. Parrish, 642 P2d 732 (Utah 1982).

either because no confidentiality was established or because the underlying subject matter is not a trade secret.[71]

Simply maintaining physical security against external intrusion is inadequate as to restraints on employees. Internal, enforced limitations on access to specific information, as well as notices pertaining to the proprietary nature of specific documents or procedures, are critical.[72] Furthermore, it is common to conduct entry and termination interviews at which the employer's secrecy claims are outlined.[73] While particular components of these procedures may not be invariably required, the standard requires reasonable effort and notice. As various internal procedures become increasingly common and widespread in secrecy programs in an industry, it may be unreasonable not to follow normal industry practice.[74]

[1] General Knowledge and Trade Secrets

In cases involving employees, a central issue involves the extent to which protection of the claimed trade secret would affect the employee's ability to use his general skill and knowledge in subsequent employment. While the employer has a right to protect commercially valuable secrets, this right does not extend to preventing the former employee from engaging in his own profession by employing his own general knowledge and skill. Drawing a distinction between general knowledge and a particular trade secret is a balancing process. Application of this balance to particular cases is inherently uncertain. However, the issue turns on several identifiable factors.

One factor involves the extent to which internal procedures notified the employee of the employer's claim and identified it with particularity. Without notice that particular information or processes are proprietary, the employee has reason to believe that skills or knowledge acquired during employment becomes part of his general background.[75] Indeed, espe-

---

[71] See Motorola, Inc. v. Fairchild Camera & Instrument Corp., 366 F. Supp. 1173 (D. Ariz. 1973); Dynamic Research Corp. v. Analytic Sciences Corp., 400 NE2d 1274 (Mass. App. Ct. 1980).

[72] See J&K Computer Sys., Inc. v. Parrish, 642 P2d 732 (Utah 1982); Telex Corp. v. IBM, 510 F2d 894 (10th Cir. 1975); Sperry Rand Corp. v. Pentronix, 311 F. Supp. 910 (ED Pa. 1970).

[73] See Sperry Rand Corp. v. Pentronix, 311 F. Supp. 910 (ED Pa. 1970).

[74] See Motorola, Inc. v. Fairchild Camera & Instrument Corp., 366 F. Supp. 1173, 1185 (D. Ariz. 1973).

[75] See Dynamic Research Corp. v. Analytic Sciences Corp., 400 NE2d 1274 (Mass. App. Ct. 1980); Jostens, Inc. v. National Computer Sys., Inc., 318 NW2d 691 (Minn. 1982).

cially in high technology industries and among scientists and other professionals, the opportunity to acquire or expand knowledge and experience may be a primary motivation for accepting employment or remaining in a position. Acquisition of personal knowledge is a protectible interest both in terms of the individual and in terms of a broader social interest in expanding the pool of technologically skilled professionals. If the employer desires to restrict subsequent use of some of this acquired knowledge, it must make that claim clearly known to the employee.

The idea of notification is closely connected to the particularity of the trade secret claim. The more general an alleged secret is, the more likely it will not be viewed as secret or, at least, as enforceable against an employee who has a right to use his general knowledge and expertise.

The specificity of the claim relates to general questions of enforceability of any restraint against the employee. It also relates to the nature of the remedy available. For example, in *J&K Computer Systems, Inc. v. Parrish*[76] the defendant was involved in the development of an accounts receivable program with his initial employer and subsequently joined a former customer's staff using a similar program. In upholding a damage award and injunction, the court noted

> [The] trial court could have reasonably determined that J&K's accounts receivable program was secret and worthy of protection by the law.... Defendants were not enjoined ... from using their general knowledge, skills, memory or experience. They were, however, enjoined from using the proprietary accounts receivable program which the plaintiff had developed.[77]

A particularized claim should permit enforcement of the original employer's rights without disabling the former employee from using his general skills in the profession.

As this suggests, mere employment does not bar the employee from subsequently entering into direct competition with the former employer.[78] Generally, this competitive employment can and will entail use of commercial insights gained while at the original job. General busi-

---

[76] 642 P2d 732 (Utah 1982).

[77] Id. at 735.

[78] See Milgrim, *Trade Secrets* 5-16, 5-17; see also Electronic Data Sys. Corp. v. Kinder, 360 F. Supp. 1044 (ND Tex.), aff'd, 497 F2d 222 (5th Cir. 1974); C-E-I-R, Inc. v. Computer Dynamics Corp., 183 A2d 374 (Md. 1962); Cybertek Computer Prod., Inc. v. Whitfield, 203 USPQ 1020 (Cal. Super. Ct. 1977); Science Accessories v. Summagraphics, 215 USPQ 1051 (Del. 1980).

ness information is not protectible.[79] Similarly, use of general, technical skills is not barred. As a result, the competitive product of the employee may closely mirror the employer's product, except that particular design elements that are substantiated as secret can not be used. For example, in *Electronic Data Systems Corp. v. Kinder*[80] the employee had helped develop a health claim processing system and subsequently left to develop a competing system. The second system involved a different design. The court noted that "Without disclosing or using plaintiff's confidential system ... Kinder's employment at SRI consisted simply of his acting in a general capacity as a data processor. To restrict him from such employment is ... unnecessary and ... unwarranted."[81] Often in such cases the provability of misappropriation requires identifying similarities in particular designs, routines, or physical elements.[82] In the absence of enforceable noncompetition clauses in a contract, subsequent competition can not be enjoined without proof of actual similarity or of a "high degree of probability that competitive employment will lead to ... wrongful use or disclosure" of trade secrets.[83]

Trade secret enforcement against a former employee also varies depending on the employee's general level of skill and role in developing the particular secret. Consistent with the view that the employee's general knowledge and ability can not be preempted in the absence of an express contract, trade secret enforcement against an employee who brought advanced skills to the job requires greater specificity in identifying the secret so that the employee remains free to use his knowledge and skill.[84] The enforceability of secrecy is counterbalanced by a desire to avoid the employer's controlling skills that it did not contribute to developing. In contrast, where the employee acquires substantial additional skill on the job, he does so in part as a result of the employer's support. Arguably, this justifies some restraint based on the employer's interests even at the expense of the employee's general mobility. Where an irreconcilable con-

---

[79] See, e.g., Trilog Assoc., Inc. v. Famularo, 314 A2d 287 (Pa. 1974); Electronic Data Sys. Corp. v. Kinder, 360 F. Supp. 1044 (ND Tex.), aff'd, 497 F2d 222 (5th Cir. 1974).

[80] 360 F. Supp. 1044 (ND Tex.), aff'd, 497 F2d 222 (5th Cir. 1974).

[81] Id. at 224.

[82] See Cybertek Computer Prod., Inc. v. Whitfield, 203 USPQ 1020 (Cal. Super. Ct. 1977); Sperry Rand Corp. v. Rothlein, 241 F. Supp. 549 (D. Conn. 1964); Structural Dynamics Research Corp. v. Engineering Mechanics Research Corp., 401 F. Supp. 1102 (ED Mich. 1975).

[83] See Milgrim, *Trade Secrets* 5–31.

[84] See Dynamic Research Corp. v. Analytic Sciences Corp., 400 NE2d 1274, 1282 (Mass. App. Ct. 1980); see also Blake, "Employee Agreements Not to Compete," 73 Harv. L. Rev. 625, 684, 685 (1960).

flict exists, at least one observer suggests that "[the secrecy interest] may be denied in cases where the secret has become such an important part of an employee's job skills that he will have difficulty in obtaining a new position if he can not take it with him."[85]

The appropriate resolution of these cases is not to generally disallow protection of acquired secrets. While the learned skills are the employee's and can not be restrained in the absence of an agreement, trade secrets should remain protectible. With any highly skilled employee it is crucial to identify and protect valid secrecy claims without unnecessary infringement on the employee's mobility and continued professional employment.

An additional factor is the extent to which the employee played a role in developing the secret process, design, or information.[86] From the employer's view, the classic trade secret case is one in which the employee is exposed to existing trade secrets. Employer protection is less clear if the employee is involved with, or responsible for, acquisition of the secret. As discussed in Chapter 4, a developmental role may give the employee ownership of the secret. However, even if ownership vests in the employer, the developer-employee has a greater interest in retaining a right to use the product of his own skills or at least the experience and ability directly gained in its development.[87] This claim is enhanced if the employer did not actively assert its proprietary rights. In contrast, the employer's position is enhanced if it supported the development, asserted rights to it, and invested with intent to exploit it.[88]

[2] Nondisclosure Agreements

Most reported employee trade secret cases involve employment contracts that limit disclosure of information or post-employment competition. The most common employee contracts are those that expressly bind the employee to nondisclosure of confidential or secret information obtained during the employee's work. Nondisclosure contracts have an important role in an internal security program. Nondisclosure clauses

---

[85] "Developments in the Law: Competitive Torts," 77 Harv. L. Rev. 888, 949 (1964).

[86] See Modern Controls v. Andreadakis, 578 F2d 1264 (8th Cir. 1978); Jostens, Inc. v. National Computer Sys., Inc., 318 NW2d 691 (Minn. 1982).

[87] See Science Accessories v. Summagraphics, 215 USPQ 1051 (Del. 1980); Amoco Prod. Co. v. Lindley, 609 P2d 733 (Okla. 1980).

[88] See Structural Dynamics Research Corp. v. Engineering Mechanics Research Corp., 401 F. Supp. 1102, 1111 (ED Mich. 1975); Amoco Prod. Co. v. Lindley, 609 P2d 733 (Okla. 1980).

serve to establish that the alleged secret holder has undertaken reasonable steps to ensure that secrecy in fact exists. A general failure to obtain nondisclosure agreements from at least those employees directly involved in secret processes may forfeit any claim to trade secret status.[89]

The importance of nondisclosure agreements in actions against an employee is more debatable. A major difficulty in enforcing any employment contract restriction lies in the context in which they are negotiated. The general judicial perception is that restrictive employment contracts are not a product of bargaining, but are imposed as a condition of employment. Even if the employee has the option of refusing a particular job, when coupled with a perceived imbalance between employer and employee this procedure may lead to a reluctance to enforce the contracts according to their express terms.

As a result, many courts view enforcement issues as essentially coextensive with basic trade secret law.[90] Thus, in a number of cases, despite contract restraints on disclosing confidential or secret information, it was necessary to establish that a trade secret was in fact involved and to distinguish protected secrets from the general knowledge and experience of the employee.[91] Commonly, the distinction between general knowledge and secrets does not derive from the contract, but from other factors including internal notifications and termination interviews.[92]

Despite this pattern, some reported cases appear to give nondisclosure clauses independent effect in enforcement actions. For example, in *Structural Dynamics Research Corp. v. Engineering Mechanics Research Corp.*[93] the court initially concluded that former employees were under no duty not to disclose or use a structural analysis program that they had developed for the plaintiff. However, the employees had signed a nondisclosure contract and this applied regardless of whether the program was a trade secret of the first employer.

> Some courts have held that such express contracts create a confidential relationship [but they] use the doctrine of trade secrets in the decisional process. This court finds such an approach too restrictive, especially in an area of knowledge and rapid technological change

---

[89] See Clark Equip. v. Harlan, 539 F. Supp. 561 (D. Kan. 1982); Cybertek Computer Prod., Inc. v. Whitfield, 203 USPQ 1020 (Cal. Super. Ct. 1977).

[90] See Motorola, Inc. v. Fairchild Camera & Instrument Corp., 366 F. Supp. 1173 (D. Ariz. 1973); Milgrim, *Trade Secrets* 3-67, 3-68.

[91] See infra ¶ 3.14.

[92] See Jostens, Inc. v. National Computer Sys., Inc., 318 NW2d 691 (Minn. 1982); Dynamic Research Corp. v. Analytic Sciences Corp., 400 NE2d 1274, 1282 (Mass. App. Ct. 1980).

[93] 401 F. Supp. 1102 (ED Mich. 1975).

such as the computer field. The express contracts in issue apply not only to trade secrets but also to privileged, proprietary and confidential information ... even though such information, knowledge or technology is not itself a trade secret.[94]

While similar language can be found in other cases,[95] it is arguable that rather than actually expanding the scope of protection these cases use a nondisclosure clause to reach a result that could have been reached by concluding that a trade secret had been misappropriated. In any event, a nondisclosure contract can not elevate nonsecret, nonconfidential material to protected status or substantially preempt an employee's right to use general knowledge and skill.[96]

The foregoing comments apply to general nondiclosure agreements, referring broadly to confidential, proprietary, or secret information. If the nondisclosure clause is more specific, it may substantially affect enforcement. For example, in *Cybertek Computer Products, Inc. v. Whitfield*[97] the nondisclosure agreement made specific reference to an on-line business computer system known as the Auto/Issue system. The signing party was a cofounder of Cybertek who left to work for another company to develop a system that would directly compete with Auto/Issue. While the trade secrecy claim included some general system design concepts, the court concluded that protection was appropriate. The particularized agreement placed the employee on clear notice as to the employer's claim and facilitated protection without broadly restricting the employee's use of general skills.

[3] Noncompetition Clauses

The second form of restrictive employment agreement used to protect trade secrets bars the employee from engaging in professional activities in competition with its former employer. The purpose of the agreement is to eliminate the close questions of fact that may arise when a former employee accepts competitive employment. A noncompetition clause can also serve as a basis for injunctive relief before an opportunity for damaging disclosures arises.

---

[94] Id. at 1113, 1114.

[95] See Cybertek Computer Prod., Inc. v. Whitfield, 203 USPQ 1020 (Cal. Super. Ct. 1977).

[96] See Trilog Assoc., Inc. v. Famularo, 314 A2d 287 (Pa. 1974); Modern Controls v. Andreadakis, 578 F2d 1264 (8th Cir. 1978).

[97] 203 USPQ 1020 (Cal. Super. Ct. 1977)

Unlike nondisclosure clauses, it is clear that noncompetition agreements significantly enhance the employer's position to the extent that the agreements are enforceable. The major issue concerns enforceability. On its surface, a noncompetition clause conflicts with policies supporting an employee's right to use general skills and experience in professional employment. The clause creates a form of economic monopoly over the employee, forcing him to stay with a particular employer or change commercial fields. This occurs in what might be described as a suspect agreement where the employee's ability to negotiate mutually acceptable terms is suspect in light of the employer's often superior bargaining position. There is substantial controversy over the enforceability of this type of employment clause. In some states such as California, noncompetition clauses are barred by statute. [98] In other states, statutory limits restrict the scope of the clauses to instances involving express protection of trade secrets. [99]

If not otherwise prohibited, noncompetition clauses are generally enforceable when supported by adequate consideration if they contain substantively reasonable restrictions. Consideration for the clause is generally found in the employment of the worker, especially if the employment is more than on an at-will or short-term basis. [100] Adequate consideration can be an issue, however, where the clause is not executed until after the employee begins work. In that circumstance, it should be determined whether the parties intended to execute a noncompetition clause from the outset or whether the employer extended additional consideration at the time of signing. [101]

The most frequently litigated questions involve whether the terms of the clause are reasonable and, if some elements are not, what the effect is on the agreement as a whole. Milgrim describes the question as "whether the protection sought by the employer is reasonable when compared with the restrictions that it might place upon the employee's ability to earn a livelihood or the disservice that might be done to the public by the restriction of competition." [102] More specifically, reasonableness focuses attention on the geographic scope, duration, and type of activity precluded. [103] Another relevant inquiry concerns the extent to which the competition

---

[98] See Cal. Bus. & Prof. Code § 16600.

[99] See Structural Dynamics Research Corp. v. Engineering Mechanics Research Corp., 401 F. Supp. 1102, 1114 (ED Mich. 1975).

[100] See Milgrim, *Trade Secrets* 3–8.

[101] See Modern Controls v. Andreadakis, 578 F2d 1264 (8th Cir. 1978).

[102] Milgrim, *Trade Secrets* 3–67.

[103] See Electronic Data Sys. Corp. v. Kinder, 360 F. Supp. 1044 (ND Tex. 1973), aff'd, 497 F2d 222 (5th Cir. 1974); Electronic Data Sys. Corp. v. Powell,

clause is designed or needed to protect valuable secrets or confidential material. In some cases, enforcement of the competition clause is contingent on establishing that the employee had access to trade secret information. At a minimum, a showing of access to confidential material is essential, but to "require the employer to prove the existence of trade secrets prior to enforcement of a covenant not to compete may defeat the only purpose for which the covenant exists."[104]

The critical issue involves the extent to which the activities foreclosed by the agreement match the employer's provable interests without unnecessarily disabling the employee from earning a livelihood. The enforceability of a noncompetition clause increases if it is narrowly drawn and the boundaries of the restraint clearly reflect the employer's particularized concerns. For example, in *Modern Controls, Inc. v. Andreadakis*[105] the court enforced a covenant not to compete against an employee who had been involved in developing a display device. The covenant was described in the following terms:

> It provides that Andreadakis would not work for a competitor of Modern Controls for two years after leaving Modern Controls if the competitor produced or developed a product which Andreadakis worked on while employed at Modern Controls. If, however, the competitor was diversified, Andreadakis could work for the competitor in a division not producing or developing the competing product.[106]

This agreement is not only limited in duration, but leaves the employee with substantial flexibility in finding future employment. It aids the initial employer by providing a barrier to direct competition independent of the need to establish that the employee had or would disclose confidential material.

The structure of the restraint is often reviewed in the context of judicial hostility to noncompetition clauses. One result is that a particular covenant may be narrowly construed in order to limit the scope of the resulting remedy. For example, in *Electronic Data Systems v. Powell*[107] a Texas court interpreted a general noncompetition clause narrowly to bar an employee only from working on data processing programs similar to those developed at Electronic Data Systems. It limited injunctive relief to

---

508 SW2d 137 (Tex. Civ. App. 1974); Modern Controls v. Andreadakis, 578 F2d 1264 (8th Cir. 1978).

[104] Id. at 1268.

[105] 578 F2d 1264 (8th Cir. 1978).

[106] Id. at 1266.

[107] 508 SW2d 137 (Tex. Civ. App. 1974).

barring use of the same data system structure, but allowed the employee to continue working at a company that marketed an independently developed, but directly competing system.

Regardless of substantive scope, a covenant not to compete may be invalid if it fails to sufficiently narrow geographic terms and duration. For example, in *Trilog Associates, Inc. v. Famularo*[108] the court invalidated a covenant that applied to employees of a data processing company who left and formed their own company. The new company obtained a contract servicing a trustee's records for a bank that had also been a customer of Trilog for processing shareholder's records. The court concluded that no confidential information was used by the former employees, although they had learned about aspects of the banking business during their employment at Trilog. It then invalidated the covenant not to compete. The covenant was limited to developing shareholder systems, to being employed by a customer of Trilog, or to being employed by an entity with which the employee came into contact as a result of his employment. The court noted

> The ... covenants have no limitation on territory and thus are broader than is necessary for the protection of Trilog. Famularo in effect promised not to practice his profession *anywhere for anyone* in developing a shareholder's record system. [The other clauses prohibit] accepting, with any customer or client of Trilog, *any employment anywhere* ... in *any* capacity. It covers employment totally unrelated to whatever work the employee performed for Trilog.... Such a covenant is a completely unreasonable restraint of trade and can not be upheld.[109]

As this indicates, whether geographic, duration, or activity elements are at issue, a critical question involves the extent to which the covenant is drafted in a manner that clearly reflects a protectible employer interest. Given a close and identifiable relationship to specific employer interests, both the interests of the former employer and the employee can be protected. In its absence, the employee's right to economic mobility is predominant.

Depending on the jurisdiction, a judicial determination that part of a covenant is unreasonable leads to differing results. In some states, an unreasonable covenant is void, leaving the employer solely with recourse to trade secret law. However, most states offer a more flexible approach under which some terms of the covenant may be enforceable if the agree-

---

[108] 314 A2d 287 (Pa. 1974).
[109] Id. at 293.

ment is divisible or otherwise subject to interpretation.[110] Where this approach is followed, most courts attempt to identify a manner of enforcement that is reasonable in light of the circumstances. Some courts have narrowed the terms of the covenant or applied the so-called blue pencil approach in which offending terms of the contract are deleted and the remainder of the agreement is enforced.[111]

¶ 3.11 NEW COMPANIES AND COMPETITIVE HIRING

[1] Third Parties: Enticement

The reported employee trade secret cases in the computer field reflect two distinct patterns. The first consists of an employee or group of employees leaving the original company to form their own company. As is discussed in the following section, to the extent that the employees do not use proprietary data the formation of a company in competition with the original employer is not actionable. The second pattern consists of an employee leaving the original employer to join an existing competitor. This is the focus of this section.

The circumstance of an employee being hired by a competitor is relatively common in the computer industry. Its significance relates to the character of the commercial product involved and the heavy reliance on personal skills. For example, in a software company commercial viability often depends only in part on existing products. Over the long term, the personal skills of the technical staff are crucial. As a result, employees are both attractive acquisitions and valuable assets independent of trade secrecy issues.

Competitors have a right to hire the employees of another company who are not under long-term contracts.[112] This is a direct corollary of the need to ensure an employee's mobility and ability to earn a livelihood, even if that involves activities in direct competition with the original

---

[110] See Electronic Data Sys. Corp. v. Kinder, 360 F. Supp. 1044 (ND Tex. 1973), aff'd, 497 F2d 222 (5th Cir. 1974); Electronic Data Sys. Corp. v. Powell, 508 SW2d 137 (Tex. Civ. App. 1974); Trilog Assoc., Inc. v. Famularo, 314 A2d 287 (Pa. 1974); see also Milgrim, *Trade Secrets* 3-41–3-44.

[111] See Blake, "Employee Agreements Not to Compete," 73 Harv. L. Rev. 625, 682–684 (1960); "Developments in the Law: Competitive Torts," 77 Harv. L. Rev. 888 (1964); see also Solari Indus., Inc. v. Malady, 264 A2d 53 (NJ 1970); Raimonde v. Van Klech, 325 NE2d 544 (Ohio 1975).

[112] See Milgrim, *Trade Secrets* § 5.04[4]; Motorola, Inc. v. Fairchild Camera & Instrument Corp., 366 F. Supp. 1173, 1180 (D. Ariz. 1973).

employer.[113] One obvious way in which the employee may exploit this mobility is by accepting a position in a competitor's company.

The ability to hire away employees is often described as a privilege available to the hiring competitor. In practice, the loss of any valuable employee represents a detriment to the original employer. This loss, however, is not recognized as protectible where the employment is at will. The expectation of future benefits established by an at-will contract is not such as to bar interference by third parties.

> As to such future hopes he has no legal right, but only an expectancy; and when the contract is terminated by the choice of the (employee) there is no breach of it. The competitor is therefore free, for his own competitive advantage, to obtain such future benefits for himself by causing the termination. Thus [the competitor] may offer better contract terms . . . without liability.[114]

From the standpoint of the original employer, the right to engage in competitive hiring may be viewed as tantamount to a license to raid. Indeed, it is the legal basis on which intraindustry employee raiding occurs. The limitations on this right are minimal and difficult to apply. In this context for example, while competitive hiring is permitted, restraints on disclosure and misappropriation of trade secrets apply.[115] Inducing an employee to breach a duty of confidentiality is "an actionable wrong."[116] This inducement can take the form of a lucrative job offer with an implicit understanding that one portion of the new employee's value derives from his disclosure of the other employer's trade secrets. The distinction between such inducement and merely hiring an employee whose value lies in general expertise and skill is difficult to draw. However, the appropriate balance must lean in the direction of ensuring that the courts do not infringe the employee's mobility by restraining competitive hiring practices. Merely offering a higher salary does not establish an intention to induce a breach of confidence. Salary increases are normal in

---

[113] See infra ¶ 3.11[2]; C-E-I-R, Inc. v. Computer Dynamics Corp., 183 A2d 374 (Md. 1962).

[114] Restatement (Second) of Torts § 768 comment j.

[115] See Sperry Rand Corp v. Pentronix, 311 F. Supp. 910 (ED Pa. 1970); Computer Print Sys., Inc. v. Lewis, 422 A2d 148 (Pa. Super. Ct. 1980); Electronic Data Sys. Corp. v. Kinder, 360 F. Supp. 1044 (ND Tex. 1973), aff'd, 497 F2d 222 (5th Cir. 1974); Electronic Data Sys. Corp. v. Powell, 508 SW2d 137 (Tex. Civ. App. 1974).

[116] See Milgrim, *Trade Secrets* 5-107; Telex Corp. v. IBM, 510 F2d 894 (10th Cir. 1975).

lateral hiring. Nevertheless, disproportionate increments may provide some indication that more than the employee's general skill is an element of the hiring decision.[117]

A conspiracy to obtain trade secrets can be inferred from the systematic practice of hiring employees of a competitor and using them in programs that consistently track or preempt secrets of the competitor. This pattern arose in *Telex Corp. v. IBM*.[118] As part of a general effort to stay abreast of IBM developments through reverse engineering and analysis of published materials, Telex also engaged in a pattern of hiring IBM employees who were involved in sensitive IBM projects. The objective was to obtain early information about IBM product developments. While the general objective was not actionable, the luring away of key employees was prohibited.

> Telex lured key employees away from IBM with the promise of greatly increased salaries, plus substantial bonuses and ... these quondam IBM employees brought with them IBM trade secrets which enabled Telex to market plug compatibles sooner than it would have otherwise been able to ... through reverse engineering. It was this "head start" or "lead time" that placed Telex in a better economic position because of its misappropriation.... Telex obtained these trade secrets from IBM by a massive and persuasive program designed to induce the breach of known obligations.[119]

In *Telex*, the information clearly related to trade secrets of a technical nature. The analysis does not apply where the main benefit obtained from competitive hiring relates to general expertise or skill. A particular application of this occurs where the competitor's objective is to obtain people with general knowledge of or contacts in a particular market. A company desiring to enter or expand in data processing for banking or health industries is not barred from hiring employees with contacts in these areas, even though the employees acquired this experience at a competitor.[120] Such general information is commonly not considered a trade secret or otherwise confidential.

---

[117] See Telex Corp. v. IBM, 367 F. Supp. 258, 321, 322 (ND Okla. 1973), aff'd, 510 F2d 894 (10th Cir. 1975).

[118] 510 F2d 894 (10th Cir. 1975).

[119] Id. at 929.

[120] See Electronic Data Sys. Corp. v. Powell, 508 SW2d 137 (Tex. Civ. App. 1974); Trilog Assoc., Inc. v. Famularo, 314 A2d 287 (Pa. 1974).

[2] Splinter Companies and Conflicting Interests

Many of the situations discussed in the previous section involve a concern about conflicts of interest between loyalty owed to the employer and the employee's natural desire for self-advancement. These conflicts also surface when the employee leaves to form a new company. The basic legal premise is that the employee has a right to compete with his former employer.[121] This right is circumscribed by restraints on the misuse of confidential material and may be barred by enforceable covenants not to compete.[122] However, especially if the employee developed the particular intellectual property, employer protection through these methods is attenuated. As a consequence, several reported cases focus directly on the potential conflicts of interest.

The employee's right to engage in subsequent competition with the former employer encompasses a parallel right to make preparations for such competition before leaving the original position.[123] These preparations may involve completing working models of an eventual product to be used by the start-up company.[124] Alternatively, it may include the recruitment of staff for the new venture.[125] The period in which the employee receives a salary, but devotes time to the preparation of a new venture entails an explicit tension between loyalty and the individual interests of the employee. While the employee has a right to make preparations to depart and to compete, this is a qualified or limited right circumscribed by requirements of fair dealing to avoid undue harm to the original employer.[126] "On the one hand there is 'concern for the integrity of the employment relationship ... that demands ... undivided and unselfish loyalty to the corporation.' However, there is an offsetting policy 'of safeguarding society's interest in fostering free and vigorous competition in the economic sphere.' "[127]

---

[121] See Motorola, Inc. v. Fairchild Camera & Instrument Corp., 366 F. Supp. 1173 (D. Ariz. 1973); Sperry Rand Corp. v. Rothlein, 241 F. Supp. 549 (D. Conn. 1964); Science Accessories v. Summagraphics, 215 USPQ 1051 (Del. 1980).

[122] See supra ¶ 3.10[3].

[123] See C-E-I-R, Inc. v. Computer Dynamics Corp., 183 A2d 374 (Md. 1962); Science Accessories v. Summagraphics, 215 USPQ 1051 (Del. 1980); Motorola, Inc. v. Fairchild Camera & Instrument Corp., 366 F. Supp. 1173 (D. Ariz. 1973); Sperry Rand Corp. v. Rothlein, 241 F. Supp. 549 (D. Conn. 1964).

[124] See Science Accessories v. Summagraphics, 215 USPQ 1051 (Del. 1980).

[125] See Sperry Rand Corp. v. Rothlein, 241 F. Supp. 549 (D. Conn. 1964).

[126] Restatement (Second) of Agency § 303 comment e.

[127] Science Accessories v. Summagraphics, 215 USPQ 1051, 1053 (Del. 1980).

The application of these competing policy interests requires close analysis of the facts of a particular case. Two general limitations are imposed on the employee. The first is related to, but not necessarily confined to, the concept of corporate opportunities. It precludes an employee from diverting opportunities from the company for personal gain if the employer is capable of and might be interested in undertaking the opportunity were it presented. In *C-E-I-R, Inc. v. Computer Dynamics Corp.*,[128] the employees had been assigned to negotiate with the government for a contract to consult on and design a data processing system. Before negotiations were completed, the employees formed and executed a plan to establish a new company to bid on the same contract. The court noted that unfair interference with customer relationships does not hinge on the existence of an actual contract. It concluded that the former employees should be enjoined from competing on this contract.

> Because of the secret plans . . . to become competitors for this same business, an unfair situation was created whereby they were able to absorb this unique experience and solidify their contacts . . . on CEIR's time and at that company's expense, and to use these advantages . . . for the benefit of a competing company. . . . The appellees owed a duty of disclosure of their plans. [CEIR] could have taken steps to preserve its own favorable . . . position by utilizing employees remaining with the company.[129]

CEIR does not support the proposition that former employees can not compete for customers of the original employer, but focuses on the method of competition. The violation in *CEIR* was undisclosed exploitation of a particular potential customer to the detriment of the employer where the employer's interest and capability to undertake the contract were apparent.

Variations on this theme in the computer industry often involve an apparent suppression of a product or process development. When this occurs, if the employer clearly manifested support for the developmental work, a conflict of interest is established. For example, in *Sperry Rand Corp. v. Rothlein*[130] a group of employees involved in silicon chip research left Sperry to form National Semiconductor Corporation. During their preparation for departure, several of the employees discouraged a company proposal to expand more fully into a particular product area that they anticipated would be a major emphasis in the company they were about to form. This explicit diversion of the employer's plans was

---

[128] 183 A2d 374 (Md. 1962).

[129] Id. at 380.

[130] 241 F. Supp. 549 (D. Conn. 1964).

one element in a finding that the employees' competitive preparations violated their obligations to the employer.

When new products or research developments are involved, distinctions must be made between wrongful conduct and the exercise of control over property owned by the employee or otherwise not available to the employer. The clearest case favoring the employer involves subject matter within the sphere of the employee's job where the employer has a clearly manifested interest and capability. In contrast, if the employer expressly disclaims interest after disclosure by the employee, the employee's subsequent efforts are not actionable.[131] Similarly, if the development can not be made available to the employer, no confidentiality breach exists if the employees exploit it for personal gain. This may occur if the invention is the product of a third party who is not willing to submit it to the employer.[132] Unavailability may also be established by inadequate financial or technical resources.

The *Sperry Rand* case noted earlier illustrates a second major limitation on the employee's right to prepare to compete. In that case, Rothlein had been hired to explore Sperry's entry into the semiconductor field and had recommended and implemented an emphasis on silicon, rather than germanium chips. Rothlein was the leader of the semiconductor research team until a corporate restructuring resulted in an administrator being appointed to supervise the team. At that point, Rothlein decided to leave and form his own company. During the several months before he resigned, Rothlein recruited key employees to join him and made plans to recruit others. These preparations were kept secret. In all, a group of 28 employees were taken from Sperry. The court concluded that this massive luring away of key technical personnel constituted violation of trade secrecy: "[The] defendants' conduct in this regard was [not] in itself separately actionable but [was] evidence of the intention and plan . . . to take . . . Sperry's production process . . . regardless of the probable damage to their employer whose best interests they were pretending to serve."[133]

Induced mass departure of critical employees is potentially actionable under either of two distinct theories. First, as in *Sperry*, it may be connected to an effort to misappropriate the employer's trade secrets.[134] Second and independent of trade secrecy issues, it may entail an unfair effort to disrupt or destroy the employer's continued ability to compete.

---

[131] See Amoco Prod. v. Lindley, 609 P2d 733 (Okla. 1980).

[132] See Science Accessories v. Summagraphics, 215 USPQ 1051, 1054 (Del. 1980).

[133] Sperry Rand Corp. v. Rothlein, 241 F. Supp. 549, 553 (D. Conn. 1964).

[134] See Telex Corp. v. IBM, 367 F. Supp. 258, 321, 322 (ND Okla. 1973), aff'd, 510 F2d 894 (10th Cir. 1975).

In this setting, the courts often refer to a conspiracy to injure the employer, implying the underlying requirement of a concerted plan of joint action. The analysis suggests an outer limit of fairness dictated by an employment relationship. Not all mass departures meet this requirement even if they are substantially disabling to the employer's business. Thus, spontaneous, independent decisions by critical employees to leave their jobs are not actionable.[135]

PART C.   PATENT AND COPYRIGHT

¶ 3.12 PREEMPTION

Trade secret law derives primarily from common-law principles. It deals with subject matter that in many cases might be susceptible to protection under federal copyright and patent law. As a result of this potential overlap, there are significant questions concerning the extent to which trade secret law is preempted by either or both of these areas of federal law.

[1] Patent Preemption

The origins of this controversy lie in two U.S. Supreme Court decisions dealing with the interface between state unfair competition sales and federal patent protection. In *Sears, Roebuck & Co. v. Stiffel*[136] and *Compco Corp. v. Day-Brite Lighting, Inc.*,[137] the Court dealt with judgments awarded based on copying mechanical devices marketed by another. Patents granted to the items had been invalidated. Under these circumstances, the Court held that state law could not be invoked to bar copying. "[When] an article is unprotected by a patent or a copyright, state law may not forbid others to copy that article. To forbid copying would interfere with the federal policy . . . of allowing free access to copy whatever the federal patent and copyright laws leave in the public domain."[138]

Significantly, in *Sears* and *Compco* the defendant had not breached a confidential relationship in creating the copies. Nevertheless, the opinions raised significant questions about the scope of federal preemption of

---

[135] See Motorola, Inc. v. Fairchild Camera & Instrument Corp., 366 F. Supp. 1173 (D. Ariz. 1973).

[136] 376 US 225, 84 S. Ct. 784 (1964).

[137] 376 US 234, 84 S. Ct. 779 (1964).

[138] Id. at 237.

trade secret law. The cases applied a form of negative preemption analysis suggesting that federal policies of disclosure and dissemination in patent and copyright might supersede countervailing state policies protecting secrecy and confidentiality.

Although this issue was widely debated for some time, it became substantially moot by the Court's decision in *Kewanee Oil Co. v. Bicron Corp.*[139] *Kewanee* dealt with a trade secret misappropriation of a crystal structure that was clearly within the subject matter of patent law, although probably not patentable under patent standards of obviousness. The secret holder had not sought patent protection. The trial court granted an injunction against several former employees based on trade secret concepts involving a confidential relationship. The Supreme Court affirmed, holding that trade secrecy law was not preempted by patent law or policy. The Court stated that "preemption occurs only if the state law erects an 'obstacle to the accomplishment' of the objectives of Congress."[140] The Court emphasized that trade secret law deals with maintaining standards of commercial ethics and encouraging invention and that although these objectives differ in part, they do not conflict with federal patent policy.

Kewanee focused on the fact that trade secret law deals with confidentiality and the breach of protected relationships, neither of which are within the subject matter of patent law. The decision clearly resolved preemption issues related to patent and trade secrets. The states can not, under the *Sears-Compco* doctrine, prevent mere copying of unpatented inventions that have been publicly disclosed. However, the states may prohibit appropriation accomplished through breach of a confidential relationship.

[2] Copyright Preemption

A similar approach to that in patent law applies to the potential preemption by federal copyright law regarding trade secrets that are also works of authorship under copyright. There should be no preemption of claims based on breach of confidentiality. However, significant controversy persists for the preemption of specific applications of trade secret law. Section 301 of the Copyright Act (Act) provides guidance for copyright preemption: "Nothing in this title annuls or limits any rights or remedies under the ... law ... of any state with respect to (3) activities

---

[139] 416 US 470, 94 S. Ct. 1879 (1974).
[140] Id. at 479.

violating legal or equitable rights that are not equivalent to any of the exclusive rights within the general scope of copyright."[141]

The exclusive rights of a copyright owner include the right to prepare, reproduce, and distribute copies of the work. The focus of protection is on the copying of the author's expression. Section 301 suggests that state law is preempted only to the extent that it deals with these exclusive rights. In most cases, equivalence is not present in trade secret actions since, while the misappropriation may involve reproduction of documents, the essence of the protected trade secret right is confidentiality and its breach, not mere copying.[142]

Beyond equivalence of protected rights, a number of reported cases focus on whether affixing copyright notice to secret material preempts any claim to trade secret protection. One argument is that distribution with a copyright notice constitutes publication and per se waives secrecy. This argument has been rejected.[143] The issue of retained secrecy is resolved based on the actual character, scope, nature, and terms of the distribution.

A related argument was rejected in *Technicon Medical Information Systems Corp. v. Green Bay Packaging, Inc.*[144] *Technicon* involved the misappropriation of secrets contained in a proprietary software manual distributed to customers. In addition to confidentiality notices, the manual contained a copyright notice, and the case arose under the former Act. The defendant argued that use of the copyright notice established statutory estoppel. Arguably, by claiming the benefits of copyright protection, the plaintiff could not claim the allegedly inconsistent benefits of trade secrecy. The circuit court concluded that statutory estoppel applied only if the plaintiff had actually received the benefits of the applicable statute and not solely as a result of affixing a copyright notice.

> Under the 1909 Act, a limited publication is, for legal purposes, no publication at all, and ... does not result in the ... investiture of statutory copyright protection.... For this reason, no benefit inures [by] limited publication with notice.... Similarly, we do not believe that the act of generally publishing ... with notice results in a suffi-

---

[141] 17 USC § 301 (1982).

[142] See, e.g., Technicon Medical Information Sys. Corp. v. Green Bay Packaging, Inc., 687 F2d 1032 (7th Cir. 1982), cert. denied, 103 S. Ct. 732 (1983; Synercom Technology, Inc. v. University Computing Co., 474 F. Supp. 37 (ND Tex. 1979); M. Bryce & Assoc. v. Gladstone, 319 NW 2d 902 (Wis. Ct. App. 1982).

[143] See, e.g., Management Science v. Cyborg, 6 CLSR 921 (ND Ill. 1978); Warrington v. Real Time Co., 522 F. Supp. 367 (ND Ill. 1981).

[144] 687 F2d 1032 (7th Cir. 1982), cert. denied, 103 S. Ct. 732 (1983).

cient benefit.... While that act is necessary to qualify ... for protection ... no actual benefit would be conferred on the copyright owner until an enforcement action was successfully maintained.[145]

The court concluded that it was not inconsistent to claim both copyright and trade secret protection, but that judicial enforcement of both claims might be barred.

The conclusion that it is not inconsistent to claim both copyright and trade secret protection is clearly correct. The two systems protect distinguishable interests. While trade secret law applies to confidential relationships, copyright restrictions apply independently of the relationship between owner and copier. Furthermore, while copyright protects against duplication of forms of expression, trade secret protects ideas and processes.

Despite these distinctions, close questions of preemption arise where the alleged act of misappropriation consists of copying secret works of authorship, especially of a design or computer program. Some decisions suggest that mere copying of the secret design or program can not be actionable under trade secret law. For example, in *Avco Corp. v. Precision Air Parts, Inc.*[146] the lower court held that trade secret protection could not apply to the copying of aircraft parts designs, since the right to preclude copying was equivalent to the exclusive rights conveyed by copyright law. In a similar decision, the district court in *Synercom Technology, Inc. v. University Computing Co.*[147] held that state misappropriation law could not be applied to bar copying of the plaintiff's input/output routines. In *Synercom,* however, the court expressly found that no confidentiality existed. It concluded that if state law applied despite the lack of confidentiality, that application was inconsistent with and preempted by copyright law.

Under Section 301 of the current Act, the central issue is whether a particular cause of action under state law deals with rights that are equivalent to those established by copyright. No difficulty arises if the copying of a document or plan is merely incidental to misappropriation of the information in the document. No preemption occurs since use of information or ideas is not an exclusive right under the Act. If the misappropriation begins and ends with copying and distribution, a more difficult question arises. One view is that the Section 301 equivalence test focuses solely on the physical act involved and preempts any state barrier to copying. The better view is that equivalence should be measured by examin-

---

[145] Id. at 1035, 1036.

[146] 210 USPQ 894 (D. Ala. 1980).

[147] 474 F. Supp. 37 (ND Tex. 1979).

ing the state cause of action in its entirety. Copying that violates trade secrecy is not equivalent to copying prohibited under copyright. The trade secrecy action focuses on culpable conduct in violation of a confidential relationship that is not essential to the copyright claim.

¶ 3.13 PATENT DISCLOSURE AND SECRECY

Patent and copyright law are oriented to public disclosure and dissemination of protected materials. As a result, at various stages in establishing protection under either system, a claimant may make public disclosure. Depending on the pertinent circumstances, this disclosure may forfeit the trade secret claim. In essence, at some point the secret holder may be forced to elect between the two forms of protection.

For patent law, a distinction must be made between the patent application and the situation following an actual grant of a patent. A patent application and attendant materials are confidential.[148] As a result, while the application may entail substantial secret material, pursuit of a patent does not amount to a disclosure waiving trade secrecy.[149] In contrast, an essential element of a patent grant is public disclosure of the invention in a form that a person with ordinary skills in the art can replicate. This constitutes disclosure for the previously secret information covered by the patent.

Patent and trade secret protection may coexist in a single product or process if only parts of the process obtain patent protection with resulting disclosure.[150] One leading authority suggests that this potential coexistence should extend one step further to permit trade secret action against misappropriation of patented aspects of an item or process where the misappropriator breached a confidence and the patent information was not in fact known in the particular trade or used by the defendant.[151] This argument is analogous to general concepts that state that the capability to learn a secret by reverse engineering does not automatically protect actions to discover it through a breach of confidence. The issue arises where the patent grant is later invalidated. As a result, the strongest argument for prohibiting breaches of confidentiality even after the patent grant is that this result encourages use of the patent system. A potentially

---

[148] 35 USC § 122 (1982).

[149] See Nashua Corp. v. RCA Corp., 431 F2d 220, 227 n.11 (1st Cir. 1970).

[150] See ¶ 2.03[2]; see also Data Gen. Corp. v. Digital Computer Controls, Inc., 357 A2d 105 (Del. Ch. 1975); M&T Chem., Inc. v. IBM, 403 F. Supp. 1145 (SDNY 1975).

[151] See Milgrim, *Trade Secrets* 2-59.

invalid grant would not automatically waive all protection. In any event, if a patent is issued before the confidential relationship is established, no trade secrecy rights can be created in the disclosed material.

¶ 3.14 COPYRIGHT DISCLOSURE AND SECRECY

Unlike patent law, copyright law applies to a work of authorship immediately upon its execution. Systems for formal public disclosure are not exacting. As a result, it is possible to claim copyright protection while maintaining the relative secrecy of information contained in the work. Under the current copyright law, affixing an appropriate copyright notice to a published work is necessary to perfect and retain exclusive rights against others unless the circumstances fall within an express exception or cure provision.[152] As a consequence, a trade secret owner who wishes to retain copyright protection for proprietary material will often affix copyright notices to works that are distributed, even if the distribution is restricted. This generates litigation concerning whether use of the copyright notice waives or estops the assertion of trade secrecy claims.[153] Appropriately, the cases consistently reject claims of waiver and estoppel, holding that trade secrecy claims are not inconsistent with a copyright notice.

Copyright is generally associated with protection of published works. Under the former Act, publication was a central concept allocating protective rights between state common-law copyright and the federal system.[154] The Act also defined the critical point at which, in the absence of appropriate notice, all copyright protection might be waived. Under the current Act publication is less important, and state copyrights for unpublished works have been preempted.[155] Publication relates to questions of when copyright notice is generally required and whether copying can be prohibited without prior deposit or registration of the work with the Copyright Office.

---

[152] 17 USC § 405 (1982).

[153] See, e.g., Technicon Medical Information Sys. Corp. v. Green Bay Packaging, Inc., 687 F2d 1032 (7th Cir. 1982), cert. denied, 103 S. Ct. 732 (1983); Synercom Technology, Inc. v. University Computing Co., 474 F. Supp. 37 (ND Tex. 1979); M. Bryce & Assoc. v. Gladstone, 319 NW2d 902 (Wis. Ct. App. 1982); Management Science v. Cyborg, 6 CLSR 921 (ND Ill. 1978); Warrington v. Real Time Co., 522 F. Supp. 367 (ND Ill. 1981); BPI Sys., Inc. v. Leith, 532 F. Supp. 208 (WD Tex. 1981). But see Crow v. Wainwright, 720 F2d 1224 (11th Cir. 1983) (copyright preempts state stolen property law dealing with record albums).

[154] See *Nimmer on Copyright* 46-59.

[155] 17 USC §§ 301, 302, 303 (1982).

A controversy exists concerning whether publication in copyright terms is consistent with the secrecy necessary for trade secret protection. Under current copyright law, "publication" is defined as "the distribution of copies . . . to the public by sale or other transfer of ownership, or by rental, lease or lending."[156] Given the statutory reference to distribution to the public, it is apparent that publication and loss of secrecy through public disclosure tend to address similar events. A software author who broadly distributes a description of its design for a program has probably published the description *and* waived trade secrecy through public disclosure. However, despite this similarity the two concepts are distinct and the question of whether adequate secrecy has been retained should not be decided by focusing on whether a copyright publication has occurred. For example, if a trade secret consists of a program design that led to a marketed software, whether that secret has been lost by marketing should not be determined based on whether the program has been published. But rather, it should be determined based on whether the secret design is discoverable in light of the copies distributed and the terms of their distribution.

Despite use of the language of publication, cases arising under the former copyright law generally reached appropriate issues. Under this law, a primary concern involved whether only a limited publication occurred. In essence, limited publication constituted no publication at all since it implied a limited, restricted distribution of the work. The issue related to whether federal copyright applied at all. Most of the cases concluded that confidential, restricted distribution of works encompassing descriptions of trade secrets constituted limited publication and did not waive secrecy.[157] The result is correct under both copyright and trade secret law. Restricted distribution of a secret under terms establishing confidential relationships does not amount to public disclosure. Under prior copyright law it also constituted a limited publication. However, even if a technical publication occurs for copyright purposes, the issue of whether secrecy and confidentiality have been retained remains pertinent and unresolved under trade secret law.

Cases under prior copyright law also contain illustrations in which both a publication and a public disclosure occurred. For example, in one case public distribution of a read only memory (ROM) chip without

---

[156] 17 USC § 101 (1982).

[157] See Technicon Medical Information Sys. Corp. v. Green Bay Packaging, Inc., 687 F2d 1032 (7th Cir. 1982), cert. denied, 103 S. Ct. 732 (1983); M. Bryce & Assoc. v. Gladstone, 319 NW2d 902 (Wis. Ct. App. 1982); Data Gen. Corp. v. Digital Computer Controls, Inc., 357 A2d 105 (Del. Ch. 1975); Digital Dev. Corp. v. International Memory Sys., 185 USPQ 136 (SD Cal. 1973).

copyright notice waived copyright protection and left the designer without a remedy against a competitor who reverse engineered and copied a marketed chip.[158] Similarly, in *Clark Equipment v. Harlan*[159] copyright publication and lost secrecy coincided. *Clark Equipment* involved the distribution of a microfilm truck parts system, and the court denied a preliminary injunction against unauthorized use. It noted that

> publication of the full set of microfilm to plaintiff's six large customers was not a limited publication so as to preserve plaintiff's rights. . . . [Authorized] dealers were required to sign confidentiality agreements [but] these agreements did not purport to bind the customers who received copies . . . and there is no evidence that [any] saw, heard of or was required to sign such . . . agreements.[160]

The holding was that under prior copyright law general publication without copyright notice waived protection. An analogous result would have been commonplace under trade secret law. Distribution of material directly disclosing the secret without confidentiality restraints relinquishes the secret nature of the information conveyed.

In addition to publication issues, the copyright-trade secret interface raises controversies about copyright deposit and registration procedures. In order to effectively enforce a copyright claim, an author may be required to register the work and deposit copies. Generally, the records containing deposited copies are available to the public.[161] Unlike in patent law, registration and deposit are not a central means for disclosure and dissemination of works of authorship. The copyright statute allows for procedures to protect secret information[162] through limited deposits and selective use of identifying materials. The Copyright Office has adopted regulations for computer programs that permit the deposit of substantially less than the entire work.[163]

Since they involve public records, registration and deposit waive secrecy to the extent that the deposit discloses the claimed secret. No reported cases have directly applied this concept in the computer area.

---

[158] See Data Cash Sys., Inc. v. JS&A Group, Inc., 628 F2d 1038 (7th Cir. 1980). Compare Hubco Data Prods. Corp. v. Management Assistants, Inc., 219 USPQ 450 (D. Idaho 1983); GCA Corp. v. Chance, 217 USPQ 718 (ND Cal. 1982) (limited distribution without notice does not lose copyright protection).

[159] 539 F. Supp. 561 (D. Kan. 1982).

[160] Id. at 569.

[161] 17 USC § 705(b) (1982); 37 CFR §§ 203, 204.

[162] 17 USC §§ 407(c), 408(c) (1982).

[163] See ¶ 1.13.

However, the language of one court that concluded that insufficient evidence was available is suggestive of the problem.

> Although the Copyright Act does not preempt Warrington's trade secret claim, the fact that it registered its User's Manual might well affect the continued secrecy of the ideas in that manual.... Thus, while Warrington's self-serving declaration that it registered the manual ... as "unpublished" does not, in itself, defeat Real-Time's claim that [the] information is in the public domain, the court cannot conclude, as a matter of law, that Warrington's proprietary materials have lost their mantle of confidentiality.[164]

As this opinion suggests, neither registration nor publication in copyright terms per se defeat a claim of trade secrecy. The questions in all cases relate to the nature of the disclosure and the restrictions under which it occurred. A general, unrestricted distribution of material directly disclosing a claimed secret defeats secrecy for the distributed material, as does deposit in a public record. However, restricted distribution and partial deposit may effectively retain relative secrecy under trade secret law.

PART D. REMEDIES AND MISAPPROPRIATION

¶ 3.15 MISAPPROPRIATION AND PROOF

Trade secret protection, if established, prohibits the infringing party from a variety of actions to obtain the benefits of the appropriated secret. The cause of action is generally stated broadly in terms of misappropriation or unfair competition. As a result, it is not necessary in all cases to establish substantial similarity between the original and the allegedly infringing copy as in copyright cases. Also, similarity of method or function is not necessarily a central issue. The focus is on whether information was wrongfully acquired and whether that information was used by the wrongdoer or at least likely to be used.

Concerning the wrongful taking, it must be established that a confidential relationship exists. Beyond that, however, it is necessary to establish that information has in fact been obtained and to link that acquisition to wrongdoing. The strongest case that establishes all of these elements consists of proof of the literal theft of documents, models, or prototypes.[165] Similarly, in many cases involving former employees ele-

---

[164] Warrington v. Real Time Co., 522 F. Supp. 367, 369 (ND Ill. 1981).

[165] See University Computing Co. v. Lykes-Youngstown Corp., 504 F2d 518 (5th Cir. 1974); Telex Corp. v. IBM, 367 F. Supp. 258 (ND Okla. 1973), aff'd, 510 F2d 894 (10th Cir. 1975).

ments of proof include that the employee wrongfully carried with him proprietary copies of documents disclosing secret information.[166] The carrying away of data tends to establish an intent to use confidential material and infers, but does not conclusively establish, actual use.

Depending on the type of misappropriation that is alleged, it is not essential that the plaintiff establish similarities in the two products or processes at issue. For example, misappropriated information may permit the wrongdoer to design compatible, but not identical, products. In such cases, the issue is not whether there are similarities in the products, but whether the appropriated information was wrongfully used to obtain a commercial advantage.[167]

The speed with which the alleged wrongdoer is able to generate competing or compatible products tends to establish wrongful use of secret information. A primary, protectible interest in a trade secret is the head start advantage that it holds for the original discoverer or designer of the secret. Especially where independent discovery may involve complex and lengthy effort, relatively rapid progress from investigation to production by a competitor not only defines the harm, but also tends to establish wrongful use.[168] It does not create a conclusive inference of wrongful use. There still remains the possibility of unexpectedly rapid, independent development, reverse engineering from a properly obtained copy, or development through the application of general experience and skill.[169]

Although not always relevant, a similarity between two products may be an element of the proof of misappropriation.[170] Unlike in copyright cases, the central issue is not whether the defendant copied the secret, but whether it was misappropriated. As a result, improvements or modifications in secret design do not avoid liability for misappropria-

---

[166] See, e.g., Sperry Rand Corp. v. Electronic Concepts, Inc., 325 F. Supp. 1209, aff'd, Sperry Rand v. A-T-O, Inc., 447 F2d 1387 (4th Cir. 1971); Dynamic Research Corp. v. Analytic Sciences Corp., 400 NE2d 1274, 1282 (Mass. App. Ct. 1980).

[167] See Telex Corp. v. IBM, 510 F2d 894 (10th Cir. 1975).

[168] See Data Gen. Corp. v. Digital Computer Controls, Inc., 357 A2d 105 (Del. Ch. 1975); Modern Controls v. Andreadakis, 578 F2d 1264 (8th Cir. 1978).

[169] See Digital Dev. Corp. v. International Memory Sys., 185 USPQ 136 (SD Cal. 1973).

[170] See Digital Dev. Corp. v. International Memory Sys., 185 USPQ 136 (SD Cal. 1973); Sperry Rand Corp. v. Rothlein, 241 F. Supp. 549, 553 (D. Conn. 1964); Sperry Rand Corp. v. Pentronix, 311 F. Supp. 910 (ED Pa. 1970); Cybertek Computer Prod., Inc. v. Whitfield, 203 USPQ 1020 (Cal. Super. Ct. 1977).

tion.[171] In fact, assuming secrecy and confidentiality, proof that the design has been modified or improved can in fact establish misappropriation.

While it is not necessary to establish literal copying, proof of copying is sufficient to prove misappropriation assuming that secrecy and confidential relationships have been established. In some cases, the elements of copying not only involve similar design choices, but also the adoption of arbitrary labels or steps.

> Plaintiff's experts ... made a careful analysis of the two programs and found not only similarity in the overall structure and organization (some of which might be explainable on functional grounds) but they found identical segments of code which were solely arbitrary and, most significantly, deviations or quasi-mistakes which, in their judgment, could only be explained by copying. ... Memory alone can not explain the specifics which according to the experts do not make sense but are explainable only by copying.[172]

Where substantial similarity is used to establish misappropriation, similarities due to functional factors or generally known concepts must be discounted. This is because trade secret law does not protect particular expression or designs per se. As a result, especially for computer programs and circuitry, close questions arise concerning whether similarities are due to misappropriation or to other factors.[173]

To the same extent that similarity builds an inference of misappropriation, identifiable and basic design dissimilarity tends to establish the absence of misappropriation. For example, in *Dynamic Research Co. v. Analytical Sciences Corp.*[174] a finding of no misappropriation by a former employee was based in large part on the conclusion that the competing program adopted data structures different from those found in the secret program.

---

[171] See Digital Dev. Corp. v. International Memory Sys., 185 USPQ 136 (SD Cal. 1973); Sperry Rand Corp. v. Rothlein, 241 F. Supp. 549, 553 (D. Conn. 1964).

[172] Structural Dynamics Research Corp. v. Engineering Mechanics Research Corp., 401 F. Supp. 1102, 1117 (ED Mich. 1975).

[173] See Automated Sys., Inc. v. Service Bureau Corp., 401 F2d 619 (10th Cir. 1968); Computer Print Sys., Inc. v. Lewis, 422 A2d 148 (Pa. Super. Ct. 1980); Cybertek Computer Prod., Inc. v. Whitfield, 203 USPQ 1020 (Cal. Super. Ct. 1977); Dynamic Research Corp. v. Analytical Sciences Corp., 400 NE2d 1274 (Mass. App. Ct. 1980).

[174] 400 NE2d 1274 (Mass. App. Ct. 1980); see also Automated Sys., Inc. v. Service Bureau Corp., 401 F2d 619 (10th Cir. 1968).

¶ 3.16 THIRD PARTIES AND NOTICE

A basic element of a trade secret action is that the defendant must be aware of the misappropriation and wrongfulness of its use of information. This reflects the concept of trade secrecy protection being linked to confidentiality and culpable behavior, without offering protection against honest or independent discovery. Milgrim suggests that this "proposition is too well established to require extensive citation."[175]

In many trade secret cases, the fact that the alleged user is aware of the source of its information is apparent from the circumstances, and proof of notice of wrongdoing is inherent in proof that the misappropriation has occurred. In other cases, however, third parties are involved in using the secret information and it may be difficult to establish actionable conduct. In general, a concomitant of the linkage between trade secrecy and breaches of confidence is that the truly innocent user of a secret misappropriated by another is not liable to the original secret holder.[176] Therefore, the trade secret holder may have no protection, at least initially, against a third party who innocently receives information stolen by an employee. Of course, the insulation of innocent third parties is subject to restriction in those circumstances where the wrongful conduct can be imputed to that party in the context of third-party inducement of trade secrecy violations.

Notice to the otherwise innocent third party may be imputed from the circumstances or directly supplied by the original secret holder. This latter principle is especially important in cases involving movement of employees into positions with competing companies. In such cases, notice to the new employer should, if possible, be supplied in writing before or during the early stages of the employee's new job.[177] When notice is given at an early stage, subsequent beneficial use of secret information by the third party may amount to knowing participation in the misappropriation of trade secrets.

The interplay between protection of innocent third parties and protection of the secret holder is more difficult to resolve where initial receipt of the secret is innocent, but the third party subsequently receives clear notice that the information was originally procured in a wrongful manner. No question arises concerning action over the third party's use prior

---

[175] Milgrim, *Trade Secrets* 5-87 n.3.

[176] See Ferroline Corp. v. General Aniline & Film Corp., 207 F2d 912 (7th Cir. 1953); Conmar Prod. Corp. v. Universal Slide Fastener Co., 172 F2d 150 (2d Cir. 1949); Sperry Rand Corp. v. Electronic Concepts, Inc., 325 F. Supp. 1209, aff'd, Sperry Rand v. A-T-O, Inc., 447 F2d 1387 (4th Cir. 1971).

[177] Milgrim, *Trade Secrets* 5-92.

to notice. Subsequent notice does not retroactively invalidate innocent use. However, the rights of the third party after receiving notice are less clear.

One approach is to view the third party in terms like the status of a good-faith purchaser. This is apparently the position of the Restatement of Torts. It provides that the third party is liable for any use after receiving notice unless "prior thereto he has in good faith paid value for the secret or has so changed his position that to subject him to liability would be inequitable."[178] In this way, the risk of misappropriation is placed on the original secret holder and, unless he acts before an innocent third party has substantially altered his position, the original holder's remedy is limited to action against the original misappropriator. The view that pre-notice reliance by an innocent third party should be protected is generally accepted. However, some authorities argue for a more flexible form of protection, permitting the secret holder to avoid future harm by allowing it to reimburse or indemnify the third party.[179]

¶ 3.17 DAMAGES

Remedies for misappropriation of trade secrets may include a combination of damages and/or injunctive relief. Reported cases indicate difficulties of proof common to any damage issue, as well as substantial uncertainty about the standard of measurement for damages that should be used. The best summary is that "the plaintiff should be made whole, and at the same time, there should be no double recovery."[180]

In developing approaches to defining a measurement standard, the courts often make general references to patent law damage measurements.[181] However, the reference should not be relied on for all purposes, since the two areas involve distinct types of harms. Among other factors, infringement of a patent cannot destroy the overall value of the patent for other uses, while misappropriation or disclosure may totally eliminate or preempt the value of a trade secret.

Another issue is whether damages should measure the plaintiff's loss or the defendant's gain. Although this distinction is often stated as an

---

[178] Restatement (First) of Torts § 758.

[179] See Sperry Rand Corp. v. Electronic Concepts, Inc., 325 F. Supp. 1209, aff'd, Sperry Rand v. A-T-O-, Inc., 447 F2d 1387 (4th Cir. 1971); Milgrim, *Trade Secrets* 5-98, 5-99.

[180] See Telex Corp. v. IBM, 510 F2d 894, 931 (10th Cir. 1975).

[181] See University Computing Co. v. Lykes-Youngstown Corp., 504 F2d 518, 536 (5th Cir. 1974).

either/or proposition, a flexible approach is preferable where both loss and gain are considered, as long as double recovery is avoided.[182] A focus on the plaintiff's loss emphasizes the compensatory character of the damage remedy.[183] However, cases arise in which this approach may be inappropriate in that no clear or identifiable loss to the plaintiff has occurred separate from a change in the competitive posture of the two parties.

The alternative approach focuses on the benefit to the defendant. It has relatively wide popularity, but involves various issues concerning the manner in which this value should be assessed. Two basic propositions should be clearly recognized in applying this approach. First, the measure of the benefit should not consist solely of comparison of developmental costs identifying the cost saving to the defendant. While this approach is occasionally used, it is too restrictive and limited. As one court noted, especially where the misappropriation is by a competitor of the original holder, the gains attained as a result of misappropriation also encompass timing and competitive advantages over potentially extended periods.[184] Second, the measurement of benefits received should not be contingent on proof that the defendant obtained commercial profit from the use of the secret. While commercial use may be an element of establishing a right to damages, measuring damages in terms of the defendant's commercial profit would place the risk of commercial success on the original secret holder, rather than the wrongdoer.

Within the focus on benefit to the defendant, a variety of approaches have been used to identify that benefit. Among these is an attempt to assess a reasonable royalty or fee for the misappropriated secret. As applied in a recent case, this requires estimation of "what the parties would have agreed to as a fair price for licensing ... at the time that the misappropriation occurred."[185]

¶ 3.18 INJUNCTION

In trade secret litigation, injunctive relief is often sought in lieu of, or in addition to, claims for monetary damages. Milgrim describes injunctive

---

[182] See Telex Corp. v. IBM, 510 F2d 894, 931 (10th Cir. 1975).

[183] See Sperry Rand v. A-T-O, Inc. 447 F2d 1387 (4th Cir. 1971).

[184] See University Computing Co. v. Lykes-Youngstown Corp., 504 F2d 518, 535–540 (5th Cir. 1974).

[185] Id. at 539; see also Telex Corp. v. IBM, 510 F2d 894, 931 (10th Cir. 1975).

relief as the "most commonly sought form of relief."[186] This relief commonly entails both prejudgment, preliminary injunctions and post-judgment, permanent injunctions.

The basic standards for preliminary injunctions track those generally available in any civil action. The plaintiff must establish a substantial probability of ultimate success on the merits of the case and the risk of inseparable harm.[187] In recent years, there has been a tendency in some courts to expand the availability of relief where, despite uncertainty as to the merits of the cases, the balance of hardship is strongly weighted in favor of injunctive relief.[188] It is not generally available, however, where substantial questions exist as to the merits of the case and where the defendant is financially able to respond to monetary damage awards.[189]

Under these standards, it is apparent that the availability of preliminary injunctive relief is related to the narrowness and clarity of the plaintiff's asserted cause of action and elements of proof. In general, this form of relief is more readily available where the cause of action is supported by clear and enforceable contractual restrictions, such as express covenants not to compete. However, since any injunctive relief is equitable in nature, overly broad and unreasonable convenants will not only fail to support preliminary relief, but may be a factor mitigating against it.[190]

Following a favorable judgment, permanent injunctions may be available. As with temporary injunctions, the standards applied generally track those found in other cases. Injunctive relief will commonly not be granted unless there is a showing of potentially irreparable harm[191] or the defendant's conduct has been flagrant and is likely to be repeated.[192] For post-judgment injunctions, significant questions arise as to the appropriate scope and duration of the injunction granted. Generally, of course, the relief should be tailored to the particular type of wrong estab-

---

[186] Milgrim, *Trade Secrets* 7-122.

[187] See Data Gen. Corp. v. Digital Computer Controls, Inc., 357 A2d 105 (Del. Ch. 1975); Modern Controls v. Andreadakis, 578 F2d 1264 (8th Cir. 1978); Sigma Sys. Corp. v. Electronic Data Sys. Corp., 467 SW2d 675 (Tex. Civ. App. 1971); Medtronics, Inc. v. Medical Design Research, Inc., 398 F. Supp. 849, 854 (CD Cal. 1975).

[188] See Milgrim, *Trade Secrets* rel. 16 at 257; Modern Controls v. Andreadakis, 578 F2d 1264 (8th Cir. 1978).

[189] See Data Gen. Corp. v. Digital Computer Controls, Inc., 357 A2d 105 (Del. Ch. 1975).

[190] See Milgrim, *Trade Secrets* 7-44.

[191] See Digital Dev. Corp. v. International Memory Sys., 185 USPQ 136 (SD Cal. 1973); Sperry Rand Corp. v. Rothlein, 241 F. Supp. 549 (D. Conn. 1964).

[192] See Telex Corp. v. IBM, 510 F2d 894 (10th Cir. 1975).

lished by the plaintiff. However, in many trade secret cases there are countervailing public policies regarding free competition and employee mobility. The general tendency then is to structure the substantive scope of the injunction, tailoring it to reasonably limited types of activity necessary to safeguard the plaintiff's interests. For example, a former employee may be enjoined from involvement with particular types of competing programs within a specified geographic area, but may otherwise be allowed to practice his profession.[193] Similarly, where a competing company has engaged in a course of conduct to discover trade secrets, the continuation of specific types of activity may be enjoined, but no further restraints may be placed on competition.[194]

The duration of the injunction has been a particular source of controversy. In general, the predominant view has been that the injunction against use of the trade secret should be limited to the period that would be necessary for independent development or discovery through proper means such as reverse engineering.[195] This approach focuses on the fact that a major commercial benefit of a trade secret lies in the head start that it gives to its owner.[196] The analysis was suggested by the court in *Analogic Corp. v. Data Translation, Inc.*[197] The court held that evidence as to the time necessary to reverse engineer a high speed data acquisition module should have been received in determining the appropriate duration of an injunction and in assessing the reasonable duration of a covenant not to compete. However, it commented

> Our holding . . . is not to be interpreted to require that the duration of an injunction be inflexibly determined by the amount of time necessary to reverse engineer the plaintiff's device. [Defendants] who have willfully attempted to profit through violation of a confidential relationship need not be placed in as good a position as . . . honest competitors [or] permitted a competitive advantage from their avoidance of the normal costs of invention. . . . [The] ultimate cessation of an injunctive order might well be conditioned on . . . payment of an appropriate sum to the plaintiff.[198]

---

[193] See Electronic Data Sys. v. Powell, 508 SW2d 137 (Tex. Civ. App. 1974).

[194] See Telex Corp. v. IBM, 510 F2d 894 (10th Cir. 1975).

[195] See Sperry Rand Corp. v. Electronic Concepts, Inc., 325 F. Supp. 1209, aff'd, Sperry Rand v. A-T-O, Inc., 447 F2d 1387 (4th Cir. 1971); Analogic Corp. v. Data Translation, Inc., 358 NE2d 804 (Mass. 1981); Data Gen. Corp. v. Digital Computer Controls, Inc., 357 A2d 105 (Del. Ch. 1975).

[196] See Restatement of Torts § 757 comment 6; Milgrim, *Trade Secrets* 7-132.

[197] 358 NE2d 804 (Mass. 1981).

[198] Id. at 808.

As the court in *Analogic* suggests, the head start effect of a misappropriation is a beginning point, but it is not necessarily decisive in fixing the length of an injunction. In some cases, the secret that is misappropriated is not generally available for reverse engineering, and a focus on the time needed for independent discovery may be misleadingly short, since knowledge of the secret provides a starting point for inquiry that might not otherwise have been seized upon.[199] Similarly, the flagrance of the defendant's conduct may be relevant. In other cases where the misappropriation involves an ongoing course of conduct that is not necessarily tied to a particular secret or bundle of secrets, even a permanent injunction against the conduct may be appropriate.[200] Furthermore, it is relevant to consider as a limiting or an extending factor the length of any enforceable covenant to which the parties have agreed.[201]

---

[199] See Milgrim, *Trade Secrets* rel. 16-V12 at 310; Brunswick Corp. v. Outboard Marine Corp., 404 NE2d 205 (Ill. 1980).

[200] See Telex Corp. v. IBM, 510 F2d 894 (10th Cir. 1975).

[201] See Milgrim, *Trade Secrets* 7-130.

CHAPTER *4*

Research, Development, and Ownership

¶ **4.01 INTRODUCTION**

The interaction between law and technological innovation is complex and defined only in part by the application of basic intellectual property law to aspects of technology. Most research and development is both joint and sequential in nature. This characteristic creates significant questions about allocating control, attributing ownership, regulating collusion, and otherwise monitoring and defining the development process.

This chapter examines the legal aspects of joint and sequential development of computer technology. The discussion encompasses intellectual property principles and includes analysis of significant antitrust and federal tax questions. The primary matters considered relate to defining an appropriate mode for encouraging innovation while not unduly sacrificing other interests.

PART A.   EMPLOYEE OWNERSHIP

¶ **4.02 EMPLOYEE DEVELOPERS**

The most common joint development setting is the employer-employee relationship. As discussed previously, especially in relation to trade secrecy, one area of concern relates to constraining the employee in order to protect the employer's rights in intellectual property owned or controlled by the employer[1] If the affected employee developed the intellectual property, however, the first question is whether and to what extent an employer has any claim to the work.

Although often viewed as solely a matter of an employer's ability to protect valuable assets developed by employees, employer-employee ownership disputes actually involve distinct policy interests and valid competing claims to the intellectual property. The employer's claim is based on financial and resource contributions. While the claim that an employer is the developer and inventor of intellectual property is often a fiction, it is essential that an employer receive the right to control in at least some circumstances. This control is a primary incentive for providing the resources for development. The product of creative employees is often the primary, most marketable asset of the employer. Unless the employer can control and exploit this asset, the economic support for basic development might dissipate.[2]

The competing view is that intellectual property rights, especially under patent and copyright law, should reward the individual inventor or author. This view acknowledges the special attributes of the individual and the fact that individual creativity is essential to technological growth. Unless an individual receives some financial benefit, the personal incentive for creative work is reduced and all potential development suffers. This does not require ongoing control of the creative property. The individual developer can realize benefits by a contractual transfer before or after creation of the property, but the individual's leverage in such contracts is affected by otherwise presumptive rights of ownership. The individual's creative potential is an employee's marketable asset, and a subsidiary issue in allocating ownership of a particular product may be the perceived need to protect the asset.

These conflicting interests arise only where the employee has made a substantial, creative contribution to development of the intellectual property. In many cases, employees are hired merely to execute mechanical construction of an invention or to operate experiments under direct supervision. In such cases, no ownership claim by the employee arises.[3] The discussion immediately following assumes that the creative impetus is the employee's, while the employer provides financial resources and a general definition of the task to be accomplished.

---

[1] See ¶ 3.10.

[2] See Milgrim, *Trade Secrets* 5-15.

[3] See 1 *Deller's Walker on Patents* 183; Rosenberg, *Patent Law Fundamentals* 11-4 (1983); Clarke v. Wilke, 203 USPQ 1101 (Bd. Patent Int'l 1978).

[1] Works for Hire and Particularity

The clearest case for attributing ownership to an employer arises where the employer contributes not only resources, but also direction and control of a particular project. One rationale for this result was suggested in an early U.S. Supreme Court patent law case: "If one is employed to devise or perfect an instrument ... [that] which he has been employed and paid to accomplish becomes, when accomplished, the property of his employer. Whatever rights as an individual he may have had ... he has sold in advance to his employer."[4] Ownership in works produced by an employee hired to invent is paralleled in copyright law by the concept of "works for hire." Under Section 201(b) of the Copyright Act (Act), the employer is the author of a "work for hire," which includes any "work prepared by an employee within the scope of his employment."[5]

In both patent and copyright law, developments made by an employee within the boundaries of the work assignment are the property of the employer. The employer invests substantial resources in the expectation of obtaining a marketable or useful product. Since both the employer and employee are aware of this, the employee implicitly conveys his rights in the property developed. Allowing the employee to claim ownership also might create conflicting interests. Both to encourage research investment and to avoid conflicting loyalties, an employer receives the predominant claim to the products of assigned and supported projects.[6]

It might be thought that all works produced by an employee are the property of the employer, but in fact, the opposite presumption is generally applied. Neither the idea of "hired to invent," nor that of "works for hire" is satisfied by the mere existence of an employment relationship. The employer's claim turns on the degree of active support and direction that it provides for the employee's work. "[No] one sells or mortgages all the products of his brain to his employer by the mere fact of employment."[7] Beyond particularized work assignments, the employee's independent interests strengthen while those of the employer weaken even if "a portion of the work was done during working hours and ... the assistance of the employer's facilities and personnel was obtained in some degree."[8]

---

[4] Solomons v. United States, 137 US 342, 343 (1890).

[5] See 17 USC § 101 (1982).

[6] See Sperry v. Pentronix, 311 F. Supp. 910 (ED Pa. 1970).

[7] Public Affairs Assoc., Inc. v. Rickover, 177 F. Supp. 601, 604 (DDC 1959), rev'd on other grounds, 248 F2d 262 (DC Cir. 1960) vacated, 369 US 111 (1962).

[8] *Nimmer on Copyright* 5-16.

Under patent or copyright law, developments outside of the general reach of a research position are not allocated to the employer in the absence of an express contract. In such cases, the fact of employment and any use of the employer's facilities are incidental. While the product may be valuable, it is difficult to argue that the employer contracted for or expected to receive developments unrelated to a primary work area. Employee ownership of such unrelated developments presents little risk of compromising the employee's efforts on behalf of the employer in more particular assignments, and attributing ownership to the employer might stifle the employee's creativity. If employer ownership encompassed unrelated developments, the employment contract would be a general conveyance of all creative work.[9]

In many cases, it is difficult to define the relationship between the creative product and the employee's work assignment. The most difficult circumstance involves an employee hired for general research work who undertakes personal research leading to a valuable development. In the absence of a contractual assignment of rights, ownership depends on the circumstances of the development and the employee's work assignment.[10] One relevant factor is the extent to which there is an actual conflict of interest in light of the thrust of the employer's research and marketing activity.[11] Work related to the employer's main interests should be given to the employer. This is most likely if the employer's resources were integral to the employee's work. The expectations of the parties implicit in the context or explicit in their behavior are also relevant. If the employee is discouraged from and not supported in the research and development, it is inappropriate to grant ownership to the employer.[12] The reported cases often appear to turn on a distinction between mere acquiescence (results owned by employee) and explicit assignment (results owned by employer).

The results and distinctions under copyright and patent law generally apply to trade secret law as well.[13] The analysis is affected by the fact that the subject matter of a trade secret may not be identifiable from documentary evidence. In some cases, this weakens the employee's claim. More often, when a claimed secret is not precisely defined the employee is accorded at least coequal rights, since a contrary result could substantially limit the employee's ability to practice his profession elsewhere.

---

[9] See Milgrim, *Trade Secrets* 5-40.

[10] See generally *Nimmer on Copyright* 5-15–5-16; Milgrim, *Trade Secrets* 5-38; 4 *Deller's Walker on Patents* 489 (1964).

[11] See, e.g., Sperry Rand Corp. v. Rothlein, 241 F. Supp. 549 (D. Conn. 1964); Science Accessories v. Summagraphics, 215 USPQ 1051 (Del. 1980).

[12] See Amoco Prod. Co. v. Lindley, 609 P2d 733 (Okla. 1980).

[13] See Milgrim, *Trade Secrets* 5-35–5-44.

In trade secrecy cases, the employer's commitment of resources and reliance on the alleged secret are especially significant. These relate to the underlying definition of whether it is a secret of the employer. In general, if an employer assigned the research and supported it, the work inures to his benefit and the employee may be barred from use outside of the original employment.[14] If the employer made no investment and did not support the work, it does not belong to him.

The employer's claim is limited by the basic concept that in the absence of noncompetition agreements the employee is entitled to use his general skill and expertise even in competitive employment.[15] Where the employee is the developer, the level of attributable general ability is often high and includes at least some ideas, information, or skills integral to the secret itself. This context requires explicit proof that isolates the secret and demonstrates that the employee remains free to use his own expertise and skill.[16] Thus, an employee who developed a particular data processing program for one employer is not barred from program development for another.[17] Similarly, designing a CAD-CAM application for an employer in one industry does not bar subsequent employment to design an improved system for another, even if the systems are in direct competition.[18]

The difficulty of distinguishing general secrets from general skill provides a rationale for explicit covenants in employment contracts. Indeed, some cases indicate that in the absence of contract restrictions the employee has a coequal right to utilize the intellectual product.[19] In *Structural Dynamics Research Corp. v. Engineering Mechanics Research Corp.*,[20] the court indicated that employee developers of a structural analysis program were barred from using a similar program only because their contract contained restrictive covenants. In the absence of such covenants, the second program could have been used even though the origi-

---

[14] See generally Cybertek Computer Prod., Inc. v. Whitfield, 203 USPQ 1020 (Cal. Super. Ct. 1977); Modern Controls v. Andreadakis, 578 F. Supp. 1264 (8th Cir. 1978); J&K Computer Sys., Inc. v. Parrish, 642 P.2d 732 (Utah 1982).

[15] See Dynamic Research Corp. v. Analytic Sciences Corp., 400 NE2d 1274 (Mass. App. Ct. 1980); Electronic Data Sys. Corp. v. Kinder, 360 F. Supp. 1044 (ND Tex. 1973).

[16] See Dynamic Research Corp. v. Analytic Sciences Corp., 400 NE2d 1274 (Mass. App. Ct. 1980).

[17] See Electronic Data Sys. Corp. v. Kinder, 360 F. Supp. 1044 (ND Tex. 1973).

[18] See Jostens, Inc. v. National Computer Sys., Inc., 318 NW2d 691 (Minn. 1982).

[19] See Wexler v. Greenbart, 160 A2d 430 (Pa. 1960).

[20] 401 F. Supp. 1102 (ED Mich. 1975).

nal was developed with the employer's active support and the second was merely a more complete implementation of the plan submitted to the original company. The court noted

> [If] the subject matter of the trade secret is brought into being because of the initiative of the employee in its creation, innovation or development even though the relationship is one of confidence, no duty arises since the employee may then have an interest in the subject matter at least equal to that of his employer or in any event, such knowledge is part of the employee's skill and experience.[21]

In the context of its particular facts, *Structural Dynamics* reached a correct result only because of its ultimate reliance on the restrictive covenant. The case illustrates a distinction between trade secrecy and patent or copyright law. The employer's interests can be protected under copyright and patent law without substantially affecting the employee's professional career, since the subject matter has an identifiable and limited scope. This is also true of trade secrets that are particularized and identified as independent of the employee's general skill or knowledge. If the secret is not so isolated, however, the potential effects on the employee are substantial and may justify coequal use of the claimed secret.

[2] Joint Use and Shop Rights

Creative work done outside of the expected scope of employment generally does not vest ownership in the employer merely by virtue of the employment contract. Where the creative work is the result of a specific work assignment and substantially supported by the employer, the employer may own the exclusive rights to control use of the resulting intellectual property. The difficulty, and substantial controversy, over ownership erupts when creative products are developed in an environment falling between these two general premises. One possible resolution is limited coownership. This approach is applied in patent law under the so-called shop rights doctrine. The idea of a shop right is essentially an equity concept. It grants the employer a nonexclusive license to use an invention patented by an employee.[22] The right is personal to the employer. It arises in cases in which concepts of absolute ownership are most difficult to apply—where employee developments involve general use of employer time and resources, but are not the result of particular, developmental assignments.

---

[21] Id. at 1111.

[22] See 4 *Deller's Walker on Patents* 507.

Shop rights decisions are not consistent and there is some uncertainty about the underlying equitable principle. Milgrim suggests that one basis for shop rights is that "since an employee has spent some of the time for which he was paid, or has used property or personnel of his employer, the employer is entitled in equity to use the invention that, in part, embodies the employer's property."[23] This view implies that shop rights are contingent on the extent of use of the employer's time and resources and that this financial contribution creates a limited right in the intellectual property. In contrast, Deller indicates that "it is not the fact alone that the company's time, materials or facilities were used by the employee, but the circumstance that after the invention was made, an inventor assented to or acquiesced in the use of the invention by the employer."[24] This view implies that the use of the employer's resources must be joined to further actions by the employee to create nonexclusive rights in the employer. Depending on the circumstances, the employee's acquiescence to use by the employer may establish an estoppel by virtue of the employer's reliance on the apparent consent or may reflect an implicit agreement that the employer may use the employee's inventions.

The shop rights approach is seldom explicitly applied in trade secrecy cases,[25] but the idea of joint rights in an alleged trade secret is not uncommon. In most trade secrecy cases, however, joint rights are achieved under other language, such as a conclusion that the secret is insufficiently novel or secret,[26] or that the secret is inextricable from the employee's general knowledge.[27] In a pure case with a definable, protected secret isolated from general skill or knowledge, no shop right is acknowledged. In patent law, shop rights entail an enforced, limited transfer from the employee-owner to the employer. This is difficult to recreate in a trade secret case. The posture of most trade secret cases involves an employer with knowledge of the secret who is currently using or planning to use the secret and who seeks to bar disclosure or use by a former employee. In the reverse situation, where the employer seeks to force the employee's disclosure of the secret to the employer, trade secrecy law arguably does not apply to the employer's claim, since the

---

[23] See Milgrim, *Trade Secrets* 5-44.

[24] See 4 *Deller's Walker on Patents* 508.

[25] See Milgrim, *Trade Secrets* 5-45, 5-46.

[26] See Jostens, Inc. v. National Computer Sys., Inc., 318 NW2d 691 (Minn. 1982).

[27] See Structural Dynamics Research Corp. v. Engineering Mechanics Research Corp., 401 F. Supp. 1102 (ED Mich. 1975); Dynamic Research Corp. v. Analytic Sciences Corp., 400 NE2d 1274 (Mass. App. Ct. 1980).

employer has not used the secret to commercial advantage prior to disclosure.[28]

The shop rights doctrine is explicitly rejected in copyright law.[29] This is based in part on a desire to avoid extrapolation of uncertain ownership doctrine into the field of copyright. As a result, exclusive copyright control of a work of authorship resides in the author or the author's assignee or licensee. If the work qualifies as an employee work for hire, authorship vests in the employer.[30]

¶ 4.03 CONTRACTUAL MODIFICATION

The uncertainties in attributing ownership and control are a strong rationale for contract resolution in the employment contract. The contract terms for ownership allocation vary, but the issues are generally two: (1) protection of developments made during the employee's tenure at the company, and (2) protection of developments completed after employment is terminated. Contracts assigning rights to the invention or other intellectual property to the employer are generally enforceable in both circumstances.[31]

Substantive standards for enforcement of contracts assigning invention or authorship rights are generally consistent in copyright, patent, and trade secrecy law. The basic standard is that the scope of the assignment and the duration must be reasonable.[32] Reasonableness standards generally parallel those for covenants of noncompetition and nondisclosure and are concerned with the type of innovation affected as well as the length or duration of the obligation to assign. Time-limited assignment clauses restricted to matters related to the work assignments or products of the employer are enforceable, while broad assignments of all of the employee's creative work product are not.[33]

Invention assignment clauses often receive restrictive interpretations favoring the employee. It is often assumed that the employee and

---

[28] See Amoco Prod. Co. v. Lindley, 609 P2d 733 (Okla. 1980); Milgrim, *Trade Secrets* 5-47.

[29] HR Rep. No. 1476, 94th Cong., 2d. Sess 121 (1976).

[30] 17 USC § 201(b) (1982).

[31] See 4 *Deller's Walker on Patents* 473; Milgrim, *Trade Secrets* 5-40.

[32] See, e.g., 4 *Deller's Walker on Patents* 475. Note, however, that various states have enacted explicit limitations on the ability of an employer to obtain a contractual restriction in employment contracts. See Milgrim, *Trade Secrets* App. D-1.

[33] See 4 *Deller's Walker on Patents* 497–498; Milgrim, *Trade Secrets* 5-41.

employer do not in fact negotiate the terms of the agreement. Rather, more often the contract terms are viewed as having been imposed by the employer.[34] As a result, reasonableness standards are a form of intervention to protect the employee against overreaching. Even absent overreaching, depending on the scope of the assignment, the employee's right to use his own creativity and skill for personal benefit may suggest a narrow interpretation. For example, in a copyright setting, "notwithstanding broad contract language the courts would often strive, if the language at all permitted, to limit its effect so as to preclude an employer claiming ownership in works which would be considered outside the scope of the employment agreement."[35]

Interpretation of employee contracts to assign intellectual work should generally follow, but slightly extend, the scope of the employer's claims in the absence of a contract. A contract limited to work resulting from particular assigned tasks should be fully enforced. The employer's interest is strongest in this context. Similarly, a broad contract should be enforced as applied to such work. Conversely, as the intellectual work is further separated from use of the employer's facilities or business and the employee's job, enforcement should be substantially restricted, since the employee's interest is great and the employer's interest is weak.[36]

Assignment or other restrictive covenants nevertheless play an important role in resolving ownership and control issues that would otherwise be uncertain. In *Structural Dynamics Research Corp. v. Engineering Mechanics Research Corp.*,[37] the court relied on a restrictive covenant to enforce nondisclosure against an employee developer. In the absence of the contract, the former employee would have had a joint right to use notwithstanding substantial investment and reliance by the employer. The ability to affect cases in this uncertain area is necessarily augmented if the contract is narrowly drawn to areas in which the employer has an identifiable interest.[38]

The benefits of a restrictive covenant are affected by narrow construction of the agreement to protect the employee.[39] One example of this is

---

[34] But see Modern Controls v. Andreadakis, 578 F. Supp. 1264 (8th Cir. 1978).

[35] See *Nimmer on Copyright* 5-16, 5-17.

[36] See Amoco Prod. Co. v. Lindley, 609 P2d 733 (Okla. 1980); Science Accessories v. Summagraphics, 215 USPQ 1051 (Del. 1980).

[37] 401 F. Supp. 1102 (ED Mich. 1975).

[38] See Cybertek Computer Prod., Inc. v. Whitfield, 203 USPQ 1020 (Cal. Super. Ct. 1977); 4 *Deller's Walker on Patents* 494–498.

[39] See, e.g., *Nimmer on Copyright* 5-17; Milgrim, *Trade Secrets* 5-40.

Amoco Production Co. v. Lindley. [40] Lindley was employed as a well log analyst with basic research tasks "in the area of developing means of using well log data more efficiently and more quickly in the search for hydrocarbons." Lindley developed a computer-based system for such analysis. Prior to completing this program, Lindley had been denied permission to develop the system and had been instructed to work on a different system Amoco had elected to emphasize. The Lindley system was completed on the employee's own time. When it proved to be superior to the system developed by Amoco, the company sought to enforce a contract that required the employee to disclose and assign "all inventions or discoveries capable of use in connection with the business of [Amoco] which the employee ... has made or may make during his employment." [41] The Oklahoma Supreme Court held that the contract did not apply to the Lindley program and, as a result, full ownership and control vested in Lindley. The court concluded that the program was not a "discovery" and not an "invention" because it was not patentable.

Lindley illustrates a method of analysis that is often used to rationalize a result motivated by other factors. Amoco's claim to the Lindley program was weakened by the fact that it had discouraged and refused to support its development. Lindley used little or no Amoco time or facilities and Amoco did not assert ownership until shortly before trial. In addition, the contract was a "fine-print form" whose use was not limited to technical employees and reflected little or no negotiation over terms. [42] In this setting, although Lindley was employed to do research and the program clearly related to Amoco's business, there was an effective waiver of interest by Amoco that was not offset by the pro forma contract. The court limited the contract to exclude works that fell outside of the actual scope of Lindley's employment.

A similarly restrictive interpretation occurred in *Science Accessories Corp. v. Summagraphics Corp.* [43] *Science Accessories* involved a contract to disclose to the employer any inventions "made or conceived" by the employees during their employment. Three employees of Science Accessories (SAC) worked in their spare time with a fourth party, who developed an idea for a "magwire digitizer" that would eventually compete with an SAC product. Although the employees constructed a working model while employed at SAC, the contract created no duty of disclosure. The court concluded that the invention was owned by the fourth party

---

[40] 609 P2d 733 (Okla. 1980).

[41] Id. at 739 n.2.

[42] Id. at 742.

[43] 215 USPQ 1051 (Del. 1980).

and that the SAC employees had merely constructed the model. The employment contract, the court held, encompassed only inventions that were the result of the employee's own creativity. It stated that to "construe the agreement . . . otherwise . . . would be clearly unreasonable and . . . would have the effect of enabling an employee without a property interest in an invention to confer property rights on his employer merely by undertaking the physical act of assembling a working model."[44]

The judicial tendency to interpret employment contracts restrictively correlates to the perceived strength of the employer's underlying claim to the particular subject matter at issue. This tendency can be offset by careful drafting specifically incorporating patentable, copyrightable, and other intellectual work products. The cases suggest, however, that the terms used in a contract are unlikely to receive expansive interpretation. As the scope of the contract terms expands, there is an increasing risk that the contract will be viewed as unreasonably broad and unrelated to identifiable employer interests.

PART B.   JOINT AND SEQUENTIAL OWNERSHIP

¶ 4.04 STANDARDS OF JOINT OWNERSHIP

In employment contracts, allocation of ownership and concomitant rights of control reflect a tension between vesting ownership rights in the creative individual and vesting those rights in the organization whose support may have been critical to the work. Other settings for allocation of control over computer software and hardware developments involve the collaboration of two or more parties in the development of the product. This setting is, if anything, more complex than employment cases because of the vast differentials that exist in the form and contractual base of the collaboration. Furthermore, the issues go beyond allocating rights based on a comparison of creative work and financial support. In collaborative development, each party can reasonably claim to have creatively contributed to the work product.

In joint work it is important to distinguish ownership and control of the product of the joint work from control of preexisting intellectual property that may or may not be integrated in the final product. In both of these situations, the rights of the participants should be determined by express contract provisions. Contract allocations of ownership and control are generally enforceable in joint ventures. Where the joint development involves an informal arrangement, however, underlying agreements

---

[44] Id. at 1056.

are frequently ambiguous, nonexistent, or simply fail to cover the particular controversy. The relative rights of the participants are then controlled by the complex, often unclear body of law dealing with joint ownership.

[1] Coauthorship and Joint Invention

Copyright, patent, and trade secret law recognize not only the possibility of absolute control or ownership in one party in a joint undertaking, but also that two or more parties might share ownership of a particular intellectual product. Standards for determining ownership are not based on the degree of resource support provided, but revolve around whether the participants contributed to the creative conception of the product in a manner intended to establish joint or exclusive ownership.

[a] Patent Law

Joint ownership questions have been litigated frequently in the context of patent law as a result of a statutory requirement that patent applications be pursued by all of the inventors.[45] The result of this litigation has been described by one court as "one of the muddiest concepts in the muddy metaphysics of patent law."[46] Deller describes the focus of analysis in the following terms

> If one man does all the inventing and another does all the constructing, the first is the sole inventor. But where two or more persons exercised their inventive faculties in the mutual production of a new or useful process . . . those persons are joint inventors. . . . In fact, the conception of the entire device may be due to one, but if the other makes suggestions of practical value . . . or contributes an independent part . . . which helps to create the whole, he is a joint inventor even though his contribution be . . . minor.[47]

While participation in or control of the creative conception or design of the end product is the central theme, there are obvious difficulties in application. For example, all inventors draw on ideas or materials of other persons, but this does not necessarily entitle the others to owner-

---

[45] 35 USC § 117 (1982); see Iowa State Univ. Research Fund, Inc. v. Sperry Rand, 444 F2d 406 (4th Cir. 1971). The failure to join the appropriate inventors is not, however, necessarily a fatal defect in the patent. See 35 USC §§ 116, 256 (1982); Sperry Rand v. Control Data, 519 F. Supp. 629 (D. Md. 1970).

[46] Mueller Brass Co. v. Reading Indus., Inc., 352 F. Supp. 1357, 1372 (ED Pa. 1972).

[47] 1 *Deller's Walker on Patents* 183; see also Rosenberg, *Patent Law Fundamentals* 11-4.

ship. The test is whether the inventor maintains "intellectual domination of the work . . . down to the successful testing, selecting or rejecting as he goes."[48] A distinction is drawn between an inventor and the skilled mechanics or lab technicians working pursuant to the inventor's design or under his control. Again, the emphasis is on intellectual or creative participation in the conception of the final product, rather than on the skilled acts necessary to test models or to reduce the design to practice.[49]

[b] Software Coauthorship

Perhaps more than any other area of technology, the software industry is characterized by product development outside of formal legal relationships, similar to the publishing industry. While some individual software authors involved in a collaborative undertaking may specify the terms under which their collaboration occurs, it is more common that the relationship is informal. As a result, the rights of the parties to the resultant product and to any aspects contributed to the program will be determined primarily by copyright doctrine concerning coauthorship.

Consisent with patent law, copyright standards emphasize creative control of the end product and the express or presumed intent of the participants involved in producing the final work.[50] In many cases, control and intent combine for expected results. For example, a secretary does not claim or deserve partial or absolute authorship of a novel by typing it, although he may make changes in the process. There is neither an intent to author jointly, nor sufficient creative control in the secretary. A similar result pertains to an editor. Although editorial contributions may be substantial, the work is intended to be that of the original writer and the writer typically retains creative control. Similarly, a client and an architect are not coauthors of an architectural plan.

In other cases, the creative input of several parties is more substantial and the intended relationship to the final product less clear. The Act recognizes the potential of joint authorship as an alternative to absolute ownership in one or the other party. A definition of "coownership" involves the concept of a joint work: A "joint work" is "a work prepared by two or more authors with the intention that their contributions be merged into inseparable or interdependent parts of a unitary whole."[51] The critical test involves intention, rather than degree or type of contribu-

---

[48] Morse v. Porter, Ausville, Wench, 155 USPQ 280 (Bd. Patent Int'l 1965).

[49] See Rosenberg, *Patent Law Fundamentals* 11-4; see also 1 *Deller's Walker on Patents* 188.

[50] 17 USC § 201(a) (1982); see also *Nimmer on Copyright* 6-2–6-17.

[51] 17 USC § 101 (1982).

tion, but the intention specifically relates to the manner in which the contributions are merged. To constitute a joint work, the merger must be into inseparable or interdependent parts.

Attribution of authorship where two or more parties contribute to the creative conception of a program is made more complex by the fact that alternative forms of coauthorship are recognized.[52] A joint product (1) may be a joint work, (2) may involve a separate, derivative work, or (3) may consist of separable contributions joined to create a collective work. These possibilities differ significantly in legal consequence. In a joint work, the coauthors are essentially joint tenants with coequal rights to license the entire work on a nonexclusive basis. In contrast, a derivative work is a new, separate work, owned by its author unless subject to a claim of infringement if not authorized by the author of the original.[53] Finally, contributors to a collective work retain rights in their contributions, while the compiler of the collection may copyright the collection as a whole.[54]

Copyright conceptions of ownership developed in the area of literary property and have uncertain application to software technology. A general point, however, should be emphasized: In both patent and copyright laws, ownership is keyed to creative input and mutual intent, rather than amount of effort. Whether a conflicting claim involves a mechanic, lab technician, editor, or secretary, ownership is reserved to the person who creates the intellectual design and expression.

Joint development of a program generally does not vest coownership unless this can be implied by the conduct of the parties or as the result of mutual contribution to the final work product. The analysis must distinguish coauthorship and editorial input. Editorial contributions generally do not rise to coauthorship even if they are substantial. The central issue involves the intent of the parties as to control of the final expressive form of the product. Where one person creates coded software and obtains editorial suggestions from another, joint authorship does not arise unless the parties intended the sequential drafting as a joint effort toward a "preconcerted common design" with both parties exercising creative control.[55]

Joint authorship does not require that the coauthors work at the same time on the same parts of the work. It is sufficient that they intend that their "contributions be merged into inseparable or interdependent

---

[52] See *Nimmer on Copyright* 6-12.

[53] 17 USC § 101 (1982); see *Nimmer on Copyright* 3-2.

[54] 17 USC § 101 (1982).

[55] See *Nimmer on Copyright* 6-6.

parts of a unitary whole." This is in contradistinction to separate works that are to be blended into a "collective work" in which "a number of contributions, constituting separate and independent works in themselves, are assembled into a collective whole."[56]

While these elusive concepts have never been explored in a technology setting associated with computer software,[57] a leading treatise suggests the following concerning joint works.

> [Joint] ownership would seem to be justified on two alternative bases. First where the respective contributions of each author are inseparable in the sense that they are not separately identifiable the only workable solution is to regard each author as the joint owner. . . . A second basis . . . occurs where the respective contributions are interdependent. Here, although . . . separately identifiable, each may be said to be written pursuant to an implied . . . agreement that the product of the several contributions will be jointly regarded as an indivisible work.[58]

In software development, either or both of these situations may arise. In the clearest case, through multiple adjustments and contributions the coding of a program inextricably blends the contributions of the parties. The only real issue then is whether creative control is clearly intended to be solely in one individual. Otherwise, joint authorship can be presumed. In contrast, where several authors contribute identifiable parts (e.g., subroutines), the touchstone is their intent at the time of writing and the issue is whether there are grounds to find an implied or express agreement to coauthor the program.

Where all software routines are developed within the joint undertaking, a joint work should be presumed unless the parties expressly agree to a different treatment. The alternative collective work concept derives from analogies to anthologies or collections of separate pieces; these models do not conform to the general understanding of software development. While subroutines (i.e., a logically separate portion of a program) are potentially useful to other program development, they are unlike book illustrations in that they generally are not separately marketable. They should be treated as interdependent parts of the whole. If this view prevails, the remaining question is the ability of each coauthor to use

---

[56] 17 USC § 101 (1982).

[57] See Aitken, Hazen, Hoffman, Miller v. Empire Constr. Co., 218 USPQ 409 (D. Neb. 1982) (client not coauthor of architectural plans); Grosset & Dunlop, Inc. v. Gulf and Western Corp., 534 F. Supp. 606 (SDNY 1982) (illustrations and text of a book did not constitute a joint work since the parties did not proceed under a preconcerted design for joint authorship).

[58] *Nimmer on Copyright* 6-4.

aspects of the program in subsequent work, even those aspects to which a coauthor's contribution is clearly predominant. Where a true, joint work is produced, this issue is moot, since each coauthor has independent rights to license or otherwise reproduce the program in whole or in part. Both coauthors retain rights to all aspects of the work and, in effect, the one who was primarily responsible for the creation of a particular portion of the program effectively conveyed away exclusive rights in that portion.

[2] Joint Venture Relationships

Within the computer industry, commercial joint ventures of two or more businesses involved in hardware and software development are common. These may involve basic research or a more focused development activity.

Joint ventures involve a joining together of separate businesses, and the transactional framework is commonly more fully defined by the parties than in an informal setting. Intellectual property concepts concerning joint control and ownership may be displaced by express agreement or made moot by the business format chosen by the participants. Nevertheless, a joint venture raises particular problems of control of the end product, the effects on other research work of the participants, and their right to maintain control of preexisting property. Despite express contracts, controversies often arise. Furthermore, since the transaction involves two or more businesses, the flexibility available in contract is constrained by antitrust restrictions.[59]

[a] Joint Ownership

The organizational structure of commercial joint ventures ranges from separate corporations to partnerships. The business format, at least initially, controls ownership of works developed in the joint venture. There are differentiations in presumed ownership in a corporate or a partnership setting.[60] Since creative development is done by employees, coauthorship issues are commonly subsumed employee-employer questions.

More important, when two businesses are involved, control of the end product is typically addressed in express agreements that vary in content from coequal and independent control of the final product to requirements of mutual consent for any use of the product on a commercial basis. These agreements are subject to scrutiny under antitrust laws.

---

[59] See infra ¶ 4.10.
[60] See Milgrim, *Trade Secrets* 5-80.

Often, however, express agreements are not all-inclusive to the rights of the parties. In such cases, it is important to examine carefully the legal relationship that pertained. There is a basic distinction between a collaborative undertaking and one in which one of the parties was an employee or an independent contractor of the other.

Institutional Management Corp. v. Translation Systems, Inc. [61] is illustrative. Institutional Management was engaged in the development of an optical scan system to read stenotype and translate it into English. The defendants helped to develop the translation software. When they terminated their involvement, a prototype had been built, based in part on a translation dictionary that was in the public domain. The defendants took various items with them, claiming ownership based on the view that the relationship was a joint venture partnership. No formal agreement clarified the status of the parties. The court acknowledged that a joint venture could exist if the actions of the parties established an implied contract to that effect, but it concluded that no joint venture partnership existed in this case.

In distinguishing a joint venture from other forms of business relationships, a sharing of potential profits is an element, but is not necessarily decisive. [62] Employees and independent contractors may be compensated through profit sharing, but this does not convey joint ownership of business assets. Instead, joint risk of loss, joint control of funds, and joint control of operations are more significant. These were not present in *Institutional Management.*

[b] Collateral Research and Development

Assuming a joint relationship exists, participants operate in a confidential relationship to each other for trade secrecy disclosures. [63] Unless controlled by the express terms of the joint undertaking, however, the participants do not waive or transfer rights to independently developed intellectual property.

In the absence of an express agreement, a joint venture does not encompass all of the research and development activities of the participant. [64] This is especially obvious in ventures joined by businesses where the partnership may be only one aspect of a multifaceted research and development process. This relatively straightforward premise can become controversial, however, where the research, development, and marketing

---

[61] 456 F. Supp. 661 (D. Md. 1978).

[62] Id. at 666.

[63] See Milgrim, *Trade Secrets* 5-80.

[64] Com-share v. Computer Complex, Inc., 458 F2d 1341 (6th Cir. 1972).

activities bear on areas closely associated with the subject matter of the joint venture. A variety of limiting issues then arise in connection with potential conflict of interest and misappropriation of confidential material.

A common motivation for joining two or more businesses involves the different expertise of the participants. It is not uncommon that during the joint undertaking one party acquires information and experience in the field that previously had been the province of the other. If there are contract restraints on the use of confidential material, each participant can be bound to nondisclosure or nonuse of trade secrets outside the venture. A similar restriction on general information or experience obtained during the venture is less clearly enforceable. As a result, where there is no agreement not to enter particular markets, it is common to find former joint participants in subsequent competition. It is then essential to distinguish between confidential material restrictively disclosed and general business information or experience rightfully obtained and used by each party.

In *Automated Systems, Inc. v. Service Bureau Corp.,*[65] the plaintiff developed software for an automobile parts control system. The developer entered an agreement with an IBM subsidiary for a test period of joint marketing. The marketing was unsuccessful and the IBM subsidiary terminated the agreement. It developed and marketed its own, competing inventory control system. The court concluded that there had been no bad faith in the marketing effort and that while the IBM subsidiary used information obtained about the auto parts business, this was general business information and not confidential or a trade secret. The court noted

> [Attempts] were made during ... the test-sell period to modify the system as further experience was gained with various dealerships; however, it is clear that the contract did not contemplate the joint development of an inventory control system, but ... was only a sales contract for ... a particular system then in existence. ... The system which defendant [later developed and sold] was quite a different one. [The buyer] was not a customer or opportunity of either party during the contract.[66]

In *Automated Systems*, as the inadequacies of the original system became apparent, the developer suggested numerous changes and was allowed to make one. The contract explicitly limited the marketing agreement, however, to a system frozen as of the time of the agreement. Against this background, the court's decision is clearly correct. If the contract or the

---

[65] 401 F2d 619 (10th Cir. 1968).
[66] Id. at 623–624.

course of performance by the parties encompassed joint development, the terms of the joint venture might have barred subsequent development and marketing of a competing system.

[c] Preexisting Works

Joint venture participants often contribute previously owned intellectual property for use in the joint work. This raises questions about the ownership of the original property after the venture is completed, and also about the right to use any modified versions that were jointly prepared. Subject to antitrust constraints, the parties may determine these effects by contract. The contract might cross-license patents, trade secrets, or copyrights insofar as their use is required in exploiting the products of the joint development, or it might specify that sole ownership and control of previously developed intellectual property is retained by the original author, even if used in a new product.

In the absence of an express agreement, mere submission of previously owned property does not convey rights in that property beyond use in the development work itself. If previously patented or copyrighted matter is incorporated in the end product of the venture, use of that product by persons other than the original patentee may require a separate license.[67] Similarly, disclosure of a trade secret in a joint program does not relinquish the secret.[68] Joint venturers are in a confidential relationship with each other, but disclosure does not necessarily allow the recipient to use the secret outside the original joint setting. A trade secret owner may make a disclosure for limited purposes. In most joint ventures, a limited purpose disclosure, rather than disclosure for all purposes, should be presumed.

The circumstances are conceptually more difficult if the original intellectual property is used to jointly develop a new product or process. This might occur if a copyrighted program is adapted to perform enhanced functions in a new hardware environment or might entail joint design of a new hardware system that incorporates previously patented inventions or the concepts encompassed in them.

Depending on the circumstances, the original owner of a copyright or patent might be estopped from denying the other parties' right to use the joint product without payment of copyright or patent license fees. However, estoppel requires a promise or representation followed by detrimental reliance by the other party. Absent other facts, mere submission

---

[67] Textron, Inc. v. Teleoperator Sys. Corp., 554 F. Supp. 315 (EDNY 1983).

[68] Com-Share v. Computer Complex Corp., 458 F2d 1341 (6th Cir. 1972); University Computing Corp. v. Lykes-Youngstown, 504 F2d 518 (5th Cir. 1974).

to a joint venture for development of a new product should not be construed as a representation for a subsequent cost-free right to use. At the outset, it generally can not be known what, if any, elements of the work will be incorporated.[69] Reliance should not be found simply in participation in the venture. In contrast, substantial post-development efforts preparing for production may create an estoppel if the original owner acquiesced or participated without comment in the need for further payment.[70] In each case, there is a need to distinguish between a purely developmental venture where the right to use the subsequent product depends on later agreement and a venture that incorporates development and use.

As an alternative, implied contract analyses may establish a license to use the products of development including separately owned patents or copyrights. Licensing law is based primarily on state contract law. Implied nonexclusive licenses have been found in some copyright cases based on the conduct of the parties.[71] Such an analysis may be appropriate where the venture is conducted in a highly informal manner. It should not be applied to a venture established by express contract that is simply silent on this particular issue.[72] The presumption is that rights in intellectual property are retained by the original owner. This presumption is not defeated by mere silence in an express contract.

Another alternative focuses on ownership in the jointly developed work per se. Although based on previously proprietary subject matter, the new work may represent new intellectual property with ownership in the joint venture, rather than in the original proprietor. Central to this result is recognition that the joint venture itself represents a distinct entity, separate from any of the particular participants.[73] This is true regardless of whether that entity is a corporation or a partnership. If the new development is owned by the venture, the organizational structure may determine the scope of ownership vested in each participant.[74]

The determination of whether the new development incorporates the original property or represents a totally new property may be complex

---

[69] See Textron, Inc. v. Teleoperator Sys. Corp., 554 F. Supp. 315 (EDNY 1983).

[70] See Lukens Steel Co. v. American Locomotive Co., 197 F2d 939 (2d Cir. 1952).

[71] See Library Publishing, Inc. v. Medical Economics Co., 548 F. Supp. 1231 (ED Pa. 1982); see also *Nimmer on Copyright* 10-36.

[72] See Textron, Inc. v. Teleoperator Sys. Corp., 554 F. Supp. 315 (EDNY 1983).

[73] See Rosenberg, *Patent Law Fundamentals* 11-2–11-4.

[74] See Milgrim, *Trade Secrets* 5-81.

and apparently differs in the three intellectual property areas. In trade secret law, the emphasis is on the substantiality of the difference between the old and the new processes. If, for example, as part of a joint development of an artificial intelligence program, the participants substantially alter the originally secret process of one party, the altered process is owned and useable by all, since it has potential competitive advantages for each. In contrast, under patent law the critical question is whether the original patent claim "reads" on the new development. This essentially requires that the patented claim or its essential equivalent be included in its entirety in the new development. The patent holder has no control over secondary developments in themselves. If the new product is a hardware system comprised of the patented elements with new peripherals added, however, the additions do not exclude the fact that the patented product is being used.[75] In contrast, products derived through use of concepts disclosed in the patent or by eliminating significant parts of the patented process are owned by the venture, or at least by the new inventor.

As for copyright claims, it is necessary to consider the concept of a derivative work. A "derivative work" is a work that is based on a prior work, but that contains sufficient elements of originality so as to constitute a new work of authorship.[76] A leading treatise on copyright explains the concept in the following terms

> A work is not derivative unless it has substantially copied from the prior work. If that which is borrowed consists merely of ideas and not the expression of ideas, then although the work may have in part been derived from the prior works, it is not a derivative work. Put in another way, a work will be considered a derivative work only if it would be considered as infringing work if the material . . . had been taken without the consent of a copyright proprietor.[77]

The copyright concept of a derivative work is not coextensive with common conceptions of deriving one product from another. The use of the ideas encompassed in an original work does not make the second work a derivative work. This occurs only where there is a substantial borrowing of the expression of the first work.[78]

Under copyright law, the preparation of derivative works is an exclusive right of the owner of a copyright. A derivative work is also recog-

---

[75] See *Deller's Walker on Patents* § 541.

[76] 17 USC § 101 (1982).

[77] *Nimmer on Copyright* 3-3.

[78] See Freedman v. Select Information Sys., Inc., 221 USPQ 848 (ND Cal. 1983); S&H Computer Sys. v. SAS Inst., Inc., 568 F. Supp. 416 (MD Tenn. 1983).

nized as a separately copyrightable work of authorship. As this suggests, the distinction between a copy that infringes and a separately copyrightable, derivative work is less than completely clear. A derivative work encompasses more than minimal independent contribution by the new author.[79] Equally important, a derivative work is an infringing copy of the original unless the new author has been authorized to prepare it. If authorization has been given, however, the new author is entitled to copyright the new elements of the work independent of statutory claims by the original author.[80]

In this framework, a modified product may be a derivative work (if it copies expression) or simply a new, joint work (if it uses only ideas from the original). Applying these concepts to the joint modification of a copyrighted computer program is exceptionally difficult in practice and occurs without the precedents of case law. What, for example, are the consequences of a joint development of an accounting program based in part on a database management system copyrighted by one participant? The initial focus is on the elements of the original that were used. The simple use of the ideas from the database system does not extend the copyright from the original to the new product. The distinction between ideas and expression is elusive, but in a highly structured technical field even small changes in coding and structure may suggest that only the idea of the original was used, rather than the expression. If this is true, ownership of the new work is wholly within the venture, since the new program is an entirely new work for copyright purposes. In contrast, if the original is virtually duplicated in literal form with only trivial changes or minor additions, the original copyright extends to it.

If there is substantial expressive similarity between old and new but the differences reflect more than minimal new contributions, the accounting system may be a derivative work. This might occur where the original was translated to a new language or to a new operating environment.[81] Submission of the work to the joint venture creates an implied license to prepare derivative works, although it does not otherwise convey control of the original work. Arguably, the venture participants contributed to the derivative work and they are coowners. However, the underlying premise of nonsubmission of preexisting copyrights should control. An implied right to prepare a derivative work is reasonable if the author

---

[79] See *Nimmer on Copyright* 3-9.

[80] See Russel v. Price, 612 F2d 1123, 1128 (9th Cir. 1979); William v. American Broadcasting Co., 538 F2d 14, 20 (2d Cir. 1977); Freedman v. Select Information Sys., Inc., 221 USPQ 848 (ND Cal. 1983).

[81] See Synercom Technology Inc. v. University Computing Co., 462 F. Supp. 1003 (ND Tex. 1978).

acquiesced, but the further implication of coownership for subsequent reproduction and distribution of the derivative work is less clear. Joint development is not in itself inconsistent with the view that the original proprietor of the copyright retains the exclusive right to distribute copies of the work.

This interpretation is consistent with *Freedman v. Select Information Systems.* [82] In *Freedman*, the developer of a text editor program submitted it to the corporation, which subsequently modified and marketed it. The argument was that an oral, nonexclusive license permitted the defendant to market the modified work without royalty payments. The court concluded that if the modified program was a derivative work, the alleged oral license was unenforceable under state law and royalty fees should be set aside for the original author.

It is particularly important that the terms of a joint undertaking specify the rights of the parties in various types of intellectual property. This is generally recognized for the final products of development, but the specification of rights must encompass use and disposition of proprietary property brought to the venture by a participant. This is true not only for use within the venture, but also for the right to use as incorporated in final developments from the venture.

¶ 4.05 CONTRACTORS AND CONSULTANTS

Joint venture activity is common in the computer industry. In the development of applications software, however, a recurrent alternative uses independent contractors to develop programs for particular applications. This alternative is distinguished from joint development in that while the party employing the contractor may supply information as to business needs and performance specifications, the design of the system is within the control and subject to the skill of the independent contractor. It is distinguished from an employee relationship in that the employer of the contractor has no control over the details of work performance. Software development contracts present significant issues concerning the quality of the delivered product that are discussed in Chapter 6. The focus here is confined to questions of ownership and control over the developed product and any subsequent modifications in it.

In a consulting or contractor transaction, a contractor often uses information disclosed to it for the purpose of the project. If the information involves trade secrets and the disclosure is made in a manner

---

[82] 221 USPQ 848 (ND Cal. 1983).

consistent with retaining proprietary claims, the independent contractor or consultant relationship imposes an obligation of confidentiality and nondisclosure.[83] This does not apply to general information or insight about the business in which the employer functions, however.[84] In fact, developed expertise in designing applications for a particular field can be a significant asset for the independent contractor and is generally not restricted unless there is an explicit, enforceable, restrictive covenant.

Similarly, assuming appropriate efforts to retain secrecy, the independent contractor can establish a confidential relationship protecting its own trade secrets used or disclosed in performing the contract.[85] Use in a particular contract, without more, does not convey to the employer a general right to use the material or a waiver of proprietary claims.

As to the developed product, it is obvious that the parties can contract for express allocation of rights to control and modify software prepared by an independent contractor. A variety of arrangements might be agreed to, including unlimited control in the employer for personal use with exclusive control over marketing in the contractor-developer. Retained control of subroutines incorporated in the delivered product is particularly important for a development firm that may benefit commercially by reutilization in subsequent contracts. If copyrighted material is involved and there is an exclusive license or an assignment to the employer, subsequent use by the developer may infringe the copyright.

In the absence of express contract provisions, the independent contractor retains control of distribution and reproduction of the software delivered to the employer. This is true even if the employer expressly assigns and commissions the work.[86] On this issue, there is a distinction between an employee and an independent contractor. In an independent contractor relationship, the employer does not control the details of work performance, but only acceptance or rejection of the eventual product. In contrast, in an employee relationship, the employer directs and controls

---

[83] See Milgrim, *Trade Secrets* 5-54, 5-55.

[84] See Trilog Assoc., Inc. v. Famularo, 314 A2d 287 (Pa. 1974).

[85] See M. Bryce & Assoc. v. Gladstone, 319 NW2d 902 (Wis. Ct. App. 1982).

[86] See Aitken, Hazen, Hoffman, Miller v. Empire Constr. Co., 218 USPQ 409 (D. Neb. 1982); BPI Sys., Inc. v. Leith, 532 F. Supp. 208 (WD Tex. 1981). In this regard, current law represents an apparently substantial shift from the thrust of the case law prior to the current Copyright Act. See HR Rep. No. 1476, 94th Cong., 2d Sess. 121 (1976); see also Meltzer v. Zoller, 520 F. Supp. 847, 854 (DNJ 1981).

work details.[87] The employer's interest in the intellectual property developments of the contractor is less than with an employee. The contractor's interests are greater because he may have significant business and employment outside of the particular contract.

The ownership issue is whether the contractor or the employer has a right to use or control use in contexts other than the particular purpose of the contract. Milgrim suggests that the contractor's right to use trade secret material should depend on the nature of the project and the implicit contract or understanding of the parties.[88] An illustration is a geologist hired to estimate oil and gas potential in a given area. The data collected is confidential to the employer and may not be disclosed, but the contractor's methods of analysis are proprietary to the contractor and may be subsequently used by the contractor.

Copyrighted works prepared under contract generally remain the property of the contractor, rather than of the employer. While ownership of works for hire vests in the employer, the Act distinguishes employee works and works prepared on a commission or contract basis.[89] A commissioned work does not constitute a work for hire unless it was done pursuant to a written agreement and the work falls within a statutory list of eligible works.[90] The only potentially applicable categories for computer programs involve translations and supplemental or explanatory works. Thus, if done pursuant to a written agreement a translation to a new programming language constitutes a work for hire. A program specially designed for a customer is not a work for hire and ownership remains in the contractor unless there is an express contractual conveyance of rights.

These restrictions recognize the distinction between an employer's relationship to an employee and its relationship to an independent consultant or contractor. Unless there is a written agreement assigning copyright or conveying an exclusive license, the contractor does not have control over subsequent copies and derivative works. Furthermore, the statute indicates that an express contract is required and that no conveyance is found by implication. The program, or parts of the program, can be reused by the contractor in a later contract with another party unless this action would involve wrongful disclosure or use of trade secrets. The

---

[87] See Aitken, Hazen, Hoffman, Miller v. Empire Constr. Co., 218 USPQ 409, 413, 414 (D. Neb. 1982) (architect is not an employee of client); Azad v. United States, 388 F2d 74 (8th Cir. 1968).

[88] Milgrim, *Trade Secrets* 5-53–5-62.

[89] See supra ¶ 4.02[1]; 17 USC § 201 (1982).

[90] 17 USC § 101 (1982); see BPI Sys., Inc. v. Leith, 532 F. Supp. 208 (WD Tex. 1981).

chief threat to this result in a particular transaction lies in practices that alter the contractor relationship. For example, a nominally independent contractor relationship may elevate to an employee-employer relationship due to the course of dealing between the parties. In a contractor relationship, the employer exercises control only over the end product and not the details of work performance. Where individuals, rather than separate businesses, perform the contracting role, excessive control by the employer may create the equivalent of employment for copyright purposes. If this occurs, the program is a work for hire and copyright vests in the employer.

Another possibility that might convey substantial control to the employer involves the creation of a joint work. In a joint work, both authors control subsequent use, marketing, and modification of the program. This result is possible in a contractor relationship because program design ordinarily is contingent on the requirements of the employer and the development work involves an interaction between the parties. The employer has substantial influence on the final character of the program. Significantly, however, joint authorship is based not only on the nature of the contribution, but on the intention of the parties. In most contractor relationships, joint authorship is not intended and the client is not a coauthor.[91]

Except for employee cases, resolution of control over the product also resolves the right of the contractor to use its work product in subsequent contracts. If control vests in the contractor, however, there are open questions about the right of the employer to modify the program for personal use consistent with the purpose of the original contract. If the program is a joint work, the former employer has this right. If not, the situation is less clear and the employer's rights are contingent on the overall character of the transaction. If the transaction is a sale of a copy of a program, the Act provides the copy owner a presumptive, limited right to make modifications for personal use in a computer system.[92] This does not apply in a lease or other transaction. As to trade secrets, the contractor's agreement with the employer must restrict use and disclosure; otherwise secrecy will have been waived. Unless the restrictions are expressly to the contrary, they should be interpreted to permit subsequent modification and use for purposes analogous to the objectives of the original transaction.

---

[91] See Aitken, Hazen, Hoffman, Miller v. Empire Constr. Co., 218 USPQ 409 (D. Neb. 1982).

[92] 17 USC § 117 (1982).

¶ 4.06 END USER MODIFICATIONS

Even where no joint development relationship is intended, modifications or derivations nevertheless may occur through alterations or new developments made by an end user or licensee. Two distinct fact patterns must be recognized. The first involves end user modifications and resulting commercial use in competition with the original product. If the modifications are trivial and the product is protected under copyright or patent law, an infringement has occurred unless the original transfer explicitly authorized reproduction and marketing. If marketing is preceded by substantial modifications, more difficult issues arise. The second pattern involves user modifications for personal use consistent with the originally intended use of the program. This might entail customization of the software to a new computer system or a modification to meet changing business needs.

These two situations affect the original proprietor very differently. In the first, there is a direct impact on the proprietor's market, since it is now in competition with a product developed based on its own proprietary system. In the second, the primary impact is on the proprietor's ability to resell to the same licensee-owner if the original owner is willing to modify its product. This interest is not clearly protected under copyright or patent law. The status of end user modifications in both cases depends on the nature of the protected property and the restraints placed on the user in the transaction in which it acquired the product. The restraints that can be established over an end user are not limited solely by the terms of a contract that can be negotiated, but by underlying intellectual property and antitrust law principles (discussed in Chapter 5).

Where property is protected exclusively under trade secret law, infringement is equatable with misappropriation. A third party who discovers the secret without misappropriation is free to use all or part of it in his own work. This is the direct significance of the idea of reverse engineering or discovery by observation.[93] An end user who discerns the algorithm or design of a program can duplicate that design as long as discovery and use do not violate confidentiality restraints. Questions of similarity in design are inapposite unless effective confidentiality restraints exist and the secret survived distribution of the product. Both of these elements are problematic in the mass market, but can be retained in custom or limited distribution software.[94]

---

[93] See also Milgrim, *Trade Secrets* 5-53.

[94] See Milgrim, *Trade Secrets* § 2.05[2]; Davidson, "Protecting Computer Software—A Comprehensive Analysis," 1983 Ariz. St. LJ 611, 727 (1983). Arguably, however, distribution in object code may prevent or at least delay disclosure of program design. See MacGrady, "Protection of Computer Software—An

The issues of patented or copyrighted property are more complex. Under both bodies of law, the proprietor has express statutory rights. Actions that conflict with those rights and are not licensed by the proprietor constitute infringement. Nevertheless, under both bodies of law, the owner of a copy of a patented or copyrighted product may have a right to make modifications for personal use, since the first sale exhausts the owner's patent or copyright to that item.[95] For example, the owner of an item may repair it without infringing the patent.[96] Similarly, the owner of a copy of a book may underline, annotate, or cut sections from the book without infringing the exclusive right to prepare derivative works. To the extent that these rights apply, the user-modifier can be said to be the owner of the modified item or product. The ownership rights are limited by the predominant statutory right and the owner may not manufacture or prepare additional copies. Furthermore, the rights of the owner of a copy do not necessarily protect third parties who prepare works that aid the owner, but also infringe the underlying copyright.[97]

There is uncertainty under copyright law about the scope of the right of a copy owner of a computer program to make modifications of the program for personal use. Section 106(2) of the Act grants the copyright proprietor the exclusive right to prepare derivative works based on the original. The copyright notion of a "derivative work" is a work that incorporates substantial portions of the expression of the original.[98] Thus, marketing a derivative work also infringes the copyright proprietor's exclusive right to make copies of the original. However, there is no requirement of reproduction for derivative works, only a requirement that a derivative work be prepared. At least one court has held that modification of a computer program by the owner of a copy is an infringement if the resulting product is displayed publicly for commercial gain.[99]

In contrast, Section 117 of the Act authorizes the copy owner of a computer program to make adaptations of the program as "an essential step in the utilization of the computer program in conjunction with a machine." On its face, this is only a limited right restricted to modifica-

---

Update and Practical Synthesis," 20 Hous. L. Rev. 1033, 1063 (1983); Grogan, "Decompilation and Disassembly: Undoing Software Protection," 1 Comp. Law. 1, 7 (Feb. 1984).

[95] 17 USC § 117 (1982).

[96] See *Deller's Walker on Patents* § 399.

[97] See Midway Mfg. Co. v. Strohon, 564 F. Supp. 741 (ND Ill. 1983); Hubco Data Prods. Corp. v. Management Assistance, Inc., 219 USPQ 450 (D. Idaho 1983).

[98] See ¶ 1.09; *Nimmer on Copyright* § 3.04.

[99] See Midway Mfg. Co. v. Artic Int'l, Inc., 704 F2d 1009 (7th Cir. 1983).

tions that are essential to use the program. The National Commission on New Technological Uses of Copyrighted Works (CONTU) report that originally proposed Section 117 suggests a potentially broader application.

> Thus, a right to make those changes necessary to enable the use for which it was both sold and purchased should be provided. The conversion of a program from one higher level language to another to facilitate use would fall within this right, as would the right to add features to the program that were not present at the time of rightful acquisition. These rights would necessarily be ... private in nature ... and could only be exercised so long as they did not harm the interests of the copyright proprietor.[100]

Under this view, the statutory reference to essential adaptations is not limited to those absolutely necessary to operate the program on a machine, but is defined in terms of essentiality to the user's optimal own use of the program. It encompasses altering language or adding features. The owner's rights parallel annotation, underlining, or altering a copy of a book for personal use. The copyright proprietor is protected by the proceeds of the initial sale and by the fact that the copy owner is barred from marketing the adapted program.[101]

This interpretation is preferable to a view that precludes any but the most limited and necessary adaptations of a program copy by the copy owner.[102] It focuses the balance of interests at the appropriate point, allowing both the user and the copyright proprietor to optimize benefits. The copyright proprietor's interest is defined in terms of the original sale and an exclusive right to market subsequent adaptations. These interests are sacrificed only for use by a single owner of a copy of those modifications made by it to optimize personal use. Distribution of copies of the derivative work by the copy owner is not a protected act.

Section 117 applies only to the owner of a copy. A person who leases a copy of the program has no statutory right to prepare adaptations, but the reference is to ownership of the copy, not the copyright. A transaction involving the sale of a disk or tape and a license to use the program is within Section 117. In distinguishing a lease from a sale of the tangible

---

[100] See *National Commission on New Technological Uses of Copyrighted Works, Final Report* 20 (1978).

[101] See *Nimmer on Copyright* 8-107.

[102] Nevertheless, the first reported decision concerning Section 117 adopted a restrictive view of the scope of the owner's rights to make a copy of the program. See Atari, Inc. v. JS&A Group, Inc., slip op. at 9 (ND Ill. 1983) (copy permitted only where media is subject to electronic or other unique forms of loss).

item on which the program is copied, the critical issue is whether the original owner of the copy retains a right to its return upon the completion of a specified term or upon another, identifiable event.

The foregoing assumes that the user modifications are a derivative work in the copyright sense. The limited rights conveyed to an owner of a copy do not encompass marketing of multiple copies of the derivative work that it prepares for personal use. As to marketing of modified forms of an original program, however, the copyright proprietor's exclusive control of the copyrighted material does not necessarily control all questions concerning user modifications. Many modifications or new program developments do not fall within copyright control, as when the user bases its program solely on the idea of the original, rather than on the expression. In technical works, the distinction between idea and expression is elusive and current case law does not provide adequate guidance. If the second program uses only the ideas of the first, however, it is not a derivative work. It is a noninfringing, new work in which the copyright is owned by the end user. It should be noted that the underlying design characteristics of software are potentially appropriate subject matter for trade secret protection. Assuming that trade secrecy can be established and that the relevant license agreement effectively constrains use of the designs, while there may be no copyright infringement, there may be a misappropriation of trade secrets.

PART C.   ANTITRUST AND INNOVATION

¶ 4.07 PRINCIPLES OF ANTITRUST LAW

Joint and sequential development of computer technology creates questions about the right to control the resulting product under intellectual property law that can be resolved by contract. Federal antitrust law is also relevant to technology research, development, and new product introduction.[103] Antitrust doctrine, like intellectual property law, supports an underlying premise that an appropriate legal system should encourage technology innovation, but creates significant difficulties in defining the best manner of encouragement and in reconciling innovation with other antitrust law concerns.

Three antitrust statutes have particular relevance to research and development issues; (1) Section 1 of the Sherman Act, which prohibits

---

[103] The most frequently litigated antitrust issues pertaining to technology involve restrictions on technology licensing. These are discussed in Chapter 5.

contracts, combinations, or conspiracies "in restraint of trade";[104] (2) Section 2 of the Sherman Act, which prohibits monopolization or an attempt to monopolize any part of "trade or commerce;"[105] and, (3) Section 2(a) of the Clayton Act, which proscribes price discrimination and certain other acts whose "effect . . . may be substantially to lessen competition . . . to create a monopoly . . . or to injure, destroy or prevent competition."[106]

While these statutes do not deal directly with intellectual property development, antitrust issues relating to research and development arise where the development affects general antitrust policies. In broad terms, these policies are directed toward promoting and preserving commercial competition free of unreasonable, unregulated restraints.[107] This broad policy statement, however, conceals a number of more specific judgments involved in antitrust enforcement. These are substantially affected by perceived characteristics of preferred social and economic structure. At least in the contemporary literature, policy analysis is shaped by application of analytical models derived from economics theory.[108] Often, the boundaries of the particular policy choice are unclear.

Current antitrust laws derive from congressional policy against monopolistic control of commercial markets.[109] In some popular perceptions, monopoly connotes size and implies that the essence of antitrust should be to preclude the emergence or continuation of large firms. In fact, this view has never been the dominant characteristic of antitrust law. While antitrust concerns are increasingly present as a potential violator's size and market dominance increases, monopoly concerns focus not only on size, but on the use of market power in a manner that unreasonably affects competition.[110]

Antitrust law distinguishes acceptable and unacceptable competitive actions. The criteria for this choice are often complex and, at least superficially, inconsistent. The underlying model is a dominant company or companies that use restrictive market techniques to exclude or drive out

---

[104] 15 USC § 2 (1982).

[105] 15 USC § 1 (1982).

[106] 15 USC § 14 (1982).

[107] See Areeda & Turner, *Antitrust Law* 1-7.

[108] See Areeda & Turner, *Antitrust Law* 1-31; Brodley, "Joint Ventures and Antitrust Policy," 95 Harv. L. Rev. 1523 (1982); Kaplow, "The Patent Antitrust Intersection: A Reappraisal," 97 Harv. L. Rev. 1815 (1984).

[109] See Standard Oil Corp. v. FTC, 340 US 231, 249 (1951).

[110] In fact, size may in many instances be the result of success in a free, competitive market. See Berkey Photo, Inc. v. Eastman Kodak Co., 603 F2d 263 (2d Cir. 1979); Areeda & Turner, *Antitrust Law* ¶¶ 110, 111.

competitors and obtain benefits in the form of higher prices as a result of the exclusion. The assumption is that, left to competition on the merits (consisting of cost, marketing, and product characteristics), natural competitive effects preclude excessive profit-taking over the long term. Actions by companies that chill these normal competitive influences rather than pursue them violate antitrust laws if the company has or may be able to obtain the market power necessary to make these actions effective.

There are two characteristics in analyses that sort between natural (permitted) competitive acts and wrongful conduct. Initially, certain conduct is defined as a per se violation of antitrust law, while other conduct comes under a broad rule of reason that considers not only conduct, but also the pertinent business and economic justifications for it. This is part of a broader concern for establishing clear evidence and substantive rules to guide business conduct and reduce complex factual issues to manageable proportions.[111] Illustrative of per se violations are agreements among competitors to fix prices, divide markets, or create group boycotts.[112] Secondly, the cases and the literature rely on economic theory and analysis to assess the alleged antitrust violation. Economic definitions of "market" and "market power" and economic theories are used to judge the competitive conduct to be prohibited or encouraged. An essential assumption is that antitrust law should generally not prohibit competitive behavior that in economic terms represents efficient competition.[113] Efficiency in this context refers to broad models of market behavior and a goal of optimizing output and consumption.

¶ 4.08 SINGLE PRODUCT INNOVATION

The distinction between improper and acceptable competitive conduct is important in discussing the antitrust implications of product development and introduction. The optimal antitrust objective is a competitive marketplace in which efficient firms compete with products and price and are unencumbered by illicit use of market power. In this model, the competing firms are involved in ongoing development and refinement of products in response to market forces. Research and development

---

[111] See Areeda & Turner, *Antitrust Law* 1-8; Brodley, "Joint Ventures and Antitrust Policy," 95 Harv. L. Rev. 1523 (1982).

[112] See Northern Pac. Ry. Co. v. United States, 356 US 1 (1958); Timken Roller Bearing Co. v. United States, 341 US 593 (1981).

[113] See Areeda & Turner, *Antitrust Law* 1-8.

leading to product innovation is clearly consistent with the overall goals of the antitrust system.

It is apparent that development and introduction of a single computer product, unencumbered by other anticompetitive activities, involves no antitrust issue. This is true even if the superiority of the new product drives other competitors from the marketplace. Areeda and Turner describe such innovation as a privileged competitive act: "A better product can impair the sales and profits of rival firms, and a dominant firm can increase its dominance by introducing better products. Nevertheless, product superiority is one of the objects of competition and cannot be wrongful, even for a monopolist."[114] This basic premise is sufficiently well accepted that it is seldom litigated. Where innovation has seemed to present antitrust concerns, it has been in situations involving physically interdependent products[115] or so-called predatory pricing activity linked to the new product.[116]

In a pure single product innovation, antitrust law provides no rationale to support abstract analyses about whether the new item is or is not technologically superior to existing products. The appropriate measure of superiority and innovation is marketplace acceptance, rather than whether the product advances the art beyond that which characterizes existing competition.[117] In a general sense applicable to antitrust law, even if there is a technological advance, a product is not superior to its competitors if there is no marketplace acceptance. For example, the introduction by IBM of a microcomputer that involves advanced, but not state of the art technology, does not present an antitrust issue merely because of IBM's size and the fact that consumers prefer this machine to more sophisticated alternatives. Marketplace acceptance indicates that product superiority to a consumer incorporates more than mere technology concerns.

¶ 4.09 INTEGRATED SYSTEMS INNOVATION

One distinguishing characteristic of the computer industry is the physical interdependence of potentially separable products and the development of market competition around these components. This involves

---

[114] Areeda & Turner, *Antitrust Law* ¶ 738.3.

[115] See Berkey Photo, Inc. v. Eastman Kodak Co., 603 F2d 263 (2d Cir. 1979); Transamerica Computer Corp. v. IBM, 698 F2d 1377 (9th Cir. 1983).

[116] See Ordover & Willig, "An Economic Definition of Predation: Pricing and Product Innovation," 91 Yale LJ 8 (1981).

[117] See Areeda & Turner, *Antitrust Law* § 738.1.

the phenomenon of plug compatibility. In a typical case, one company markets a basic system, but various enhancements and elements of the system are subject to independent manufacture and sale by competing firms. In many cases, these firms do not directly compete with the basic system, but establish a substantial competitive market for system components and a submarket develops. This competitive submarket is dependent on continued popularity of the basic system and on the competitors' ability to maintain compatibility with pertinent elements of the basic system.

Innovations or changes in the underlying or basic system may compromise, at least for a time, the compatibility of competing peripherals or components. The particular antitrust risk is that the original manufacturer will use its control of the basic machine to force out competition in the market for peripherals or components by making unnecessary changes. Under appropriate market conditions, the original firm may obtain excessive profits from its now dominant position in the compatibles market, at least until competitors are able to adapt to the new designs. Arguably, under some circumstances a design change in the basic unit unreasonably restrains peripheral and component competition.

Both antitrust and general law should encourage competition and efforts at product improvement in the basic system as well as in the components. Product improvement is a characteristic of a competitive market and is desirable even if there is a harmful effect on competitors who are unable to match the product enhancements. In the instant case, however, the relevant competition is not limited to the basic unit, but incorporates the peripheral or component market in which the original manufacturer also competes. While improvements in the basic system may be privileged and should be encouraged, the risk is that the original manufacturer may use its control to make arbitrary changes designed solely to compromise compatibles competition, rather than to improve the basic product.

This might suggest a relatively simple proposition for analysis of interdependent system innovation: Improvements in the basic system are privileged competitive acts, but mere design changes intended to reduce peripheral competition may entail an antitrust violation. The reported cases accept the first element of this view.[118] Furthermore, it is clear that no greater restraint on product innovation is justified beyond that expressed in the second element. The second element of this proposition, however, might create an undesirable restraint on research and development activity. Establishing a dichotomy between mere changes and product improvements imposes an antitrust risk in all research and develop-

---

[118] Id.

ment in an integrated environment. The overall objective of antitrust should be to encourage product innovation. To the extent that there is a legal risk involved, the dichotomy may chill innovative development and tend to lock in the original manufacturer to the original design of the basic system to avoid liability for competitive harm to the compatibles competitors.[119] This risk is especially high because of the difficulty of distinguishing product improvements from their alternative, arguably anticompetitive, counterpart. Such distinctions might require complex analyses of system capabilities or of corporate motivations in introducing changes in the basic system. Either approach creates substantial uncertainty and potentially adverse effects on innovation that are inconsistent with basic antitrust policy.

The appropriate alternative is to regard all changes in the basic system as presumptively privileged and legally protected.[120] This would promote innovation in the basic system as much as possible. Furthermore, unless there are substantial time and cost barriers to competitors adapting their product to the design change, natural market restraints will preclude the hypothetical use of arbitrary design changes in an anticompetitive manner. For each change, the original manufacturer incurs costs in development and in adapting its own products. Unless the effect on competitors overcomes these costs, there is a natural disincentive for predatory design change. A substantial effect on competitors only occurs if the competitor's ability to adapt is questionable and the design change is accompanied by actions that remove the original system from the marketplace.[121] This is even more relevant with competition for the basic unit. Recurrent, arbitrary design changes in the basic unit make it less desirable to buyers who have an interest in broad compatibility and this negative market effect provides another natural restraint on arbitrary design change. Of course, if the design changes make the new system more attractive in the market, they are properly described as improvements and are protected despite their impact on competitors.

In most cases, natural market factors provide sufficient restraints against predatory design changes in an integrated or interdependent

---

[119] See Ordover & Willig, "An Economic Definition of Predation: Pricing and Product Innovation," 91 Yale LJ 8 (1981); Sidak, "Debunking Predatory Innovation," 83 Colum. L. Rev. 1121 (1983); Ordover, Sykes & Willig, "Predatory Systems Rivalry: A Reply," 83 Colum. L. Rev. 1150 (1983).

[120] See generally Sidak, "Debunking Predatory Innovation," 83 Colum. L. Rev. 1121 (1983).

[121] See Areeda & Turner, *Antitrust Law* ¶ 738.4; Ordover & Willig, "An Economic Definition of Predation: Pricing and Product Innovation," 91 Yale LJ 8 (1981).

system environment.[122] Attempting to deal with the relatively few cases in which these restraints do not operate may have a substantial impact on the pace of innovation. The cost exceeds the benefit. As a result, the preferable approach entails at least a presumptive, if not an absolute, privilege to alter design. While per se legality of design changes has substantial appeal, it has not been adopted in the reported cases. Instead, the courts assume that product changes in an integrated environment may involve antitrust violation, but approach individual cases in a circumspect, protective manner. The result is that integrated system changes generally incur no antitrust liability, but the risk of liability nevertheless continues.

[1] Product Superiority

Even in an integrated system environment, introduction of a superior new product or of design changes in existing products that constitute improvements is a privileged act, free from antitrust liability.[123] This is true even if there is a substantial impact on competitors and even if the manufacturer is or intends to become a monopolist. One rationale for this view was expressed by the circuit court in *Telex Corp. v. IBM*[124] *Telex* involved alleged efforts by IBM to monopolize peripheral markets by a combined strategy including price cuts, marketing format changes, and central processing unit (CPU) design changes. In concluding that no antitrust violation occurred, the court noted

> There must be some room to move for a defendant who sees his market share acquired by research and technical innovations being eroded by those who market copies of its products. It would seem that technical attainments were not intended to be inhibited or penalized by a construction of Section 2 of the Sherman Act . . . to so interpret the Act to prohibit such actions is to protect the others in the market from ordinary competition.[125]

---

[122] See Ordover, Sykes & Willig, "Predatory Systems Rivalry: A Reply," 83 Colum. L. Rev. 1150 (1983).

[123] See California Computer Prods., Inc., v. IBM Corp., 613 F2d 727 (9th Cir. 1979); Transamerica Computer Co. v. IBM Corp., 481 F. Supp. 965 (ND Cal. 1979), aff'd as modified, 698 F2d 1377 (9th Cir. 1983); Berkey Photo, Inc. v. Eastman Kodak Co., 603 F2d 263 (2d Cir. 1979); ILC Peripherals Leasing Co. v. IBM Corp., 458 F. Supp. 423 (ND Cal. 1978), aff'd sub nom., Memorex Corp. v. IBM Corp., 636 F2d 1188 (9th Cir. 1980).

[124] 510 F2d 894 (10th Cir. 1975).

[125] Id. at 927.

Acceptance of the right to improve a product even in an interdependent system environment is not only essential to encourage innovation, it is an elemental characteristic of the permissible range of competition even by a monopolist. The contrary view would amount to a position that protects other firms at the expense of, rather than in furtherance of, competition. The essence of an antitrust claim is use of monopoly power, not of technological or research and development expertise.

This basic premise leaves open the question of what criteria determine if the product change is an improvement or an anticompetitive mere design change. It is pertinent that the concept of improvement or product superiority is a variable, contextual issue rather than an absolute one. The technical journals in computer and other areas are replete with disputes about the superiority of various microprocessors, programming languages, applications software, and other elements of technology. This is characteristic of a dynamic technology. Furthermore, technical superiority does not necessarily equal market superiority as can be witnessed by the current viability of microcomputers whose technology is clearly not equatable with the state of the art.

In measuring superiority, one approach refers to the views of engineers and other technocrats to determine if one product is superior to another. This creates a test of technological superiority. While this approach has been argued in all of the innovation antitrust cases,[126] the test has been rejected as the sole or even the primary measure. Instead, the cases emphasize market judgments. This was most clearly expressed in *Berkey Photo, Inc. v. Eastman Kodak Co.*[127] In *Berkey*, the alleged violation involved simultaneous introduction of a new camera and new film in an alleged attempt to use a monopoly in one market to augment competitive advantage in another. The court rejected arguments that the new film was technically inferior to other film products manufactured by Kodak. There was a dispute about shelf life and other characteristics of the new film.

> In this context . . . the question of product quality has little meaning. [Consumer reactions to different capabilities will vary.] In such circumstances no one can determine with any reasonable assurance whether one product is "superior" to another. Preference is a matter of individual taste. The only question that can be

---

[126] See, e.g., Berkey Photo, Inc. v. Eastman Kodak Co., 603 F2d 263, 287 (2d Cir. 1979); ILC Peripherals Leasing Co. v. IBM Corp., 458 F. Supp. 423, 440 (ND Cal. 1978), aff'd sub nom., Memorex Corp. v. IBM Corp., 636 F2d 1188 (9th Cir. 1980).

[127] 603 F2d 263 (2d Cir. 1979).

answered is whether there is sufficient demand . . . to make its production worthwhile, and the response, so long as the free choice of
consumers is preserved, can only be inferred from the reaction of
the market.[128]

Berkey involved a consumer market with a high volume of sales. As such,
market judgment was an appropriate standard in the absence of effective
actions by Kodak to render other film unavailable to buyers. Market evidence is frequently less clear cut, especially where a relatively small volume of expensive items are involved, and in this context technological
judgments are pertinent.

Where technological judgments are a major variable, the primary
issue concerns the degree to which there must be a provable consensus
that the innovation is technically superior. To avoid inhibiting innovation, it is necessary to stop short of close scrutiny of technical disputes
and to avoid any requirement that a consensus exist.[129] A colorable
dispute about whether the change is an improvement is in itself sufficient to establish immunity from antitrust liability.[130] This point was
made by the district court in *ILC Peripherals v. IBM*,[131] another case
dealing with IBM design changes that adversely affected peripheral
competitors.

Where there is a difference of opinion as to the advantages of two
alternatives which can both be defended from an engineering standpoint, the court will not allow itself to be enmeshed "in a technical
inquiry into the justifiability of product innovations." . . . At most,
Memorex has only been able to show that there was an alternative
approach available. Where the approach chosen was at least as justifiable as the alternative . . . courts should not get involved in second
guessing engineers.[132]

The applicable test is whether a colorable dispute exists about the superiority of a design.[133] In this test, the fact that one alternative more seriously affects competitors should be irrelevant.

---

[128] Id. at 286–287.

[129] Telex Corp. v. IBM Corp., 367 F. Supp. 258, 347 (ND Okla. 1973), aff'd,
510 F2d 894 (10th Cir. 1975).

[130] Areeda & Turner, *Antitrust Law* ¶ 738.1.

[131] 458 F. Supp. 423, 440 (ND Cal. 1978), aff'd sub nom., Memorex Corp. v.
IBM Corp., 636 F2d 1188 (9th Cir. 1980).

[132] ILC Peripherals v. IBM, 458 F. Supp. 423, 439–441 (1978).

[133] See Transamerica Computer Co. v. IBM Corp., 481 F. Supp. 965, 1002–
1005 (ND Cal. 1979), aff'd as modified, 698 F2d 1377 (9th Cir. 1983).

[2] Ancillary Restraints and Market Power

Whether or not a new design or product is superior to the old, no antitrust violation occurs unless the product is introduced into a market with restrictions that unreasonably affect competition and constitute an exercise of monopoly power or an attempt to attain it. This requires analysis of the relevant market structure and of the position of the alleged violator and its competitors within that market.

A minor actor in a market, or a competitor in a highly elastic market with relative ease of entry, is free to make design changes without antitrust risk. Natural market factors restrain and market demand evaluates the changes. There are sufficient market alternatives or new entrant possibilities to minimize the competitive effect of the change and to eliminate the incentive for predatory conduct. In contrast, the collateral circumstances in which design changes occur may create an antitrust problem if: (1) the company making the change has sufficient market power to control prices and force others out; (2) the related manufacturers are dependent on compatibility with the basic unit and in a situation in which reentry or adaptation is precluded or, at least, extremely difficult; and (3) the design change is accompanied by adaptations in existing products that effectively eliminate buyer choice between the old and the new, thereby denying competitor access to the existing market.

The relevant market may be defined either by the basic system or by the market for peripherals or compatibles. Monopoly control in the basic unit market can be used as a lever to attain dominance in the peripheral market. Most of the reported cases have involved mainframe or minicomputer systems. In these markets, while IBM and several other companies have a significant market share of basic systems, substantial competition nonetheless exists and it is likely that no one firm occupies a monopoly position.[134] Peripherals or compatibles markets on the other hand may involve more explicit market control since they are outgrowths or submarkets from particular basic units. Colloquially, it is clear that in the computer industry, markets for IBM compatibles, Apple compatibles, and the like are well-recognized phenomena. Nevertheless, in cases not involving illegal tying of two products,[135] the courts consistently refuse to accept this market definiton, opting instead for a broader conception of the relevant market.[136] The net effect is that the original manufacturer

---

[134] See Telex Corp. v. IBM Corp., 367 F. Supp. 258, 347 (ND Okla. 1973), aff'd, 510 F2d 894 (10th Cir. 1975).

[135] See ¶ 5.04.

[136] See Telex Corp. v. IBM Corp., 367 F. Supp. 258 (ND Okla. 1973), aff'd, 510 F2d 894 (10th Cir. 1975); Transamerica Computer Co. v. IBM Corp., 481 F.

who retains a substantial share of sales of components and peripherals for its own basic product is often immunized from antitrust by a finding that it does not have and is not likely to obtain dominance of the relevant market.

The antitrust definition of a relevant market for analysis is a complex issue[137] and full consideration is beyond the scope of this book. However, the cases reflect a consistent conclusion that peripherals and components for a *particular system* are not a cognizable market for the purposes of antitrust law. This conclusion is based on a relatively straightforward concept. In antitrust, one purpose of defining a market is to assess the extent to which a company can control prices and competition without effective competitive restraints. It is thus pertinent to determine not only whether a popularly conceived market exists, but to what extent there is cross-elasticity or potential interchangeability in supply or demand with similar products.[138] If interchangeability exists, monopolistic acts are naturally constrained. As prices for one product rise, consumers will turn to interchangeable products of other manufacturers and these should be defined as part of the same market. Alternatively, as prices rise, new manufacturers are likely to enter competition. In either case, the original firm's power or ability to act is constrained by these other factors.

Applying this notion of interchangeability to component or peripheral markets, the market encompasses at least all peripheral products of a particular type, rather than solely those currently compatible with a specific type of basic machine. This analysis was followed in *Telex Corp. v. IBM.*[139] Focusing primarily on supply or manufacturing substitutability, the court concluded that the relevant market encompassed all peripherals and not merely IBM compatibles.

> Manufacturers of peripherals were not limited to those which were plug compatible with IBM CPU's. These manufacturers were free to adapt their products ... to plug into new IBM systems. It also followed that ... manufacturers could modify their interfaces so that their own peripheral products could plug into IBM. ... Factually, then, there existed peripheral products of other CPU manufacturers

---

Supp. 965 (ND Cal. 1979), aff'd as modified, 698 F2d 1377 (9th Cir. 1983); ILC Peripherals Leasing Co. v. IBM Corp., 458 F. Supp. 423 (ND Cal. 1978), aff'd sub nom., Memorex Corp. v. IBM Corp., 636 F2d 1188 (9th Cir. 1980).

[137] See Areeda & Turner, *Antitrust Law* ¶¶ 501-507.

[138] United States v. Dupont de Nemours & Co., 351 US 377 (1956).

[139] 367 F. Supp. 258 (ND Okla. 1973), aff'd, 510 F2d 894 (10th Cir. 1975).

which were competitive with IBM.... The fact that Telex ... devoted itself to ... IBM ... cannot control.[140]

Central to this conclusion is that either or both consumers and suppliers will cross product lines given the appropriate incentive. A central issue involves the cost barriers in such conversion. For computer peripherals, the court in *Telex* concluded that costs of adaptation were low.

Financial or other barriers to entry are important in defining the relevant market. They are also pertinent in directly assessing whether design changes by a monopolist violate antitrust norms. There is a tendency to define antitrust violations in terms of context and potential effect, rather than solely in terms of often ambiguous corporate intent. In the context discussed here, the antitrust concern involves design changes made to force competitors out of a market so that the monopolist can obtain monopoly profits on subsequent sales. This can not be achieved if the competitor's cost of adaptation to the change is low. In such situations, existing or potential competitors are likely to adapt before the monopolist obtains the benefit of its actions. Predatory design changes involve both design and internal adaptation costs. These are unlikely to be undertaken in the absence of reentry barriers to competition and, if they are, are likely to be ineffective.[141]

Both anticompetitive feasibility and intent can be inferred from circumstances related to demand elasticity. If, after the introduction of the new redesigned product, the monopolist continues to make the old basic product available to buyers on competitive terms, there is no antitrust risk.[142] Peripherals or compatibles manufacturers may elect to continue to concentrate on the old product that will retain its market share if the new product is not an improvement. Absent steps to make the old product less attractive or unavailable, if the new product nevertheless dominates the market, it is a superior product and its introduction is not actionable. A redesign is anticompetitive only if accompanied by efforts to eliminate the old product from the market by substantial price increases or discontinuation.[143]

---

[140] Id. at 917.

[141] See Ordover & Willig, "An Economic Definition of Predation: Pricing and Product Innovation," 91 Yale LJ 8 (1981).

[142] See Areeda & Turner, *Antitrust Law* ¶ 738.4; Ordover & Willig, "An Economic Definition of Predation: Pricing and Product Innovation," 91 Yale LJ 8 (1981).

[143] See Ordover & Willig, "An Economic Definition of Predation: Pricing and Product Innovation," 91 Yale LJ 8 (1981); Sidak, "Debunking Predatory Innovation," 83 Colum. L. Rev. 1121 (1983); Ordover, Sykes & Willig, "Predatory Systems Rivalry: A Reply," 83 Colum. L. Rev. 1150 (1983).

[3] Predisclosure

One risk of applying antitrust law to design changes might be to preclude any such introductions or, at least, to require the basic unit manufacturer to maintain production of the old unit to avoid anticompetitive effects. Unless implemented under carefully defined and limited criteria, either alternative will substantially chill innovative activity.[144] This potential is one explanation for the permissive approach adopted in the case law to this point.

Plaintiffs in antitrust innovation cases have argued for imposition of a less restrictive alternative requiring the dominant firm to make a predisclosure of product plans to competitors.[145] The objective is to permit innovation, but also to allow competing firms an opportunity to adapt their products before substantial market losses occur. A duty of predisclosure has been consistently rejected by U.S. courts even where the innovator is a monopolist in one of the markets involved.[146] In part, this result is due to the fact that in the context of integrated systems, predisclosure does not respond to the antitrust problem involved in redesign of a basic unit. By hypothesis, redesign is anticompetitive only if the design change is not an improvement and there are substantial barriers to competitors remaining in the market or adapting to the new product. Presumably, these barriers would preclude effective response to the predisclosure. As a result, predisclosure would be effective only in cases in which no antitrust issue in fact exists—that is, a superior product or economically acceptable adaptation costs.

In addition, while predisclosure might appear to have minimal impact, it strikes directly against a primary financial incentive for ongoing innovation. Especially where the new product or technology does not qualify for patent or copyright protection, a major financial reward lies in the benefits of the head start that the new product gives to the innovating firm. A duty to disclose would reduce or eliminate this incentive and lessen the pace of innovation.[147] Since even a monopolist has a right to compete through innovation, this result would directly contradict antitrust goals.

---

[144] See Sidak, "Debunking Predatory Innovation," 83 Colum. L. Rev. 1121 (1983).

[145] See Areeda & Turner, *Antitrust Law* ¶ 738.4d; ILC Peripherals Leasing Co. v. IBM Corp., 458 F. Supp. 423 (ND Cal. 1978), aff'd sub nom., Memorex Corp. v. IBM Corp., 636 F2d 1188 (9th Cir. 1980).

[146] See Berkey Photo, Inc. v. Eastman Kodak Co., 603 F2d 263 (2d Cir. 1979).

[147] Id. at 281; see Areeda & Turner, *Antitrust Law* ¶ 738.4d.

¶ 4.10 JOINT VENTURE RESEARCH AND DEVELOPMENT

In one-party innovations, antitrust issues do not focus directly on research and development, but on the impact of new product introductions. In contrast, research and development involving two or more entities present direct antitrust issues. Joint research involves a combination of commercial parties for at least a portion of their business operations. Combined or joint activity has historically been more suspect under antitrust laws than individual conduct.[148]

The relationship between antitrust policy and joint venture research has been controversial for a number of years. Although there are a few reported decisions, antitrust considerations have been a major factor in designing joint research programs where the participants have more than a de minimis share of the market to which the research is directed.[149] In many cases, the influence of perceived antitrust liability has negatively affected the decision to join resources for research and development or, at least, altered the manner in which the joint activity was undertaken.

In 1984, Congress enacted legislation that exempted joint research and development ventures from aspects of antitrust liability and defined the standard required to establish antitrust liability as a rule of reason analysis.[150] The National Cooperative Research Act of 1984 (Cooperative Research Act) was intended to substantially reduce the perceived and actual antitrust barriers to collaborative research and to remove any international competitive disadvantages.

[1] Rule of Reason or Per Se Tests

The impact of antitrust on joint venture research is determined in part by the standard of review applied. In essence, the choice is between tests that apply per se liability based on the inherently anticompetitive nature of the activity or a rule of reason that examines the purpose and effect of the conduct. Historically, the choice between these standards involves an assessment of the degree to which the alleged activity clearly violates competitive norms or, in the alternative, has a justifiable, procompetitive impact.

---

[148] See Monsanto Co. v. Spray-Rite Serv. Corp., 104 S. Ct. 1464 (1984).

[149] See HR Rep. No. 656, 98th Cong. 11–12 (1984); S. Rep. No. 427, 98th Cong. (1984).

[150] Pub. L. No. 98-462 (1984); reported at Cong. Rec. H.9939 (Sept. 21, 1984).

Joint ventures involve several distinct antitrust issues. Initially, there is a potential of collusive activity among the participating firms.[151] Collusion consists of a tendency to cooperate, rather than compete, and may relate to the subject matter of the joint program or may encompass spillover effects resulting from cooperation established in one context being extended to others. However, collusion is or can be merely a relabeling of joint involvement or cooperation. As a consequence, this issue often entails an assessment of the need for or purpose of the joint program and of the extent to which information exchange and other mutual agreements extend beyond this core.

A second antitrust risk concerns potential direct effects on competition.[152] Competition may relate to end product markets or to research and development itself. The peculiar character of a joint research venture is that it may both add and detract from competitive activity. Two competing firms may forego independent research programs, but a new, joint entity is created. Balancing these competing effects is central to antitrust law. The existence of competing effects in itself distinguishes joint ventures from mergers or acquisitions. Unlike in the latter, the creation of new competitive capability is inherent in the idea of a joint venture.

Finally, joint venture programs may involve a risk of market exclusion or joint control of access to injure nonparticipating companies.[153] Joint refusal to deal is an antitrust violation even in circumstances in which individual firms may be individually free to refuse.[154] The consequences or risks of joint action to exclude others increase as the joint actors control a greater share of significant, competitive resources.

In contrast to these risks, it is clear that joint venture research has a number of advantages over the counterpart of individual entities pursuing independent research programs. In part, these relate to the scale of the resources that can be brought to the particular research program. The

---

[151] See Brodley, "Joint Ventures and Antitrust Policy," 95 Harv. L. Rev. 1523, 1530 (1982); Dep't of Justice, *Antitrust Guide Concerning Joint Venture Research* (1980).

[152] Brodley, "Joint Ventures and Antitrust Policy," 95 Harv. L. Rev. 1532; Dep't of Justice, *Antitrust Guide Concerning Joint Venture Research* 3 (1980). To the extent inconsistent with the legislative record involved in the Cooperative Research Act of 1984, the provisions in this Department of Justice policy manual have been superseded.

[153] See Berkey Photo, Inc. v. Eastman Kodak Co., 603 F2d 263, 301 (2d Cir. 1979); see also United States v. Realty Multi-List, Inc., 629 F2d 1351 (5th Cir. 1980).

[154] See Monsanto Co. v. Spray-Rite Serv. Corp., 104 S. Ct. 1464 (1984); Brodley, "Joint Ventures and Antitrust Policy," 95 Harv. L. Rev. 1523, 1534 (1982).

joining of resources in a joint venture obviously responds to the possibility that the individual companies would be unable to act independently.[155] Similarly, even if financial resources exist, relevant technical expertise may be insufficient to accommodate the work. A joint venture may be an effective alternative to one firm purchasing or hiring such additional expertise. Finally, even if a single entity might be able to conduct the research itself, a joint program may speed both the work effort and the rate at which research results are disseminated and used.[156]

Even under prior law, these considerations justify a flexible rule of reason analysis and indicate that the antitrust posture should be permissive, especially for ventures involving basic research separate from product development and marketing.[157] The Cooperative Research Act clarified the approach under which joint venture research and development is examined. It provides that in any action under federal antitrust laws or any similar state laws, no joint research and development venture shall be deemed per se illegal.[158] Instead, antitrust liability for such ventures must be tested under a rule of reason. Furthermore, the legislative history of the Cooperative Research Act makes clear an intent that the rule of reason standard be applied in light of an extensive congressional commentary favorable to joint research in the conference committee report dealing with this act.[159]

[2] Detrebling of Damages

The Cooperative Research Act did not totally exempt research joint ventures from antitrust liability, but does reduce perceived and actual antitrust liability risk. Given the preexisting legal environment, it is arguable that express adoption of a rule of reason test has more of a psychological than substantive role in encouraging joint research.[160] In contrast, a second aspect of the Cooperative Research Act provides significant insulation against antitrust risks.

---

[155] See Areeda & Turner, *Antitrust Law* ¶ 703; Brodley, "Joint Ventures and Antitrust Policy," 95 Harv. L. Rev. 1523, 1570 (1982).

[156] See Areeda & Turner, *Antitrust Law* ¶ 703; Brodley, "Joint Ventures and Antitrust Policy," 95 Harv. L. Rev. 1523, 1571–1573 (1982).

[157] Dep't of Justice, *Antitrust Guide Concerning Joint Venture Research* 3 (1980); Brodley, "Joint Ventures and Antitrust Policy," 95 Harv. L. Rev. 1523, 1571–1573 (1982).

[158] The Cooperative Research Act § 3.

[159] HR Rep. No. 98-1044, at Cong. Rec. H.9941 (Sept. 21, 1984).

[160] HR Rep. No. 656, 98th Cong. 11–12 (1984); S. Rep. No. 427, 98th Cong. 2–4 (1984).

A significant aspect of antitrust enforcement is in the availability of treble damage awards in private antitrust actions. Such damage awards create substantial deterrence effects and are intended to provide incentive for private actions that enforce antitrust norms. Prior to 1984, treble damage provisions were a major element determining the impact of antitrust law on joint venture research. The Cooperative Research Act provides for a detrebling of damages in selected cases. Section 4 of this act provides that notwithstanding provisions of the Clayton Act or similar state law, treble damages are not available against joint venture research as defined in the Cooperative Research Act if the parties to the research venture comply with a notification procedure established by the Cooperative Research Act. While the threat of antitrust liability remains, this provision substantially alters the degree of risk and the likelihood of private actions against the venture.

This statute is in the nature of a safe-harbor provision. Statutory insulation from treble damages applies to any conduct that is "within the scope" of notifications that are provided for and given under the Cooperative Research Act.[161] The procedures for notice permit any party to a joint research and development venture to file notice with the Department of Justice and the Federal Trade Commission (FTC) on behalf of the venture. The notification to these federal agencies must be filed within 90 days after the parties enter into a written agreement to form the venture.[162] It is to be relatively limited in content and need only contain the identities of the parties and disclosure of the nature and objectives of the venture. The Cooperative Research Act provides for updating the notification no later than 90 days after any change in the membership of the venture.

The "guiding principle is that R&D conduct within the scope of a . . . venture is never subject to more than actual damage recovery where there is compliance" with the notification procedures.[163] The federal agencies to which notification is provided play a ministerial role in this process. They do not engage in a substantive review and are not given authority to deny protection to joint ventures for which adequate notification is provided.

The notification to the federal agencies by the parties to the venture leads to a published notice in the Federal Register. The Cooperative Research Act requires publication within 30 days after the notification is received by the Attorney General or the FTC. The detrebling protection

---

[161] The Cooperative Research Act § 4.

[162] Id. at § 5(b)(c).

[163] HR Rep. No. 98-1044, at Cong. Rec. H.9942 (Sept. 21, 1984).

provided in the Cooperative Research Act attaches at the point of publication. If no publication occurs within the 30-day period, the protection attaches from the time that the notification was given to the government.

The damage limitations under the Cooperative Research Act apply to any conduct within the scope of notification given to the governmental agencies. Obviously, this provision has not been subject to judicial interpretation. Arguably, the reference to the scope of the notification suggests an intention to require relatively elaborate or detailed disclosure that can be compared to particular challenged conduct. In fact, the legislative history of the Cooperative Research Act indicates that detailed specification of included activity is not required. Instead, unless otherwise excluded, congressional reports indicate that the venture notification is assumed to encompass all of the types of activity defined as ordinarily included within the definition of a joint research and development venture by Section 2 of the Cooperative Research Act. Only a general notification is required. The protected scope of the detrebling provision is broadly applicable within the particular subject of the research and development venture.

[3] Scope of the Research Venture

A wide variety of activity might be included in the concept of "joint research and development." While the Cooperative Research Act insulates joint research and development, it does not broadly validate all joint ventures under antitrust laws.[164] Accordingly, the scope of application of the Cooperative Research Act is significant and identifies the type of activity incorporated under the label of research and development and included in the congressional policy to encourage and facilitate joint action.

A determination that joint conduct or agreements are within the Cooperative Research Act's definition of joint venture research triggers several distinct results. For antitrust liability in all cases, the Cooperative Research Act requires application of rule of reason rather than any per se illegality analysis. If there has been compliance with notification procedures, the Cooperative Research Act insulates the activity from treble damage awards if it is found to be illegal. In practice, this may lead to virtually complete protection from antitrust liability. In concept, however, even if the conduct is within the Cooperative Research Act, an antitrust liability risk remains. Even for this residual risk, however, the fact that particular conduct is within the Cooperative Research Act definition

---

[164] See The Cooperative Research Act § 2(b); HR Rep. No. 98-1044, at Cong. Rec. H.9941 (Sept. 21, 1984).

suggests relevant inferences as to whether or not antitrust liability should be imposed.

Several approaches might be used to distinguish between protected and potentially illicit actions in joint research. Variations in potential definition involve two factors. The first focuses on the principle aim and intended immediacy of the commercial benefits from the research. This entails a distinction between basic research and applied research or product development. Since basic research is substantially more removed from competitive markets, it represents a lesser risk of restraining competition than does applied research and development. In basic research unconnected to product development or marketing, antitrust concerns relate solely to effects on research competition.[165] While some level of competition or potential competition is conducive to more active and effective basic research,[166] the relationship is less clear than in other business areas.[167] As a consequence, pure basic research ventures have never been challenged.[168] In contrast, as the joint venture encompasses more applied developmental or distribution activity, the level of antitrust risk increases. A research venture to develop *and* jointly market a product does not only affect research competition, but also entails antitrust risks related to marketing.

The second factor focuses on the secondary restraints placed on participants in the joint venture.[169] In most cases, the restraints placed on the parties parallel their view of the objectives of the venture. A basic research venture commonly involves few restraints on marketing and presents little antitrust risk for *both* reasons. Conversely, an applied research venture may attempt to bind the parties to a preagreed marketing format that might be separately viewed as an antitrust violation involving, for example, an improper apportioning of a market or a joint refusal to deal. Arguably, the fact that the restrictions are linked to research is not relevant unless they are objectively necessary to the research program. The alternative view is that the research goal provides

---

[165] See Brodley, "Joint Ventures and Antitrust Policy," 95 Harv. L. Rev. 1523, 1572 (1982).

[166] See Turner, "Patents, Antitrust and Innovation," 28 U. Pitt. L. Rev. 151 (1966); Ginsburg, *Antitrust, Uncertainty and Technological Innovation* 8 (1980).

[167] Ginsburg, *Antitrust, Uncertainty and Technological Innovation* 9–19 (1980); Hay & Morris, *Industrial Economics* 454–464 (1979).

[168] See Department of Justice, *Antitrust Guide Concerning Joint Venture Research* 2 (1980).

[169] See Louis, "Restraints Ancillary to Joint Ventures in Licensing Agreements: Do Sealy and Topco Logically Survive Sylvania and Broadcast Music?" 66 Va. L. Rev. 879 (1908); McCracken, "Joint Ventures: Evaluating the Risk Under Existing Antitrust Laws," 1 Comp. Law. 12 (1984).

at least a partial justification for secondary restrictions or that protecting the marketing agreements is necessary to provide practical incentives for joint research ventures.

The definition of joint research and development venture in Section 2 of the Cooperative Research Act incorporates the foregoing factors. The legislative history of this act makes clear that there is no intent to insulate peripheral or unrelated restraints imposed on venture participants through the venture. However, this result is balanced against a desire to provide clear and clearly perceived protection for research ventures to encourage this form of activity. This primary goal is implemented under provisions that extend protection beyond basic research to incorporate a full range of research, development, and marketing for subject matter developed within the research venture.

The Cooperative Research Act adopts a subject matter test for including conduct and agreements in the protection applicable to joint venture research. The Cooperative Research Act expressly incorporates basic research defined as "theoretical analysis, experimentation [and] development or testing of basic engineering techniques," as well as the exchange of research information.[170] It also includes applied research in the extension of findings or theory into practical applications for demonstration purposes. Finally, and potentially most significant, a joint research venture also incorporates and provides protection for the prosecution of patent applications and joint licensing of the products of the venture.

This definition adopts a broad subject matter view of joint venture research. Most actions related to the creation, testing, and licensing of technology are protected if linked to a joint venture. The legislative history of the Cooperative Research Act suggests that joint marketing of products is customarily within the venture protection. This result applies regardless of whether or not extension of joint control to marketing was objectively necessary to the creation of the joint venture.

In contrast, Section 2(b) of the Cooperative Research Act expressly excludes various joint actions that do not directly relate to the subject matter of the venture. For example, the basic definition excludes actions involving exchange of cost, profitability, or other information among competitors not reasonably required to achieve the joint research and development objective. Similarly, agreements that restrict or control production or marketing of products or technology not developed in the venture are excluded from protection. Agreements that restrict sale, license,

---

[170] The Cooperative Research Act § 2.

or exchange of inventions or developments not developed in the venture are also excluded.

The definitions are practically and conceptually significant. They provide an express indication of the constituent features of a protected research and development venture. While compliance with the Cooperative Research Act does not totally insulate from antitrust liability,it creates a substantially reduced level of risk that in many cases is commercially acceptable to parties contemplating a joint venture. The Cooperative Research Act definitions provide a drafting guide in formulating a proposed venture.

[4] Rule of Reason Standards

Even prior to the enactment of the Cooperative Research Act, there was relatively little reported litigation concerning research and development joint ventures.[171] The Cooperative Research Act and, especially, the exclusion of treble damages makes it even more unlikely that significant challenges will arise regarding joint venture research and development. Nevertheless, it is important to examine the standards of review under a rule of reason analysis in light of the Cooperative Research Act and prior case law.

In this regard, perhaps to a greater extent than in any other recent federal legislation, congressional documentation concerning the Cooperative Research Act was intended to provide express guidance to the courts in rule of reason analyses regarding joint venture research. Indeed, the conference committee report regarding the Cooperative Research Act admittedly goes beyond mere explanation of the statute and incorporates a wide discussion of appropriate standards for the rule of reason approach. "By providing guidance to the courts and the general public in Section 3 [of the Act] and in [the conference] report, the conferees seek to remove any misperception and thereby encourage the formation of lawful ventures."[172]

[a] Research and Other Relevant Markets

The basic thrust of the Cooperative Research Act as outlined in the conference report is an express recognition that joint venture research has procompetitive effects that must be considered in applying antitrust standards. The standard of review suggested was that if "a joint R&D pro-

---

[171] See Brodley, "Joint Ventures and Antitrust Policy," 95 Harv. L. Rev. 1523, 1572 (1982).

[172] HR Rep. No. 98-1044, at Cong. Rec. H.9941 (Sept. 21, 1984).

gram has no anticompetitive effects or if any such effects are outweighed by its procompetitive effects, then it should not be deemed to violate the antitrust laws."[173] The initial analysis in this standard is an identification of the competitive market in which the research and development venture functions.

Depending on the structure of the joint venture, the pertinent markets for examining competitive effects will necessarily vary. Importantly, however, the analysis is not limited to commercial markets defined in terms of the sale or marketing of products. As noted in Section 3 of the Cooperative Research Act, "properly defined, relevant research and development markets" are pertinent. The premise is that no antitrust problem arises for research unless the joint program substantially reduces competitive research.

An appropriate definition of a research and development market is not always readily obtained. It is not clear that the definition is necessarily limited to entities currently in competition for *products*. The conference report suggests a standard oriented to the ability and incentive of firms to engage in particular *research*.

> To be included in the relevant R&D market, firms must have the ability and incentive, either individually or in collaboration . . . to undertake R&D comparable to that of the joint venture. . . . [Ability] and incentive are measured by an objective standard. Central to evaluating these factors are a firm's business objectives, facilities, technologies and other available assets. Firms need not be actual competitors at the production or marketing stage. Market shares in existing markets [are] not determinative.[174]

The conference report emphasizes that due to the mobile nature of knowledge and the relevance of international competition, overseas "R&D competitors will usually be significant factors in properly" defined markets.

If the joint venture extends beyond pure research, additional markets must be considered. For example, in a venture that includes joint marketing, the relevant market for the product or technology is pertinent, rather than simply the research and development market. A venture that has no anticompetitive impact on an R&D market may have a significant impact on the resulting product market.

If a relevant market is identified, there are further questions related to the relationship of the parties within that market. As applied to

---

[173] HR Rep. No. 98-1044, at Cong. Rec. H. 9941 (Sept. 21, 1984).
[174] Id.

research and development markets, one issue focuses on the competitive relationship of the participants in the joint venture and the characteristics of other firms in the market. A joint undertaking by firms who are not in direct competition or substantially likely to become competitors[175] involves no significant impact on competitive research.[176] In fact, this form of joint activity is an optimal bringing together of diverse skills. Nevertheless, under the standards suggested in the conference report, a reference to product competition is misplaced, since the appropriate inquiry focuses on firms that have the ability and incentive to participate in research ventures.

The mere fact that the venture involves actual competitors does not result in an antitrust prohibition under rule of reason analyses. One approach to determining the validity of agreements among competitors focuses on the size and market power of the parties. A venture among firms that have a sufficiently small market share or limited power such that an actual merger would be allowed will not violate antitrust norms; "absent unreasonably restrictive collateral restraints, such ventures are presumptively lawful."[177]

Antitrust concerns increase if the venture includes participants with substantial market shares pertaining to the likely end products of the research and development.[178] However, even if the market share of the venturers is large, there may be no antitrust objection *to the research element* in the absence of restrictive collateral provisions. The clearest instance is where a number of competitors or potential competitors are capable of similar research and, especially, where such research is already underway. The degree of research market concentration and the existence or absence of substantial barriers to beginning research are relevant. In the context of low barriers to begin research, the joint program may in fact enhance research competition. In contrast, assuming high barriers to research activity, a joint project may effectively reduce the number of competitors and, at least on a preliminary basis, raise an antitrust issue. Even then, the procompetitive effects of the venture must be weighted against the potential reduction in research competition.[179]

---

[175] See United States v. Penn-Olin Chem. Co., 378 US 158 (1964).

[176] See 3 Areeda & Turner, *Antitrust Law* ¶ 703(c).

[177] Department of Justice, *Antitrust Guide Concerning Joint Venture Research* 7 (1980).

[178] See Turner, "Patents, Antitrust and Innovation," 28 U. Pitt. L. Rev. 151, 158–59 (1966); Sullivan, *Handbook of the Law of Antitrust* 298–303 (1970); Berkey Photo, Inc. v. Eastman Kodak Co., 603 F2d 263, 301 (2d Cir. 1979).

[179] HR Rep. No. 98-1044, at Cong. Rec. H.9941 (Sept. 21, 1984).

A potential for a reduction in research competition does not necessarily preclude the project under antitrust law, since "cooperation . . . limited to research does not eliminate a firm from the marketplace [and] may even promote a more competitive market . . . by [providing] new goods or services that" would not otherwise have been developed.[180] In this context, however, there may be a more particularistic analysis of the research activities. A central factor is that only an unjustified, substantial impact on research competition should be barred under antitrust law.

One issue is whether the companies would have been able to conduct the research independently. If the parent firms are not otherwise able to do the research, the joint project adds to, rather than detracts from, the competitive pool. In contrast, a joining of independently capable firms may be unjustified if it has a substantial, adverse impact on research competition. Similarly, the capability of the remaining nonparticipants to conduct similar research independently or cooperatively is pertinent. This, of course, is a direct measure of the effect of the venture on research competition.

If there is a definable effect on competition, additional issues arise about the scope and duration of the research venture. "Scope" in this sense means both the number or variety of research issues and the extent to which participation in the venture is industry-wide. A venture encompassing all or most research questions in the industry and involving industry-wide participation is susceptible to antitrust objection. The effect substantially reduces incentive for independent creativity among participants who simply draw from a common pool.

In the computer industry, these standards interact to the effect that few if any research ventures will involve antitrust violations due to their impact on research competition. For software development, entry barriers to research are low and the number of participating companies in the industry is high. The risk of substantially reducing research competition is low in an environment dependent on product development.

The greatest antitrust issues arise for large hardware systems, microprocessors, robotics, and the like where research activity is characterized by substantial capital requirements. In this environment, joint ventures among a number of major participants may raise some concern since the number of potential and actual competitors is relatively low. The analysis of any such ventures may vary over time. At this writing, however, viewed as an *international* market, the number of participants and the intensity of research competition indicate that all but the broadest ventures neverthe-

---

[180] Department of Justice, *Antitrust Guide Concerning Joint Venture Research* 8 (1980).

less leave significant, competitive forces in the marketplace. This is particularly true for basic issues, rather than product development.

[b] Secondary Restrictions

Especially after the enactment of the Cooperative Research Act, the
central consideration in antitrust law as applied to research joint ventures
is to recognize the distinction between the research itself and the related
restraints or obligations that the venture agreement imposes on participants. There is an antitrust interest in promoting research competition
that is consistent with joint research ventures. In many cases, joint
research is more effective than independent work. Beyond the interest in
effective research, however, there are clear antitrust risks in joint action
that extend beyond the research activities. In many joint ventures, these
are the crux of the antitrust problem. The research itself is not anticompetitive, but the additional restraints may be anticompetitive. In discussing
secondary restraints, even assuming the core objective of encouraging
joint venture research, there are critical questions about the extent to
which this objective requires acceptance of other restrictive behavior by
the parties. The issue is how far should the law go in validating joint
action associated with joint research and development?

Secondary restraints can be usefully divided into three general categories for discussion. The first concerns the exchange of information
and proprietary rights. In a joint research venture some such exchanges
are essential to the research. For example, in developing a new concept
of data processing software, two firms might reasonably cross-license
use of their own proprietary products for research purposes and
exchange data derived from prior or parallel work on the same issue.
Generally, such necessary exchanges of information and rights raise no
antitrust issue beyond that present for the research activity. Indeed, the
exchanges are an inherent part of the research.[181] In any joint venture,
there is a risk that legitimate core purposes may be used or may
develop into a context for broader, collusive activity. As exchanged
information or rights extend beyond those necessary for the research,
they entail increased antitrust risk. Illustrative are sharing of production costs or other business information not pertinent to particular
research or an agreement to license all patents or copyrights including
those not developed in or necessary to the research venture.[182] These

---

[181] See United States v. Realty Multi-List, Inc., 629 F2d 1351 (5th Cir.
1980).

[182] See, e.g., Department of Justice, *Antitrust Guide to International Operations* 20 (1977).

collateral restraints do not violate antitrust law in all cases, but their legality is not tied to the research venture. It must, instead, be assessed for more general antitrust doctrine.

This distinction between necessary sharing and potentially illicit exchanges is recognized with the Cooperative Research Act definition of joint research. Section 2 expressly includes the "collection, exchange, and analysis of research information" in the protected joint venture activities. However, the Cooperative Research Act excludes protection for exchange of information about cost, profitability, and the like to the extent that it is not reasonably required to conduct the research venture. Similarly excluded are agreements restricting sale, licensing, and sharing of inventions unrelated to the venture. The objective is to exclude the areas of the highest risk of spillover into collusive activity.[183]

The second category of restrictions involves marketing or exploitation of the products of the joint research and development. Agreements for joint marketing involve greater antitrust risk than agreements permitting separate marketing. This is particularly true if the venture involves participants with significant market power in the market for the resulting product. Joint agreement on marketing is an antitrust problem independent of the research involvement. While an individual firm may refuse to deal with another company, a joint refusal or boycott may be a per se antitrust violation.[184] As a result, agreements giving each party a right to veto licensing any nonparticipant may be suspect.[185]

Information sharing and marketing restraints in a research venture have never been treated as per se invalid, but are justifiable based on the legitimate research purpose only if they are closely related to that purpose. The distinction is commonly described in terms of ancillary and collateral restraints.[186] A restraint that is collateral to the legitimate research purpose must be justified on its own terms.[187] In contrast, a restraint or obligation that is inherent (ancillary) in the research

---

[183] HR Rep. No. 98-1044, at Cong. Rec. H.9941 (Sept. 21, 1984).

[184] See Monsanto Co. v. Spray-Rite Serv. Corp., 104 S. Ct. 1464 (1984); United States v. Krasnov, 143 F. Supp. 184 (ED Pa. 1956), aff'd, 355 US 5 (1957).

[185] See, e.g., Associated Press v. United States, 326 US 1 (1945); United States v. Topco Assoc., Inc., 405 US 596 (1972).

[186] See Brodley, "Joint Ventures and Antitrust Policy," 95 Harv. L. Rev. 1523, 1543 (1982); Louis, "Restraints Ancillary to Joint Ventures in Licensing Agreements: Do Sealy and Topco Logically Survive Sylvania and Broadcast Music?" 66 Va. L. Rev. 879 (1908); McCracken, "Joint Ventures: Evaluating the Risk Under Existing Antitrust Laws," 1 Comp. Law. 12 (1984).

[187] See Timken Roller Bearing Co. v. United States, 341 US 593, 598 (1981).

venture is supported by that research purpose unless it is excessively broad.[188]

In this regard, the Cooperative Research Act suggests a potentially significant shift of analysis as applied to joint venture research. Section 2 of this act protects joint agreements for the granting of licenses on the products or technology of the venture. The scope of a research venture is ordinarily presumed to encompass joint marketing of results even if this entails more than licensing the technology. As a result, the rule of reason analysis and antitrust risk is limited not merely to secondary, nonresearch restraints, but only to those secondary restraints that extend beyond the products of the venture.

[c] Access and Participation

A third category of restriction involves third-party access to the joint venture and its results. Especially if proprietary property rights emerge from the joint research, some access questions parallel issues concerning marketing and other secondary restraints. From an antitrust perspective, individual control of the intellectual property is optimal, while joint marketing characterized by veto power creates antitrust liability.

Beyond joint marketing, access involves a tension between two competing antitrust concerns. The first originates in cases involving joint control of materials or services essential to competitive involvement in a market.[189] If the services are essential, the joint controllers of the service may have an obligation to provide access to competitors on reasonable terms even though an individual firm would not have this obligation. This concept is relatively clear in cases of tangible bottlenecks, but is less clearly applicable to research. Nevertheless, it has been argued that where the research is not "practicably or effectively duplicable by the excluded firms, access to the venture [or its results] may be mandated."[190] In contrast, there is a possibility that access must be limited in order to avoid anticompetitive effects. This arises because industry-wide cooperation may substantially lessen research competition. A joint venture that is freely available to all participants in the industry and that encompasses a

---

[188] See Broadcast Music, Inc. v. Columbia Broadcasting Sys., Inc., 441 US 1 (1979); United States v. Realty Multi-List, Inc., 629 F2d 1351 (5th Cir. 1980).

[189] See United States v. Terminal Ry. Ass'n, 224 US 383 (1912); Associated Press v. United States, 326 US 1 (1945); Silver v. New York Stock Exchange, 373 US 341 (1963); United States v. Realty Multi-List, Inc., 629 F2d 1351 (5th Cir. 1980).

[190] See Department of Justice, *Antitrust Guide Concerning Joint Venture Research* 21 (1980).

substantial range of the research issues pertinent to that industry presents a substantial antitrust risk.

Although not directly covered in the Cooperative Research Act, the legislative discussion of this act indicates that the critical problem in reference to access is in avoiding excessive, rather than too limited, entry into the joint venture. The conference report notes that the "greatest potential for harm to R&D competition exists when a joint R&D venture is overly inclusive."[191] A significant benefit of excluding some firms lies in the fact that competing research is made more likely. The conference report notes that one standard for legality of a joint venture is the existence or potential for competing research. A decision to exclude some competitors does not injure research competition if a potential for competitive research exists. In contrast, joint venture provisions that provide for access by all other firms in the field are suspect and are justified only if costs, scope limitations, or other factors make them necessary or desirable.

Access issues require close analysis. This is another context in which research elements should be distinguished from other features of a joint venture. As to research activities, access is not required unless nonparticipants are unable to mount similar research. Of course, however, if such inability exists, the venture entails significant antitrust risk. Access may be a method for permitting the combined work while minimizing anticompetitive effects. In contrast, if a proprietary product arises, the issue is less a question of access and more a question of joint marketing. If the parties desire to retain joint control of a patent or copyright that is essential to competing in the industry over the long term, there may be an obligation to license to others on reasonable terms.

[d] Joint Ventures and Monopolists

A legitimate joint research effort may circumstantially elevate to an antitrust violation. This is especially true if one of the participants is a monopolist in the market to which the research pertains. This point is illustrated in *Berkey Photo, Inc. v. Eastman Kodak Co.,*[192] one of the few cases dealing with joint research and development. A major thrust of *Berkey* concerned innovation in an integrated systems environment. However, *Berkey* also involved two joint development projects concerning flash camera products. In both of these projects, Kodak was approached by an independent company with a flash device to be used on Kodak cameras. In the first case, Kodak and Sylvania executed a development

---

[191] HR Rep. No. 98-1044, at Cong. Rec. H.9941 (Sept. 21, 1984).

[192] 603 F2d 263 (2d Cir. 1979).

agreement with covenants of nondisclosure. Kodak introduced the camera and flash cube system three years later. In the second project, Kodak received a proposal from General Electric (GE) for a different flash system. To avoid simultaneous introduction of two new systems, Kodak encouraged GE but did not execute an agreement for several years. When the agreement was signed, it provided for nondisclosure and led to a product introduction two and one-half years later. The appellate court affirmed the jury conclusion that this course of conduct constituted an unreasonable restraint of trade.

Two characteristics of the case were central to this result. First, Kodak occupied a monopoly position in the relevant markets. As a result, although neither GE nor Sylvania were direct competitors, Kodak's market control created a substantial potential for exclusion of competing development projects. In essence, the GE and Sylvania proposals were unlikely to have been made to other camera manufacturers and were not so made. Similarly, other manufacturers may have lacked independent development potential. As a result, the nondisclosure provisions in the development contracts excluded competitors. Second, the evidence supported the fact that Kodak used its position and the agreements to delay development of the new system, creating a sequential introduction that maximized its profits. For the GE proposal, the court noted

> Kodak did not wish to introduce two new flash systems at the same time.... The jury's verdict could reflect its belief that Kodak embarked on a carefully balanced campaign. Kodak desired to cool GE's ardor . . . sufficiently to delay introduction . . . for several years, and, at the same time, to avoid the appearance of deferment so that [GE] would not seek another camera maker.[193]

Viewed in these terms, Kodak's conduct before and during the joint venture could not be justified by a general social interest in innovation, since Kodak's conduct actually delayed innovation.

The court in *Berkey* noted that joint venture research involving a monopolist is not per se an antitrust violation. However, such activity is subject to closer scrutiny than are ventures not involving a monopolist.[194] In *Berkey*, this scrutiny included an examination of the purpose in creating the venture and the monopolist's conduct in the project. Close scrutiny of delay would be inappropriate in cases involving less extreme market power or research and development less closely connected to an identifiable product. Absent its market power, Kodak's effort to delay and orchestrate product introduction would be ineffective. Other firms

---

[193] Id. at 300.
[194] Id. at 303.

would be capable of independent development. Similarly, to the extent that more basic research is involved, delays are an inherent risk in the undertaking and are not anticompetitive.

In each of these situations, the antitrust risk must be balanced against the effect on innovation of subjecting joint ventures to closer scrutiny. In the absence of monopoly characteristics, this balance weighs against close review of the purpose and conduct of the venture. The potential benefits of joint research in a nonmonopolized market outweigh the harm caused by potential delay. The market characteristics themselves eliminate or, at least, substantially reduce the potential for delay.

PART D.   TAXATION AND INNOVATION

¶ 4.11   RESEARCH AND RESOURCE EXPENDITURES

Beyond joint ownership doctrine and antitrust restrictions, the pace of technical innovation and the scope of investment in innovation are related to questions about the federal tax consequences of actions pertaining to technology development. The impact of tax laws on innovation is both more direct and more pervasive than is the impact of other fields of law. Federal tax provisions have a direct impact on balance sheets and financial projections central to the initiation and maintenance of programs for ongoing technical development. Indeed, especially for the use of research and development partnerships, it is clear that tax considerations often play a major role in determining the manner in which developmental work is conducted.

As indicated previously in the discussion of the antitrust implications of joint venture research, there is an increasing congressional recognition that the federal government should play a role in creating incentives for innovation and removing preexisting, nonessential barriers. This same perspective applies to federal tax policy. There are clear manifestations within the federal tax code documenting a federal effort to formulate tax policy to encourage innovation and research and development. Nevertheless, especially in technology related to computer software, the implementation of this policy has been halting and uncertain.

[1] Depreciation and Investment Property

The Internal Revenue Code contains generally applicable provisions for deduction of depreciation[195] of tangible property and for investment

---

[195] IRC § 168.

tax credits (ITC)[196] associated with the acquisition of tangible assets for use in a business. For depreciation, prior law provided for deductions over a period of time generally reflecting the useful life of tangible property. Under more recent federal tax legislation, an accelerated cost recovery system has been instituted with specific time periods for depreciation assigned to particular property without necessary reference to the actual or predicted useful life.[197]

The ITC is computed as a percentage of the acquisition cost of a tangible asset and is available as a credit against tax liability in the year of acquisition of the asset. The percentage allowed to be taken depends on the recovery time period allotted for depreciation purposes.[198] The total ITC is also subject to various limitations based on the overall tax liability of the business claiming the credit. If the applicable asset is sold by the taxpayer prior to the expiration of the applicable period for depreciating the value, a portion of the tax benefit from the credit is subject to recapture.[199]

In broad terms, these provisions encourage asset acquisition and replacement as well as recognize the economic reality that the value of assets decreases over a period of use. They apply to tangible property. As a result, computer hardware is clearly encompassed within depreciation and ITC provisions. In general, most hardware will fall within the cost recovery category creating a five-year recovery period. However, a special exception exists for hardware used "in connection with research and experimentation."[200] Reflecting the enhanced need that often exists to maintain state of the art equipment for this purpose, the recovery period is specified to be three years. While the inclusion of hardware within depreciation and ITC rules is clear, substantial uncertainty exists for computer software. In general, the problems relate to the characterization of software for federal tax purposes. ITC and depreciation rules generally apply only to tangible property. Arguably, at least, software is an intangible. As a result, the availability of depreciation or ITC benefits is not uniformly recognized.

The result of this uncertainty is that the tax treatment of software acquired by a taxpayer may depend on the manner in which the acquisition occurred. In general, software is treated as an intangible, the cost of which may be subject to amortization "ratably over a period of five

---

[196] IRC § 46(c).
[197] IRC § 168(c)(2).
[198] IRC § 46(c)(7).
[199] IRC § 47(a)(5).
[200] IRC § 168(c)(2)(A).

years."[201] In contrast, however, where the software is acquired with hardware and the price is not separately stated, the entire cost is depreciable under appropriate rules.[202] Software acquired alone is not covered by the ITC.

[2] Research and Experimentation Expenses

While depreciation and ITC provisions are significant, a more direct impact on innovation involves federal tax treatment of research and experimental expenses relating to computer technology. The nature of this treatment has been controversial, especially for computer software expenditures. The issues do not focus on whether research and experimental expenditures are appropriate or whether the costs will eventually be considered in computing tax liability. Rather, the concerns center around two distinct special provisions designed to enhance incentives for research and experimentation.

An initial issue involves the extent to which research and experimental expenditures can be treated as current expenses for purposes of tax deductions in the year incurred. Prior to 1954, research and experimental expenses were required to be capitalized based on the view that they conveyed a long-term benefit to the business.[203] This treatment differed dramatically from other expenditures and tended to defer and reduce tax benefits for research expenses. As a consequence, Section 174 was added to the Internal Revenue Code providing that a taxpayer may elect to treat research and experimental costs in connection with a trade or business as current deductible expenses and not chargeable to the capital account.[204]

Subsequent to the adoption of Section 174, Congress took further action designed to provide incentives for increased research and experimental activity. Section 221 of the Economic Recovery Tax Act of 1981 (ERTA) established a 25 percent tax credit for incremental increases in qualified research expenses.[205] In general, qualified research is to be interpreted as consistent with the interpretation of research and experimental expenses under Section 174, although the ERTA expressly excludes expenditures outside of the United States and expenditures for social science research. It encompasses both certain in-house research and

---

[201] Rev. Proc. 69-21, 1969-2 CB 303.

[202] Id.

[203] See In re Red Star Yeast & Prod. Co., 25 TC 321 (1955).

[204] IRC § 174.

[205] IRC § 44F(a).

contract research expenses conducted by a nonemployee on behalf of the taxpayer.[206]

The tax benefits established by these provisions involve numerous, complex issues. For purposes of this discussion, the primary matters focus on the statutory reference to research and experimental expenses. This phrase is basic to qualifying for either form of special tax treatment. For both the research credit and the provisions of Section 174, the intent is to create special treatment designed to encourage and stimulate socially important activity. The difficulty in applying both provisions involves an underlying uncertainty about the nature of the activity to be encouraged.

The content of research and experimental expenditures was established by the Internal Revenue Service (IRS) in an early regulation under Section 174. That regulation suggested that the term included "research and development costs in the experimental and laboratory sense."[207] As this indicates, the term distinguishes basic development from normal operating expenses. It excludes "ordinary testing or inspection . . . for quality control."[208] Like many legal distinctions, however, distinguishing ordinary testing from research and experimental activity is often difficult.

Recurrent difficulties also arise in distinguishing research and experimental expenditures from costs in the manufacture of a product or asset. The cost of the actual construction or manufacture of a depreciable asset is not deductible under Section 174, while research costs are deductible. At some stage in the move from idea to product or manufactured asset, there is a transformation from research and experimental work to manufacturing expenditures. This distinction has been stated in terms of a transformation from investigation to construction activity. "[It was reasonable] to limit deductions to those expenditures of an investigative nature expended in developing the concept of a model or a product [as compared to] actual construction."[209] A similar distinction is made between experimental expenditures and manufacturing start-up expenses. Here, it is arguable that the scope of experimental work is exceeded when the product is operationally feasible and only economic risks remain in its production.[210]

Research and experimental expenditures include situations in which third-party contractors perform the work, but do not include the pur-

---

[206] IRC § 44F(b)(3).

[207] Treas. Reg. § 1.174-2(a)(1).

[208] Id.

[209] In re Martin Mayrath, 41 US 582 (1964), aff'd, 357 F2d 209 (5th Cir. 1966).

[210] Treas. Reg. § 1.174-2(a).

chase of technology from another.[211] As with other distinctions in this field, in some cases the difference in the two formats is apparent, but in others characterization of the transaction is dependent on the particular facts. The distinction relates to determining which party undertook a risk of failure in the development of new technology. A contract to deliver a product for a specific price is a purchase, but a contract to pay for services applied to a particular task is a research contract even if a product is eventually delivered.[212]

Standards for distinguishing research and experimental expenditures from other expenses have created difficulty for computer software expenses. In an early ruling in 1969, it was concluded that software development costs could be treated as current expenses under "rules similar to those applicable under Section 174."[213] While this implied broad inclusion of software costs in the scope of Section 174, subsequent developments suggest a more limited scope.

In several rulings, the IRS indicated that while some software development costs could be in Section 174, many expenditures would not be included. For example, it was held that a contract for third-party development of custom software was not within Section 174 where "neither the operational feasibility nor the cost . . . were in doubt [and] the only risk borne by the taxpayer was that [the program] would not be a commercial success."[214] In contrast, in a contract for third-party development of software where charges were billed on an hourly basis without any warranty that the contracting party could produce the software, Section 174 was applicable.[215]

There are a number of practical difficulties in implementing Section 174 in a software environment. These are due to the manner in which software is developed and the fact that is often modified while in use. Based in part on these difficulties, in 1982 the IRS issued a proposed regulation that would have substantially limited the extent to which software expenses are within the concept of research and experimental expenditures. The primary concern involved the extent to which software-related expenses could qualify for research credit treatment. The proposed regulation noted

---

[211] Treas. Reg. § 1.174-2(a)(1).

[212] Treas. Reg. § 1.174-2(b)(3).

[213] Rev. Proc. 69-21, 1969-2 CB 303.

[214] LTR 7804007.

[215] LTR 8136024.

> Generally, the costs of developing computer software are not research and experimental expenditures. . . . However . . . Section 174 includes the programming costs . . . incurred for new or significantly improved computer software. [It does not] include . . . development of software the operational feasibility of which is not seriously in doubt. The costs of modifying previously developed computer software . . . do not constitute research or experimental expenditures. [216]

This regulation drew distinctions based on factors related to the quality of a program ("new and significantly improved") or the degree of risk at the outset of the undertaking. While these are not completely inappropriate, they go beyond standards applied to other forms of research and development. They do so in a manner that would severely restrict the application of Section 174 to software. The anomaly, of course, is that there would be a resulting exclusion of a major field of significant research activity. As a result of substantial criticism, the proposed regulation was withdrawn for reconsideration.

¶ 4.12 RESEARCH AND DEVELOPMENT PARTNERSHIPS

As discussed previously for antitrust, there are frequent circumstances in which efficient research and development requires a combination of two or more entities. [217] In many cases, this occurs where the parties have complimentary technical abilities or resources. An alternative motivation for bringing together various entities entails the acquisition of financing for research activities. Obviously, financial support can be obtained from various sources. However, at least since 1974, one significant form of financing involves research and development limited partnerships. The frequency with which this format is used relates in large part to federal tax regulations that enhance the attraction to individual and other investors.

Research and development limited partnerships may be structured in various forms. Common to each, however, is the joining together of investors and research operators. [218] In the most common format, the limited partners are individual or other investors who provide funding for research in return for tax benefits and potential profits deriving from sales or licens-

---

[216] Prop. Treas. Reg. § 1.174-2(a).

[217] See supra ¶ 4.10.

[218] See Garahan, Fuller, Chilton, "Research and Development Limited Partnerships," in PLI Research and Development Limited Partnerships 9, 11 (1983).

ing of any resulting product or technology. The sponsor of the partnership is typically a corporation interested in conducting the particular research or product development. The sponsor provides initial ideas or concepts and, often, key research or development staff. The general partner is most often an affiliate of the sponsor, but may be an independent financial services company or an affiliate of a research contractor.

From the standpoint of the investor-limited partners, the attraction of the research and development partnership lies in the tax benefits and ultimate profit from the partnership product. The tax benefits involve the availability of Section 174 current expense deductions for substantial portions of the partnership expenses. In general, preoperating or start-up expenses of a new business (the partnership) must be capitalized. However, Section 174 provides an exception for research and experimental expenditures. In 1974, this exception was held to apply to start-up partnerships that had not previously engaged in the operation of a business.[219]

While a research and development partnership qualifies for Section 174 treatment, it typically does not qualify for research credits. This is due to the different language of Section 174 and the research credit statute. Section 174 applies to expenditures incurred "in connection with the taxpayer's trade or business." In contrast, the tax credit applies only to incremental expenses incurred in "carrying on" a trade or business and this is intended to exclude start-up operations.[220]

Implicit within most research and development partnerships is not only the expectation of current tax deductions, but the possibility of profit from the developed technology. The eventual transfer of any product rights or technology is commonly prearranged in the initial structure of the partnership with the objective of conveying the technology to the sponsor of the partnership. Ideally, the transfer will involve conveyance of a capital asset with resulting tax benefits. In general, the final conveyance may be in any of four forms: (1) incorporation of the partnership,[221] (2) exchange sale of all rights to patented technology,[222] (3) sale of unpatented technology that constitutes property held for over one year,[223] or (4) sale of partnership assets.[224]

---

[219] Snow v. Comm'r, 416 US 500 (1974).

[220] IRC § 44F.

[221] IRC § 351; see Garahan, Fuller, Chilton, "Research and Development Limited Partnerships," in PLI Research and Development Limited Partnerships 9, 61–88 (1983).

[222] IRC § 1235.

[223] IRC § 1231.

[224] IRC § 741.

PART II

Transactions and Third-Party Liability

PRECEDING CHAPTERS examined ownership and control of intellectual property pertinent to computer technology. An underlying premise of these chapters is that the legal system should encourage and reward technological innovation, but this view can lead to incomplete and potentially contradictory results when all commercial and scientific interests are recognized. Innovation is not typically a unidimensional or isolated activity. Rather, it commonly involves a number of people and businesses functioning either in tandem or in competition. Within the resultingly complex environment, rewarding and encouraging innovation requires a balance of multiple contributions and the recognition that additional, competitive innovations will also demand accommodation.

The following chapters assume that intellectual property rights are vested in one party. The focus is on the implications of transactions with third parties involving technology or information. The desirability of encouraging and rewarding innovation remains relevant. It provides some justification for circumspection in imposing restraints or liability in such transactions, but this justification encounters significant countervailing policies. These involve the desire to protect competitive markets and third-party users or purchasers, creating a climate of reasonable protected reliance to encourage use of technology.

Part II ranges from basic contract law to antitrust and international law. The questions involve the social and personal responsibilities of the person who delivers technology or information in transactions with third parties. The boundaries of the issues vary according to the transaction. For example, the supplier of an electronic database for third-party use may undertake to warrant the accuracy and completeness of the data, but not its relevance to a particular application. Conversely, the software designer who prepares automated programs may have undertaken obligations to warrant both accuracy and suitability for a particular purpose.

In many of the topics considered in this part of the book, computer technology fits smoothly into existing bodies of law. In others, however, the transactions created by the technology represent unique circumstances for which appropriate doctrine is not yet clearly developed and the issue may still be emerging. The purpose of these chapters is to identify those contexts and to suggest directions for coping with the issues that they present.

CHAPTER 5

Technology Licensing

¶ 5.01 INTRODUCTION

Domestic contract issues relating to computer technology involve two major topics: One addresses the quality and performance of the technology and resulting products (discussed in Chapters 6 and 7) and the second concerns restrictions imposed on the recipient of the technology. These restrictions typically are found in licensing agreements, and technology licensing contracts are the focus of this chapter.

Historically, technology licensing contracts have involved transactions among businesses, often in relation to marketing or manufacturing relationships. As a result, the norm in licensing law is to presume a contractual freedom that reflects the relatively equal bargaining power and business expertise of the contracting parties. This contractual freedom is limited by antitrust law and other doctrines that define the range within which intellectual property rights may be used to leverage commercially advantageous business relationships.

Transactions among businesses continue to be the primary context for application of licensing law in the computer industry. Microcomputers and the commercial software industry, however, have interjected licensing law issues into a new, mass-market environment characterized by substantially different technical expertise and bargaining power. Although there is little case law pertinent to licensing in this new environment, the different factual circumstances suggest that different constraints on contractual freedom are relevant. This chapter discusses aspects of traditional and this newer form of technological licensing.

PART A.   GENERAL ISSUES

¶ 5.02 NATURE OF THE TRANSACTION

In discussing technology licensing, it is necessary to distinguish several aspects of the relevant transaction. When a license involves a marketing agreement, for example, the two distinct considerations are (1) the delivery or promise to deliver products from the manufacturer to the marketing agent under terms that may or may not convey ownership of the product; and (2) an agreement by the marketing agent to promote, distribute, or use the product within specified restraints, making payments to the original owner. In practice, these are commonly included in a single agreement and are interdependent. Nevertheless, different legal doctrines apply to each. The first or product element of the agreement commonly involves issues of product quality and ownership resolved under the Uniform Commercial Code (UCC) and related contract or personal property law. The second, distributorship element entails performance issues and restraints often tested under antitrust and related doctrines.

While many transactions in the computer industry involve only these two elements, additional questions arise when intellectual property rights are part of the transaction. These rights create an intangible corpus of the transaction involving exclusive rights and information. The agreement necessarily allocates those rights, and the manner in which this occurs affects both product quality issues and questions relating to the validity of distributorship and use restraints beyond the intellectual property rights involved.

[1] Assignment, License, and Lease

Conveyance of intellectual property rights may be by an assignment or a license. An "assignment" consists of an absolute conveyance of the intangible rights and is analogous to a sale. For statutory forms of intellectual property, assignments may require compliance with registration and other formalities.[1]

In contrast, a "license" is an agreement in the form of permission to practice the technology in a manner that would otherwise be reserved exclusively by the original proprietor.[2] It is governed by general contract law. For example, a patent license might convey a right to use the patented process, while a copyright license might grant the licensee a right to reproduce (copy) the work. While exclusive licenses are common, the normal license transaction conveys less than all of the proprietor's exclusive rights. Restrictions on the licensee might be viewed as reservations in the licensor. Subject to antitrust considerations, these reservations may be premised on a wide variety of factors such as field of use, volume of distribution, or geographic area.

Both an assignment and a license deal with intangible attributes or rights. Depending on the circumstances, they are not necessarily related to the disposition or ownership of tangible property involved in the transaction. Thus, a license is distinguishable from a lease. For example, a proprietor of a copyrighted program might lease or sell a copy of the program to another person but, except for certain statutory limitations, the characterization as a lease or a sale is independent of any license of the copyright owner's exclusive, though intangible, right to reproduce the program. A lease of one copy might be accompanied by a license to reproduce the program in volume for resale or by a more limited license

---

[1] See infra ¶ 5.13[1][b].

[2] See *Deller's Walker on Patents* § 538.

to reproduce solely for archival purposes. Similar alternatives exist if the copy is sold.

[2] Patent and Copyright Licenses

A technology license is one form by which the exclusive rights associated with intellectual property can be conveyed. These exclusive rights for patents and copyrights are enumerated by statute. These rights are divisible in the licensing context in that the copyright or patent owner may selectively license one or several of the enumerated rights without conveying the others. For example, one person may be licensed to reproduce and distribute copies of the copyrighted work, while the right to prepare derivative works may be withheld or conveyed by license to another party.

While the ability to license exclusive rights selectively is inherent in copyright and patent law, in many cases the enumerated categories provide inadequate flexibility for commercial use. As a result, license restrictions commonly do not conform to the basic statutory categories. Thus, the right to use a patented process may be conveyed in several different licenses, each license restricted to a particular field of use or specified geographic area. Depending on the transaction, there may be both a subdivision of the statutory categories and, in other instances, an extension beyond them. Either context raises potential issues as to the enforceability or legality of the license restraint.

The most problematic license provisions are those that effectively extend beyond the scope of the statutory rights. This can occur in a variety of ways. A license to use a patented process might be conditioned on the licensee's use or purchase of nonpatented items. This conditioning or tying leverages intellectual property rights into a market advantage in another commodity or item. It raises severe antitrust issues.[3] A less explicit extension occurs where the license restricts activities that are not within statutory exclusive rights. A copyright license to reproduce copies might also restrict the use of the copies, for instance. Similarly, since a sale of an item (machine or copy) effectively exhausts certain patent or copyright controls as to that item, a license that restricts these uses after a sale in effect extends the patent or copyright beyond the statutory scope.[4]

The fact that a license extends beyond statutory protections does not necessarily imply that the contract is invalid or unenforceable. Especially where the parties have relatively equal bargaining power, the agreement

---

[3] See infra ¶ 5.04.
[4] See United States v. Univis Lens Co., 316 US 241 (1942).

might reasonably be viewed as presumptively valid. This presumption is not consistently applied, however, and such agreements are subject to challenge under antitrust doctrine or related intellectual property law doctrine.

[3] Trade Secret Licenses

Trade secret and industrial know-how licenses are even more common within the computer and other technology fields than are pure patent or copyright licenses. They are often included along with their statutory counterparts in a single licensing transaction. While properly described as technology licenses, trade secret licenses are in fact a very dissimilar type of conveyance. Unlike copyright and patent, trade secret licensing does not consist of granting permission to perform actions otherwise exclusively vested in the proprietor of the secret. The exclusive rights granted by copyright and patent laws have no direct analogies in trade secret doctrine. The trade secret proprietor's rights are premised on reasonably protected secrets disclosed under circumstances establishing expectations of confidentiality. In essence, the proprietor is protected solely against wrongful appropriation by another.[5]

A conveyance of a trade secret is not a mere license, but a restricted disclosure coupled, perhaps, with technical assistance concerning use. Some license restrictions are necessary to establish confidentiality and retain the secret itself. In essence, the trade secret license is a basic element in the continuation of the underlying proprietary right. Given the nature of the transaction and the relatively imprecise scope of many trade secrets, however, it may be difficult to distinguish provisions central to proprietary interests from more collateral restraints. Presumably, the more central restraints are those relating to confidentiality and nondisclosure, but it may not be necessary to draw fine distinctions. A patent or copyright proprietor is in a position to leverage and extend statutory rights that are relatively fixed. In contrast, the trade secret interest is subject to defeasance based on independent discovery. This reduces the potential leverage that can be exercised since, at some point, burdensome restraints create an incentive to refuse the license in lieu of independent development.[6]

As in copyright and patent law, there may be an interaction between the effectiveness of conditions in a trade secret license and the manner in

---

[5] See generally Milgrim, *Trade Secrets*. See also ¶ 3.02.

[6] Milgrim, *Trade Secrets* § 6.05.

which tangible products embodying the secret are conveyed. Under some circumstances, general distribution of a product may be tantamount to public disclosure of the secret. More specifically, while sale of a product that embodies the secret does not relieve the buyer of restrictions placed on information disclosed confidentially, a public policy allows third-party discovery of secrets encompassed in objects that have been sold. Attempted restrictions on reverse engineering the item may be inconsistent with the sale. To enforce a restraint in this context would tend to elevate a trade secret to a quasi-patent status without procedural and substantive limitations.

¶ 5.03 ANTITRUST AND RELATED RESTRICTIONS

In principle, technology licensing should be characterized by enforceable freedom of contract, at least where relatively equal bargaining parties are involved. In practice, however, while this principle has widespread application, technology licensing historically has been subject to external limitations derived from federal antitrust and intellectual property law.

[1] Antitrust Policy

Antitrust laws are directed toward eliminating unreasonable restrictions on competition and precluding monopolization. When considering the interface between antitrust and intellectual property doctrine as applied to technology licensing, the two bodies of law appear inconsistent. While antitrust law seeks to minimize competitive restrictions and monopolization, intellectual property law seemingly encourages restrictions and monopoly-like control. Indeed, intellectual property rights are often described as monopolies. This inconsistency has created a long history of doctrinal tension.[7]

Properly viewed, intellectual property law merely establishes property rights in intangible property, rather than a monopoly. A normal aspect of any property right is the right to exclude others or to restrict their use of the property. This is precisely what occurs in a technology

---

[7] See Kaplow, "The Patent-Antitrust Intersection: A Reappraisal," 97 Harv. L. Rev. 1815 (1984); Stedman, "The Patent-Antitrust Interface," 58 J. Pat. Off. Soc'y 316 (1976); Turner, "The Patent System and Competitive Policy," 44 NYU L. Rev. 450 (1969); Baxter, "Legal Restrictions on the Patent Monopoly: An Economic Analysis," 76 Yale LJ 267 (1966).

license. The mere exercise of those rights presents no particular antitrust risk.

Of course, the simple fact that a restriction is made possible by a legal and vested property right does not insulate that restriction from antitrust liability. Most antitrust violations are made possible by vested property rights. In copyright and patent law, however, exclusive property rights are created by federal legislation of coequal stature with antitrust law. Restrictions directly authorized by those laws should be insulated from antitrust risk in the absence of contrary circumstantial factors. Beyond this, the key issue is identifying and distinguishing restrictions that allow competition or are neutral from those that unreasonably restrain competition or illicitly monopolize a relevant market and are not directly authorized by intellectual property law.[8]

Most of the appellate cases to date involve patent licensing; prior to the advent of computer software technology, copyright licensing was largely confined to nontechnology environments.[9] In patent licenses, antitrust cases generally apply a rule of reason analysis to technology license provisions, rather than any per se illegality.[10] The starting point of analysis involves identifying the relevant market and the alleged violator's position within it. The aim is to determine whether the licensor has sufficient control to extract monopoly prices or restrain competition. In most cases this analysis incorporates assessment of an array of relatively interchangeable, similar products and producers.[11] At least with patents, the case law indicates that intellectual property rights presumptively are equivalent to economic power, since they imply a right to total exclusion of others from a particular technology.[12] This premise is debatable for patents, since related, noninfringing technology is not controlled, and it is

---

[8] Kaplow, "The Patent-Antitrust Intersection: A Reappraisal," 97 Harv. L. Rev. 1815, 1818–1820 (1984).

[9] See generally Kaplow, "The Patent-Antitrust Intersection: A Reappraisal," 97 Harv. L. Rev. 1815, 1818–1820 (1984). Compare Broadcast Music v. CBS, Inc., 441 US 1 (1979).

[10] See, e.g., Continental TV, Inc. v. GTE Sylvania, 433 US 36 (1977); Bela Seating v. Poloron Prod., Inc., 432 F2d 733 (7th Cir. 1971). However, the presence of exclusive copyright or patent claims creates a closer analysis of alleged tying claims. See infra ¶ 5.04.

[11] See United States v. EI Dupont & Co., 351 US 377 (1956).

[12] See Jefferson Parish Hosp. Dist. No. 2 v. Hyde, 104 S. Ct. 1551, 1560 (1984); United States v. Loew's, Inc., 371 US 38, 83 S. Ct. 97 (1962); Int'l Business Mach. Corp. v. United States, 298 US 131, 56 S. Ct. 701 (1936); Digidyne Corp. v. Data Gen. Corp., 734 F2d 1336 (9th Cir. 1984); see also Johnston, "Product Bundling Faces Increased Specter of Illegality Under the Antitrust Laws," 1 Comp. Law. 1 (Sept. 1984).

weaker still for copyright or trade secret licenses, since the scope (copyright) and durability (trade secret) of the exclusive rights are less extensive than in a patent.[13]

Assuming requisite market power, particular restrictions in a technology license are reviewed on the basis of several variables related to the connection between the restriction and the underlying intellectual property right. The first is whether the restriction is ancillary or collateral to a primary, lawful purpose of the license. Ancillary implies a close or, at least, reasonably related connection. In a license, the lawful objective is to commercially develop the technology and receive compensation for its use. Restrictions ancillary to this purpose are not antitrust violations.[14] In contrast, collateral restrictions, restrictions less closely connected to the technology transfer purpose, are assessed under general antitrust standards focusing on their purpose and competitive effect.

A second variable is the extent to which license provisions are obtained by leveraging exclusive rights to produce anticompetitive effects beyond the scope of the intellectual property. The economic power represented by control of the technology rights cannot be used to restrain competition in other contexts. This premise has been controversial and provides a focal point for a basic political and policy dispute as to how best to promote technology development in a competitive marketplace. Regardless of this dispute, not all leveraged restrictions are antitrust violations, and there is a need to distinguish among restrictions under relatively uncertain guidance and in light of an assessment of their purpose and effect.[15]

The perceived antitrust status of technology license restrictions is subject to wide variation, depending on the prevailing political and enforcement environment. Based solely on reported cases, technology license law has been relatively stable, if somewhat ambiguous, for a number of years. During the 1970s, however, informal pronouncements by the Department of Justice established policy positions explicitly hostile to relatively common provisions in technology licenses. The number

---

[13] As discussed in Chapter 2, the patent grant excludes even independent discovery and use of the patented technology, while both copyright and trade secret protections only extend to forms of misappropriation. See Milgrim, *Trade Secrets* § 6.05.

[14] See United States v. General Elec. Corp., 272 US 476, 490 (1926); Brodley, "Joint Venture and Antitrust Policy," 95 Harv. L. Rev. 1523 (1982); Louis, "Restraints Ancillary to Joint Ventures and Licensing Agreements: Do Sealy and Topco Logically Survive Sylvania and Broadcast Music," 66 U. Va. L. Rev. 879 (1980).

[15] See Arnold et al., "An Overview of U.S. Antitrust and Misuse Law," Technology Licensing 43, 151 (1982).

of enforcement actions filed increased and, not surprisingly, so did the number of private lawsuits.[16] The policy announced at this time included the view that certain clauses in patent licenses were or tended to be unlawful. Described as the "Nine No-No's," these included:[17]

1. Requiring a licensee to purchase unpatented materials
2. Requiring a licensee to assign back subsequent patents
3. Restricting a purchaser of a patented product in its resale
4. Restricting licensee's dealing in products and services outside the patent scope
5. Agreeing to not grant additional licenses without the licensee's consent
6. Licensing a group of patents only as a package
7. Conditioning the license on royalties computed in a manner not related to licensee sales or use
8. Restricting sale of products made with a patented process
9. Specifying a minimum price for the licensee's sale of licensed products

The common thread is an arguable leveraging of the patent into products or activities outside the patent grant. While the listed clauses identify contract terms in which antitrust problems may arise, the Department of Justice policy position that such clauses were per se illegal reflected a narrow interpretation of the patent owner's right to exploit his technology commercially. The interpretation was that, in all cases, the patent itself established sufficient market power to cause antitrust concern and that only restrictions closely related to express patent rights are permissible. Broader restrictions involve an unacceptable risk of unreasonable competitive restraint due to control of the intellectual property. The patent holder was permitted to function within the precise terms of the patent grant, but encountered extreme antitrust risk whenever he sought license provisions extending beyond the grant.

The reported case law during this period did not fully implement this extreme view. With a change in administration in the 1980s, a dramatically different antitrust posture emerged. For example, in 1982, the Chief of the Intellectual Property Division of the Department of Justice commented

Few technology licenses are likely to raise any significant issues under the antitrust laws. . . . A per se illegal approach should be lim-

---

[16] Andewelt, "Department of Justice Antitrust Policy," 1 Domestic and Foreign Technology Licensing Law 401 (1982).

[17] See 5 Trade Reg. Rep. 50, 146 (CCH 1972); Arnold, "An Overview of U.S. Antitrust and Misuse Law," Technology Licensing 43, 151 n.1 (1982).

ited to those provisions in technology licenses that [are] manifestly anticompetitive and lack any redeeming virtue. A restraint otherwise per se unlawful . . . cannot be shielded . . . by its inclusion in a technology license.[18]

In a series of speeches and publications, the preexisting policy was systematically attacked and explicitly revised.

While most reported licensing cases have involved patent licenses, trade secret and know-how licenses also raise significant antitrust issues. Special antitrust concern about anticompetitive leverage based on the market power held by a patent's proprietor is not present for trade secret licenses. The trade secret holder does not have absolute proprietary control, but only control over confidential relationships and disclosures. Since the secret is not protected against independent discovery, natural market factors restrict the leverage that can be exerted. Excessive demands create an incentive for the third party to refuse a license and conduct independent research.

Nevertheless, trade secret licensing has gone through a period of policy fluctuation analogous to that experienced by patent license policy, presumably derived from similar philosophical roots. One view, articulated in the 1970s, is that since trade secrets are not protected by federal statute, they are particularly suspect as a purported basis for license restraints.[19] This view is not supported in the reported cases. Indeed, there is ample authority sustaining both the commercial and social value of such licensing contexts.[20] The better view is that trade secrets are clearly a sufficient basis for technology licensing free of antitrust objection and that the cause for antitrust concern is more limited in this context than where patent or copyright licenses are involved. The primary additional issue where restraints are justified as ancillary to the technology transfer is the determination of whether a technology transfer is involved or whether the claimed license is merely a subterfuge to justify otherwise anticompetitive provisions.[21]

These shifting and conflicting positions raise important questions as to the manner in which antitrust policy is articulated and pursued. Equally important, however, they reflect an underlying debate about the

---

[18] Andewelt, "Department of Justice Antitrust Policy," 1 Domestic and Foreign Technology Licensing Law 401, 411, 412 (1982).

[19] See Department of Justice, *Antitrust Guidelines for International Operations* (1976).

[20] See Aaronson v. Quick Point Pencil, 440 US 257 (1979).

[21] See A&E Plastik Pak Co. v. Monsanto Co., 396 F2d 710 (9th Cir. 1968); Shin Nippon Koki Co. v. Irvin Indus., Inc., 186 USPQ 296 (NY Sup. Ct. 1975).

appropriate role of antitrust and intellectual property in developing technology. In one view, intellectual property laws are regarded as aberrants in an otherwise open, competitive system. Their scope should be closely constrained. Competition, minimally affected by leverage exerted from vested intellectual property rights, is viewed as the optimal environment for the development of technology. The contrary view regards intellectual property as integral to a truly competitive environment. Intellectual property rights provide the economic incentives for technology innovation. These incentives are central to the qualitative and cost improvements indicative of a competitive economy. Under this view, maximum licensing flexibility enhances the economic incentives created by intellectual property law and contributes to overall competition. The main thrust of antitrust law should be to identify only those cases in which a technology license is used as a subterfuge for anticompetitive conduct.

This latter view clearly represents the preferable perspective on the interface between antitrust and intellectual property licensing law. Presently, it also represents the perspective of the Department of Justice. In any event, in the reported cases, the divergent views are reflected in differing conceptions of the market power necessary to invoke traditional antitrust concepts such as prohibitions on tie-in arrangements.

[2] Patent and Other Abuses

Antitrust law is not the sole source of external restrictions on the terms of a commercial technology license. Since the 1940s, a parallel doctrine has been applied to limit the enforceability of particular license provisions based on equitable considerations grounded primarily in notions of defining the appropriate limitation of patent and copyright grants.

The doctrine of patent abuse was first articulated by the Supreme Court in *Morton Salt Co. v. G.S. Suppinger Co.* [22] In that case, the licensee of a patented salt tablet dispenser was contractually bound to purchase all of its salt tablets from the licensor. The tablets were not patented. The licensee refused to comply with this part of the license and was sued for infringement based on its continued use of the dispenser patent. Although an antitrust tying issue was raised, the Supreme Court denied enforcement of the patent on equitable grounds independent of antitrust violation. In essence, the patent rights had been misused by conditioning the license on acceptance of obligations on unpatented, generally avail-

---

[22] 314 US 488 (1942). Milgrim argues that, in general, concepts of intellectual property misuse should not apply to the proprietor of a trade secret, since unlike patent and copyright trade secrecy conveys no monopoly over the property. Milgrim, *Trade Secrets* § 6.05[4].

able items. This misuse amounted to unclean hands justifying denial of equitable enforcement.

Patent misuse is a defensive doctrine, rather than an affirmative cause of action. It precludes enforcement of a patent right until the misuse has been corrected (purged). Since its inception, the misuse doctrine has been applied to a variety of contexts and has been subject to doctrinal or policy variation similar to that found in the antitrust area. Since it arises from equitable concepts, the misuse doctrine is ultimately amorphous and relatively flexible. The common thread in most misuse cases, however, is a use of the patent to leverage transactional results that extend beyond the patent grant.[23] Properly construed, the misuse doctrine only applies where an element of coercion is involved so that the grant of the license is conditioned on the licensee's acceptance of the extended terms.

PART B.   INTEGRATED AND LEVERAGED SYSTEMS

¶ 5.04 TYING ARRANGEMENTS

A major issue in licensing law involves the extent to which the proprietor may leverage intellectual property rights to control other aspects of a transaction or other products. This issue has broad implications in the computer and software industry, especially with reference to integrated or bundled system sales. It represents a portion of a broader antitrust concern with the use of so-called tying arrangements to restrain competition.

A tying arrangement may exist if one party conditions a license or sale of one product on the buyer's acceptance of a license or sale of another product. The essential characteristic of an arrangement that violates antitrust law is not merely that the sale of one product is conditioned on purchase of another, but "lies in the seller's exploitation of its control over the tying product to force . . . the purchase of a tied product."[24] This forcing restrains competition in the tied product. Transactions in which a sale or license is conditioned in this way constitute a per se violation of antitrust law if the circumstances are such that the existence of the forcing element of the transaction is probable.[25] Otherwise, they constitute a violation of antitrust law only if it can be established

---

[23] See 2 Rosenberg, *Patent Law Fundamentals* 16-22.

[24] Jefferson Parish Hosp. Dist. No. 2 v. Hyde, 104 S. Ct. 1551, 1558 (1984).

[25] Id. at 1560.

that the seller's behavior unreasonably restrains trade under an antitrust rule of reason analysis.

Four factors are necessary to establish a per se violation: (1) the existence of at least two distinct products or services; (2) the sale of the tying product or service conditioned on the purchase of the tied product or service; (3) the defendant has sufficient economic power over the tying product to restrain competition for others; and (4) the amount of commerce involved is not insubstantial.[26] A tying arrangement under this definition violates antitrust law unless it can be justified by a lawful business purpose that cannot be attained by less restrictive means. Tying arrangements involving patent licenses may also constitute a patent abuse.[27]

Allegations of illegal tying are common in the computer industry.[28] In part, this is because computer systems are sold or licensed at varying levels of integration. Equally important, the industry is characterized by a number of manufacturers who focus on markets for component or peripheral equipment compatible with popular systems. These competitors are uniquely affected by integrated system or conditioned sales by the vendor of the underlying, basic system, since their markets depend on finding buyers for the components rather than entire systems. Furthermore, at least on the surface, the vendor of the underlying system has significant, preexisting advantages in this market environment. Arguably at least, these advantages can be exploited to force prospective purchasers or licensees to accept two products in order to obtain desirable elements of the basic system.

As a result of this pattern, antitrust issues pertaining to tying have two significant effects within the computer industry. First, they tend to shape the extent to which this secondary industry is protected. In essence, cases that restrict on the basic manufacturer's ability to force linking of products establish a protected market environment for the secondary

---

[26] Fortner Enter. v. United States Steel Corp., 394 US 495, 499 (1969); Foremost Pro Color, Inc. v. Eastman Kodak Co., 703 F2d 534, 540 (9th Cir. 1983).

[27] But see Dawson Chem. Co. v. Rohm & Haas Co., 488 US 176 (1980).

[28] See, e.g., Digidyne Corp. v. Data Gen. Corp., 734 F2d 1336 (9th Cir. 1984); Telex Corp. v. IBM, 367 F. Supp. 258 (ND Okla. 1973), rev'd on other grounds, 510 F2d 894 (10th Cir.) cert. dismissed, 423 US 802 (1975); ILC Peripherals Leasing Corp. v. IBM, 448 F. Supp. 228 (ND Cal. 1978), aff'd sub nom., Memorex Corp. v. IBM, 636 F2d 1188 (9th Cir. 1980), cert. denied, 452 US 972 (1981); Response of Carolina, Inc. v. Leasco Response, Inc., 537 F2d 1307 (5th Cir. 1976); Innovation Data Processing v. IBM, 585 F. Supp. 1470 (DNJ 1984); In re IBM Peripheral EDP Device Antitrust Litigation, 481 F. Supp. 965 (ND Cal. 1979).

manufacturers, arguably at the expense of the intellectual property rights of the manufacturer. Second, decisions on tying issues relate directly to the degree of risk entailed in varying types of marketing arrangements in the computer and software industry.

Because the allegations of tying are so common, it is important to identify what acts do not constitute tying. Initially, the most significant, a tying arrangement does not exist simply because one manufacturer offers to sell or license two or more products as an integrated system.[29] For example, IBM is free to offer an integrated personal computer system consisting of a central processing unit (CPU), monitor, disk drives, printer, and the like. This is true even if, as is likely in this case, the integrated system is more commercially attractive than the individual parts sold separately and the integration negatively affects a component manufacturer's ability to compete. The missing element central to an allegation of tying is a compulsory linkage of all or some of the components. That is, a tying arrangement exists only if the potential licensee or buyer is required to take two or more of the products or none at all.

Even a compelled linking of products does not necessarily establish a per se antitrust violation. Instead, there must be at least a potential or probable cause and effect relationship. "Application of the per se rule focuses on the probability of anticompetitive consequences."[30] In essence, aspects of the market or the seller's position regarding one product must be such that in light of the circumstances, anticompetitive forcing is probable. This is often put in terms of one product's (the tying product) economic power that is sufficient to affect the second (tied) product.

Especially with regard to economic power, important policy and doctrinal issues are litigated concerning the role of antitrust and intellectual property laws as applied to technology and tying. The case law suggests that the existence of intellectual property rights in one product creates a presumption of the special economic or other position sufficient for a per se antitrust violation.[31] The restrictive view of technology licensing that dominated in the 1970s would elevate this presumption to a conclusion that any conditioned sale involving an intellectual property product

---

[29] See Response of Carolina, Inc. v. Leasco Response, Inc., 537 F2d 1307 (5th Cir. 1976); Innovation Data Processing v. IBM, 585 F. Supp. 1470 (DNJ 1984).

[30] Jefferson Parish Hosp. Dist. No. 2 v. Hyde, 104 S. Ct. 1551, 1560 (1984).

[31] See Jefferson Parish Hosp. Dist. No. 2 v. Hyde, 104 S. Ct. 1551, 1560 (1984); United States v. Loew's, Inc., 371 US 38, 83 S. Ct. 97 (1962); IBM v. United States, 298 US 131, 56 S. Ct. 701 (1936); Digidyne Corp. v. Data Gen. Corp., 734 F2d 1336 (9th Cir. 1984).

represents a per se violation. The contrary view is that the presumption is rebuttable in cases where viable substitute products or other alternatives are available to the potential purchaser.[32]

[1] Product Differentiation

A necessary element of proof of a tying arrangement is that a transaction involve two or more distinct products. In a computer environment, a decision as to whether two or more products are involved may be unclear because of the modularity of many contemporary computer systems. To a lay observer, this is most apparent in peripheral devices such as monitors, printers, terminals, modems, and the like that can often be purchased apart from the CPU. It is clearly possible to design systems that physically integrate otherwise peripheral devices into a single unit, however. The farther into the core of the system, the less obvious is the separability of elements to the lay user, although it is equally common. Although affected by industry custom or standards, which elements are physically separable often is determined by design choices made by the manufacturer. The potential separability of internal elements such as memory boards and disk drive controllers does raise the question of whether these elements constitute separate products. If they do, antitrust implications may attend a decision to link their sale or, even, to select a design that physically integrates the two products. At one level, the situation itself is analogous to any complex contemporary machine: It reflects the technological capability to differentiate many elements in a complex system.

In the computer industry, substantial markets have developed around these various elements. The existence of these markets establishes potential antitrust issues that would not be present if no pertinent market regarded elements of a system as separable and subject to separate marketing. The markets include those competing to supply the elements themselves to traditional manufacturers, as well as the so-called original equipment manufacturer (OEM) market of manufacturers who acquire products or licenses from others and assemble them for resale. In the microcomputer environment, the competition also extends to retail sales. Thus, an IBM personal computer may be initially sold or subsequently

---

[32] The issue will turn on whether or not the court is permitted or required to view market circumstances in broad terms reflecting the interchangeability of the product. In most instances, a broad marketplace conception engenders a finding of no liability. See Stern, "Restricting Customer's Use of Software to Particular Computers," 1 CLR 194 (1982); Johnston, "Product Bundling Faces Increased Specter of Illegality Under the Antitrust Laws," 1 Comp. Law. 1 (Sept. 1984).

outfitted with a memory board by AST Corporation and disk drives by CDE Corporation. In addition, there is a considerable competitive market for systems compatible with currently popular systems marketed by other manufacturers. Compatibility typically entails the ability to operate existing applications software developed for other systems. The tying issue arises because it may be necessary, or at least desirable, to use some component of the primary system to obtain complete compatibility, but the manufacturer may be unwilling to license or sell that component apart from the main system.[33]

The existence of these markets raises a question of the extent to which antitrust law constrains design choices made by the manufacturer of the basic system. Specifically, are there antitrust risks in a decision to integrate physically previously separable elements of a computer system? A second critical question focuses on the circumstances under which physically separable portions of a system can or should be regarded as separate products so that a forced linkage of them may represent an antitrust violation if other conditions are met.

One approach to both questions centers on whether it is technologically possible to separate elements of a system. Separate products would be present if the components *could be* designed to allow their separate acquisition. This view has been advocated in some computer cases,[34] and has properly been rejected. Given the flexible technology in the computer industry, this analysis would discourage innovation in the integration of functions to optimize performance or marketability.[35] It would tend to require particular manufacturers to adopt a modular design solely to create or maintain a market for elements of the system. Even where existing markets have developed and the designed integration of functions effectively eliminates the separate elements on which the markets are based, a focus on potential separability is inappropriate. As one district court observed, such a focus would in effect "use the antitrust laws to make time stand still and preserve" markets profitable to certain producers.[36]

Where a particular manufacturer markets a physically integrated system so that the components cannot be separated without damage to the

---

[33] See Digidyne Corp. v. Data Gen. Corp., 734 F2d 1336 (9th Cir. 1984); Innovation Data Processing v. IBM, 585 F. Supp. 1470 (DNJ 1984).

[34] See Telex Corp. v. IBM, 367 F. Supp. 258 (ND Okla. 1973), rev'd on other grounds, 510 F2d 894 (10th Cir.), cert. dismissed, 423 US 802 (1975).

[35] See ILC Peripherals Leasing Corp. v. IBM, 448 F. Supp. 228 (ND Cal. 1978), aff'd sub nom., Memorex Corp. v. IBM, 636 F2d 1188 (9th Cir. 1980), cert. denied, 452 US 972 (1981); see also ¶ 4.09.

[36] ILC Peripherals Leasing Corp. v. IBM, 448 F. Supp. 423, 444 (ND Cal. 1978).

system, no antitrust tying issue exists, since only one product is involved. Rather than in terms of technological feasibility, the existence of separate products should be determined based on the configuration in which the product is in fact marketed. This approach has been followed consistently in computer-related antitrust cases. In *Telex Corp. v. IBM*, the court held that an integration of memory and control functions in a CPU constituted a single product.

> Control of memory function has been integrated with processing functions over a long period of time in varying degrees. [Progress] in ... miniaturization has made possible the integration of additional memory and control functions.... The integration ... involves ... no tying.... To rule otherwise would enmesh the courts with technical and uncertain inquiry ... and cast unfortunate doubt on the legality of product innovations.[37]

Antitrust doctrine concerning technological change and design should avoid inhibiting innovation. Separability should be tested in light of how an item is designed, not how it might have been designed.[38]

While the technological feasibility of producing separable elements is not an appropriate test, neither is it sufficient to establish simply that particular elements of a system are physically separable in fact. In many situations involving both consumer and commercial markets, products are sold with constituent elements that could be removed and sold separately. It is not, however, an antitrust violation for General Motors to refuse to sell Chevrolets without the engine and transmission allocated to that particular model. As this suggests, the designation that separate products exist is not resolved purely by technological considerations. Rather, it reflects the economic purposes of antitrust law. Distinct products do not exist for purposes of antitrust law unless there is a possibility that the economic effects sought to be prevented by antitrust may arise from the sale transaction.

For antitrust purposes, the criteria for determining the existence of separate products are necessarily contextual and economic in character. Separable components should not be considered separate products unless there is a "coherent economic basis" for treating the products as dis-

---

[37] Telex Corp. v. IBM, 367 F. Supp. 258, 347 (ND Okla. 1973), rev'd on other grounds, 510 F2d 894, 906 (10th Cir.), cert. dismissed, 423 US 802 (1975).

[38] See Foremost Pro Color, Inc. v. Eastman Kodak Co., 703 F2d 534, 540 (9th Cir. 1983); Response of Carolina, Inc. v. Leasco Response, Inc., 537 F2d 1307 (5th Cir. 1976).

tinct.[39] In most instances, this requires proof of the existence of two distinct product markets for the items linked in the sale. "[The] answer to the question whether one or two products are involved turns not on the functional relation between them, but on the character of the demand for the two items."[40] Thus, the appropriate standard focuses on industry and consumer recognition that the elements are distinct products. This does not suggest that they are always sold separately, but merely that the sale of one without the other is not unexpected. Of course, such recognition ordinarily requires at least the perceived feasibility of separating the items. More importantly, however, industry and market recognition would reflect that separate marketing is not only technically feasible, but that it has occurred and represents a viable commercial undertaking.

In a technology-driven market environment, this emphasis requires a focus on the existence of submarkets for components and for basic units independent of the particular components. As a result, to some extent the basic manufacturer's range of action in marketing its product may be constrained by the nature of the competition that has arisen concerning related products. Products viewed by some consumers as single products may nevertheless be considered to consist of separate products for purposes of this antitrust analysis. For example, in a technology context pertinent to contemporary computer markets, it has been held that components of a community television antenna system were separate products. The court noted

> Others who entered the . . . field offered all the equipment necessary for a complete system, but none of them sold their gear exclusively as a single package as [defendant did. The] number of pieces in each system varied considerably so that hardly any two versions of the alleged product were the same. [The] customer was charged for each item of equipment. . . . Finally, [defendant sold] cable and antennas . . . manufactured by other concerns [but] required that the electronic equipment be bought from it.[41]

---

[39] See Jefferson Parish Hosp. Dist. No. 2 v. Hyde, 104 S. Ct. 1551, 1572 (1984) (dissenting opinion of Justice O'Connor).

[40] See Jefferson Parish Hosp. Dist. No. 2 v. Hyde, 104 S. Ct. 1551, 1562 (1984); MDC Data Centers v. IBM, 342 F. Supp. 502, 352 F. Supp. 63 (ED Pa. 1961), aff'd per curiam, 365 US 567 (1961); Telex Corp. v. IBM, 367 F. Supp. 258, 347 (ND Okla. 1973), rev'd on other grounds, 510 F2d 894, 906 (10th Cir.), cert. dismissed, 423 US 802 (1975); Cole v. Hughes Tool Co., 215 F2d 924 (10th Cir. 1961).

[41] United States v. Jerrold Elec. Corp., 187 F. Supp. 545, 559, aff'd, 365 US 567, 81 S. Ct. 755 (1961).

As this implies, the strongest case for concluding that components are separable products exists where the defendant, and not only others in the industry, engages in marketing patterns that reflect a perceived market for the separate items.

Under this argument, a variety of computer components must be considered separate products at least with respect to current technology and marketing patterns. For example, it has been held that memory board and operating system software are separate from the underlying CPU in a minicomputer system.[42] Similarly, reflecting earlier technology, computer systems and computer punched cards have been held to constitute separate products,[43] and separate routines within a complex operating system program were separate products due to marketing practices.[44] In contrast, a disk drive unit and a head-disk assembly were found to be a single product.[45]

[2] Economic Power and Bundling

For purposes of antitrust law, a tying arrangement exists only if a vendor of technology exercises leverage from one product market into another. The Supreme Court has phrased this in terms of the vendor's use of the typing product in such a manner as to "force" a prospective buyer or licensee to acquire a tied product or service that it would otherwise not desire to acquire from this vendor.[46] This conception of forcing requires more than that the buyer merely find it convenient or less costly to acquire both products from one vendor or that the vendor's involvement in one product convey benefits of reputation to the second. Instead, forcing for the purposes of antitrust law does not occur unless the vendor or licensor possesses "sufficient economic power" over one product to have a substantial adverse effect on competition for the other.

The nature of the economic power required to establish a tying arrangement has been controversial, particularly the definition of actions that constitute per se antitrust violations. Thus, this issue is caught up in the general, contemporary uncertainty about whether there should be any per se antitrust violations. One purpose of a per se rule is to avoid the

---

[42] See Digidyne Corp. v. Data Gen. Corp., 734 F2d 1336 (9th Cir. 1984).

[43] IBM v. United States, 298 US 131, 56 S. Ct. 701 (1936).

[44] Innovation Data Processing v. IBM, 585 F. Supp. 1470 (DNJ 1984).

[45] See ILC Peripherals Leasing Corp. v. IBM, 448 F. Supp. 228 (ND Cal. 1978), aff'd sub nom., Memorex Corp. v. IBM, 636 F2d 1188 (9th Cir. 1980), cert. denied, 452 US 972 (1981).

[46] See Jefferson Parish Hosp. Dist. No. 2 v. Hyde, 104 S. Ct. 1551, 1558 (1984).

costly and uncertain market analyses characteristic of antitrust rule of reason cases in circumstances where the risk of anticompetitive conduct is sufficiently great as to warrant simplification of analysis.[47] An arrangement conditioning the sale of two products or services constitutes tying only if the vendor has sufficient economic power to force the buyer's conduct. As a result, some economic or market analysis is necessary to establish the per se violation, but a comprehensive assessment of market power is inconsistent with a per se rule. The net effect is an uncertain conception in which some market analysis is necessary, but this analysis is less than that required in a full rule of reason case.[48]

The essential ingredient of tying is that the vendor use control over the tying product to obtain access to and control of at least a segment of the tied product market. This requires both that the vendor control the tying product and that this control is such as can be converted into leverage to force a transaction involving a distinct product. The pertinent doctrinal issue is the extent to which these factors require proof of monopoly control or economic dominance over the tying product market and the extent to which the tying market can be defined solely in terms of the particular product.

Consistent with the nature of the per se rule in this context, it is clear that control over the tying product can exist even in the absence of a finding that the vendor has a monopoly over the product market. The Supreme Court has held that it is sufficient if the unique attributes of the tying product affect the decision of buyers. "Even absent a showing of market dominance, the crucial economic power may be inferred from the tying product's desirability to consumers or from uniqueness in its attributes."[49] Furthermore, the unique characteristics of the tying product need not appeal to all people or entities; it is sufficient that the product establish power only with some buyers in the market, as long as a substantial volume of commerce is foreclosed as a result.[50]

This conception of the per se rule avoids application of a full rule of reason market analysis. It leaves unanswered significant questions per-

---

[47] Id. at 1560 n.25; see also Northern Pac. Ry. Co. v. United States, 356 US 1, 5 (1958).

[48] See United States Steel Corp. v. Fortner Enter., Inc., 429 US 610, 620 (1977); United States v. Loew's, Inc., 371 US 38, 45 (1963); see also Note, "The Logic of Foreclosure: Tie-In Doctrine After Fortner vs. U.S. Steel," 79 Yale LJ 86, 93–94 (1969).

[49] United States v. Loew's, Inc., 371 US 38, 45 (1963).

[50] See Jefferson Parish Hosp. Dist. No. 2 v. Hyde, 104 S. Ct. 1551, 1560 (1984); United States Steel Corp. v. Fortner Enter., Inc., 429 US 610, 620 (1977); see also Areeda & Turner, *Antitrust Law* ¶ 1134 (1980).

taining to the sufficient economic power adequate for antitrust violation. Absent market dominance, what are the characteristics of the vendor's position concerning the tying products that are sufficient for antitrust liability? Both the extent of product uniqueness and the sufficient number or scope of buyers affected by the control over the product are issues that remain unclear, and the result has been decisions that reflect individualized judgments about appropriate marketing practices, rather than coherent doctrine.

These issues have been litigated with reference to computer industry practices involving bundling hardware and software products. Although the term "bundling" has several connotations, the meaning here is marketing that links into a single system hardware and software not physically integrated. The benign marketing purpose is to appeal to end users who do not desire to make the variety of decisions needed to individualize systems. When a bundled system is offered as only one of several market options, no antitrust issue arises. Potential antitrust concerns are present, however, when the bundled system is the only configuration that is marketed and the independent pieces are not available separately. For purposes of a tying arrangement, economic power or leverage might exist for either product. A hardware system may be used to leverage sales of software bundled with it. Conversely, unique characteristics of the software may serve to leverage the sale of the CPU or other hardware. Under either arrangement, the presence of two distinct products is relatively clear. The primary task is to determine whether the defendant has sufficient economic power in the tying product to affect sales or licensing of the other product. The significant criteria used to assess market power in this context ultimately relate to the character of competition protected by antitrust and misuse law in the computer industry.

[a] Intellectual Property

Questions concerning sufficient economic power for application of per se tying violations arise in two distinct technology licensing environments. The most significant is that in which a transaction involves intellectual property controlled by the vendor. Most commonly, the alleged antitrust violation entails use of the intellectual property control to influence the purchaser's decision concerning another product. The conception of economic power applied in such cases determines, in large part, the extent to which flexibility in intellectual property licensing is permitted or curtailed under antitrust law.

The existence of statutory intellectual property protection for one product in an alleged tying arrangement is, in itself, sufficient to establish a presumption of the requisite market power for application of the per se rule.[51] The basis for this conclusion lies in the presumed uniqueness of the protected product. The courts "presume that the inability to buy the product elsewhere gives the seller market power."[52] Conceptually, at least, this result is not contingent on or related to the vendor's overall position in any relevant market, since it is based totally on the unique character of the product and the statutorily invoked barrier to duplication of the product by any other source.

Although arguably independent of the vendor's market position, the presumption of economic power based on intellectual property protection does not in itself resolve questions about the appropriate treatment of intellectual property licensing. The significant questions remaining relate to the extent to which the presumption can be rebutted or overcome and the factors that can be used to achieve this result in appropriate cases. Even given acceptance of the underlying presumption of economic power, resolution of these questions will determine the actual impact of antitrust tying law on intellectual property licensing. The mere existence of the presumption, however, affects licensing practices. Since a patent or copyright implies economic power, any license conditioned on purchase or license of unpatented products encounters an antitrust risk.[53]

Under one view, the presumption of economic power can not be rebutted. This view parallels the restrictive view of intellectual property licensing described earlier by regarding statutory intellectual property grants as limited deviations from a more general model of entirely open competition. In essence, any conditioning of an intellectual property license upon acceptance of another product is viewed as an improper effort to extend the scope of the underlying patent or copyright.

The alternative perspective regards the underlying presumption of economic power as rebuttable. From an antitrust perspective, the significant fact is that intellectual property rights grant exclusive control over a particular process or product, precluding access by a competitor and, thus, conveying to the proprietor power over any purchaser who desires the specific product. Arguably, however, the competitive importance of the exclusive process and the availability of noninfringing but suitable substitutes are relevant in the analysis of whether a per se tying violation has occurred.[54] If a purchaser has access to a suitable substitute, the vendor's ability to force acquisition of the tied product is constrained by the

---

[51] See International Salt Co. v. United States, 332 US 392, 68 S. Ct. 12 (1947); United States v. Loew's, Inc., 371 US 38, 45 (1963).

[52] Jefferson Parish Hosp. Dist. No. 2 v. Hyde, 104 S. Ct. 1551, 1560 (1984).

[53] See Dawson Chem. Co. v. Rohm & Haas Co., 488 US 176 (1980).

[54] Jefferson Parish Hosp. Dist. No. 2 v. Hyde, 104 S. Ct. 1551, 1572 n.7 (1984) (dissenting opinion of Justice O'Connor).

fact that the purchaser will, at some definable point, elect to refuse to purchase either product and proceed to use the substitute. The extent to which a substitute in fact exists for this purpose depends on analysis of costs and relative performance involved in the transition. Absent consideration of these, a conclusion of market power based solely on the intellectual property claim is equivalent to uniformly restraining the proprietor's marketing options to foster competition in a narrow band defined by its own intellectual property and independent of overall market considerations.

Although this broader consideration of market factors is appropriate, judicial support for this view has been intermittent at best. For example, in an early case the Supreme Court rejected proof of competitively analogous products available in lieu of the patented item.[55] More recently, however, there has been some tendency to reject per se illegality for a more complete analysis of the market and the economic effects of a tying arrangement. For example, in *United States v. Studiengesellschaft Kohle m.b.h.*,[56] the district court rejected a per se approach and examined general market effects where a process patent was used to leverage restraints on the distribution of the unpatented product. Similarly, in the most recent Supreme Court decision dealing with a tying arrangement, four justices voted to abandon a per se approach as applied to any alleged tying and suggested that, in any event, neither a patent nor a copyright on one product is sufficient to establish the requisite market power for a tying violation.[57]

On the issue of presumptive economic power, a distinction should be recognized among the various types of intellectual property. A patent conveys the most complete control over a process or product in that even independent development is precluded. In contrast, trade secrecy does not foreclose independent discovery; access by competitors is precluded only to the extent they are unable or unwilling to invest in independent development. Copyright only bars copying or substantially similar reproduction. In trade secret and copyright, the assumption of economic power will often misperceive reality.

The existence of copyright protection for an operating system program was sufficient to establish a per se tying arrangement in *Digidyne Corp. v. Data General Corp.*[58] Data General was a dominant manufac-

---

[55] See International Salt Co. v. United States, 332 US 392, 68 S. Ct. 12 (1947).

[56] 670 F2d 1122 (DC Cir. 1981).

[57] Jefferson Parish Hosp. Dist. No. 2 v. Hyde, 104 S. Ct. 1551 (1984).

[58] 734 F2d 1336 (9th Cir. 1984).

turer of minicomputers. It marketed its product primarily through OEMs who used the Data General CPU (NOVA) and operating system software (RDOS), along with acquired or developed applications software and peripherals to market complete systems. Data General was sued by various manufacturers of CPUs that emulated the NOVA. These manufacturers wanted to sell to and through the same OEMs, but claimed that the OEMs were locked into Data General because they had developed software to run on NOVA and RDOS. The cost of reworking this software allegedly precluded the OEMs from adopting another system unless it was fully compatible with the Data General system. This could not be achieved without access to the RDOS software. Allegedly, there were technical and cost barriers to developing fully compatible alternative software. However, Data General refused to license RDOS for use on any CPU other than its own NOVA system.

The lower court in *Data General* had reversed a jury verdict in favor of the emulator manufacturers. Based on an analysis of the overall markets for operating system software and for CPUs, the court concluded that Data General lacked sufficient market power to force purchases of the CPUs or to affect appreciably the CPU market. In this analysis, the court considered a market defined by potentially interchangeable products including other, noncompatible operating systems and CPUs. The Ninth Circuit Court of Appeals reversed, rejecting both the conclusion and the focus of the lower court's analysis. It held that sufficient economic power for purposes of a per se tying can exist despite the absence of monopoly power in either product market. The court defined the central issue as whether the copyrighted RDOS operating system was "sufficiently unique and desirable to an appreciable number of buyers to enable defendant to force those buyers also to buy a substantial volume of defendant's ... CPUs."[59] The existence of copyright protection for RDOS created a presumption of economic power and the burden was on Data General to rebut this presumption. It failed to do so and, indeed, the facts presented to the jury tended to reinforce the presumption of power.

The court's discussion of economic power arising from the copyrighted software focused on three aspects of the case as supporting the presumed power. The basic consideration was the fact that the RDOS system could not be replicated without infringing the Data General copyright or after the investment of millions of dollars over a number of years. In addition, the facts presented to the jury indicated that an appreciable number of buyers were influenced by the desirability of RDOS to pur-

---

[59] Id. at 1345.

chase Data General CPUs. While these factors were sufficient to support the jury verdict, the court concluded that the economic power of Data General was enhanced by the "lock-in" of OEM distributors. The evidence suggested that the OEMs who had previously opted to develop and market software for Data General systems were in a position such that it was not economically feasible to shift away from the RDOS system. Data General had argued that this was the result of a choice earlier exercised by the OEMs. The court suggested that this choice was forced on the OEMs by virtue of the tying arrangement and the attractiveness of the RDOS system. Thereafter, the initial leverage was magnified by the lock-in, which made it economically unfeasible to avoid acquiring additional CPUs for subsequent needs.

The final factor considered by the court involved the relevance of substitute programs. The conclusion was that Data General possessed sufficient economic power in RDOS to force sales of the NOVA systems. The market analysis of the lower court focused on whether there were reasonably interchangeable substitutes for RDOS. The appellate court expressly rejected this approach as improperly transporting an analysis of monopoly power into an analytical environment in which the issues were much different. The existence of competitive substitutes is not, the court held, pertinent to whether sufficient economic power exists.

> If a seller's product is distinctive, not available from other sources, and sufficiently attractive to some buyers to enable the seller by tying arrangements to foreclose a part of the market for a tied product, the adverse impact on competition in the tied product is not diminished by the fact that other sellers may be selling products similar to the tying product.[60]

Under this approach, the existence of reasonable alternatives is not relevant unless the tying product is itself fungible and can be identically reproduced from other sources. By definition, this condition can never be met if the product is protected by statutory intellectual property rights. Similarly, the attractiveness or relative performance of available alternatives is not relevant as long as the particular product is more attractive to some customers to a degree sufficient to enable forcing the purchase of other products.

The *Data General* decision reflects an extreme application of the view that the exercise of any leverage from intellectual property rights into another product is prohibited under antitrust laws. Under *Data General*, this result will obtain in any case in which the plaintiff can establish that more than a de minimus number of buyers regard the proprietary

---

[60] Id.

system as desirable or preferable to other alternatives. The approach lacks any sensitivity to market conditions and provides no criteria for resolving those cases in which the attraction to potential buyers is offset by tying arrangements such that the buyers will make neither purchase, rather than both. This situation, of course, most clearly arises where available substitutes are reasonable alternatives for the affected buyers.

[b] General Economic Analysis

In cases not involving copyrights or patents, judicial inquiry concerning the existence of illegal tying arrangements focuses more clearly on unique characteristics of particular products and the structure of relevant markets. Predictably, in the absence of intellectual property factors, significant flexibility in technology marketing has been allowed.

One issue recurrently raised in this context has already been noted with reference to copyrighted products. This argument attempts to define the vendor's economic power and the relevant market in terms of lock-in and system compatibility.[61] This view emphasizes that once a user, OEM, or distributor commits to a particular system, it will tend to purchase or license only products compatible with that system. The user is, in effect, locked in by an understandable desire to avoid the cost and disruption of reworking existing procedures and software to accommodate a new incompatible product line. The implication is that there is a discrete market or submarket associated with the primary product and that this market is protected by antitrust law.

This phenomenon does occur within the industry. Compatibles markets are common. In an antitrust context, however, the analysis is more than a benign factual description; it incorporates a significant policy choice. Given the narrow description advocated under this view, the primary manufacturer inevitably has substantial market power based on the fact that it is the sole manufacturer of the basic product. As a consequence, whenever it combines the sale of that product with the sale of another, there is an antitrust risk. The result is that the primary manufacturer's marketing, development, and other activities are constrained to protect and preserve compatibles competition.

---

[61] See ILC Peripherals Leasing Corp. v. IBM, 448 F. Supp. 228 (ND Cal. 1978), aff'd sub nom., Memorex Corp. v. IBM, 636 F2d 1188 (9th Cir. 1980), cert. denied, 452 US 972 (1981); Telex Corp. v. IBM, 367 F. Supp. 258, 347 (ND Okla. 1973), rev'd on other grounds, 510 F2d 894, 906 (10th Cir.), cert. dismissed, 423 US 802 (1975); Innovation Data Processing v. IBM, 585 F. Supp. 1470 (DNJ 1984).

A lock-in analysis has been used to buttress a finding of sufficient economic power in litigation involving an alleged tying arrangement by Data General Corporation,[62] but this narrow view of the appropriate market has never been adopted as the primary basis for decision.[63] Instead, the market view adopted by the courts has been significantly broader and more fluid, with the predictable result that inadequate economic power is often found. The broader approach emphasizes the elasticity of supply and demand as well as the interchangeability of products in the industry. Market divisions may be based on the size or processing power of systems or on particular, generic types of peripherals. Within this environment, however, a decision to focus on a particular system by either competitors or users is viewed as reversible and inadequate to establish a protected market, even though a changeover may entail costs. The result is rejection of the notion that competitors' decisions to concentrate on a narrow, product-defined market give rise to a protected interest under antitrust law.

This broad market view validates a heterogeneous market structure in the industry. It properly limits antitrust regulation primarily to ensuring competition among systems, rather than within them. The protected competitive model consists of competition among primary systems such as Data General, Digital Equipment, Honeywell, and so forth or between RDOS and the approximately 100 other operating systems. Within these, compatibles may be developed and become competitors, but the choice to do so is not protected by antitrust law.[64] The result is an appropriate placement of the risks and rewards of technology innovation. The risks consist of direct competition with distinct products with high levels of innovation or performance; the rewards consist of at least a theoretical ability to control the market niche carved out in this competition. This level of reward, in turn, supplies the needed incentive for continuing innovation.

---

[62] See supra ¶ 5.04[2][a].

[63] See ILC Peripherals Leasing Corp. v. IBM, 448 F. Supp. 228 (ND Cal. 1978), aff'd sub nom., Memorex Corp. v. IBM, 636 F2d 1188 (9th Cir. 1980), cert. denied, 452 US 972 (1981); Telex Corp. v. IBM, 367 F. Supp. 258, 347 (ND Okla. 1973), rev'd on other grounds, 510 F2d 894, 906 (10th Cir.), cert. dismissed, 423 US 802 (1975); Kaplan v. Burroughs Corp., 611 F2d 286 (9th Cir. 1979), cert. denied, 447 US 924 (1980); MLC, Inc. v. North Am. Phillips Corp., 1983-1 Trade Cases ¶ 65,351 (SDNY 1983); General Business Sys. v. North Am. Phillips Corp., 699 F2d 965 (9th Cir. 1983); Warner Management Consultants, Inc. v. Data Gen. Corp., 545 F. Supp. 956 (ND Ill. 1982).

[64] See Apple Computer, Inc. v. Franklin Computer Corp., 714 F2d 1240 (3d Cir. 1983), cert. dismissed, 104 S. Ct. 690 (1984); Apple Computer, Inc. v. Formula Int'l, 725 F2d 521 (9th Cir. 1984).

[3] Justifications and Exceptions

Even if a tying arrangement is established, it is possible to avoid liability by establishing an adequate business justification for the practice. Since the basic conditions for tying have not been met in most reported computer cases, there is little directly applicable case law. Nevertheless, a brief review of justifications is desirable.

In practice, one frequent rationale for establishing a tying arrangement is to recoup the costs of research and development invested in a particular product. This motivation is most commonly present in cases in which market conditions make adequate pricing of the product prohibitive. Recovery of investment cost has been expressly excluded as a justification for a tying arrangement, however.[65] In virtually all cases, recovery of costs can be achieved, if at all, by the less restrictive alternative of pricing the particular product properly to reflect investment.

A second commonly alleged justification is that the tying is necessary to retain or establish a reputation for quality and resulting customer goodwill. The tying arrangement precludes introduction of inferior or inappropriate elements into a system. For example, if an operating system software and a CPU are not tied as a single system, the operating system might not perform as effectively with a different processing unit. This reduced performance would adversely affect the general reputation of quality of the system. While this motivation has some superficial appeal, its acceptance as a legal justification is uncertain. The clearest case for accepting motivations relating to assuring performance arises where health or safety dangers are present in the absence of tying, or where there is proof of reduced performance and resultant customer dissatisfaction in the absence of tying.[66] In most cases, however, less restrictive alternatives are available to protect the manufacturer's interests. For example, advertising and packaging can warn prospective purchasers of a risk of reduced performance if other suppliers' products are used. Similarly, warranty provisions can be drafted to limit relevant risks and disclaim performance warranties when other products are brought into the system.

---

[65] See United States v. Jerrold Elec. Corp., 187 F. Supp. 545, 559, aff'd, 365 US 567, 81 S. Ct. 755 (1961); Digidyne Corp. v. Data Gen. Corp., 734 F2d 1336 (9th Cir. 1984).

[66] See United States v. Jerrold Elec. Corp., 187 F. Supp. 545, 559, aff'd, 365 US 567, 81 S. Ct. 755 (1961); Tripoli Co. v. Wella Corp., 425 F2d 932 (3d Cir.), cert. denied, 400 US 831 (1970); Dehydrating Process Co. v. AO Smith Corp., 292 F2d 653 (1st Cir.), cert. denied, 368 US 931 (1961); Electronic Pipeline, Inc. v. Fluid Sys., Inc., 231 F2d 370 (2d Cir. 1956).

In patent licensing, one form of tying to unpatented products is permitted as a concomitant of the underlying patent. This arises where the tied, unpatented product is necessary to practice the patented technology and has no other commercially viable applications.[67] In that setting, a tied license is permissible.

¶ 5.05 PACKAGE LICENSING

Tying arrangements that involve patent licenses are commonly construed not only as violations of antitrust law, but also as instances of patent misuse. They clearly involve an impermissible effort to extend the patent by leverage to control unpatented items. A relatively small conceptual step from tying arrangements in misuse law leads to the issue of package licensing. Package licensing arises when a group of patents or copyrights are licensed as a group, rather than independently. In general, multilicense packages are treated in a manner analogous to tying arrangements. The basic issue is whether the package is compulsory or voluntarily created.[68]

Voluntary package licensing is common and is often essential to effective use of the licenses due to commercial considerations or because the subject matter is interdependent. In contrast, compulsory packaging in which one license is conditioned on acceptance of another constitutes patent misuse and may also contravene antitrust law.[69] Conceptually, there is a direct analogy to tying law. The main, additional difficulty in this context revolves around proof of conditioning or coercion, especially where the licensed subject matter is interdependent.[70]

¶ 5.06 NEW AND DERIVATIVE WORKS

Significant ownership issues arise where technology is jointly or sequentially developed, as the discussion in Chapter 4 illustrates. Regardless of the form of intellectual property involved, ownership of the original technology does not necessarily convey ownership or control of

---

[67] Dawson Chem. Co. v. Rohm & Haas Co., 488 US 176 (1980).

[68] See, e.g., Automatic Radio Mfg. Co. v. Hazeltine Research, Inc., 339 US 827 (1950).

[69] Zenith Radio Corp. v. Hazeltine Research, Inc., 395 US 100 (1969); Beckman Instruments, Inc. v. Technical Dev. Corp., 433 F2d 55 (7th Cir. 1970), cert. denied, 401 US 976 (1971).

[70] North Am. Phillips Co. v. Stewart Eng'g Co., 319 F. Supp. 335 (ND Cal. 1970).

improvements or derivations from that original. Licensing agreements therefore ordinarily deal with the relative rights of the parties in the event of the development of new technology based on the old. The manner by which this issue is resolved, of course, depends on the circumstances of the licensing transaction, but provisions to deal with new technology developments can create antitrust and misuse law problems.

[1] Grant-Back Agreements and New Developments

One method of dealing with new developments made by a licensee is to require the transfer back of all or some rights in the new development to the original licensor. Such provisions are described as "grant-back clauses." They are found in several forms. In some instances there is an absolute assignment of exclusive rights to the licensor, while in others there is only a nonexclusive license back. Similarly, the clauses vary in the extent to which the obligation to grant back includes developments not directly related to the original subject matter of the license.

There is a superficial similarity between grant-back clauses and tying arrangements if the grant-back is a condition for granting the license. The licensor's exclusive rights to the original subject matter extend to encompass additional developments beyond the limits of the original rights. Despite the similarity, grant-back provisions in patent licenses are not per se antitrust violations, but are examined under a rule of reason approach.[71] This results from the presence of valid business motivations for the clauses, including the desirability of ensuring access to improvements on technology originally controlled and relied on by the licensor.

Although not illegal per se, grant-back provisions have had a controversial antitrust history. The controversy focuses on provisions that convey exclusive rights back to the original licensor, leaving the innovator-licensee with only a limited license to use its own innovation or, in the most extreme case, required to pay royalties for such use. In this form, a grant-back clause has a substantial chilling effect on the licensee's incentive to innovate and a clear effect in expanding the licensor's patent-based control of an area of technology. During the 1970s, the Department of Justice stated the position that exclusive clauses were per se illegal.[72]

---

[71] See Transparent Wrap Mach. Corp. v. Stokes & Smith Co., 329 US 637 (1947).

[72] See Department of Justice, *Antitrust Guide to International Operations*, Case 1 (1977).

Various commentators suggest that, at a minimum, an exclusive grant-back creates a substantial risk of antitrust illegality.[73]

In a rule of reason analysis, there is a significant distinction between an exclusive grant-back and provisions calling for a nonexclusive license back of new technology. Nonexclusive clauses reduce the extension of the original patent and retain substantial incentive for the original licensee to engage in innovation.[74] As a result, the greater the rights retained by the licensee, the greater the likelihood of validity.[75]

Additional factors in a rule of reason analysis include the extent to which the original licensor has a dominant market position. Where dominance is based in part on existing patents and a pattern of grant-back licensing develops, the overall effect and purpose may be to perpetuate and expand a monopoly.[76] Similarly, a preexisting dominance or a lack of such dominance affects the extent to which the licensee may be forced effectively to accept grant-back terms.[77] Finally, the scope of grant-back may be relevant. A narrowly drawn provision is more likely to be acceptable than one drawn broadly to encompass all or most of a licensee's innovative activity, including that unrelated to the subject of the license.[78]

In an overall assessment of drafting patent grant-back clauses, two authorities noted that steps should be taken to ensure that

> (1) any rights to be transferred are solely by way of nonexclusive licenses; (2) the subject matter of the grant-back is no broader in scope than the subject matter of the underlying license; and (3) no further royalties are imposed on the licensee for the use of his own improvement patents or technology.[79]

---

[73] See, e.g., Sullivan, *Handbook of the Law of Antitrust* (1970); Chevigny, "Validity of Grant-Back Agreements Under the Antitrust Laws," 34 Fordham L. Rev. 569, 576 (1966).

[74] See McCarthy, "Patent Grant-Backs: A New Look," 2 APLA J. 67, 78 (1974).

[75] See, e.g., Banks Mfg. Co. v. Ransberg Electro-Coating Corp., 281 F2d 252 (9th Cir. 1960); Robintech v. Chemidus Wavin, 450 F. Supp. 817 (DDC 1978).

[76] See United States v. ALCOA, 91 F. Supp. 333, 410 (SDNY 1950); United States v. General Elec. Co., 80 F. Supp. 989, 1005 (SDNY 1948).

[77] Sante Fe Pomeroy, Inc. v. P&Z Co., 569 F2d 1084 (9th Cir. 1978).

[78] See Duplan Corp. v. Deering Milliken, Inc., 444 F. Supp. 648 (DSC 1977), aff'd in part, 281 USPQ 641 (4th Cir. 1979).

[79] Arnold & Swartz, *The Patent-Antitrust Interface* 53 (1976).

[2] Grant-Backs and Derivative Works

The case law pertaining to grant-back agreements involves patent licensing. In the contemporary computer industry, copyright and trade secret protections are more significant to software developments. At first glance, it might appear that grant-back agreements in copyright or trade secret licensing should be handled in the same manner as patent licenses. That is, the courts should apply a rule of reason in which exclusive conveyances back are suspect. At least in regard to trade secret licensing, this was apparently the position taken by the Department of Justice in the 1970s.[80]

On closer inspection, significant distinctions do exist between patent licensing and copyright and trade secret protections under grant-back agreements. In trade secret licensing, the nature of the underlying rights significantly reduces the leverage that the licensor can exercise to obtain the grant-back.[81] Furthermore, the essence of the transaction is a protected or restricted disclosure. An exclusive grant-back reserving the licensee's right of personal use may be necessary to maintain the underlying secret.

The differences are even more apparent in contrasting patent and copyright licenses. A patent encompasses only the particular subject matter and extends to improvements only if they incorporate the patented technology. In contrast, copyright expressly grants an exclusive right to prepare derivative works.[82] While there are limited exceptions for the owner of a copy to make adaptations of that copy for personal use, it is clear that even the sale of a copy does not convey an unfettered right to make adaptive works or improvements.[83]

As a result, the licensor's control over improvements of copyrighted software is implicit in the statutory rights conveyed by copyright, with the possible exception that the owner of a copy has rights for personal use. The terminology of a grant-back is inappropriate. Often, vesting control in the original licensor is not a grant, but merely an affirmation of basic copyright law, at least where the copyright license does not incorporate grant-back of unrelated technology.

---

[80] See Department of Justice, *Antitrust Guide to International Operations* (1977).

[81] See Milgrim, *Trade Secrets* § 6.05.

[82] See ¶ 1.09.

[83] 17 USC § 117 (1982); see Freedman v. Select Information Systems Inc., 221 USPQ 848 (ND Cal. 1983).

[3] Contract Terms

Grant-back provisions in technology licenses often present questions of interpretation about the inclusion of a particular improvement or new development. With the possible exception of copyrighted derivative works, grant-back clauses are subject to restricted, rather than expansive interpretation. This results from the fact that the clauses run counter to common assumptions concerning ownership and control of technology innovations. Furthermore, even when drafted to avoid antitrust problems, the effect of the clause is to reduce the licensee's incentives for innovation that are established by law.

In the context of restrictive interpretation, it is pertinent to focus on the derivation and generic limitations of the language commonly employed in grant-back provisions. Historically, most technology licensing has revolved around patent or trade secret law and discoveries of physical science. As a consequence, terminology referring to inventions and discoveries is common. These terms are interpreted in light of their origin. They do not, for example, encompass software refinements in programs that are not patentable.[84] Conversely, a contract reference to derivative works reflects a copyright base, but does not include patentable inventions or the development of new ideas or formulas.

No case law exists on interpretation of copyright licensing in a technology context. In general, however, a contract reference to derivative works is inadequate. The application of the term depends on the extent to which the new work incorporates the expression of the old.[85] More important, the phrase excludes improvements based on the underlying *idea* of the original. Alternative language is needed to incorporate software developed on the basis of the original idea.

PART C.   LICENSE DURATION AND ROYALTIES

¶ 5.07 DURATION OF LICENSE AND ESTOPPEL

The preceding discussions considered a variety of circumstances in which proprietary rights are leveraged to obtain control of other products or technology. Where the transaction involves statutory rights, such leveraging raises substantial antitrust and misuse law concerns. It may be

---

[84] See Amoco Production Co. v. Lindley, 609 P.2d 733 (Okla. 1980).

[85] See Freedman v. Select Information Sys., Inc., 221 USPQ 848 (ND Cal. 1983); S&H Computer Sys. v. SAS Institute, Inc., 568 F. Supp. 416 (MD Tenn. 1983).

improper to use protected rights to obtain advantages in areas beyond the defined subject matter of the exclusive rights. The duration of the technology license presents an analogous circumstance. Copyright and patent protections are limited to a specified term of years.[86] Agreements by which the technology proprietor leverages its rights beyond the specified term of years involve an extension of the statutory grant beyond its clear limits. While this issue may have little practical significance in copyright in view of the length of the statutory period, it has been the subject of patent licensing litigation. The use of the underlying patent to extend control is, in pertinent respects, comparable to a tying arrangement and has been held invalid.[87]

Antitrust and misuse law combine to limit patent and copyright licenses to no more than the statutory term of years. Beyond that, the Supreme Court has identified a public policy to encourage earlier testing and, perhaps, invalidation of the statutory grant in the patent field. In *Lear, Inc. v. Adkins*,[88] the Court held that contractual doctrine estopping a licensee from contesting the title or validity of the licensor's patent was inconsistent with federal policy encouraging the dedication of inventions to the public domain. Under *Lear*, the licensee is not estopped from contesting the patent and, if the patent is declared invalid, cannot be required to pay further royalties.[89]

While patent and copyright licenses are limited to a maximum term defined by the underlying statute, an analogous proposition limiting trade secret licenses to the period in which the underlying subject matter remains secret has not been adopted. Instead, trade secret licenses are treated as purely contractual. They may continue in force despite disclosure of the subject matter.[90] The rationale is twofold. First, due to the nature of the underlying rights, the risk of overreaching and leverage is less than under patent and copyright licenses, and an agreement is more likely to reflect arm's length bargaining. Second, unlike in patents and copyrights, in trade secrets there is no federal or state defined limit of validity beyond which it can be said that the license extends.

---

[86] See *Deller's Walker on Patents* § 410.

[87] See, e.g., Brulette v. Thys Co., 379 US 29 (1964).

[88] 395 US 653 (1969).

[89] The applicability of this doctrine to copyright licenses is less clear, since the public interest in dedicating the subject matter of a copyright to the public domain is less obvious and grounds for challenge are less commonly encountered. See Erie Technological Prods., Inc. v. JFD Elec., 198 USPQ 179 (EDNY).

[90] Aaronson v. Quick Point Pencil Co., 440 US 257 (1979); Sinclair v. Aquarius Elec. Co., 42 Cal. App. 3d 216 (1974).

¶ 5.08 ROYALTY DURATION

Royalty payment in a technology license may be made in a variety of ways. Among the most common are "single payment" royalties, which are similar to a literal purchase of the rights conveyed and involve no ongoing obligation to make continuing payments. No antitrust or other constraints directly limit the amount charged. An alternative form of royalty involves periodic payments computed on specified formulas relating to use or product sales. This format involves potential legal issues relating both to the duration of the obligation to pay and the manner by which payments are computed.

[1] Post-Expiration Royalties

The duration of periodic royalty obligations may be directly related to considerations of the duration of the license itself. Indeed, in many licenses, the royalty obligation is the most significant, ongoing restraint on the licensee. Invalidating the license but allowing the royalty obligation to continue after expiration of the patent would be inconsistent. As a result, extension of royalties beyond the term of the underlying patent has been held to be per se unlawful.[91] In contrast, royalties in a trade secret or know-how license are permissible beyond the term of actual secrecy.[92]

While this underlying legal doctrine is clear, circumstances arise in which payments validly may be continued beyond the term of a patent. The clearest case involves payments that represent deferred payment of a lump sum royalty. One indicia of this approach is the specification of a total license payment independent of ongoing use or sales. A second justification for extended royalties arises where the licensor continues to perform services for the licensee and the payments may be reasonably construed as payment for those services.

[2] Multiple Technology

In practice, many technology licenses blend the major intellectual property types, and the dissimilar expiration terms for various elements in the transaction potentially create confusion. In light of doctrine concerning extension of royalties beyond the term of an intellectual property right, they also involve significant legal risks.

---

[91] See, e.g., Brulette v. Thys Co., 379 US 29 (1964); Technograph Printed Circuits, Ltd. v. Bendix Aviation Corp., 218 F. Supp. 1 (D. Md.), aff'd per curiam, 327 F2d 497 (4th Cir. 1963).

[92] Aaronson v. Quick Point Pencil Co., 440 US 257 (1979).

Two distinct forms of multiple technology licenses must be considered. The first involves a transaction in which multiple copyrights or patents are licensed in one transaction. Where the package license is obtained by conditioning the license of one on acceptance of all, a form of impermissible tying occurs.[93] Beyond this, potential problems arise with royalty computation where the licensed technologies expire at different times, but the package license involves a uniform, unchanging royalty rate. If the royalty extends beyond the term of the last patent to expire, the extension is invalid.

The status of a continuing royalty rate where one or more of the packaged patents expires is less clear. While this circumstance might be compared to impermissibly extending an expired patent, a continuous rate is valid if it was not obtained by *conditioning* the license of any patent on acceptance of the continuous rate.[94] This results from the fact that in practice royalty rates on a package of patents are not and often can not be computed as a rate for each of the constituents of the package. While the basic doctrine suggests validity, however, the difficulty of distinguishing between illicit conditioning and mere negotiation places a severe practical restraint on the use of uniform rates.

The second form of multiple technology license is an agreement combining statutory rights with a trade secret license. The issue concerning duration is most likely to arise in patent and trade secret licensing. Federal policy concerning the expiration of patent royalties prevails over contract law concerning extension of trade secret license royalties unless it is possible to implement both. Specifically, the alleged inclusion of trade secret elements in a license does not in itself justify royalties beyond the patent term. Where the parties provide a separate, reduced rate in the event a patent expires or is invalid, however, this reduced rate is enforceable.[95] Where no explicit differentiation is made, the court will not supply one.[96]

¶ 5.09 ROYALTY COMPUTATION

[1] Extended Basis

Where a periodic royalty is adopted in a technology license, both the dollar amount and the basis for computation are negotiable and vary with

---

[93] See supra ¶ 5.05.

[94] Beckman Instruments, Inc. v. Technical Dev. Corp., 433 F2d 55 (7th Cir. 1970), cert. denied, 401 US 976 (1971).

[95] Aaronson v. Quick Point Pencil Co., 440 US 257 (1979).

[96] St. Regis Paper Co. v. Royal Indus., Inc., 552 F2d 309 (9th Cir. 1977).

the particular technology, the status of the parties, and the intended patterns of use. In concept, selection among potential arrangements is a matter solely at the discretion of the parties. In practice, however, these decisions involve at least latent antitrust and misuse law issues.

The most problematic issue is the selection of a basis to compute a royalty. Involved in the decision are considerations of ease of monitoring and reporting, as well as accurate reflections of the value of the license to the licensee. In addition, of course (especially where a license restricts or indirectly affects the ability of the licensor to grant other licenses), there is a clear issue from the licensor's perspective of ensuring at least a minimum return on the technology investment. In many cases, these business considerations can be met by computations directly connected to the rate of sale of the patented or copyrighted product. This is true where the license covers the right to manufacture or reproduce a patented or copyrighted product that is marketed essentially intact and not incorporated into another item. For example, a software distribution license might reasonably compute royalties based on the number of sales. These sales not only reflect the value to the licensee, but also are relatively easy to monitor. In other cases, however, the appropriate standard is less clear. For example, in a license of a process or of software to control a manufacturing plant, the standard may involve a variety of possibilities including royalties computed on the basis of net or gross profitability of the plant or royalties based on net reductions in processing costs per unit processed.

Royalty computations based on products other than the particular, licensed technology present potential antitrust and misuse law issues. Where the expanded computation base is the result of coercion or leverage of the underlying proprietary rights, it may be analogous to a tying arrangement. This was true in the leading Supreme Court case of *Zenith Radio Corp. v. Hazeltine Research, Inc.*[97] In that case, Hazeltine held patents on a variety of components that could be used in the manufacture of television sets. It refused to license these patents except on a royalty basis computed in terms of all televisions sold by Zenith, regardless of whether the licensed technology was used. The Court held that this constituted patent misuse.

The illegal conduct in *Zenith* involved conditioning or leveraging the underlying patent or copyright. No illegality occurs where the royalty basis is selected for the convenience of the parties or by the necessity of the circumstances.[98] For example, in cases involving manufacturing pro-

---

[97] 395 US 100 (1969).

[98] 4 *Deller's Walker on Patents* § 602.

cesses, royalties based on net volume are appropriate even though nonlicensed technologies play a role in determining volume. Similarly, an indirect measure of sales may be a mutually convenient means of reducing monitoring costs. In *Western Electric Co. v. Stewart Warner Corp.*,[99] royalties measured by sales of a semiconductor device were held to be valid in a license of a microchip patent where the patented item was merely one component of the unpatented device. In that case, there was proof that the method of computation was jointly selected, rather than forced on the licensee.

[2] Differential Rates

Assuming a computational base, selection of a royalty rate does not implicate antitrust or misuse law unless differential rates are specified for two or more licenses. Differential rates may reflect valid business considerations. The apparent market value of a particular technology may change over time, for instance, and the intended use by the licensee may affect the royalty to be charged. Differential rates may also be used, however, to substantially impair competition among licensees or between licensees and licensor. As a result, differential royalty practices are often subjected to antitrust analysis where the rates are applied to competitors.[100]

In this analysis, general hostility to price discrimination is often manifest. As a result, the actual status of differential royalties to competitors is suspect. In fact, one court has held that the burden is on the licensor to establish a valid reason for the difference.[101] In contrast, a second appellate court has held that an action would lie only on proof that the licensees were similar in all pertinent respects, the royalty rate was an important expense factor, and the discrimination substantially impaired competition.[102]

The latter approach is clearly preferable. Differential royalty rates in technology licenses are not precluded directly under the Robinson-Patman Act.[103] They are invalid only under rule of reason analyses revealing a purpose and effect to restrain competition. This does not justify requir-

---

[99] 631 F2d 333 (4th Cir.), cert. denied, 450 US 971 (1980).

[100] See, e.g., Allied Research Prod., Inc. v. Heatbath Corp., 300 F. Supp. 656 (ND Ill. 1969); Bela Seating Co. v. Poloron Prods., Inc., 438 F2d 733 (7th Cir. 1971); Honeywell, Inc. v. Sperry-Rand Corp., 180 USPQ 673 (D. Minn. 1973).

[101] See Bela Seating Co. v. Poloron Prods., Inc., 438 F2d 733 (7th Cir. 1971).

[102] See Honeywell, Inc. v. Sperry-Rand Corp., 180 USPQ 673 (D. Minn. 1973).

[103] 15 USC § 13(a) (1982).

ing a licensor to prove a valid purpose for differential rates. Such an approach tends to presume illegality and would significantly constrain commercial use of proprietary property. The burden should be on the complaining licensee to establish a similarity of circumstances to rebut a presumably valid business judgment.

[3] Most Favored Licensees

Although differential royalty rates are not an antitrust violation or a misuse, the risk that others will receive more favorable license terms is a substantial threat to any licensee of technology. As a result, many technology licenses contain provisions designed to ensure access by one licensee to any more favorable terms granted to later licensees. Described as "most favored" clauses, these contract provisions may provide for any of a variety of remedies in the event of a later, more favorable license, ranging from automatic adjustment of the original license to refund of coverages previously paid.

Most favored licensee clauses are enforceable on their own terms as long as they are not an element of a price-fixing scheme.[104] Although commonly included in relatively elaborate contracts, the clauses nevertheless often generate significant litigation as a result of inadequate attention to drafting.

In many cases, most favored clauses are broadly drafted to include any form of subsequent license. Where this occurs, issues often arise in cases involving infringement or alleged infringement by a third party. The allegations may lead either to a judicial finding of an implied license due to nonaction by the proprietor or a settlement leading to a payment for past use.[105] Unless expressly excluded, these may trigger application of the clause, even though the probable intent of the parties was only to cover consensual licenses for future use.

Even where there is no issue arising from infringement-related disputes, many most favored clauses fail to adequately define the manner in which subsequent license terms will be compared to the original. "Court decisions, not surprisingly, have not established even general criteria for determining the relative worth of different licenses."[106] The result is sub-

---

[104] Technograph Printed Circuits, Ltd. v. Bendix Aviation Corp., 218 F. Supp. 1 (D. Md.), aff'd per curiam, 327 F2d 497 (4th Cir. 1963).

[105] See, e.g., Shatterproof Glass Corp. v. Libby-Owens-Ford Glass Co., 482 F2d 317 (6th Cir. 1973); Searle Analytic, Inc. v. Ohio-Nuclear, Inc., 398 F. Supp. 299 (ND Ill. 1975).

[106] Brunsvold & Payne, "Five Important Clauses: A Practical Guide," 2 PLI Technology Licensing 367, 374 (1982).

stantial uncertainty where differing royalty rates are coupled with different geographic, volume, or use restrictions. While the better view is that a court should look beyond mere percentages or dollar figures and to the entire contract,[107] a judicial forum is inappropriate for full consideration of business factors. Furthermore, unless the license specifies the relevant criteria for comparison, there is a risk that the clause will be activated despite material differences in the remainder of the license.

PART D.　VERTICAL RESTRICTIONS AND DISTRIBUTORS

¶ 5.10　RESALE PRICE

A technology license may impose various restrictions on the use of the technologies by a licensee. The clearest cases in which antitrust issues arise as a result of such restrictions involve attempts to fix the price at which products are resold. An agreement or conspiracy to fix prices is a per se violation of antitrust law.[108] In general, this result pertains whether the agreement is expressly limited to price fixing or is in the form of a license that specifies resale price controls. Despite this, it is clear that a vendor may unilaterally establish and announce prices for sale of its products and not encounter antitrust liability when it subsequently makes sales at the announced prices.[109]

These general propositions apply to licensing agreements. The case law also supports a limited exception for patent and copyright licensing. The major case is *United States v. General Electric Co.*[110] This case upheld the right of a licensor to set the price at which a manufacturing licensee sold a patented product. Although it has been subject to substantial criticism, *General Electric* apparently remains valid.[111] A similar rule applies to copyright licensing, at least until the first sale of a copy has occurred.[112]

----

[107] Prestol Corp. v. Tinnerman Prods., Inc., 271 F2d 146 (6th Cir. 1959), cert. denied, 361 US 964 (1960).

[108] See Monsanto Co. v. Spray-Rite Serv. Corp., 104 S. Ct. 1464 (1984); Dr. Miles Medical Co. v. John D. Park & Sons Co., 220 US 373, 31 S. Ct. 376 (1911).

[109] See United States v. Colgate & Co., 250 US 300, 307 (1919).

[110] 272 US 476 (1926).

[111] See In re Yarn Processing Patent Validity Litigation, 541 F2d 1127, 1135 (1976); United States v. Huck Mfg. Co., 214 F. Supp. 776 (ED Mich. 1963), aff'd, 382 US 197 (1965) (affirmed on a split vote).

[112] Bobbs Merrill Co. v. Strauss, 210 US 339 (1908).

Although *General Electric* provides a limited avenue for licensing price control, it must be carefully read as limited to particular facts. *General Electric* involved a single license between one licensor and one licensee. The involvement of more parties or multiple licenses restricting price may convert the facts into an antitrust violation.[113] Similarly, in *General Electric* the price restraint was on the first sale of the patented product. The case does not support use of a process patent to control the price of a resulting, unpatented product. After the first sale, patent rights in the item are exhausted, as are some copyright rights. *General Electric* would not authorize resale price restraints on a buyer of the product.

¶ 5.11 NONPRICE VERTICAL RESTRICTIONS

Various antitrust issues may arise concerning restrictions not dealing with resale price. Although these restrictions vary, the most common clauses in a marketing and manufacture setting restrict the territory or the commercial field of use of the technology. Antitrust and misuse issues must be examined at two levels for both settings. The first concerns the general validity of territorial or field of use restrictions. The second involves the role of proprietary property in the transaction.

A distinction between horizontal and vertical restraints is pertinent to field of use and territorial restrictions. An agreement among competitors to apportion a market geographically or otherwise, a classic horizontal restraint, is a per se violation of antitrust law.[114] In contrast, most technology licensing is vertical, at least in form. It involves restrictions imposed on parties down the distribution line. Since the Supreme Court's decision in *Continental T.V., Inc. v. GTE Sylvania*,[115] the validity of vertical restraints (even if imposed on products sold to another) is tested under an antitrust rule of reason focusing on the purpose and competitive effect of the restriction. Thus, restricting distributors to particular geographic areas is not per se illegal. In determining the validity of restrictions under a rule of reason, however, the cases currently conflict as to whether the analysis should be limited to intrabrand competition or should assess the impact on competition between brands.[116]

---

[113] See United States v. New Wrinkle, Inc., 342 US 371 (1952); United States v. Line Materials Co., 333 US 287 (1948).

[114] See, e.g., Northern Pac. Ry. Co. v. United States, 356 US 1 (1958).

[115] 433 US 36 (1977).

[116] Compare Valley Liquors, Inc. v. Renfield Importers, Ltd., 678 F2d 742, 745 (7th Cir. 1982) with Carlson Mach. Tools, Inc. v. American Tool, Inc., 678 F2d 1253, 1262 (5th Cir. 1982).

Superimposed over this structure is the potential effect of proprietary property rights on the restrictive clauses. These rights either tend to support or weaken the validity of a particular restraint. Some restraints are inherent in or obviously ancillary to such licensing. For example, patent law clearly supports the patentee's right to grant geographically limited licenses. Conversely, other restrictions clearly extend beyond the statutory grant. For example, extension of a process patent to control the unpatented product clearly exceeds the grant.[117] Similarly, in patent and copyright law, a first sale of a product or copy exhausts some rights to that item. Reimposition of these controls by a license exceeds or extends the grant.

In general, territorial restrictions in patent and copyright licenses are valid.[118] In fact, these arrangements may enhance interbrand competition. The general validity of such restrictions is subject to two significant restrictions, however. First, a patent or copyright license does not validate an agreement among competitors to apportion the marketplace. Second, and equally important, the validity of the restraint may be limited to the subject matter of the proprietary property itself. Thus, geographic restraints extending beyond the first sale of a patented product may constitute patent misuse, since the sale exhausted the patent rights in the product.

Territorial restraints in a trade secret license are subject to a rule of reason analysis. To the extent that the restraint is based on valuable subject matter and limited to the life and scope of the trade secret, it may be justifiably viewed as ancillary to the license.[119]

A similar analytical structure should apply to commercial field of use restrictions. A use restriction that does not apportion naturally competitive markets should be valid as long as the restriction focuses on the actual subject matter of the protected technology.[120] The restriction may not be supportable in a copyright or patent license, however, after these rights have been exhausted by a first sale.[121] As for trade secret licenses,

---

[117] See supra ¶ 5.04; see also Dawson Chem. Co. v. Rohm & Haas Co., 488 US 176 (1980).

[118] See United States v. Chicago Tribune New York News Syndication, Inc., 309 F. Supp. 1301 (SDNY 1970).

[119] See Shin Nippon Koki Co. v. Irvin Indus., 186 USPQ 296, 298 (NY Sup. Ct. 1975).

[120] See General Talking Pictures Corp. v. Western Electric Co., 305 US 124 (1938).

[121] See United States v. Glaxo Group, Ltd., 302 F. Supp. 1 (DDC 1969), aff'd in part, 410 US 52 (1973).

manufacturing restrictions reasonably ancillary to the subject matter and limited in time are valid. Extension of the restriction to a purchaser or to unrelated activities is not supported by the underlying license.[122]

¶ 5.12 DISTRIBUTORS

Beyond issues directly related to technology licensing, contemporary systems for marketing computer-related products are affected by various constraints associated with distributorships and franchise relationships. Many of the issues involved are not unique to the computer environment and are beyond the scope of this book, but two general considerations are of particular interest in microcomputer marketing: exclusive dealerships and mail order terminations.

[1] Exclusive Dealerships

The current market for microcomputers employs both multiple product distributors and exclusive dealing relationships. Manufacturers such as Tandy use a marketing approach characterized by single product line dealers. In contrast, the more common retail format for other vendors entails multiproduct dealers offering several hardware systems and multiple programs.

Agreements for exclusive dealing are not per se illegal under current antitrust laws.[123] Where, however, one of the participants in the arrangement possesses substantial market power, an exclusive dealing agreement is tested under a rule of reason analysis that has been summarized in the following terms

> An exclusive dealing arrangement . . . does not violate [antitrust law] unless . . . the contract will foreclose competition in a substantial share of the line of commerce affected. . . . To [make this determination] it is necessary to weigh the probable affect . . . on . . . competition, taking into account the relative strength of the parties, the proportionate volume of commerce involved in relation to the total volume of commerce in the relevant market area, and the probable immediate and future effects [of] preemption of that share.[124]

---

[122] See Munters Corp. v. Burgess Indus., 450 F. Supp. 1195 (SDNY 1977).

[123] See Jefferson Parish Hosp. Dist. No. 2 v. Hyde, 104 S. Ct. 1551 (1984); United States v. Colgate & Co., 250 US 300, 307 (1919).

[124] Tampa Elec. Co. v. Nashville Coal Co., 365 US 320, 327–329 (1961).

A different analysis has been used where the exclusive dealing relationship involves a leveraging of patent or copyright protections.[125] Precluding a licensee from dealing in competing products is clearly beyond the statutory grant and not necessary or ancillary to the license. It constitutes misuse and may represent an antitrust violation.[126]

[2] Mail Order and Terminations

Mail order distribution is virtually unknown in marketing large computer systems, but it has achieved a substantial market share in the small systems market. In fact, mail order sales are the dominant form of mass marketing some forms of software, even to small businesses. Where a given producer uses this format as a primary system of marketing, no concern arises about distributorships. Indeed, mail order marketing reduces an otherwise severe bottleneck to entry in the mass market. Given the array of hardware and software products, most retailers can not carry more than a small fraction of the potentially available products. Direct mail sales circumvent this limitation.

Where a manufacturer or software publisher distributes through both retail stores and mail order, two distinct problems arise. First, given the entry of computers into a market comprised of unsophisticated buyers, there is both a perceived and actual need to provide service, technical support, and advice to the buyer. This can be accomplished most effectively with retail stores and is extremely difficult in a mail order context. In fact, many mail order vendors do not attempt to provide support. Second, since mail order operations dispense with retail service staff and salesroom overhead, they are able to provide products at prices substantially below those of the stores and, often, below the manufacturer's suggested retail price.

In concept, and assuming that there are no monopolistic or price-setting motivations, the proprietor of a computer product is free to refuse to establish mail order distributors, at least insofar as this can be accomplished through control of the first product sale. Similarly, the proprietor may establish and enforce service and other requirements for dealerships. An agreement intended to fix resale prices, however, is invalid.

In the current marketing environment, these principles coalesce into relatively close factual questions where a proprietor seeks to terminate

---

[125] See, e.g., Berlinbeck v. Anderson Thompson Ski Co., 329 F2d 783 (9th Cir. 1964); Park-In Theatres, Inc. v. Paramount Richards Theatres, Inc., 90 F. Supp. 730 (D. Del. 1949), aff'd per curiam, 185 F2d 407 (3rd Cir. 1950).

[126] See Milgrim, *Trade Secrets* § 6.05[4].

existing mail order distribution channels. This issue was reflected in litigation ensuing from Apple Computer's attempt to terminate mail order distribution of its systems. [127] The issue arises because both a lack of service and downward price pressure are commonly present where mail order and retail store distribution coexist. If the termination of mail order distribution is preceded by complaints from retail store operators about mail order price discounting, the termination may constitute an illegal agreement or conspiracy between proprietor and retail store distributor to fix prices. Such an agreement is a per se antitrust violation. [128] In contrast, however, termination solely for concerns about service or support do not violate antitrust norms.

These doctrinal conclusions are not widely disputed, but there has been substantial controversy over the extent to which complaints and termination are in themselves sufficient to establish an antitrust violation. The law on this issue was recently clarified by the U.S. Supreme Court in *Monsanto Co. v. Spray-Rite Service Corp.* [129] In *Monsanto*, the Court held that beyond the combination of complaint and termination, "there must be evidence that tends to exclude the possibility of independent action by the manufacturer and [other] distributor." [130] This standard recognizes and attempts to protect the primary producer's right to establish prices or other distribution standards acting independently. Antitrust violation is present only if the evidence beyond the termination reasonably establishes a "conscious commitment to a common scheme . . . to achieve an unlawful objective." Standing alone, complaints and mail order termination are too ambiguous to establish joint action.

PART E.   SOFTWARE PUBLISHING

¶ 5.13 THIRD-PARTY AUTHORS

Software publishing and distribution is a major industry characterized by diverse methods through which software products are marketed. Products involving substantial development work by a company's regular staff are common, as are custom designed programs for particular end users. Software publishers often play a role similar to that of book and

---

[127] OSC Corp. v. Apple Computer, Inc., 1983-2 Trade Cases ¶ 65,493 (CD Cal. 1983).

[128] See Roesch, Inc. v. Star Cooler Corp., 712 F2d 1235 (8th Cir. 1983); Battle v. Watson, 712 F2d 1283 (8th Cir. 1983).

[129] 104 S. Ct. 1464 (1984).

[130] Id. at 1473.

periodical publishers, however, especially in developing small systems software. Programs are received from third-party authors, edited by staff, and distributed through traditional retail markets.

The use of third-party authors or the acquisition of programs from other companies creates issues that have not previously been encountered in the industry. The typical acquisition contract involves an assignment of rights or an exclusive license from the author to the publisher. These transactions vest exclusive rights in the assignee and are analogous to a sale of the intellectual property. Under the Copyright Act, transfers of ownership must be in writing.[131] In contrast, a nonexclusive license does not convey ownership.[132] In either format, problems arise in defining the rights transferred and the rights the author retains to use the work to produce distinct, future works. Another significant issue is the obligations of the publisher, who typically agrees to pay the author at least in part on the basis of royalties computed as a percentage of sales.

[1] Title Considerations

In any transaction between a software author and a publisher, the core issue is the nature of the title possessed and conveyed by the author. In most cases, the transaction is an assignment or license of exclusive rights to the publisher. Commonly, the assignment pertains to rights under copyright law. Three distinct title risks are relevant.

The first risk is whether enforceable copyright protection exists in the program. Copyright vests immediately on authorship in works within statutory subject matter.[133] There is dispute about the ability to copyright some programs.[134] Equally important, however, copyright protection may be lost on publication without notice under circumstances precluding cure. Under either eventuality, while a transfer to the publisher conveys the information in the program, the publisher is without legal recourse to exclude reproduction by others. The result may be an inability to recoup a substantial investment.

The second risk is that a portion of the rights in a program may be vested in person or entity other than the author making the assignment.

---

[131] 17 USC § 204(a) (1982).

[132] See *Nimmer on Copyright* 10-101.

[133] Id. at §§ 7.12, 7.13.

[134] See Apple Computer, Inc. v. Franklin Computer Corp., 714 F2d 1240 (3d Cir. 1983), cert. dismissed, 104 S. Ct. 690 (1984); Apple Computer, Inc. v. Formula Int'l, 725 F2d 521 (9th Cir. 1984).

This may occur where coauthors are involved.[135] Alternatively, an author may have executed a prior license to a third party. In either case, while an assigned copyright conveys the right to exclude other potential users, it may be no more than coequal to rights vested in the third party. Again, the publisher's ability to recoup investment may be compromised.

The final title risk is that reproduction by the publisher will infringe a copyright of a third party. This risk is most obvious where the alleged author plagiarized the work. However, the author may have created an original work, but have previously conveyed an exclusive license or assignment to it. Beyond intentional misrepresentation, the copyright may vest in an employer by operation of law or contract under circumstances that may or may not have been apparent to the author. This is especially a risk with university-based authors, since college policies on software copyrights are uncertain and in flux.

These risks are encountered in traditional book publishing, but the environment in which they arise is significantly different in ways that reduce the publisher's ability to protect its interests. In ordinary books or articles, the subject matter is visible to any reader after publication. With computer software this is not necessarily the case in relation to program code. Indeed, a serious effort to independently detect plagiarism may be impossible except in the most obvious cases. In addition, given the technical environment in which software is often developed, works for hire and coauthorship are substantially more common than in traditional book publishing.

Existing legal systems that deal with these title risks are inadequate. Unless an author is in fact a financially viable defendant, publishers of third-party works proceed at substantial risk of liability or lost investment, even with a carefully drawn contract.

[a] Warranties and Fraud

Although title issues are present in traditional publishing, there is surprisingly little case law concerning title representations in a publishing contract. This is due to the common practice of including express warranties or covenants of good title in most publishing contracts.

Even in the absence of an express covenant, the better view is that every publishing contract contains an implicit representation that the work is not in the public domain and that it is in fact substantially an original work by the person represented to be the author.[136] While it is

---

[135] See ¶ 4.04.

[136] See *Nimmer on Copyright* 10-100.

possible to draft an assignment in the form of a quitclaim representing that the transferor is conveying only such rights as he may have, in the absence of express disclaimers, the opposite should be presumed. Title representations are at the core of any publishing agreement unless disclaimed. An analogy to the provisions of the UCC is apt even though the transaction may not be a sale or conveyance of goods.[137] Under the UCC, every sale conveys a warranty that the "title conveyed [is] good, and its transfer rightful."[138]

Although title and infringement warranties might be implied, their scope is uncertain and issues of title should be dealt with in express terms. For example, the essence of the transaction is that the author has good title and a right to convey it; this warranty may be implied. This does not necessarily exclude the possibility that another party, such as a coauthor or a nonexclusive licensee, has coequal or analogous rights, however. In either case, the author can still make a valuable conveyance, but the existence of these parties may materially reduce the value of the acquisition to the publisher.

A similar issue involves the existence of title disputes and the resulting cost of defense even if they prove invalid. Although there is some authority to the contrary, in general there is "no implied warranty of marketable title" in a copyright transfer.[139] This is due to the fact that title registration and tracing systems in copyright law are incomplete and a warranty that there are or will be no substantial title disputes would place a great burden on the author. Couple this with the fact that the costs of litigation are not commonly chargeable to the author in the absence of agreement, and the result is a substantial, but perhaps justifiable, allocation of risk to the publisher that should be considered in the agreement.

[b] Registration Systems

Express or implied warranties ultimately may be no more than a paper remedy, accessible only after costly litigation. From the publisher's viewpoint, the optimal alternative is a system under which title issues can be identified and resolved before substantial resources are committed. This can not be accomplished through reliance on the author. Further-

---

[137] This transfer, of course, differs from the subsequent transaction involving a sale or lease of a copy of the program to an end user. See ¶ 6.02. In this context, it is clear that the essence of the transfer is delivery of the intellectual property rights, rather than merely a copy of the software.

[138] UCC § 2-312.

[139] *Nimmer on Copyright* 10-101.

more, while investigation and inquiry might discover title problems, cost and incompleteness make this prohibitive. The preferable alternative is a registration or notice system. Unfortunately but perhaps inevitably, existing copyright systems are inadequate.

On the surface, the current copyright laws seem to provide substantial notice protections. Registration of copyrighted works is centralized and registration is encouraged by the statute. The Copyright Act establishes a recording statute and priority system for resolving conflicts of ownership.[140] The recording system is based on a concept of constructive notice. It provides that a transfer that is recorded within a one- or two-month grace period[141] has priority over any subsequent transfer or copyright in the same work if the copyright has been registered.[142] If the first transferee does not record the transfer within the grace period, the second transferee takes priority if it took in good faith, for valuable consideration, without notice, and is the first to record and register.

This recording system provides some protection, but is inadequate even when records are checked and the good-faith and other requirements are met. Initially, recording relates only to competing transfers. There is no protection against direct infringement or against the possibility that a work is in the public domain. Since copyright registrations are incomplete and provide relatively inadequate data, no central resource is available to investigate these risks. Furthermore, a first recording of competing transfers may not convey priority if a prior transfer is later recorded within the applicable grace period. Finally, the Copyright Act does not include nonexclusive licenses in its definition of "transfer."[143] Nonexclusive licenses need not be recorded, but have priority over subsequent assignments or exclusive licenses.

[2] Qualitative Considerations

Contracts providing for the conveyance of software rights to a publisher involve significant questions concerning the quality of the work conveyed. This is most clearly true where the assignment provides a substantial payment on delivery of a completed program. Even if payment is in royalties on the sale of copies of the work, however, quality issues are important. Not only is the profitability of the product contingent on qual-

---

[140] 17 USC § 205 (1982).

[141] 17 USC § 205(c) (1982).

[142] 17 USC § 205(e) (1982).

[143] 17 USC § 101 (1982).

ity, distribution of a program with defects exposes the publisher to liability risks. These risks cannot be passed back to the author in the absence of warranty or indemnity rights.

In the absence of express contract terms, virtually no case law deals with implied qualitative representations made by an author to a publisher. In traditional publishing, the question seldom arises. To the extent that quality is an issue in the form, style, or content of a manuscript, controls are generally encompassed in the publisher's right to accept or refuse manuscript and in the normal editing process.

Warranty protections for software publishers should be examined in light of the particular facts. For example, there is little justification for qualitative warranties where the author is an individual not normally in the business of selling programs and the publisher is an experienced software producer. Similarly, it is pertinent whether the publisher controls the final content of the program or merely accepts the author's submission.

An analogy can be drawn to the framework of the UCC regarding implied warranties. The basic warranty in the UCC is that the product is merchantable. Unless disclaimed, this warranty is implied if the seller is a merchant engaged in selling goods of the particular kind. The merchant status of the seller creates at least a minimal right for the buyer to rely on product quality. However, the warranty is limited, assuring merely that the item would pass without objection "under the contract description" and that it is "fit for the ordinary purposes" for which it is used.[144] Warranties that the product is fit for a particular purpose are not implied unless the buyer is known to be acting in reasonable reliance on the seller's skill and judgment.[145]

While a warranty of merchantability might be implied in a software publishing contract involving experienced authors, a warranty of fitness for particular uses should not be imposed in the absence of express contract terms. In most cases, the publishing company has equal or superior skill in software. The publisher is seldom in a position to argue that it relied solely on the author's skill and judgment concerning the suitability of a particular program. This is especially true if there is a period of joint editing and modification in which the publisher participates.

An implied warranty of merchantability provides minimal protection to a publisher. In the current state of the industry, a contract to deliver a word processing program can be satisfied by products having widely

---

[144] UCC § 2-314(2)(a)(c).
[145] UCC § 2-315.

divergent capabilities as to ease, speed, and availability of various editing and printing capabilities. A program that is not able to store and recall text reliably would be inadequate. Even then, however, the publisher should have an obligation to inspect and test the program before marketing it. No liability should fall on the author for readily discoverable defects.

[3] Express Warranties and Indemnity

Uncertainty about the scope or existence of qualitative warranties places a significant premium on express contractual definition of the obligations of the author in delivery of the program. Two distinct issues are involved. The first involves defining the performance characteristics of the program assigned to the publisher. The performance of a program is central to marketability. Furthermore, in the absence of specific definition, a variety of performance levels might reasonably fall within a general label such as word processor or spreadsheet. These variations may not be discernible from preliminary inspection. In most cases, even a well-written program contains latent defects or "bugs." In this environment, contract specification is central to defining the product that the publisher acquires.

The second issue involves indemnification for liabilities due to deficiencies in a marketed program. Publishing houses can reasonably anticipate a risk of contract lawsuits based on allegedly faulty performance, especially in commercial applications software. In the absence of contract reallocation, the risk of loss is on the publisher, particularly where a period of editorial work has been involved in preparing the program for the market. In appropriate cases, this risk might be reallocated to the author in whole or in part by indemnification agreements.

[4] Publisher Obligations

Where the exclusive assignment or license to a software publisher encompasses an obligation to make royalty payments based on sales of the program, the author is placed in a position in which his return on the program is contingent on the publisher's marketing efforts. Case law deriving both from literary licenses involving copyright and from technology licensing imposes an obligation on the publisher to act in good faith to market the product.

In the literary area, the publisher's obligation has been phrased as an implied covenant to "use reasonable efforts to make the work as productive as the circumstances warrant."[146] This concept includes not only an obligation to develop and promote the particular product, but also some restraint on marketing of competitive software products by the same publisher. The combination of a conveyance of exclusive rights and a promise to pay royalties creates a limited fiduciary relationship between author and publisher. Absent contract clarification, however, the scope of the restraint on the publisher is unclear. The issue requires balancing the publisher's right to carry a complete and commercially viable line of products against the author's right to be treated fairly in development of his program. One court addressing this issue suggested that the publication of competing books on the same subject did not violate the obligation unless the competing work and its marketing are "manifestly harmful" to the author and known by the publisher to be harmful.[147]

The case law in technology licensing raises similar arguments. In general, where a license is exclusive and the licensor is compensated by royalties contingent on the licensee's use or sale, an implied obligation to exploit the technology arises.[148] In the absence of contractual clarification, however, the scope of this obligation is unclear and there is disagreement about the basic standard. For example, some courts describe the core obligation as involving a good-faith effort.[149] Other courts refer to an obligation to use "best efforts" or "due diligence" to exploit the technology and focus on appropriate business judgment in marketing a product in particular circumstances.[150]

The implied obligation to exploit the technology is not confined to marketing. It extends to the development efforts necessary to perfect the program and place it in the marketplace.[151] By analogy, it may require at least some effort to modify the initial program in response to perceived or reported defects and deficiencies. The obligation to undertake such efforts is not absolute; the publisher does not ensure the marketability

---

[146] *Nimmer on Copyright* 10-96.

[147] See Van Valkenburgh, Nooger and Nevill, Inc. v. Hayden Publishing Co., 281 NE2d 142 (NY 1972).

[148] See Eastern Elec., Inc. v. Sieburg Corp., 427 F2d 33 (2d Cir. 1970); Vacuum Concrete Corp. v. Am. Mach. and Foundry Co., 321 F. Supp. 771 (SDNY 1971); Wood v. Lucy, Lady Duff Gordon, 118 NE 214 (NY 1917).

[149] See Western Geophysical Co. v. Bolt Assoc., Inc., 285 F. Supp. 815 (D. Conn. 1968), aff'd, 200 USPQ 1 (1969).

[150] See Perma Research and Dev. v. Singer Co., 542 F2d 111 (2d Cir. 1976); Willis, Inc. v. Ocean Scallops, Inc., 356 F. Supp. 1151 (EDNC 1972).

[151] See Perma Research and Dev. v. Singer Co., 542 F2d 111 (2d Cir. 1976).

of the software. The basic obligation is a good-faith effort to develop and market technology entrusted to the publisher. Where the publisher lacks technical expertise for such work and this was known to the author-licensor at the outset, no obligation to develop or modify the program further should be implied.

¶ 5.14 END USER RESTRICTIONS GENERALLY

Software distribution contracts reflect the origins of the industry. Although many of the products are distributed to a mass market, virtually all transfers to end users are cast in the form of an intellectual property license. Software license agreements with end users impose various restrictions on the use of the software. Reflecting the diversity of the industry, the terms and enforceability of these restrictions vary. Among the most common clauses are prohibitions against reverse compilation of the program, limitations on use to single user CPUs or designated systems, restrictions on modification of the program, and restraints on alienation.

In discussing these restrictions, it is necessary to understand their purpose and effect on transactions. This, in turn, requires a distinction between mass-market software transactions and transactions involving software that is custom designed or distributed only on a limited basis. Contracts involving custom software typically are negotiated on an individual basis between parties that, at least in the particular transaction, establish a substantial connection and potential confidentiality. In contrast, most mass-market transactions are remote and undifferentiated contracts involving little or no negotiation or contact between end user and publisher. The market environment may cause the intellectual property rights in the particular programs to differ. Custom software generally involves trade secret and copyright licensing. In contrast, mass-market transactions are more apt to involve only copyright licensing to the substantial exclusion of other rights.

Because of the different configuration of underlying rights and the character of the parties involved, greater freedom of contract is warranted in custom or limited distribution software licenses. The contrast between these contracts and mass-market transactions is virtually total and substantively relevant. As a result, while nominally similar subject matter is involved in mass-market software transactions, the transactions themselves are sufficiently dissimilar that analogies drawn from one context to the other are perilous or misleading.

¶ 5.15 END USERS OF CUSTOM SOFTWARE

Custom or limited distribution software agreements commonly involve both trade secret material and material that may be copyrighted. In some cases, the parties may agree that the end user receive exclusive rights in the program. More commonly, the publisher retains the significant intellectual property rights in the program, merely licensing the end user to use the product. When this is the case, restrictions in a license serve various purposes, the most obvious of which is to ensure the continuation of trade secret rights.[152] Assertion of trade secret claims is contingent on successful efforts to retain the relative secrecy of the subject matter and establish confidential relationships with those to whom the secret is disclosed.[153] The license agreement and, especially, nondisclosure and use restrictions are essential to this purpose.

A second purpose relates more to copyright claims and involves both authorizing and limiting the user's exercise of rights otherwise exclusively vested in the licensor. Presumably, the objective is to optimize commercial advantage to the licensor while delivering acceptable value to the end user. Thus, the license can withhold, partially grant, or completely grant a right to prepare and distribute copies of the work. The license may extend beyond copyright categories. For example, the software developer may intend to reuse modules in a program in creating other programs, and the license may restrict use that is in competition with the original licensor.

In any intellectual property license, the contractual flexibility of the parties is constrained by antitrust and misuse law considerations. These are especially significant if the intellectual property rights are used to leverage or force acceptance of terms beyond the intellectual property grant.

In a typical custom software agreement, issues of control are direct concerns in negotiation. Further issues of ownership and control of the media on which the software is delivered may be perceived as inconsequential and encompassed within negotiation of the relevant license restraints. In some cases, no media is involved; the program is designed at or directly entered into the user's computer. In cases where the software is delivered on tape or disk, the presumption is that rights in the media are controlled by the terms of the license. In essence, the media are leased under terms identical to those of the license, and the assumption prefer-

---

[152] See Sum of Squares, Inc. v. Market Research Corp., 401 F. Supp. 53 (SDNY 1975); Milgrim, *Trade Secrets* § 6.05.

[153] See ¶ 3.05.

ably expressed in the agreement is that on termination of the license copies of the program will be returned.

[1] Restricted Disclosure and Reverse Compilation

In a software license involving trade secrets, a basic term in the agreement is a prohibition on disclosure of the secret subject matter beyond a specified use. Such restraints are essential to maintaining trade secrecy and are clearly ancillary restraints in custom software licenses.[154]

Software licensing provides an opportunity to extend secrecy restraints one step further. Commercially effective conveyance of the software can occur without actual disclosure to the licensee of secret program design and logic considerations. To utilize the program effectively, it may not be necessary that the end user know the design of a program or the coding. In this technology, it is possible to deliver a program in working order without directly disclosing these elements even though access to the program code is clearly desirable for the end user to avoid total reliance on the publisher to update or maintain the program.

Custom software agreements may contain provisions that preclude the end user's discovery of the underlying design. Most often, this involves prohibition of disassembly or reverse compilation of the program. The effect is that the licensee may use a product containing trade secrets, but is contractually barred from employing that product to discover the secrets themselves. To the extent that trade secret licenses commonly involve restricted disclosure of secret information, this is not such a license.

Reverse compilation restraints in custom software licenses involve no antitrust or misuse law violation. They contractually remove a traditional restraint on trade secret protection—the possibility that the secret may be legally discovered by reverse engineering a product. Despite this, such restraints are enforceable in most custom software licenses in the absence of a sale of a product incorporating the secrets. Restrictions on commercial use have been upheld where the transaction involves actual disclosure of information[155] or where a product has been leased.[156] Most custom software licenses implicitly or expressly encompass a lease of the tangible media, and when they do so, restraint on reverse engineering is

---

[154] See Sum of Squares, Inc. v. Market Research Corp., 401 F. Supp. 53 (SDNY 1975); Milgrim, *Trade Secrets* § 6.05.

[155] See Data Gen. Corp. v. Digital Computer Controls, Inc., 357 A2d 105 (Del. Ch. 1975).

[156] See K&G Oil Tool & Serv. v. G&G Fishing Tool, 314 SW2d 782 (Tex. 1958).

enforceable.[157] In contrast, such restrictions are unenforceable as to products sold to a third party.[158]

[2] Single System or Location Restraints

Many custom software licenses expressly restrict the location and type of system in which the licensed program can be used. Such restrictions may create antitrust issues respecting alleged tying of software and hardware systems where the restriction effectively links two products sold by the publisher. A condition in a license limiting use to a hardware environment provided by or only available through the publisher may be an element of an illegal tying arrangement.[159]

This result does not apply to clauses that restrict locale or system, but are generic and do not tie the software license to acquisition or use of a particular hardware system. Thus, for example, a license may be granted to operate the software on a single user CPU selected by the user, but not on a networked system involving multiple users. This arrangement does not create an illegal tying.

Restrictions of this type have a variety of purposes. Perhaps most significant where trade secrets are involved is the augmentation of the monitoring of nondisclosure and confidentiality restraints. Thus, restriction to a single system designated by the user may aid in controlling the number of people who have access to the secret material. Furthermore, unauthorized proliferation of copies or contact with the material may at least indirectly be discovered by observed usage in unauthorized systems or locales.

System or location restrictions are enforceable where the license involves trade secret subject matter and the restrictive clause is not used as an unreasonable restraint on competition. It is less clear whether location restraints are supportable by copyright when a copy of the program is sold. Such restrictions are less relevant to monitoring copyright compliance and may even be viewed as illicit leveraging of the copyright grant in the form of requiring multiple purchases even where only one copy will be used at a time. The existence of copyrightable elements in custom software, however, does not preempt the coexistence of trade secrecy claims. The protection of these claims provides a viable support for the restraint. In the first reported case dealing with single system license restrictions, a

---

[157] See Sum of Squares, Inc. v. Market Research Corp., 401 F. Supp. 53 (SDNY 1975).

[158] See ¶ 3.07[1].

[159] See supra ¶ 5.04.

district court held that the contract clause was supportable under copyright principles. In *S&H Computer Systems v. SAS Institute, Inc.,*[160] a statistics program was delivered to the defendant under a license agreement restricting use to a single CPU identified by serial number. There was a dispute about the validity of a copyright in the program. The court held that if the copyright were valid, "use . . . on a non-designated CPU [and] the making of unauthorized copies [for such use] constitute a form of copyright infringement."[161]

[3] Restraints on Secondary Conveyances

Custom software licenses often preclude conveyance of the licensee's rights in the program to third parties without the consent of the licensor. In most cases, this restriction is enforceable. Most such transactions do not involve sale of a copy of the program. The intellectual property rights involved include trade secret material. Restricting the licensee's right to sublicense or otherwise convey the subject matter bears an obvious and direct relationship to protecting secrecy. The confidentiality necessary to maintain secrecy is established with the initial licensee, but may be lost through a conveyance or other action.

[4] Adaptations and Derivations

A software license should deal with the various issues of ownership that arise when the user makes modifications in licensed software, as Chapter 4 discusses. One approach requires that the licensee disclose and grant back rights in any modification.[162] A more extreme restriction prohibits the user of the custom software to make any modifications in the delivered program. The purpose of this is to limit access to the secret material. More important, the restriction maintains the quality of the operating product and ensures access to a secondary market for maintaining and updating licensed programs. To the extent that the program is protected by copyright and the transaction does not involve the sale of a copy, prohibiting modification is supported by the author's exclusive right to make adaptations or derivative works.[163] Where a program copy has been sold, however, the validity of the clause is more suspect. The Copyright Act grants the owner a right to make adaptations for personal

---

[160] 568 F. Supp. 416 (MD Tenn. 1983).

[161] Id. at 422.

[162] See supra ¶ 5.06.

[163] See ¶ 1.09.

use.[164] Control of such derivative works by contract may be preempted by copyright law.

A more basic issue concerns interpretation of any such clause in light of the transaction as a whole. In many cases, at least a limited right to make minor modifications is implicit. This is true, for example, where a license of an expensive program allows use in any system owned by the licensee, but modifications are needed to adapt to different hardware configurations. In such cases, unless the express clause is absolutely clear and to the contrary, it is appropriate to imply a right to make the necessary coding modifications.

¶ 5.16 MASS-MARKET END USERS

[1] Nature of the Transaction

The contrast between custom transactions and mass marketing of software is such that while nominally the same subject matter is involved, analogies drawn from one context to the other can be misleading. In most cases in the mass market, the end user has not dealt in any significant respect with the software publisher or developer. Instead, the software has simply been made available to potential users through mail order, retail, or wholesale outlets. Characteristic of mass marketing, software availability is indiscriminate: A purchaser need only have sufficient funds. The potential user's intended use or willingness to comply with transactional restrictions is not important in the purchase. In most cases, when purchased, the program is delivered in disk or cassette form. The delivery is commonly accompanied by a document purporting to be a license defining the limitations under which the software is to be used.

In this context, it is important to characterize the contract between the vendor and the end user. There is substantial current uncertainty, but as discussed in Chapter 6, regardless of the language used in papers transmitted with the program diskette or tape, most mass-market transactions are properly characterized as a sale of a copy of the program that attempts to establish an enforceable license agreement pertaining to intellectual property rights and warranty disclaimers. There is uncertainty about the enforceability of licenses included within marketed software packages.[165] It is necessary, however, to identify carefully what is and is not at issue in the enforceability of a mass-market license. The existence of an enforceable license is relevant to whether the purchaser's rights in

---

[164] 17 USC § 117 (1982); see ¶ 4.06.
[165] See ¶ 6.02.

the copy have been effectively expanded or restricted beyond those inherent in the purchase itself and whether warranty and remedy disclaimers are enforceable. As to copyright protections, the owner of a copy has a limited right to make copies or adaptations for personal use and to reconvey the copy.[166] If there is no enforceable license agreement, these define the user's rights against copyright interests. An enforceable license agreement might expand these rights; more often the agreement seeks to restrict them.

[2] Protected Interests

Assuming that a license agreement exists, the type of intellectual property involved affects the enforceability of particular license provisions. It is clear that some aspects of most mass-market programs can be protected under copyright law. Indeed, copyright is the most significant source of protection in the mass market. While it extends only to the form of expression in a program, copyright encompasses the exclusive right to reproduce and distribute copies and is directly relevant to widespread software piracy.

The availability of trade secret protection for mass-market software is less clear. Since unauthorized reproduction of mass-market software is a copyright issue, the potential importance of trade secrecy in the mass market involves protection of aspects of a program such as the idea or design content. While never tested in the courts, it is unlikely that trade secret protection of idea or design remains in aspects of a program discoverable by end users. Trade secrecy protection is built on effective efforts to maintain relative secrecy of commercially valuable subject matter and to establish confidential relationships binding those to whom the secret is disclosed.[167] A confidential relationship can be established by a license agreement, but the requisite confidentiality is difficult to reconcile with mass marketing in which the product is generally available to all purchasers. Furthermore, in many cases, binding restrictions on the buyer are not established in the mass market. These factors weigh against a requisite finding of confidentiality and suggest that to the extent that distributed software encompasses previously secret information, trade secrecy protection is lost.

As a result, a critical factual issue is whether distribution of a program in fact discloses otherwise secret subject matter. There is case law support for continued secrecy protection where the secret is difficult or

---

[166] 17 USC § 117 (1982).

[167] See ¶ 3.05.

virtually impossible to discern from the distributed product.[168] Applied to mass-market software, this requires assessment of whether an allegedly secret design can be discerned from the product by reverse engineering (compiling) the program. The answer depends on the complexity of the design and the technical feasibility of reverse compilation of the program, as well as the existence of barriers to prevent reverse engineering.

The ability to discover trade secret designs from a copy of the program is often confused with the ability to reproduce another copy. The particular expression (coding) of a program and its reproduction are the domain of copyright law in the mass market and not trade secrecy. The common tendency to "copy protect" a program potentially provides practical augmentation of copyright law by making more difficult the preparation of new copies. It is not relevant to trade secrecy, however, unless it also affects the user's ability to reverse compile the program and thereby discern its design.

[3] License Provisions

Mass-market software license forms are less complex than their counterparts in the custom development area. While the licensing agreements are not subject to individual negotiation, the forms currently used differ substantially in philosophy and in the degree of restraint imposed on the end user. For example, the licensing agreement for one of the most popular microcomputer programs indicates that the transferred copy remains the property of the publisher, implying a combined lease and license format.[169] In contrast, the license for another popular program expressly defines the transaction as a sale of a copy subject to a copyright license.[170] Despite the diversity, most licenses deal with four issues. The enforceability of various approaches to each issue are considered in subsequent sections. As a prelude to that discussion, it is useful to note briefly the recurrent factors that bear on the enforceability of the restrictive clauses.

In a mass-market transaction, one approach is that if the transaction is such that the user can be said to have agreed to the license, the terms of

---

[168] See Milgrim, *Trade Secrets* § 2.05[2]; Davidson, "Protecting Computer Software–A Comprehensive Analysis," 1983 Ariz. St. LJ 611, 727 (1983). Distribution in object code may delay or prevent relinquishing secrecy as to persons under enforceable confidentiality restraints. See MacGrady, "Protection of Computer Software–An Update and Practical Synthesis," 20 Hous. L. Rev. 1033, 1063 (1983).

[169] *Ashton-Tate License Form* 3 (1983).

[170] *Lotus Dev. Co. License Form* 123 (1983).

the agreement should be enforced as written. This represents traditional legal doctrine in which contract law is concerned primarily with enforcement of the written terms of a contract. In mass-market transactions, however, there are at least two general bases on which this approach may be rejected as to particular clauses.

The first source of offsetting legal doctrine arises from the manner in which a mass-market transaction occurs. The terms of the license are seldom negotiated, but rather are imposed by the software publisher and its selling agent. While a vendor may condition transactions on acceptance of its terms, in the mass-market software environment, the license terms are often not disclosed until after a purchase has been made. Although the purchase then can be reversed, the entire process raises potential issues associated with the commercial law doctrine of unconscionability and the general judicial reluctance to enforce fully contracts of adhesion characterized by clearly unequal bargaining power.

Unconscionability is an issue primarily in consumer purchases, although efforts to apply it to small businesses have been intermittently successful.[171] The doctrine arises from Section 2-302 of the UCC. It has been described in the following terms by a leading appellate case: "Unconscionability has generally been recognized to include the absence of meaningful choice on the part of one of the parties together with contract terms which are unreasonably favorable to the other party."[172] The language suggests that this doctrine combines procedural concerns about how the contract was entered and substantive concerns about the one-sidedness of a particular clause.[173] Upon a finding of unconscionability, a court may refuse to enforce or limit the effect of a particular contract clause or, even, refuse to enforce the contract as a whole.[174] Unconscionability is most commonly applied to excessive prices and efforts to restrict remedies or disclaim warranties,[175] but the procedural characteristics of the analysis will often be met. The substantive applicability would necessarily be decided on a clause-by-clause basis.

The second source of potential limitations on license terms may be inferred directly from copyright and trade secret law. In general, these limitations relate to the rights of a buyer of a copy of a program. If the transaction is a sale, the attributes of ownership of a copy may insulate

---

[171] White & Summers, *Uniform Commercial Code* 170 (2d ed. 1980).

[172] Williams v. Walker Thomas Furniture, 198 A2d 914 (DC App. 1964).

[173] Leff, "Unconscionability and the Courts—The Emperor's New Clause," 115 U. Pa. L. Rev. 485, 487 (1967).

[174] UCC § 2-302.

[175] White & Summers, *Uniform Commercial Code* 155.

the owner from certain restraints. This is especially likely where the alleged contract restraints are imposed rather than negotiated. Whether this is described as an instance of unconscionability or, simply, preemption of contract terms inconsistent with copyright and trade secret policy, the effect is that some license restrictions are unenforceable.

The Copyright Act states an affirmative policy conveying limited rights of reproduction and modification of a program to the owner of a copy.[176] The owner may make such copies and adaptations of the program as are essential for use in a computer or as are used solely for archival or backup purposes. This provision is an adaptation of the copyright principle that the first sale of a copy terminates some of the proprietor's rights in that copy. It establishes a balance between protection of the copyright holder and the ownership rights of the copy owner. In other words, the copyright proprietor is protected by retaining exclusive rights to make and distribute copies, while the owner of a copy has exclusive control of that copy as to its use and resale. The analogy in computer programs is that the proprietor retains all reproduction and distribution rights, except those essential to the copy owner's use and resale of the original.

Arguably, the Copyright Act creates an umbrella of rights that can not be reduced by a mass-market contract imposed with little or no opportunity to negotiate. By a marketing decision, the publisher effectively can attempt to broaden copyright protection through a purported contract. In the absence of negotiation, the attempt may be precluded. Even if it is not barred by copyright law, attempts to force acceptance of broader restraints on the use of a program may reflect misuse.

[a] Single Terminal Use

Although mass-market licenses vary substantially, one element is present in virtually all licenses. This restricts the purchaser to use of the program in a single computer with, perhaps, authorization for use in "subsequent but not additional" machines.[177] The restraint is variously phrased. Although in some cases the terms are ambiguous, in others the restriction is clearly stated as referring to one single user and a single terminal system.[178] Use in multiterminal or multiuser systems allegedly requires a special license for that purpose or the payment of multiple license fees.

---

[176] 17 USC § 117 (1982).

[177] *Ashton-Tate License Form* (1983).

[178] *IBM License Form* (1982) ("single machine"); *Micropro Int'l License Form.*

The license provisions essentially reflect the posture adopted by the publishers that there is a right to sell or license one software copy for each combination of a user and a terminal or CPU. The economic attraction of this model is apparent. For example, in an office containing five micro-computers, the publisher anticipates five sales. Independent of whether the program will ever be used simultaneously on more than one system, the literal terms of the license require five purchases. The same result applies in at least some licenses where five terminals are linked to one computer or five microcomputers are part of a network and share a single program file. All of these settings contain a presumed right to five sales, although many publishers offer multiunit discounts.

The contrasting proposition is that the buyer has a right to use the copy as it chooses as long as it does not make multiple copies beyond those essential to use in a machine. Thus, for example, the owner might one day read the program into the memory of machine number one and the next day into machine number two. No infringement occurs unless several copies coexist. A more extreme proposition is that the owner has a right to make as many copies as are necessary for use in all machines that it owns, as long as they are not used simultaneously.

It is important to recognize that copyright does not convey an exclusive right to *use* a program, but only to reproduce it. The distinction may be relevant to whether there is a basis for the limit against use in systems involving shared use of a single CPU. The legislative history of copyright indicates that loading a program into a computer memory is a preparation of a copy in that the program is then fixed for more than an ephemeral period in a tangible medium from which it can be reproduced.[179] Loading a disk-resident program into a microcomputer may, thus, be an act of copying the program and be controllable through a copyright license. This analysis was apparently accepted by the court in *S&H Computer Systems v. SAS Institute, Inc.*[180] In that case, the court concluded that a license restriction on use in a single, designated CPU was enforceable as a copyright license restriction. Use in other CPUs violated the license and thus would constitute copyright infringement.

S&H did not deal with a situation in which a copy had been sold to a user. Section 117 of the Copyright Act gives the owner of a copy a right to make such additional copies as are essential to use in "a machine." Arguably, Section 117 affects the enforceability of a restriction premised on the view that loading the program in a computer constitutes making a

---

[179] See *National Comm'n on New Technological Uses of Copyrighted Works.*
[180] 568 F. Supp. 416 (MD Tenn. 1983).

copy. Regulation by contract on that basis may be preempted by the statute.

Ultimately, however, neither analysis aids in establishing a balance between the rights of a copyright holder and the owner of a copy. The statutory reference in Section 117 to use in a machine is ambiguous, since it does not necessarily imply a restriction to a single user machine or even to a single CPU. The extremes of the appropriate policy seem relatively clear. The copy owner should not be prevented from using the program on replacement or alternative machines in a sequential pattern of use. Conversely, the purchase of a single copy should not authorize a corporation to reproduce sufficient copies for use in the 1000 machines that it owns. That use would substantially reduce the author's market, while allowing a sequential pattern of use is essential to maintain flexibility and not artificially expand a natural market. The manner in which uses falling between the extremes should be resolved should depend on careful assessment of policy, rather than on technical assessment of arcane technological features. Clearly, the issue should not be resolved by imposed contract terms unless it is initially determined that they fall within the range of appropriate copyright policy.

[b] Restricted Copying

Mass-market licenses contain various provisions relating to the preparation of backup copies of programs. In general, programs distributed in a form that precludes easy copying (copy protection) buttress this physical restraint with license provisions that limit copying by the end user to entry into a computer memory for use. Most other licenses, however, expressly authorize backup or archival copies for personal use. Some licenses, however, contain an express limit on the number of backup copies that can be in existence at any particular time.

Those licenses that permit backup copies are enforceable whether or not the underlying transaction is a sale or a true lease of a copy of the program. In general, they track the rights of an "owner" as outlined in Section 117 of the Copyright Act, except where a specific number of backup copies are indicated. The benefit of including provisions that trace statutory rights is that they clarify that no greater rights are conveyed and establish a contractual basis for action. In addition, the contract may notify the purchaser of the subsisting copyright restrictions.

Licenses that preclude backup copies conflict with Section 117 if the underlying transfer involved a sale of a copy. A conclusion that Section 117 is not subject to contract variation would invalidate such restraints. More appropriately, the validity of the restraint should be determined in light of the entire transaction. Section 117 recognizes that possession of a backup copy of a program is important to the user. A transaction that seeks to preclude this violates the purpose of the Section. If, however, the publisher supplies a backup copy, the restriction may be supportable. Copy protection is a potentially effective extralegal means to safeguard against program piracy. A license restraint coupled with the provision of a backup is reasonably tailored to effectuating this protection.

The first case to discuss Section 117 generally supports the view that the scope of the Section is determined by the purpose of the rights conveyed to the copy owner. In *Atari, Inc. v. JS&A, Inc.,*[181] however, the court focused on the nature of the copy conveyed, rather than on whether the transaction as a whole satisfied a user's need for a backup copy. It held that the right to prepare a backup exists only if the tangible copy entails a unique risk of destruction distinguishable from loss of other copyrighted works.

[c] Transfer Restrictions

Most mass-market licenses deal expressly with the end user's right to transfer rights in the program. In a number of licensing forms, the right to transfer the copy is expressly granted, subject to the restriction that all rights are conveyed and that all archival copies are conveyed or destroyed. This language generally conforms to Section 117 of the Copyright Act and is enforceable.[182]

In some mass-market programs, however, conveyance of the copy is expressly prohibited or severely limited. For example, the license form accompanying Micropro's word processing program describes the license as "non-transferable" while the Ashton-Tate license form accompanying a database management program states that the program copy will not be transferred "in any form . . . without the prior written consent of Ashton-Tate." These transfer restrictions are unenforceable if the transaction is a sale of a copy of the program. In such cases, they are in direct conflict with copyright law regarding the effect of a first sale of a copyrighted work and permitting the copy owner to convey its rights. Not surprisingly, therefore, the licensing forms that purport to preclude reconveyance make explicit efforts to define the underlying transaction in terms consistent with a lease of the copy with a license to use it.[183] Further-

---

[181] Copyr. L. Dec. (CCH) ¶ 25,613 (ND Ill. 1983).

[182] See ¶ 1.11[1].

[183] *Ashton-Tate License Form* (user acknowledges that program remains the "sole and exclusive property of Ashton-Tate" and that the user does not become the "owner of the materials").

more, these forms also make express claims of trade secrecy for elements of the program.

If the transaction is a lease and involves trade secrets, the restrictions on subsequent conveyance may be enforceable. The difficulty lies in equating this characterization with the circumstances of most mass-market transactions. Most purchases in the mass market convey title and it is highly unlikely that purchasers of software proceed with any different expectation about title to the software copy. Furthermore, the publisher's description of the transaction as a lease is on a form that is reviewed, if at all, only after the fact of the acquisition. The expectations of the buyer and, perhaps, the retail seller should prevail over the contrary terms of a form, especially where efforts to enforce the lease are virtually nonexistent.

[d] Nondisclosure

Several mass-market licensing forms expressly bind the end user to nondisclosure of materials and designs present in the program copy. Not surprisingly, these provisions are found only in licenses that assert claims to trade secret protection in aspects of the mass-marketed program. Nondisclosure is clearly outside the range of copyright protection. Nondisclosure restraints may even be said to be in direct conflict with traditional concepts of copyright in published works.

Since it is supported solely by trade secrecy claims, a nondisclosure restriction arguably is unenforceable unless at least a colorable claim to trade secrecy persists at the time of the license transaction. The likelihood of this occurring with a true mass-market product is low. In the absence of a colorable trade secret claim, the restraint should be unenforceable.

[e] Progam Modifications

In most cases, the mass-market end user has a right to make adaptations necessary to operate the program in a computer of his selection. Few license agreements in fact attempt to limit or exclude this personal right; none expressly expand the adaptation right. In the likely event that the mass-market transaction is viewed as a sale, copyright law expressly conveys the right to make personal adaptations, independent of language in the license agreement. If the transaction is treated as a lease, the right to make essential personal adaptations arguably is implicit in the transaction, unless expressly prohibited.

Even if the license agreement is not enforceable, transactions conducted in the mass market do not convey a right to prepare derivative works and commercially distribute them. Section 117 grants the owner of a copy a right to make adaptations, but is expressly limited to personal use. It does not encompass marketing of the adaptations without authorization from the copyright proprietor.[184] This limitation on the end user's rights must be qualified, however, by recognizing that it is grounded in copyright law. Copyright law does not protect the ideas of an author, only his expression of those ideas. Thus, an end user who is able to discern the underlying ideas expressed in a mass-market product may use those new ideas in producing his own software. While the concept or idea as contrasted to expression in a software environment has not been delineated in the cases, it is clear that the idea of a work is more specific than, for example, the mere concept of creating a program to handle the recording and editing of text, while it is less specific than the particular coded program used to implement a word processing program.

Restrictions on use of the ideas underlying a program in the creation of a competing program can only be enforced through trade secret or similar intellectual property grounds. This, of course, is one of the purposes behind the use of licensing forms that attempt to characterize the transaction as a lease of a product containing trade secret information. In a mass-market environment, it is unlikely that any trade secret protections continue in secrets that can be discerned from the product itself. It is even more unlikely that secrecy protections can be enforced against the typical mass-market purchaser. Pertinent questions of fact relate to the degree of difficulty involved in discerning the secret from the distributed product and the existence of effective confidentiality imposed in the product distribution. As to discovery and use by the end user, the significant question would seem to focus on the confidential nature of the purchase, since by contextual definition the end user has in fact discovered the secret from the software product.

While appropriate language may be included within license agreements accompanying a mass-market transaction, the mass market would seem to be the direct opposite of a confidential disclosure. There is no prescreening of purchasers and no direct relationship between publisher and end user. In most cases, the transaction is effectively anonymous and undifferentiated from the vast bulk of retail sales. Furthermore, no current case law supports the imposition of secrecy restraints on the buyer of a product, and it is likely that any such restraints would contradict concepts of ownership and the basic role of reverse engineering as a limit on the scope of trade secrecy protections.

---

[184] 17 USC § 117 (1982).

CHAPTER **6**

Computer Contracts: Leases and Sales Agreements

¶ 6.01 INTRODUCTION

This chapter examines contract law issues in transactions dealing with computer technology and information services. Contracts to acquire technology present significant issues of quality, performance, and the allocation of loss if a product fails to conform to expectations. These expectations and the manner in which they are enforced are defined by the specific contract terms and in light of traditional contract law.

Describing a product as an innovative technology does not guarantee that it performs the functions desired. Indeed, given the complexity of the technology and often overenthusiastic expectations, new technology frequently falls short of end user expectations. In such cases, the cost of the disparity between performance and expectation must be apportioned between the parties in a specific transaction. More broadly, decisions apportioning loss accumulate to affect the manner in which technology transactions are conducted. This effect transcends particular transactions. The risks that the manufacturer or vendor undertakes shape its willingness to participate in the market. Similarly, the degree of risk borne by the end user affects the willingness of technology consumers to participate in transactions.

There are few doctrinal questions unique to computer contracts, but the character of the technology creates a unique environment that requires close attention in defining the actual bargain and the manner in which it is implemented. Computer software and hardware have broader potential application than other products and current marketing stresses their flexibility. This contributes to the potential impact of computer products, but also creates transactional problems in expressing and enforcing contractual expectations. Expectations should be resolved in the contract, but in practice contracts are often ambiguous so that contract law doctrines must be applied to reconstruct the intentions and expectations of the parties.

PART A.   DEFINING THE BARGAIN

¶ 6.02 GOODS, SERVICES, AND INTANGIBLES

[1] Contract Characterization Issues

Computer-related contract rights can be significantly affected by the characterization of the agreements. As discussed in further sections, computer hardware and software acquisitions may be structured in the form of a lease or in the form of a sale. The choice affects the rights of the end user and the supplier of the delivered system.[1]

[a] Services or Goods

A second, frequently discussed distinction exists between contracts for goods and contracts for services. This distinction determines the body of law that applies to the transaction. The Uniform Commercial Code (UCC) applies to goods, while common law and other statutes apply to services. Computer hardware constitutes goods under the UCC. Software contracts are more questionable. However, the difficult issues are largely confined to contracts-involving custom-designed software. Software that is mass marketed or otherwise prepackaged is analogous to any generally marketed product for purposes of UCC sales law. The product may involve substantial, original effort to design and develop, but it is now generally manufactured and reproduced.

Ultimately, the characterization of a particular transaction as involving services or goods in any close case should reflect the body of law that contains substantively pertinent standards. The UCC was drafted for transactions involving the conveyance and delivery of products. In contrast, common law and statutes dealing with personal service agreements are concerned primarily with labor issues in the broad sense. Their main focus concerns matters such as control over work performance.

The distinction between goods and services does not lie in whether significant human labor or creativity is involved in preparing the final product of the agreement. The UCC definition of "goods" encompasses any object that is movable at the time of identification to the contract.[2] The reference is to the end product; transactions in goods include contracts in which substantial effort is involved in specially manufacturing a product for delivery. The purchase of a custom-designed, handcrafted table is a sale of goods even though the seller's performance involves personal work of a high degree of creativity and skill. Similarly, the fact that the contract involves custom-designed software does not define a per-

---

[1] See infra ¶ 6.14.

[2] UCC § 2-105.

sonal services contract. If the essence of the agreement is the delivery of a product, a sale of goods is involved even though development of the product involves substantial creative work by the vendor.

Any argument that all contracts for custom software are personal service agreements does not accurately apply the distinction between a services contract and a contract for goods whose construction requires substantial work effort. The principal question is what constitutes the essence of the agreement and, essentially, what performance satisfies the contract. If the contract calls for a product to be delivered, the software agreement constitutes a transaction in goods and the program represents the movable corpus of the transaction, even if transferred in electronic rather than tangible form. Many custom software contracts involve specially manufactured goods, but while this might affect remedial and other rights of the parties, it does not alter the basic characteristic of the transaction. It is not surprising that in most reported cases involving contract issues[3] the status of the software contract as a sale of goods under the UCC has been stipulated by the parties or not substantially contested.[4]

Nevertheless, many computer-related contracts are service agreements, rather than transactions in goods. This is true, for example, if an individual is hired as a programmer or consultant and the essence of the agreement is that the individual's services are retained. His obligation is satisfied by the performance of work, whether or not a program is delivered. While a completed program may be one product of the services, it is incidental to the main activity. The transaction is a service agreement, but the UCC may apply to those aspects of performance that involve delivery of a product.

A similar circumstance exists in the typical service bureau contract where one party contracts with another for the use of the other's computer resources. For example, a party may deliver information to a data processing company which then processes this information on its own system and returns specified reports. Although reports are delivered, the essence of the transaction is the data analysis. A service contract is involved.

> The fact of the matter here is that the alleged contract was simply not for the sale of goods. . . . Rather it was that certain services be provided the defendant by the plaintiff. The written proposal states that it is an agreement "for performance of data processing services."

---

[3] Compare infra ¶ 6.02[2].

[4] See, e.g., Jones, Morrison, Stalnaker, PA v. Contemporary Computer Servs., Inc., 414 So. 2d 637 (Fla. Dist. Ct. App. 1982); National Cash Register Co. v. Adell Indus., Inc., 225 NW2d 785 (Mich. Ct. App. 1975); WR Weaver Co. v. Burroughs Corp., 580 SW2d 76 (Tex. Civ. App. 1979); cf. Triangle Underwriters, Inc. v. Honeywell, Inc., 604 F2d 737 (2d Cir. 1979).

The proposal indicated that there would be a separate charge for supplies. . . . The payment contemplated was for the analysis, storage, and reporting of certain data supplied the plaintiff by the defendant.[5]

[b] Tangible or Intangible Property

Beyond the distinction between services and goods, confusion also arises over whether a software contract involves a sale of tangible or intangible property and whether this distinction affects the liability of the vendor for defects in the program. The issue is commonly mentioned in conjunction with intellectual property rights. The inference is that the involvement of intellectual property may insulate the vendor from responsibility for faulty performance of a delivered product.

In fact, the two issues are separable and routinely separated. Intellectual property rights involve matters such as disclosure of information and the right to reproduce copies. To the extent that these are conveyed, the UCC does not apply directly to that aspect of the conveyance.[6] This does not alter contract responsibility for delivering a product that performs to expectations. The sale of a program on a disk does not merely convey an inert plastic disk, but a product claimed to have particular performance characteristics. These characteristics are determined by copyrighted expression in the program, but this does not change the nature of the product conveyed or the vendor's obligation that it perform adequately. By analogy, the vendor of a television set is not insulated from claims that the set does not receive a picture by the fact that the receiving component is patented.

[2] State Tax Law

Characterizing a particular transaction as involving goods, services, or intangibles may affect the body of law that applies to determine the rights of the parties to the contract and to determine the framework for analysis of various contract issues. In many instances, however, this has little effect on substantive rights, since each of the potentially applicable bodies of law applies analogous criteria for determining contract rights.

Classifying the subject matter of the transaction is also necessary when applying state tax laws to the transfer. In most states, a major source of tax revenues consists of sales or use taxes imposed on property sold within the state or used in the state following acquisition in another

---

[5] Computer Servicenters, Inc. v. Beacon Mfg. Co., 328 F. Supp. 653, 655, aff'd, 443 F2d 906 (4th Cir. 1971).

[6] But see UCC § 2-312.

jurisdiction.[7] While such laws could be extended to encompass intangible property or services, in most jurisdictions sales and use taxes are limited to transactions involving tangible items. Given this state tax law structure, it is frequently important to determine whether aspects of a computer-related transaction fall within sales or use tax provisions. Clearly, computer hardware is tangible property for this purpose, but whether software transactions involve transactions in tangible or intangible property for purposes of state tax laws is debatable.

The relevant state laws are rapidly developing and expanding, particularly since the availability of software as a potentially valuable source of tax revenue is increasingly obvious. In responding to this opportunity, however, the various state laws differ widely in effect and in the underlying conceptual framework for defining the scope of existing tax provisions. Summaries of state tax provisions relating to software are published annually by several sources.[8]

The overall pattern of state tax law generally recognizes a basic distinction between "packaged" or "canned" software and custom-developed software. A substantial majority of all states in which sales or use taxes exist impose this tax on prepackaged software.[9] The analogy between this product and other forms of mass-produced products is obvious and generally followed for tax liability. In contrast, however, state regulations concerning custom-developed software are widely divergent. In several jurisdictions, the personal service and intangible characteristics of such software are treated as predominant and the transactions are not included within a general tax law structure pertaining to transfers of tangible property.[10] In other jurisdictions, even custom-developed software is included within the tax system.[11]

Other aspects of the software and data processing industry may also be subject to sales, use, or service taxes. In several states, for example, the

---

[7] See *State Tax Guide* 6012, 6013, 6014 (CCH); Hollman, "Sales Taxation of Software," 1 Comp. Law. 31 (March 1984).

[8] See Bigelow & Saltzberg, *State Computer Tax Report—1983; ADAPSO*, ADAPSO Tax Service (1983).

[9] See, e.g., Ark. Stat. Ann. § 84-1903; Cal. Rev. & Tax Code § 6010.9; Mass. Sales & Use Tax Reg. 830 CMR § 64H.06; Okla. Tax Code § 1354(H); NC Gen. Stat. §§ 105-164.4, 105-164.6; Ga. Code § 48-8; Idaho Tax Reg. 12-2B(ii); Comptroller v. Equitable Trust Co., 464 A2d 248 (Md. 1983); Chittenden Trust Co. v. Comm'r, 465 A2d 284 (Vt. 1983).

[10] See, e.g., Cal. Rev. & Tax Code § 6010.9; Fla. Stat. Ann. § 12A-1.32; Ga. Code § 48-8; NC Gen. Stat. § 105.164.4; Comptroller v. Equitable Trust Co., 464 A2d 248 (Md. 1983).

[11] See Ark. Stat. Ann. § 84-1903; Conn. Gen. Stat. § 12-407; Idaho Tax Reg. 12-2B(ii); Kan. Stat. Ann. § 79-3603(s); Ky. Rev. Stat. § 139.120; Chittenden Trust Co. v. Comm'r, 465 A2d 284 (Vt. 1983).

tax systems encompass data processing services. In others, maintenance contracts are also included.[12]

¶ 6.03 RESOURCES AND SOLUTIONS CONTRACTS

[1] Defining the Obligation

In any contract, the parties should define the subject matter of the bargain and the circumstances that constitute adequate performance of the agreement. This general proposition has added importance in computer hardware or software contracts. Critical to computer contracting is the determination of whether the purchaser is contracting merely for *resources* with which it may solve a business problem or for a *solution* to the problem itself. This can be clarified in the contract, but the distinction may be ephemeral in many cases even to the parties themselves. If the contract is ambiguous, this ultimately will be the prime question raised in interpreting contract warranties.

The difference between resources and solutions contracts can be captured in relatively simple terms. At one extreme, the purchaser may anticipate no more than delivery of the tools with which it will subsequently design a computer system for internal needs. For example, a small law firm may acquire five microcomputers and word processing software, intending to use these resources to develop a word processing system.[13] This is a pure resource transaction. In contrast, the buyer may express a need for a word processing system for a small law firm and accept the vendor's recommendation of five microcomputers with specially designed word processing software. This is a solutions contract. Assuming that the vendor shares the buyer's expectations, the two transactions impose dissimilar performance obligations.[14]

[2] Role of Contract Specifications

The dissimilar obligations can and should be defined in the agreement through acceptance standards, contract specifications, express war-

---

[12] See "State Tax Law Summary," 3 CLR 862 (1984).

[13] See Aplications, Inc. v. Hewlett-Packard Co., 501 F. Supp. 129, aff'd, 672 F2d 1076 (2d Cir. 1982); International Business Mach., Inc. v. Catamore Enter., Inc., 548 F2d 1065 (1st Cir. 1975); Honeywell v. Lithonia Lighting, Inc., 317 F. Supp. 406 (ND Ga. 1970).

[14] See Sperry Rand Corp. v. Industrial Supply, 337 F2d 363 (5th Cir. 1964); Lovely v. Burroughs Corp., 527 P2d 557 (Mont. 1974); National Cash Register Corp. v. Adell Indus., Inc., 225 NW2d 785 (Mich. Ct. App. 1975).

ranties, and the like. When the contract terms and the behavior of the parties are ambiguous, UCC provisions for implied and express warranties operate to reconstruct the transaction. A standard against which a particular agreement is measured must be developed. Is the presumed expectation that the contract provide a solution, or merely resources to subsequently develop that solution? In general, the net effect of standard contract terms and UCC warranty provisions creates a resource transaction unless a contrary intent is clearly expressed or otherwise manifest. Of course, this enhances the importance of the ability of the buyer to obtain contract terms that delineate more if, in fact, that is the nature of the bargain between the parties.

These issues are more apparent in computer contracting than in many other acquisition contracts due to the nature of the technology and the expectations that the parties have for it. The technology is malleable in experienced hands. As a consequence, even in relatively small transactions there is a tendency toward customization of hardware and software. In addition, especially among inexperienced users there is often a conception that the mere presence of a computer generates solutions for operational needs. Thus, even though a contract merely involves acquiring computer resources, the purchaser may perceive it as a solution to a perceived problem. In fact, however, the technology is sensitive to gross disparities in performance based on a multitude of factors, many of which may be integral to the technology and outside the common expertise of most purchasers. Many deal explicitly with software characteristics. Others involve the ability to obtain, train, and keep qualified system operators.

Often, one issue in a contract dispute is whether contract specifications were inadequate or whether performance was deficient. This is especially important given the extent to which deficiencies in a computer system can adversely affect a business. Obviously, the importance of any system depends on its use, but computer systems tend to become central to business operation, especially in small businesses. A system failure may contribute to the demise of the business itself.[15]

While often discussed from the standpoint of the purchaser, contract specifications can also substantially enhance the position of the vendor, especially where the contract involves a customized applications system. Contract specifications provide explicit benchmarks for the vendor's performance. As discussed in a further section,[16] system requirements are often modified in development contracts during the period in which con-

---

[15] See The Glovatorium, Inc. v. NCR Corp., 684 F2d 658 (9th Cir. 1982).
[16] See infra ¶ 6.21.

tract performance occurs.[17] Specifying the elements of the contracted-for system aids in identifying the extent to which modifications alter the terms and chargeable cost of the contract.

The literature on computer contracting[18] suggests various methods to define the bargain of the parties. While many of these involve identifiable costs that often preclude their use, they provide a basis or framework for discussion. The following sections examine several of the most frequently discussed methods with a focus on the contract law concepts concerning their effect and the risks involved. Whether a particular method should be adapted to a transaction must be decided by the parties involved in the transaction itself in light of cost and time constraints.

¶ 6.04 REQUESTS FOR PROPOSAL

One method for initiating a computer acquisition and specifying the terms of the agreement involves use of a request for proposal (RFP). In concept, in an RFP, specification of contract objectives begins prior to the time that the buyer contacts a prospective vendor. The buyer conducts a needs analysis and specifies the system performance that it requires. These decisions are reduced to relatively specific terms and circulated to prospective vendors. The vendors submit prices and detailed specifications for proposed systems that respond to the buyer's request.

The RFP procedure provides a structured foundation and significantly reduces the buyer's reliance on the vendor. By predefining its own needs, the buyer reduces the risk of being induced to acquire a system that is not optimal merely because a particular vendor is the most persuasive. Of necessity, however, use of an RFP implies that the buyer has the resources and expertise to conduct an adequate analysis of its needs and that the size of the transaction justifies the cost and effort involved. In many cases, internal resources are not in fact adequate. Lacking either system design or technological expertise, many buyers must use a consultant to examine internal procedures, assess needs, and evaluate proposals that are received. As a result, the buyer shifts reliance from the vendor to a consultant, potentially gaining in terms of the neutrality of the advice received.

Although a structured RFP is preferable to a totally unstructured approach to a computer acquisition, it has identifiable weaknesses, the

---

[17] See Bernacchi & Larsen, *Data Processing Contracts and the Law* (1974).

[18] See, e.g., Brandon & Segelstein, *Data Processing Contracts* (1976); Bernacchi, Davidson & Grogan, "Computer System Procurement," 30 Emory LJ 395 (1981).

most obvious of which is the time and cost of predesigning the system. This expenditure makes the procedure economically unavailable to many purchasers. In addition, an RFP tends to reduce the input of vendors who may be the most knowledgeable about particular systems. The RFP defines the relationship between the parties in a manner that is significantly different than that of more traditional purchases. Two of the differences merit comment here: reliance on third-party consultants and the extent to which initial specifications are incorporated into the final bargain.

[1] Consultants and Reliance

When an RFP is used, it is clear that the buyer elected to rely primarily on its own or a consultant's expertise, rather than on a vendor's. The extent of the shift away from reliance on a vendor varies. For example, an RFP that provides merely that the buyer desires a "local area network consisting of ten microcomputers" is sufficiently general to permit substantial clarification in reliance on the particular vendors. In contrast, an RFP that outlines "all relevant technical specifications for a local area network" establishes a transaction in which the buyer places no reliance on the seller to design a system suitable for a particular task.

If a buyer relies on the seller to design or recommend a system, the vendor's obligations may include implied or express warranties that the delivered system be suitable for the buyer's needs. In contrast, absent reliance the vendor's sole responsibility is to supply products that meet the contract specifications. If the RFP is detailed, this latter result is likely. Furthermore, even if there are modifications from the original, detailed RFP based on the seller's recommendations, it is likely that there is no enforceable reliance on the seller. Overall, the buyer's conduct in an RFP procedure demonstrates a reliance on its own or its consultant's expertise. In this situation, the vendor does not undertake to supply a system that meets the needs of the buyer, but merely to supply the resources defined as necessary by the buyer and this is not altered if the buyer elects to follow the vendor's suggestions.

The altered reliance affects the risk of nonperformance due to inadequate or inappropriate system design. Where the RFP was prepared solely by an inhouse staff, the buyer assumes the risk of such error. If a consultant is involved, responsibility for ineffective design may be shifted to the consultant. The consulting relationship, however, is a service contract, typically involving an independent contractor. In that relationship, the client may have bargained for the consultant's effort, not for an assurance of a workable design. Absent negligence or fraudulent representations, the consultant has no liability for merely misestimating the needs of the buyer-client.

Where there is no reliance on the seller's judgment, errors by the consultant do not place the buyer in a position to reject or otherwise avoid the purchase contract. The buyer is required to complete the transaction and seek a remedy, if at all, from the consultant. This result may change if the buyer has sufficient leverage to obtain representations or warranties that its particular application needs will be met by the delivered system. Such representations are unlikely unless the vendor is able to participate in defining the needs and the responsive system designs.

[2] Specifications and Parol Evidence

An RFP procedure is a request that potential vendors submit offers for a contract in general compliance with the specifications of the RFP. The RFP does not itself constitute an offer and can not lead directly to an agreement. Outside of public (governmental) contracting, the potential buyer is not bound to accept a low bid or, indeed, insist on particularized compliance with the specifications in the RFP. The purpose of the RFP is to provide guidance for potential vendors in responding to the needs of the buyer. As a result, the terms of the RFP do not automatically become a part of an eventual contract between the parties.[19]

The RFP is a preliminary document rather than an element of the contract, unless it is expressly incorporated in the contract. The result is a possible discontinuity between the terms of the contract and the original system defined in a RFP. Parol evidence rules may foreclose use of the terms of the RFP to clarify or alter the final bargain. As a result, to the extent that they are intended to carry forward, it is important that elements of an RFP specifically be incorporated in the contract.

Absent express incorporation, the specifications of the RFP might be inconsistent with the final written agreement and their use barred by parol evidence rules. Under UCC § 2-202, the terms of the written agreement may not be contradicted by "any prior" agreement.[20] This preclusion applies whether or not the contract is intended as the exclusive statement of the agreement, but requires that the terms of the RFP are *directly* inconsistent with the written contract.

---

[19] This, of course, assumes that the RFP is structured in relatively standard form, expressing the potential interest of the buyer in acquiring a system like the one described. It would be possible, although seldom desirable, to structure an RFP in the form of an offer in which a contract is complete on acceptance by a potential vendor. See UCC § 2-206.

[20] UCC § 2-202(a).

A second possibility is that the RFP may be viewed as evidence of "consistent additional terms." Under the UCC, this evidence is allowable unless the contract was intended to be "a complete and exclusive statement of the terms of the agreement."[21] This formulation of the parol evidence rule is triggered by the inclusion in the eventual contract of a so-called integration or merger clause,[22] which is a routine part of most vendor agreements.

¶ 6.05 ACCEPTANCE STANDARDS AND TESTING

Unless otherwise agreed, under the UCC a seller is required to tender delivery of the goods, but is not required to complete delivery until the buyer makes payment.[23] The buyer's obligation to pay is deferred, however, until the buyer "accepts" the goods.[24] Acceptance in this context is a technical term not associated with the idea of accepting an offer. Rather, it is essentially the converse of rejecting goods that do not conform to the contract. Acceptance alters the buyer's remedies in the event that a defect is subsequently discovered.[25]

Acceptance procedures can be used to clarify the terms of the bargain. Under the UCC, acceptance is preceded by a limited right to inspect, unless the parties otherwise agree.[26] One frequently recommended approach to major system contracting expands on this by contractually specifying detailed acceptance standards and calling for extensive testing to determine compliance with the standards prior to acceptance. Compliance with the specified standards and resulting acceptance of the system is a precondition to the buyer's obligation to pay.

Acceptance standards and testing serve two distinct functions. First, they protect the buyer against being required to pay for an inadequate delivery. By conditioning the obligation to pay on compliance with particular standards, the buyer retains leverage to ensure compliance with those specifications for which testing is required. Withholding payment is a more effective incentive for the seller's compliance than the threat of a lawsuit. Second, standards and testing provide the seller with benchmarks

---

[21] UCC § 2-202(b).

[22] See Earman Oil Co. v. Burroughs Corp., 625 F2d 1291 (5th Cir. 1980).

[23] UCC §§ 2-503, 2-507.

[24] UCC § 2-607.

[25] See Fargo Mach. & Tool Co. v. Kearney & Trecker Corp., 428 F. Supp. 364 (ED Mich. 1977); Stahl Management Corp. v. Conceptions Unlimited, 554 F. Supp. 890 (SDNY 1983); Neilson v. MFT Leasing Co., 656 P2d 454 (Utah 1982).

[26] UCC § 2-513.

that are especially significant in contracts involving substantial customization or development work. The acceptance standards define the system and performance that satisfy the contract.

In practice, standards and testing procedures vary in scope and content depending on the type of transaction and leverage or objectives of the parties. For example, many standard form hardware contracts provide de minimis acceptance standards based on the amount of time that a system is operable during a particular interval ("up time"). The buyer is obligated to pay whenever the installed system functions for a specified percentage of available time. The standard is protective of the seller. It may be adequate for the buyer if the transaction merely involves an agreement to deliver resources, although even then issues concerning the speed and capacity of the system are also pertinent. In more complex transactions, these standard provisions are inadequate. Negotiated standards and testing should track at least the major aspects of the system expected by the buyer.

Ideally, acceptance standards are adjuncts to the overall agreement, their provisions being subordinate to the terms of the contract. Where relatively elaborate standards are employed, however, the acceptance standards may have significantly greater importance. In many cases, they provide a definitive statement of what is considered to be adequate performance of the contract and clarify ambiguous language in the remainder of the agreement. Acceptance standards frequently define, rather than simply implement, the bargain.

At a minimum, acceptance based on compliance with express standards and relevant testing alters the remedial posture of the parties if defects are subsequently discovered. The buyer is responsible for the purchase price unless it is able to revoke acceptance.[27] Revocation based on discoverable defects, however, is not permitted unless acceptance was induced by assurances that the defect would be corrected.[28] The discoverability of the defect is reviewed in terms of the degree of testing actually conducted. As to discovered defects, depending on the circumstances, it can also be argued that acceptance constitutes a waiver of the problem.[29]

---

[27] UCC § 2-607(1) provides: "The buyer must pay at the contract rate for any goods accepted."

[28] UCC § 2-608(1).

[29] The idea of waiver is implicit in the UCC treatment of discovered and discoverable defects. Unless there is a reservation of rights, the accepting buyer loses the ability to sue for damages based on discovered defects for which there were no assurances of cure. Beyond waiver, however, it can be argued that acceptance in the face of less than complete performance constitutes an accord and

More important, standards and testing alter the character of the underlying bargain and apportion the risk of certain forms of nonperformance between the parties. Significant testing of the system before acceptance may contradict subsequent claims that the buyer relied on warranties or other representations of the seller.[30] Implied warranties of merchantability and fitness for a particular purpose are removed from the transaction "with regard to defects which an examination ought in the circumstances to have revealed to him."[31]

Comprehensive acceptance standards may totally define the underlying bargain. This result is suggested in *Sha I v. City of San Francisco.*[32] *Sha I* involved a contract for the delivery of an innovative hospital clinic laboratory information system. The system was to be developed and delivered as part of this contract, but the seller anticipated broader marketing based on the prototype. The contract required a three-stage installation of successively more sophisticated components of the system. Each stage was characterized by a separate acceptance test defined in elaborate detail in the contract. The system passed the first two stages and passed the third-level test after an initial failure. Subsequently, however, its performance proved inadequate for the buyer's actual needs. The court nevertheless held that the buyer was obligated to pay the purchase price of the system.

> It is therefore irrelevant that, subsequent to the test, the system may have developed problems and ceased to operate satisfactorily. In creating state-of-the-art data processing systems, there is, of course, a risk that the system will not function as originally hoped. Other things being equal, however, the parties are free to allocate this risk in their contract as they mutually choose. [Seller] assumed the risk that its system would not be able to pass the acceptance test. [Buyer] bore the risk and became obliged to pay the contract price and suffer the consequences if the system did not perform to expectations.[33]

Due to the procedural posture of the case, it is possible that the court meant that through the acceptance tests the buyer relinquished the right to revoke acceptance and to refuse to pay the purchase price. This applies UCC acceptance and revocation provisions. The buyer retains the theo-

---

satisfaction. This argument was raised, but rejected in Stahl Management Corp. v. Conceptions Unlimited, 554 F. Supp. 890 (SDNY 1983).

[30] Investors Premium Corp. v. Burroughs Corp., 389 F. Supp. 39 (DSC 1974).

[31] UCC § 2-316(3)(b).

[32] 612 F2d 1215 (9th Cir. 1980).

[33] Id. at 1218.

retical right to sue for damages for breach, although proof of breach would be difficult in light of the elaborate testing that the system had passed.

The more likely interpretation of *Sha I* is that the comprehensive acceptance tests defined the obligation of the seller in full. The contract was not to deliver a system that would solve particular applications needs in the buyer's hospital, but to deliver a system that would pass acceptance tests at the contractually specified 95 percent performance level. By installing a system that passed the specified tests, the seller not only established the buyer's obligation to pay the contract price, but also completed its contractual obligation. The test standards defined the contract.

In practice, the degree of difference between the two interpretations of *Sha I* may not be large. Under either view, it is unlikely that a buyer will subsequently be able to collect damages, avoid paying, or otherwise reverse a transaction in which the delivered system passes elaborate acceptance testing. Where testing matures to encompass a substantial portion of the relevant characteristics of the purchased system, the acceptance procedure should be viewed as an allocation of risk, binding on the parties. *Sha I* does not refute the desirability of acceptance standards and testing in major acquisition contracts. It does, however, indicate that acceptance procedures are not a one-way transaction conveying benefits solely to the buyer. In fact, comprehensive standards, properly drawn, may protect both parties. If comprehensive standards are used, it is essential that the standards in fact reflect the full bargain, or there should be an express exclusion and reservation of those aspects of performance not incorporated in the testing. In the absence of these steps, the risk is that performance of the standards will be taken as adequate performance of the entire agreement and omitted terms will be ignored.

¶ 6.06 SOFTWARE AND HARDWARE INTERDEPENDENCE

In many transactions, the purchaser acquires both a hardware system and relevant applications or system software. These elements of a complete system may be acquired from a single vendor or purchased separately from independent suppliers. In either instance, hardware and software are often covered in separate contracts, even when the parties clearly understand and intend that an integrated system is being acquired. In such cases, the parties can expressly define the two agreements as interdependent or as separable depending on the character of their transaction. Either arrangement may be commercially acceptable, as long as an illegal tying arrangement is not involved.

When a business simultaneously acquires hardware and software for a particular application, however, failure to define the two as interdependent creates a risk that one element of an expensive system will be delivered and paid for, but will remain idle and unusable because the other is not a workable product. This result is acceptable only where the purchaser intends merely to acquire problem-solving resources. Arguably, it is in the purchaser's best interest expressly to link performance of both elements in the overall transaction.[34]

In the absence of express provisions, the reported cases at least indirectly enforce an interdependence between software and hardware contracts if the circumstances clearly indicate that this relationship was intended by the parties.[35] This approach is most readily applied in transactions in which a single vendor supplies both hardware and software and the software is custom-designed by the vendor. In this situation, the clear inference is that the transaction contemplates delivery of a complete system. Thus, in *Burroughs Corp. v. Century Steel, Inc.*[36] the Nevada Supreme Court upheld a trial court decision that a hardware lease agreement had been breached by the vendor's failure to make timely delivery of a "workable computer software system."[37] Similarly, in *Carl Beasley Ford, Inc. v. Burroughs Corp.*[38] the court did not expressly link the two contracts in the sense of implying a breach of one based on a breach of the other, but its damage award achieved a similar result

---

[34] See Diversified Environments v. Olivetti Corp., 461 F. Supp. 286 (MD Pa. 1978).

[35] Given that the two agreements are separated, an initial issue may arise concerning parol evidence barriers. Arguably, an oral software agreement may represent excluded, additional terms of a hardware contract if the written contract is definable as the full expression of the parties. See UCC § 2-202. This argument is avoided if the software agreement is referenced in the written contract. Furthermore, even in the absence of such a reference, a failure to mention software in a written agreement has been held sufficient to establish that the writing was not intended to be the exclusive statement of the agreements between the parties. This interpretation is appropriate whenever software is clearly integral to the overall transaction. See Carl Beasley Ford, Inc. v. Burroughs Corp., 361 F. Supp. 325 (ED Pa. 1973); Diversified Environments v. Olivetti Corp., 461 F. Supp. 286 (MD Pa. 1978).

[36] 664 P2d 354 (Nev. 1983).

[37] Id. at 357; see also Olivetti Leasing Corp. v. Mar-Mac Precision Corp., 459 NYS2d 399 (NY S. Ct. 1983) (flaws in software lease performance bar recovery under separate hardware lease). Compare Westfield Chem. Co. v. Burroughs Corp., 21 UCC Rep. 1298 (Mass. Super. Ct. 1977) (hardware and software contracts are separable).

[38] 361 F. Supp. 325 (ED Pa. 1973).

> [The] E-4000 machine was virtually worthless without proper pro-
> gramming. . . . [At] the time of the sale, Burroughs sold the equip-
> ment at a "bundled" price, i.e., the price was the same whether or not
> the customer had Burroughs do the programming. . . . [T]he two were
> virtually inseparable insofar as the utility of the equipment was con-
> cerned. It appears appropriate, therefore, to allow the return of the
> entire purchase price as an element of damage for breach of the
> agreement to furnish proper programming.[39]

In *Carl Beasley*, the transaction involved indicia that the two elements of
the system were interdependent since they were sold at a "bundled" price
and, apparently, little or no other software was available for the Burroughs computer.

The question in all such cases is whether the parties regarded the two
transactions as interdependent. This focuses on whether the parties anticipated a possibility that the purchaser would be left with an unpro-
grammed hardware system for which it was required to pay. In most cases
involving a single vendor and an obligation to develop software for the
buyer, the appropriate presumption is that the two elements are interdependent. This inference is even easier to draw when the transaction
involves a single price for bundled hardware and software products that
can not be acquired separately.

A presumption of interdependence may not apply if the contract
involves prepackaged software not specially developed for the purchaser. The vendor may be a retail outlet for other vendors. It may not
have undertaken to provide a completed, operational system, but
merely the resources to create one.[40] The fact that both hardware and
software are provided by one vendor may be more a matter of convenience than of an express linkage or conditioning of the two transactions. At least, the fact that this pattern may exist should lead a court
to require a clearer showing that the two aspects of the transaction
were in fact interdependent.

A similar analysis applies if the hardware system has multiple applications but the vendor provides programming for only one of the applications to which the purchaser will devote the machine. This is a common
situation in the microcomputer market where, for example, a system may
be used for accounting and word processing, but the seller provides only
accounting software. Unlike in *Carl Beasley*, it would be difficult either to
establish that the hardware is worthless without the particular program or

---

[39] Id. at 334.

[40] See IBM v. Catamore Enter., Inc., 548 F2d 1065 (1st Cir. 1975); Honeywell v. Lithonia Lighting, Inc., 317 F. Supp. 406 (ND Ga. 1970).

that the essence of the transaction was that neither hardware nor software would be retained unless both performed to expectations. To the extent that the buyer intends these results, it must expressly incorporate them in the agreement or establish them by clear evidence, rather than by presumption based on the nature of the transaction.

While hardware and software acquisitions are often made from a single vendor, it is also common to obtain software from a third party. Third-party programming obviously involves significantly different issues in terms of the interdependence of the agreements. Absent an express agreement or a symbiotic relationship between programmer and the hardware vendor, the two agreements are not interdependent. One vendor cannot be presumed to be responsible for the performance of the other party. This is true even if the purchaser is referred to the programmer by the other vendor, although representations made in the referral might provide an independent basis for action. For example, a representation that particular hardware is capable of operating a specific applications program may raise a claim for fraud or an express warranty as to the capacity of the underlying hardware.[41]

¶ 6.07 EXPRESS WARRANTIES

In defining the essence of a bargain, express warranties are among the most significant factors in litigation under the UCC. An express warranty is any affirmation, promise, description, or sample that "becomes part of the basis of the bargain" between the parties.[42] It must be affirmatively created by action or statement. Any representation that creates an express warranty is, by definition, an element of the agreement and enforceable.

Issues about express warranties frequently arise in the context of contract terms that seek to eliminate or reduce the effect of the representations. While the UCC recognizes that express warranties can be negated by the written agreement and thus in a sense disclaimed, the standards for effective disclaimer are exacting. UCC § 2-316 provides:

> Words or conduct relevant to the creation of an express warranty
> and words or conduct tending to negate or limit warranty shall be

---

[41] See Suntogs of Miami, Inc. v. Burroughs Corp., 433 So. 2d 581 (Fla. Dist. Ct. App. 1983) (asserted fraudulent representation that system can operate software purchased from third party); Schatz Distrib. Co. v. Olivetti Corp., 647 P2d 820 (Kan. Ct. App. 1982) (inadequate capacity breaches warranty even though system not defective).

[42] UCC § 2-313.

construed wherever reasonable as consistent with each other; but subject to the provisions ... on parol or extrinsic evidence ... negation or limitation is inoperative to the extent that such construction is unreasonable.[43]

If a particular term, promise, or representation amounts to an express warranty, the UCC presumes that the warranty will remain a part of the bargain. Inconsistent language in a disclaimer or other limitation is to be construed in a manner consistent with the warranty if possible, but is discarded if no reasonable, consistent reading exists.

This approach is consistent with the definition of an express warranty, a definition whose significance is often not fully recognized by the courts. In a literal sense, an express warranty cannot be disclaimed since it is part of the basis of the bargain. To the extent that contrary language is pertinent, it must either be consistent with that bargain or establish that the express warranty was not part of the agreement. In this latter event the limiting language effectively establishes that no warranty was made. To do so, pro forma language in the agreement disclaiming any additional representations or warranties is insufficient.

Express warranties may be based on language in the written contract or on representations extraneous to that document. In practice, many express warranties are part of an overall limitation on the purchaser's remedies. This is true, for example, when an express warranty against defects of workmanship is coupled with a clause limiting the seller's obligation to replace the product or repair the defect. There is rarely any question about the enforceability of the express representation.[44] The controversial issue is whether the purchaser's other remedies are effectively limited.[45]

[1] Contract Specifications

Representations in the written agreement concerning the specifications of the product and other obligations of the vendor are often described as express warranties. They are enforceable despite language disclaiming and excluding warranties.[46] This result is independent of the

---

[43] UCC § 2-316(1).

[44] But see Bruffey Contracting Co. v. Burroughs Corp., 522 F. Supp. 769 (D. Md. 1981) (effective remedy limitation excluded the particular defect alleged by buyer).

[45] See infra ¶ 6.12.

[46] See Consolidated Data Terminal Co. v. Applied Digital Sys., Inc., 708 F2d 385 (9th Cir. 1983); Fargo Mach. & Tool Co. v. Kearney & Trecker Corp., 428 F. Supp. 364 (ED Mich. 1977).

relative sophistication of the parties, their economic strength, or technical expertise. Warranty terminology can be misleading concerning these representations. They are the basic, express terms of the agreement that can not be disclaimed. Even if the representations are warranties, UCC standards for negating them will not be met by a general disclaimer. The representations should be excluded only if the facts and the language of the contract specifically indicate that they were not a part of the basic bargain.[47]

Difficulties arise in moving away from representations in the written contract. A common pattern in computer transactions involves published technical specifications that are not directly included in the contract. For example, published specifications may describe a computer with a particular processing speed or software able to process a specified number of data files, but the contract merely refers to the product by name. In such cases, the threshhold issue is whether the specifications became part of the bargain, that is, were relied on by the buyer.

In the absence of parol evidence barriers, technical specifications considered by the buyer before purchase create enforceable express warranties despite general exclusionary language in the contract. In *Consolidated Data Terminal v. Applied Digital Systems, Inc.,*[48] a distributor purchased terminals from Applied Digital for resale based in part on written specifications indicating that the terminals would operate at a speed of 19,200 baud. When delivered, faulty design made the terminals incapable of operating at speeds that high. Since operational speed was a significant factor, the distributor sued for damages. Applied Digital relied on a provision in the contract purporting to limit its liability and exclude express warranties other than a limited warranty against defects of workmanship. The Ninth Circuit rejected the defense, noting simply that "the express statements warranting that the Regent 100's would perform at a 19,200 baud rate prevail over the general disclaimer."[49]

Similarly, *Fargo Machine & Tool Co. v. Kearney & Trecker Corp.*[50] involved automated machinery that failed to perform to its published specifications. As in *Consolidated*, the contract contained a limited warranty and an exclusion of all other warranties. Nevertheless, the court enforced express warranties based on the technical specifications.

---

[47] See WR Weaver Co. v. Burroughs Corp., 580 SW2d 76 (Tex. Civ. App. 1979).

[48] 708 F2d 385 (9th Cir. 1983).

[49] Id. at 391.

[50] 428 F. Supp. 364 (ED Mich. 1977).

> [The] express representations made in the sales literature and the provisions of [the contract] may be construed consistently. The language in [the contract] warranting the product free from defect in material and workmanship is entirely consistent with the promotional literature's description of what the machine could do. The tandem effect of these writings [is] that the sales material and technical specifications on the order established the standards of the product's performance when free of defects in material and workmanship.[51]

In *Fargo,* portions of the specifications were included by reference in the purchase order and agreement. Warranty disclaimer language referring to these is inappropriate. In addition, subject to parol evidence concerns, if the remaining specifications were relied on, the resulting express warranties do not yield in the face of conflict with limitation language in the contract. To the contrary, the warranties prevail and the limiting language is inoperative unless consistent with the warranties. As *Fargo* suggests, in many cases the two are consistent.

Technical specifications such as speed of performance and storage capacity are basic to the contract. They are not excludable by general language. Requiring a vendor to deliver the capacity that it claims for its product establishes an important framework for the development of technology. Furthermore, in contrast to predictions about suitability of a system for a particular application there is little risk that a vendor will be unwittingly held to inappropriately high technical performance standards. Where the vendor defines the technical capacity of a system in concrete form, it should be held to those representations.

[2] Suitability and Performance

As agreements move away from pure technical specifications and general disclaimers, the enforceability of any alleged express warranties is less clear. The buyer retains an interest in obtaining what has been agreed to or, at least, apparently promised. From the seller's perspective, however, there are increasing concerns about protecting a vendor's ability to establish the boundaries of its risk in a marketing environment where it is not possible to monitor all statements made by sales representatives. There is an interest in allowing the technology vendor to define contractually the limits of its undertaking and avoid being bound by unauthorized representations or by unfounded expectations of the buyer.

Specific exclusionary language in an agreement is effective to eliminate express warranties that extend beyond technical specifications and

---

[51] Id. at 371.

into issues of suitability for a particular application. *Bruffey Contracting Co. v. Burroughs Corp.*[52] illustrates this result. *Bruffey* involved a contract for the sale of a computer accounting system in which Burroughs supplied the hardware and an independent vendor was to develop appropriate software. In the face of a failure to provide a suitable system, the court enforced Burroughs' limited warranty and remedy provisions to bar any express warranty as to the suitability of the system for the buyer's intended application. The case did not involve technical specifications. The court noted

> Although ... testimony might otherwise establish an express warranty that the computer system was suitable for his needs, the contract specifically provides that no affirmations or other statements of fact ... are to be considered warranties. [In contrast to the case in *Fargo*] this contractual provision ... precludes an attempt to read the warranty limitation with other statements made to Bruffey. The reasonable reading of the warranty is that only what are termed manufacturing defects [are covered].[53]

Given the language of the contract and the fact that the buyer acknowledged awareness of the exclusion, it was reasonable to conclude that representations about suitability for a particular application were not part of the bargain and, hence, not express warranties. The case involved a contract between merchants. The court's conclusion is consistent with allowing the vendor to limit the terms under which its product is delivered in a purely commercial transaction.

[3] Warranties and Parol Evidence

Representations that are not included in the written agreement may be eliminated not only by exclusionary language, but also by parol evidence rules that foreclose proof of the alleged warranty. UCC § 2-316(1) establishes a restrictive standard for exclusion of express warranties but is expressly subject to parol evidence rules. UCC § 2-202 precludes the use of parol or extrinsic evidence to contradict the terms of a written agreement intended to be the final agreement of the parties. It permits evidence of consistent, additional terms unless the "court finds the writing to have been intended also as a complete and exclusive statement of the terms of the agreement."[54] Properly construed, this language generally should not preclude proof of extrinsic technical specifications. Such spec-

---

[52] 522 F. Supp. 769 (D. Md. 1981).

[53] Id. at 772.

[54] UCC § 2-202.

ifications neither contradict the written agreement nor provide additional terms. Rather, they clarify the language used in the agreement to describe the system. This is pertinent and provable even when the parties agree that the written contract is the exclusive statement of their agreement and the specifications are not directly included in the agreement.

Parol evidence barriers are significant for warranties of the suitability of the system for particular applications, warranties in which the alleged representations usually are "additional" contract terms. Extrinsic evidence of the warranty is admissible unless the court finds that the parties intend the written contract to be the sole and exclusive expression of the agreement. [55] This commonly requires consideration of both the terms of the agreement and the circumstances under which the contract was entered.

In *Jaskey Finance & Leasing v. Display Data Corp.,* [56] the seller allegedly made express warranties that the system would be a "turnkey" system requiring minimal maintenance and that it was particularly suitable for the buyer's business. These representations were not in the written contract, but were in the seller's advertising and promotional literature. The contract restricted the seller's liability to an attempt to correct any programming errors discovered within one year from delivery and also included a merger clause providing that the written agreement "contains the entire agreement between the parties." The court concluded that proof of the warranties was barred by parol evidence rules, since the parties intended the written agreement to be the comprehensive and exclusive statement of their agreement. Significantly, the court did not rely solely on the merger clause but considered other factors, including the fact that the contract involved two merchants who were sophisticated in contracting and had relatively equal bargaining power.

Especially in a contract between merchants, a merger clause integrating the terms of the transaction into a single document creates a presumption that no extrinsic representations were intended. This presumption disappears if the circumstances clearly indicate that the writing was not the all-inclusive expression of the agreement. For example, if software development is a major element of a transaction but the contract does not refer to software issues, a merger clause should not be given effect. [57] Evidence of additional terms in the form of express warranties or separate agreements is not barred.

---

[55] Compare the relationship between fraud and parol evidence. See ¶ 7.02[2].

[56] 564 F. Supp. 160 (ED Pa. 1983).

[57] See Diversified Environments v. Olivetti Corp., 461 F. Supp. 286 (MD Pa. 1978); Teamsters Sec. Fund v. Sperry Rand Corp., 6 CLRS 951 (ND Cal. 1971).

¶ 6.08 IMPLIED WARRANTIES

In addition to express warranties, the terms of the transaction may be defined by implied warranties imposed by law or through the actions of the parties. Two implied warranties are most commonly involved in cases under the UCC.[58] The first is the implied warranty of merchantability, which is presumptively present in any transaction in which the seller is a merchant engaged in selling goods of a particular type. The warranty is that the delivered products would pass without objection in the trade under the contract description and are fit for the ordinary purposes to which such goods are used.[59] The second implied warranty is the warranty that the delivered goods are fit for a particular purpose.[60] Unlike merchantability, this warranty exists only if the seller has reason to know of the intended application of the buyer and that the buyer is relying on the seller's skill or judgment to furnish suitable goods. The two warranties focus on distinct aspects of a transaction and protect distinct interests of the buyer. The implied warranty of merchantability ensures that the resources obtained in the contract are functional. The fitness warranty protects reasonable expectations of the buyer that the seller's skill and judgment have been used to furnish appropriate solutions to particular applications needs.

Implied warranties have been significant in consumer contracts and related litigation under the UCC, but they play a minor role in litigation between businesses because of the relative ease with which implied warranties can be disclaimed and replaced by more specific contractual terms. Unlike express warranties, implied warranties can be disclaimed by appropriate and conspicuous language in the contract. Most standard form sales agreements contain the appropriate language.

Under UCC § 2-316(2), analysis of the effect of a disclaimer does not require attention to whether the disclaimed obligation was a part of the basis of the bargain. Instead, in a more traditional contract law analysis the contract language is given presumptive effect. The primary statutory requirement is that the language disclaiming the warranty must be conspicuous and, in the case of merchantability, that it expressly mention merchantability.[61] These requirements protect the buyer from "unex-

---

[58] In addition to the warranties of merchantability and of fitness for a particular purpose, the UCC provides a warranty of title for any sale of goods. See UCC § 2-312.

[59] UCC § 2-314.

[60] UCC § 2-315.

[61] See generally White & Summers, *Handbook of the Law Under the Uniform Commercial Code* ch. 12 (2d ed. 1980).

pected and unbargained" disclaimers. [62] Beyond these requirements, however, questions are frequently raised about whether the disclaimer can be challenged as unconscionable. In most commercial transactions conscionability arguments fail. [63]

[1] Merchantability Standards

Since merchantability is readily and commonly disclaimed, there is virtually no case law applying standards of merchantability to either software or hardware. The UCC lists six criteria for determining whether a particular product is merchantable. The most commonly used are that the goods would pass without objection in the trade under the contract description and that they "are fit for the ordinary purpose for which such goods are used." [64]

Merchantability law defines quality in terms that are expressly independent of the particular use that the buyer makes of the goods. Suitability for particular applications is the domain of express warranties, specific contract terms, or the implied warranty of fitness. Thus, the buyer of a microcomputer does not have a claim under merchantability standards if it uses the microcomputer for mass data processing beyond the ordinary application of similar machines.

The concept of ordinary use and condition entails the possibility that the product is not in perfect condition. A classic illustration is the sale of a used car where at least minor defects are ordinarily expected. An analogy in the computer environment may be found in software products. In the software industry, it is not uncommon that distributed products contain flaws ("bugs"). While this does not suggest that all defective products are acceptable, it establishes a standard that recognizes the presence of some defects in a new product. [65] In particular cases, of course, the issue involves distinguishing reasonably acceptable flaws from flaws adequate to define the product as defective. [66]

---

[62] See Jaskey Fin. & Leasing v. Display Data Corp., 564 F. Supp. 160, 165 (ED Pa. 1983) (failure to mention merchantability precludes disclaimer even if parties had equal bargaining power and business experience).

[63] See infra ¶ 6.13.

[64] UCC § 2-314(2)(a). See generally White & Summers, *Handbook of the Law Under the Uniform Commercial Code* 353 (2d ed. 1980).

[65] See Alderman & Dole, *A Transactional Guide to the Uniform Commercial Code* 95 (1983).

[66] See infra ¶ 6.10; National Cash Register Corp. v. Adell Indus., Inc., 225 NW 2d 785 (Mich. Ct. App. 1975).

The implied warranty of merchantability is most often disclaimed in commercial sales transactions. In most cases, however, it is replaced by express warranties regarding the existence of defects of workmanship and the seller's obligation to replace or repair defective products.[67]

[2] Fitness Warranties and Consulting Sellers

Unlike the warranty of merchantability, the warranty of fitness for a particular purpose does not relate to general standards of performance of a particular product. This warranty is built around transactional expectations and its content is based on the particular needs of a specific buyer. The warranty both protects and results from the buyer's reasonable reliance on the seller's skill and judgment in a particular transaction.

The existence of a warranty of fitness depends on four considerations:

1. The seller must have reason to know the particular needs of the buyer.[68]
2. The seller must be aware that the buyer is relying on the seller's particular skill or judgment to select appropriate products.
3. The buyer must, in fact, rely.[69]
4. The warranty must not have been effectively disclaimed.

The warranty of fitness for a particular purpose fills a gap between those circumstances in which there is no reliance by the buyer and those in which the seller's recommendations are in the form of express warranties. For the buyer, this entails a reliance interest in classic form. In the prototypical transaction, the buyer is at the mercy of the seller regarding the quality of the goods and their suitability, since the seller served at least informally as a consultant. This form of reliance is common in the computer industry, since in many transactions an inexperienced buyer is unable or unwilling to obtain outside advice.

The buyer's reliance interest is obvious. The countervailing interest of the seller is most clearly present where there is a less explicit reliance or the seller is less willing to assume the role of advisor. The interest involves limiting liability in a sales environment and acknowledging differences between an enterprise that consults about or designs systems and one that merely sells them. If expanded obligations are implied in a transaction,

---

[67] See, e.g., Bruffey Contracting Co. v. Burroughs Corp., 522 F. Supp. 769 (D. Md. 1981).

[68] UCC § 2-315.

[69] UCC § 2-315, Comment 1.

control has passed from the seller. The interest is in retaining the power to define the extent to which it is willing to provide advice on which the buyer might reasonably rely.

In many microcomputer transactions, hardware and software acquisitions occur in a traditional retail setting. The buyer acquires name brand merchandise over the counter from a local store. Ordinarily, there is some questioning and seeking of advice from the vendor, but the transaction involves no extended investigation by the seller into the needs of the buyer. While the buyer might rely on the salesperson, the setting is inappropriate for an implied warranty. The environment itself tends to refute any claim of reasonable reliance. The seller's interest is strongest in this setting since there are no means for thorough assessment of needs, and this is apparent to both parties. Furthermore, imposing an implied warranty in this retail setting would tend to reduce normal levels of advice and customer assistance where the nature of the product makes such assistance particularly important.

A more appropriate application of the implied warranty arises in transactions in which there is extensive involvement by the seller in advising on the buyer's system. In many business purchases, buyers ask sellers to recommend software and hardware. Often, the vendor retains a professional sales staff to assist in designing system configurations as a way of enhancing sales. The contract law issue involves the extent to which the seller in these circumstances must deliver a system that satisfies the buyer's needs or merely a system free of defects, albeit poorly matched to the purposes of the buyer. Unless disclaimed, the implied warranty of fitness plays a significant role and may be the sole recourse for the buyer.

An implied warranty of fitness was applied in *Sperry Rand Corp. v. Industrial Supply Corp.*[70] In *Industrial Supply*, Sperry Rand and other vendors were invited to examine Industrial Supply's business operations and propose systems to automate accounting, inventory, and other functions. The Sperry Rand proposal was in a relatively extensive brochure recommending its equipment as the "one best suited to a tailor made job." The brochure described the proposed software and hardware system along with various options as to cost and structure. The eventual sales contract, however, did not discuss the suitability of the system to be delivered, but did contain an integration clause and the statement that the "entire Agreement [is] contained in this Agreement."[71] The delivered system was not suitable for the buyer's application although, apparently, the system was not defective and met the specifications in the contract.

---

[70] 357 F2d 363 (5th Cir. 1964) (decided prior to adoption of the UCC).
[71] Id. at 370.

The integration clause imposed a parol evidence barrier to the express representations in the Sperry proposal. As a result, while the transaction depended on plans and recommendations provided by the seller, the suitability of these proposals might not have been a factor in the contract. The court held that parol evidence did not preclude an implied warranty, however. While there was no provable express warranty of suitability, an implied warranty to that effect existed and provided relief.

Beyond parol evidence, *Industrial Supply* involved two issues that recur in the application of the fitness warranty. The first was that the transaction involved a sale of name brand products sold by their trade names. Prior to adoption of the UCC, the law in a number of states was that fitness warranties were not present if a transaction involved name brand merchandise. The presumption was that the buyer relied on the brand name or its known capacity rather than on the skill of the seller. Under the UCC this absolute rule is rejected, but the purchase of name brand products by their trade names may be relevant to the issue of whether the buyer relied on the expertise of the seller.[72] If a buyer insists on an IBM personal computer for an application in which a different computer would be more appropriate, the seller is not responsible for the error.

Industrial Supply involved a significant variation on this theme. The purchase not only involved a name brand product, but a configuration of several products. Even given insistence by the buyer on the basic product, a warranty of fitness may arise from the seller's design of a system incorporating the merchandise.

> The transaction [involved] ten items . . . incorporated into a system. . . . The operational functions of these ten machines were keyed together in a manner intended to meet the . . . requirements of the buyer. They were tailored by Sperry Rand's know how. . . . There is no difference in principle between the incorporating of specifically described machines into an integrated system and the building of a specially designed single piece of equipment for a like purpose.[73]

Properly construed, the issue involves a factual determination of whether a buyer relied on the seller's judgment or whether it relied on the brand name. Where a system is designed with numerous brand name items, reliance concerning the system design is the critical factor. This is true

---

[72] UCC § 2-315, Comment 5.

[73] Sperry Rand Corp. v. Industrial Supply Corp., 357 F2d 363, 371 (5th Cir. 1964).

whether several computers are involved or whether, as is common with microcomputers, items from different suppliers are used as add-on features for a single machine.

A second issue involves the extent to which an opportunity to inspect obviates the implied warranty. UCC § 2-316(3)(b) provides that when the buyer inspects or declines an opportunity to inspect prior to entering the contract, no implied warranty exists for defects "which an examination ought in the circumstances to have revealed to him." This result does not relate to inspection at the time of delivery, but to examination of items before entering the contract and to the responsibilities assumed by the buyer and the seller. Where there is a precontract opportunity to inspect, it is reasonable that the buyer's reliance should be on the inspection rather than solely on the seller's skill. Indeed, presentation of samples is one method of testing whether the seller's product in fact meets the buyer's needs. Of course, the inspection obviates reliance only for discoverable problems viewed in light of a reasonable inspection and the abilities of the buyer. As the court in *Industrial Supply* noted

> Industrial Supply did not know and could not be expected to ascertain, except by use and experiment, the functional abilities and capacities of the electronic equipment, with its transistors, tubes and diodes, its varicolored maze of wiring, its buttons and switches.... And, of course, the personnel of Industrial Supply could not be expected to understand the processes by which a set of these modern miracle makers perform their tasks.[74]

The requirement of actual reliance by the buyer on the seller's skill and judgment presents significant fact issues if there is substantial prespecification of the system or substantial acceptance testing. In either context, it is unlikely that an implied warranty of fitness survives the active role of the buyer.[75] A contract opportunity to inspect before accepting the goods may obviate reliance concerning discoverable performance characteristics of the system.

Even more important, the implied warranty of fitness is most often disclaimed in mercantile contracts.[76] As with the merchantability warranty, pro forma contract language is often sufficient to exclude the warranty and is commonly used in standard contracts.

---

[74] Id. at 370.

[75] UCC § 2-316, Comment 9.

[76] See, e.g., Bakal v. Burroughs Corp., 343 NYS2d 541 (NY S. Ct. 1972); Office Supply Co. v. Basic/Four Corp., 538 F. Supp. 776 (ED Wis. 1982); WR Weaver Co. v. Burroughs Corp., 580 SW2d 76 (Tex. Civ. App. 1972).

[3] Conspicuous Disclaimers

In commercial, nonconsumer sales, implied warranties can be disclaimed with relative ease. In the absence of arguments about conscionability, the primary UCC requirement for disclaiming implied warranties is that the disclaimer be conspicuous.[77] A conspicuous disclaimer is often associated with the use of large, capital letters, perhaps in boldface type. This is the manner in which disclaimers are commonly incorporated in sales agreements and is expressly described in the UCC as meeting the requirement of conspicuous disclaimers. The actual standard, however, is that the clause be "so written that a reasonable person against whom it is to operate ought to have noticed it."[78] Under this more general standard, conspicuousness may be based on circumstantial factors even if the agreement does not use disclaiming language in capital letters.

There is a noticeable tendency to apply this broader conception in cases involving businesses.[79] The relevant line of cases enforces otherwise inconspicuous disclaimers when circumstances suggest that the buyer was in fact aware of the contract language. This might occur if there was actual discussion of the disclaimer[80] or if the sophistication of the buyer, coupled with relatively equal bargaining power, implies that significant terms have been considered.[81]

¶ 6.09 COLLATERAL OBLIGATIONS

System acquisition transactions pertaining to computer hardware and software commonly entail obligations on the part of the supplier-developer beyond delivery of the particular product. These collateral obligations range from limited promises to provide training for selected personnel to long-term agreements to provide maintenance and support. In general, however, the collateral obligations involve service-related activity to assist in the start-up and continued use of the system.

---

[77] UCC § 2-316; see also National Cash Register Corp. v. Adell Indus., Inc., 225 NW2d 785 (Mich. Ct. App. 1975).

[78] UCC § 1-201(10) defines "conspicuous" as a term "so written that a reasonable person against whom it is to operate ought to have noticed it."

[79] White & Summers, *Handbook of the Law Under the Uniform Commercial Code* 444 (2d ed. 1980).

[80] See Office Supply Co. v. Basic/Four Corp., 538 F. Supp. 776, 784 (ED Wis. 1982).

[81] See Fargo Mach. & Tool Co. v. Kearney & Trecker Corp., 428 F. Supp. 364 (ED Mich. 1977); Jaskey Fin. & Leasing Co. v. Display Data Corp., 564 F. Supp. 160, 165 (ED Pa. 1983).

There is little case law dealing with these collateral obligations, but some general observations may be made based on the character of the transaction involved. In many transactions, the collateral obligations are major facets of the overall transaction and are critical to the buyer's selection of one vendor over another. Nonperformance or inadequate performance of the collateral obligation is often a major source of frustration and loss for the purchaser.

One risk is that agreements for support, training, or installation may be subject to the same limitations applied to express warranties. In fact, in some cases collateral promises regarding support or service are described as warranties rather than separate contracts.[82] This is especially significant when considering parol evidence issues. If agreements to provide maintenance, error correction, training, or access to the source code of a program are collateral to the main contract, but not incorporated in it, proof may be barred if the sales contract contains a merger or integration clause.[83] The collateral obligations should be referenced in the sales contract. Absent a reference, however, there is at least some support for the view that the integration clause can be ignored where the related obligations are so clearly material that failure to mention them in the contract indicates that the contract was not intended to be all-inclusive.[84] Finally, depending on the scope and duration of the collateral obligation it might properly be viewed as a separate transaction, unaffected by the parol evidence barriers of the sales agreement.

[1] Training and Data Transfer

In many transactions essential services for the purchaser include not only physical installation of the system, but also training and data transfer services to facilitate implementation of the system. Absent express agreement, the vendor has no obligation to train the purchaser's staff. Neither does the vendor assume an obligation to assist in transferring data or creating operational procedures to accommodate use of the new system. To the extent that such obligations arise, they must come from an express agreement or from established trade use or course of dealing.

---

[82] See, e.g., WR Weaver Co. v. Burroughs Corp., 580 SW2d 76 (Tex. Civ. App. 1979).

[83] See supra ¶ 6.07[2].

[84] Diversified Environments v. Olivetti Corp., 461 F. Supp. 286 (MD Pa. 1978).

[a] Documentation

The technology vendor assumes responsibility for supplying information sufficient to bring the user to a level of familiarity adequate to make at least ordinary use of the product. Computer technology is distinguishable from more traditional products since, in most cases, even minimal competence in operating a system requires information in addition to mere physical availability. While it is relatively easy to discern the manner in which a radio or television operates, the operation of a computer or particular software may be less apparent.

While documentation is a necessary adjunct of the sales agreement, the amount or type of documentation sufficient to satisfy the seller's obligation varies. The determining factors include the type of transaction, the terms of the agreement, and the general expectations or trade usage relevant to the transaction. The expertise of the buyer is also a factor. The basic assumption should be that the seller must supply documentation that will reasonably enable the buyer to operate the system consistent with ordinary use. Excluded is any requirement that the seller undertake to ensure the buyer's ability to implement advanced or unusual applications unless this purpose is expressed or is implicit in the transaction and the resulting obligation can be implied (as with a warranty of fitness for a particular use).

Perfect or absolutely complete documentation is virtually never necessary to complete the seller's obligation, especially in an industry in which documentation manuals notoriously reflect widely divergent information levels. On the other hand, it is reasonable to require documentation commensurate with general expectations in the trade. To this end, absent contrary agreement the purpose of documentation is to allow the ordinary use of the system, not to provide detailed schematic representations that are not essential to such operation but that may risk loss of trade secret protection. Unless otherwise agreed, it is not necessary to describe the design of the software, even where the software was specially developed rather than mass-marketed.

In *Law Research Service, Inc. v. General Automation, Inc.,*[85] the Second Circuit Court of Appeals concluded that documentation pertaining to the design of legal research software was not required as part of a transaction involving the delivery of a prototype system. Although documentation might have enabled operation and modification of the system independent of the original vendor, the court noted

---

[85] 494 F2d 202 (2d Cir. 1974).

[There] was no evidence to show that in this type of special application software, material in addition to that actually supplied, is required to be furnished, either by the custom of the trade or under the terms of the contract or its supporting documents. The contract itself called only for providing "the initial software to enable you to operate your prototype system."[86]

In *Law Research*, operator's manuals and programmer's manuals were provided and were adequate to explain how to operate the software in the research application.

Law Research involved the user's desire to have access to documentation of the source code or design of the software to enable modification and updating of the system independent of the availability of the original vendor. This type of documentation should be available only if expressly contracted for or provided as a matter of course in the trade. In many cases, of course, it is desirable from the buyer's standpoint to insist on availability, even if third-party custody is necessary to protect the seller.

A related use of documentation concerns the ability to maintain and service a hardware system. It is arguable that the seller has an obligation to provide sufficient documentation for normal maintenance. While this is common for large systems, it is not for microcomputers, a market in which service oriented documentation may require a separate agreement. In any event, the failure to provide such documentation is actionable only if it is established that it resulted in a failure to obtain necessary service.[87]

[b] Installation

The responsibility of the vendor to install the delivered system and make it operational depends on the type of transaction and the particular delivery terms involved. In most instances, by analogy to transactions in other types of goods, the seller's obligation is satisfied by tender of delivery. Any obligation to install or make a product operational requires an explicit undertaking in the contract or surrounding transaction.[88] This undertaking might be found in language in the agreement calling for testing and adjustment prior to acceptance by the purchaser. It should be

---

[86] Id. at 204.

[87] See Fargo Mach. & Tool Co. v. Kearney & Trecker Corp., 428 F. Supp. 364, 375 (ED Mich. 1977).

[88] UCC § 2-308 provides that, absent a contrary agreement, delivery of goods occurs at the seller's location. Of course, in many cases this basic norm is varied by contract and the question, in the event of ambiguity, involves the extent to which contract terms require installation. Consistent with the underlying UCC structure, however, installation should be part of the transaction only if there is explicit agreement to install the system.

implied in cases in which trade use establishes installation as normal practice.

In the absence of express agreement, the seller has no obligation to prepare the work site, train personnel, or convert data or programs to operate with the new system. The pertinent standard is that the goods become the buyer's responsibility after delivery. In many cases, however, this does not meet the expectations or needs of the parties; express agreements require the seller to provide this form of advanced support for the installation and implementation of the system. These undertakings are in the nature of service agreements and require some level of cooperation between the buyer and seller.[89] This makes the attribution of fault in the event of dispute difficult. Where a transaction fails, the seller's nonperformance of training or data conversion promises may be evident because significant parts of the required services remain incomplete. In other cases, difficulties arise in assessing the qualitative sufficiency of the seller's performance.

A primary illustration of this involves obligations to provide personnel training for a new system. Clearly, the seller does not guarantee that the buyer's personnel in fact learn to operate the system. Unless expressly agreed to the contrary, the primary obligation is merely to provide training ordinarily adequate to that purpose. Adequacy in this context should involve consideration of the time devoted to the training and the credentials of the person assigned to the task by the seller.

Where data transfer, training, or similar obligations are involved, both parties have responsibilities. The buyer's responsibility is to cooperate by providing a reasonable opportunity to complete the training or other activities. Refusal to provide access to staff or data may be an anticipatory repudiation that obviates the seller's obligation unless the buyer's refusal is in itself motivated by the seller's nonperformance.[90]

[2] Maintenance and Repair

The most common collateral obligation related to computer hardware is an obligation to provide maintenance or, at least, replacement and repair of defective parts. Maintenance obligations are commonly in a separate contract that extends the seller's involvement beyond that required in a normal sales agreement. In contrast, replacement and repair obligations are often incorporated in the sales contract and associated with lim-

---

[89] See Diversified Environments v. Olivetti Corp., 461 F. Supp. 286, 291 (MD Pa. 1978).

[90] Id. at 292.

ited warranties that reduce the seller's obligations under implied warranties.[91]

Perhaps because maintenance and repair disputes are often subsumed in disputes about performance of the underlying sales contract, there is very little case law dealing with the obligations established by such agreements.[92] These contracts, however, raise obvious issues related to the objective of the contract in terms of the performance of the system.

Courts commonly presume that the purpose of replacement or repair warranties within a sales contract is to produce a defect free, operational product.[93] An analogous presumption is inappropriate for separate maintenance and repair contracts, which are associated with, but not part of, the sales agreement. The more reasonable presumption is that the contracting party does not undertake to guarantee the performance or quality of the product. This is most clearly the case when the maintenance is provided by a third party. The maintenance provider is merely providing specified services delineated in the maintenance contract.

At issue is delineation of promised service and replacement activities, especially commitments concerning response time and the availability of replacement parts. This issue was indirectly the basis for the decision in *Fargo Machine & Tool Co. v. Kearney & Trecker Corp.*[94] In *Fargo*, the seller of a computerized machine agreed to assume sole responsibility for replacement of defective parts. The machine in question was critical to the buyer's production schedule and had been designed in modular form to permit ready replacement of defective parts. Among the difficulties that arose in the transaction, one claim was based on a delay of 18 days in replacing a defect. The delay was allegedly due to the failure of the seller to maintain an adequate supply of spare parts. The court held that this delay breached the express undertaking and contradicted a significant, fundamental feature of the bargain.

A fundamental purpose of modular components is to enable the user to keep costly down time to a minimum by simply substituting a replacement module when something goes wrong . . . without having to locate and repair the defect. Where the manufacturer simply does not have spare parts in stock, that advantage disappears and the entire principle of single point responsibility for replacement of

---

[91] See infra ¶ 6.12.

[92] See Bernacchi, Davidson & Grogan, "Computer System Procurement," 30 Emory LJ 395, 435 (1980).

[93] See Chatlos Sys., Inc. v. National Cash Register Corp., 635 F2d 1081, 1085 (3d Cir. 1980); Office Supply Co. v. Basic/Four Corp., 538 F. Supp. 776 (ED Wis. 1982).

[94] 428 F. Supp. 364 (ED Mich. 1977).

defective parts is of no value.... Kearney & Trecker's apparent inability to provide spare parts breached its express undertaking of sole responsibility for replacement.[95]

Although affected by the use of modular system design to increase speed of replacement, *Fargo* states a principle that is applicable for any maintenance and repair contract. For the buyer, the essence of the agreement is an effort to control service costs and obtain assured access to reliable repair and replacement services. As a result, the agreement often specifies response time or maximum time to repair. Even in the absence of specification, these variables are significant. The contractor must respond in a reasonable time in light of the known use of the machine and resulting need for promptness.

Implicit in defining both the objective of the agreement and the allowable time to respond is a clear understanding of the type of problems covered by the agreement. No standard form exists for scope of coverage. *Bruffey Contracting Co. v. Burroughs Corp.*,[96] illustrates the issues encountered if a narrow definition of scope is used. In *Bruffey*, the seller disclaimed implied and express warranties, replacing them with a written warranty that the delivered computer and software would be free from defects in material or workmanship for a period of one year. The buyer's remedy was limited to enforcing Burroughs' obligation to correct such defects by repair or replacement and the obligation excluded parts which "by their nature are expendable." The case turned on whether the buyer could prove that faulty performance of the office system was due to malfunctions in nonexpendable parts. The court accepted Burroughs' definition of expendable parts, which included not only items used up in normal operations but also the printed circuit boards and chips in the machine. Burroughs had an obligation to replace and repair, but excluded those parts of the system most likely to require replacement and repair. The limits were enforceable and the buyer was unable to establish the cause of the malfunction with sufficient precision to bring it within the contract obligation.

PART B.   DISPUTES AND REMEDIES

¶ 6.10   DEFINING A BREACH OF CONTRACT

When a dispute arises concerning performance of a sales contract, the initial question is whether a breach of contract has occurred. This

---

[95] Id. at 374.

[96] 522 F. Supp. 769 (D. Md. 1981).

question, of course, is directly linked to the obligations the seller has undertaken in the agreement. In many cases, the issue is relatively straightforward, the facts being characterized by substantial nonperformance of relatively clear-cut obligations. In other settings, difficult issues arise concerning both whether there are provable defects in the delivered product and, more basically, under what standard the performance is to be measured.

[1] System Defects and Perfect Tender

The parties to any contract may define the level of performance that is acceptable under the agreement. When two businesses so agree, there is little doubt that the contract definition will be enforced. This definition is one function of the acceptance standards and testing procedures discussed earlier.[97] If the parties provide that a hardware system will be accepted if it maintains no less than 90 percent up-time over a specified period of operation, this is the level of continuous performance required by the agreement. The buyer will not be able to claim a breach of contract based on the failure of the system to maintain operation for 95 or 100 percent of the available time.

In many contracts, this level of precision does not exist. When it does not, it remains necessary to define the level of performance required by the contract in the event of a dispute. The basic UCC standard is that if the goods "fail in any respect to conform to the contract" the buyer may reject the delivery.[98] This suggests that the UCC adopts a perfect tender rule that the buyer is not obligated to accept substantial but imperfect performance of the contract.[99] In fact, however, the buyer's right to refuse imperfect goods is limited by a variety of considerations that include the seller's right to cure an imperfect delivery.[100]

The buyer can not reject if the imperfect performance, in fact, constitutes acceptable tender in the particular transaction. This is especially relevant in the computer industry. Consider, for example, the rights of the buyer of software when a defect or bug is discovered that limits, but does not disable, performance of the program. Under prevailing industry practices, design and programming bugs are not uncommon and it is at least arguable that the imperfect program nevertheless constitutes perfect tender under the contract.

---

[97] See supra ¶ 6.05.

[98] UCC § 2-601.

[99] See Alderman & Dole, *A Transactional Guide to the Uniform Commercial Code* 253, 254 (1983).

[100] UCC § 2-508.

While the UCC presumes a requirement that the seller deliver products that fully conform to the contract, it does not define the level of performance required in any particular transaction. In the absence of contract specification, the courts must interpret the meaning of particular contract descriptions in light of baseline industry expectations. At least for new systems, something less than immediate, perfect performance is anticipated and acceptable. One court described this in the following terms

> Certainly, however, every mechanical failure in a new and complex machine does not constitute a breach of warranty. [It] is necessary to distinguish and segregate those defects which merely required that work be performed and those legally significant defects. . . . [The buyer] does not contend that it was entitled to a perfect machine, nor that the installation and break-in period should have been completely service free.[101]

If the circumstances suggest that the buyer is entitled to something less than a perfectly performing machine or software package, the pertinent question is how much less than perfect is adequate under the agreement. This question can arise in the context of the seller's right or obligation to cure defects, but more basically, it defines whether any remedial action is required. If the products fall within reasonably anticipated ranges of performance there has been no breach of contract.

An initial period of debugging and adjustment is to be expected for new and specially developed products; no breach occurs except for defects not cured after a reasonable opportunity.[102] It is relatively clear that in most commercial markets there is no enforceable expectation of perfect performance. This does not, of course, resolve the more basic question of whether or under what circumstances minor flaws in a program or hardware system constitute a breach of contract. The level of imperfection that is tolerable is a product of trade expectations coupled with any known and mutually accepted special circumstances in the intended use of the system. For example, it is clear that mass-marketed software is subject to less exacting standards than systems delivered for control of medical operations. Similarly, a greater degree of imperfection should be anticipated from newly created, complex systems than from programs or hardware that have been in the market for an extended time.

---

[101] Fargo Mach. & Tool Co. v. Kearney & Trecker Corp., 428 F. Supp. 364, 370 (ED Mich. 1977).

[102] See infra ¶ 6.11[1].

[2] Causation

Assuming that an appropriate standard of performance is identified for a particular product, whether nonperformance in an operational environment is attributable to system defects may remain in question. The answer involves the full spectrum of evidence and proof considerations of any problematic complex transaction. Several recurrent issues of causation in computer transactions merit separate attention, however.

In most cases the buyer need only establish that a delivered system fails to perform at a required level, regardless of the cause for such failure within the system.[103] The essence of the transaction is to deliver a particular product and failure to do so is actionable, whether caused by programming or other errors. Negligence is not at issue. Despite this general principle, it may be essential to establish the particular source of a problem or, at least, to exclude certain possibilities. This is important where several vendors are involved and action is taken against only one. A similar need for more specific proof might arise where the vendor effectively limits its liability to certain types of defect.[104]

The most common causation case involves distinguishing system defects from problems caused by operator or environmental errors in the control of the buyer. The existence of operator error must be established by the defendant-seller.[105] In most cases, if inadequate performance is caused by operator error, no cause of action lies against the seller. This simple proposition, however, is not necessarily applicable where the seller has undertaken to train the buyer's personnel in use of the system and the operator problems relate to the faulty training. Similarly, errors caused by inadequate documentation may be chargeable to the seller.

¶ 6.11 PERFORMANCE ISSUES

While the UCC provides limited guidance for determining whether a particular product conforms to a contract, it does provide an extensive framework for the options of the parties when performance problems occur. The UCC establishes the buyer's presumptive right to insist on perfect tender in many cases.[106] The overall structure of the UCC, how-

---

[103] Carl Beasley Ford, Inc. v. Burroughs Corp., 361 F. Supp. 325, 331 (ED Pa. 1973).

[104] See Bruffey Contracting Co. v. Burroughs Corp., 522 F. Supp. 769 (D. Md. 1981).

[105] Carl Beasley Ford Co. v. Burroughs Corp., 361 F. Supp. 325, 331 (ED Pa. 1973).

[106] See supra ¶ 6.10[1].

ever, enhances the likelihood that parties will resolve problems with imperfect goods in the context of the particular transaction without resort to judicial action. This result is achieved through an interaction of acceptance, cure, and rejection standards.

On tender of nonconforming goods by the seller, the buyer has the option of rejecting the goods or accepting them in whole or in part.[107] Acceptance does not waive a right to action for damages caused by defective goods, but does place the buyer in the position of retaining the delivered product. The buyer is legally responsible for the purchase price unless he is later able to revoke acceptance (i.e., rescind). The remedy for defects in accepted goods consists of an action for the difference between the value of the goods as promised and the value as delivered.[108]

If the buyer rejects the goods, the seller may have a right to cure the defective delivery.[109] The right to cure arises if the seller had reason to expect that the delivery would be acceptable. It provides the seller with a reasonable time to correct any defects by substituting conforming goods. The policy is to create a legal context that encourages informal efforts to resolve performance problems between the parties. In the absence of a cure, rejection effectively returns the goods or leaves them with the seller. The buyer may recover any part of the price already paid plus relevant contractual damages.

The differentiation between rejection and cure or acceptance is often not clear in complex or major transactions. Even where initially manifest, the distinction might blur as the seller makes efforts to cure over a period of time. Since the buyer's position is altered materially in the contrasting situations of rejection and acceptance, substantial litigation has focused on when or if an effective rejection is made or, alternatively, whether the buyer has a right to revoke a prior acceptance.

[1] Rejection and Debugging New Systems

Many reported cases involving computer sales raise the issue of whether a buyer has implicitly accepted the delivered product by delaying rejection of the goods for too long a period. The UCC defines "acceptance" to include not only explicit action signifying acceptance, but also a failure to make an effective rejection.[110] Under this standard, the recur-

---

[107] UCC § 2-601.

[108] See Chatlos Sys., Inc. v. National Cash Register Corp., 670 F2d 1304 (3d Cir. 1982).

[109] UCC § 2-508.

[110] UCC § 2-606.

rent issue is the effect of the buyer's participation in an extended period of modification of the delivered system by the seller. It is often not clear whether this activity involves acceptance by the buyer or an effort by the seller to cure in response to a rejection of the goods. Most often, in fact, the adjustment effort is simply a response to a buyer's complaint without the benefit of a particular legal label applied to either the complaint or the response.

The UCC model for rejection and cure presumes a transaction in what might be described as static goods, whose suitability for the particular delivery can be determined with relative ease. The implicit expectation is that minor defects will be repaired or the item replaced and that, in fact, the necessity for long-term adjustment is not part of the anticipated transaction. This model is consistent with delivery of relatively uncomplex systems, and in many computer transactions such as those involving mass-market software or hardware it is quite appropriate.

Many computer transactions, however, do not fit the model. Indeed, in transactions characterized by custom-designed software and hardware a contrary expectation can be presumed. The expected transaction does not entail only the delivery of perfect items, but also an anticipated period of time in which problems are identified, worked on, and resolved. When the transaction is of this kind, the buyer's participation in the period of adjustment does not waive its right to reject the system.[111] Properly viewed, this period of adjustment does not derive from the seller's right to cure, but is an inherent part of the transaction. It does not exist simply because the transaction involves computer hardware or software, but because the transaction involves items that are so commonly subject to adjustment and repair that a period of post-delivery adjustment is reasonably within the contemplation of the parties at the time of the contract.[112]

The observation that a period of product adjustment and refinement is implicit in many computer contracts does not answer how long the period is and when the buyer's or seller's actions pass beyond expected levels of tolerance or delay. Whether arising under cure provisions or inherent contract expectations, a limit of forbearance is appropriate in fact and in law. The issue is best considered from the perspective of two distinct questions pertinent to extended periods of adjustment.

_____

[111] See, e.g., Chatlos Sys., Inc. v. National Cash Register Corp., 479 F. Supp. 738 (DNJ 1979), aff'd, 635 F2d 1081 (3d Cir. 1980); Carl Beasley Ford, Inc. v. Burroughs Corp., 361 F. Supp. 325 (ED Pa. 1973) (eight months).

[112] Carl Beasley Ford, Inc. v. Burroughs Corp., 361 F. Supp. 325, 330 (ED Pa. 1973).

The first question concerns the point at which the buyer is free to terminate the effort, declare a breach of contract, and proceed to other remedies. Clearly, there is a limit to the degree of tolerance required of a buyer who has not received an operational system. Under UCC cure provisions, the seller must provide an effective cure within a reasonable time after notification of the problem.[113] It is also clear that a limit exists in inherent contractual expectations. As one court explained: "Here, the malfunctioning was continuous. Whether the plaintiffs could have made it functional is not the issue. The machine's malfunctions continued after the plaintiff was given a reasonable opportunity to correct its defects. [The] warranty was breached."[114]

The buyer must allow the seller a reasonable opportunity to adjust or repair the system and to satisfy the bargain. The length of time that must be accorded necessarily varies, depending on the circumstances of the transaction. If the system is central to the buyer's business and the malfunction substantially disables the system, the buyer's exigent circumstances indicate that less latitude is required than if no immediate harm is occurring. Similarly, any extension of time is contingent on the seller in fact making an effort to correct the problem. Finally, there must be some reasonable likelihood that a solution is possible; a hopelessly defective system should be replaced.

The second question concerns the point at which inaction by the buyer compromises the buyer's position by constituting an acceptance of the goods or a waiver of the alleged problem in performance. In essence, at what point must the buyer act? A balance is necessary. There is a policy interest in bringing transactions to a close and establishing the rights of the parties that argues for an outer limit beyond which alleged inaction converts into a fixed waiver of rights. On the other hand, informal settlement of contract disputes is desirable. This argues for permitting the buyer to wait for a cure without risk of jeopardizing its own position.

Substantial periods of delay and continuing adjustment are permitted if characterized by relatively continuous efforts to correct problems. In computer cases, intervals of over eight months after delivery have been held to be reasonable preceding rejection of the tendered goods, if the interval is characterized by continuous complaints and efforts to correct the problems that had developed.[115]

---

[113] UCC § 2-508.

[114] National Cash Register Corp. v. Adell Indus., Inc., 225 NW2d 785, 787 (Mich. Ct. App. 1975).

[115] Carl Beasley Ford, Inc. v. Burroughs Corp., 361 F. Supp. 325 (ED Pa. 1973); Lovely v. Burroughs Corp., 527 P2d 557 (Mont. 1974).

> While the plaintiff did retain possession for almost eight months, the evidence clearly shows that they did not accept the computer in its defective condition. The record is replete with repeated complaints . . . resulting in numerous service calls directed at remedying the many problems. Plaintiffs' actions amount to a good-faith attempt to permit defendant to remedy the defects, not an acceptance of them.[116]

As long as there are continuous adjustment efforts, the buyer's election to continue to work within the transaction should not result in a penalty by denying the right to reject. The continuous activity avoids any problem of notice or closure. In contrast, when there has been a significant period of use without complaint, the seller is justified in believing that its corrective effort has succeeded and that the transaction is complete. Similarly, even with a continuing effort, at some point it may become apparent that there is no realistic hope of correction of the defects and it might be incumbent on the buyer to elect to accept the defective product or reject.

[2] Revocation

When a buyer signifies by express notification or silent use that computer products delivered under a contract are acceptable, the buyer assumes ownership and is legally chargeable with the purchase price. Acceptance does not foreclose action to collect damages, but such action requires that the buyer notify the seller of the defects within a reasonable time after it should have been aware of them.[117] Furthermore, unless the buyer is able to revoke acceptance, collection of damages does not entail the return of the goods and recovery of the purchase price.

The UCC treats acceptance as a substantial closure to the sales transaction, at least insofar as location and ownership of the goods is concerned. The standards to revoke acceptance are restrictive. As discussed earlier, where substantial testing precedes acceptance it is unlikely that any subsequent developments will permit revocation.[118] More generally, revocation is precluded unless the defect substantially impairs the value of the goods. Furthermore, the defect must have been unknown due to a difficulty of discovery at the time of acceptance unless the acceptance was based on a reasonable assumption that the seller would cure the problem.[119] Finally, revocation must occur within a reasonable time after

---

[116] Lovely v. Burroughs Corp., 527 P2d 557, 561 (Mont. 1974).

[117] UCC § 2-607(3)(a).

[118] Sha I v. City of San Francisco, 612 F2d 1215 (9th Cir. 1980).

[119] UCC § 2–608(1).

discovery of the problem and before there is a material change in the goods.

The combined effect of these standards is illustrated in *Iten Leasing Co. v. Burroughs Corp.*[120] *Iten* combined contract causes of action with allegations of fraud. Iten acquired an accounting system from Burroughs consisting of an accounting machine, software, and various peripherals including an "R/F/S device" to read, feed, and stack data entering into the system. When the R/F/S device and a data storage device malfunctioned, Iten sought to revoke acceptance of the overall system. Although Iten was awarded damages for the reduced value of the system in light of these malfunctions, revocation was disallowed on the basis that the defects did not substantially impair the value of the system and that Iten had failed to give timely notice of revocation. There was a four-month period in which, although the problems were known to Iten, there was no contact with the seller seeking correction of the defects or replacement of the machine.

As to the issue of substantial impairment, the court concluded that although the malfunctions substantially reduced the speed of the system in producing data reports, the overall system remained valuable to Iten.

> Plaintiff operated defendant's system for several months before the R/F/S was delivered, and for several months after [it] ceased using the R/F/S because of its defects.... Plaintiff wanted to eliminate delay in obtaining financial information. [While] the R/F/S was an important factor in influencing plaintiff to decide to purchase the system, neither it nor the data-save device was at the heart of the decision to undertake a new accounting system.[121]

In essence, despite the malfunction the buyer substantially achieved the results desired from the new system.

¶ 6.12 LIMITED WARRANTIES AND REMEDIES

Virtually all form contracts used by computer vendors contain language limiting the warranties and the remedies available to the buyer in the event of a breach by the seller. In some cases, these provisions are in fact negotiated by the parties. In most instances, especially those involving consumers or small businesses, the language is incorporated in the final agreement without substantial opportunity for modification.

---

[120] 684 F2d 573 (8th Cir. 1982).
[121] Id. at 576.

Commonly, limitation packages involve three distinct contract provisions; the law relating to each differs. The first disclaims implied and express warranties substituting a limited, express warranty covering, for example, "defects in material and workmanship for a period of one year." The essential element is the disclaimer.[122] If the disclaimer is effective, the limited, express warranty is the primary obligation and potential liability for the seller. Absent breach of that warranty, there is no liability. If the disclaimer is ineffective, the express warranty is an additional, rather than a replacement, provision and liability may exist under it or any other applicable warranty.

The second and third provisions in the typical limitation package involve the buyer's remedy in the event of a breach of contract. Remedy limitations commonly appear in either or both of two forms. The first limits the buyer's remedy in the event of breach to replacement and repair of defective systems or parts. The purpose of the limitation is to ensure that the buyer receives an operating product and to protect the seller against extended liability relating to factors outside of its control. The second remedy limitation disclaims responsibility for consequential damages. As with the replace and repair remedy, the objective is to provide the buyer with a viable remedy while protecting the seller from potentially broad liability in the event of a breach.

The basic premise of the UCC and general contract law is that the parties are free to negotiate the remedies available in the event of breach. This flexibility, however, is constrained by several factors that differ according to the transaction, the breach involved, and the particular contract clause at issue.

[1] Failure of Purpose in Replacement and Repair Remedies

Under UCC § 2-719, the parties may modify the remedies available in the event of breach by providing remedies in addition to or in substitution for the remedies under the UCC. The ability to contract for substitutes to UCC remedies is limited, however. First, UCC § 2-719 provides that a contract remedy is presumed to be cumulative and in addition to UCC remedies, unless it is expressly defined as the exclusive remedy. As a result, to replace traditional remedies, the replacement remedy must be explicit to the effect that it will be the sole and exclusive recourse in the event of breach.[123]

---

[122] See supra ¶ 6.08.

[123] UCC § 2-719; see also Garden State Food Co. v. Sperry Rand Corp., 512 F. Supp. 975 (DNJ 1981).

The second restriction on contracting for an exclusive substitute for traditional UCC remedies is less subject to the seller's control and more frequently litigated. Under UCC § 2-719, where "circumstances cause an exclusive or limited remedy to fail of its essential purpose, remedy may be had as provided in this Act."[124] The defense of "failure of purpose" is often premised on events after the contract is formed. The rationale for the failure of purpose limitation lies in the policy decision that "at least minimum adequate remedies be available." The failure of purpose defense applies "where an apparently fair and reasonable clause because of circumstances fails in its purpose or operates to deprive either party of the substantial value of the bargain."[125]

The failure of purpose standard requires that a court define the purpose of a remedy limitation and then assess whether that purpose is fulfilled in the particular case and in light of all the circumstances.[126] The purpose obviously varies with the type of clause at issue. The common thread is that the remedy limitation allocates particular risks away from the party receiving the benefit of the limitation. In most cases, this is clearly achieved. In turn, the clause must provide at least a basic, minimum remedy for the other party, which often is expressed in the limitation clause itself. The analysis then is extended to the conclusion that one purpose of the limitation is to convey this minimum remedy to the buyer. In the reported cases, the main focus of analysis is on whether the clause effectively conveys at least the requisite minimum of protection to the buyer.

The most common limiting clause restricts the buyer's remedy in the event of breach to replacement and repair of defective parts by the seller. In some cases, there is a further constraint requiring that defects be discovered and reported within a limited time period. The purpose of these provisions from the seller's perspective is relatively clear. They eliminate the risk of broad liability for resulting damages from breach, provide that a completed transaction will not be upset by defective goods, and, in the case of a time limit, establish a cut-off point beyond which the transaction can be treated as fully complete. One court described the package as follows

> Several goals of the limited remedy of repair may be envisioned, but its primary objective is to give the seller an opportunity to make the goods conform while limiting exposure to risk by excluding liability

---

[124] UCC § 2-719(2).

[125] UCC § 2-719, Comment 1.

[126] See Eddy, "On the Essential Purpose of Limited Remedies: The Metaphysics of U.C.C. Section 2-719(2)," 65 Calif. L. Rev. 28 (1977).

for damages that might otherwise be due. Viewed from the buyer's standpoint, the repair remedy's aim is to provide goods that conform to the contract for sale.[127]

Given this definition of purpose, the analysis typically centers on whether the purpose of providing conforming goods was achieved. The limited remedy is enforced if the seller makes an active effort to correct defects and the buyer in fact obtains substantial use of the product. This might occur either because the defect is repaired or because the continuing problems involve peripheral considerations.[128] In *Bruffey Contracting Co. v. Burroughs Corp.*,[129] the remedy limitation was enforced where the buyer had used the system for seven months, five of which followed the last effort to resolve the performance problems that had been encountered.

The replacement and repair remedy fails to achieve its purpose when repair efforts are not made or have not provided the buyer with adequate beneficial use of the product.[130] Both the ultimate success and the timing of the repairs are at issue. The known character of the transaction and the buyer's expressed needs are considered in determining a reasonable time for the repairs. The court in *Chatlos Systems v. National Cash Register Corp.*[131] noted

> To be effective the repair remedy must be provided within a reasonable time after discovery of the defect. [As] long as the buyer has the use of substantially defect free goods, the limited remedy should be given effect. But when the seller is either unwilling or unable to conform the goods to the contract, the remedy does not suffice. . . . In this case we consider a product programmed specifically to meet the customer's individual needs. Time was of substantial importance because added efficiency was needed at that time.[132]

In *Chatlos*, ongoing efforts to complete programming continued over a period of one and one-half years, but the majority of the contracted func-

---

[127] Chatlos Sys., Inc. v. National Cash Register Corp., 635 F2d 1081, 1085 (3d Cir. 1980).

[128] Earman Oil Co. v. Burroughs Corp., 625 F2d 1291 (5th Cir. 1980); Garden State Food Co. v. Sperry Rand Corp., 512 F. Supp. 975 (DNJ 1981); Westfield Chem. Co. v. Burroughs Corp., 21 UCC Rep. 1298 (Mass. Super. Ct. 1977).

[129] 522 F. Supp. 769 (D. Md. 1981).

[130] See, e.g., Office Supply Co. v. Basic/Four Corp., 538 F. Supp. 776 (ED Wis. 1982); Teamsters Sec. Fund v. Sperry Rand Corp., 6 CLSR 951 (ND Cal. 1971).

[131] 635 F2d 1081 (3d Cir. 1980).

[132] Id. at 1085.

tions had not been satisfactorily completed. While there was no dispute that eventual completion was possible and that the seller had been making efforts, the delay in itself substantially deprived the buyer of the benefit of its bargain.

Other circumstances may cause a remedy to fail. Time limits on discovery of defects have been held to fail of their purpose when applied to latent defects not discoverable within a brief period allocated by the contract.[133] The remedy limitation also fails when the defect is of a type that neither replacement nor repair will provide the buyer with the product that it bargained for. No amount of repair and replacement, for example, will conform to the contract when a design defect contradicts express warranties of performance since the product is incapable of that performance.[134] This does not suggest that cases of design failure or ongoing repair problems are such that no limitation of remedy is enforceable. The point is that a limitation to replacement and repair fails when replacement and repair do not convey a substantially conforming product to the buyer within a reasonable time. Alternative remedy limitations might nevertheless be valid and enforceable.

When repairs do not produce a conforming product, the ultimate failure in the remedy is that it forces the buyer to pay for and retain defective merchandise. A limited remedy that includes a right to return the defective product and recover the purchase price is enforceable despite the seller's inability to repair.[135] From the buyer's perspective, the purpose of the remedy limitation includes not only that a conforming product will be delivered, but that, in the event that it is not, the buyer can withdraw from the transaction. This purpose is not defeated by the simple fact that repair is impossible or long delayed. Of course, this remedy is potentially enforceable simply because it does convey greater rights to the buyer at the expense of the seller.

[2] Consequential Damage Limitations

Absent contractual modification, the UCC provides that the buyer in most cases may recover consequential damages arising from any breach of contract. "Consequential damages" are defined to include "any loss resulting from general or particular requirements and needs of which the

---

[133] Alderman & Dole, *A Transactional Guide to the Uniform Commercial Code* 234 (1983).

[134] Consolidated Data Terminals v. Applied Digital Data Sys., 708 F2d 385, 392 (9th Cir. 1983).

[135] Garden State Food Co. v. Sperry Rand Corp., 512 F. Supp. 975 (DNJ 1981).

seller at the time of contracting had reason to know ... and injury to person or property proximately resulting from any breach of warranty."[136] In general, consequential damages encompass the effects resulting from the breach, such as lost profits or unrealized but anticipated personnel savings.[137] Although the precise scope of consequential damages is unclear in particular cases, the general thrust is that direct damages encompass losses incurred naturally and ordinarily from a breach, whereas consequential damages are contingent on the existence of external or circumstantial factors.[138] Consequential damage awards entail the greatest risk of substantial assessments against the seller.[139] As a result, it is commonly in the seller's interest to disclaim responsibility for such losses. This exclusion shifts the risk of consequential loss to the buyer if the clause is enforced.

UCC § 2-719(3) provides that "consequential damages may be limited or excluded unless the limitation ... is unconscionable." The presumption, applicable except to goods sold to consumers, is that the parties may specify their own arrangement, but that enforcement will be denied if it would contradict basic concepts of providing at least some adequate remedy for the buyer. Thus, exclusion of consequential damages will not be enforced where it will operate in an "unconscionable manner." Unconscionablity may be present from the outset or may arise only as an exclusion is applied to a particular case. It is clear, however, that the mere fact that the buyer is denied compensation for otherwise provable loss can not be the standard of unconscionability. The purpose of the clause is to allocate risk; it should not be invalidated simply because the risk allocation matured.

Standards of unconscionability are discussed in the next section, but it is pertinent to note that few cases find a consequential damage exclusion or limitation unconscionable in mercantile sales. The allocation of known risks is too central to the commercial environment to be readily discarded by a court. In fact, in commercial sales, exclusion or limitation

---

[136] UCC § 2-715(2).

[137] Teamsters Sec. Fund v. Sperry Rand Corp., 6 CLRS 951 (ND Cal. 1971).

[138] Applied Data Processing Co. v. Burroughs Corp., 394 F. Supp. 504 (D. Conn. 1975).

[139] This relationship does not always hold true in the computer environment. For example, in computing direct damages for the seller's failure to deliver a complete system, even though consequential damages had been disclaimed effectively, at least one court approved a computation system that included lost future benefits even above the contract price. Chatlos Sys., Inc. v. National Cash Register Corp., 670 F2d 1304 (3d Cir. 1982).

of consequential damages should be presumed valid, subject to contrary proof.[140] While most consequential damage exclusions are enforced, various circumstances arise in which the effect of the clause is essentially avoided. This may reflect that the courts are uneasy with denying the buyer a full recovery despite the buyer's own bargain. One manifestation of this is found in cases that strictly construe the scope of an exclusionary clause.

In *Carl Beasley Ford, Inc. v. Burroughs*,[141] a clause excluding consequential damages and contained in the written sales contract between the parties for equipment was held to be inapplicable to an oral contract for software entered as one part of the same transaction. In *Consolidated Data Terminals v. Applied Digital Data Systems*,[142] a consequential damages exclusion was held to be inapplicable to design defects in the delivered products. The clause provided that Applied Digital "will not be liable for any consequential damages, loss or expense arising in connection with the use of or the inability to use its products or goods for any purpose whatsoever." The court held that the clause covered only damages arising from the use of defective products. The design-defective products presented a wholly different issue.

A consequential damages clause may be invalidated in a commercial sales transaction when an accompanying exclusive remedy "fails of it essential purpose." Although the better view is that the consequential damages provision and the replacement and repair remedies are distinct portions of an agreement,[143] there is some authority for viewing the provisions as essentially part of a single package that is effective or invalid in its entirety.[144] The flaw in this result is that it elevates a failure of repair efforts not only to allow the buyer to recover the purchase price and other directly caused damages, but to reallocate totally the distribution of risk that occurred.

---

[140] See Office Supply Co. v. Basic/Four Corp., 538 F. Supp. 776, 778 (ED Wis. 1982); Chatlos Sys., Inc. v. National Cash Register Corp., 635 F2d 1081 (3d Cir. 1980); Alderman & Dole, *A Transactional Guide to the Uniform Commercial Code* 240 (1983); White & Summers, *Handbook of the Law Under the Uniform Commercial Code* 473–475 (2d ed. 1980).

[141] 361 F. Supp. 325 (ED Pa. 1973).

[142] 708 F2d 385 (9th Cir. 1983).

[143] Office Supply Co. v. Basic/Four Corp., 538 F. Supp. 776 (ED Wis. 1982); Chatlos Sys., Inc. v. National Cash Register Corp., 479 F. Supp. 738, aff'd, 635 F2d 1081 (3d Cir. 1980).

[144] Alderman & Dole, *A Transactional Guide to the Uniform Commercial Code* 236, 237 (1983).

¶ 6.13 UNCONSCIONABILITY

When Article Two of the UCC was initially promulgated, one of the most controversial provisions was UCC § 2-302, regarding unconscionable contracts or contract clauses. This section provides that a court may refuse to enforce any contract or clause of a contract on a finding that the contract or clause was unconscionable at the time that it was made. The comments to UCC § 2-302 indicate that the purpose of this doctrine is to prevent "oppression and unfair surprise and not [to disturb an] allocation of risks because of superior bargaining power."[145] The intention was to authorize judicial policing of the terms of litigated contracts.

The doctrine of unconscionability concerns two distinct types of overreaching or oppressive behavior in contracting. The first generally is described as procedural unconscionability and focuses on the use of pressure or deceptive tactics, the presence of extreme bargaining inequality, and significant differences in the sophistication of the parties. The second form generally is described as substantive unconscionability and encompasses terms that are unreasonably favorable to one party.[146] A clause or contract normally is not refused enforcement unless both forms of unconscionability are present.

Unconscionability has played a major role in the law regarding risk allocation for remedy limitations and warranty disclaimers.[147] The successful litigation, however, has been almost entirely confined to consumer contracts in which conscionability coalesces with concerns about enforcing contracts of adhesion against unsophisticated buyers who are in no position to bargain for favorable contract terms. In consumer contracts today, most of the concerns underlying conscionability have been taken over by deceptive trade practice and other consumer legislation.[148]

While there have been no reported computer contracting cases dealing with the doctrine of unconscionability in the context of con-

---

[145] UCC § 2-302, Comment 1.

[146] See Leff, "Unconscionability and the Code—The Emperor's New Clause," 115 U. P. L. Rev. 485, 487 (1967); White & Summers, *Handbook of the Law Under the Uniform Commercial Code* 4-2 (2d ed. 1980).

[147] The extent to which unconscionability arguments are properly applied to warranty disclaimers that meet the express provisions of the UCC has been the subject of substantial debate. Arguably, at least, the specific provisions regarding the creation of an effective warranty disclaimer should prevail over the general unconscionability concept. This view has not, however, been universally accepted. See White & Summers, *Handbook of the Law Under the Uniform Commercial Code* 392 (2d ed. 1980); Alderman & Dole, *A Transactional Guide to the Uniform Commercial Code* 123 (1983).

[148] See infra ¶ 6.18[1].

sumer transactions, there has been significant controversy over the application of unconscionability to contracts with small businesses who acquire computer systems, especially when the small business is a first-time user. Consistent with the primary, general use of the doctrine, the controversy centers on warranty disclaimers[149] and exclusion of liability for consequential damages.[150]

The argument to apply conscionability in the context of the small business users involves several facets of such transactions. Few small businesses in fact negotiate the remedy or warranty terms of form contracts. The transactions involve an economic imbalance not substantially different from that in many consumer transactions.[151] This imbalance exists regardless of whether a contract involves a computer transaction, however, and courts have been generally unreceptive to conscionability arguments in commercial sales.[152]

The arguable distinction in a computer environment involves the lack of sophistication of most small business, first-time users concerning computer technology and their resulting reliance on the recommendations and advice of the seller.[153] The argument is that even an otherwise sophisticated business person can not reasonably appreciate the significance of warranty and damage limitation language in this context. While this argument has generally been rejected, there are some exceptions in

---

[149] Badger Bearing Co. v. Burroughs Corp., 444 F. Supp. 919 (ED Wis. 1977).

[150] Earman Oil Co. v. Burroughs Corp., 625 F2d 1291, 1299 (5th Cir. 1980); Office Supply Co. v. Basic/Four Corp., 538 F. Supp. 776 (ED Wis. 1982); Westfield Chem. Co. v. Burroughs Corp., 21 UCC Rep. 1298 (Mass. Super. Ct. 1977); WR Weaver Co. v. Burroughs Corp., 580 SW2d 76 (Tex. Civ. App. 1979). But see Horning v. Syncom, 556 F. Supp. 819 (ED Ky. 1983) (unconscionability applied to choice of law provision in contract involving a dentist).

[151] See Marzouk, Rinkerman, Porter, "Unconscionability in Computer Contracts With Small Businesses," 2 CLR 214 (1983).

[152] Alderman & Dole, *A Transactional Guide to the Uniform Commercial Code* 123 (1983); White & Summers, *Handbook of the Law Under the Uniform Commercial Code* (2d ed. 1980).

[153] See generally Marzouk, Binkerman, Porter, "Unconscionability in Computer Contracts With Small Businesses," 2 CLR 214 (1983). Among the most widely discussed lower court applications of unconscionability to a computer environment was in The Glovatorium, Inc. v. NCR Corp., 684 F2d 658 (9th Cir. 1983). In *Glovatorium*, the buyer relied on a model and the seller's assurances that did not in fact reflect the true performance limitations of the business records system. The lower court indicated the limitations language was unconscionable in the face of this clear reliance by an inexperienced buyer. However, the appellate court affirmed a substantial damage award based on the lower court's finding of fraud, without expressly dealing with the conscionability claim.

lower court decisions subsequently affirmed on other grounds.[154] One recent exception involved invalidation of a choice of forum clause.[155]

While unconscionability is relevant to business contracts, mere lack of sophistication in computer technology should be an inadequate basis to conclude that the terms of a contract allocating risk are oppressive or unfair.[156] The argument favoring application of unconscionability to small business computer contracts mistakenly equates lack of sophistication in the technology to lack of sophistication in general contract bargaining and business practices. If anything, the buyer's lack of sophistication in the technology should alert it to a need to exercise additional caution in the terms of the agreement. This is especially relevant where the purchased equipment will play a major role in business operations. The fact that form agreements are common in this industry does not distinguish it from many others in which the courts have shown no disposition to extend unconscionability protection. As one court noted, businessmen are presumed to act at arm's length and mere technological naivete is inadequate cause to disrupt this presumption on issues relating to assumption of risk and the like.[157] Although a businessman may not be sophisticated in computers, the presumed sophistication in commercial matters coupled with an ability to obtain legal and other assistance is ordinarily decisive.[158]

PART C.   COMPUTER LEASING

¶ 6.14 FORMS OF LEASING

While many computer system acquisitions involve direct purchases of equipment and software, a common alternative is acquisition under a

---

[154] See Chesapeake Petroleum & Supply Co. v. Burroughs Corp., 6 CLRS 768, aff'd, 384 A2d 734 (Md. Ct. Spec. App. 1978); The Glovatorium, Inc. v. NCR Corp., 684 F2d 658 (9th Cir. 1983).

[155] Horning v. Syncom, 556 F. Supp. 819 (ED Ky. 1983) (case involved a solo dentist and had aspects of consumer law concerns present).

[156] Earman Oil Co. v. Burroughs Corp., 625 F2d 1291 (5th Cir. 1980) (unconscionability can not be based on computer inexperience); Chatlos Sys., Inc. v. National Cash Register Corp., 635 F2d 1081, 1087 (3d Cir. 1980) (damage limit not unconscionable); Badger Bearing Co. v. Burroughs, 444 F. Supp. 919, (ED Wis. 1977); Office Supply Co. v. Basic/Four Corp., 538 F. Supp. 776 (ED Wis. 1982); WR Weaver Co. v. Burroughs Corp., 580 SW2d 76 (Tex. Ct. App. 1979).

[157] Earman Oil Co. v. Burroughs Corp., 625 F2d 1291, 1300 (5th Cir. 1980).

[158] Badger Bearing Co. v. Burroughs Corp., 444 F. Supp. 919, 923 (3D Wis. 1977).

leasing arrangement. Computer lease transactions may involve a two-party lease in which the roles of the parties are analogous to buyer and seller, except that the transaction does not convey title of the product to the lessee. An equally common format is a three-party transaction. The equipment and software are conveyed by the original owner-seller to a third party, which then leases the property to the end user lessee. In most such transactions, the third party is a financing entity or, at least, a business established to serve as a conduit for such transactions. A variation on this is the leveraged lease in which the lessor's investment in the lease is financed at least in part by a lending institution. In any form, leasing is most common for larger systems where it is a significant, frequently encountered method of acquiring computer hardware.

One motivation for use of a lease in lieu of a sale subject to a security interest lies in the redistribution of tax advantages to the parties that occurs if the characterization of the transaction as a lease is upheld. In a lease used in lieu of a more traditional financing arrangement, the lessor functionally extends credit to the lessee, or at least permits the lessee to acquire the property without immediately paying the purchase price of the computer equipment. Ordinarily, a purchase money loan of this nature would result in transfer of ownership to the lessee (debtor) and the creation of a credit obligation for that party. In contrast, a transaction that qualifies as a lease does not result in a credit obligation on the lessee's financial records. The lessee is able to treat lease rental expenses as current deductible expenses for tax purposes. If the transaction is characterized as a lease, the lessor (creditor) is the owner of the computer equipment and is able to claim tax benefits associated with ownership, including investment tax credits and depreciation. In a particular case, these results may be advantageous to the parties and may allow the lessor to complete the transaction with less cost to the lessee than would be required for a traditional financing transaction.

Regardless of whether a transaction involves two or three parties, an initial issue in computer leasing is whether the transaction is treated as a true lease or as a purchase agreement under contract or tax law. In a true lease, the intention of the parties is that ownership and substantial elements of risk remain in the lessor. The lessee-end user is expected to return the equipment and/or software at a future date. The rights of the parties are determined by the terms of the lease and a body of law dealing with bailments for mutual benefit. For tax purposes, ownership benefits remain in the lessor while the lessee can treat monthly payments as current expenses.

In contrast, in a lease that is in fact a purchase transaction the intention is that the lessee retain the equipment even though the contract may contain an obligation to return the property. This intention may be implemented by establishing a lease term that exceeds the useful life of the equipment. More commonly, the lease provides an option to purchase the equipment at a nominal price at the expiration of the lease.[159] In such cases, the lease substitutes for a security agreement and the monthly rentals are in effect equivalent to loan payments.[160] Ownership of the computer vests in the nominal lessee and the rights of the parties are determined by the terms of the written agreement, mediated or circumscribed by UCC provisions relating to the sale of goods and security interests. For tax purposes, the lessor is treated as a seller and ownership benefits vest in the lessee.

The characterization of the transaction chosen by the parties is not determinative, and a court may look beyond the label to determine the true character of the transaction. The result is that the nature of the transaction in financing leases may remain uncertain until an adjudication. This affects tax planning. It also lends uncertainty to the rights of the parties in the event of problems in the performance of the contract, such as delivery of defective goods, default on rental payments, and so forth.

[1] Contract Law Standards

One measure for distinguishing between a true lease and a lease that is a security device is suggested in the UCC and focuses on the character of any option to purchase provided to the lessee. UCC § 1-201(37) provides that a personal property lease is to be treated as a security interest if it provides an option to purchase for nominal additional consideration. This entails a comparison between the option purchase price and the market value of the computer at the time that the option will be exercised. A sale subject to a security interest is present if the option price is so disproportionately low as to leave no reasonable alternative but to exercise the option.

Under this standard, a variety of fractional prices have been held to conclusively equate with a security interest, rather than a true lease. In general, purchase options at or below 10 percent of the market value of

---

[159] UCC § 1-201(37).

[160] See Coogan, "Leases of Equipment and Some Other Unconventional Security Devices," 1A Coogan, Hogan, & Vagts, *Secured Transactions Under the U.C.C.* 4A-151 (1980).

the computer at the time of exercise establish a security interest.[161] Such a differential reflects the understanding of the parties that completion of the term of the lease is equivalent to having paid the substantial bulk of the price of the computer and having amassed equity in the property. Conversely, an option price that approximates the market value of the computer establishes a true lease.[162] The lessee's performance of the rental obligations has not established an equity position in the property or substantially accounted for payment of the purchase price.

A comparison of option price and market value is inadequate to resolve many cases in which only a fraction of current market value is to be paid, but that fraction is more than a nominal price. Under these circumstances, a variety of factors are considered as the entire transaction is reviewed to determine its true nature, independent of the label provided by the parties. The court in *Burroughs Corp. v. Century Steel, Inc.*[163] summarized these in the following terms

> (a) that the lessee bears the entire risk of loss, theft, damage of destruction and no such loss relieves the lessee of his obligation to pay rent; (b) that the lessee must provide insurance against loss . . .; (c) that the lessee is required to indemnify the lessor against and hold him harmless from all claims and liabilities arising in connection with the equipment; (d) that the lessee must pay all charges, taxes and fees on the leased equipment; and (e) that the lessor disclaimed all warranties.[164]

Additional considerations include whether the lessor was a manufacturer or dealer in the type of equipment involved in the transaction and whether or not it inspected or selected the equipment that it purportedly purchased and subsequently leased to the eventual end user.[165]

[2] Tax Law Standards

Since a substantial part of the computer leasing industry depends on the tax implications of a lease transaction, it is not surprising that substantial litigation and discussion has been devoted to determining the cir-

---

[161] See American Fin. Corp. v. Computer Sciences Corp., 558 F. Supp. 1182 (D. Del. 1982); HMO Sys., Inc. v. Choicecare Health Servs., 665 P2d 635 (Col. Ct. App. 1983).

[162] See WL Scott, Inc. v. Madra Aerotech, Inc., 653 P2d 791 (Idaho 1982).

[163] 664 P2d 354 (Nev. 1983).

[164] Id. at 356.

[165] Atlas Indus., Inc. v. National Cash Register Corp., 531 P2d 41 (Kan. 1975).

cumstances under which a transaction is characterized as a true lease for purposes of tax law. This characterization is often central to the entire economic base of a lease transaction since it permits the lessor to obtain investment tax credits and other tax benefits associated with ownership.[166] The significance of these benefits are such that virtually all leases include provisions to protect the lessor against economic loss that would result if the lease is characterized as a sale and security interest for tax purposes.

The standards for lease characterization for purposes of federal tax law generally parallel those applied by the courts in contract cases. In recent years, however, the federal tax standards have undergone substantial changes as leasing has become a major focus of legislative efforts to reorient tax law pertaining to investment and asset acquisition.

The basic standards for determining whether a transaction is a true lease for federal tax purposes are outlined in Revenue Ruling 55-540. This ruling characterizes a lease in terms of the intent of the parties as reflected by a consideration of all of the facts that existed at the time of the original transaction.[167] The ruling suggests several areas for consideration without elevating these to the status of particularized rules. In general, a lease is treated as a sale subject to a security interest based on a number of factors including:

1. "Rental" payments accrue equity for the lessee,
2. Required rental payments lead in themselves to a transfer of ownership,
3. The rent exceeds fair market value of the equipment; or
4. A nominal or relatively low purchase option is granted to the lessee.

These standards have resulted in substantial litigation and informal review that has proceeded generally under standards similar to those of contract law.[168]

Beyond the basic criteria of Revenue Ruling 55-540, the Internal Revenue Service (IRS) provides guidelines for advance rulings pertaining to leveraged lease transactions. The guidelines suggest a number of specific criteria relevant to leveraged leases that establish a framework within which to structure most such leasing. They include:

---

[166] See supra ¶ 6.14[1].

[167] Rev. Rul. 55-540; see Contino, "Current Developments in Computer Leasing," *PLI Computer Finance and Leasing* 217 (1982).

[168] See supra ¶ 6.14[1].

1. Lessor must maintain an "at risk" investment of 20 percent of the cost of the equipment.

2. The equipment must have a fair market value of at least 20 percent of cost at the end of the lease.

3. The equipment must have a remaining useful life at the end of the lease equal to 20 percent of the original useful life.

4. Lessee must not have a contract right to purchase for less than fair market value and the lessor must not have the right to require purchase.

5. The lessee may not guarantee the lessor's debt.

6. The lessor must demonstrate that it will derive a profit independent of tax benefits.

7. The lease must not involve limited use property where use by any other end user is not feasible.[169]

Since 1981 federal tax leasing law has been subject to dramatic changes. Initially, the enactment of the Economic Recovery Tax Act of 1981 (ERTA) established a so-called safe-harbor lease.[170] The safe-harbor rules were designed to expedite the transfer of tax benefits and to reduce the uncertainty that existed about the characterization of a lease transaction for tax purposes. ERTA's safe-harbor provisions were repealed for leases entered into after 1983, however, and the Tax Equity and Fiscal Responsibility Act (TEFRA) restricted the tax benefits of leasing.[171] TEFRA placed limits on the extent to which a taxpayer can claim ownership benefits from lease transactions treating the taxpayer's business as a whole.[172]

Despite the repeal of safe-harbor leasing, there has been a significant change in tax law related to equipment leases. This involves the recognition of a finance lease for purposes of federal tax law.[173] The finance lease substantially alters the criteria for determining whether a transaction is treated as a lease for tax purposes. Contrary to preexisting IRS guidelines, the finance lease provisions permit treatment as a lease notwithstanding the existence of a fixed purchase price option of no less than 10 percent of the original cost of the equipment. This is significant both because of the percentage that is permitted and because the provisions

---

[169] Rev. Rul. 55-540; Rev. Proc. 76-30 (limited use property).

[170] Pub. L. No. 97-34, 95 Stat. 172 (1981).

[171] Pub. L. No.98-248, 96 Stat. 324 (1982).

[172] See Curatola, et al., "An Analysis of Safe Harbor Leasing After TEFRA," The Tax Executive 261 (July 1983).

[173] See Rizzi, "Tax Leasing After TEFRA," 1 Comp. Law. 29 (March 1984).

allow a fixed price, rather than a price determined with reference to fair market value at the time of the purchase option. Equally important to the computer industry, the finance lease provisions permit leases for limited use property that in essence may be suitable only for use by the particular lessee.

Despite this change, the underlying structure of review remains oriented to the basic intention of the parties and the economic reality of the transaction. Thus, it remains important to determine if the lessor has a realistic opportunity for profit independent of tax benefits. This might entail, for example, a consideration of the expected residual value of the leased equipment as well as other characteristics of the overall transaction.[174]

¶ 6.15 SUBSTANTIVE LAW DIFFERENCES

Whether a transaction is a true lease is critical to an acquisition transaction, affecting the transaction's tax implications and the steps that the lessor must take to safeguard its interest against creditors of the nominal lessee.[175] Beyond these effects, the determination of whether the transaction constitutes a true lease affects the relationship between the parties and their respective rights if the transaction malfunctions. This includes the rights of the lessor in the event of a default by the lessee. Under either characterization of the transaction, a default gives the lessor a right to retake possession of the computer, but the rationale for taking possession in the two situations is distinctly different. The obligations of the repossessing lessor may also differ, depending on the characterization of the transaction.

If the transaction is a security interest, the lessor is a repossessing secured creditor foreclosing against the pertinent debtor's property. The disposition of the computer after foreclosure is in part determined by the terms of the agreement, but the lessor's options for the property are sub-

---

[174] See Rice's Toyota World, Inc. v. Comm'r, 81 TC No. 16 ¶ 81.16 P-H Memo TC (1983).

[175] Essentially, if a lease is construed as a security interest, in most cases not involving consumer goods a filing must be made to perfect the resulting security interest as against claims of other creditors and, especially, a trustee in bankruptcy. 11 USC § 544(a) grants the trustee the status of a judgment lien creditor as of the day the bankruptcy case is filed. Under UCC § 9-301, the lien creditor has priority over an unperfected "security interest." This, in turn, effectively invalidates the lease-security interest in bankruptcy. See generally "Money, True Lease or Lease 'Intended as Security'–Treatment by the Courts," 1C Coogan, Hogan, & Vagts, *Secured Transactions Under the U.C.C.* 2915, 2925 (1980).

stantially constrained by the provisions of Article Nine of the UCC. In most cases, the property must be sold in payment of the debt with any surplus receipts conveyed to the debtor-lessee.[176] The lessor may retain the property only if it implements a UCC procedure described as "strict foreclosure" in which the collateral is held by the creditor in full satisfaction of the outstanding debt.[177] This procedure requires the post-repossession consent of the debtor. At any time prior to resale of the property, the debtor-lessee has a right to recover possession of the property by tendering satisfaction of outstanding liabilities and redeeming the collateral.[178] The entire post-default process presumes that the creditor (lessor) is in possession of the debtor's property solely for the purpose of using it to satisfy outstanding indebtedness owed to it by the debtor.

If the transaction is a true lease, the lessor reclaims possession of its own property and has greater flexibility in its disposition or subsequent use. Absent an obligation to mitigate damages caused by the breach of the lease agreement, the lessor has no obligation to sell or otherwise dispose of and recover from the reclaimed computer. It may elect to re-lease the property.

In a true lease, any amounts owing to the lessor are in the form of unpaid rental and a claim for damages based on breach of the lease agreement. In many cases, the lease provides that the rentals for the term of the lease are accelerated and due on a breach. If the lease is a security agreement, the rentals are equivalent to monthly note payments and there is no conceptual problem with an acceleration. If the transaction is a true lease, however, these provisions are in the nature of liquidated damages, regardless of language referring to acceleration of amounts due. The enforceability of the liquidated damages provision should be tested under general standards pertaining to such provisions. The provision should be enforceable only to the extent that it represents a reasonable effort to estimate actual loss rather than impose a penalty.

If the transaction is a true lease, the lessor has no obligation to sell or otherwise dispose of the property since ownership of the computer is and always has been the lessor's. This general principle, however, is subject to responsibilities to mitigate damages. The lessor's claim is for damages that presumably include unpaid rental as well as losses in the form of lost profit from future rentals.[179] While there is no obligation to sell the prop-

---

[176] UCC § 9-504.

[177] UCC § 9-505 (strict foreclosure).

[178] HMO Sys., Inc. v. Choicecare Health Servs., 665 P2d 635 (Col. Ct. App. 1983).

[179] Honeywell v. Lithonia Lighting, Inc., 317 F. Supp. 406, 413 (ND Ga. 1970).

erty, the lessor might be required to take steps to re-lease or otherwise obtain alternative income from it to mitigate loss from breach of the lease. The lessor must act in a commercially reasonable manner to recover from the property.[180] While this does not require that the lessor sell the property, if the lessor makes a decision that a sale is appropriate the terms and manner of the sale should be reasonably calculated to optimize recovery from the property. A standard approximation applicable in cases involving the resale of repossessed collateral under Article Nine is appropriate if the lessor elects to sell.

¶ 6.16 WARRANTY AND THIRD-PARTY LIABILITY

Computer leasing transactions occur as either two- or three-party transactions. The substantive liabilities of the parties to the transaction, particularly the allocation of warranty liability in a lease agreement rather than a sale transaction, are examined in the following discussion.

[1] Leases and Warranties

Warranties based on Article Two of the UCC may not be applicable to the relationship between lessor and lessee in transactions in which the lease is considered to be a true lease.[181] Despite this, analogous warranty provisions are often applicable. For example, any true lease conveys a limited warranty that the goods will be suitable in general terms for their known, intended use.[182] This common-law warranty is less comprehensive than the equivalent UCC warranty, since it does not imply that the goods will be the most suitable or even convenient to the particular applications. The warranty is more analogous to the warranty of merchantability under the UCC.

If a lease is viewed as a security interest rather than a true lease, the underlying transaction is a sale and the full panoply of warranties are applicable.[183] Similarly, in a three-party transaction UCC warranties pertain to the transaction between the seller and the intermediate lessor and may also be conveyed to the end user in the form of a third-party beneficiary relationship.

---

[180] WL Scott, Inc. v. Madras Aerotech, Inc., 653 P2d 791 (Idaho 1982).

[181] Teamster Sec. Fund v. Sperry Rand Corp., 6 CLRS 951 (ND Cal. 1977).

[182] See Lovely v. Burroughs Corp., 527 P2d 557 (Mont. 1974).

[183] Schatz Distrib. Co. v. Olivetti Corp., 647 P2d 820 (Kan. Ct. App. 1982).

[2] Third-Party Lessees

Three-party lease transactions are common in computer acquisitions. While the ultimate end user may select and negotiate for a particular system, the actual sale is a conveyance of that system to a third party who provides the system to the end user under a lease agreement. The overall transaction is designed to provide a form of financing with particular tax benefits and other advantages to the parties.

Under the three-party arrangement, complex issues may arise in enforcement of warranty and other substantive obligations. In form at least, the end user's only contract is the agreement with the lessor. Typically, this lease expressly disclaims any liability on the part of the lessor. The disclaimer is consistent with the role that the lessor plays in the overall transaction. Even if there is no disclaimer, if the transaction is a true lease only limited warranties are involved. In addition, to the extent that maintenance and the like are relevant considerations the lessor-intermediary may be in no position adequately to perform or otherwise protect the lessee's interests or needs. As a result, it is important that the end user be able to refer to the original seller of the computer for support and, eventually, for remedial action in the event of a system failure. This desire to reach back to the actual vendor of the system is consistent with the actual nature of the transaction. The lessor is only a conduit in a transaction between two parties. Nevertheless, the transaction is structured as two distinct, separable transfers, the first involving a sale from the vendor to the lessor and the second, the lease from lessor to lessee. This structure impedes access to the vendor.

The apparent lack of contractual privity between the vendor and the lessee can be circumvented. In the clearest case, the contract between the lessor and the vendor designates the lessee as a third-party beneficiary of the sale. The purchase order submitted by the lessor may expressly say that the system will be leased to the named lessee and specify that the vendor's warranties are enforceable by the lessee.[184] Supplementing these provisions of the original sale agreement, the lease agreement should disclaim all warranties by the lessor and expressly provide that the lessee has the benefit of the manufacturer's warranties, if any exist.[185] Under these circumstances, the lessee has access to remedies against the vendor but is appropriately restricted in remedies available against the lessor.[186]

---

[184] Uniflex v. Olivetti Corp., 445 NYS2d 993(1982).

[185] Badger Bearing Co. v. Burroughs Corp., 444 F. Supp. 919 (ED Wis. 1977).

[186] Earman Oil Co. v. Burroughs Corp., 625 F2d 1291 (5th Cir. 1980); Uniflex v. Olivetti Corp., 445 NYS2d 993 (1982); Badger Bearing Co. v. Burroughs Corp., 444 F. Supp. 919 (ED Wis. 1977).

While an express reference to the lessee as the intended third-party beneficiary reflects the transaction normally intended by the parties, in a number of cases the references are omitted. In many jurisdictions the failure to mention the intended lessee in the sale papers, or at least to mention that there was a third-party beneficiary involved, is fatal. While Corbin argues that third-party beneficiary status can be established wholly from evidence extrinsic to the written contract,[187] this view is not uniformly followed.[188] The use of extrinsic evidence is especially uncertain when the original sale agreement contains a merger and integration clause, providing that the written agreement contains the entire agreement between the parties. In this regard, it is important to note that to establish third-party beneficiary status it is not sufficient that one party intend the third-party benefit; both parties must so intend.[189] Where extrinsic evidence is allowed to establish beneficiary status, the fact that all of the documentation for the transaction was executed at roughly the same time tends to indicate that the entire transaction should be considered as a whole.[190]

Establishing a contract directly between lessee and seller may be an independent basis for finding warranty representations enforceable by the lessee against the original vendor. This result is possible when negotiations between the end user and the vendor are reduced to a written agreement before the sale to the lessor. While a subsequent sale and lease arguably supersede the original contract, at least one court has found an absence of an intent to replace the original agreement and, thus, direct privity between vendor and lessee.[191]

PART D.   MASS-MARKET CONTRACTS

¶ 6.17 SALE CONTRACTS AND LICENSES

Part of the computer industry has moved from the sophisticated context of expensive systems into a mass, consumer-oriented market. This shift creates unique and often unsettling issues for the industry and especially for software distribution. It affects the use restrictions that might be

---

[187] 4 *Corbin on Contracts* 776 (1971).

[188] See American Fin. Corp. v. Computer Sciences Corp., 558 F. Supp. 1182 (D. Del. 1982).

[189] Restatement (Second) of Contracts § 302(1) (1981).

[190] Earman Oil Co. v. Burroughs Corp., 625 F2d 1291 (5th Cir. 1980).

[191] Burroughs Corp. v. Century Steel, Inc., 664 P2d 354 (Nev. 1983). Compare Kali Bottling Co. v. Burroughs Corp., 619 P2d 1055 (Ariz. Ct. App. 1980).

placed on software products, as well as the form of intellectual property protection that is most appropriate for commercial products. The shift into the mass market also affects contract allocations of liability.

Earlier portions of this chapter discuss issues that arise in fully negotiated contracts in which various contract clauses allocate risk and define terms. Many of these options are limited to transactions in which the parties have equal bargaining power and there are sufficient economic stakes to justify the cost of negotiation. In contrast, in mass-market transactions with consumers or small business users who deal with retail vendors and not the developer, manufacturer, or publisher, the contract terms (price included) are not negotiated. Often, no contract is signed. The transaction is recorded solely in a retail receipt or cancelled check.

In the mass market, there is an underlying tendency in courts and legislatures to protect at least limited expectations of the buyer, since this is an environment where traditional negotiated protections are not present. The tendency is manifest in legislation and case law dealing with consumer protection. Although at present there is no case law applying consumer protection laws to the computer industry, there is no doubt that cases will emerge. From a consumer's perspective, software and hardware purchases are relatively large items with substantial potential for actual or perceived malfunction.

[1] Sale and License

One source of confusion in mass-market software transactions is a failure to distinguish issues involving a sale or lease of tangible property from those involving a license of intellectual property rights. A common tendency is to assume that a license agreement equates with a particular disposition of the tangible item. In fact, the presence of a license agreement is analytically and functionally independent of whether the transaction involves a sale or lease of a tangible product. Any tendency to equate licensing with disposition of rights in the tangible item derives from practices in custom software. It is not appropriate in a mass market where the expectations of vendor and buyer are significantly different.

Current mass-market publishers are divided in the manner in which they define the transaction with an end user. Some publishers append a license form to the software package describing the transaction as a lease of the software disk accompanied by a license to use the intellectual property contained on the disk. Typically, these same publishers assert that elements of the program are protected trade secrets. The end user is purportedly bound to nondisclosure of the secret information and to destroying or returning all copies of the program if the lease-license is terminated. The term of the license is indefinite, but "terminates automatically" if the licensee violates any provisions of the "agreement."

While this characterization of the transaction is consistent with patterns for limited distribution software, in the typical mass-market transaction it is highly suspect. Initially, while the license agreement describes the transaction as a lease of the disk or cassette, commercial advertising does not emphasize or in most instances mention this characterization. Neither do the retail vendors of the product. Against this background, it is unlikely that consumers regard their purchases of software as different in any manner from purchases of phonograph records, televisions, or other consumer items. Furthermore, no serious effort is made by software publishers to enforce those aspects of the transactions that purportedly characterize them as leases. The attempt to alter the expectations of the common purchaser by virtue of a printed form included within the product package is unlikely to be successful.

Properly viewed, mass-market transactions in software involve the sale of a program copy accompanied by an attempt to establish a license of related intellectual property rights. Indeed, this is the characterization expressly adopted by a second group of mass-market publishers. It is a characterization that most closely fits the real expectations of consumers and other mass-market purchasers. These publishers correctly emphasize that while the buyer obtained ownership of a copy of a program, the buyer remains subject to intellectual property (copyright) restrictions.

Prepackaged software distributed in cassette or diskette form involves a transaction in goods; the cassette or disk clearly meets the definition of goods. As is true of any generally marketed product, the disk or cassette has certain performance characteristics that in this case are determined by the design and coding of a program. The fact that these encoded characteristics may be subject to intellectual property protection does not alter the underlying character of the product. The same holds true whenever a copyrighted novel is sold or loaned. In either case, the disposition of the particular product is independent of any license to practice intellectual property rights otherwise exclusively reserved to the copyright proprietor.

Most mass-market software transactions involve a sale of a copy of a program coupled with an attempted license of related intellectual property rights. Under the UCC, a "sale" is a transaction "passing title from the seller to the buyer for a price."[192] It can be contrasted to a lease agreement in which the lessor retains ownership subject to the lessee's qualified right to remain in possession. Although some mass-market

---

[192] UCC § 2-106(2).

licenses characterize the transaction as a lease, it is relatively apparent that consumers view the transaction as a sale. A subsequently interposed form that is not realistically enforced does not change this.

The distinction between a sale and a license is blurred when the mass-market transaction is conducted without intervention of tangible media. This might arise, for example, where the software is electronically delivered into the end user's computer. Arguably, this transaction involves a pure conveyance of information for which the law has no clear precedent. Analogies to information delivered verbally are inapposite here, since in electronic delivery the program is used in the form delivered by the vendor without interpretive intervention by the user and recipient. Conversely, it is a strained analogy to equate electronic impulses with "things that are movable" at the time of the contract—the classic definition of "goods." The relevant issue is whether the user expects and, in fact, receives a right to possess the program, albeit in electronic form, that is not conditioned on a fixed period of time or the performance of specified obligations.

[2] License Agreements

Despite the sale of a copy of a program, the proprietor of intellectual property rights retains substantial rights in certain uses of the program. These rights are the appropriate subject matter of a mass-market software license. To the extent that an enforceable license or other agreement can be established, it can provide a context for risk allocation through disclaimer of warranties and remedy limitations. It is necessary, however, to determine if an enforceable license agreement exists.

In most mass-market transactions, a license agreement is included among the materials delivered to the buyer at the time of sale. In a few cases, agreement to a license is an integral element of the transaction: The cassette or disk is delivered and the agreement is executed at the time of acquisition. In these cases, the existence of an enforceable agreement is clear. The consideration that supports the sale encompasses the license agreement. The primary issue concerns the enforceability of particular license provisions.

More often, a sale is made, the end user pays a purchase price, and the license contract is simply included among the variety of materials (e.g., disks, manuals) delivered. Indeed, in many such transactions, the terms of the license are not even discussed or seen prior to delivery.

These circumstances produce serious questions as to whether an enforceable agreement has been created. It is important to identify carefully what is and is not at issue. In the mass market, it is clear that the existence of an agreement is not germane to whether a transaction involved a sale (assignment) of all intellectual property rights in a program. Neither the seller nor the buyer contemplates an assignment of all intellectual property rights through an over-the-counter sale. An analogy to book sales is appropriate. The purchaser of a copy of the latest bestseller does not acquire the entire copyright to the book, but only a single copy. Similarly, the existence of an enforceable license is not germane to the publisher's or developer's right to enforce certain proprietary rights. Specifically, the exclusive right to reproduce the work in copies is largely retained under copyright. The existence of an enforceable license is relevant solely to the issue of whether the purchaser's rights in the copy have been effectively expanded or restricted beyond those inherent in the purchase itself and whether a reallocation of risk has been effectively implemented through disclaimer of warranties.

[a] Included Licenses

In many mass-market sales, a license agreement is simply included with the software, and the purchaser is requested to execute the contract and return an acknowledgment to the publisher. The end user's right to continued use and possession of the program is not expressly conditioned on execution of the license agreement. The existence of a license then depends on the response of the purchaser. A contract for the sale is completed upon payment of the price and delivery of the copy. The included license agreement is in the form of a proposal for additional terms, modification, or additional contract.[193] If the purchaser executes the license and returns it or a valid acknowledgment, there is an effective modification of the contract.[194] The absence of consideration for the license is immaterial under the UCC unless the license is treated as totally separate from the sale. In that event, consideration must be found in an expansion of some of the purchaser's rights or, perhaps, in access to update or other services. Of course, concluding that a license agreement has been made does not necessarily imply that all of the license provisions are enforceable.

If the license agreement is not executed by the purchaser, it is not enforceable. The license is, in effect, a proposal for additional terms in the contract. Under UCC § 2-207, in the absence of express consent such additional terms do not become part of the agreement if the purchaser is a consumer.[195] Where the purchaser is a merchant, silence for a reasona-

---

[193] UCC § 2-207.

[194] UCC § 2-209.

[195] UCC § 2-207(2).

ble time may elevate the terms into the contract, but only if they do not materially alter the bargain. Since most licenses restrict the rights of a purchaser or disclaim otherwise existing warranties, the proposed terms ordinarily are a material alteration. In the case of either a merchant or a consumer, merely proceeding to use the software is an ambiguous act insofar as acceptance of this form of proposed license is concerned. Acceptance requires a more explicit, overt act.

[b] Tear-Open License

Most purchasers of mass-market software fail either to execute a license agreement or otherwise acknowledge agreement to it. Because of this and the perception that a license agreement aids in protecting the publisher, many mass-market software transactions are structured in a manner designed to infer acceptance of the license based on use of the program. Commonly, this involves license forms that purport to condition the purchaser's right to use the program on acceptance of the license or forms that indicate that the act of opening the software package constitutes acceptance of the license provisions.

Under the UCC, a contract may be formed in any manner "sufficient to show agreement, including conduct by both parties which recognizes the existence of such a contract."[196] The argument in support of finding an enforceable license agreement is that opening the package or using the program represents conduct that "recognizes" the existence of the contract and is sufficient to show an agreement. From the publisher's standpoint, of course, the benefit of this analysis is obvious. Without any monitoring or other enforcement costs, it can claim that all users have agreed to the licenses since the act of use in itself constitutes agreement.

This argument is based on a formalistic view of the transaction and essentially seeks to elevate the purchaser's silence and acceptance of the program to acceptance of license terms that in most cases were not discussed prior to receipt of the program. The argument is valid only if it is clear that the purchaser was aware of the consequences of its actions and of the terms of the agreement to which it was allegedly agreeing. This attempt to superimpose license terms is thus contingent on conspicuous notice and disclosure of terms. The difficulty is that even with conspicuous notice it is likely that many purchasers do not read the license or the conditioning language. Silence and use are ambiguous responses inadequate to establish a contract. As one authority has noted "Common law contract principles have never permitted offerors to generally provide

---

[196] UCC § 2-204(1).

that silence is acceptance, and there is nothing in [the UCC] that would support the argument that the buyer accepted all of the seller's terms by accepting the goods."[197] The reluctance to elevate silence to acceptance would be particularly strong in sales to consumers where UCC provisions on offer and acceptance would be buttressed by general principles of unconscionability and avoiding full enforcement of adhesion contracts.

Although not yet resolved by the courts, the effect of conditioned licenses in the sale of a copy of software parallels a classic commercial law problem often described as the "battle of the forms." This issue is dealt with in UCC § 2-207, which should also apply here. The net effect of this section is that additional terms proposed after an oral or other contract, or contained in what is in form a counteroffer, do not become part of the contract unless expressly consented to by the party initiating the transaction.[198]

Under UCC § 2-207, two factual patterns may arise where an ambiguity exists because the forms state terms inconsistent with each other or with other communications but the parties have proceeded as if a contract exists. The first pattern involves a prior oral contract followed by a confirming memorandum that contains terms not agreed to initially. In most over-the-counter sales, the license agreement fits this model since, although it purports to condition agreement to the sale, the license does not appear until an agreement has already been made. Under these facts, the license is a proposal for additional terms. These are not part of the contract unless they are expressly accepted by the other party or the party is a merchant who does not object and the terms do not materially alter the contract.[199] The second fact pattern arises where, in the absence of a prior contract, acceptance of the buyer's offer is expressly conditioned on acceptance of the new terms. This is, in effect, a counteroffer. The situation arises in many mail order sales where an order (offer) to purchase is followed by delivery with a conditioned license. In this setting, conduct that recognizes the existence of a contract is sufficient to show agreement, but the contract includes only "those terms on which the writings of the parties agree."[200] Even where the purchaser placed an offer by telephone, the clear thrust is that the terms of the license do not become part of the contract unless expressly accepted.

---

[197] Alderman & Dole, *A Transactional Guide to the Uniform Commercial Code* 24 (1983).

[198] See White & Summers, *Handbook of the Law Under the Uniform Commercial Code* §§ 1, 2 (2d ed. 1980).

[199] UCC § 2-207(2).

[200] UCC § 2-207(3).

¶ 6.18 WARRANTY AND REMEDY LIMITATIONS

[1] Consumer Protection and State Law

The effort to superimpose license terms on a mass-market transaction is based on two concerns. The first relates to use and secrecy restrictions intended to protect intellectual property rights. This issue was discussed in an earlier chapter.[201] The second involves an effort to disclaim warranties and to restrict the publisher's liability in the event of significant malfunctions by the delivered product.

Warranty disclaimers and remedy limitations are common in all hardware and software markets. To the extent that they actually are negotiated or agreed to by a party with the ability to negotiate, disclaimers and remedy limitations are acceptable ways to allocate risk. In transactions involving business buyers, disclaimers and remedy limitations are commonly enforced according to their own terms.[202] The presumption is that businesses have the sophistication to allocate risks rationally and courts should not undertake to alter a contract-based allocation. This has been true even in cases involving business persons with little or no computer sophistication. That such persons may have been misled or enthralled by the technology is an inadequate basis to readjust a contract.

Courts are far less willing to enforce risk allocation in contracts involving consumers. Based on doctrines such as unconscionability, contracts of adhesion, and so forth, there is a greater willingness to monitor and readjust the distribution of risk. In part, this is due to the presumed naivete of a consumer who may not appreciate the risks involved and arguably allocated in the contract. There is also a presumption that even if the risk is perceived, the consumer lacks adequate bargaining power to effect the terms specified by the seller in the agreement. This attitude is reflected not only in judicial decisions, but in various forms of state legislation. For example, although essentially a commercial statute the UCC provides that exclusion of consequential damage remedies for personal injury is presumptively unconscionable and unenforceable in consumer transactions.[203] Similarly, several states either have altered the UCC or passed separate legislation to preclude or substantially restrict warranty disclaimers and remedy limitations in consumer transactions.[204]

---

[201] See ¶ 5.16[2].

[202] See supra ¶ 6.12.

[203] UCC § 2-719(3).

[204] See generally Rothschild & Carroll, *Consumer Protection Reporting Service* chs. 18–20 (1978).

The general principles for consumer mass-market transactions are equally applicable when the transaction involves computer hardware or software. Indeed, if anything, the complex character of the technology and the intricate choices involved in purchasing even relatively simple systems heighten the need for consumer protection. Furthermore, at least under the present marketing and pricing practices for personal computers and related software, the acquisition involved is likely to be a major purchase to the consumer, akin to acquiring a car. It is apparent that even in the absence of applicable legislation considerations of unconscionability and the like are relevant to consumer transactions involving computer products and will significantly undermine disclaimer and remedy limits.

Unconscionability challenges to warranty disclaimers and damage limitations in typical consumer sales of software and hardware are especially likely in light of the manner in which the purported restrictions are obtained in the transaction. Unlike automobile and other major consumer sales, the terms of a purchase contract and any accompanying warranty and remedy limitations are not even discussed pro forma prior to delivery. The terms are contained instead on license agreements included in the delivered package. Even where an enforceable contract results, coupling this procedure with the substantive effect of the clauses and the lack of bargaining is tailor-made to support a conclusion that the terms are unconscionable. As already indicated, this is the presumed conclusion relative to damage limits involving personal injury.[205]

[2] The Magnuson-Moss Warranty Act

Entry of computer products into the mass market not only exposes the manufacturer-publisher to risks of judicial nonenforcement of contractual limitations, but also to regulation by state and federal statutes limiting the scope of contractual flexibility available in consumer contexts. The federal legislation most directly applicable to issues concerning warranty liability and risk allocation in mass-market transactions is the Magnuson-Moss Act (Magnuson-Moss).[206] Magnuson-Moss does not require that the publisher or manufacturer make any warranties at all, but it does impose limitations on the ability to disclaim warranties in any case in which an express written warranty is given. Since most mass-market transactions involve some form of limited remedy at least, Magnuson-Moss does indirectly have the effect of limiting warranty disclaimers.

---

[205] See supra ¶ 6.12[2].

[206] 15 USC §§ 2301 et seq. (1980).

[a] Consumer Goods

An initial point of reference in Magnuson-Moss is the scope of coverage. In broad terms, Magnuson-Moss applies to suppliers and warrantors who provide a consumer product to a consumer under terms involving a written warranty or service contract. Although each of these terms has significance in defining the scope of Magnuson-Moss, the definitions of "consumer products" and of "suppliers" are most directly pertinent to the computer industry.

Section 2301 of Magnuson-Moss defines a "consumer product" as "any tangible personal property which is distributed in commerce and which is normally for personal, family or household purposes."[207] As this indicates, a distinction between goods and services is required in assessing application of various portions of Magnuson-Moss. The definition would appear clearly to exclude contracts involving training and maintenance from the definition of consumer products. Similarly, it is at least arguable that some custom software contracts are excluded, but the description of tangible personal property clearly applies to the typical mass-market software product distributed on disk or tape.

While this aspect of the definition is not unlike that of consumer goods in the UCC and other contexts, the remainder of the definition diverges significantly from that of the UCC. The statute specifies that a product is a consumer product if it is "normally used for personal, family or household purposes." As this indicates, the characterization of a particular item is not dependent on the uses of that item by a specific buyer, but on the normal patterns of use.[208]

> This means that a product is a "consumer product" if use of that type ... is not uncommon. ... For example, products such as automobiles and typewriters which are used for both personal and commercial purposes come within the definition of consumer products. Where it is unclear ... any ambiguity will be resolved in favor of coverage.[209]

The emphasis of this standard is on the generic labeling of particular products as consumer products, independent of the intended or actual use by any specific buyer. This approach is adopted by the Federal Trade Commission (FTC) in the implementing regulations under Magnuson-Moss.[210] As a consequence, judgments about whether a particular type of

---

[207] 15 USC § 2301(1) (1980).

[208] 42 Fed. Reg. 36,112, 36,113 (July 13, 1977).

[209] 16 CFR § 700.1(a).

[210] But see Balser v. Cessna Aircraft Co., 512 F. Supp. 1217 (ND Ga. 1981).

product falls within Magnuson-Moss are made on a wholesale, broad-based level. For example, after a significant period of debate the FTC concluded that new aircraft sales were not within Magnuson-Moss because "no appreciable portion . . . are sold to consumers, for personal, family or household use."[211] This approach, of course, is most conducive to a regulatory system oriented to a mass-market environment.

The orientation away from defining coverage in terms of the actual use by the buyer is reinforced by Magnuson-Moss' definition of a "consumer" as "a buyer (other than for resale) of any consumer product."[212] The definition excludes intermediate transactions leading ultimately to the end user market. Assuming that a product is defined generically as a consumer product, however, the definition of consumer encompasses even a business buyer who clearly intends to use the product solely for business purposes.

While the definition of consumer excludes coverage of intermediate sales, Magnuson-Moss' definitions of supplier and warrantor make it clear that the disclosure and antidisclaimer provisions of Magnuson-Moss apply not only to the retailer, but also to the manufacturer or publisher of the product. For example, a "supplier" is defined to include any person engaged in the business of making a consumer product directly or indirectly available to consumers.[213]

Although these provisions have not yet been applied to the software industry, it is apparent that the provisions of Magnuson-Moss will affect a large number of software transactions. The most obvious of these are the variety of educational and game software sales that have become a major element of the microcomputer industry. Beyond those, it becomes extremely difficult to predict the scope of coverage for products such as accounting, inventory, spreadsheet, and other forms of software. The obstacle to predictions is that it is not clear what degree of differentiation will be applicable in defining consumer products in a mass-market environment. For example, is it appropriate to lump all microcomputer software into a single category or is it permissible to distinguish business and other applications? Although the answer is unclear, it is arguable that broad distinctions should be made. If true, most microcomputer and, hence, mass-market software is covered by Magnuson-Moss. The second obstacle is a lack of definitive interpretation for determining when consumer-related use is "not uncommon" for particular types of products. There is, perhaps, an intuitive distinction between inventory software and

---

[211] 41 Fed. Reg. 26,757 (June 29, 1976).

[212] 15 USC § 2301(3) (1980).

[213] 15 USC § 2301(4) (1980).

spreadsheet software, with personal use of spreadsheets relatively common. Establishing a basis for the distinction nevertheless will be difficult.

[b] Disclosure and Labels

The primary thrust of Magnuson-Moss is the disclosure of terms. Magnuson-Moss' primary provision states that any warrantor of a consumer product sold to a consumer with a written warranty "must fully and conspicuously disclose . . . the terms of such warranty" to the extent required by the regulations of the FTC.[214] The FTC has promulgated regulations mandating the inclusion of certain information and the use of particular language concerning exclusion of consequential damages, time limitations of warranties, and so forth. A thorough examination of these standards is beyond this discussion, but several standards have particular relevance to software transactions as currently conducted.

Magnuson-Moss requires presale disclosure of warranty terms in any transaction in which a written warranty is made to the consumer.[215] Since it is unrealistic in most mass-market transactions to expect retailers to outline the terms of warranties prior to sale, the FTC has specified a variety of alternative methods for establishing requisite disclosure. These include conspicuous displays near the products in the store and displaying packages on which the text of the warranty is visible.[216] Absent these or other in-store alternatives, the predisclosure requirement is not met merely by making the warranty known before use of the product as in a tear-open, plastic container.

Additional disclosure and substantive terms are built around Magnuson-Moss' distinction between full and limited warranties. Magnuson-Moss requires that a written warranty be labeled as either "full" or "limited."[217] To qualify for the description as a full warranty, the warranty must meet specific minimum standards, including imposing no limitation on implied warranties and making no exclusion of consequential damages except by conspicuous language. The intent of this structure is to establish a degree of uniformity for use of the phrase full warranty and to encourage warranty competition. Presumably, this competition will benefit consumers in that manufacturers will build up warranty protections for competitive advantage.

One significant aspect of a full warranty under Magnuson-Moss is that it can not be conditioned expressly or impliedly on the return of so-

---

[214] 15 USC § 2301(a) (1980).
[215] 15 USC § 2302(b)(1)(A) (1980).
[216] 16 CFR § 702.3.
[217] 15 USC § 2302 (1980).

called warranty or registration cards.[218] The manufacturer may encourage the return of a card for informational purposes, but if it does so and describes the warranty as a full warranty, it must clearly indicate that a failure to return the card will not affect the consumer's rights under the warranty. In this respect, however, it must be recalled that Magnuson-Moss does not require the manufacturer to meet these requirements in all cases, but merely makes them conditions for the use of the label full warranty if a written warranty is in fact given.

|c| Disclaimers and Remedy Limits

One of the primary objectives of Magnuson-Moss was to eliminate, or at least reduce, the extent to which consumer transactions were characterized by written warranties that in effect diminished rather than expanded the rights of the consumer buyer, while giving the contrary impression. The House Report described this as a practice in which "the paper operated to take away ... implied warranties ... arising by operation of law leaving little in its stead."[219]

Magnuson-Moss therefore imposes direct limits on the ability of a supplier of a consumer product to disclaim implied warranties in any transaction in which a written warranty is given. Specifically, the supplier may not disclaim or modify "any implied warranty" to a consumer, regardless of whether the written warranty is described as a full warranty.[220] In a limited warranty, the supplier may limit the duration of the implied warranties to the same duration as the express written warranty. Significantly, a disclaimer, modification, or limitation that fails to comply with this provision is invalid under state law as well as under Magnuson-Moss.[221]

While these provisions limit the ability of the supplier to disclaim implied warranties, it is significant that they do not apply to limitations on the remedies available for breach of warranty. Indeed, Magnuson-Moss recognizes the enforceability of remedy limitations in a variety of ways, including the fact that exclusion of consequential damages is permissible even in the context of a full warranty.[222] Thus, the enforceability of remedy limitations is a matter of state law not preempted by Magnuson-Moss.[223]

---

[218] 16 CFR § 700.7(b).

[219] HR Rep. No. 1107, 93d Cong., 2d Sess. 13 (1974).

[220] 15 USC § 2308(a)(b) (1980).

[221] 15 USC § 2308(c) (1980).

[222] 15 USC § 2304(a)(3) (1980).

[223] 15 USC § 2311(b)(1) (1980).

PART E. DEVELOPMENT CONTRACTS

¶ 6.19 DESIGN IMPOSSIBILITY

The converse of mass marketing in the contemporary computer industry is either the sale of specially prepared systems developed for a particular contract or the distribution of newly developed or developing technology. Both situations require consideration of responsibility for partial or complete failure to deliver the promised technology on a timely basis and allocation of resulting loss when delays or nondelivery occur. Contractual allocation is possible and is generally enforced between merchants within the framework of existing contract law.

Problems in the delivery of newly developed hardware or software systems may arise when the initially tendered system is imperfect and a significant period of refinement (debugging) is necessary before an operational system exists. This situation was discussed earlier in this chapter.[224] It requires judicial sensitivity to the inherent probability that adjustments to a system that is being specially designed will be required after delivery. Problems may also entail an essential inability to deliver some or all of a promised system. If the inability reflects simple nonperformance by the vendor, the primary issue becomes remedies under the contract of the parties. More difficult issues arise when the nonperformance is traceable to technological impossibility or to technological problems as a result of which completion of the system requires significantly more time, effort, and expense than the vendor initially estimated. In these cases, the underlying question is the extent to which the vendor remains responsible for nonperformance despite technological considerations beyond its control.

When both parties are aware that the contract involves a system to be developed, rather than an existing system, potential technological impossibility is merely one issue of risk allocation in the transaction. Either party may undertake the risk of unforeseen technological barriers. If there has been a conscious allocation of risk by the parties, it should be enforced. For example, when the parties establish comprehensive acceptance standards for a new software system, once those standards are met the risk that the technology does not reach beyond the specified performance is allocated to the buyer.[225] In the context of software development, use of performance and acceptance standards is designed at least in part to allocate the risk of noncompletion. Conversely, of course, a contract

---

[224] See supra ¶ 6.11[1].

[225] See supra ¶ 6.05.

might be designed to provide for payment by the buyer after the seller's best efforts, even if there is a failure to complete the system.

Technological impossibility issues are raised in many contract disputes involving developmental technology. In a number of situations, the essence of the dispute is alleged fraud based on the seller's overenthusiastic claims or predictions as to the capability and availability of new systems. The industry is characterized by rapid development and even more rapid advancement of new products. In the gap between announcement and actual completion of a new product, there is ample opportunity to mislead, in fact or in appearance, a potential customer into detrimental reliance.[226]

Basic contract law issues are also relevant to nonperformance induced by technological difficulties not explicitly dealt with at the time of the contract. In the absence of contract resolution, it might be possible to take the approach that the loss resulting from technologically induced nonperformance should be shared by the parties, arguably to promote experimentation in new systems and product development. This approach could be implemented by interposing technological barriers as a sustainable excuse for nonperformance, relieving the putative seller from liability for nonperformance. While this approach is somewhat attractive, absent contract provisions creating the excuse, technological difficulties and even impossibility do not generally excuse nonperformance. The seller is responsible for any damages. This approach promotes the development of new technology by creating an environment in which purchasers are able to rely on receiving the systems described in the purchase contracts. The seller, in essence, is presumed to take the risk that the system promised becomes more costly or impossible to deliver.

In practice, technological impossibility issues commonly arise in terms of time and cost overruns rather than pure impossibility.[227] This affects the outcome of litigation. UCC standards for excuse based on commercial impracticability are not satisfied by increased cost alone. In an environment of rapid technology advances, however, it is difficult to argue that literal impossibility barred delivery of a product, at least while simultaneously asserting that promises made by the seller were not fraudulent. USS § 2-615 provides the relevant framework for consideration of the circumstances under which technological barriers excuse performance. In relevant part, it provides that "delay in delivery or non-delivery

---

[226] See The Glovatorium, Inc. v. NCR Corp., 684 F2d 658 (9th Cir. 1982) (seller actively misled buyer about performance of a system in which defects had not yet been corrected); see Chapter 7 generally for a discussion of fraud claims.

[227] See Stahl Management Corp. v. Conceptions Unlimited, 554 F. Supp. 890 (SDNY 1983).

in whole or in part . . . is not a breach of . . . a contract for sale if performance as agreed has been made impracticable by the occurrence of a contingency the non-occurrence of which was a basic assumption on which
the contract was made."[228] By its literal terms, the statute does not
require that performance be totally impossible. It does, however, limit
excuse to situations in which an unforeseen contingency occurs that renders performance impracticable.

While UCC § 2-615 is potentially flexible, the courts considering
impracticability defenses often apply a strict interpretation, even when
the inability to perform is caused by factors clearly outside of the seller's
control.[229] The comments to UCC § 2-615 clarify that an excuse is not
available based merely on increased costs to the seller. The statute does
not guarantee profitability to a seller who has underestimated the costs of
performance. A significant limitation on UCC § 2-615 arises from the
requirement that the impracticability involve events the nonoccurrence of
which was a basic assumption of the contract. This requires an element of
unforeseeability in the type of events that excuse performance. Foresee-
ability is considered in light of the commercial circumstances and the
transaction involved. The risk of foreseeable events is assumed to have
been allocated in the agreement and is not a basis for excused nonperformance.

> [Given] the commercial circumstances in which the parties dealt:
> Was the contingency which developed one which the parties could
> reasonably be thought to have foreseen as a real possibility which
> could affect performance? Was it one of that variety of risks which
> the parties were tacitly assigning to the promisor by their failure to
> provide for it explicitly?[230]

The Second Circuit Court of Appeals directly faced the question of
technological impossibility in *United States v. Wegematic Corp.*[231]
Wegematic submitted a detailed proposal for an intermediate-sized computer in response to an invitation for proposals distributed by the Federal
Reserve Board. The proposal offered to deliver an innovative computer
within nine months from the date of acceptance of the bid. The computer
had not been completely developed when the contract was awarded to
Wegematic and engineering problems eventually resulted in a failure to

---

[228] UCC § 2-615(a).

[229] Alderman & Dole, *A Transactional Guide to the Uniform Commercial
Code* 280 (1983).

[230] Mishara Constr. Co. v. Transit-Mixed Concrete Corp., 310 NE2d 363
(Mass. 1974).

[231] 360 F2d 674 (2d Cir. 1966).

deliver the product within the scheduled time period. Pursuant to a clause in the contract, the government cancelled the contract and obtained an alternative machine from another supplier. The court held that Wegematic was not excused from performance by the engineering barriers, which greatly increased the cost of completion and the time needed to produce an operational system. The court noted

> We see no basis for thinking that when an electronics system is promoted by its manufacturer as a revolutionary breakthrough, the risk of the revolution's occurrence falls on the purchaser; the reasonable supposition is that it has already occurred or, at least, that the manufacturer is assuring the purchaser that it will be found to have when the machine is assembled. As Judge Gravinen said: "The Board . . . did not request invitations to conduct a development program for it. The Board requested . . . the furnishing of a computer machine."[232]

In most cases, the appropriate assumption in a development contract is that the contingency of technology problems is or should have been foreseen by the parties. Unless the terms of the contract expressly excuse performance or adjust contract terms in the event of such problems, the appropriate assumption is that the promiser-seller has undertaken the risk that these barriers will render the agreement uneconomical or impossible to complete.

¶ 6.20 SHARED DESIGN RESPONSIBILITY

Software development contracts are seldom one-directional in character, but commonly demand interaction of design and performance. This may create issues of ownership and control of the software and lead to difficulties in allocating responsibility for any performance failure and in determining whether performance has been inadequate.

[1] Contingent Responsibilities

When the mutual development of design and performance characteristics in software contracts involves parties who are experienced in computer applications and the shared development consists of allocating responsibility for particular modules or stages in the creation of a module, any difficulties can be considered by analysis of the performance of each party in their particular tasks and the relationship of those tasks to

---

[232] Id. at 676.

each other. For example, *Teamsters Security Fund v. Sperry Rand*[233] involved a contract for development of an on-line insurance claims processing system. Sperry Univac was supposed to furnish adequate hardware and a functional operating system and share responsibility with Teamsters in the development of applications software. When the contract encountered serious performance problems, Sperry asserted that its failure to perform was excused by the nonperformance of Teamsters in providing design and programming of the applications software. The court rejected this defense.

> These applications programs were primarily the responsibility of [Teamsters] with Univac to assist.... The delay in the application programming attributed ... to [Teamsters] and serving as virtually the sole basis upon which Univac seeks to be relieved of contractual performance, while an important factor in the overall project did not, in itself, prevent the effective development of the hardware and systems software, the exclusive responsibility of Univac. The problem with applications programs was not a hindrance of performance that would totally excuse Univac from further performance.[234]

Assuming a proven failure to perform a shared responsibility, the effect of this failure on the performance of the other party or alternatively the existence of potential excuses for nonperformance depends on the character of the performance and the relationship among the shared tasks. Nonperformance provides a defense or an excuse when the failed performance by one party is factually or contractually a condition precedent for the performance of the other. Given this relationship, nonperformance by the first hinders, precludes, or excuses performance by the other. In *Teamsters*, the development of applications software was not a condition precedent to completing the underlying hardware or systems software by Sperry-Univac and the excuse did not apply. A converse result is justified if the unperformed applications design is essential to structuring the hardware or systems software. In that situation, the second party is within its rights to await performance by the other and, failing that, to treat the contract as having been breached.

In some circumstances, nonperformance by one party can be described as a repudiation of the entire agreement. In *Diversified Environments, Inc. v. Olivetti*,[235] the buyer allegedly hindered performance of the vendor's training and data transfer obligations by denying access to pertinent individuals and facilities. The defense failed, however, when the

---

[233] 6 CLRS 951 (ND Cal. 1977).
[234] Id. at 971.
[235] 461 F. Supp. 286 (MD Pa. 1978).

court concluded that the refusal was reasonable since it did not occur until after the substantial efforts to complete the activities and after suit had been filed for nonperformance. Conversely, of course, a preemptive refusal to perform or cooperate might constitute a repudiation justifying nonperformance by the other party.

Short of an actual repudiation or a material breach, uncertainty about the other party's ability or willingness to perform may justify a suspension of performance. In any contract, the essence of the commercial bargain is not the right to sue for damages, but the assurance that performance will be forthcoming as contracted between the parties. On this underlying premise, the UCC establishes an intermediate remedy for those circumstances short of a repudiation in which there is substantial uncertainty about whether the other party will perform. UCC § 2-609 permits one party to suspend performance based on "reasonable grounds" for insecurity about the other's performance. The suspension can continue until the other party responds with adequate assurances. This provides an alternative especially useful in cases in which shared responsibilities are not clearly sequential and, thus, the contingent relationships are unclear. Failure to respond adequately to a justifiable demand for assurances within a reasonable time constitutes a repudiation of the contract.[236]

The right to demand assurances of performance does not permit the uncertain party to suspend performance for which it has already received an agreed-upon exchange, however. Thus, where the developer of the software has been prepaid for its work, UCC § 2-609 does not excuse its suspension of development efforts.

[2] Nonexpert End Users

In many software development transactions the end user is inexperienced at software design and often is inexperienced in any use of computer systems. It might then seem anomolous to refer to a shared responsibility for design of software since by definition the end user-buyer does not have expertise in system design. Nonetheless, shared responsibilities are characteristic of software development because software systems are tailored to the particular application and performance needs of the end user.

The buyer's responsibility commonly entails specifying the general business functions of the system, the particular data or data analyses required, and the volume, accessibility, and other characteristics needed

---

[236] UCC § 2-609(4).

to establish an acceptable system. While not involved in the actual process of designing the internal functioning of the software, specifications for such design characteristics are central to the overall developmental effort. Providing these specifications is also an undertaking for which the novice end user has no direct training or expertise.

Conditional performance analyses are pertinent to transactions involving shared responsibilities, regardless of the relative sophistication of the parties. In most transactions with end users, the buyer's role in specifying system characteristics is initially critical, since it is not possible to design software without an understanding of the application and the needs of the user. The buyer must define at least some performance needs or applications to trigger the vendor's obligation to begin design work. Of course, the designer may elect to proceed with minimal information. In such cases, the designer assumes the risk of inaccurate predictions of the cost and time involved.[237]

Transactions involving inexperienced end users impose higher obligations on the vendor in the interactive design of the system. In many cases, the buyer can not define the system that it requires in sufficient detail to support software development. This can be remedied by consultants or the use of technical staff, if any are available to the buyer. Often, however, neither of these options is used by the parties. The buyer relies on the seller to assist in defining functions and this reliance is apparent from the outset of the transaction. When this occurs, the seller is both a vendor and a consultant. It assumes obligations to advise the buyer and to direct the buyer reasonably in structuring the system.

This enhanced obligation has not been fully explored by the courts, but was suggested by the court in *NAPSCO International, Inc. v. Tymshare, Inc.*[238] NAPSCO sought an on-line system for inventory control, accounting, and related functions. Tymshare agreed to develop custom software for NAPSCO to be used through computer facilities owned by Tymshare. When it failed to complete the system in the time promised, Tymshare claimed an excuse based on the large number of design changes requested by the end user and the impracticability of some of the requested changes. The court rejected this view. Tymshare had a duty not only to attempt to implement the requests, but an obligation to advise as to the difficulty, cost, and feasibility of the requested design changes. The duty arose from the substantial expertise of Tymshare as contrasted to the limited knowledge of the buyer.

---

[237] See Stahl Management Corp. v. Conceptions Unlimited, 554 F. Supp. 890, 893 (SDNY 1983).

[238] 556 F. Supp. 654 (ED La. 1983).

In fact, Tymshare had a substantial duty to respond. [They] were ostensibly the experts in this transaction; they knew how their computer system operated, what its capabilities were, and how long requested modifications would take. Or, at least, they should have known. . . . Napsco's accounting system was woefully inadequate . . . its data compilation was handled somewhat roughly . . . and it probably asked for a number of things . . . which were either impossible, ridiculously expensive, or far too time-consuming. . . . Tymshare had a duty to alert Napsco . . . by focusing Napsco on precisely how long a modification would take, how much a modification would cost and how certain modifications could not be performed because the technology had not been developed in the . . . system.[239]

In other cases, a similar failure to inform the buyer of the capabilities and limits of the system amounts to fraud.[240]

This duty to advise arises according to the tenor of the transaction. It can be viewed as equivalent to a warranty concerning the suitability of the end product to be designed. As a practical matter, the buyer may insist upon particular design characteristics if it is willing to pay for them. The software developer who plays the role of both seller and consultant must adequately perform both roles. It is not excused simply because the end user is unaware of the implications of the requests that it makes or the underlying system inadequacies present in its business operation. The buyer in such cases places explicit reliance on the developer. This reliance creates an enforceable obligation. To avoid this effect, the designer must expressly refuse to undertake the obligations that are involved in serving in a joint capacity.

¶ 6.21 MODIFICATIONS

In part as a result of the interactive nature of software designing and in part because of the multifaceted capabilities of programmed systems, development contracts are often characterized by frequent modification of design and specifications. Modifications occur while the system is in development. Optimally, of course, the implications of all such modifications should be outlined and specified by contract or other written memoranda. In practice, this is unlikely and the implications of the various changes on cost and performance create questions.

---

[239] Id. at 660, 661.

[240] See The Glovatorium, Inc. v. NCR Corp., 684 F2d 658 (9th Cir. 1982); Strand v. Librascope, Inc., 197 F. Supp. 743 (ED Mich. 1961).

Recurrent modification can amount to a breach of contract if the buyer has basic responsibility for specification of system characteristics, since it hinders the seller's ability to perform. In assessing whether this has occurred, it is necessary to consider not only the scope and character of the changes, but also the relative relationship between the vendor and buyer. Repeated, major changes without express provision for compensatory price adjustments would in most cases be an adequate basis for the seller to discontinue its own performance.

Assuming that the modifications do not amount to a breach of the underlying agreement, questions arise as to the attributable charges for the extra cost or time resulting from the modifications.[241] In the absence of contract terms, this issue requires close analysis of the facts of the transaction. There is a significant difference between changes that occur during the design phase of a development contract and changes that occur after designs have been settled and coding or actual program construction has begun. During the design phase, it is essential that the parties be free to modify the structure and detail of the design. The assumption is that changes in this phase are within the contemplation of the parties and involve no added costs. Changes occurring later in the actual development of the system are subject to a reverse presumption. Unless the changes are trivial or there is reason to believe that a mutual benefit is derived, the assumption should be that these changes are at a cost to the buyer rather than gratuitously provided by the designer.

---

[241] See Stahl Management Corp. v. Conceptions Unlimited, 554 F. Supp. 890 (SDNY 1983).

CHAPTER *7*

Computer-Related Torts

¶ 7.01 INTRODUCTION

This chapter examines liability issues of computer systems manufacture, distribution, and use where liability arises independent of contract and is based on general concepts of tort law such as fraudulent misrepresentation, negligence, and product liability. The field of computer-related torts is largely unexplored. Most of the reported cases involve fraudulent representations in contractual relationships. Over the long term, however, tort principles establish basic minimum obligations and liability risks that can not be modified or avoided entirely by contract. The combination of relatively unexplored doctrine and a potential for substantial impact on industry and user practices makes the tort liability setting extremely significant.

The three distinct contexts of tort liability involve: (1) that between two parties in a direct contractual relationship; (2) that pertaining to remote parties, such as manufacturers and consumers; and (3) that involving user reliance on information supplied by the computer system. The first context raises questions of fraud, although allegations of negligence and malpractice are intermittently raised. Regardless of the label, in this setting tort law imposes sanctions on active deception and grossly harmful behavior. Less directly, it may also impose minimum obligations on the parties, notwithstanding contrary contractual specification. Tort doctrine, in effect, establishes limitations on freedom of contract.

The second context, liability issues pertaining to remote parties, deals with the responsibility of the manufacturer, designer, or distributor for damages caused to people with whom it has not directly dealt. This is the classic environment for what has been loosely described as product liability law, but in fact encompasses both negligence and strict liability considerations applied to the technology marketplace.

The third and final context is potentially the most significant over the long term. It involves emerging questions pertaining to the liability of the user of a computer system for action taken in reliance on information supplied by that system. Under what circumstances will a claim of "computer error" justify or excuse conduct? The critical question is the manner and extent to which society can become computer reliant.

PART A.   FRAUDULENT REPRESENTATIONS

¶ 7.02   GENERAL CONSIDERATIONS

In broad outline, the boundaries of an action for fraud are relatively well understood. Common-law fraud requires proof of a party's knowing misrepresentation of material fact, made with the intent to deceive, where the misrepresentation is in fact relied on by the deceived party to its detriment.[1] This is the core definition of fraud in all jurisdictions. Under this definition, the doctrine provides a civil remedy for cases of active deception. If this were the sole definition and application of fraud applicable to computer transactions, however, the doctrine would be important, but not as central as it is to the development of the overall responsibilities of the parties.

In most states, the tenor of the cause of action has been broadened substantially. A virtually universal variant imposes fraud liability where the representation was made recklessly in a manner not justified by the facts, even though the defendant did not know that a representation was false.[2] A more significant modification extends beyond this: A substantial minority of all jurisdictions have adopted a theory of negligent misrepresentation, dispensing with the requirements that the defendant intend to deceive and that it know or be reckless regarding the falsity of the representation.[3] Under this variation, a party is in effect the insurer of the accuracy of any factual statement that is material to the transaction and is relied on by the other party.

[1]   Fraud and Contract Law Policy

As these developments reflect, the contemporary law of fraud has expanded well beyond mere concern with imposing liability against clear wrongdoers. In its contemporary guise, fraud law frequently serves to police contract relationships by establishing minimum standards of fair dealing and honesty in a contract. The extent to which this role should be expanded or constrained is debatable. In one view, fraud doctrines provide a desirable opportunity for judicial scrutiny of contractual relationships, acting as a safeguard and restraint on agree

---

[1] Prosser, *The Law of Torts* § 105.

[2] Dunn Appraisal Co. v. Honeywell Information Sys., Inc., 687 F2d 877 (6th Cir. 1982).

[3] See, e.g., Clements Auto Co. v. Service Bureau Corp., 444 F2d 169 (8th Cir. 1971); Burroughs Corp. v. Hall Affiliates, Inc., 423 So. 2d 1348 (Ala. 1982); Cal. Civil Code §§ 1709–1710 (West 1973).

ments. In many cases, in fact, agreements are nonnegotiated, form contracts. On the other hand, fraud arguments often override contractual provisions. The effect is an attack on freedom of contract that is arguably unwarranted when applied to cases in which the parties have relatively equal bargaining power.

The relationship between allegations of fraudulent inducement and disputes associated with express contractual warranties is growing. Allegations of fraud are common in computer contract lawsuits. The allegations are often intended to circumvent restrictive remedy and warranty clauses in the written agreement. This use creates a need to distinguish between a mere contract dispute, presumably controlled by the terms of a written agreement, and a dispute concerning fraud, presumably not controlled by the document that was allegedly obtained fraudulently.[4] The distinction is relatively clear in situations involving knowing and intentional misrepresentation,[5] where contractual freedom policies clearly are overridden by considerations of fraud prevention. Such situations are often characterized by active efforts to describe a system inaccurately or mislead as to the system's suitability. These are actions that tend to obviate the presumption of consent to the eventual terms of a contract.

The distinction blurs, however, as emphasis shifts to less blatant misrepresentations. Ultimately, the distinction between fraud and contract may no longer be definable for particular alleged actions, especially in cases of allegedly innocent, but nevertheless actionable misrepresentations.[6] A decision about whether the particular conduct and representations constitute fraud involves defining the minimum standards of fair dealing in a contract relating to disclosure and representation of facts. From a policy standpoint, imposition of fraud liability in this contract setting is an affirmative statement that the defrauded party was entitled to rely on factual representations made by the other party, notwithstanding contractual disclaimers.

Computer fraud cases tend to establish at least a minimum level of absolute responsibility on the part of the computer vendor for representations about the current operability and suitability of a particular system for the buyer. This approach does not imply or impose representations of operability and suitability when they were not in fact made. Rather, the

---

[4] Westfield Chem. Co. v. Burroughs Corp., 21 UCC Rep. 1298 (Mass. Super. Ct. 1977).

[5] See, e.g., The Glovatorium, Inc. v. NCR Corp., 648 F2d 658 (9th Cir. 1982); Strand v. Librascope, Inc., 197 F. Supp. 743 (ED Mich. 1961).

[6] See Clements Auto Co. v. Service Bureau Corp., 444 F2d 169 (8th Cir. 1971); Closed Circuit Corp. v. Jerrold Elec. Corp., 426 F. Supp. 361 (ED Pa. 1977); Investors Premium Corp. v. Burroughs Corp., 389 F. Supp. 39 (DSC 1974).

cases clarify that a vendor who has made representations presumably designed to obtain the contract is bound to their accuracy in any case where the buyer's reliance is justifiable. Fraud liability thus provides a functional backstop to allegations that express or implied warranties of suitability were made in the transaction. Indeed, in many cases, the vendor's responsibility could have been established under the contract standards, especially in the absence of pro forma disclaimers.

One distinction between contract disputes and the law of fraud as applied to contractual relationships is that fraud requires proof of inaccurately stated, present facts.[7] Contract breach may, of course, relate to subsequent nonperformance of agreed terms. The functions of fraud doctrine are thus limited within the overall contract spectrum.

The historical emphasis on misrepresentation of present facts is based in part on questions about the provability of a misrepresentation and more significantly, on decisions concerning the degree of protection that should be extended to a person who acts in reliance on the statements of another. The emphasis on present facts provokes a number of difficult problems in the law of fraud. Among the most significant are the difficulties of differentiating between statements of fact, expressions of opinion, and mere advertising or "puffing."[8] Actionable misrepresentation must relate to present facts and be more specific than mere sales talk and opinion. An individual's reliance on sales talk is not legally protected in the absence of express contract terms.

Significant room for dispute concerning the classification of particular representations remains. In many cases, the alleged fraud involves statements that incorporate both present facts and predictions as to probable future performance. The question of fraud must be resolved on a case-by-case basis through a consideration of the relative expertise of the parties and the extent to which a position of trust has been assumed by the alleged defrauder.[9] In general, a party is more likely to rely on statements, and will receive greater protection when relying on statements, made by someone with superior knowledge of the technology who has undertaken an advisory function in the transaction. Thus, fraud analyses consider inequality of technological expertise more directly than contract analyses do.

---

[7] See, e.g., Centronics Fin. Corp. v. El Conquistador Hotel, 573 F2d 779 (2d Cir. 1978); Clayton Brokerage Co. v. Teleswitcher Corp., 555 F2d 1349 (8th Cir. 1977); Prosser, *The Law of Torts* § 106.

[8] See Badger Bearing Co. v. Burroughs Corp., 444 F. Supp. 919 (ED Wis. 1977), aff'd mem., 588 F2d 838 (7th Cir. 1978); Teamsters Sec. Fund v. Sperry Rand Corp., 6 CLRS 951 (ND Cal. 1977).

[9] See infra ¶ 7.03[3].

[2] Contract Barriers and Fraud Claims

While the use of fraud claims in contract litigation involves significant doctrinal and policy issues, the practical significance lies in the extent to which fraud liability is used to circumvent otherwise restrictive contractual provisions. As discussed in Chapter 6,[10] warranty disclaimers in contracts between merchants are generally enforceable against implied warranties. A combination of contract disclaimer and parol evidence is effective to exclude most oral express warranties collateral to basic product specifications. As a result, the vendor can control its contract liability risk through carefully drafted agreements. In concept, these agreements are negotiated allocations of risk between parties with relatively equal bargaining power. In fact, they are often form agreements to which the buyer acquiesced without significant negotiation.

In the absence of a fraud claim, the buyer often has little effective recourse in transactions that have malfunctioned and generated losses beyond those provided for by the limited remedies in the contract.[11] Fraud allegations provide an alternative in business cases not unlike conscionability for consumers. Conversely, of course, the availability of such arguments in the face of contract limitations weakens the ability of the seller to limit and predefine its liability exposure. To the extent that contract freedom has the positive social value of loss allocation, fraud claims used beyond active deception create a potentially serious problem.[12]

The view that fraud liability can exist in spite of contract limitations is grounded in the argument that fraud induced the contract that is now asserted to bar the claim.[13] This is reasonable in cases of active fraud and deception. The swindler can not escape liability by inducing not only a transfer of property, but also execution of an exculpatory contract by the victim. This same viewpoint is questionable, however, when applied to fraud allegations that merely restate contract causes of action and are grounded in the failure of the seller to perform purported promises in the transaction.[14]

---

[10] See ¶¶ 6.07, 6.08.

[11] See Walker, "Computer Litigation and the Manufacturer's Defenses Against Fraud," 2 CLR 199 (1983) ("fraud . . . is a prominent legal theory used in an attempt to avoid these contract provisions").

[12] See "Report of the Special Committee of the Association of the Bar of New York City on Computers and the Law, Tort Theories in Computer Litigation" (1984).

[13] Id. at 11.

[14] See National Cash Register Corp. v. Modern Transfer Co., 302 A2d 486 (Pa. Super. Ct. 1973); Westfield Chem. Co. v. Burroughs Corp., 6 CLRS 438 (Mass. Super. Ct. 1977).

Parol evidence and warranty disclaimers do not necessarily bar the assertion of fraud allegations relating to the transaction. This rule is uniformly applied to *general* disclaimers and *general* merger clauses.[15] The primary exception arises where the contract expressly disclaims or contradicts the alleged, unwritten misrepresentation. "Only if the written contract included a specific disclaimer of the very representation later alleged to be the foundation for [fraud] would such proof be barred."[16] Direct contradiction of an alleged misrepresentation in the written agreement calls into question whether the representation was in fact made. Furthermore, reliance on the verbal statement is not reasonable in light of the express disclaimer or contradiction. If the contract "explicitly states a fact completely antithetical to the claimed misrepresentations," a fraud claim is barred.[17]

A similar analysis ordinarily applies to damage and remedy limitations.[18] Contract limitations on damages do not apply to fraud claims. At least one commentator argues that an election of remedies approach may be appropriate.[19] While the contract remedy limit does not per se apply to fraud claims, a buyer who elects to retain the benefits of the contract arguably is bound to accept the remedy limitation inherent in that agreement.

¶ 7.03 MISREPRESENTATIONS

The application of fraud law to computer contracts is determined by which representations of fact are considered potentially actionable. This determination necessarily depends on the facts of individual cases. Gen-

---

[15] See, e.g., Applications, Inc. v. Hewlett-Packard Corp., 501 F. Supp. 129 (SDNY 1980), aff'd, 672 F2d 1076 (2d Cir. 1982) (fraud recovery barred because of buyer's expertise); Centronics Fin. Corp. v. El Conquistador Hotel, 573 F2d 779 (2d Cir. 1978); Suntogs of Miami, Inc. v. Burroughs Corp., 433 So. 2d 581 (Fla. Dist. Ct. App. 1983).

[16] Centronics Fin. Corp. v. El Conquistador Hotel, 573 F2d 779, 781 (2d Cir. 1978).

[17] Clements Auto Co. v. Service Bureau Corp., 444 F2d 169, 179 (8th Cir. 1971); see also National Cash Register Corp. v. Modern Transfer Co., 302 A2d 486 (Pa. Super. Ct. 1973) (the ineffectiveness of general parol evidence and disclaimer clauses may be avoided where, while the clauses are general, the contract in fact deals expressly with the subject matter of the alleged misrepresentation and does so in a way that contradicts the allegedly fraudulent representation).

[18] See generally Clements Auto Co. v. Service Bureau Corp., 444 F2d 179 (8th Cir. 1971).

[19] See Walker, "Computer Litigation and the Manufacturer's Defenses Against Fraud," 2 CLR 199, 204–205 (1983).

eralization is difficult, but the reported cases reflect some consistency in the types of statements that provide a basis for a claim of fraud.

[1] Existing System Capabilities

The most readily understood cases of alleged fraud are those in which the vendor's description of the capabilities of its system or software is false from the outset. The reference here is to objective capability, rather than to the suitability of a system for the needs of the buyer. With this focus, representations pertaining to system characteristics are clear assertions of present facts.[20] If material and relied on by the other party, they provide a basis for an action of fraud.[21] Included are assertions about the response time of a hardware system[22] or the current ability of a particular system to operate specific software.[23] The representation might also constitute an express warranty. This does not preclude a properly pleaded fraud allegation, even if the express warranty claim is barred by parol evidence or similar considerations.

There is an important distinction between existing and projected capabilities. A vendor is properly held to relatively high standards of accuracy in describing the performance of an existing system. Response time or operating speed and compatability with particular software are often material to a buyer's purchase decision. In cases where representations about these facets of a system can be established, proof that there was a relatively immediate failure to meet expectations is itself substantial proof of the falsity of the representation and the validity of allegations of fraud.[24]

In most cases, it is improper to impose liability for fraud when the product that is the subject of an alleged misrepresentation involves capabilities that are anticipated, but admittedly not yet present in the system.

---

[20] See Applications, Inc. v. Hewlett-Packard Co., 501 F. Supp. 129 (SDNY), aff'd, 672 F2d 1076 (2d Cir. 1982); The Glovatorium, Inc. v. NCR Corp., 684 F2d 658 (9th Cir. 1982); Strand v. Librascope, Inc., 197 F. Supp. 743 (ED Mich. 1961); Suntogs of Miami, Inc. v. Burroughs Corp., 433 So. 2d 581 (Fla. Dist. Ct. App. 1983).

[21] See Applications, Inc. v. Hewlett-Packard Co., 501 F. Supp. 129 (SDNY), aff'd, 672 F2d 1076 (2d Cir. 1982) (misrepresentations did not constitute fraud due to buyer's expertise and resulting lack of reasonable reliance).

[22] See Applications, Inc. v. Hewlett-Packard Co., 501 F. Supp. 129 (SDNY), aff'd, 672 F2d 1076 (2d Cir. 1982); The Glovatorium, Inc. v. NCR Corp., 684 F2d 658 (9th Cir. 1982).

[23] See Suntogs of Miami, Inc. v. Burroughs Corp., 433 So. 2d 581 (Fla. Dist Ct. App. 1983).

[24] The Glovatorium, Inc. v. NCR Corp., 684 F2d 658 (9th Cir. 1982).

When a system is to be developed, anticipated capabilities are properly construed as matters on which only opinions or expectations can be expressed. The potential buyer has no protectible right to rely on these projections unless that reliance is expressly in the contract.[25] In the absence of proof that the vendor intended from the outset not to perform the promised programming or other system development,[26] allocation of the risk of incomplete or nonperformance properly is left to the contract of the parties. The very nature of a developmental undertaking implies that early difficulties and performance inadequacies are within the realm of contemplation and are not indicative of fraudulent intent.

[2] New Systems: Misrepresentation and Incomplete Disclosure

Misrepresentation in any setting can assume a variety of forms. For purposes of fraud liability, attention is correctly focused on explicit misstatements of existing capacity. Nevertheless, circumstances often arise in the computer field in which a failure to disclose sufficient facts about a system amounts to misrepresentation and is sufficient to support fraud allegations. This situation often arises with newly developed systems in which full performance capability has not yet been achieved.

Misrepresentations about newly developed systems can take place in two distinct forms. Clearly the easiest to resolve under traditional fraud doctrines is the case of a vendor who undertakes to mislead and cover up information about the initial, perhaps permanent, flaws in the existing system. This, in essence, constitutes a premature marketing of a product as fully developed and operable. The incentive for such conduct is manifest in an industry characterized by rapid technological advances. Premature marketing is not in itself objectionable, but it becomes fraud when the producer actively attempts to deceive customers. Such active misrepresentation occurred in *Glovatorium, Inc. v. NCR Corp.*[27] where the vendor of a system that performed at unacceptably slow speeds produced a demonstration model specially designed for faster performance. The use of this sales model to induce purchases demonstrated knowledge of the system's flaws. It was also an active misrepresentation.

More difficult situations arise if the vendor makes no effort to misrepresent defects in the system, but does not disclose them to a buyer. Under these circumstances, the failure to make full disclosure may constitute fraud in that it renders affirmative statements about the system mis-

---

[25] United States v. Wegematic Corp., 360 F2d 674 (2d Cir. 1966).

[26] Dunn Appraisal Co. v. Honeywell Information Sys., Inc., 687 F2d 877 (6th Cir. 1982).

[27] 684 F2d 658 (9th Cir. 1982).

leading. However, a determination of whether a fraud has occurred is necessarily contingent on a variety of factors. For example, depending on the nature of the transaction, undisclosed information may not be material to the buyer's decision, and there is then no actionable fraud. Similarly, there is no duty to disclose unless the vendor knows or has reason to know of defects.

One potential limit on equating nondisclosure with fraud in a new technology environment appears with proprietary information that is the subject matter of ongoing research. Such was the case in *Strand v. Librascope, Inc.* [28] *Strand* involved the sale of "magnetic read-record" heads by the developer of the product to a manufacturer of computer systems. At the time of delivery, the newly developed heads had ongoing problems with interference in the form of "noise" and "cross talk," which substantially restricted their performance in particular applications, including applications that the buyer in this case intended to make. Librascope did not disclose these problems when Strand made its purchase. Indeed, it did not disclose the problems after Strand had undertaken substantial testing to discover the nature and cause of performance problems in its systems using the heads supplied by Librascope. The court concluded that the failure to disclose constituted fraud in light of the fact that Librascope held itself out as an expert in the transaction and its advice had been instrumental in the decision to make the purchase. A seller is under an obligation, even in the absence of a fiduciary relationship, to make complete disclosure where partial disclosure may be materially misleading. This principle applied in *Strand* because of the expertise of the seller and the known reliance and intended use of the product by the buyer.

> When Strand made inquiry concerning the availability of read-record heads to fit his specifications, he relied upon the superior knowledge and expertise of Librascope, as Librascope well knew. . . . The facts vital to Strand's needs were exclusively . . . within the possession of Librascope—facts which, if disclosed . . . might have dissuaded him from entering into the transaction. . . . Under these circumstances, the law did not compel Librascope to divulge all its confidential . . . information, but standards of fair dealing did require complete disclosure of the state of development of this new product. [29]

Where nondisclosure is motivated by concerns about proprietary information, it is reasonable to scrutinize the transaction more closely to determine the need for full disclosure. To what extent does partial disclo-

---

[28] 197 F. Supp. 743 (ED Mich. 1961).
[29] Id. at 747.

sure of performance information convey a misleading impression material to the buyer's decision? If a relevant connection is established, the claim of proprietary information is subordinate to the need to avoid misleading and material factual impressions. If the product can not be marketed without materially misleading others, the vendor must choose between full disclosure or delaying entry into the market.

Overall, then, fraud concepts have a significant application to early marketing of developing computer and software systems. They establish a basic restraint on the commercial incentive to enter the market early and aggressively with new technology. This entry must be accompanied by disclosure of known, material performance limits and defects. Of course, such disclosure might hinder marketing. Nevertheless, this effect is a fair cost and necessary restraint on premature market entry.

[3] Suitability for Intended Use

Perhaps the most difficult task in applying fraud concepts to computer transactions is determining the extent to which fraud liability attaches when the delivered system fails to perform in a manner suitable for the buyer's intended application. The general problem of defining the seller's responsibility for furnishing a suitable solution for a buyer's need has been discussed in relation to express and implied warranties and other contractual terms.[30] In a contract setting, a central issue is distinguishing transactions that contemplate delivery of resources to the buyer and transactions contemplating delivery of solutions to particular needs. This distinction is relevant to fraud claims, but the issue changes to expose the seller more commonly to liability if other elements of fraud are met. Even if the contract contemplates mere acquisition of computer resources, it is difficult to conclude that the buyer is unconcerned about the suitability of the system for its own needs. As a result, misstatements about the suitability of a system for a particular application usually are material to the overall transaction. If other criteria are met, the misrepresentation is fraudulent.

Assuming materiality, cases involving representations of suitability raise difficult questions about whether a particular representation is a statement of fact or an opinion relating to future events. Since a fraud action may be maintained only for misrepresentation of existing facts, this question is frequently dispositive of the cause of action. The difficulty is that representations about suitability involve composite judgments incorporating both representations about the capacity of a system and the

---

[30] See ¶ 6.08[2].

needs of the purchaser, as well as opinions about whether that system fits with the perceived application need. The issue may be considered primarily a question of fact, requiring close analysis of what the vendor in fact represented to the potential buyer.[31] In most cases, however, the composite nature of the representations means the ultimate decision more accurately derives from legal policy and assessment of appropriate boundaries of fair dealing.

At least in some cases, an overriding policy interest binds vendors to representations about the suitability of their systems, notwithstanding contract language that is adequate to disclaim liability under traditional commercial law doctrine. This is most clearly true in transactions in which the vendor has significantly superior technological or economic capability. The buyer with little or no technological sophistication relies heavily on the seller's recommendations. This reliance should be protected, but is often not by standard form contracts. Fraud law provides an alternative remedy.

The reported cases generally support the view that an overriding policy interest in enforcing such representations exists where the buyer lacks technological sophistication. Illustrative of this result is *Clements Auto Co. v. Service Bureau Corp.*[32] In *Clements*, the central representation was that the data processing system "would ... be capable of providing ... sufficient information in a form" that would provide an efficient and effective inventory control tool for the plaintiff automobile dealer. The court concluded that this represented a fraudulent statement about the inherent capabilities of the product. In reaching this result, the court noted that Minnesota decisions traditionally impose a high standard on the statements of manufacturers about their products. The court concluded that this standard was particularly appropriate where, as in *Clements*, the delivered system was important to the buyer's business operations and the buyer relied on the seller's expertise. This tended to distinguish *Clements* from other cases in which only a statement of opinion was present in representations such as that a new air conditioning system would "do the job."[33] In addition, as is most often the case, the central representation about suitability was accompanied in *Clements* by several statements concerning the capacity of portions of the system.

The major factor in *Clements* was the justifiable reliance by the less experienced purchaser. As the court noted, the purchaser "sought inven-

---

[31] See Iten Leasing Co. v. Burroughs Corp., 684 F2d 573 (8th Cir. 1982) (misrepresentation as to one element of a system did not create fraud with reference to entire transaction).

[32] 444 F2d 169 (8th Cir. 1971).

[33] See First Acceptance Corp. v. Kennedy, 194 F2d 819 (8th Cir. 1952).

tory control and was told by an expert in the field that the system designed would provide it."[34] The use of fraud law to protect this reliance interest demonstrates the interrelationship between fraud and basic contract law warranties. The *Clements* result is replicated in other decisions. In *Burroughs v. Hall Affiliates, Inc.*,[35] liability was imposed for an inaccurate representation that a particular computer had sufficient capability to support a custom program to be developed for the buyer's application needs. Similarly, in *Dunn Appraisal Co. v. Honeywell Information Systems, Inc.*[36] the Sixth Circuit Court of Appeals noted

> [The] implied representation that the 62/40 would be suitable for the intended use . . . was a statement regarding a present fact rather than an opinion about the future, because it was a statement regarding the inherent, existing capabilities of the product. General representations that data processing equipment will be suitable for a customer's operations, based on familiarity with both the equipment's capabilities and the customer's needs, are statements concerning present facts.

As the court in *Dunn* indicates, since the analysis is premised on expertise and reliance, the inference that a representation about suitability is a representation of fact is contingent on the party's knowledge about both the system and the apparent needs of the customer.[37]

[4] Time and Cost Savings

Inaccurate representations about the suitability of a system for the buyer's application may result in liability under fraud theories, but the essential concept of a suitable system encompasses elements of prediction and expectation that, standing alone, do not support fraud or express warranty liability. These elements include estimates concerning the benefits that will be derived from implementing a system, such as increased information flow or time or cost savings. A representation that use of a particular system will lead to certain results is a prediction or opinion relating to future events and not properly the subject of fraud liability.

The rationale for excluding liability for predictions about the eventual effect of a new system can be considered in several ways. Consistent with traditional fraud doctrine, predictions of future events are not

---

[34] Clements Auto Co. v. Service Bureau Corp., 444 F2d 169, 183 (8th Cir. 1971).

[35] 423 So. 2d 1348 (Ala. 1982).

[36] 687 F2d 877, 882 (6th Cir. 1982).

[37] See The Glovatorium, Inc. v. NCR Corp., 684 F2d 658 (9th Cir. 1982).

actionable because, by definition, the defendant does not know that the prediction is false when made. Beyond this, even if a system is appropriate for a given purchaser, a variety of intervening factors determine the effect of the system and these intervening factors are not within the control of the vendor. Imposing liability for the nonoccurrence of cost and manpower savings would create liability that is in part at least determined by the actions of others. These aspects of the problem were captured by the court in *Westfield Chemical Corp. v. Burroughs*,[38] a case in which allegations of fraud were rejected as stating no more than mere contract claims.

> Any representations made by the defendant here necessarily related to the future. [Man-hour] savings are dependent on such variables as the program actually decided upon, the cooperation and efficiency of the operators . . . the volume of business being processed, etc., none of which were susceptible of knowledge when the proposal was written.[39]

Westfield apparently did not involve a total malfunction of the delivered system, but merely a failure to achieve expected benefits. Similar circumstances arose in *Badger Bearing Co. v. Burroughs*.[40] The court in *Badger Bearing* rejected a fraud claim based on the conclusion that representations that a new system would afford "more work in less time and more meaningful management information than ever before" were not false, despite the fact that the delivered system had frequent mechanical failures.[41] The purchaser's preexisting data system had provided virtually no management information. Against this background, even a partially functional computer system represented a significant improvement. Especially where management effects are partially contingent on the buyer's operation of its own system, the courts should be reluctant to impose fraud liability where the primary complaint is that although the system performs, it failed to fully meet expectations.

¶ 7.04 RELIANCE ISSUES

Implicit in any allegation of fraud is the requirement that the allegedly false representation resulted in justifiable reliance by the defrauded party, to its detriment. Reliance issues are considered either as a direct

---

[38] 6 CLRS 438 (Mass. Super. Ct. 1977).

[39] Id. at 442.

[40] 444 F. Supp. 919 (ED Wis. 1977), aff'd mem., 588 F2d 838 (7th Cir. 1978); see also Iten Leasing Co. v. Burroughs Corp., 684 F2d 573 (8th Cir. 1982).

[41] Badger Bearing Co. v. Burroughs, 444 F. Supp. 919, 924 (ED Wis. 1977).

element of the proof of fraud or as implicit in the requirement that a misrepresentation be material to the transaction; that is, reasonably susceptible of affecting the decision of the other party.

In computer-related cases, the clearest form of reliance occurs when the buyer is technically unsophisticated and relies on the opinions of the vendor to implement an appropriate system. This characterizes several of the reported decisions. Of course, reliance based on differential expertise extends only insofar as there are actual differences in the knowledge and experience of the parties. An imbalance of technical expertise might suggest that the buyer relies on technological assessments of processing power, but does not justify reliance on the technical expert's judgment about the type and timing of reports needed for a business.[42]

When the relative expertise of the parties is reversed, the likelihood that reasonable reliance will be found is significantly reduced, but not necessarily eliminated. The issue turns on the nature of the representation and the extent to which its inaccuracy could have been perceived from the outset. In *Applications, Inc. v. Hewlett-Packard Co.*,[43] the buyer's representative was experienced in computers and was more knowledgeable than the seller's representatives. In these circumstances, the buyer could not reasonably have relied on publicity concerning the multi-user performance of a system. In contrast, an action for fraud was proper in *Strand v. Librascope*[44] where, although both parties were experienced in the technology, the buyer was forced to engage in extensive testing and analysis to discover problems about which the seller had detailed information that it did not disclose.

The requirement of justifiable reliance indicates that liability will not arise where the buyer relies on its own investigation or knowledge to reach a conclusion that proves to be incorrect.[45] In the case of thorough testing by the buyer or actual knowledge of a particular defect, this is relatively clear and uncontroversial. Illustrative of this situation is *Fruit Industries Research Foundation v. National Cash Register Co.*[46] In that case, the buyer allegedly relied on the seller's representation that a slow printout rate was not significant for the operations of a computer service bureau. The claim of reliance was rejected where the buyer was aware of

---

[42] See Clements Auto Co. v. Service Bureau Corp., 444 F2d 169 (8th Cir. 1971); Fruit Indus. Research Found. v. National Cash Register Corp., 406 F2d 546 (9th Cir. 1969).

[43] 672 F2d 1076 (2d Cir. 1982).

[44] 197 F. Supp. 743 (ED Mich. 1961).

[45] Restatement (Second) of Torts § 546 (1977).

[46] 406 F2d 546 (9th Cir. 1969).

the slow printout rate. Given this knowledge, the buyer was in an equal or superior position to determine the impact on its own business operations.

A more difficult issue is present if there was no (or an inadequate) investigation, but the defect would have been discovered by a reasonable investigation. Absent facts that create suspicion, the buyer has no duty to investigate. The potential discoverability of the flaw is not a defense to an action for fraud.[47] When notice of a potential problem is present, however, some investigation may be a prerequisite to establish "reasonable" reliance.[48] This is especially true in cases involving negligent but innocent misrepresentation where the better view is that even a negligent failure to investigate by the buyer bars recovery.[49] Even where the fraud is intentional, the defrauded party at least should not be allowed to disregard warning factors deliberately and refuse to undertake a reasonable investigation.[50] In determining whether warning signs existed, however, the actual expertise and sophistication of the buyer must be considered. Events that would warn a computer expert may be meaningless to a novice.

PART B.   NEGLIGENCE ISSUES IN MANUFACTURING AND MARKETING

¶ 7.05 NEGLIGENCE, MALPRACTICE, AND CONTRACT CLAIMS

The negligent design or manufacture of computer products may entail liability under negligence and related theories in two settings. The manufacturer, programmer, or vendor may be liable to people with whom they have a direct contractual relationship. Alternatively, design and manufacture may create liability to third parties. Liability to third parties encompasses the law of product liability and is examined in the next section. The focus of the discussion that follows immediately is the extent to which negligence and similar liability claims are available within a relationship defined by a contract for the delivery of computer products or services.

---

[47] Prosser, *The Law of Torts* § 108.

[48] Walker, "Computer Litigation and the Manufacturer's Defenses Against Fraud," 2 CLR 199, 211 (1982).

[49] Restatement (Second) of Torts § 522A comment a (1977).

[50] Walker, "Computer Litigation and the Manufacturer's Defenses Against Fraud," 2 CLR 211 (1982).

[1] Negligent Contract Performance

As with fraud claims, issues about the availability of negligence, malpractice, and related liability arise in part because of their potential impact on otherwise effective contract warranty disclaimers and remedy limitations. While contract law, especially the Uniform Commercial Code (UCC), recognizes the effectiveness of general disclaimers, claims based on negligence and similar theories are less likely to be barred by agreement. In the normal mercantile agreement in which warranty disclaimers and remedy limitations have been interposed, negligence may be alleged in an effort to avoid contract restraints.

There is a threshold need to distinguish negligence-related and contract-related claims. Unlike fraud, negligence is not conceptually bound by a singular focus on misstatements of fact, but potentially derives from any failure to exercise care in the execution of an enforceable duty. To the extent that negligence concepts are applied to contractual relationships, then, there is a risk that they will preempt standards for measuring contract obligations and performance standards. This result generally has been considered inappropriate. Also apparently inappropriate, however, is the total elimination of the concepts of negligence and duty of care from contract relationships. The net result has been a process of balancing and selection that does not in all cases proceed according to clear standards.

Three approaches have been used to distinguish negligence and contract claims. The first, described by Prosser as the traditional approach of the courts, distinguishes between misfeasance and nonfeasance of contract obligations.[51] Both negligence standards and express contract standards apply to allegedly improper performance of contract obligations, but negligence standards are not applicable to pure nonperformance on a contract obligation. In essence, performance of any contract obligation carries an implied legal duty to exercise reasonable care, a view that has its broadest application in cases involving service contracts (as opposed to contracts for the sale of goods). Negligence standards of reasonable care have a primary role in defining performance obligations in the face of the traditional doctrine that contracts for the delivery of services do not convey implied warranties.[52]

The second approach to distinguishing contract law and negligence, or tort law, is to separate the two by the inherent nature of the claimed wrongdoing. The distinction between tort and contract law duties is said to be that contract law enforces obligations taken on by consent, while

---

[51] Prosser, *The Law of Torts* § 92.
[52] See Sanitary Linen Serv. v. Alexander, 435 F2d 292 (5th Cir. 1970).

tort law is designed to protect the individual's freedom from particular harms or risks.[53] Corbin suggests:

> If the defendant's conduct would have been tortious even if he has made no contract whatsoever and the establishment of the plaintiff's case does not require the proof of any contract, it is open to him to allege and prove his case as being solely for tort [despite the existence of a contract].[54]

This approach is most commonly applied to contracts involving transactions in goods. Under its terms, the distinction between a tort and a contract claim lies in the nature of the substantive allegations. Allegations that trace the mere nonperformance of contractual obligations do not stand separately as negligence claims. Thus, an allegation that a defendant-vendor negligently failed to design an appropriate system for a buyer's business and negligently delivered defective equipment is not a negligence claim but a restatement of breached contract duties.[55] The claim is actionable, if at all, under contract doctrines and is subject to traditional contract limitations.

The third approach to contract and tort law distinctions supplements the first two and is most commonly applied to transactions involving goods. It focuses on the nature of the alleged injury in determining whether a tort claim independent of the underlying contract has been established. Economic loss, as compared to personal injury, is treated as subject to contract law and not appropriate for separate claims of negligence.[56] This originated in the law of product liability, historically confined to cases involving personal injury.[57] It is based on the view that the

---

[53] Prosser, *The Law of Torts* § 92.

[54] 5 *Corbin on Contracts* 119.

[55] See Investors Premium Corp. v. Burroughs Corp., 389 F. Supp. 39 (DSC 1974); Closed Circuit Corp. v. Jerrold Elec. Corp., 426 F. Supp. 361 (ED Pa. 1977).

[56] See, e.g., Office Supply v. Basic Four Corp., 538 F. Supp. 776 (ED Wis. 1982); Jaskey Fin. & Leasing v. Display Data Corp., 564 F. Supp. 160 (ED Pa. 1983); Chesapeake Petroleum & Supply Co. v. Burroughs Corp., 6 CLRS 768 (Md. County Ct.), aff'd, 384 A2d 734 (Md. Ct. Spec. App. 1978). But see Air Prods. & Chem., Inc. v. Fairbanks Morse, 206 NW2d 414 (Wis. 1974); Cova v. Harley Davidson Motor Co., 182 NW2d 800 (Mich. Ct. App. 1970).

[57] But there have been a number of cases imposing economic loss liability in the third-party context associated with product liability. See Nobility Homes of Texas v. Shivers, 557 SW2d 77 (Tex. 1977) (liability based on negligence or contract warranty theory even absent privity); Santor v. A&M Karagheusian, Inc., 207 A2d 305 (NJ 1965). This imposition of economic loss, however, has been described as the "minority view." See "Report of the Special Committee of the Association of the Bar of New York City on Computers and the Law" 4 (1984).

economic consequences of a contract are the defining characteristics of the bargain of the parties. The existence and scope of any loss from this bargain are contingent on the terms of the agreement and properly determined according to contract law.[58] There is also less social interest in protecting against such contractual economic loss than in personal injury and its consequences.

For parties involved directly in a contractual relationship, the availability of negligence-related causes of action is contingent on the type of allegation and the type of transaction that underlies the claim. In most cases in which services, rather than goods, are involved and the allegation involves misfeasance, standards of reasonable care are enforceable under tort law. This is clearly the case for personal injury or property damage. It may also apply for economic loss since, in the absence of contract warranties, tort standards are the primary qualitative underpinnings of the agreement. In contrast, in most computer-related transactions in goods, negligence claims are not available. They are preempted by UCC warranties and contract terms.[59]

[2] Reasonable Care and Malpractice

Whenever a negligence claim is properly raised, the critical issues concern the appropriate standard of care. While the computer industry encompasses sophisticated and complex activities, traditional negligence standards stand: The computer designer, programmer, or service bureau must exercise the care that a reasonable man would exercise in the same or similar circumstances.

Two difficulties are present in applying this basic premise. The first is encountered in any industry. Reasonable care is contextual in character; the level of caution required varies according to the circumstances, which include general industry standards. Thus, for example, largely unanswered questions about the appropriate level of care to be followed in developing a custom computer program or in maintaining a database remain. The answer depends on the nature and intensity of the perceived risk flowing from an error. It is appropriate, for example, to expect greater levels of care and pretesting in a program to operate manufactur-

---

[58] Prosser, *The Law of Torts* § 101.

[59] See Office Supply v. Basic Four Corp., 538 F. Supp. 776 (ED Wis. 1982); Jaskey Fin. & Leasing v. Display Data Corp., 564 F. Supp. 160 (ED Pa. 1983); Chesapeake Petroleum & Supply Co. v. Burroughs Corp., 6 CLRS 768 (Md. Cir. Ct.), aff'd, 384 A2d 734 (Md. Ct. Spec. App. 1978); Westfield Chem. Co. v. Burroughs Corp., 6 CLRS 438 (Mass. Super. Ct. 1977).

ing equipment with a high risk of personal injury than for a program designed merely to produce management report graphics.

In applying standards of reasonable care in a software or database context, it is also appropriate to acknowledge the common fact that most completed systems retain significant performance deficiencies ("bugs"), perhaps for several years after initial completion.[60] With the possible exception of certain high risk environments, therefore, a reasonable level of care does not require that all errors be removed immediately from a completed program, nor does it imply that a database be absolutely free of all errors. The appropriate standard involves not the end product, but the level of care exercised in creating or delivering the service in terms of quality assurance.

The second difficulty in applying the basic premise of reasonable care in a computer environment is the possibility that an enhanced standard of care will be enforced under a concept of computer "malpractice." The essence of a malpractice claim is that the alleged tort occurred in the context of a contract for the delivery of *professional* services. If such a claim is allowed, a higher standard of care is imposed on professionals, with the result of increased willingness to permit recovery for pure economic loss. Also, by statute in several jurisdictions, a malpractice claim is subject to different statutes of limitation than a mere negligence action.[61]

The issue in the context of computer operations is whether and under what circumstances malpractice liability is appropriate. In general, discussion has focused on the possibility that computer programmers might be viewed as professionals, subject to a higher standard of care. Presumably, the basis of this possibility pertains to the technological complexity of high quality programming and the common tendency to refer to practitioners as "professionals." Notwithstanding the complexity, however, computer programming lacks the indicia commonly associated with professional status for purposes of imposing higher standards of reasonable care. While programming requires significant skill, the ability to practice programming is not restricted by state licensing. If anything, programming skills are proliferating, rather than being restricted to specifically trained professionals. Unlike most professions, while practitioner associations exist, there is no substantial self-regulation within the programming profession.

---

[60] See Editors Note, 1 CLR 192 (1982); Datapro Research, *1982 User Ratings of Computer Systems.*

[61] See Triangle Underwriters, Inc. v. Honeywell, Inc., 604 F2d 737 (2d Cir. 1979).

Under these circumstances, it is not surprising that the few cases bearing on the issue have rejected the idea that programmers should be regarded as professionals. For example, a district court concluded that computer programmers did not qualify for an exemption from labor standards concerning overtime for people employed in a professional capacity.[62] Similarly, in a footnote, the court in *Chatlos Systems, Inc. v. National Cash Register Corp.* rejected the argument that a tort of computer malpractice should be developed. The court correctly and simply noted that "because an activity is technically complex does not mean that greater potential liability must attach."[63]

In a similar manner, a federal court applying New York law in *Triangle Underwriters, Inc. v. Honeywell, Inc.*[64] refused to apply a "continuous treatment" exception to a statute of limitations bar in a case involving computer programs. The continuous treatment analysis had been applied to various transactions involving clients of professionals and, in essence, defers the beginning of the limitations period until the professional-client relationship is ended. In rejecting application to the seller of a computer system, the court noted that the concept was based on a relationship of trust and reliance that was "wholly lacking" in the case at bar.[65]

One objective of contemporary law should be to encourage innovation and development within the computer and other technology industries. Imposition of an enhanced standard of care with resulting higher levels of liability risk would be counterproductive and unnecessary. Computer industry practitioners are not absolved from basic standards of reasonable care, but they should not be subject to higher levels of responsibility merely because they have undertaken to work in an advanced technology industry.

¶ 7.06 THIRD-PARTY PRODUCT LIABILITY

As the preceding discussion indicates, in addition to potential liability under contractual theories, negligence, malpractice, and fraud may provide a basis for recovery in some cases. The fact that one party to a contract owes at least some obligations of care in performance to the

---

[62] Pezzillo v. General Tel. & Elec. Information Sys., 414 F. Supp. 1257 (MD Tenn. 1976), aff'd, 572 F2d 1189 (6th Cir. 1978).

[63] Chatlos Sys., Inc. v. National Cash Register Corp., 479 F. Supp. 738, 741 n.1 (DNJ 1979), aff'd, 635 F2d 1081 (3d Cir. 1980).

[64] 604 F2d 737 (2d Cir. 1979).

[65] Id. at 745.

other is relatively clear and is not controversial. In contrast, product liability law deals with situations in which, at least historically, there has been some doubt about whether any obligation of care was owed by one party to another. The term "product liability" is the general label commonly applied to the various legal theories through which a manufacturer or distributor of a chattel may be liable to third parties with whom it has no direct contractual relationship.[66] The legal theories supporting this third-party liability include negligence, contract warranty theories, and concepts of strict liability.

Early development of product liability focused on the availability of warranty or negligence actions against third-party sellers or manufacturers and on the extent to which liability could be imposed in the absence of contractual privity. This early uncertainty has been resolved, however, at least for personal injury claims. It is now generally settled that the manufacturer or seller of a product is liable in negligence for foreseeable harm caused by the sale, manufacture, and distribution of any product that is reasonably capable of inflicting substantial harm if defective.[67]

The primary controversy in product liability law pertains to the scope of so-called strict liability. Despite numerous variations in terminology and emphasis, the following definition of strict product liability from the Restatement (Second) of Torts is the most widely used:

> One who sells any product in a defective condition unreasonably dangerous to the user or consumer or to his property is subject to liability for physical harm thereby caused [even though] the seller has exercised all possible care in the preparation and sale of his product, and ... the user or consumer has not bought the product from or entered into any contractual relation with the seller.[68]

Imposition of negligence liability on the distributor of a product is based on the proposition that a duty of care arises because of the seller's affirmative conduct. Strict liability theories carry this proposition farther, based on the difficulties of establishing negligence in a manufacturing environment remote from the injured party and on the ability of the manufacturer to ensure against and spread the risk of loss. Strict liability is intended to provide incentive for the exercise of care in the design and manufacture of the product.

Product liability law involves an array of conceptually and factually complex issues, many of which are beyond the scope of this discussion.

---

[66] Prosser, *The Law of Torts* § 96.

[67] Id.

[68] Restatement (Second) of Torts § 402A (1977).

There has been no substantial relevant litigation in the computer industry to date. As a result, the primary issues pertain to the potential application of negligence and strict liability concepts to the unique products and services created in the industry.

As the Restatement formulation indicates, product liability law in most jurisdictions is limited to cases involving physical injury, rather than mere economic loss. This is based on the assumption that economic loss reflects a failure of the bargain and is best handled through contract law. The fact that historically the manufacturer and the injured party have commonly not dealt with each other erected barriers derived from a lack of contractual privity. Consistent with the development of strict liability, however, privity barriers increasingly are disregarded. In some states, at least, this has led to imposition of liability for remote economic loss based on contract theory.[69]

Current industry patterns show that product liability claims involving physical damage tend to be limited to cases involving computer-assisted machinery, robotics and guidance, and diagnostic or informational systems used in activities that involve a foreseeable risk of physical injury to users and others.[70] The issue is whether the manufacturer, designer, programmer, and seller of such products are exposed to significant levels of liability risk based on contract negligence or strict liability.

[1] Computer-Assisted Machines

The initial question is the applicability of product liability law to machines, including robots, whose functional operation is assisted or controlled by computer systems. The issue is perhaps better phrased as whether there are any reasons to exempt such products from general standards of care and allocation of risk in prevailing product liability law. With the exception of programming defects, there is no apparent reason

---

[69] See Nobility Homes of Texas v. Shivers, 557 SW2d 77 (Tex. 1977) (liability based on contract warranties even though no privity); Santor v. A&M Karagheusian, Inc., 207 A2d 305 (NJ 1965). There remains a majority view to the contrary however. The most frequently cited case in this regard was authored by Justice Traynor in Seely v. White Motor Co., 403 P2d 145, 45 Cal. Rptr. 17 (Cal. 1965); see also Southwest Forest Indus., Inc. v. Westinghouse Elec. Co., 422 F2d 1013 (9th Cir. 1970), cert. denied, 400 US 902 (1970).

[70] Historically, strict liability was limited to items that were "unreasonably dangerous" to the consumer. While this restriction continues in most states, there is substantial disagreement about whether it should be retained. See Restatement (Second) of Torts § 402A comment g (1977); Keeton, "The Meaning of Defect in Product Liability Law—A Review of Basic Principles," 45 Mo. L. Rev. 579, 589 (1980); Prosser, *The Law of Torts* § 99.

to exempt computer-operated machines from basic product liability principles. Arguably, because robotics is a significant, developing industry whose growth should be promoted, some form of exemption might provide encouragement, but it is appropriate not merely to encourage the development of new technologies, but to ensure their safe development and use. Beyond this, computer-assisted machines differ from less automated products only in their capabilities, not in the pertinent risks that attend their distribution.

Consistent with this, the few reported cases dealing with product liability and computer-assisted machinery provide no indication that special treatment will be appropriate.[71] For example, in *Lewis v. Timco, Inc.,*[72] strict tort liability was imposed in connection with an injury sustained from a malfunction of computer-controlled hydraulic tongs. The court did not consider the case to be unique in terms of the type of product involved.

[2] Software and Product Liability

The application of product liability law to cases involving alleged physical injury as the result of defective computer programs raises significant questions about liability standards of programming the control of machinery, diagnostic systems, and other forms of software.

It is important to clarify what is and is not at issue. Negligence standards for foreseeable third-party victims are present in any undertaking that affects third parties, including computer programming. Although there may be difficult questions about what level of care is adequate and what range of victims are reasonably foreseeable, it is clear that the computer programmer owes a basic obligation of due care to third parties that is actionable when breached and the breach results in injury to another.

The threshold question in product liability for computer programs is whether a negligence standard is sufficient or a strict liability approach is appropriate. Resolution of this question should not result in an industry-wide, indiscriminate response, but should reflect an analysis of the particular facts of specific cases and program applications. This requires a two-fold focus on: (1) the appropriate characterization of the programming in

---

[71] See Lewis v. Timco, Inc., 697 F2d 1252 (5th Cir. 1983) (injury caused by computer-controlled hydraulic tongs); Scott v. White Trucks, Inc., 699 F2d 714 (5th Cir. 1983) (computerized brake system); Krammer v. Lamb-Grays Harbor Co., 639 P2d 649 (Ore. Ct. App. 1982) (injury caused by computer-assisted conveyor).

[72] 697 F2d 1252 (5th Cir. 1983).

terms of products or services, and (2) the type of defect involved in programming.

[a] Programming and Products

Historically, strict liability applies only in cases involving defective products or goods. The rationale is that transactions in goods rather than in services involve the greatest area of risk of third-party injuries. In the contemporary retail environment, they also involve the greatest likelihood that proof of negligence will be difficult because the victim is far removed from the setting in which performance occurred.

> Professional services do not ordinarily lend themselves to [strict liability] because they lack the elements which gave rise to the doctrine. There is no mass production of goods or a large body of distant consumers whom it would be unfair to require to trace the article they used along the channels of trade to the original manufacturer and there to pinpoint an act of negligence remote from their knowledge. . . . [As suggested by Traynor, J.] those who sell their services for the guidance of others . . . are not liable in the absence of negligence or intentional misconduct. . . . Those who hire [others] are not justified in expecting infallibility, but can expect only reasonable care and competence.[73]

This posture is important because of the relatively familiar argument that computer programming involves the provision of services and not a sale of products.[74] In at least some jurisdictions, however, the distinction between products and services pertaining to strict liability has been weakened or abandoned in favor of an analysis examining the cause of the injury and the third party's reliance.[75] Furthermore, at minimum, negligence standards apply to injuries caused by defective programming.

Assuming that a distinction between services and products is relevant, it is clear that some programming will lead to a distributed product that is susceptible to strict liability. The distinction between these and other cases in which no product is involved should be made in light of the policies of the tort liability doctrine. Where a program is distributed on a mass basis to consumers, the analogy to any other product is clear and direct, although few current mass-market programs entail a physical injury risk if used in reasonably foreseeable ways. The element of *mass*

---

[73] La Rossa v. Scientific Design Co., 402 F2d 937, 942 (3d Cir. 1968).

[74] See Nycum & Lowell, "Common Law and Statutory Liability for Inaccurate Computer-Based Data," 30 Emory LJ 445, 460–462 (1981).

[75] See, e.g., Newmark v. Gimbel's, Inc., 258 A2d 697 (NJ 1969); Michalko v. Cooke Color & Chem. Co., 451 A2d 179 (NJ 1983).

distribution is not essential to strict liability principles, but the factor of *distribution* may be critical. Most completed programs distributed to more than a single client possess sufficient characteristics of a product to fall under strict liability principles. In all such cases, the individuals functioning within foreseeable risk zones rely on the product's safe construction and design. The manufacturer and designer can spread the risk of loss through pricing. Furthermore, the victim's ability to trace defects to the programming operation and establish negligence in that remote enterprise is rendered difficult or impossible by the context. It is only when the output of the services is restricted to a single client that the programmer's undertaking lacks the affirmative commitment of a product to the marketplace that establishes potential liability for defects.

The fact that a particular program can be classified as information rather than as a traditional form of goods does not affect the issue of whether product liability principles apply. For example, a product liability analysis was applied to an "information product" in *Aetna Casualty & Surety v. Jeppeson & Co.*[76] *Jeppeson* involved instrument approach charts distributed for pilots making instrument approaches to various airports. A defect in a chart allegedly caused a crash. The court concluded that the charts were products for purposes of strict liability principles. Misleading graphics constituted an actionable defect on which strict liability could be based, even though the underlying information used in the chart was accurate.[77] The analogy to software products is relatively clear, assuming a similarly clear connection with a risk of physical injury from a defective product. The essential point is that as the software industry moves into areas involving exposure to risk of injury, it assumes the risk that its product defects will expose it to substantial personal and property injury claims.

[b] Design and Manufacturing Defects

Product liability law incorporates causes of action based either on a defectively manufactured product or a product whose design was defective. While both forms of potential liability arise from the same general body of law, they involve different standards of liability. Especially as applied to software products, determination of whether a design or a manufacturing defect is involved in a particular case may be difficult.

Liability for manufacturing defects is based on what amounts to an absolute obligation to deliver defect-free products to the marketplace whenever a defect would be significantly dangerous to consumers. The

---

[76] 642 F2d 339 (9th Cir. 1981).

[77] Id. at 343.

standard of liability in most cases is strict. The determination of whether there is a defect in the product focuses on a comparison between the condition of the particular product and the design specifications of the manufacturer.[78]

In contrast, design defects are both potentially broader in scope and less clearly identifiable in particular cases. The essence of the liability is not that of avoiding particular defects, but of producing relatively safe designs for computer products. Liability is based on the assumption that the product is defect-free according to design specifications adopted by the manufacturer, but that those design specifications contain unreasonably dangerous decisions or choices.

Liability for design defects involves some inquiry into the choices made by the manufacturer developing the product. Such an inquiry entails difficult factual and conceptual issues in identifying when or if a defect in design is present. In many states, the predominant test was first announced in the Restatement (Second) of Torts and focuses on consumer expectations. Under this test, liability attaches if a product is sold in a defective condition unreasonably dangerous to the end user or consumer. This standard is met if the product is "dangerous to an extent beyond that which would be contemplated by the ordinary consumer who purchases it with ordinary knowledge common to the community or to its characteristics."[79] This approach has been widely criticized because of its apparent uncertainty.[80]

The predominant alternative test focuses on the designer's choice and, essentially, attempts to balance the safety risk involved in the choice against the utility of the choice as made. This standard was phrased in the following terms in a 1979 draft of a proposed uniform product liability law

> In order to determine that the product was unreasonably unsafe in design, the trier of fact must find that ... the likelihood that the product would cause the claimants harm ... and the seriousness of those harms outweighed the burden on the manufacturer to design a product that would have prevented those harms [as well as] the adverse effect that alternative design would have on the usefulness of the product.[81]

---

[78] Model Uniform Product Liability Act § 104(a), 44 Fed. Reg. 62,714, 62,724 (1979).

[79] Restatement (Second) of Torts § 402A comment i (1977).

[80] Keeton, "The Meaning of Defect in Product Liability Law—A Review of Basic Principles," 45 Mo. L. Rev. 579, 589 (1980).

[81] Model Uniform Product Liability Act § 104(b)(1), 44 Fed. Reg. 62,714, 62,724 (1979). See Caterpiller Tractor Co. v. Beck, 624 P2d 790 (Alaska 1981).

Applying this standard requires consideration of: (1) the current state of the technology, (2) the comparative costs and feasibility of alternative designs, and (3) the extent to which the questioned design choice pertains to the characteristics that made the product a commercial success. This approximates normal analyses for determining the degree of ordinary care required under negligence standards; design defect law is more analogous to negligence than to strict tort liability.

While the distinction between manufacturing and design defects of software driven products is often apparent, a number of cases might be expected in which the distinction is less clear. For example, it is analytically possible to distinguish the development of a program design or concept (algorithm) from the task of coding the program in an appropriate programming language and implementing that program in an appropriate medium. In practice, however, most software development does not so neatly distinguish these phases. Furthermore, software development involves a substantial period of what is commonly described as debugging the program—that is, finding and correcting operational flaws. Given this blending of activities, a continuum exists that begins at the stage of abstract conceptualizing of the program and moves to the mechanical task of reproducing copies of the program for distribution. The mechanical stage is clearly the manufacturing, while the abstract conceptualization stage is the design work. The status of the intermediate stages is less clear.

For product liability law, design activity encompasses any activity that contemplates modification of the program by human decisions pertaining to its operability. This is consistent with the focus on whether or not there was a reasonable design choice. The effect is that debugging is part of the design process. Strict liability would be limited to packaged systems in which production problems created defects—an effect consistent with the underlying conception of strict product liability.[82] The alternative characterization of debugging as part of the production process would interject strict liability concepts into a manifestly human and uncertain process.

Assuming that a program defect involves design rather than manufacture, difficult questions arise about the nature of the design choice. One test of the reasonableness balances the utility of the choice against the risks involved.[83] In most situations in which product liability is a potential issue in software, the utility of the product involves effects such

---

[82] See Brannigan & Dayhoff, "Liability for Personal Injuries Caused by Defective Medical Computer Programs," 7 Am. J. L. & Med. 123, 137 (1981).

[83] See Wheeler, *Product Design Liability* (1982).

as reducing paper work, creating displays of systems, controlling numerous mechanical or other operations at a single source, and interjecting rapid, multivariable analyses not possible for humans. The trade-off, however, is that in many cases these results reduce the individual's opportunity to interject personal judgment and analysis. The system either moves too rapidly or the documentation for that judgment is reduced, eliminated, or condensed by the program itself. The balancing involved in such contexts goes to the heart of policy judgments about automating functions in society and the extent to which automation inherently involves dehumanization of various decision-making. In cases not involving product liability claims, courts have rejected any argument that automation justifies adverse effects on other consumers and clients.[84] A similar interpretation is appropriate for design choices that effectively eliminate the opportunity for human intervention, but fail to furnish a system that avoids injury to consumers.

PART C.   COMPUTER USERS AND LIABILITY RISKS

¶ 7.07   USER LIABILITY RISKS

As with product liability, currently there is very little case law dealing with the liability of end users of computer systems for actions mistakenly taken on the basis of computer-generated information. It is apparent that as computer use increases, however, the manner and extent to which a computer system user can safely rely on computer-based information in making decisions and taking actions that affect third parties must be defined.

The possible variety of settings is bounded only by the nature and variety of uses to which computer systems can be put. In each setting, the problem involves defining the extent to which traditional doctrines of negligence, estoppel, and waiver apply in an automated environment. This, in turn, defines the degree of care and risk that pertains to the use of computer systems in various business and professional activities. The appropriate approach is to apply traditional doctrine, rather than develop computer-oriented concepts of user liability, but the changed circumstances characterized by extensive use of computer systems must be carefully considered. While reasonable care may be the relevant standard, for example, it may have different connotations where computer-generated advice or data is relied on than in cases involving decisions based on direct personal observation. In the computer-based systems, the pertinent

---

[84] See infra ¶¶ 7.10, 7.11.

initial question is whether reliance on the data system is reasonable. Similarly, concepts of waiver or estoppel are relevant in an automated system, but may require adaptation in an environment in which particular actions are in fact controlled by machines.

As this implies, the standard of liability involved in the use of or reliance on a computer system depends on the traditional standard of care or liability associated with the action involved. The use or nonuse of a computer does not alter the underlying judgment about the degree of care required or the obligations imposed in a given environment. It may, however, require a reassessment of the manner in which these obligations can be discharged.

¶ 7.08 NEGLIGENT USE OF A COMPUTER

Use of a computer does not alter the standard of care or liability to which an individual is bound, but may affect the manner in which that standard is applied. This is most clearly applicable in the myriad situations in which computer users are subject to standards of reasonable care or negligence. This includes the use of robotics in a workplace, home, or commercial environment. Alternatively, it may arise in the context of the use of computer systems to assist or direct professional decision-making. At present, the most common illustrations of this are systems for computer analysis of tests and diagnostic information in the medical profession and the variety of computer-based control systems, such as that associated with air traffic control in commercial aviation. In each of these uses, the computer translates, displays, and perhaps interprets information for human action.

Use of these and similar systems does not alter standards of care, but injects additional levels of analysis. The care used in selection, maintenance, administration, and reliance on the system is at issue. For example, data entry errors do not absolve the user of reliance on the inaccurate output of the system if the processes for data entry and verification reflect inadequate care in light of the nature of the system involved.[85] Similarly, knowing selection or continued reliance on a system that produces recurrent errors or is unable to perform a vital function may in itself violate applicable standards of reasonable care.[86]

In fact, three distinct forms of system-related negligence may be identified. Negligence may occur: (1) in data entry procedures or proce-

---

[85] See Phillips v. Texas, 650 SW2d 396 (Tex. App. 1983) (computer filing error does not absolve denial of statutory speedy trial in criminal case).

[86] See Swiss Air Transp. Co. v. Benn, 467 NYS2d 341 (NY Civ. Ct. 1983).

dures for verifying the accuracy of entered data; (2) in the selection of a particular system, assuming that aspects of the system known to the user create pertinent, unreasonable risks; or (3) in the manner in which computer information is reacted to or relied upon by the user. Data entry negligence is the least complex issue. Regardless of the function of the system, the data entry stage is critical. It may consist of mechanical data entry or entry by humans, but in either event, to the extent that the user of the system intends to and in fact does rely on the system, the user is properly charged with undertaking to establish and maintain reliable data entry procedures and with any loss resulting from a failure to do so. The term "computer error," more and more commonly heard, does not excuse negligent actions. In many cases, it in fact describes human error arising in the context of a machine system. Data inaccuracies are properly chargeable to those who control the entry systems, at least insofar as issues of negligence are involved.[87]

The premise that the use of a computer does not alter standards of care potentially cuts in both directions, favoring liability in some cases and absolving or reducing the user's liability in others. For example, in *Johnson v. Continental Insurance Co.,*[88] a six-week failure to deliver worker's compensation claims was related to a data entry error in the insurer's computer system. Although the information relevant to issuing the checks remained in the insurer's possession, the delay was found not to have been willfull since there was negligence in data entry. As a result, a lesser liability was appropriate.

If negligence is the liability standard, merely asserting reliance on a reasonably maintained computer system is insufficient to absolve what would otherwise be negligent behavior. The significant question for long-term development of computer-supported systems is the extent to which reliance on computer systems absolves the user from taking additional action. When must the user go beyond the limits of an operational, but not necessarily complete, computer system? Where there have been reasonable decisions regarding the data to incorporate into a system for analysis and support of particular decisions, it is not uncommon that less than all data available to the user will be included. The decision as to whether the user is justified in relying on the limited data or must incorporate information not in the base system reflects on the permitted scope of automation and condensation of data. This may arise in a variety of contexts requiring different analyses, depending on the standard of responsibility applied to the actor's conduct. In the context of a negli-

---

[87] See infra ¶ 7.11.

[88] 410 So. 2d 1050 (La. 1982).

gence standard, the basic point was addressed in *Pompeii Estates, Inc. v. Consolidated Edison Co.* [89]

Pompeii involved the termination of electrical services to an unoccupied residence during winter months. Although the case involved questions about the design of computer-supported bill collection systems, it is relevant that Consolidated Edison was held to have violated standards of reasonable care in relying on the computer data in terminating services. It acted without examining noncomputer files that would have indicated the existence of an owner to whom pretermination notice should be sent at a different address than that of the residence. The court noted

> While a computer is a useful instrument, it can not serve as a shield to relieve Consolidated Edison of its obligation to exercise reasonable care when terminating service. The statute gives it discretionary power to do so, and this discretion must be exercised by a human brain. Computers can only issue mandatory instructions—they are not programmed to exercise discretion. [90]

Significantly, there was no data entry error in *Pompeii*. The pertinent information was in a hard copy file that was not used in deciding to issue termination orders. The court's decision is, essentially, that when the utility would otherwise be required to examine and react to such data before terminating services, the fact that the system has been computerized does not absolve it from fulfilling that obligation.

Decisions such as *Pompeii* establish standards of care that reduce the utility of computer systems, since they require human intervention and research before final action. Similar results are present in decisions pertaining to debt collection systems. The observation that the standard reduces the utility of computer systems does not imply that the decision is wrong. Rather, the lost efficiency is offset by the substantive benefits of reducing the potential for inaccurate decisions by interjecting human decision-making into the otherwise mechanical system. [91] This is appropriately a matter of balancing social costs and benefits. An organization relying on incomplete computer data must do so at its risk. Does human intervention in a computer-supported system reduce the likelihood of errors or their impact? This will necessarily depend on the type of activity involved, the importance of rapid (machine-based) action, and the reasonably anticipated accuracy level of the system, absent human intervention. A second question is whether the presumed gains from human inter-

---

[89] 397 NYS2d 577 (NY Civ. Ct. 1977).

[90] Id. at 580.

[91] See Palmer v. Columbia Gas Co., 342 F. Supp. 241 (ND Ohio), aff'd, 479 F2d 153, modified, 503 F2d 607 (6th Cir. 1974).

vention outweigh costs and time delays. Essentially, is it reasonable to require that the intervention occur in light of all of its effects?

Underlying the decision in *Pompeii* should have been a judgment that there would be gains in accuracy from human intervention (in the form of reviewing hard copy files before ordering termination) and that these gains offset costs. Simply observing that discretion can not be exercised by a machine is beside the point, since it is arguable that a system could readily be designed to incorporate all factors that the human actor, in his discretion, desired to include. Even though based on an unexamined presumption, however, the substantive decision of the court in this particular case is probably correct.

Pompeii was not approached as a case of reliance on an inappropriate computer system that failed to incorporate all pertinent data, but this approach was adopted by a New York court in a case involving liability for alterations of airline tickets. In *Swiss Air Transport Co. v. Benn*,[92] the altered tickets originally had been issued for a trip within Switzerland, but were altered to apparently represent a round trip between Europe and New York. They were used by an innocent third party who purchased them in altered form from a purported travel agent. The airline argued that it was unable to discover the alteration before the tickets were used because its reservations computer database was not tied to the database for its sales computer. Thus, the names and flight destinations could not be cross-checked. Although the court concluded that the buyer was not protected by standards of bona fide purchase or holder in due course status because of the nature of the airline tickets, it adopted estoppel to protect the purchaser who relied on the cost of the altered tickets. The estoppel was based on a breach of a duty to exercise reasonable care in detecting this form of forgery.

> Plaintiff could have prevented the passengers from using altered tickets by maintaining a system capable of confirming which passengers are scheduled for a particular flight. In light of the advanced computer technology available today, this is not an unreasonable burden to place on the plaintiff. . . . I do not recognize Swiss Air's reliance on its computer system as a legally cognizable defense. Had [it] been properly equipped with a more sophisticated computer system, it could have promptly discovered [the alteration]. I hold that an airline owes a duty to use reasonable precautions when inspecting and confirming a passenger's flight ticket [and that this duty was breached].[93]

---

[92] 467 NYS2d 341 (NY Civ. Ct. 1983).
[93] Id. at 344–345.

Although it did not deal with a situation involving negligence in its normal form, *Swiss Air* suggests an analysis that may become increasingly significant in the allocation of liability in a computer environment. As the case indicates, the choice of a computer system design and the data that it does and does not utilize are equally subject to scrutiny. The conclusion that an insufficient or inadequate system has been adopted must, of course, be based on a reasoned assessment of alternatives and relative costs. [94] At some level, however, the choice of a computer-supported system that affects the interests of other people includes an obligation to use reasonable care in selecting a suitable system. [95] A decision about whether this obligation has been met requires analysis of the risks involved in operating the system and the degree to which alternative, more accurate or comprehensive systems are available.

¶ 7.09 NEGLIGENT NONUSE OF A COMPUTER

As computer use expands, it is probable that at least in some professions or areas of business, computer selection, operation, and reliance will be a standard against which ordinary care is measured. In essence, given widespread availability and usability, it may constitute negligence to fail to use computers. The argument is not that a failure to use computer systems may breach a duty developed solely because computer technology exists. Rather, a duty of care exists, and at some point in the development and use of technology, the failure to use the technology may in itself violate that duty.

The most likely environments for this in the near future are those professional or commercial activities that already involve extensive computation and instrumentation. In particular, computer assistance as a professional norm is likely in the medical profession. The process by which technology use blends into professional norms involves an interaction between the courts and the profession.

As new developments in medical practice become more widely accepted, standards of required conduct [for] medical profession-

---

[94] See Exceptional Children's Home & Nursery, Inc. v. Fortuna, 414 So. 2d 1130 (Fla. Dist. Ct. App. 1982).

[95] Compare Allen v. Beneficial Fin. Co., 531 F2d 797 (7th Cir. 1975). A failure to comply with Regulation Z requiring disclosure of credit information in a "meaningful sequence" was not justified by the creditor's desire to comply with a national computer data system. In essence, as in other contexts, given a legal standard justified on other grounds, computer systems must be designed to protect the interests legally defined as protectible.

als ... gradually evolve to embrace these new developments. Usually, the medical profession itself alters these standards to fit new developments. Occasionally, however, the courts have become impatient. ... [Several well-known cases illustrate] the courts' willingness to take the lead in setting minimum legal standards of care. [As] the use of computers becomes more common in medical practice, possibly the medical profession, but if not later the courts, are likely to decide that the use of computer systems in certain clinical practice situations is part of the "legal" standard of "due care."[96]

The essential element is whether a superior and reasonably available technology exists and should have been known to the particular actor.

Questions pertaining to nonuse of computer systems are difficult when the allegedly negligent actor does not have access to a system. Where a system is available, but the pertinent data or analyses are not used, the issue is less complex. Without altering standards of negligence or malpractice, the failure to use potentially relevant data and analytic services reflects on whether alternative actions adequately meet the duty of care. In many cases, a failure to use amounts to negligence even if it would not be negligent not to install the system to begin with.[97] A technologically sophisticated or advanced business or professional operation should be held to standards of performance that reflect the advanced environment in which it operates.

¶ 7.10 WRONGFUL BILL COLLECTION

To many people, computerization is epitomized by an increasing difficulty in dealing with bill payment and records systems maintained by service agencies, creditors, and utilities. The extensive use of computers in the business community has led to advances in efficiency, but also to increasingly impersonal relationships with creditors. The result is high levels of frustration in cases in which malfunctions in the system require that the computer be adjusted and corrected to reflect actual transactions. "The computer is down" has become a frustrating refrain for many.

In a computer billing and service environment, one fear of any consumer is that the computer will, in some manner, erase the person's iden-

---

[96] Norris & Szabo, "Foreward: Removing Some Impediments to Development of America's Third and Fourth Generation Health Care Delivery Systems," 7 Am. J. L. & Med. v (1981).

[97] See Bechnel v. Answer, Inc., 428 So. 2d 539 (La. Ct. App. 1983) (failure to issue paycheck within statutory time limit is actionable negligence where access to data exists).

tity. In a more realistic and more common situation, inaccurate data in a computer leads to action or threatened action by the creditor, agency, or utility to the substantial detriment of the consumer and without giving him an opportunity to correct or dispute the information. From the standpoint of businesses, maximum administrative efficiency requires substantial reliance on the data in a computer system. Commonly, this equates with implementation of many actions taken directly by the machine or with no more than minimal human intervention. This very fact, however, creates a potential for incorrect actions and for substantial customer frustration. The consumer generally prefers to deal with another human, rather than with an impersonal system.

In cases involving actions to collect debts based on incorrect computer data systems, the initial question involves determining the appropriate standard to be applied. This will differ according to the action that the creditor has taken. For example, in cases dealing with wrongful termination of gas, electricity, or other public utility services, a negligence standard may apply to termination notices and require that some examination of hard copy files be made before final action is taken.[98] Even more basic, under government regulation, due process standards may require some opportunity for a hearing prior to terminating utility services.[99] Under either analysis, at least in the context of utility services, automation efficiencies are constrained by a required level of human decision-making and access.

In contrast to public utilities, general creditors are not subject to due process standards. The extent to which they may rely safely on computer data concerning bill payments and collection activities varies with circumstances. The most commonly litigated questions pertain to reliance on incorrect computer data by private creditors to enforce security interests in the face of what their data indicated was a default in the underlying agreement.

The basic standard of liability for actions for wrongful repossession does not require proof that the creditor acted negligently or maliciously. It is sufficient that there be an intentional taking of the collateral under circumstances in which the debtor's right of possession remains in force because there has been no default. The wrongful action is a conversion of the debtor's property. The fact that the conversion was motivated by

---

[98] Pompeii Estates, Inc. v. Consolidated Edison Co., 397 NYS2d 577 (NY Civ. Ct. 1977).

[99] Palmer v. Columbia Gas Co., 342 F. Supp. 241 (ND Ohio 1972), aff'd, 479 F2d 153, modified, 503 F2d 607 (6th Cir. 1974).

inaccurate computer data may bear on the extent of damages, but not on the fact of liability.[100]

> Ford explains that this whole incident occurred because of a mistake by a computer. Men feed data to a computer and men interpret the answer the computer spews forth. In this computerized age, the law must require that men in the use of computerized data regard those with whom they are dealing as more important than a perforation on a card. Trust in the infallibility of a computer is hardly a defense.[101]

While the underlying repossession is not justifiable by a computer error, the question of whether computer-induced repossession exposes the creditor to punitive or other special damages arises. The argument favoring such exposure is that damages provide incentive for careful monitoring of data systems and circumspection prior to taking action against the property. The traditional standards for such damage claims have required intentional wrongdoing, however, or at least recklessness. In some cases, extreme laxness in maintaining computer records may qualify. In general, however, mere reliance on inaccurate data and resulting repossession without more is not adequate to support special or punitive damage claims.[102]

Despite this general proposition, in many cases involving an inappropriate repossession the creditor's actions beyond mere reliance on the inaccurate computer data justify punitive damage awards. In *Price v. Ford Motor Credit Co.*,[103] a repossession occurred based on inaccurate data in two different records systems and an apparently lost money order. Punitive damages were allowed in part because the creditor had violated its own promise to defer action until the alleged errors could be examined and corrected if necessary. Similarly, in *Ford Motor Credit Co. v. Swarens*,[104] the repossession occurred even though the debtor had shown the creditor's agents cancelled checks that had not been recorded in the database and that indicated the debt was not overdue. A punitive damage claim was based on the fact that after admitting error in retaking the car,

---

[100] See Ford Motor Credit Co. v. Hitchcock, 158 SE2d 468 (Ga. Ct. App. 1967); Price v. Ford Motor Credit Co., 530 SW2d 249 (Mo. Ct. App. 1975).

[101] Ford Motor Credit Co. v. Swarens, 447 SW2d 53, 57 (Ky. Ct. App. 1969).

[102] See First Wisconsin Nat'l Bank v. Nicolaou, 335 NW2d 390 (Wis. 1983) (computer and data errors mentioned as within bona fide error defense re repossession); Johnson v. Continental Ins. Co., 410 So. 2d 1050 (La. 1982) (data entry error and resulting failure to issue a check were inadvertent, not willfull).

[103] 530 SW2d 249 (Mo. Ct. App. 1975).

[104] 447 SW2d 53, 57 (Ky. Ct. App. 1969).

the creditor refused to release it back to the debtor unless the debtor agreed to sign a liability release form.

¶ 7.11 WAIVER AND ESTOPPEL BY COMPUTER

Reliance on computer data to guide debt collection activities leads to direct liability exposure for wrongful conduct if the data is inaccurate. Situations also arise in which the user of the computer system fails to assert rights that are available because the conditions triggering those rights are inaccurately recorded in the pertinent system. When this occurs in juxtaposition to regulations that establish time or other limitations on the assertion of rights, the computer error does not excuse inaction. The right has been effectively waived.

While computer error does not excuse noncompliance with absolute limitations, in other settings computer errors raise significant questions of waiver and estoppel for contractual rights. The initial waiver issue concerns the relevant standard to be applied. In general, a waiver consists of a *knowing* relinquishment of a right. Knowledge in this context involves both knowledge of the existence of the right and knowledge that the actions performed relinquish enforcement of it. As a result, the cases dealing with waiver properly focus on whether an organization or individual has knowledge of a fact, considering the errors or delays in the underlying computer system on which it relies. A variety of factual circumstances may exist. The clearest case is where no human had actual knowledge of pertinent facts and, at the time for decision, those facts had not yet been entered in the computer system. Absent detrimental reliance by a third party constituting an estoppel, the only basis for waiver is that the data should already have been entered. Assuming a reasonable procedure to collect and enter data, the argument is without merit.[105] This result should hold unless the data collecting system is so poor that reliance on it can be considered to be reckless.

A more difficult situation exists where the data has been collected by the computer user, but is incorrectly entered or interpreted by the computer system. There is a relevant distinction between cases involving possession of raw information and cases involving possession of full, relevant facts by members of an organization. When raw data requiring significant computer processing is involved, knowing waiver should not be presumed if the computer user exercises reasonable care to avoid the mistake and

---

[105] See Kennedy v. Hospital Serv. Corp., 455 NE2d 206 (Ill. App. Ct. 1983) (processing system did not reflect that insurance limit exceeded, but not waiver because no knowledge).

there is no detrimental reliance by the other party. Absent the computer processing, the data conveys no pertinent information. As a result, inaccurate entry or processing in effect precludes knowledge. An example of this result is *Lincoln v. Bud Moore, Inc.*,[106] where a public utility's computer miscalculated monthly bills based on accurate data from meters located at the service site. The error was due to a programming problem that failed to account for the fact that the meters turned over periodically as the maximum on the gauge was reached. The utility was permitted to recover the unbilled amounts resulting from this error.

In the more difficult case, some members of an organization have all the pertinent information, but it has not been transmitted to the computer system or decision makers approving the action that allegedly constitutes a waiver. The ultimate issue in these cases is the extent to which reliance on computers requires a reconsideration of concepts of imputed and actual knowledge in a business environment. This issue is reached only when the party claiming lack of knowledge maintains an adequate system with reasonably effective procedures to maintain the accuracy of the data in the system. In such cases, knowledge within the organization does not occur until the time that the information would normally have been entered into the data system.[107] Only after that point can an action disregarding a contractual right be reasonably described as a knowing waiver by the organization, unless of course a person in the organization with actual knowledge of the facts makes the decision. In contrast, a business that relies on an inadequate or poorly maintained system should not be absolved of the consequences of its actions based on what amounts to internal negligence. Knowledge is then properly imputed to the organization based on notice to an individual with a reasonable time for its transmission.

One case applying this analysis is *State Farm Mutual Automobile Insurance Co. v. Bockhorst*.[108] Bockhorst had permitted an automobile insurance policy to expire. After some time, he attempted to renew the policy on the morning after being involved in an accident. Bockhorst informed the insurance agent of the accident and was told that it was not clear whether the reinstated policy would be retroactive to cover the accident. The agent mailed the check for the policy, but did not mention that the accident had preceded receipt of the renewal check. Borkhorst then took the damaged car to the State Farm claims adjuster and, after describing the facts, was informed that there was doubt that the accident was covered. Neither the claims supervisor nor the selling agent informed

---

[106] 316 NW2d 590 (Neb. 1982).

[107] See UCC § 1-201(27) (notice to an organization).

[108] 453 F2d 533 (10th Cir. 1972).

the policy issuing center of the timing question. Accordingly, the State Farm computer issued a retroactively dated policy, predating the accident. The court held that issuance of the policy was a waiver of the right to defer renewal until after the date of the accident.

The result in *Bockhorst* was premised on a conclusion that there had been no fraud or collusion in processing the claims and the renewal. Furthermore, the computer issuance of the policy on a retroactive basis could have been avoided by including in the data sent to the system either the fact of the intervening accident or the actual time that the renewal check was received. Neither item was included. Under these circumstances, the knowledge of the selling agent and the claims superintendent was imputed to the company (or its computer).

> [The] insured should not be charged with the failure to input this critical data. Holding a company responsible for the actions of its computer does not exhibit a distaste for modern business practices as State Farm asserts. A computer operates only in accordance with the information and directions supplied by its human programmers. . . . The reinstatement of Bockhorst's policy was the direct result of the errors and oversights of State Farm's human agents and employees. The fact that the actual processing of the policy was carried out by an unimaginative mechanical device can have no effect on the company's responsibilities for those errors and oversights.[109]

Although the State Farm system generally may not have been inadequate for tracking pertinent data, in this particular case the data collection and management were substantially ineffective. Under these circumstances, the court chose to ignore the fact that no knowledge was in fact brought to the attention of either the data system or the relevant decision makers and it imputed knowledge based on a view that it should have been communicated.

Concepts of waiver, of course, can readily mature into issues of estoppel when the third party detrimentally relies on the output and actions induced by the computer system. In cases of estoppel, the central issue is whether the third party relied to its detriment[110] Action sufficient for an estoppel may be based on knowledge that the other party may rely, but may also be found in the operation of an inadequate computer system in circumstances in which there is a duty to exercise care in dealing with others.[111] This latter behavior may involve awareness of a risk of undue reliance.

---

[109] Id. at 536–537.

[110] See Stutelberg v. Farrell Lines, Inc., 529 F. Supp. 566 (SDNY 1982).

[111] See Swiss Air Transp. Co. v. Benn, 467 NYS2d 341 (NY Civ. Ct. 1983).

CHAPTER *8*

International Trade Considerations

¶ 8.01 INTRODUCTION

It is not possible to discuss the economics or law related to the computer industry without considering international competition and the issues of import/export law and policy. Access to foreign markets can be critical to the economic health of a particular company or to an entire segment of the technology industry, while foreign competition can be the single most significant threat to a domestic concern. The rapid, and now virtually complete, dominance of the home electronics market by foreign competitors signals the possibility of similar competition and dominance in other technology markets.

Whether viewed in terms of commercial opportunity or competitive threat, the international dimensions of computer technology transfer are quite clear. The result is a complex spectrum of commercial law and technology issues such as intellectual property protection and qualitative performance of contracts. More significantly, the international environment interjects a variety of national and transnational policy conflicts. Foreign and international law may be inconsistent with traditional U.S. conceptions of competition and commercial development.

In broad terms, two uniquely international issues are involved in computer technology. The first stems from national military security. In this country and elsewhere, computer technology is a vital element of military development. To the extent that computer technology is transported out of the country, there is a risk that it will benefit nations that are currently or potentially unfriendly to U.S. interests. This threat justifies governmental intervention in some export transactions, but the extent and character of the justifiable intervention is unclear. In light of the commercial importance of the industry, national security issues must be balanced against the often substantial effect that intervention has on business dealings and the consequent ability of domestic companies to compete in international markets. These issues surface primarily in the character and scope of U.S. export control laws.

The second issue involves policies of other countries that are inconsistent with traditional U.S. law and concepts about promoting commercial growth or, at least, inconsistent with the perceived interests of U.S. industry. Such inconsistency is neither surprising nor troublesome in itself. To the same extent that U.S. law and policy appropriately support the U.S. view of how best to promote domestic interests, the law of other countries can be expected to reflect and promote the interests of those countries. The difficulties pertain to operating within the frameworks created by these varying interests and, when desirable, moderating or eliminating inconsistencies.

PART A.   IMPORT CONSIDERATIONS

¶ 8.02 ISSUES

International law issues pertinent to the computer industry require an initial distinction between import and export policies. The dominant import issue involves the degree and nature of protection that domestic industries receive in national markets. Protection in this environment often involves importation barriers or fees that alter the availability and competitive character of foreign products that compete with national industry. Obviously, decisions about appropriate barriers and levels of protection are made by all countries involved with technology, but the focus in this discussion is on the decisions made by the United States.

The political and economic arguments supporting some form of protection for national industries are multifaceted. Since these arguments achieve varying levels of acceptance at different points in time, the character of import control policy is not stable, but subject to substantial political variation. At the core of most commercially focused import restraints, however, is a judgment that it is desirable to insulate national industry from particular forms of international competition.[1] The ultimate objective is to establish a form of national "safe harbor" for the development and continued vitality of the local business. The terms of the safe harbor vary widely according to the competitive pressures from which the local industry is to be protected.

In broadest form, this safe-harbor approach can be described as protectionism. In its extreme, protectionism is a national policy that can be functionally defined as the insulation of local industry from *all* forms of international competition without particular regard to whether elements of competitive unfairness are otherwise present. The objective is to stimulate internal economic growth by providing a complete, safe-harbor market. This approach to import policy for certain industries is characteristic of a number of countries. Arguably, it is shortsighted and disruptive in that it may lead to comparable protectionism in other countries, while removing competitive incentives that might stimulate innovation and development in the local industry. The line at which these adverse effects outweigh local interests in establishing and maintaining business operations is seldom clear.

---

[1] Of course, various noncommercial motivations support restrictions on imports, including national health protection and national security. The most controversial restraints not concerned with commercial interests are those pertaining to foreign policy issues. See infra ¶ 8.06[2] concerning export limits on foreign policy grounds.

The current position of computer technology in the United States is sufficiently strong that pure protectionism has not been a major objective. While the national industry does not lead in all aspects of the technology, it is competitive in most. Furthermore, the industry is growing at a sufficient rate that the protective arguments that have arisen for older industries such as steel and automotives have not been raised. Instead, the major themes of import restrictions pertaining to technology focus on defining the type of internationally competitive actions that merit protective responses. Two forms of competition have been viewed as appropriate for import regulation and interdiction: unfair pricing acts and intellectual property piracy.

¶ 8.03 IMPORTS AND PRICE CUTTING

In a free market, product price and quality are primary factors determining commercial success. In a pure, competitive model, the ability to compete in terms of price is related to manufacturing and marketing costs and to the underlying efficiency of a particular company. Given equal levels of efficiency, competitive pricing provides a form of protection for domestic companies, since they do not bear the transportation costs of foreign imports.

In many domestic markets, however, U.S. companies have experienced increasingly severe price and quality competition from foreign manufacturers. When this increased competition is based on greater efficiency or lower costs because of advantages in labor or technology, the situation represents an international manifestation of basic marketplace concepts. In fact, in many industries, foreign manufacturers have major advantages in lower labor costs and more advanced automation. Any direct restraints on their competition in U.S. markets cannot be justified by concepts of unfair competition. Direct restraints are justifiable only based on a decision simply to protect domestic industry against competition that would be considered fair if present in U.S. industries. This political decision may reflect a desire to preserve current employment or to provide a period in which a domestic industry is able to restructure and regain international competitiveness.

A different situation exists when the price advantage of the foreign producer is not based on efficiency or labor economics, but on governmental support or an artificial allocation of costs and pricing designed to affect national industries adversely in our own local markets. In either case, the competitive advantage of the foreign producer may be defined as unfair and is a basis for offsetting measures to avoid material injury to the domestic industry that is adversely affected. There is a potential analogy in efforts to apply U.S. antitrust law to predatory pricing by a monopolist where subsidized, low prices are initially designed to drive competitors out of a market to achieve subsequent, exaggerated profits.[2] Governmental subsidies and predatory pricing have similar implications on an international level and are considered unfair competition.

[1] Dumping

Predatory pricing in an international environment is most often described as dumping a product in a foreign marketplace. Despite the implication that the product is simply being liquidated, consistent patterns of dumping can have substantial, long-term effects on the marketplace and the profitability of the company that undertakes the dumping activity. As described by one observer, the objective of dumping a product in foreign commerce is long-term profit through subsequent monopoly or, at least, less competitive markets.

> The economics of dumping arise from a producer's opportunity to compartmentalize the overall marketplace for his goods, thus permitting him to offer the product for sale at different prices in different sectors. . . . Only if trade barriers or other factors insulate each market sector . . . is there an opportunity to substantially vary the product's price [since other conditions lead to market competition setting the price]. The objective of dumping may be to increase long-term marginal revenues or to ruin a competitor's market position.[3]

"Dumping" is defined as a situation in which a product is sold in a target country at a price below the fair market value of that product and, in some cases, even below the costs of production.[4] Thus defined, dumping has been the subject of prohibition in the General Agreement on Tariffs and Trade (GATT) that governs much of international trade[5] and in the multinational trade negotiation round conducted pursuant to GATT in 1979 in Tokyo.[6] Within the United States, dumping is subject to two distinct statutory regulations beyond direct presiden-

---

[2] Compare ¶ 4.09.

[3] Wilson, *International Business Transactions* 149 (1981).

[4] See "Implementing Article VI, the 1979 Tokyo Round, Antidumping Code," XVIII *International Legal Materials* 621.

[5] General Agreement on Tariff and Trade, Oct. 30, 1947, 61 UST 5, TIAS No. 1700, 55 UNTS 194, as amended, IV General Agreement on Tariffs and Trade, Basic Instruments & Selected Documents (1958).

[6] See Staple, "Implementing 'Tokyo Round' Commitments: The New Injury Standard in Antidumping and Countervailing Duty Laws," 32 Stan. L. Rev. 1183 (1980).

tial intervention:[7] the Revenue Act of 1916, which allows for private actions by an injured party against the competitor,[8] and the Trade Agreements Act of 1979, which provides for the imposition of anti-dumping duties against the foreign products.[9]

[a] The Revenue Act of 1916

The Revenue Act of 1916 (1916 Act) provides for direct personal action with the potential of treble damage awards for people injured by the dumping of a foreign product in U.S. markets. Under Section 72 of the 1916 Act, actionable dumping includes systematic importation or selling of products in this country at a price below the market price at the point of origin with an intention to injure industry within the United States or to prevent its development.[10] The 1916 Act "mandates a comparison of the prices at which articles are imported . . . with the actual market value or wholesale price . . . in the principal markets of the country of their production."[11] The 1916 Act is effectively a price discrimination statute oriented to international trade.

Although it has been in force for many years, the 1916 Act has seldom been employed against alleged dumping practices. Historically, this pattern of nonuse related to the dominant and naturally insulated position enjoyed by most U.S. industries. In addition, tariff and other remedies were used to enhance or ensure national protection whenever an issue arose. In many industries, neither condition currently prevails. Foreign producers are substantially more competitive, and the potential to injure national industries by dumping products is clear. Politically, the ability to implement tariff and similar remedies is suspect. In this environment, litigation under the 1916 Act has arisen.

Nevertheless, it is unlikely that the 1916 Act will provide a viable remedy for predatory dumping from foreign producers. U.S. courts have not generally been receptive to arguments alleging anticompetitive acts based on predatory pricing.[12] Furthermore, to establish a case the plaintiff must contend with relatively difficult questions of fact and intention.

---

[7] 19 USC § 2252 (1982).

[8] 15 USC § 72 (1982).

[9] 19 USC §§ 1671–1673 (1982).

[10] 15 USC § 72 (1982).

[11] Zenith Radio Corp. v. Matsushita Indus. Co., 494 F. Supp. 1161 (ED Pa. 1980).

[12] See Ordover & Willig, "An Economic Definition of Predation: Pricing and Product Innovation," 91 Yale LJ 8 (1981); Areeda & Turner, "Predatory Pricing and Related Practices Under Section 2 of the Sherman Act," 88 Harv. L. Rev. 697 (1975); Chapter 4.

Predictably, while an intent to injure is required under the 1916 Act, this intent may be inferred from the defendants' actions.[13] To establish price discrimination sufficient to constitute dumping, however, the products sold in two markets must be proven to be comparable. Either comparability or actual market price may be difficult to establish in cases where there is no local market or where there are substantial differences in items sold in the origin market and items sold in the United States.[14]

[b] The Trade Agreements Act of 1979

Historically, the more significant remedy for injuries caused by foreign dumping of products in the United States has been administrative action under the Trade Agreements Act of 1979 (Trade Act) and its predecessors.[15] The Trade Act does not provide a private remedy for injured parties, but does permit the imposition of offsetting duties on the imported goods in an amount equal to the amount by which the value of the items exceeds their U.S. price. Antidumping duties are imposed following a two-stage process involving decisions by both the Department of Commerce and the International Trade Commission (ITC). Offsetting duties may be imposed if it is found that (1) the products are being sold at less than their fair market value in the United States, and (2) the result of these sales is a material injury, or threat of material injury, to an industry in the United States or that the establishment of an industry in the United States is being materially retarded.[16]

As with the private remedy previously discussed,[17] both elements of this standard present difficult questions of fact in particular situations, but in contrast to the private action, the facts relating to dumping are collected by concurrent investigations by the Department of Commerce and the ITC. The statute imposes time limits on the speed with which action must be taken, requiring in general no more than 240 days between commencement and completion of proceedings.[18]

The issues of comparative value and price are often at the heart of antidumping proceedings.[19] The statute requires a finding that the injury

---

[13] Zenith Radio Corp. v. Matsushita Indus. Co., 494 F. Supp. 1161 (ED Pa. 1980).

[14] See Outboard Marine Corp. v. Pretezel, 461 F. Supp. 384 (D. Del. 1978).

[15] 19 USC §§ 1671–1673 (1982).

[16] 19 USC § 1673 (1982).

[17] See supra ¶ 8.03[1][a].

[18] See generally Note, "United States Import Relief Options: A Comparison of Procedures," 13 NYU J. Int'l L. & P. 1049 (1981).

[19] Wharton, "Treasury Runs the Maze: LTFV Determination Under the Antidumping Act of 1921," 8 Ga. J. Int'l & Comp. L. 919 (1978).

to U.S. industry is caused by sales at "less than . . . fair value." In making this determination, administrative regulations specify two measurement procedures or tests.[20] The first assesses value based on a determination of the market value in a foreign market. In general, this refers to the producer's home market, but a third-country market may be substituted if the producer's home market is not a feasible standard. This might occur, for example, when the item is produced solely for export or when a state controlled economy obviates any assumption that the home market is a reasonable comparison.[21] The alternative test is a constructed value test. This attempts to project back to actual value based on judgments assigning presumed costs to labor, materials, and related contributions to the value of the product. As with third-country market assessments, the constructed value approach is used primarily when circumstances indicate that the home market is not a reliable measure of value. One such circumstance involves a state controlled economy where costs and prices are controlled with no necessary relationship to fair market values.

[2] Governmental Subsidies

Closely related to the issue of predatory pricing through dumping are situations in which the price of foreign products is artificially low as a result of governmental subsidies designed to enhance the competitive posture of the industry. Governmental support of local industry in the international marketplace is neither uncommon, nor necessarily objectionable. Its obvious purpose is to stimulate domestic economic growth by enhancing the competitive circumstances of the industry. While this is an acceptable governmental objective, the form of subsidization may vary widely. At least on the surface, some governmental supports are unfair forms of competition in international markets.

The propriety of responses by one country to subsidies granted by another to its own industry has been the subject of substantial debate. Most recently, in the Tokyo round of multinational trade negotiations, the ability of the target countries to respond was expressly acknowledged in the Agreement on Subsidies and Countervailing Measures.[22] Within the United States, the Trade Act establishes that countervailing import duties are available in certain cases where U.S. distribution prices reflect a foreign government subsidy.[23] As with antidumping

---

[20] 19 CFR §§ 353.1–353.23.

[21] 19 CFR § 353.8.

[22] "Agreement on Subsidies and Countervailing Measures, the 1979 Tokyo Round," XVIII *International Legal Materials* 579.

[23] 19 USC §§ 1671 et seq. (1982).

duties, countervailing duties are initiated by a two-agency decision process requiring action by both the Department of Commerce and the ITC. In essence, the statute requires findings that (1) there has been a foreign government subsidy of the product, and (2) "by reason of imports of" the subsidized product, a U.S. industry is materially injured, threatened with material injury, or the development of the industry is materially retarded.[24]

Application of the countervailing duty statute is complex; two issues are of particular importance. The first concerns establishment of material injury as a result of imports of the subsidized product. In determining whether there has been a material injury under this or the antidumping statute, the ITC is required to consider the volume of imports, the effect of the imports on prices for similar products in the United States, and the direct impact of the import on U.S. producers.[25] Since these involve questions of fact, judicial review of ITC findings on these factors has generally been limited.[26]

A more conceptually complex and significant issue is the determination of what forms of governmental support constitute a subsidy for purposes of imposing countervailing duties. Clearly, the statute is not intended to provide offsetting duties for any governmental action that improves the competitive posture of foreign industry. The emphasis is on support in an international setting. As a result, generally applicable tax benefits, low interest loans, or other subsidies that are not tied to engaging in foreign commerce are not generally adequate bases for countervailing measures.[27] Even among supportive actions clearly directed at international trade, however, the courts and the agencies have had substantial difficulty in identifying the forms of support that constitute fair competition and the forms that are subsidies sufficient to trigger countervailing responses. *Zenith Radio Corp. v. United States*[28] is illustrative. *Zenith* dealt with a Japanese tax imposed on consumer electronics products manufactured in Japan. The tax was waived or remitted to the Japanese producer if the produced goods were exported. The Supreme Court upheld an agency decision that this tax rebate was not an actionable subsidy where the amount rebated was not excessive.

---

[24] 19 USC § 1671 (1982).

[25] 19 USC § 1677 (1982).

[26] See Armstrong Bros. Tool Co. v. United States, 483 F. Supp. 312 (Cust. Ct. 1980) (discusses eight factors to be considered).

[27] See ASG Indus., Inc. v. United States, 467 F. Supp. 1167 (Cust. Ct. 1979). Compare ASG Indus., Inc. v. United States, 467 F. Supp. 1200 (Cust. Ct. 1979).

[28] 437 US 443 (1978).

¶ 8.04 INTELLECTUAL PROPERTY AND IMPORT INFRINGEMENT

Adverse effects from dumping or governmentaly subsidized imports have yet to materialize in the computer industry. Nevertheless, substantial industry concern exists about unfair competition from imported products. This focuses on products brought into the country in a form that infringes or contributes to the infringement of U.S. patents, copyrights, or trademarks. Infringing imports are especially significant for relatively small systems sold for home or business use. The lower end computer and software market is price sensitive. Given lower costs for materials and labor coupled with development costs truncated by copying, the imported products can be sold at prices substantially below those of the original. Partially in consequence (at least prior to recent decisions by the I.T.C.), infringing imports have been a visible and significant portion of the microcomputer market.

The target country of infringing products has a right to enforce its own intellectual property laws against items already in the country. As a consequence, import infringements create the same issues that arise for any intellectual property infringement, but the fact that the infringing products were produced in a foreign country creates significant additional issues of enforcement. Discovery and seizure of copies within the United States may be inadequate, since the productive capacity of the infringer and most of its resources are in another country. This is especially true where the scope of the infringement problem is large and the infringing companies are a mini-industry, as has been the case in the microcomputer industry. Individual civil actions against such alleged infringement may be too time-consuming and inadequate to protect the industry or even a particular victim.

Enforcement of U.S. intellectual property rights against alleged infringers in their own countries is both costly and problematic. A primary aim of efforts to enforce U.S. rights within domestic borders is therefore on the use of import restrictions, which are based on an imported product's infringement, or contribution to infringement, of U.S. rights.

Section 337 of the Tariff Act of 1930, as amended, provides

> Unfair methods of competition and unfair acts in the importation of articles ... or in their sale ... the effect or tendency of which is to destroy or substantially injure an industry, efficiently and economically operated in the United States, or to prevent the establishment of such an industry, or to restrain or monopolize trade ... are declared unlawful.[29]

---

[29] 19 USC § 1337 (1982).

This provision establishes a broad basis to impose import restrictions designed to prevent unfair competition. The language of Section 337 is sufficiently broad to encompass acts that would otherwise violate U.S. antitrust provisions, as well as importation acts that amount to dumping products within the country. More significant to this discussion, however, Section 337 has been interpreted to encompass import restrictions based on violation of U.S. intellectual property rights including patent, trademark, and copyright.[30]

Section 337 does not establish a private, civil right of action, but creates criteria for regulation of imports by the ITC.[31] The benefits of a proceeding under Section 337 are that federal enforcement is enlisted against the infringing products and that infringements can be detected and acted against before they are dispersed into the marketplace. Enforcement of Section 337 begins with an ITC investigation that may be initiated sua sponte or pursuant to a complaint filed by an interested party. As is true with most investigative agencies, the decision to undertake an investigation pursuant to a complaint is discretionary, based at least in part on a decision as to the significance of the alleged unfair practices to U.S. industries.[32] If an investigation is undertaken, unless the matter is determined to be "more complicated," the investigation must be completed within one year from initiation. Following completion of the investigation, the initial determination and recommendations in most cases are made by an Administrative Law Judge, whose recommendations are then reviewed by the ITC.[33]

If a violation of Section 337 is found, the ITC may issue orders placing restrictions on the importation and sale of products. The most significant sanction is an order totally excluding a product or type of product from the United States.[34] This order operates as an in rem preclusion, applicable to all importers. Under the statute, an exclusion is ordered only if, after finding a violation, the ITC finds further that exclusion will not adversely affect the public health and welfare or competition in the United States to an extent that should preclude the exclusion order. The order is enforced through the U.S. Customs Office.

---

[30] See Bally/Midway Mfg. Co. v. United States Int'l Trade Comm'n, 714 F2d 1117 (Fed. Cir. 1983).

[31] 19 USC § 1337(a) (1982).

[32] See Easton & Neely, "Unfair Competition in U.S. import Trade Developments Since the Trade Act of 1979," 5 Int'l Trade LJ 203, 219 (1980).

[33] 19 CFR § 210.51.

[34] 19 USC § 1337(d) (1982).

The alternative to an exclusion order is a cease and desist order.[35] Unlike the exclusion order, a cease and desist order operates in personam against particular individuals. It is directed to ordering them to cease the unfair acts that violate Section 337. Significantly, Section 337 not only precludes unfair importation, but also the sale and distribution of products unfairly brought into the country. Thus, the cease and desist order affects not only products to be brought in, but also products that already are in the country. As with the exclusion order, a cease and desist order requires a judgment that health, welfare, and competitive considerations do not preclude its issuance.

Decisions by the ITC finding a violation of Section 337 are submitted to presidential review for a period of 60 days. The President has express authority to reject any sanction imposed by the ITC.[36] During this period of review, products subject to exclusionary sanctions may continue to be imported upon payment of a bond in an amount determined by the ITC.

In addition to issuing cease and desist or exclusion orders, the ITC is also empowered to issue orders for temporary relief pending completion of its investigation.[37] This relief is analogous to preliminary injunctive relief. In general, the temporary order requires a "reason to believe" that a violation has occurred and that the complainant will be immediately and substantially harmed if a temporary order is not issued.[38]

[1] "Industry" Defined

Unless the unfair importation materially retards the development of a domestic industry, Section 337 requires proof that the unfair acts have the effect or tendency to substantially injure "an industry, efficiently and economically operated, in the United States."[39] Thus, a threshold inquiry concerns whether a domestic industry exists and whether that industry is efficiently operated.

While the existence of a domestic industry is often obvious, difficulties arise in some cases because of the definition of "industry" customarily followed by the ITC in decisions pertaining to technology. This definition was suggested in *Bally/Midway Manufacturing Co. v. United States*

---

[35] 19 USC § 1337(F)(1) (1982).

[36] 19 USC § 1337(g)(1982).

[37] 19 USC § 1337(e)(1982).

[38] See In re Certain Coin-Operated Audiovisual Games and Components, No. 337-TA-105 (ITC 1982).

[39] 19 USC § 1337(a) (1982).

International Trade Commission.[40] In *Bally*, the ITC reviewed allegations by Bally that infringing copies of copyrighted video game programs were being imported in violation of U.S. copyrights. Two different games (PAC-MAN and Rally-X) were involved. The ITC concluded that there were two separate industries, each associated solely with the part of the complainant's business devoted to exploiting each separate intellectual property right.[41] The ITC further concluded that while the PAC-MAN industry had been harmed by the imports, the Rally-X industry had not.

The ITC definition of "industry" is most often protective of intellectual property rights. A narrow definition of what constitutes an "industry" facilitates the conclusion that importation of infringing products harms or has a tendency to harm the domestic industry. In contrast, a more expansive definition that encompasses the entire video game industry might be more intuitively correct, but could lead to conclusions that particular imports have too small of a market share to be actionable.

In *Bally*, however, the limited definition of an "industry" initially produced an unexpected result. Rally-X was a less successful game than PAC-MAN. During the ITC proceedings, sales and production of Rally-X essentially had stopped for lack of a continuing market. As a result, when it made its final decision, the ITC concluded that, at the time of decision, no industry existed that was being affected by the imports. This result was arguably justified by the fact that ITC sanctions apply only prospectively and there was no further, ongoing commercial activity to protect. Nevertheless, the decision was properly reversed by the Federal Circuit Court of Appeals. Although the majority of the court did not challenge the underlying definition of "industry," it concluded that sanction considerations are separate from a determination of whether there was a violation. For that determination, the appropriate time for assessment is when the complaint is filed.[42]

As *Bally* suggests, while a narrow definition of "industry" enhances protection of individual copyright and patent holders, it creates potential difficulties where the circumstances of a specific producer are unique. A related illustration is found in *Shaper Manufacturing Co. v. United States International Trade Commission.*[43] In that case, enforcement was denied in favor of a toy manufacturer against foreign copies where the entire manufacturing and most of the packing and quality control concerning

---

[40] 714 F2d 1117 (Fed. Cir. 1983).

[41] Id. at 1120.

[42] Id. at 1121.

[43] 717 F2d 1368 (Fed. Cir. 1983).

certain toy vehicles were conducted in Hong Kong. There was an insufficient effect on a U.S. industry.

[2] Substantial Harm and Tendency for Harm

Assuming that a requisite domestic industry exists, Section 337 requires that the unfair actions have the effect or the tendency to destroy or substantially injure that industry.[44] The issue of substantial injury or tendency to injure is not necessarily limited to the impact on a domestic industry's actual, current sales, but does in fact most often focus on the impact on a product's domestic market. The issue commonly is to what extent it can be concluded that sales of the infringing product are, in effect, lost sales opportunities for the domestic industry. Unless there is reason to conclude that import sales were in substitution for some other product, the mere fact of distribution in the United States is a basis for inferring harm.

Section 337 apparently requires not only proof of injury, but proof of substantial injury or destruction of the domestic industry. The impact of this language, however, is reduced by the alternative grounds provided for relief: that the imports have a tendency to destroy or substantially injure the domestic industry. This result is suggested by the court in *Bally*

> Although the number of infringing imports was not a high percentage of Bally's total sales of the Rally-X game, it was enough to establish injury to a domestic industry under Section 337(a). That section prohibits . . . acts that have a tendency to [injure]. Where the unfair practice is the importation of products that infringe a domestic industry's copyright, trademark, or patent right, even a relatively small loss of sales may establish . . . the requisite injury to that portion of the complainant's business devoted to exploitation of the intellectual property rights.[45]

[3] Exclusion and Incomplete Products

The triggering event for ITC action against import practices in the situations discussed here is that the imported product infringes on an existing U.S. intellectual property right. In the context of technology imports, notwithstanding ITC orders or other reasons to prevent importation on this basis, there are substantial practical barriers to enforcement. Unlike other forms of intellectual property infringement, software copy-

---

[44] 19 USC § 1337(a) (1982).

[45] Bally/Midway Mfg. Co. v. United States Int'l Trade Comm'n, 714 F2d 1117, 1124 (Fed. Cir. 1983).

right and hardware patent infringements can be detected only through close, technologically assisted inspection that is not always possible.

The difficulties of enforcement are exacerbated by the fact that especially for smaller systems, it is possible to disassemble infringing and noninfringing parts of a product and ship them separately. As to the infringing parts (read only memory (ROM) chips and the like), the ability to issue and attempt to enforce exclusion orders is clear. As to the disassembled, noninfringing parts of the ultimate product, however, a more difficult question arises. On the one hand, exclusion of the disassembled parts is important to an effective effort to control infringement by imported products. Often the noninfringing parts are more susceptible to detection. On the other hand, interest in free trade and open markets indicates that circumspection is necessary in issuing exclusionary sanctions against these items.

The excludability of disassembled parts of computers under Section 337 was addressed by the ITC in proceedings instituted by Apple Computer seeking general exclusion of machines that infringed its copyrights and patents in several microcomputer systems.[46] At the time of this decision and of the alleged unfair acts, Apple was one of the major producers of personal computers for the home and hobbyist market. During the investigation and hearing, Apple established that ROM chips in a number of imported microcomputers infringed the copyrights to various portions of Apple's proprietary operating system.[47] In most of the cases, there were exact duplications of the Apple programs with only slight modifications designed to display the importer's, rather than Apple's, brand name. Based on these data, an exclusion order was issued against all computers incorporating programs substantially similar to Apple's copyrighted works.[48]

Apple also proved that computers shipped by certain respondents were imported in incomplete form but were later outfitted with programs that infringed the Apple copyrights. The ITC approached this situation under two distinct analyses, both of which led to the conclusion that an exclusion order should issue against the incomplete products.

The first analysis focused on machines that were imported with a motherboard circuit configuration identical to that used in the Apple systems, but that were not equipped with ROM chips containing the infringing programs at the time of importation. For these products, the issue was

---

[46] In re Certain Personal Computers and Components Thereof, No. 337-TA-140 (ITC 1984).

[47] See ¶ 1.03[5].

[48] In re Certain Personal Computers, No. 337-TA-140 (ITC 1984).

treated as a copyright question pertaining to contributory infringement.[49] Based on the U.S. Supreme Court decision in *Universal City Studios, Inc. v. Sony Corp. of America*,[50] the ITC concluded that the critical test was whether the incomplete computers *as imported* had a commercially significant, noninfringing use. Based on the conclusion that the motherboard circuitry could only be used in connection with copyrighted Apple programs, the ITC concluded that contributory infringement was proven.[51] It issued an exclusion order against incomplete computers with a motherboard identical to any of those used by Apple.

The second situation involved cases of incomplete imports under circumstances in which the product being brought into the country could have been used for noninfringing purposes. That is, as imported, the configuration of the product did not require that infringing programs be used. In fact, however, Apple established that the importing company did later install infringing programs. Based on this, the ITC concluded that the importation of the incomplete machines was merely one step in a direct infringement of Apple's copyrights.[52]

[4] Customs Enforcement Beyond Section 337

Exclusion orders issued by the ITC are enforced through the U.S. Customs Service. Especially in light of the practical problems involved in identifying excluded products as they are brought into the country, many potential complainants forego action under Section 337 because of the time and effort entailed. Furthermore, because of the limited resources of the ITC, not all complaints of infringing imports lead to investigation and the imposition of sanctions.

Short of proceedings and orders under Section 337, exclusionary action against infringing products may be obtained from the Customs Service by direct action under the authority of the Copyright Act (the Act). Sections 602 and 603 of the Act prohibit importation of unauthorized copies of a work without the consent of the copyright holder.[53] Articles imported in violation of these provisions are subject to seizure by the government and to forfeiture.[54] In general, these provisions are

---

[49] Id. at 28.

[50] 104 S. Ct. 774 (1984).

[51] In re Certain Personal Computers, No. 337-TA-140 (ITC 1984).

[52] Id. at 36.

[53] 17 USC §§ 602, 603 (1982).

[54] 17 USC § 603(c) (1982).

enforceable by the U.S. Customs Service under regulations promulgated by the Secretary of the Treasury.

The regulations implementing this enforcement option provide for recording the copyrighted work with the Customs Service.[55] They then provide for seizure of any piratical copy of the recorded work, pending determination of whether it constitutes a copyright infringement.[56] A "piratical work" is defined in terms that are substantially equivalent to the copyright definition of a "copy." Following seizure, administrative procedures are instituted to determine if the work does violate the copyright.[57]

Under current regulations, the Customs-Service interprets its enforcement power as limited to directly infringing works. Absent ITC exclusionary orders, Customs will not act against noninfringing items that ultimately may be used to construct an infringing product.[58] This apparently restrictive position is consistent with statutory language and, particularly, with the broader exclusionary power given to the ITC. Furthermore, unlike the ITC, which acts only after extensive factual investigation, the Customs Service is not in a position to determine the eventual use of noninfringing products.

PART B.   EXPORT CONSIDERATIONS

¶ 8.05 POLICY AND COMMERCIAL ISSUES

Increasingly, U.S. industries, especially those associated with computer technology products, are involved in an international marketplace in which competition for domestic markets involves both domestic and foreign producers. In fact, in some domestic consumer electronics markets, dominant market shares are now controlled by foreign companies. As discussed previously, elements of domestic importation law are designed to protect domestic industries from competition that is deemed unfair or contrary to U.S. industrial and legal policy. U.S. companies also compete in foreign markets. There is a commercial emphasis on exportation of technology and technology-related products. Furthermore, contrary to historical precedent in many fields, U.S.-based technology is no longer technologically dominant in all international markets.

---

[55] 19 CFR §§ 133.2, 133.32.

[56] 19 CFR § 133.42.

[57] 19 CFR §§ 133.43–133.44.

[58] Blatt, "The 'ROMless' Dilemma: U.S. Customs Enforcement of Contributory Copyright Violations," 1 Comp. Law. 22 (July, 1984).

While export agreements involve many of the same issues previously discussed for technology licensing, [59] exportation also introduces a variety of issues unique to the foreign marketplace. One major issue is the reconciliation of national security and foreign policy interests with interests in commercial exploitation of technology. The transfer of products to a foreign market may introduce national security questions in a variety of ways. These are most obvious when the export involves state of the art technology that has obvious potential military applications and is not generally available from other sources. While such technology is commercially valuable to the exporting business, it involves great risk because it could fall directly or indirectly into the hands of foreign entities not friendly to U.S. interests. This risk results in relatively extensive U.S. export regulations. [60] It is also manifest in international joint action among Western countries to limit certain exports. In both settings, there is an acknowledged governmental right to prohibit export of certain items and information in furtherance of national security.

More broadly, there is a tension between competing views of domestic technology in an international context. From one perspective, domestic technology (and other products) is viewed as a national resource subject to governmental control. The alternative, more commerical, view is that the international marketplace is not to be treated as essentially different from the domestic market. This view emphasizes private ownership and free trade independent of governmental control. It postulates a commercial right of access to foreign markets and objects to any noncommercial restriction or disruption of this access. The tension between these competing views is manifest in governmental control of exports based on foreign policy considerations and in the scope and form of controls justifiable by national security. The right of the government to exercise foreign policy-based restrictions on exports is established, [61] but it is controversial because of its disruptive effect on commerce. Unlike national security concerns, foreign policy controls are not predictable or necessarily stable over the life of an agreement. At a minimum, the commercial view of international trade argues for limited governmental intervention in a form that preserves the predictability and timing that are essential to maintain access to foreign markets.

A second set of issues, more directly associated with private law concerns, involves the extent to which technology protections can be carried forward into the international marketplace. In general, copyright and pat-

---

[59] See generally Chapter 5.

[60] See 50 USC §§ 2401 et seq. (1982).

[61] See infra ¶ 8.06[2].

ent protections, subject to several multilateral treaties,[62] are territorial in application in the sense that U.S. patent rights, for example, do not extend protection into a foreign market. Equally significant, the intellectual property controls of each country reflect local judgments about the appropriate scope of protection; these judgments are not uniformly consistent with contemporary protections under U.S. law.

¶ 8.06 EXPORT REGULATION

Based on national security and foreign policy interests, the United States has maintained export regulation since the 1940s. As presently structured, regulation exists under two primary statutes. The first is the Arms Export Control Act (Arms Export Act).[63] As indicated by its title, the Arms Export Act deals primarily with the control of export of products and technology related to arms and munitions. Its provisions are administered by the Department of State, which establishes a munitions list. Technology and products on this list may be exported only pursuant to a license obtained from the Department of State. Indirect controls are also established on other products or technologies to the extent that they may be used to produce items on the munitions list.

More significant for most exports is the Export Administration Act of 1979 (EAA).[64] When enacted, EAA was a substantial reform of existing export control legislation and a clarification of standards pertaining to controls and was meant to decrease the uncertainties of prior law.[65] Although the terms of the EAA provide the structure under which export controls are administered, the EAA itself has expired and export administration in fact occurs under emergency powers available to the President. Legislative efforts to replace the export statute reflect a significant conflict over the extent to which executive power should be constrained in deference to commercial needs for speedy decision-making and relative predictability. Given the uncertain status of the EAA, it is important to discuss not only the existing structure of export regulation, but also the policy issues that pertain to computer technology export.

The stated objectives of the EAA consist of four distinct and potentially conflicting goals

---

[62] See infra ¶ 8.07.

[63] 22 USC §§ 2571 et seq. (1982).

[64] 50 USC §§ 2401 et seq. (1980).

[65] 50 USC § 2402 (1980).

[1] to minimize uncertainties in export ... policy and to encourage trade with all countries ... except those ... with which such trade has been determined ... to be against the national interest; [2] to restrict the export of goods and technology which would make a significant contribution to the military potential of any other country; [3] to restrict the export of goods and technology where necessary to further significantly the foreign policy of the United States; [and] [4] to restrict the export of goods when necessary to [prevent] the excessive drain of scarce materials.[66]

Pursuant to these policies, export controls consist of a complex licensing system that is keyed to classification lists administered primarily through the Office of Export Administration (OEA) of the Department of Commerce. The system also involves the Department of Defense. Two lists are pertinent. The first is the Commodity Control List, which encompasses hardware components of computer exports.[67] Inclusion in the Commodity Control List imposes the requirement of an export license for export to any country to which controls are applicable. In general, items on this list require a "validated license," which essentially is a license for the particular export only, as compared to a series of exports.[68] This license requires application to the OEA. This routine requirement for virtually all computer hardware exports leads to substantial delays that are disruptive of computer technology commerce. Limited alternatives to the validated license requirement exist for single shipments of small value requiring only a general license[69] or for cases in which a distribution license is available because of multiple shipments.[70]

The second control list pertains to technical data.[71] This list reflects a focus at least in part away from products and on information or process transfers. "Technical data" is broadly defined to include information that "can be used, or adapted for use, in the design, production, manufacture, utilization, or construction of articles or materials."[72] Beyond obvious application to design information, this concept encompasses computer software in most cases. As with the commodities list, inclusion in this list requires a license for export. Unless the software is associated with sensi-

---

[66] 50 USC § 2402 (1980).

[67] 15 CFR § 399.1 (computers listed in ECCN 1565A; disks in 1572A(d)).

[68] 50 USC § 2403(a) (1980).

[69] 15 CFR § 371.5.

[70] 15 CFR § 373.2. These provisions are currently under reconsideration in a form designed to increase direct governmental control over individual transactions. See McKenzie, "Proposed Export Regulation Amendments," 1 Comp. Law. 24 (1984).

[71] 15 CFR § 379.

[72] 15 CFR § 379.1[a].

tive applications in areas such as munitions, however, the terms of the license will vary according to assessments of the general availability of the data in foreign countries. The least complex license, requiring no compliance steps, applies to General Technical Data Available.[73] The more commonly used variant applies to technical data not generally available, but not within specified sensitive areas. This General Technical Data Restricted license requires that the exporter obtain assurances from the recipient that it will not re-export the software or its direct products to prohibited countries.[74]

[1] National Security and Foreign Availability

Implicit in the regulatory structure are a variety of judgments about the need to implement controls on technology exports and the extent to which this need outweighs observable and inevitable disruption of commercial relationships. One of the issues involved in this balancing process is the relationship between controls, national security, and the international availability of comparable goods. Protecting national military security is recognized as a basic objective of the export regulation system.[75] Export restrictions are in fact most readily defensible when there is a clear relationship between the technology or product and military applications. The goal of export regulation is to deny, or at least delay, access to that technology by restricting its flow outside of the United States. As discussed in a following section,[76] this approach requires attention to re-exporting or indirect shipment to unfriendly countries.

The EAA provides a structure in which foreign availability of militarily sensitive technologies must be considered in determining whether and for how long export controls are appropriate. Section 2403(c) provides

[The] President shall not impose export controls for foreign policy or national security purposes on [items] which he determines are available without restriction from sources outside the United States in significant quantities and comparable in quality to those produced in the United States, unless the President determines that adequate evidence has been presented . . . that the absence of such controls would be detrimental to the . . . United States.[77]

---

[73] 15 CFR § 379.3.

[74] 15 CFR § 379.4.

[75] 50 USC § 2402(2) (1980). A stated objective of the Export Act was to "restrict the export of . . . technology which would make a significant contribution to the military potential of any other country. . . ." Id.

[76] See infra ¶ 8.06[3].

[77] 50 USC § 2403(c) (1980).

The EAA establishes relatively elaborate procedures for the determination of foreign availability, including the appointment of a technical advisory committee and an obligation to review periodically the content of the list.[78] Regulations promulgated under this statute are directed to ensuring that controlled technologies are deleted from the control list when they have become generally available. Perhaps significantly, however, the President is authorized to impose controls even in the event of clear foreign availability.

As this regulatory structure suggests, a central judgment in export controls was that national security interests apply only as long as the technology is not available from other sources. The outer limits of export control of militarily sensitive technology are relatively clear. There is little disagreement that state of the art weapons technology unique to the United States should not be freely exported. National security clearly outweighs private commercial interests. Conversely, there is little debate that widely known technologies with no potential military application should be freely exported. In this case, commercial interests predominate.

There are difficulties, however, in defining the appropriate balance in less extreme cases and identifying when or if a particular technology is in fact generally available.[79] These questions are especially difficult in the contemporary computer industry since the technology is subject to rapid change. Furthermore, the essential character of the technology is that it has general application susceptible to a variety of often unpredictable uses. As a result, while the EAA provides a framework in which foreign availability is considered, particular decisions often turn more on underlying bias as to how freely export systems should function. From one vantage, any risk of a militarily significant application should be sufficient to restrict export. The converse view, of course, is that there is a national interest in allowing domestic technology companies to compete in international markets and that this requires relatively free export structures unless there are clear ties to potentially unique military applications.

[2] Foreign Policy Controls

While the administration of national security controls can become controversial, they are premised on an underlying policy that commands widespread acceptance. In contrast, the view that the government has a right to exercise export controls in response to general conceptions of

---

[78] 50 USC § 2404(d)(f)(g) (1980).

[79] See Note, "The Export Administration Act of 1979: An Examination of Foreign Availability of Controlled Goods and Technologies," 2 NW J. Int'l L. & Bus. 179 (1980).

national foreign policy is in itself controversial. Nevertheless, the EAA expressly recognizes this basis for export regulation. Section 2403(a)(1) provides "[The] President may prohibit or curtail the exportation of any goods, technology, or other information . . . to the extent necessary to further significantly the foreign policy of the United States.[80]

A major difficulty is that export controls based on foreign policy vary over time as policy considerations change. As a result, there is a lack of predictability in the ability of U.S. businesses to export to particular countries. Dramatic examples arise in cases where international events, such as the Russian invasion of Afghanistan, lead to sudden changes in trade relationships. Such changes directly affect future dealings with the affected country and raise questions about the ability of U.S. businesses to honor existing contracts. They also create an aura of uncertainty in dealing with other countries that places U.S. industries at a competitive disadvantage. Arguably, in light of the growth of foreign business expertise, the controls are often ineffective, since the commodities or technology barred on policy grounds can be produced or obtained elsewhere.[81]

While the EAA recognized the validity of foreign policy export regulations and that these regulations are necessarily discretionary with the executive branch, it attempted to place restraints on the scope or exercise of the controls that would lessen their effect on U.S. industry. Under the EAA, foreign policy controls expire within one year after their issuance unless expressly renewed.[82] In addition, the EAA also establishes criteria to be considered by the President in imposing controls. These include the probability that the controls will have the intended effect in light of foreign availability of the controlled items and the likely effect of the controls on the export performance of U.S. industries.[83] These criteria have little real effect, however. In practice, if not in intent, the EAA resolved the debate about foreign policy controls by expressly validating them with few real controls or limitations.

[3] Re-export Controls

Whether based on foreign policy or national security, the essence of export controls on technology is to restrict or eliminate access to the technology by certain countries. In concept, at least, this objective can be achieved by literally denying any export. For various reasons, however,

---

[80] 50 USC § 2403(a)(1) (1980).

[81] See Bertsch, "U.S. Export Controls: The 1970s and Beyond," 15 J. World Trade L. 67 (1981).

[82] 50 USC § 2405(a)(2) (1980).

[83] 50 USC § 2405(b) (1980).

including a need to maintain the commercial viability of domestic indus-tries, this option is seldom chosen except for the most sensitive technolo-gies.

The more common alternative involves controlling exports by limit-ing them to specific destination countries. This is at best a partial mea-sure. It entails the possibility that the recipient of the technology will subsequently transfer it to a country to which U.S. export laws would have barred shipment. This is commonly referred to as re-export. It presents issues concerning the ability of the United States to control the actions of an entity that is not a citizen and underscores a need to obtain multilateral cooperation in export control policy.

Efforts to deal directly with re-export within the U.S. regulatory sys-tem tend to focus on obtaining agreements by the technology recipients not to re-export without permission. Such assurances are required for export under a General Technical Data Restricted license.[84] Similarly, various assurances and reliability measures for recipients have been pro-posed as a requirement for obtaining a multiple export, distribution license.[85] The enforceability of these assurances in the absence of cooper-ation by the recipient country is not clear, but it is presumably within the rights of the OEA to deny subsequent licenses where a diversion to another country has previously occurred.[86]

The responsibility of the U.S. exporter in any case involving re-export to a prohibited country is clear only in the obvious case of a con-spiracy. The EAA imposes both criminal and civil sanctions for its willful violation.[87] These sanctions apply in any case in which the exporter had knowledge that the export would "be used for the benefit of any country to which exports are restricted." The constitutionality of criminal penal-ties for export to communist countries has been upheld.[88] In cases in which the re-export is without the complicity of the exporter, however, no liability arises.

[4] Multilateral Controls

Even in cases of clear national security concerns, unilateral controls implemented solely within the United States are not likely to restrict fully

---

[84] 15 CFR § 379.4(f). See supra ¶ 8.06[1].

[85] See McKenzie, "Proposed Export Regulation Amendments," 1 Comp. Law. 24 (1984).

[86] 50 USC § 2404(1) (1980).

[87] 50 USC § 2410 (1980).

[88] See United States v. Brumage, 377 F. Supp. 144 (EDNY 1980).

the flow of technology or products. In such cases, multilateral action is necessary.

The major multilateral organization concerning technology transfers to communist countries is the International Coordinating Committee on Strategic Trade with Communist Countries (COCOM), of which the United States is a member. A total of 15 countries are members of COCOM, including most of the North Atlantic Treaty Organization (NATO) countries and Japan. The primary function of COCOM is to establish a confidential list of items of military significance for which the member countries will agree to restrict or preclude trade with prohibited countries.

Although COCOM has been in operation since 1950 and functions well for clearly sensitive technologies, the administration of COCOM control lists has been a source of continuing tension, especially for the computer industry. Although the organization has no formal enforcement power, it does review export licenses for items on the control list. This adds to the time needed to obtain export clearance. Equally significant, member states in the organization do not uniformly interpret the terms of the control list. The result is that arguably at least the industries of some of the participating countries obtain a competitive advantage.

¶ 8.07 PROPRIETARY RIGHTS PROTECTION

Even assuming that export licenses are obtained, export of computer technology and related products involves a variety of complex legal issues analogous to the contracting questions about domestic technology licensing discussed in Chapter 5. The issues involve questions of defining the agreement of the parties and, more importantly, the extent to which intellectual property rights available within the United States are available in foreign jurisdictions. In addition, antitrust and monopoly laws have an impact on the licensing agreement. While U.S. antitrust laws may pertain to elements of the technology export, foreign antitrust laws are the major and more significant issue. It is clearly beyond the scope or capability of any single book, however, to examine the technology laws of all countries into which U.S. exports might be directed. It is important to discuss, at least generally, the problems and foreign law considerations in any technology export transaction.

Initially, and central to the entire range of issues to be discussed, intellectual property laws are limited in application to the territorial confines of the initiating country.[89] Thus, while most industrial countries

---

[89] See Deepsouth Packing Co. v. Laitram Corp., 406 US 518, 531 (1972).

have laws analogous to U.S. patent or copyright laws, the scope and rationale of the legal systems often differ substantially. In any event, there is no guarantee that a product or technology protected in the United States will necessarily receive protection in another country.

For both copyright and patent, international treaties or conventions establish a degree of protection against international discrimination in protecting the rights of authors and inventors of one country from actions taken in another. The primary patent law treaties are the Patent Cooperation Treaty[90] and the Paris Convention.[91] The Paris Convention (Convention) is administered by the World Intellectual Property Organization (WIPO). The Convention expressly recognizes that patents granted in one country are independent of those granted in another (the underlying premise of territoriality in patent law), but the Convention further provides that nationals of any contracting country must be granted access to the same patent protections that are available to nationals of the other country, provided that all local formalities are complied with.[92] Furthermore, a limited international priority of patent is established in that a patent filing in one participating country establishes a right of priority for 12 months in all others.[93]

International copyright protections are governed by two distinct treaty systems. The first is the Bern Convention of 1971.[94] The United States is not a party to this agreement because the Bern Convention requires no formalities as a precondition to establishing copyright. The second agreement is the Universal Copyright Convention[95] that requires contracting countries to offer the same protection for works of foreign nationals of other contracting countries as are provided for works of their own nationals.[96] While participating states may require that formalities be followed before the foreign work is protected, for published works these formalities are limited to copyright notice that is accompanied by the year of publication.[97] Protection without formalities is required for unpublished works. Additional requirements such as registration and deposit are permitted as a condition precedent to an infringement suit,

---

[90] TIAS No. 8733, June 19, 1970.

[91] 1883 Convention of the Union of Paris, as revised June 2, 1911, 38 UST 1645, amended November 6, 1925, 47 UST 1789, amended October 31, 1958, TIAS No. 4931, amended July 14, 1967, TIAS No. 6923, 7727.

[92] Paris Convention, art. 2.

[93] Paris Convention, art. 4.

[94] Bern Convention of 1971, Paris text, 7/24/71.

[95] Universal Copyright Convention, July, 1971.

[96] Universal Copyright Convention, art. II, § 3.

[97] Universal Copyright Convention, art. III, § 1.

but these can not be treated as challenging the basic validity of the copyright.

While these international agreements establish some consistency, there are wide variations in national laws. The legal systems of most industrial countries have had to face issues analogous to those encountered within the United States in the protection of computer hardware and software technology. The uncertainty has been especially acute for software protection. The issues necessarily arise under the particular terms of the national legislation involved. Few foreign countries have express statutory provisions that bring computer software within copyright law protection. Even though the degree of protection available under U.S. law is unsettled, the software protection law in most other countries is even less well developed. In general, however, with exceptions confined mostly to a lower court level and subsequently reversed,[98] the trend has been toward protection for software under copyright law.

¶ 8.08 THE EUROPEAN ECONOMIC COMMUNITY

In technology exports to European countries that are members of the European Economic Community (EEC), it is necessary to consider both the scope of protection available under the law of a specific country and the network of rights and restrictions established through the various EEC agreements and treaties.

No intellectual property rights for computer software vest under patent law in EEC countries. Article 52(2c) of the European Patent Convention provides that no patent shall be granted for programs for data processing.[99] Conversely, copyright law protection is available in most EEC countries. For example, in France computer programs have received protection through both copyright and trade secret law, with the latter also encompassing criminal law sanctions for unauthorized disclosure.[100] Copyright protection apparently extends to both source code and object code forms of programs and encompasses both operating systems and

---

[98] See "Protection of U.S. Computer Hardware and Software in Australia," 1 Comp. Law. 5 (1984); Heidrich, "Protection of Computer Programs Under German Copyright Law," 2 CLR 41 (1983).

[99] Dratler, Daunt, Davidson, *Distribution of Computer Products to the Common Market and Japan* 15, in USC 4th Annual Computer Law Institute, May 11–13, 1983.

[100] See Note, "French Law Provides Protection for Computer Software," 1 Software Protection 15 (March-April 1984).

applications programs.[101] In West Germany, there is no specific statutory coverage. While the decisions of German District Courts were initially conflicting, the decision against software copyrights was subsequently reversed on appeal and is currently pending in the German Federal Supreme Court.[102] In other EEC countries such as Italy and Switzerland, copyright protection is not generally available and the protection of computer software is primarily available only through national laws of unfair competition.[103]

Regardless of copyright protection, exporters of technology to EEC countries must consider the application of EEC competition laws to the contracts adopted for technology transfer. EEC competition laws are contained primarily in Articles 85 and 86 of the Treaty of Rome establishing the Common Market. These competition law provisions override any contrary laws in the participating countries and are enforced by a Commission of the Economic Community (Commission) with judicial enforcement actions occurring in the Court of Justice of the EEC.

Article 85(1) prohibits "agreements ... which may affect trade between member states and which have as their object or effect the prevention, restriction or distortion of competition within the common market."[104] The provisions of Article 85 apply to agreements that directly or indirectly fix purchase or sales prices, control production, markets, or investment. Article 85 excludes relatively small agreements where competition within the common market will not be affected to a significant degree. In 1977, the Commission indicated that an agreement is minor and is not covered by Article 85 if it does not cover products constituting more than 5 percent of the total product market and the participants in the agreement do not have an aggregate annual turnover of 50 million units of account.[105] Beyond the exclusion of minor agreements, Article 85 provides for exemptions to be granted by the Commission for individual agreements that have been "notified." In addition, the Commission may by regulation provide for block exemption of groups of similar types of agreements. The grounds for exemption vary, but involve a balancing in which the exemption is granted if the agreement has "appreciable

---

[101] TGI, 21 Septembre 1983, reported in *Expertises 1983*, no. 56, at 257; TGI, 8 Decembre 1982, reported in *Expertises 1983*, no. 48, at 31.

[102] See Heidrich, "Protection of Computer Programs Under German Copyright Law," 2 CLR 41 (1983).

[103] See Dratler, Daunt, Davidson, *Distribution of Computer Products to the Common Market and Japan* 15, in USC 4th Annual Computer Law Institute, May 11–13, 1983.

[104] Treaty of Rome, art. 85(1), March 25, 1957, 298 UNTS 3.

[105] OJ Eur. Comm. (No. C313) 3 (Dec. 29, 1977).

objective advantages of such a character as to outweigh the disadvantages which it causes on . . . competition. [The agreement] has to merit positive assessment from the point of view of the economy as a whole [and not merely to the participating companies]." [106]

Article 86 prohibits actions by "one or more firms to abuse a dominant position in the common market." This article has been applied to various activities of dominant firms, including the imposition of unfair pricing or trading conditions, limiting production or markets to the detriment of consumers, and imposing tying arrangements. As is true in the analogous U.S. antitrust law, the definition of what constitutes a "dominant position" in a particular case is difficult and involves substantial uncertainty. The term implies sufficient economic power to "prevent effective competition being maintained on a relevant market by giving it the power to behave to an appreciable extent independently of its competitors." [107] A market share of 40 percent may be held to constitute a dominant position. [108] Significantly, there is case law in both the Commission and the European Court of Justice indicating that a firm can be considered in a dominant position in a market defined by its own products, a proposition generally rejected in U.S. antitrust case law. [109] In line with this, major antitrust charges were pursued against IBM for the compatibles markets with one remedy being predisclosure of any system changes.

The status of exclusive licenses and various other license restrictions in software and hardware transactions is uncertain. The EEC is strongly oriented toward free movement of goods among countries, but in a recent decision it was established that an exclusive license of a patent in a particular territorial area did not violate Article 85 since a licensor can agree to not compete with its licensee. [110] In addition, the Commission has by regulation exempted certain forms of exclusive distributorship agreements that limit the dealer's market on a territorial basis. [111] These agreements may restrict the manufacture and distribution of competing products by the distributor, require the purchase of an entire line of goods, and preclude an active sales effort outside of a given geographic area. The exemption, however, only applies where there is significant intrabrand competi-

---

[106] Schlieder, "European Competition Policy," 50 Antitrust LJ 661, 663 (1982).

[107] United Brands v. EC Comm., Case 27/74 [1978] ECR 207.

[108] See OJ Eur. Comm. (No. L95) 1 (April 9, 1976).

[109] See Hugin Kassaregister AB v. EC Comm., Case 22/78 [1979] ECR 1869; see also OJ Eur. Comm. (No. L22) 23 (Jan. 25, 1978).

[110] Nungesser v. EC Comm., Case 258/78 [1982] ECR 2015.

[111] OJ Eur. Comm. (No. L173) 1 (June 30, 1983); Reg. No. 1983/83.

tion available to the consumer. The regulation forbids any measures, including use of exclusive intellectual property rights, to restrict such competition unduly.

Draft regulations are under consideration to block exemption of certain intellectual property licenses.[112] With an exception made for certain small and medium-sized companies, the proposed drafts generally permit restrictions on the initial manufacture of a product, but once manufactured within the EEC the product must be free to move among member countries. The draft also permits restrictions in licenses such as prohibitions on sublicensing, limitations on the field of use of the technology, and required observation of minimum quality restrictions. On the other hand, the proposed exemption does not apply if clauses prohibit a challenge to the validity of the patent, extend the agreement beyond the term of the intellectual property rights, set a maximum quantity to be manufactured, and restrict the licensee's assignment rights to any improvements made in the technology.[113] Individual exemptions may be available.

¶ 8.09   JAPAN

The primary protection for computer software in Japan is copyright law. As in the United States, Japanese copyright law applies to works of authorship that are defined to include: "a thing in which an idea or feeling is expressed in a creative way and which comes within the realm of literature, science, fine art or music."[114] Although no direct mention of computer software appears in the Japanese copyright law, the earliest decisions on the issue have concluded that programs contained in ROM fall within the definition of literary works under this statute.[115]

In contrast, current indications are that in most cases patent protection in Japan will not be available for computer software.[116] The Japanese patent law apparently is in the same position as U.S. patent law. No

---

[112] See Jerrard, "Applying the Rules of EEC Competition Law to Software Distribution and Licensing," 1 Comp. Law. 35, 37 (1984).

[113] Id. at 38.

[114] Law No. 48 of 1970 as amended, art. 2(1)1.

[115] See, e.g., Taito, Co. v. ING Enter. Co., 1979 Case No. 10867 (Tokyo Dist. Ct. Dec. 6, 1982); Grogan, "Status of Legal Protection in Japan," 1 Comp. Law. 25 (1984) (also discusses competing proposals of Japanese agencies to change protection for software); Davis, Greguras, Kawashima, "Legal Protection of Computer Software in Japan," 1 CLR 559 (1982).

[116] Davis, Greguras, Kawashima, "Legal Protection of Computer Software in Japan," 1 CLR 559 (1982).

express exclusion of computer software is applied, but there is a tendency toward substantially restricting availability to avoid granting patent protection to mathematical algorithms and mental processes.

Beyond issues of coverage of software under Japanese intellectual property laws are significant issues that arise when the terms of a technology agreement confront the prevailing Japanese law dealing with competitive practices. Questions of industrial policy and competitive practices are handled by two distinct agencies in Japan. The Ministry of International Trade (MITI) is primarily responsible for establishing general industrial policy. The Japanese Fair Trade Commission (JFTC) is primarily responsible for the enforcement of Japanese antimonopoly laws.

Under current law, any agreement between Japanese firm and a foreign company must be submitted for review by JFTC within 30 days after its execution.[117] This early submission permits both monitoring of business activities and early review for possible monopoly violations. The scope of Japanese antimonopoly law is broader than the equivalent U.S. law. It does not necessarily depend on a finding that particular contract terms have been imposed as a result of substantially uneven economic power. JFTC guidelines pertaining to international licensing agreements indicate that monopoly violations may occur

1. in territorial restrictions on the licensee's export of products except insofar as the restrictions pertain to areas in which the licensor is actively engaged in sales or licensed distribution;
2. restrictions on the Japanese licensee's purchase of competing products or technology, except in cases involving an exclusive license and any requirements as to from whom the licensee may purchase raw materials or components;
3. restrictions on distribution within Japan or on the resale price;
4. grant-back provisions pertaining to improvements on the licensed technology unless the licensor "bears similar obligations and the obligations of both parties are equally balanced in substance."
5. payment of royalties on products not using the technology unless this is a necessary computational device.[118]

---

[117] Law Relating to Prohibition of Private Monopoly and Methods of Preserving Fair Trade, Law No. 59, 1947.

[118] See Dratler, Daunt, Davidson, *Distribution of Computer Products to the Common Market and Japan* 32, in USC 4th Annual Computer Law Institute, May 11–13, 1983. Davis, Greguras, Kawashima, "Legal Protection of Computer Software in Japan," 1 CLR 559 (1982).

¶ 8.10 LESSER DEVELOPED COUNTRIES

The term "lesser developed country" (LDC) has become a synonym for a loosely defined, but large group of countries that are underdeveloped industrially, but may or may not have economically significant natural resources. The term connotes a spectrum of issues pertaining to the role of third world countries in international economic transactions. In large part, these stem from the fact that apart from natural resources such countries tend to be consumers, rather than producers of industrial or technological resources.

As applied to issues of technology trade and licensing, the law pertaining to individual LDCs is predictably diverse, reflecting the variety of cultural, geographic, and financial circumstances that are encompassed by this heterogeneous group. Despite this diversity, technology licensing as commonly practiced in international markets often presents a common set of issues central to the potential development of LDCs in technology industries. The result is that in several LDCs restrictive laws have been enacted pertaining to the terms of licensing agreements involving local industries[119] and a proposed international code of conduct (UNCTAD) has been drafted reflecting the LDC concerns.[120]

The issues posed by LDCs concerning technology agreements deal with the extent to which all or portions of developed technology can be regarded as a national asset and retained within the country. The thrust of the position favored by LDC policymakers is that, at least in part, local development defines a local asset. As a practical matter, technology in LDCs regularly will be at the mercy of developed countries and multinational corporations unless the LDCs are able to obtain some vested rights in technology developed in whole or in part within their borders.[121]

In most technology licensing involving an LDC, the licensee is a domestic company. Consequently, from the perspective of the LDC, licens-

---

[119] See Kantor, "Restrictions on Technology Transfer in Latin America," 68 TMR 552 (1978); Note, "Japan and the Introduction of Foreign Technology: A Blueprint for Less Developed Countries," 6 Stan. J. Int'l L. 171 (1981).

[120] UN Conference on Trade and Development, *Code of Conduct on Transfer of Technology*. See Joelson, "United States Law and the Proposed Code of Conduct on the Transfer of Technology," 23 Antitrust Bull. 835 (1978).

[121] Silverstein, "Sharing United States Energy Technology with Less-Developed Countries: A Model for International Technology Transfer," 12 J. Int'l L. & Econ. 363 (1978); Matsui, "The Transfer of Technology to Developing Countries: Some Proposals to Solve Current Problems," 59 J. Pat. Off. Soc'y 612 (1977); Note, "Multinational Corporations and Lesser Developed Countries—Foreign Investment, Transfer of Technology and the Paris Convention: Caveat Investor," 5 Dayton L. Rev. 105 (1980).

ing provisions that restrict export by the licensee and that require the licensee to grant back exclusive rights in any newly developed technology or modifications of the old technology tend to perpetuate the technology imbalance that currently exists. Thus, the pressure is toward domestic and, perhaps, international laws that limit the use of such agreements. At least to the extent that the protection is implemented individually in particular countries, however, the willingness of technology licensors to engage in transactions may be affected where these clauses are barred.

¶ 8.11 TRANSBORDER DATA FLOW

The increasing international importance of information, data analysis, and computer services to basic commercial and governmental functions, when coupled with advances in telecommunications, raises significant issues concerning the transmission of data other than technology across international borders.

The international issues associated with the movement of nontechnical data are commonly encompassed under the general term "transborder data flows."[122] The ultimate issue is the reconciliation of the international mobility of information assets with the desire of national governments to control valuable assets and critical processes related to their own operations and social systems. This understandable national interest is counterbalanced by the potentially significant impact on international financial and commercial operations if a technologically mobile asset is immobilized by parochial and competing national restrictions.

The issue of nontechnical data flow grows with the increasing capability for efficient transmission of nontechnical data internationally.[123] As a result of telecommunications, industries located in France, for example, need not conduct data processing and storage in that country. Efficiency and centralization for a multinational corporation may instead indicate the processing of data in a Canadian location with transmissions occurring via satellite.[124] Alternatively, the French company may hire a

---

[122] See generally House Comm. on Gov't Operations, Subcomm. on Gov't Information and Individual Rights, Int'l Information Flows: Forging a New Framework, HR Rep. No. 1535, 96th Cong., 2d Sess. (1980); Patrick, "Privacy Retrictions on Transnational Data Flows: A Comparison of the Council of Europe Draft Convention and OECD Guidelines," 21 Jurimetrics J. 405 (1981); Gotlieb, Dalfen, Katz, "The Transborder Transfer of Information by Communications and Computer Systems," 68 Am. J. Int'l L. 227 (1974).

[123] See HR Rep. No. 1535, 96th Cong., 2d Sess. 17 (1980).

[124] The effects of multiple, inconsistent regulations of data on an international basis are especially acute for multinational companies. See generally

data service bureau to process customer, inventory, and account data. That service bureau might be located in Sweden. A German bank considering a loan for an Italian company may desire financial information about other loans made in the United States or Japan to the same company. Alternatively, the German bank may desire to interest a U.S. bank in participating in the loan and, accordingly, communicate the relevant financial data to that bank. As these illustrations suggest, information is a uniquely mobile commodity and, unshackled from geographic limits by efficient telecommunications systems, it becomes an elusive asset to control or direct. There are several international concerns involved here. Consider, for example, the position of a country, large or small, in which all basic information about its own industries is processed in a neighboring country. There is a perceivable risk that the first country, despite being the host of the industries, will be in fact dependent on policy decisions of the second, information processing entity.

The risk of de facto dependence on data processing or information-rich countries is increasingly significant as information services grow in international importance. Given the sophisticated technology involved, it is unlikely that all countries could, under any circumstances, develop and maintain parallel capabilities in information services. The international community has little or no experience in dealing with information imbalance, however, and has been slow in responding to the need to develop a clear understanding of the issues that are posed.[125] The instinctive reaction may be to limit the extent to which nontechnical data can be transmitted outside of the originating country. Such an alternative would interfere substantially with international commercial and financial systems.[126] More importantly, over the long run, attempts to contradict and legislate away the direction of new technology and social change are almost certain to fail.

One manifestation of data flow problems involves the development of inconsistent international privacy protection for electronically stored or transmitted data. Chapter 12 will discuss the current status of privacy protection in the United States, but it is sufficient to note here that with the exception of certain fields of data collection the primary methods of privacy protection in the United States are relatively weak. They are

---

Coombe & Kirk, "Privacy, Data Protection and Transborder Data Flow: A Corporate Response to International Expectations," 39 Bus. Law. 33 (1983).

[125] Nanda, "The Communication Revolution and the Free Flow of Information in a Transnational Setting," 30 Am. J. Comp. L. 411 (1982 Supp.).

[126] See Coombe & Kirk, "Privacy, Data Protection and Transborder Data Flow: A Corporate Response to International Expectations," 39 Bus. Law. 33 (1983).

organized around individual action in administrative or judicial forums to enforce individual rights. In contrast, at least some Western countries have established more elaborate administrative and licensing systems for personal data creation and use in computer systems.[127] These systems apply to both governmental and private sector data systems and often establish relatively rigorous protection of individual privacy interests. The legislation adopted in most West European countries and in Canada is not consistent. Although a set of guidelines and draft legislation have been promulgated by an international organization, they have had little effect on national laws.[128] It is important to note that the systems specify in many cases what information may be retained about an individual and, in some countries, even the form in which the data may be stored. Given these limitations and assuming a lack of full consistency among countries, several obvious problems are apparent.

One basic consideration is how a country may effectively enforce privacy regulations in an environment in which information is an internationally transient asset. Given the mobility of the data, restrictions can be circumvented by transmission to other countries with either less restrictive regulations or, at least, regulations more in line with the data processing structure of the relevant company. Similarly, inquiries originated in one country in which data restrictions impede an answer might be directed through another jurisdiction in which the data can legally be stored and is available.

Even the methods for controlling data flow for privacy concerns have not been adequately identified. Two factors are clear, however, and significantly enhance the difficulty of the issues. First, to an extent far greater than in any other commercial context, the current and potential transnational mobility of information is a factor in policy-making. Restrictive legislation, unless matched in most potential locations for the data, will tend to drive the information processing and retention systems to more congenial locales. Second, national restrictions that disrupt available transmission capabilities have a potential for significantly disrupting international commercial and financial operations.

---

[127] See Burkert, "Institutions of Data Protection: An Attempt at a Functional Explanation of European National Data Protection Laws," 3 Comp. LJ 167 (1982); Novotny, "Transborder Data Flow Regulation: Technical Issues of Legal Concern," 3 Comp. LJ 105 (1982).

[128] See OECD, *Guidelines on the Protection of Privacy and Transborder Flows of Personal Data* (1981); Patrick, "Privacy Restrictions on Transnational Data Flows: A Comparison of the Council of Europe Draft Convention and OECD Guidelines," 21 Jurimetrics J. 405 (1981).

PART III

Information Age Issues

THE ADVENT OF WIDESPREAD use of powerful computer systems affects many functions in society. As earlier chapters indicate, significant legal and social policy issues surround the application of tax, contract, antitrust, and intellectual property principles to new forms of commercial value, intellectual development, and property transactions. Over time, resolution of these issues will substantially affect both the character of these areas of law as a whole and the manner of development within the computer and related industries.

While these issues are of vital significance, a further array of questions may ultimately have a greater effect on society and daily life. Categorizing these questions is difficult, but their effects are potentially ubiquitous and long-range, requiring not only the adaptation of existing legal concepts, but also the development of entirely new concepts of law, property, and civil rights. While these issues are referred to as questions of the "information age," that is only a label for multifarious and numerous issues of substance.

The chapters that follow begin an exploration of the legal issues involved in these social developments. The legal issues inherent in the characteristics of an information age are ultimately open-ended and unpredictable. As a consequence, Part III of this book is equally open-ended. These final chapters will expand as the information era advances.

CHAPTER *9*

Computer Crime

¶ 9.01 INTRODUCTION

The "information age" or "computer age" is characterized by the storage of vast amounts of information in major computer systems that are subject to remote access by telephone lines and other communications systems. Inherent in the systems are significant opportunities and very substantial risks: The most obvious risk is the potential for unauthorized access to and manipulation of information. The development of legal, as opposed to technological, responses to this unauthorized access is the subject of this chapter.

Unauthorized access or manipulation generally implicates criminal law and privacy law. (Chapter 12 discusses computer privacy.) Criminal law historically focuses on defining the limits of socially acceptable behavior. It imposes sanctions on acts that infringe property and personal interests of others and that are deemed sufficiently serious to call for criminal, in addition to civil, responses. Thus, the law of crimes concerns the taking of another's property (theft), inflicting personal injury on others, or the use or distribution of substances that have been defined as dangerous to society. Many criminal statutes have direct parallels in the law of torts or contracts dealing with personal remedies rather than public (criminal) sanctions.

In practice, criminal law can be reduced to two distinct questions: (1) Under what conditions is a particular act or sequence of conduct definable as criminal behavior? (2) How are criminal actions detected and prosecuted or defended? This chapter focuses on the first of these questions, an issue that involves, at least in part, defining the protectible scope of property in an electronic environment. Answers to this, in turn, will go far toward defining the ultimate character of the information age in relation to the legal system.

PART A.   DEFINITIONAL ISSUES

¶ 9.02 DEFINITIONAL PROBLEMS

The term "computer crime" has become a major concern of legislatures and administrations. It has been the subject of major federal legislative consideration.[1] Since 1976 over 25 states have enacted computer

---

[1] See Hearings on S.1766 Before the Subcommittee on Criminal Laws & Procedures of the Senate Committee on the Judiciary, 95th Cong., 2d Sess. 77 (1978); Hearings on S.240 Before the Subcommittee on Criminal Justice of the Senate Committee on the Judiciary, 96th Cong., 2d Sess. (1980); 130 Cong. Rec. H 1570 (March 13, 1984) (remarks of Rep. Hughes).

crime legislation.[2] In addition, computer crime has been the subject of a number of books and empirical studies.[3] The general perception is that computer crime is a major social concern whose incidence and economic importance are large and rapidly increasing. This general perception and the widespread activity that it has engendered are matched, however, by the lack of a clear consensus about the term "computer crime" and the appropriate response of the criminal law system to such crime. The definitional problem is at once the most frustrating and the most directly indicative aspect of the difficult social policy issues that are raised by unauthorized access to and use of computer systems.

Unauthorized access and use is a multifaceted phenomenon, with few parallels or connections among the various acts that might reasonably be described as computer crimes. At one end of the scale is a variety of traditional criminal acts that seemingly retain their criminal character when implemented through a computer. This might entail, for example, an embezzlement scheme made more lucrative by virtue of the high speed transmissions made possible by a computer. The pertinent question here is whether the criminal system is structured to provide for effective deterrence and prosecution in the new electronic environment. Detection and proof problems are exacerbated by electronic media. Clearly, however, criminal law is appropriately applied to these cases based on years of experience with theft-related crimes.

Conversely, a substantial portion of what is often described as computer crime is in fact new behavior that is socially troubling. This might include, for example, the actions of people who access a computer without authority, but do no damage and infringe no identifiable privacy right. The policy judgments are much more complex than those of traditional crimes "enhanced" by computers. They include whether and under what conditions a crime has occurred.[4] Similar issues pertain when the access is used to alter or destroy information. To what extent are or

---

[2] See infra discussion of state legislation at ¶¶ 9.04, 9.05, 9.06.

[3] See Parker, *Fighting Computer Crime* (1983); Bequai, *Computer Crime* (1978); Parker, *Crime by Computer* (1976); SRI Int'l, *Computer Crime: Criminal Justice Resource Manual* (1979); Turnick, "Computer Law: An Overview," 13 Loy. LAL Rev. 315 (1980); Comment, "Addressing Computer Crime Legislation: Progress and Regress," 4 Comp. LJ 195 (1983); Nycum, "The Criminal Law Aspects of Computer Abuse: Part I," 5 Rutgers J. Comp. & L. 271 (1976); Sokolik, "Computer Crime—The Need for Deterrent Legislation," 2 Comp. LJ 353 (1980).

[4] A particularly significant illustration concerns behavior involving unauthorized access to a computer without proven intent to defraud or commit theft. As discussed infra in ¶ 9.06, a number of states have enacted legislation that potentially applies criminal sanctions to this unauthorized conduct.

should criminal laws be extended to protect information as property? Furthermore, if these actions are to be criminalized, with what degree of severity should the law regard them and what factors, reasonably considered, would mitigate or aggravate the level of crime?[5]

Within an environment of substantially variant risks and vulnerabilities, therefore, what actions might be described as computer crime? There have been various efforts, generally unsuccessful, to achieve a consensus definition. Writing in 1978, Bequai commented

> There is no widely accepted definition of computer crime. Some authorities define it as making use of the computer to steal large sums of money. Others include theft of services within this definition. Some take an open approach [encompassing] the use of a computer to perpetrate any scheme to defraud others of funds, services or property.[6]

Some commentators have concluded that it is nonproductive to attempt a definition, suggesting instead that all computer crime falls into traditional criminal categories such as fraud or theft and differs from traditional crimes only in that it is computer-assisted.[7]

Nevertheless, a thread of certain actions would, by consensus, be described as computer crime[8] and the dispute concerning definition is

---

[5] One straightforward approach to assessing the level of criminal severity is to use traditional measures against analogous crimes. This leads to an emphasis on the value of the property affected by the criminal act. See infra ¶ 9.04[2]. Other alternatives may be more useful or more directly reflective of the level of concern. For example, there is an arguable difference in unauthorized access and meddling with the client records or treatment data of a hospital and with the information in an entertainment database. Greater criminal sanctions might apply to access of medical, national security, and other sensitive data. See 130 Cong. Rec. S633 (February 27, 1984) (remarks of Rep. Wyden) (introducing a bill to create the Medical Computer Crimes Act of 1984).

[6] Bequai, *Computer Crime* 3 (1978).

[7] See Taber, "On Computer Crime (Senate Bill S240)," 1 Comp. LJ 517 (1979).

[8] See Bequai, *Computer Crime* 3, 9 (1978). Parker suggests a four-part classification in which the computer is, respectively, the object, the environment, the instrument, or the symbol of the criminal act. Parker, *Fighting Computer Crime* 17 (1983). In contrast, Nycum suggested a classification based on the manner in which computer software is abused. See Nycum, "The Criminal Law Aspects of Computer Abuse: Part I," 5 Rutgers J. Comp. & L. 271 (1976). Another analyst suggests a categorization in terms of the stages of a computer operation that are susceptible to abuse or negligent error. Thus, distinctions would be made in terms of input of data, programming functions, central processing unit operations, output, and communications of data. See Bequai, *Computer Crime* 9–11 (1980). A federal study classified computer crime into (1) introduction of false data into a

beside the point. Although aspects of computer use in society create vulnerabilities or opportunities for abuse, these are not always qualitatively different from vulnerabilities that exist independently of computers. In many cases, however, the degree of risk and the nature of conduct are sufficiently different to raise questions about basic social decisions concerning levels of criminality for computer-related actions and the ability to discover and prosecute them under current law. Whether these are discussed under the heading of computer crime or merely as general criminal law problems is not important. The basic issue for the criminal justice system, as for so many aspects of society, is the manner in which the system should respond to new or altered patterns of conduct made possible or affected by computer technologies.

The discussion that follows concentrates on those actions most closely associated with the vulnerabilities created by computer use. To the extent it is necessary, the working definition of "computer crime" is that it consists of any abusive conduct definable as criminal behavior and concerning, facilitated by, or made more damaging or lucrative by the vulnerabilities created by increasing use of computer systems.

¶ 9.03 VULNERABILITY TO CRIME

In discussing computer crime, it is useful to identify the types of abusive activity that can be associated with computers and might be described as criminal acts or, at least, acts that could be labeled as crimes. One approach is to focus on the aspects of computer systems that have some level of vulnerability to third-party access and misuse.[9] Under this approach, five aspects of a computer system have been commonly described as susceptible to unauthorized intrusion or use: data input, programming, central data processing, data output, and electronic communications. Each of these is subject to manipulation of data (e.g., false input, modification of the existing data), direct theft of stored information (e.g.,

---

system, (2) unauthorized use of computer facilities, (3) altering or destroying data, and (4) taking money or services through a computer. GAO, *Computer Related Crimes in Federal Programs* 1 (1976); see also Comment, "A Suggested Legislative Approach to the Problem of Computer Crime," 38 Wash. & Lee L. Rev. 1173 (1981).

[9] A variety of different classification schemes have been suggested for analysis purposes. See Bequai, *Computer Crime* 3, 9 (1978); Parker, *Fighting Computer Crime* 17 (1983); Nycum, "The Criminal Law Aspects of Computer Abuse: Part I," 5 Rutgers J. Comp. & L. 271 (1976); GAO, *Computer Related Crimes in Federal Programs* 1 (1976); Comment, "A Suggested Legislative Approach to the Problem of Computer Crime," 38 Wash. & Lee L. Rev. 1173 (1981).

appropriation of trade secrets, unauthorized use of services), or destructive actions.

These various forms of intrusion may occur, however, with differing motivations or objectives, which presumably affect the treatment of the act under criminal laws. For example, in the classic computer-related fraud case, an embezzler may alter accounts or deposit data in the system to transfer funds to a personal account or to cover a prior act of embezzlement. Alternatively, a disgruntled employee may alter the content of an accounting system with the intention of disrupting the employer's business operations. A college student may access an IBM Corporation computer for pure enjoyment or to use the processing power for a computer game, or a competitor may access the same system intending to copy existing, proprietary data or programs.

The range and volume of computer-related vulnerabilities and threats are thus widely variant. For this reason, many discussions of computer crime eventually become essentially laundry lists of the diverse possibilities, perhaps with colloquial labels provided for the novice. This approach, however, tells little about the essential issues and how they relate to defining and enforcing criminal law sanctions against particular computer abuses. To approach this question more directly it is necessary to focus not on the technology, but on the manner in which computers are used. Essentially, four characteristics about the way in which computers are used create a vulnerability to abusive acts. These, in turn, constitute activity that society may wish to define as criminal or otherwise attempt to deter.

First, an increasingly large amount of valuable information is placed in computers and is often inaccessible in more traditional forms. The information may be valuable to persons other than the particular proprietor and a motivation for information copying may arise. In direct proportion to its value and unavailability in other forms, such information is also a tempting target for sabotage and other destructive actions against the proprietor. Although the fact that the information is stored in a computer or pertains to a computer does not change the motivation for destruction or copying, computer storage makes massive, rapid copying or destruction more feasible and a greater practical risk.[10]

Second, significant decisions and actions concerning business, financial, and other activities are increasingly made in whole or in part through a computer system with no immediate human validation. The vulnerability here is that the impersonal nature of the new decision-making system is prone to manipulation involving the transfer of assets or the like by

---

[10] See Ward v. Superior Court, 3 CLRS 206 (Cal. Super. Ct. 1972).

unauthorized means.[11] Traditional means of discovering unauthorized transfers before the fact do not operate in this environment. Furthermore, the speed of the processing and transfer of information accommodates large, rapid transfers. As a result, a greater vulnerability to fraudulent actions concerning property represented in or controlled by computer systems is at least perceived. The fraud may occur through the false input of data into a system or the manipulation of existing data.

Third, as computers become increasingly important, the availability of computer processing and storage capacity becomes an increasingly valuable asset in itself. Any analogy to real estate or personal property is insufficient, since appropriation of the property is not limited to actual theft of the computer hardware. More important, appropriation of processing power can occur through use—without any physical carrying away of the system or information. This, indeed, is not only a less risky form of appropriation, but may also be more efficient for the unauthorized user.[12] Significantly, perhaps, this theft can occur without ever denying the owner access to the same asset.

Fourth, although computers can operate as self-contained, stand-alone systems, computers that can access central processors from remote locations and transfer data (communicate) from one computer or system to another are increasingly prevalent. Communication can occur through telephone lines, private satellite-based systems, or other means. Ultimately, it is characterized by the ability of one computer user to access the system or intercept the transmission of another, given knowledge about appropriate access numbers and the like. Communications are central to the growing importance of computer use. They create, however, the clear vulnerability that third parties may access systems or intercept transmissions without authorization. The vulnerability of sensitive information, of decision-making systems, and of processing time thus extends beyond employees and other persons with physical access to the premises at which the central processing unit is stored. It includes virtually the entire world of computer users with access to telephone lines, subject only to the individuals' limitations of breaking through access codes and data coding techniques.[13]

Taken together, these various vulnerabilities create the anomalous picture of an increased capacity for rapid performance of complex tasks

---

[11] See Bequai, *Computer Crime* 13 (1978); Survey, "White Collar Crime: Computer Crime," 18 Am. Crim. L. Rev. 370, 372 (1980).

[12] See, e.g., Lund v. Virginia, 232 SE2d 745 (Va. 1977).

[13] Concerning illustrative remote access crimes, see Ward v. Superior Court, 3 CLRS 206 (Cal. Super. Ct. 1972); United States v. Seidlitz, 589 F2d 152 (4th Cir. 1978).

and a dramatically increased exposure of valuable property to abusive actions. Various technology-based actions can serve to reduce vulnerability, however. For example, while satellite transmission of data creates an environment in which competitors "overhear" transmissions with relative ease, private coding of data may reduce the ease of access and limit the risk of interception by unauthorized parties.[14] Similarly, secret access codes with multiple layers may deny the occasional or casual thief access to financial and other systems. Secret codes are themselves subject to unauthorized acquisition, however, that is increasingly probable as more people gain access to the systems. Although it may not be possible in practice to prevent access to all unauthorized people, neither has it been possible fully to protect noncomputer systems from unauthorized intrusion.

These vulnerabilities suggest the boundaries of risk involved in a computer-based environment. They are exacerbated by the extreme difficulty of discovery and prosecution of computer criminals, even when the computer crime is within the well-recognized scope of criminal law. Computer theft from financial institutions, for example, may leave no paper trail through which a thief can be discovered or identified in court. Similarly, eye witnesses are unlikely where a crime involves remote access of processing systems and tampering with data. Finally, any prosecution of a computer-related crime necessarily requires evidence and argument concerning an electronic world with which prosecutors, judges, and juries may not be familiar. These prosecution and detection problems increase the need for a well-defined conception of computer crime.

PART B.   STATE LAW

¶ 9.04 FINANCIAL FRAUD

Estimates of the total value of all computer crime-related losses in the U.S. economy vary widely, but an often-cited figure is that the value exceeds $10 billion annually.[15] It is clear that the dollar value of criminal computer abuses is high. It is equally clear that many computer-related

---

[14] See Chapter 12.

[15] See Volgyes, "The Investigation, Prosecution, and Prevention of Computer Crime: A State-of-the-Art Review," 2 Comp. LJ 385, 389 (1980); Parker, Nycum, Aura, *Computer Abuse* (Stanford Research Institute 1976); GAO, *Computer Related Crimes in Federal Programs* (1976); Problems Associated with Computer Technology, Computer Abuses, Sen. Comm. on Gov't Operations, 94th Cong., 2d Sess. 71–91 (1976).

crimes represent computer-assisted variations of traditional crimes such as theft and embezzlement.

The frequence of financial fraud as a form of computer crime arises in part from the reliance of financial institutions on computer processing systems. This reliance began almost from the onset of commercial computer use and has been paralleled by widespread adaptation of computers in corporate accounting functions by major and, increasingly, medium-sized and smaller businesses. As a result, criminal law concern about the untrustworthy employee in a financially sensitive position has assumed a computer-related dimension.

The introduction of computer systems did not create a new form of criminal behavior. Theft, fraud, misrepresentation, forgery, and other fraudulent activities remain. Computer systems are like traditional book-keeping systems in that they are subject to manipulation and to disbursement of funds based on fraudulent documents. Arguably, however, computer systems create a new methodology for ancient crimes and amplify the ability of the embezzler or fraudulent individual to obtain large sums of money or to operate undetected over a long period of time.

[1] Traditional Theft Crimes

Financial fraud involving computers can be prosecuted under state law by applying traditional theft-related criminal statutes. In many states, the criminal code retains common-law theft offenses, in whole or in part, providing for separate crimes of larceny, embezzlement, false pretenses, forgery, and similar crimes. These statutes focus on distinct forms of criminal behavior and may be mutually exclusive. As with noncomputer-based crime, electronic crime creates difficulties of classification in applying criminal law concepts.

One potential difficulty is in distinguishing larceny from embezzlement where the funds in question are represented in an electronic records system. The distinction between these crimes has historically focused on whether or not the employee-wrongdoer had lawful possession of the funds (embezzlement) before the crime.[16] Possession in an electronic environment may be difficult to determine. It should turn on control over disbursement of the funds. In most instances, however, the distinction between larceny and embezzlement has been eliminated under the modern theft statutes that combine these and other common-law property crimes into a single offense.

---

[16] See Lafave & Scott, *Criminal Law* § 89; Bequai, *Computer Crime* 31 (1978).

A second classification problem arises in distinguishing false pretenses (fraud/false representation) from forgery (false instrument/false signature). In a computer environment, checks might be issued directly by machine pursuant to data that a wrongdoer forges or otherwise fabricates. In such cases, the resulting crime is not forgery since the check was properly executed. Rather, a crime of fraud or false pretenses has occurred.[17] False data provided to a machine is assumed to be equivalent to misrepresentations to a human being. Given the use of computer systems that directly execute transactions, this assumption is both necessary and conceptionally justified to retain criminal sanctions against fraud.

The nature of the misappropriation is a potential issue even in states that have adopted modern theft statutes that replace the common-law crime categories. In these statutes, concepts such as "effective consent" are used to distinguish voluntary transfers of property from transfers accomplished by force, threat, fraud, and the like.[18] Clearly, the proprietor of the check disbursing system consents only to disbursing checks based on valid information. There is no difference in fact or law between a misrepresentation that involves taking property through a machine or one that involves taking directly from the person or an employee.[19]

[2] Computer Fraud

While there are extreme difficulties in prevention, discovery, and prosecution, financial fraud cases do not require a general reconceptualization of the criminal law pertaining to fraud and theft. Despite this, computer fraud has been a major focus for legislative action.[20] Computer fraud legislation is most commonly coupled with legislation dealing with misuse of computers independent of financial objectives; both types of criminal statute involve unauthorized access to a computer or computer

---

[17] United States v. Jones, 553 F2d 351 (4th Cir. 1977), cert. denied, 431 US 968 (1977).

[18] See Tex. Penal Code Ann. §§ 31.01(4), 31.03 (1974).

[19] Although this proposition seems relatively clear, at least one state has concluded that it required express recognition by statute. See Alaska Stat. § 11.46.990 (1980) ("In a prosecution . . . that requires 'deception' as an element, it is not a defense that the defendant deceived or attempted to deceive a machine [including a] computer.").

[20] See 5A Ariz. Rev. Stat. Ann. §§ 13-2301(E), 13-2316; Cal. Penal Code § 502 (West 1983); Del. Code Ann. tit. 11, §§ 857, 858 (1982); Ga. Code Ann. §§ 26-9951(a)–26-9953; Mich. Stat. Ann. §§ 752.791–752.797; NM Stat. Ann. §§ 30-16A-1–30-16A-4; NC Gen. Stat. §§ 14-453–14-456; ND Cent. Code §§ 12.1-06, 12.1-08; RI Gen. Laws §§ 11-52-1–11-52-4; Tenn. Code Ann. §§ 39-3-1401–39-3-1406; Utah Code Ann. § 76-6-703.

system. The distinguishing characteristic of computer fraud is that access occurs with the intent to execute a fraudulent scheme. The Delaware statute is illustrative: "Whoever knowingly . . . without proper authorization, accesses . . . any computer . . . for purpose of: (1) devising or executing any scheme to defraud [another], or (2) obtaining money, property or services . . . by means of false or fraudulent pretenses, representations or promises shall be guilty of computer fraud."[21] Computer fraud under these statutes is commonly treated as a felony. As is common in theft-related crimes, several computer fraud statutes scale the criminal sanction to the value of the property that is the subject of the fraud.[22]

As applied to financial crimes, computer fraud statutes serve two purposes. First, the statutes contain definitions of computer-related terms such as "access" and "network." The result is a modern statute that aids the prosecution by avoiding the problem of explaining to a jury both technical computer jargon and its awkward fit with common-law language. Second, the statutes create an offense based on proof of access with a particular intent, rather than proof of success in carrying away the property (money) that is the objective of the offense. This facilitates prosecution, but creates clear issues concerning proof of intent where the fraudulent acquisition of funds is not completed. This approach is designed to reflect the proof that is most likely to be available in computer fraud cases. Tracing the flow of proceeds without paper records is likely to be difficult and access may be the only clearly provable event.

In most states, computer fraud is a form of an "attempt crime" in that the object of the fraud need not be achieved to establish criminal liability. Furthermore, fraudulent representations need not have been made or communicated to another human being. Access, rather than representation, is the act defined as criminal. The emphasis on access as a criminal act is consistent with the related crime computer misuse that, discussed below, establishes criminal liability based on unauthorized access.[23] The net effect is a policy that views the computer as a protected asset. The protection is independent of actual loss to the proprietor as a result of an intrusion.

Computer fraud statutes are recent enactments whose ultimate interpretation will remain uncertain for many years. Significantly, however, one of the few variations among the state computer fraud statutes involves the requirement that access be "without authorization." Four

---

[21] Del. Code Ann. tit. 7 § 858a (1982).

[22] See, e.g., Mich. Stat. Ann. § 752.797; Utah Code Ann. § 76-6-703; NM Stat. Ann. § 30-16A-3.

[23] See infra ¶ 9.06[2].

states make the lack of authority an explicit aspect of the crime.[24] Arguably, this excludes cases in which the fraudulent individual is an employee whose wrongdoing is incidental to authorized use of the system.[25] If this interpretation holds, the result is to focus computer fraud on remote access crimes but the untrustworthy employee may be prosecuted under other criminal provisions. In contrast, employees are covered by computer fraud in the states using language without the requirement that access to the system be unauthorized. In those states, however, significant problems of proof arise in distinguishing operator error from intentional efforts to commit fraud where the alleged criminal is an employee with authorized access to the computer.

¶ 9.05 INFORMATION THEFT

Computer fraud statutes apply traditional concepts to a new environment. They are characterized by dealing with criminal behavior designed to obtain money or property. The methodology alone is new. In contrast, the increasing use of computer systems and the attendant movement of society into an information age have created a variety of new situations for criminal law in which the pertinent issues are not only whether enforcement can be conducted efficiently and with effective deterrence, but also whether and under what circumstances the acts in question are properly characterized as criminal.

One situation in which this issue arises concerns what can be described as "information theft." Information theft encompasses circumstances in which there has been access to and copying or taking of information in the form of data, computer programs, formulas, and the like. The affected conduct concerns not only the unauthorized use of computer systems, but also a broader array of unauthorized behavior. There is, however, a significant connection between information theft and the contemporary use of computers. The connection consists of both the increased value of information and the increased accessibility of that information through mechanical means.

[1] Tangibility, Tradition, and Policy Choices

It may be appropriate to describe a type of activity as information theft. Nevertheless, it is important to distinguish that activity from crimes

---

[24] See 5A Ariz. Rev. Stat. Ann. §§ 13-2301(E), 13-2316; Del. Code Ann. tit. 7, §§ 857, 858 (1982); Ga. Code Ann. §§ 26-9951(a)–26-9953; ND Cent. Code §§ 12-106, 12-1-08.

[25] See People v. Weg, 450 NYS2d 957 (NY Crim. Ct. 1982).

that involve obtaining money, real estate, or other tangible property formerly owned and controlled by the victim. On a technical level, there is a difference in the type of property involved. Cash and personal property are tangible, identifiable items. In contrast, the criminal who accesses a computer database and obtains secret information takes intangibles—the idea or information involved. This creates potentially important differences in the ability to establish that an appropriation occurred, rather than an independent development of the idea or information.

There is also a distinction in the effect of the theft on the victim. In the case of tangibles, the theft effectively deprives the original owner of the property itself, unless it is recovered. In contrast, unless accompanied by a destruction of the records, theft of information provides a gain to the wrongdoer but does not deprive the original owner of the property. Instead, the original owner may be deprived of the exclusivity and secrecy that had otherwise attached to the information. At a minimum, the owner is deprived of the presumed right to deny access to the particular wrongdoer who has accessed and taken the material. In the clearest case, prior to the theft, the owner of the information has exclusive control of secret information with the ability to use or license it for value. After the theft, the owner retains possession and use, but no longer exclusivity. Instead, the information is shared with the wrongdoer.

These differences do not necessarily suggest that the theft of tangibles and the theft of information should be treated differently. Obviously, it is easy to construct hypotheticals in which the theft of tangibles is far less disruptive than the theft of information. Such hypotheticals are increasingly valid as the importance of information and information-providing systems expands. Furthermore, it is clearly true that the civil law recognizes the importance of protecting the interest in exclusivity, at least where the subject material fits common-law concepts of trade secrecy.

The distinction between tangibles and intangibles is incorporated in traditional criminal law. Under traditional definitions in most states, larceny, embezzlement, and the more modern theft statutes exclude acts involving intangibles.[26] In part, this is accomplished through statutes that define "property" subject to theft as including only goods and chattels.[27] This, of course, creates difficulties in applying the laws to crimes such as accessing information bases or copying computer programs. Indeed, in states that retain traditional definitions of theft without

---

[26] See Nycum, "The Criminal Law Aspects of Computer Abuse: Part I," 5 Rutgers J. Comp. & L. 271, 275 (1976).

[27] See Lund v. Virginia, 232 SE2d 745 (Va. 1977); Lafave & Scott, *Criminal Law* 634.

modification, the ability to apply a criminal statute to a case of information appropriation is contingent on fortuitous characteristics of the act or an expansive interpretation of particular language in a statute.[28]

Because they are not directed at the type of behavior involved in information theft, traditional theft laws are difficult to apply to this environment. A basic characteristic of theft law in its traditional forms is the requirement that the defendant take and carry away or exercise control over the property of another or at least attempt to do so by illegal means.[29] This so-called asportation requirement has obvious relevance when the subject of the theft is tangible and moveable property. It has little direct applicability to a pure information theft, especially through a computer, since reading, copying, or memorizing the information is sufficient to appropriate its value. Nevertheless, there is at least a widespread belief that information theft is a crime that should be prosecuted under theft statutes in the face of other clear alternatives. The results are strained attempts to extend the idea of taking to effectively exclude the necessity that the original owner be deprived of the property.[30] Some decisions focus on peripheral involvement of tangible copies that can fit the carrying away requirement.[31] In contrast to such interpretations is the direct finding that taking information or services is not theft.[32]

A related difficulty in applying traditional theft statutes to information theft involves intention. Again, consistent with the focus of these statutes on tangible property, a requirement that the defendant intend to steal is typical. In many statutes, this is clarified as an intent permanently to deprive the other party of the property.[33] Under this definition, mere copying of a program or data is not sufficient since the original owner,

---

[28] See Ward v. Superior Court, 3 CLRS 206 (Cal. Super. Ct. 1972) (unnecessary carrying away of printout sufficient to meet tangibility); Hancock v. State, 402 SW2d 906 (Tex. Ct. App. 1966) (program is within statutory reference to "writing"). See generally Bender, "Trade Secret Protection of Software," 30 Geo. Wash. L. Rev. 909, 945, 946 (1970); Lafave & Scott, *Criminal Law* 633 (not all state law exclude intangible property).

[29] See Lafave & Scott, *Criminal Law* 631.

[30] See Gemignani, "Computer Crime–The Law in '80," 13 Ind. L. Rev. 681, 683 (1980); Nycum, "The Criminal Law Aspects of Computer Abuse: Part I," 5 Rutgers J. Comp. & L. 271, 284 (1976). Bequai suggests that in the taking requirement "what matters is that the wrongdoer has set in motion any agency, either animate or inanimate, with the design of effecting an illegal transfer of possession of some property of another to him." Bequai, *Computer Crime* 29–30 (1978).

[31] See Ward v. Superior Court, 3 CLRS 206 (Cal. Super. Ct. 1972).

[32] See Lund v. Virginia, 232 SE2d 745 (Va. 1977).

[33] Lafave & Scott, *Criminal Law* 637–638.

while deprived of some value, is not permanently deprived of the program or data itself.[34]

In reviewing these difficulties, it has become common for computer experts to conclude that traditional statutes are archaic and inadvertently exclude an important area of theft under contemporary conditions. In fact, regardless of current needs to change or expand focus, the emphasis of traditional theft law represents an explicit decision to exclude criminal prosecution for theft of intangibles. This express, traditional choice is the source of current difficulties in applying the statutes to information crimes. The difficulties in applying traditional criminal law to information theft can be and have been solved in many jurisdictions through legislative action, but these solutions do not resolve archaic loopholes in contemporary law. Rather, expansion of theft-like criminal sanctions to include information theft represents a clear policy decision that creates a new form of crime.

The protectible interest supporting this decision is clear. The value of information is high and increasing but need not always be protected by criminal law sanctions. Contract and tort law are also available as private sanctions. The policy question is the extent to which public sanctions should be added. The legislative answers have not been consistent or necessarily supportable. There is a need to recognize that some information is valuable and not adequately protected through civil law remedies, while other information is less vulnerable or valuable. This distinction is vital for the development of the law of crimes in an information society.

[2] Modified Theft Statutes

One common response to a perceived inadequacy of existing theft law applicable to information crimes is to redraft the theft-related statutes to encompass information-related actions.[35] On its surface, redefinition of existing theft laws appears to be the most direct response to information theft and has been accomplished in several states by restating the

---

[34] See Gemignani, "Computer Crime—The Law in '80," 13 Ind. L. Rev. 681, 693 (1980); Bequai, *Computer Crime* 30 (1978).

[35] See statutes redefining "property" under theft statutes to include computer data and software. Md. Ann. Code art. 27, § 340; Ohio Rev. Code Ann. §§ 2901.01, 2913.01 (Page); Va. Code §§ 18.2–98.1; Wash. Rev. Code Ann. § 9A.56.010; Colo. Rev. Stat. § 18-5.6-101(8) (property includes "information, including electronically produced data, and computer software . . . in either machine readable or human readable form.") Accord Wyo. Stat. § 6-3-502; RI Gen. Laws § 11-52-1; Mont. Code Ann. § 45-2-101(54); Minn. Stat. § 609.87 (1984); see also Alaska Stat. § 11.46.985 (defining deception to include deceiving a computer).

definition of "property" subject to theft (or larceny) under applicable laws.[36] The current definition of "property" in the Ohio Criminal Code is illustrative: 'Property' includes but is not limited to electronically processed, produced or stored data, data while in transit, computer programs in either machine or human readable form, and any original or copy of a document associated with computers."[37] This definition covers information theft pertaining to computers, but may not encompass trade secret thefts unrelated to computer data or documents. In several states, this omission is directly cured in the property definition.[38]

An initial problem with the property redefinition approach lies in the fact that the remainder of the theft or larceny statutes are commonly left intact. As a result, while the definitional change expresses a clear legislative intent to include information crime, ambiguities arise in the nature of the intent required for the act and in the extent to which asportation requirements continue to be relevant.[39] In some cases, these ambiguities are resolved along with the definitional issue. For example, in Washington an intent to deprive the owner of property is required for theft, but "deprive" has been redefined: "In addition to its common meaning ["deprive" means] to make unauthorized use or an unauthorized copy of records, information, data, trade secrets, or computer programs, provided that the aforementioned are of a private proprietary nature."[40] Thus, an intent to use or copy is included within the definition of "theft" if it relates to private, proprietary materials.

The more significant policy issue lies in determining the scope of the legislation. In themselves, theft-related statutes provide no clear limitations on the type of information that might be subject to redefined theft. Absent further qualification, redefining property to include data creates the potential of a theft prosecution for accessing widely known information, for information available to the public but for which a particular defendant was not authorized to search, or for unauthorized access to information for which there was no effort to retain secrecy.

---

[36] In a number of states, the redefinition of basic theft statutes is also accompanied by additional legislation relating to computer fraud or misuse. See Colo. Rev. Stat. § 18-5.6-101(8) (property includes "information, including electronically produced data, and computer software ... in either machine readable or human readable form."). Accord Wyo. Stat. § 6-3-502; RI Gen. Laws § 11-52-1; Mont. Code Ann. § 45-2-101(54); Minn. Stat. § 609.87 (1984).

[37] Ohio Rev. Code Ann. § 2901.01(J)(1).

[38] Md. Ann. Code art. 27, § 340(h)(11).

[39] See supra ¶ 9.05[1].

[40] Wash. Rev. Code Ann. § 9A.56.010(e)(5).

The extent to which any of these should be considered criminal conduct has been insufficiently examined. Particularly for widely known information, the argument for imposing criminal liability is weak since the loss to the proprietor is relatively limited. As a result, restrictions whereby criminal sanctions are applied only if the data is of a private proprietary nature are both common and appropriate, although they are not universal. For example, the Ohio legislation encompasses electronic data but defines the intent to deprive the owner as including the intent to "use . . . property . . . with the purpose not to give proper consideration in return . . . and without reasonable justification or excuse for not giving proper consideration."[41]

Redefining information theft within traditional theft law establishes that the severity of the sanctions for the crime are determined by the value of the property involved. The determination of the value of intangibles presents potential problems that affect not only these statutes, but other situations in which value is an aggravating factor for computer or information-related crime.[42]

[3] Trade Secret Theft

Although not necessarily limited to computer-related cases of information theft, an increasingly significant state law response to information crimes occurs in the form of statutes prohibiting theft of trade secrets. As of this writing, 25 states have adopted trade secret or intellectual property theft statutes.[43] In general, theft of trade secret statutes track common-law concepts in defining the subject matter to which the statute applies. As discussed in Chapter 3, the underlying definition of "trade secret" in terms of civil liability relates to material of relative novelty and secrecy that conveys a commercial benefit or advantage to its possessor.[44] Within this definition, common-law trade secrecy is not limited to tangible items; the criminal law counterpart shares this scope. The California Penal Code definition of a trade secret is illustrative. A "trade secret" is "any scientific or technical information, design, process, procedure, formula, computer program or information stored in a computer . . . which is secret and is not generally available to the public and [which] gives one who uses it an

---

[41] Ohio Rev. Code Ann. § 2913.01(C)(3).

[42] See supra ¶ 9.05[4].

[43] The states include Alabama, Arkansas, California, Colorado, Delaware, Florida, Georgia, Illinois, Maine, Massachusetts, Michigan, Minnesota, Missouri, New Hampshire, New Jersey, New Mexico, New York, North Carolina, Oklahoma, Pennsylvania, Tennessee, Texas, Wisconsin, and Wyoming.

[44] Restatement (First) of Torts § 757.

advantage over competitors who do not know of or use the trade secret."[45]

Although oriented toward theft of intangibles, trade secret legislation reflects a conflict in the type and degree of protection that is designed into the process.[46] Thus, some trade secrecy statutes include a requirement that a tangible embodiment of the secret information be taken. In *Ward v. Superior Court*,[47] this aspect of the California statute was held to preclude prosecution based solely on telephone impulses conveying a computer program, but included the carrying away of a tangible, hard copy. The tangibility requirement here, insofar as it is reasonable, serves to require physical evidence of misappropriation.

The trade secret legislation limits criminal sanctions to cases in which the information was held in relative secrecy and had identifiable commercial value. This excludes information made available to the public, even under subscription agreements. The pertinent interest of the victim that is being protected by such legislation is the commercial advantage that flows from secret information or processes. This interest is lost, at least in part, with surreptitious acquisition. By definition, an interest in secrecy or exclusivity cannot be taken when the information is public knowledge.

The nature of the secrecy, novelty, or other characteristics required to establish a sufficient proprietary claim creates potential ambiguities that may be acceptable in civil law, but are uncommon and undesirable in criminal law. In an effort to avoid this uncertainty and redirect trade secret legislation, several statutes contain presumptions as to the trade secret status of particular information. These focus on the efforts of the proprietor to maintain secrecy. For example, the California statute establishes a presumption that the information is "secret" if the owner "takes measures to prevent it from becoming available to other persons other than those selected by the owner."[48] The Wyoming statute is broader. It builds a presumption that all elements of trade secrecy are present if the owner takes measures to prevent the information from becoming available to other than selected persons who have access for limited purposes.[49] With these statutory presumptions, the focus of the criminal pro-

---

[45] Cal. Penal Code § 499(c)(9) (West 1983).

[46] See Bender, "Trade Secret Protection of Software," Geo. Wash. L. Rev. 909, 944 (1970); Nycum, "The Criminal Law Aspects of Computer Abuse: Part I–State Penal Laws," 5 Rutgers J. Comp. & L. 271, 276 (1976).

[47] 3 CLRS 206 (Cal. Super. Ct. 1972). Compare Hancock v. State, 402 SW2d 906 (Tex. Ct. App. 1966).

[48] Cal. Penal Code § 499(c).

[49] Wyo. Stat. § 6-3-502(xi).

vision shifts. The essence of the statute is oriented to imposing criminal sanctions to enforce and reward efforts of the proprietor of information to maintain its secrecy.

[4] Valuation

In a number of information theft and computer fraud statutes the value of the property that has been taken is a determining factor in affixing the severity of the criminal act.[50] This is consistent with traditional forms of affixing criminal severity in theft. For intangible property, however, valuation questions can produce quixotic and troublesome issues.

The most quixotic of these is whether the value of the information can or should be segregated from the value of the medium on which it is recorded. Thus, it might be argued that where a secret formula of commercial significance is taken, the value of the property stolen can be computed based on the value of the notebook paper on which it was written.[51] The mere statement of this position illustrates its inherent weakness. Such an analysis fails to reflect the true value of the theft to either the thief or the original owner. Consequently, it is not surprising that the first court to consider the question directly for computer software held that the value of the theft must be computed in consideration of both the tangible and intangible property that was taken.[52]

Assuming that the intangibles are properly considered, there remain questions about the appropriate reference for determining the value of the property. Three alternatives are available and the choice is largely determined by specific statutory language in a given jurisdiction. The first focuses on the market value of the property.[53] In general, this standard directs attention to the price that a willing buyer and seller would arrive at on the open market. Obviously, this market pricing includes the value of the information. In fact, for significant secret information there may be no real market value and at best only a hypothetical market reference, if

---

[50] See, e.g., SD Codified Laws Ann. § 43-43B-4,5,6,7; Ill. Rev. Stat. § 16-9; Mo. Ann. Stat. § 569-095 (Vernon); NM Stat. Ann. §§ 30-16A-3, 30-16A-4; Comment, "Addressing Computer Crime Legislation—Progress and Regress," 4 Comp. LJ 195 (1977).

[51] See Gemignani, "Computer Crime—The Law in '80," 13 Ind. L. Rev. 681, 693 (1980); Bender, "Trade Secret Protection of Software," Geo. Wash. L. Rev. 909, 947 (1970).

[52] Hancock v. State, 402 SW2d 906 (Tex. Ct. App. 1966), aff'd sub nom., Hancock v. Decker, 379 F2d 552 (5th Cir. 1967). Compare Lund v. Virginia, 232 SE2d 745 (Va. 1977) (where no market value is proven, actual value applies to printout and does not include the cost of producing the printout).

[53] See Minn. Stat. § 608.87(10); 18 USC 641 (1982).

any, can be found. The second standard consists of actual value in the form of cost to create or replace.[54] Finally, a number of statutes have directed attention squarely to the harm caused to the victim through a measurement of value in terms of the loss to the original owner. The Minnesota definition is illustrative:

> [The] value of electronic impulses . . . data or information, computer software or programs . . . shall be considered to be the amount of the economic loss that the owner of the item might reasonably suffer by virtue of the loss of the item. The determination of the amount of such economic loss includes but is not limited to consideration of the value of the owner's right to exclusive use or disposition.[55]

¶ 9.06 ACCESS AND USE CRIMES

The combination of computer fraud and information theft statutes do not exhaust the potential criminal justice issues in unauthorized activities concerning computer systems. These statutes focus on conduct that is most readily compared to historical conceptions of criminal activity, but beyond theft-like actions, a range of intrusive conduct might and, at least in some jurisdictions, has been subjected to criminal sanctions. In general, these involve activities such as unauthorized access and use of computer systems as well as intentional, unauthorized modification of computer data.

These actions are the most difficult to fit into traditional criminal categories. Nevertheless, they are among the most significant in defining the level of protection for the developing role of computer systems. By establishing a criminal law umbrella over acts involving access and use, a general expectation of the importance of maintaining the integrity of computer systems might be established. Even stripped of an intention to injure, the act of intruding into a computer system may be disruptive.

> The aspect of wrongful intrusion into a processing queue, which is most difficult to fit into traditional charging language, is therefore the one that most justifies statutory description. The intrusion engenders a ripple effect, which can disrupt or even destroy property. The property, though in the form of impulses invisible to the

---

[54] See Gemignani, "Computer Crime—The Law in '80," 13 Ind. L. Rev. 681, 700 (1980); Bender, "Trade Secret Protection of Software," Geo. Wash. L. Rev. 909, 947 (1970).

[55] See Minn. Stat. § 45-2-101(69)(a)(iii) (1984).

keenest microscope . . . nonetheless can represent and affect personal endeavor and individual rights.[56]

The policy questions, of course, are whether and to what extent access, with or without an intention to injure the system, should constitute a criminal offense.

[1] Criminal Access to a Computer

At least 10 states have enacted criminal statutes that define unauthorized access to a computer as a criminal offense.[57] In these statutes, "access" is commonly defined to mean "to approach, instruct, communicate with, store data in, retrieve data from, or otherwise make use of any resources of, a computer or computer system."[58] The criminal penalties attach regardless of the intention of the unauthorized user and regardless of whether any damage is done to the system involved or the data that it contains. Thus, for example, the Arizona statute defines "unauthorized access" as a form of computer fraud in which: "A person commits computer fraud in the second degree by intentionally and without authorization accessing . . . any computer . . . or any computer software, program or data contained in such computer."[59] In most other states that have adopted this form of criminal sanction, the offense is described as computer abuse, but is defined in virtually the same manner.

Criminalization of access separate from any damage, theft, or intent to damage or take can be viewed in either of two ways. One interpretation is that the crime is regarded as a lesser included offense of the crime of computer fraud or information theft. This is supported by the fact that criminal access statutes are commonly found in states that also have adopted fraud statutes. Furthermore, the crime of computer fraud is defined in terms of access with a particular intention.[60] The lesser included crime then excludes a need to prove intent.

---

[56] Tunick, "Computer Law: An Overview," 13 Loy. LAL Rev. 315, 326 (1980).

[57] See 5A Ariz. Rev. Stat. Ann. § 13-2316; Del. Code Ann. tit. 11, § 858; Ga. Code Ann. § 26-9952(a); Mich. Stat. Ann. § 752.795; NM Stat. Ann. §§ 30-16A-3, 30-16A-4; NC Gen. Stat. § 14-454; ND Cent. Code § 12.1-06.1-08; RI Gen. Laws §§ 11-52-1–11-52-4; Tenn. Code Ann. § 39-3-1404; Utah Code Ann. § 76-6-703.

[58] Del. Code Ann. tit. 11, § 858(b)(6). This definition is repeated in virtually all of the computer fraud legislation and legislation dealing with misuse through unauthorized access.

[59] 5A Ariz. Rev. Stat. Ann. § 13-2316(B).

[60] See supra ¶ 9.04.

The alternative interpretation is that the access statutes represent a legislative judgment that unauthorized access, without more, is a serious, socially disruptive act. Clearly, there is factual support for this positon. As the use of computer databases increases in importance, its value as an asset increases. Unauthorized intrusions attain a significant level of seriousness. Stripped of the intent to take information, modify records, or devise and execute a fraudulent scheme, the focus of the statute is on a form of privacy interest. Thus, the apparent conclusion is that there is an interest protected by criminal law in maintaining the integrity of a computer system even against people with no further intent at disruption.

Stated in these terms, it is arguable that criminalizing mere access may be an overreaction, insofar as more than relatively minor sanctions are imposed. The statutes may have more to do with the threat of damage or other more abusive acts once access has occurred. In any event, the existing statutes reflect a wide divergence in the apparent degree of seriousness that legislators have attached to access per se. The statutory penalties for crimes of mere access range from a felony with a sentence of from zero to fifteen years in Georgia to a misdemeanor offense in North Carolina.[61]

[2] Computer Use Crimes

Given the definition of access discussed in the preceding section, it is apparent that those states that have adopted a criminal sanction for the crime of unauthorized access have, in effect, also criminalized most aspects of unauthorized use of a computer system. An additional number of states have adopted criminal legislation pertaining to unauthorized use of a computer or computer system.[62] Often, the definition of unauthorized "use" consists of unauthorized access to the computer system.[63]

In cases of unauthorized use of computer services, it is apparent that in most states the defendant's conduct will not fall within traditional larceny or theft statutes, since the services (e.g., data processing) are clearly intangible property. The same, of course, could be said for any other form of services that might be obtained through artifice. As a consequence, most states have adopted general theft of services statutes that, in most

---

[61] Ga. Code Ann. § 26-9952(a); Mich. Stat. Ann. § 752.795; NM Stat. Ann. §§ 30-16A-3, 30-16A-4; NC Gen. Stat. § 14-454.

[62] See, e.g., Wyo. Stat. § 6-3-504; Fla. Stat. Ann. § 915-06; Mo. Ann. Stat. § 569.095; Colo. Rev. Stat. § 18-5.5-102; Ill. Ann. Stat. § 16-9; Mont. Code Ann. § 45-6-311.

[63] See Wyo. Stat. § 6-3-504; Ill. Ann. Stat. § 16-9.

cases, appear to encompass theft of computer services through unauthorized use.

A common pattern in the adopted legislation that deals specifically with use of a computer is to address two distinct criminal actions concerning computer use. The Wyoming statute is illustrative.

> A person commits a crime against computer users if he knowingly and without authorization: (i) Accesses a computer. . . . (ii) Denies computer system services to an authorized user of the computer system services which, in whole or part, are owned by, under contract to, or operated for, on behalf of, or in conjunction with another.[64]

The significance of this two-tiered structure is that it manifests an explicit legislative judgment about the importance of computer services. The statute penalizes unauthorized use, but also prohibits actions that deny access to an authorized user in situations involving time share or other data processing service systems. The policy judgment manifest in such statutes is that reliance on computer system access and use is an important, protected interest.

[3] Criminal Modification of Data

Computer systems in which significant operational and research data are stored represent valuable assets, but they are also assets that are peculiarly vulnerable to external intrusion. In many cases, unauthorized access or use is connected to an intention to appropriate information or implement a fraudulent scheme. The other major threat is that the unauthorized user will intentionally or negligently destroy or alter the data in the system. Such actions might immediately disable the system and the activities conducted in reliance on the data. Alternatively, if data modification rather than destruction is involved, the intrusion may lead to continuing business operations based in part on inaccurate information that may not be discovered for some time.

Manipulation or destruction of data is a significant threat to computer systems independent of fraudulent or other schemes. Such action, however, does not readily fit into common crimes such as vandalism since the material involved is intangible. As a result, over 15 states have direct criminal sanctions for unauthorized alteration, modification, or destruction of computer data, including computer programs.[65]

---

[64] Wyo. Stat. § 6-3-504.

[65] See, e.g., RI Gen. Laws § 11-52-3; SD Codified Laws Ann. § 43-43B-5; Mont. Code Ann. § 45-6-311; Colo. Rev. Stat. § 18-5.5-102; Ill. Ann. Stat. § 16-9(b)(2); NC Gen. Stat. § 14-455; Del. Code Ann. § 858(b); Ga. Code Ann. § 26-

In many cases, data vandalism is defined as criminal in the same statute that prohibits unauthorized access or use of a computer. In most cases, the level of penalty for access and for vandalism are identical. Thus, there is a wide variation in the degree of severity attached to unauthorized, knowing alteration of computer data, ranging from misdemeanor treatment to characterization as a felony with a maximum sentence of 15 years in prison. In cases where the alteration or destruction of data pertains to a scheme to defraud or commit theft, the more specific computer fraud, information theft, or general theft statutes apply, with a higher sentence range.

[4] Severity and Information Type

Statutes regarding computer access, use, or vandalism reflect overall judgments about the social need to protect against abuse of information processing systems independent of theft-related intentions. The general recognition of this social interest, however, presents questions of whether the severity of the criminal behavior varies depending on the type of data or system that has been abused.

As presently drafted, most state statutes related to these crimes make no distinctions between types of information systems. Neither do they generally provide different sanctions for mere access or for data destruction. Instead, to the extent that distinctions are drawn, they differentiate between access and vandalism on the one hand, and access with the intent to defraud on the other.[66] Thus, the computer hacker who merely accesses a university student records system is treated no differently in the statutes than one who accesses and modifies hospital patient records.[67]

PART C.   FEDERAL CRIMES

¶ 9.07 FEDERAL CRIMINAL LAW

Traditionally, the federal government has taken a secondary role in the definition of property crimes except insofar as they infringe on identi-

---

9952a(b); ND Cent. Code § 12.1-06.1-08; Cal. Penal Code § 502(a)(8)(d); Ariz. Rev. Stat. Ann. § 13-2316(B); Mich. Stat. Ann. § 752.795.

[66] See Ariz. Rev. Stat. Ann. § 13-2316; Del. Code Ann. § 858; NC Gen. Stat. § 14-455; ND Cent. Code § 12.1-06.1-08.

[67] See 130 Cong. Rec. E633 (February 27, 1984) (remarks of Rep. Wyden introducing the proposed Medical Computer Crimes Act of 1984).

fiably federal institutions or interests.[68] However, since computer crime often involves communication with remote computers or transfers within the banking industry, the nature of the criminal activity often directly affects areas that have had substantial federal involvement. As a result, a significant number of prosecutions for computer offenses have occurred under federal law.

[1] Theft of Government Property

One statute frequently used for computer-related offenses is Section 641 of the federal code, which prohibits theft, embezzlement, or conversion of property of the United States.[69] As this indicates, the statute applies only where the United States has a property interest in the subject of the theft. Within this limitation, however, it appears that the statute applies even though the subject matter is intangible in the form of information theft though a computer.

Since Section 641 encompasses theft of any "thing of value" that belongs to the United States, the computer crime issue turns on whether a thing of value encompasses intangibles such as information, data, and computer programs. The cases considering this issue have concluded that the statutory terms extend beyond common-law theft concepts of tangible property. For example, in *United States v. Girard*[70] the Second Circuit Court of Appeals interpreted Section 641 expressly to include intangible information. *Girard* involved the misappropriation of information in Drug Enforcement Administration files. Other decisons have indicated clearly that the concept of intangible things of value is workable under Section 641. For example, in *United States v. Sampson*[71] a district court applied Section 641 to encompass computer time services.[72]

[2] Communications Abuses

One historical aspect of federal law consists of a concern about interstate transportation and communications. Consistent with this, two separate federal statutes pertain to criminal fraud activities that extend on an interstate basis or involve federal forms of communications. Section 1341

---

[68] See generally Lafave & Scott, *Criminal Law.*

[69] 18 USC § 641 (1982).

[70] 601 F2d 69 (2d Cir.), cert. denied, 444 US 871 (1979); see also United States v. Truong Dinh Hung, 629 F2d 908 (4th Cir. 1980).

[71] 6 CLRS 879 (ND Cal. 1978).

[72] See Nycum, "The Criminal Law Aspects of Computer Abuse: Part II—Federal Criminal Code," 5 Rutgers J. Comp. & L. 297 (1976).

prohibits mail fraud and applies to any use of the mails to execute or attempt a scheme to defraud. [73] Section 1343 applies to any use of wires, radio, or television communication to accomplish a fraudulent purpose across state lines.

Both of these statutes may apply to computer crimes that involve interstate communications. The statutes are restricted to crimes that involve the pertinent form of communications as well as the existence of a fraudulent scheme. In *United States v. Seidlitz*, [74] for example, the wire fraud statute was applied to a misappropriation of computer software through a remote terminal in which the electronic impulses representing the appropriated information crossed state lines.

Not all uses of interstate wires in a fraudulent scheme are sufficient to invoke federal criminal law, however. The wire fraud statute is limited to cases in which the interstate transmission is an "essential element" of the fraudulent scheme. [75] As a result, the mere fact that an interstate transaction involving interstate wires is involved in the fraud is insufficient. In *United States v. Computer Services Corp.*, [76] the statute was held inapplicable to a fraudulent overbilling scheme involving computer services provided by wire across state lines. The transmission of data by wire was not pertinent to the fraud. The court noted that "[the] only involvement of the interstate wires in this case was the use of the wires to provide this service. There is no allegation that the service was in any way deficient or fraudulent. None of the false representations are alleged to have been communicated over the interstate wires." [77] In contrast, a fraudulent scheme involving airline tickets in which the tickets were controlled by a remote computer situated across state lines was held to fall within the wire fraud statute. [78]

A related concern involves the extent to which private, unauthorized interception of data transmissions falls within federal criminal law. The major federal legislation pertaining to interception and theft of information are the wiretapping provisions of the Omnibus Crime Act. [79] As discussed in Chapter 12, this statute apparently does not apply to nonaural interceptions of information [80] or to interceptions from stages of data

---

[73] 18 USC § 1341 (1982).

[74] 589 F2d 152 (4th Cir. 1978).

[75] United States v. Giovengo, 637 F2d 941 (3d Cir. 1980).

[76] 511 F. Supp. 1125 (ED Va. 1981).

[77] Id. at 1135.

[78] United States v. Giovengo, 637 F2d 941 (3d Cir. 1980).

[79] 50 USC § 1809 (1982).

[80] See United States v. New York Tel. Co., 434 US 159, 167 (1977); ¶ 12.04.

communications that do not involve wires but are accomplished through radio or other broadcast technology.

[3] Interstate Stolen Goods

Interstate transportation of stolen goods is prohibited under federal criminal law.[81] The significant limitation of this statute for computer-related offenses is the limitation to transportation of "goods," which seemingly limits the application of the statute to cases in which a tangible item is transported across state lines. One observer suggests that this should apply to cases in which a copy of data or a program is transported.[82] The leading case concerning computer crimes under this statute, however, confirms that interstate transmission of electronic impulses representing a computer program is not within the statute.[83]

[4] Electronic Funds Transfer Crime

In light of the current and increasing use of electronic financial services,[84] it is likely that significant computer crimes involving the automated systems of financial institutions will continue. As a result, criminal legislation dealing directly with such offenses is of great potential effect. Electronic funds transfer (EFT) systems have, almost from the outset of their development, come under federal control at least in part. For the purposes of this discussion, the pertinent statute relating to criminal and other activites is the Electronic Funds Transfer Act (EFTA).[85] This statute defines an electronic funds transfer as any "transfer of funds ... which is initiated through an electronic terminal, telephonic instrument, or computer ... [to] authorize a financial institution to debit or credit an account."[86]

In addition to consumer and other provisions, the EFTA contains criminal provisions relating to the misuse of an EFT system. The EFTA applies to the misuse of a debit instrument, which is defined to include any "card, code, or other device, other than a check ... by the use of

---

[81] 18 USC § 2314 (1982).

[82] See Nycum, "The Criminal Law Aspects of Computer Abuse: Part II—Federal Criminal Code," 5 Rutgers J. Comp. & L. 297, 308 (1976).

[83] United States v. Seidlitz, 589 F2d 152 (4th Cir. 1978).

[84] Electronic transactions and their legal implications are discussed in Chapter 12.

[85] 15 USC § 1693 (1982).

[86] 15 USC § 1693(a)(6) (1982).

which a person may initiate an electronic fund transfer."[87] The EFTA imposes federal criminal liability on any fraudulent use of a debit instrument to obtain services, money, goods, or anything of value.[88]

[5] Federal Computer Crime

After many years of legislative debate and consideration, in October of 1984 Congress enacted the first federal criminal code provisions dealing specifically with computer crime.[89] The enacted legislation stops short of providing a comprehensive criminal law framework for computer abuse in interstate environments, but does deal with significant aspects of previously unregulated abuse.

The federal computer crime legislation deals with three distinct forms of computer abuse. First, the Federal Computer Crime Act (Computer Crime Act) deals with computer abuse involving national security issues. The prohibition extends to obtaining and intending to use information from the computer. Specifically, Section 1030(a)(1) provides that it is a criminal offense to access a computer without authorization (or to use a computer beyond authorization) to obtain information falling within specified security categories[90] with the intent or "reason to know" that the information so obtained is "to be used to the injury of the United States or to the advantage of any foreign government."

The second type of computer abuse covered by the Computer Crime Act pertains to the use, modification, destruction, or disclosure of information in a computer system accessed without authority or used beyond the purposes of the authorized access.[91] These activities, however, are criminal only if they occur in a computer "operated for or on behalf of the Government of the United States." Furthermore, the activity is criminal only if it "affects" the governmental operation of the computer.

The third form of criminal computer abuse covered by the Computer Crime Act is perhaps the broadest in eventual impact. It provides a basis for enforcing individual financial privacy against unauthorized access in a computer environment. Under Section 1030(a)(2), it is a criminal offense

---

[87] 15 USC § 1693(n) (1982).

[88] 15 USC § 1693(n)(3) (1982).

[89] 18 USC § 1030 (1984).

[90] The categories in the statute are: "information that has been determined by the United States Government pursuant to an executive order or statute to require protection against unauthorized disclosure for reasons of national defense or foreign relations, or any restricted data as defined in paragraph r of section 11 of the Atomic Energy Act of 1954."

[91] 18 USC § 1030(a)(3) (1984).

to access a computer without authorization and obtain information contained in a "financial record of a financial institution, as such terms are defined in the Right to Financial Privacy Act . . . or contained in a file of a consumer reporting agency on a consumer, as such terms are defined in the Fair Credit Reporting Act." The national security offense under the Computer Crime Act is defined as a felony punishable by a maximum of 10 years in prison and a $10 thousand fine. In contrast, the other two violations are punishable by up to one year in prison.[92]

Under this federal legislation, no criminal sanctions are available for abuse of the various private databases that are operated independently of consumer financial protections and not under contract with the U.S. government. Presumably, even though computer abuse concerning these systems might entail interstate commerce effects, it must be dealt with under more general federal statutes or under state law.

Regarding these three areas, the Computer Crime Act premises liability on unauthorized access to the computer. However, it expressly incorporates situations in which access was authorized, but the individual "uses the opportunity such access provides for purposes to which such authorization does not extend." Violations based on this language and not involving national security are expressly limited to cases involving more than mere use of the computer in an unauthorized manner. Access and unauthorized use are offenses only if the access itself is originally unauthorized or the use relates to the national security offense.

---

[92] 18 USC § 1030(c) (1984).

CHAPTER *10*

The Electronic Transaction Environment

¶ 10.01 INTRODUCTION

Since their earliest commercial use, computers have had the capacity to receive, process, and communicate vast amounts of numerical information. As a result, among the first commercial activities affected by computers was the financial industry in which the processing of numerical information is central to daily operations. The effect has been especially significant in the nation's banking system, construed in its broadest sense. Despite the long-standing use of computer-based financial systems, for years the phenomenon was confined largely to the banking industry. Recent years, however, have witnessed significant and lasting changes beyond the banker's door and directly into the lives of most citizens. While properly considered as a manifestation of electronic banking, these developments have broader importance. They contribute to an "electronic transaction environment" that differs in both degree and type from the paper-based environment of the past in which contract, consumer, and other law developed.

An electronic transaction environment is multifaceted and is currently in an incipient, rather than developed stage. It is visible primarily in the form of electronic funds transfer (EFT) systems. EFT is an umbrella term that covers various devices and procedures by which transfers of funds and credits can be conducted through the transmission of electronic impulses, rather than through the transfer of paper documentation. EFT systems involving automated teller machines (ATMs) are already commonplace for most banks and savings and loans. An electronic transaction environment includes use of EFT, but moves beyond the funds transfer aspect of a transaction to encompass selection and ordering of goods and services electronically. In some cases, the services or goods may even be delivered electronically, particularly when they are in the form of information rather than tangible products.

The technology for an electronic transaction environment already exists. The direction of social change is clear. Home and in-store use of computer retailing systems is increasing. Similarly, there is substantial interest among financial institutions in developing and deploying electronic terminals for direct customer access to accounts. The purpose of this chapter is to explore some of the developmental legal issues encountered as society moves toward an electronic transaction environment.

¶ 10.02 TERMINOLOGY AND TECHNOLOGY

An electronic transaction environment is not only feasible, but likely within a lifetime. A variety of operating and experimental systems for funds transfers are already in place. In discussing an electronic environment from a legal perspective, it is necessary to become acquainted with several basic, generic terms used in these systems that describe technological and transactional options in the electronic environment.

[1] Automated Clearing House Systems

One widely used form of electronic funds transfer is the automated clearing house (ACH) system. While ACH encompasses a diverse technology, one use focuses on systems for direct deposit of payroll and social security checks from accounts of a payor into individual, depository accounts held by employees or other recipients.[1] In this form, ACH is the electronic extrapolation of early systems of direct cash payments to employees. These cash-based systems have long since been displaced by payroll checks, a shift to paper-based payments based on security and cost concerns. Similarly, the move from payroll checks to direct deposit arguably benefits both parties by improving security and reducing the costs of delivery. A related system transfers preauthorized debits from consumer and other depository accounts into the accounts of utilities and creditors. As with payroll ACH Systems, the direct debit systems arguably avoid security problems inherent in payment by mail. They reduce the cost to both the payor and the payee in the system and, from the recipient's perspective, the speed of the system reduces the delay inherent in checking processes. From the consumer's perspective, there is a benefit in being relieved of the need to remember due dates. Under the direct debit system, the banking process, more particularly the computer system, recalls and acts on significant dates.

As the ACH illustrations suggest, the advantages of electronic systems over paper systems include a reduction in traditional security risks associated with the theft of cash or negotiable instruments and an apparent increase in the speed and assurance of the transfer of final credits.

---

[1] See Penny & Baker, *The Law of Electronic Funds Transfer Systems* 3-6 (1980); *National Commission on Electronic Fund Transfer, EFT and the Public Interest* 36–40 (1977).

Electronic systems have the capability of acting virtually instantaneously once the appropriate access codes and data have been entered.

[2] Automated Teller Machine Systems

Automated teller machine systems involve a more direct interchange with individual consumers than do ACH systems. The typical ATM system consists of a machine capable of accepting deposits, issuing cash to depository customers, and providing limited information about the customer's account.[2] As the name implies, ATMs are electronically simulated bank tellers. The essential character of an ATM transaction is that there is no intervening human actor in the disbursement of funds. In issuing or accepting funds, the ATM does not, under current technology, require traditional forms of identification.[3] Instead, an ATM is accessed with a plastic card and personal identification number (PIN). Transactions initiated in this manner may be made on-line with the account immediately debited or the transaction may be stored in the computer memory for subsequent batch processing along with other transactions.

ATM systems began in the form of wall units or stand-alone machines located in traditional banking locations and their commercial success was directly related to enhanced customer convenience. During normal business hours, ATMs outside of the building provide an efficient alternative to drive-up or inside teller stations; after hours, they permit access to accounts at virtually all times without requiring the depository institution to provide human staffing. Subsequent developments have led to widespread adaptation of ATMs well beyond depository institutions. Indeed, with systems run by nondepository organizations such as American Express, the limitation to a bank location has become commercially, if not legally, inappropriate.[4] ATMs are located in retail stores to provide cash advances or withdrawals mechanically when needed. More recently, groups of institutions have organized national ATM networks such as "PLUS," "NATIONET," and "CIRRUS" in which participating ATMs are linked electronically.[5] The national networking allows customers of

---

[2] See Penny & Baker, *The Law of Electronic Funds Transfer Systems* 6-2–6-10 (1980). As discussed in subsequent sections, the ATM systems have been the most popular to date and have attracted a substantial share of regulatory and judicial activity. See Brandel & Hawke, *Electronic Financial Services* 121–150 (1984).

[3] See infra ¶ 10.09.

[4] See infra ¶ 10.04.

[5] See Burchfield, Martin & Reed, "ATM Networks Go 'Live' Nationwide: Cirrus, Nationet, and Plus," Brandel & Hawke, *Electronic Financial Services* 121–150 (1984).

the system to access depository functions of a member institution in any state in which the network is located, even if the customer's depository institution has no operations in that state. Depending on the view of the appropriate structure of the nation's depository institutions, this represents either an optimization of depositor convenience or an illicit creation of interstate banking that may ultimately destroy local banks.

[3] Point of Sale Systems

The elements of cost savings, increased security, and customer convenience seemingly merge in EFT systems that provide electronic access to depository accounts at the retail point of sale.[6] In contrast to ACH and ATM systems, point of sale (POS) systems have been relatively slow to achieve commercial acceptance. Replacing payment by cash or personal check, POS systems are electronic surrogates that record immediate electronic debits and credits to the customer and the retail merchant. Ultimately, POS is the core of a cashless society. As with ATM systems, POS involves access through identifying cards and personal identification numbers. Unlike an ATM, POS does not receive or disburse cash and is not located off-line of the retailer's normal checkout operation. Instead, POS systems are directly integrated into checkout procedures, replacing traditional cash registers.

POS has not yet been widely adopted in part because there are relatively large capital costs involved in installing POS stations in sufficient numbers at retail locations for a commercially viable system. The growth of POS has also been retarded by unresolved commercial issues in integrating it with traditional retail credit cards. Various legal issues also remain unresolved. Finally, consumer acceptance of basic changes in their manner of conducting business may be slow in coming.

[4] Home Computer Systems

A fourth, potentially significant electronic system must be mentioned as a constituent of an electronic transaction environment. This system involves the personal or home computer linked to external systems

---

[6] See Bequai, *The Cashless Society: EFT at the Crossroads* (1981); *National Commission on Electronic Fund Transfers, EFT and the Public Interest* 7–24 (1977); National Science Foundation, *The Consequence of Electronic Fund Transfer* (1975). Concerning the effect of POS on traditional forms of making retail and other payments, see Scott, *New Payment Systems: A Report of the 3-4-8 Committee of the Permanent Editorial Board of the Uniform Commercial Code* (1978); Nimmer, "Consumer Payment Systems: Leverage Effects Within an Electronic Funds Transfer System," 17 Hous. L. Rev. 487 (1980); infra ¶ 10.10.

through telephone lines. Unlike the foregoing systems, which involve facilities established by banks, card systems, and investment houses, the home computer system involves technology that in most cases is acquired by the consumer for purposes other than transacting financial or other business. In a sense, the home computer can be viewed as a multipurpose system, one ultimate function of which may be to conduct transactions in goods, services, or payments.

Home banking and home purchasing systems other than database access are currently available in only limited form in this country. The potential is clearly present, however, to issue disbursements directly from a debtor's account to a creditor's account and to select and pay for goods or other services from on-line vendors accessed by computer.

PART A.   INDUSTRY STRUCTURE

¶ 10.03 GENERAL ISSUES

Electronic funds transfer systems are developing in the context of significant changes within the financial industry that are characterized by a blurring of traditional service and institutional environments and by significant deregulation.[7] Banks offer brokerage services; savings and loans offer the equivalent of checking accounts; brokerage firms offer depository services through money market funds; traditionally labeled and restricted product lines and services arise in indistinguishable forms among various commercial vendors. These changes are driven by economic and technological change, but also provide a feedback loop that tends to promote development of new technologies. The overall pace of change contributes to an environment of regulatory and judicial inconsistency in which vestiges of an older system continue to be applied to a dramatically altered environment.[8]

Basic questions concerning the eventual structure of an electronic transaction environment and the type and source of services are unanswered. For example, if point of sale electronic cash systems come into general use, will they be operated primarily by retail merchant organizations as an extension of the cash register, by credit card systems as a service alternative, or by bank-depository institutions as an extension of

---

[7] See generally Huber, *Bank Officer's Handbook of Government Regulation* (1984).

[8] See Huber, *Bank Officer's Handbook of Government Regulation* ch.3 (1984); Scott, "The Dual Banking System: A Model of Competition in Regulation," 30 Stan. L. Rev. 1 (1977).

the deposit contract? Will national or regional sharing and marketing be involved, or will the systems be essentially local in nature? Resolution of these structural issues will eventually shape a billion dollar industry and the transactional alternatives available to future consumers. Obviously, economic forces will play a significant role in determining the eventual structure, as will various legal issues.

While it is not clear that depository institutions will have a dominant role in electronic funds transfer systems in the future, most of the early controversy about EFT development has focused within the depository industry. Significant litigation and regulatory activity have arisen around two basic issues pertaining to depository institutions and their role in EFT. The first involves branch banking and the related ability of individual depository institutions to extend across state lines for deposit and other activities. The second focuses on antitrust issues relating to joint venture EFT systems.

Issues of shared resources and control are in fact involved in both antitrust and branch banking problems in EFT. As a practical matter, at least in the early development of EFT, shared systems have been virtually essential to experimentation and use of POS systems. Sharing has also been significant in expansion of ATM systems beyond the parking lot of a particular bank.[9] At one level, shared resources is a form of controlling costs and allocating financial risk among participating institutions. This risk allocation is especially significant in a new, developing technology that involves substantial capital expenditure before consumer reaction can be fully ascertained. More significant over a long-term period, sharing in some form may be essential to the commercial viability of consumer oriented POS systems. Arguably, at least a basic "critical mass" of retail acceptance is essential before consumers are willing or likely to adopt PIN cards to retail purchases. A wide market penetration would be aided by a shared system and simply may not be feasible with totally disparate, unshared services for which one POS system is available from a particular merchant, but not available from another.

The fact that shared control and resources are important in the growth of at least a portion of the EFT industry does not necessarily determine the form that the sharing will take or the extent of the legal regulation that is appropriate. A variety of commercial and technological sharing options exist. For example, in a POS system a group of banks

---

[9] See Burchfield, Martin & Reed, "ATM Networks Go 'Live' Nationwide: Cirrus, Nationet, and Plus," Brandel & Hawke, *Electronic Financial Services* 121–150 (1984); see also *National Commission on Electronic Fund Transfers, EFT and the Public Interest* 49–64 (1977).

might share ownership of terminals or simply share use of a terminal owned by the retail merchant. Alternatively, the supporting banks might limit shared control to the computer switching systems needed to direct electronic signals to appropriate accounts. Another option would involve sharing advertising and the entire customer base.

Obviously, these variations will substantially affect the degree of control and the resultant legal issues encountered. The issue of shared involvement in EFT is not a unitary or simple one and not only involves determining whether shared control or resources is appropriate, but if so, in what form. To begin to resolve that question, it is necessary to examine briefly the legal environment in which financial services function.

¶ 10.04 BRANCH BANKING AND REMOTE SERVICES

Under current market and regulatory conditions, the banking industry is merely one element in a heterogeneous and complicated network of institutions providing credit, deposit, and transactional services for consumers and commercial entities. Portions of this network remain largely unregulated in terms of the ability to provide particular intrastate and interstate financial services. This is true, for example, for retail credit card systems and various brokerage or multi-service financial organizations. In contrast, despite substantial, recent efforts at deregulation, banking and other depository organizations function under significant local and national restrictions.[10]

The disparate levels of regulation create potential competitive imbalances that are especially important as the types of services that the various organizations offer become increasingly indistinguishable. For example, the absence of prohibitions on interstate mutual funds was not a major issue until money market funds became a major consumer product offering interest-bearing deposits and check writing privileges. Given such changes, however, questions arise about whether continued restriction of interstate banking elevates form over substance to the detriment of a major industry. The question is exacerbated by the fact that regulation among types of depository institutions is not consistent, nor does it originate in the same agencies. Thus, while savings and loans and banks compete for similar consumer accounts, the range of action allowed to

---

[10] See generally Huber, *Bank Officer's Handbook of Government Regulation* (1984); Hill, "Electronic Funds Transfer and 'Competitive Equality': A Doctrine That Does Not Compute," 32 Ark. L. Rev. 347 (1978); Mortimer, "Current Legal Problems Facing Commercial Banks Participating in Electronic Funds Transfer Systems," 95 Banking LJ 116 (1978).

each is controlled by different substantive regulations. This inconsistency and the growing complexity of the marketplace generate a need to reassess the overall financial services structure from a legal perspective. This reassessment is discussed in other publications and is not the primary concern here,[11] but aspects of regulation do directly affect the structure of an electronic transaction environment and are reviewed below.

[1] Intrastate Branching Restrictions

To the extent that ATM and POS systems are operated by financial institutions rather than retail merchants, they represent an outreach in services that would not have been commercially feasible without automation. This outreach encounters legal issues based on long-standing conceptions about the appropriate shape and nature of the banking industry. One set of concerns involves the possibility that these actions constitute unauthorized banking activities.[12] Another involves the extent to which secondary or branch service locations are permissible and, if restrictions apply, to what extent these pertain to ATM or POS terminals. This involves traditional state and federal policies that restrict branch banking.

In broad terms, "branching" refers to the ability of a financial institution to provide services from more than one location in a state. Under current law, branching issues are an explicit illustration of the competitive imbalance created by legal doctrine and regulatory systems developed in a less active financial services environment. As applied to EFT, branching issues involve the possibility that an EFT terminal will be considered a branch.[13]

As for financial institutions other than banks, the direction of contemporary developments is that secondary electronic locations in a state violate no federal or state policy. No current limitations are imposed on brokerage and similar financial institutions with multiple locations. Similarly, under federal law mutual savings banks are allowed to provide intrastate branch offices, despite contrary state law.[14] Also, federally

---

[11] See generally Huber, *Bank Officer's Handbook of Government Regulation* (1984); Penny & Baker, *The Law of Electronic Funds Transfer Systems* 3–6 (1980).

[12] See supra ¶ 10.04[3].

[13] See Independent Banker's Ass'n v. Smith, 534 F2d 921, 948 (DC Cir. 1976); Independent Banker's Ass'n v. Marine Midland Bank, 583 F. Supp. 1042 (WDNY 1984).

[14] Financial Institutions Regulatory and Interest Rate Control Act of 1978, Pub. L. No. 95-630, 92 Stat. 3641, amending 12 USC § 1461.

chartered savings and loan associations are federally authorized to operate EFT stations as "remote service units."[15]

In contrast, the right of banks to operate ATM or POS systems involves an interaction between federal and state law. The current U.S. banking industry involves a two-tiered structure with separate banks chartered, respectively, under federal or state law. The major sources of law on the relationship between state and federally chartered banks with reference to branching are the McFadden Act[16] and regulations adopted by the Comptroller of the Currency.

The McFadden Act was designed to establish "competitive equality" between federally and state chartered banks.[17] It defines a "branch" as any location at which "deposits are received, or checks paid, or money lent."[18] This definition is a matter of federal law,[19] but the effect of defining a particular operation as a branch is a matter of state law. Federal banks may establish a branch only if a state bank could do so.[20] This is inherent in the idea of competitive equality in the banking industry, which denies a competitive advantage to federally chartered banks. The concept has created a lack of national uniformity, however. While some states permit branch banking or the operation of EFT terminals, others prohibit them.[21] Thus, to the extent that an EFT system in a prohibitory state is defined as a branch bank, use is prohibited to both federally and state chartered banks.

Cases dealing with the application of the federal definition of branch bank to EFT systems generally have focused on ATM systems. An early ruling by the Comptroller of the Currency that ATMs operated by nationally chartered banks did not constitute a branch under the McFadden Act was rejected by the appellate court in *Independent Banker's Ass'n v. Smith*,[22] based on the premise that an ATM provides the services of receiving and disbursing cash. This meets two of the three definitions of a branch under the McFadden Act. Subsequent cases at the appellate level establish that to the extent that the ATM is established and operated by

---

[15] 12 CFR § 545.4-2 (1983), renumbered as 12 CFR § 545.140 at 48 Fed. Reg. 23032 (1983).

[16] 12 USC § 36 (1982).

[17] First Nat'l Bank of Logan v. Walker Bank & Trust Co., 385 US 252, 261 (1966); First Nat'l Bank in Plant City v. Dickinson, 396 US 122 (1969).

[18] 12 USC § 36(f) (1982).

[19] First Nat'l Bank in Plant City v. Dickinson, 396 US 122 (1969).

[20] Id. at 130–133.

[21] See Diamond & Sweet, "Special Problems of ATM Systems and Services" 151, 161, Brandel & Hawke, *Electronic Financial Services* (1984).

[22] 534 F2d 921 (DC Cir. 1976), cert. denied, 429 US 862 (1976).

the bank, it represents a branch under the McFadden Act.[23] The situation is less clear in cases in which the ATM terminal is owned by the retail merchant or other third party. In such cases, it is difficult to argue that the bank has established and is operating a branch. Current regulations of the Comptroller of the Currency authorize a bank to permit customers to access and withdraw funds from a terminal owned and operated by another entity.[24] This regulation is based in part on the lack of bank ownership and control of the secondary operation. The validity of the regulations is in doubt. In the first court decision dealing with third-party ATM terminals, a federal district judge concluded that the terminal was a branch prohibited under state law.[25] The conclusion of the court was that an emphasis on the ownership of the terminal elevated form over substance. The existence of the branch depends on the performance of the remote services.

The relationship between POS terminals and branching is undecided. In most POS applications the terminal neither disburses nor receives funds for deposit. As a result, the McFadden Act definition should not apply. The terminal merely implements remote transfers between accounts.

The regulatory and judicial structures place national (and affected state) banks at a competitive disadvantage even though these depository institutions may be the most appropriate source for developing EFT. The prohibition on branching is rooted in historical concerns that lack contemporary relevance in the face of proliferating financial service institutions, many of which operate in multiple locations as a matter of course. This is especially true since the effect of branching restrictions on the banks themselves is often blurred by the fact that large bank holding companies are effectively able to achieve many of the effects of branching through the ownership of multiple banks in a state.[26] As a result, it is not surprising that there have been frequent efforts to repeal limitations on national bank branching through ATM terminals.[27] It is likely that a competitive balance will be achieved in this context in the near future.

---

[23] See Illinois v. Continental Illinois Nat'l Bank and Trust Co. of Chicago, 536 F2d 176 (7th Cir. 1976); Colorado State Banking Bd. v. First Nat'l Bank of Fort Collins, 540 F2d 497 (10th Cir. 1976); Kostman v. First Nat'l Bank in St. Louis, 538 F2d 219 (8th Cir. 1976), cert. denied, 429 US 941 (1976).

[24] 12 CFR § 5.31(g)(4) (1983).

[25] Independent Banker's Ass'n of NY State v. Marine Midland Bank, NA, 583 F. Supp. 1042 (WDNY 1984).

[26] Huber, *Bank Officer's Handbook of Government Regulation* ¶ 10.04 (1984).

[27] See HR Rep. No. 4101, 97th Cong. (1983).

[2] Interstate Branching Restrictions

Traditional restrictions on intrastate branching by depository institutions were based partially on a fear that large banks would capture disproportionate market shares to the detriment of local banks. This is an even more substantial fear for the interstate market, where geographically remote banks potentially can take control of local financial operations, draining control and resources from the state. As a result, there are express prohibitions on national banks and mutual savings banks establishing branch operations across interstate lines.[28] In some states, federal regulations to this effect are buttressed by state legislation prohibiting the establishment of ATM or other banking services by out-of-state companies.[29]

The prohibitions on interstate operations are curiously limited in scope, however, and often ineffective even in regard to regulated banks. Thus, no interstate restraints, direct or indirect, are placed on the various financial service conglomerates that now compete in depository and similar banking markets. Equally important, the direct restraints on banks themselves are often overcome through bank holding companies, loan processing offices, and various other devices. One commentator has observed

> The often stated proposition that interstate banking is prohibited means something quite specific and narrow: Banks may physically accept deposits only in a single state. Even this limitation is becoming less universal. . . . Arguably, the limitation of banks and [bank holding companies] to a single state does not prevent banks from undertaking desirable activities, but only requires that they be accomplished in an indirect manner and at increased cost.[30]

The fact of interstate banking is part of the reality of the financial services market—a virtually unavoidable fact especially in an electronic environment. The pertinent policy issues are not whether interstate financial transactions are allowable, but in what manner they and the institutions that implement them should be structured and controlled.

---

[28] 12 USC § 36(f) (1982); First Nat'l Bank in Plant City v. Dickinson, 396 US 122 (1969).

[29] See, e.g., NJ Stat. Ann. § 17-9A-19.L; Fla. Stat. Ann. § 658.65(9); Conn. Gen. Stat. § 36-193(F). The validity of these statutes that single out interstate commerce is questionable at least under prevailing standards for interstate commerce. In some states, interstate sharing is expressly permitted. See Md. Code Ann. § 12-207(a).

[30] Huber, *Bank Officer's Handbook of Government Regulation* 10-18 (1984).

The limitations on interstate banking are inconsistent with present markets and, in any event, are indirectly avoided in many cases. This does not imply that the limitations have no effect on EFT and other activities. Under current law, the validity of interstate ATM operations is uncertain. There is little possibility that such a system could be established and operated by a single bank. ATMs that receive or dispense funds have been held to constitute branches under federal law and their establishment across state lines would directly contravene prohibitions on interstate banking.[31] On the other hand, economies of scale, consumer convenience, and even the willingness of consumers to accept particular systems indicate that nationally based ATM systems are commercially desirable and feasible.

The response to this situation might entail a variety of legally defensible structures. Indeed, within the past several years a number of interstate ATM networks have been initiated. These systems depend for their legality in part on the fact that individual banks own local ATMs that are then connected to a national network. Rather than a branch of an out-of-state bank, each ATM is a local branch with services made available as an accommodation for other members.[32] However, to the extent that reliance is placed on ownership of the terminal by a local bank, courts may bypass form and focus on the substance that the ATM network provides deposit and withdrawal services on an interstate basis and, consistent with the definition in the McFaddan Act, constitutes a branch bank.[33] Furthermore, casting interstate networks in the form of a joint venture may encounter antitrust issues that would not be present if the network were established and operated by a single entity.

[3] Unauthorized Banking Services

Federal legislation in the form of the Glass-Steagal Act prohibits any company from accepting customer deposits unless chartered as a deposi-

---

[31] See Independent Banker's Ass'n v. Smith, 534 F2d 921 (DC Cir. 1976), cert. denied, 429 US 862 (1976); Illinois v. Continental Illinois Nat'l Bank and Trust Co. of Chicago, 536 F2d 176 (7th Cir. 1976); Colorado State Banking Bd. v. First Nat'l Bank of Fort Collins, 540 F2d 497 (10th Cir. 1976); Kostman v. First Nat'l Bank in St Louis, 538 F2d 219 (8th Cir. 1976), cert. denied, 429 US 941 (1976).

[32] See Burchfield, Martin & Reed, "ATM Networks Go 'Live' Nationwide: Cirrus, Nationet, and Plus," Brandel & Hawke, *Electronic Financial Services* 121–150 (1984).

[33] Independent Banker's Ass'n of NY State v. Marine Midland Bank, NA, 583 F. Supp. 1042 (WDNY 1984).

tory institution and subject to examination by banking authorities.[34] Based on this and related state law, when a POS or ATM system is owned and operated by an organization other than a bank, a question exists as to whether unlicensed banking activity is being conducted. This is most clearly raised in situations where the ATM is located in a retail store and owned and operated by a retail merchant. This is becoming increasingly common as various retail merchants offer access to cash as an accommodation for customers and a method of reducing reliance on personal checks as a payment system. Often, the terminal is owned by the merchant as a means of avoiding branching regulations and allocating responsibility for maintenance and repair. The question is whether this ownership places the merchant in a position of performing banking activities.

The earliest case on this issue was *Nebraska ex rel. Meyer v. American Community Stores Corp.*,[35] where the owner of the ATM was a grocery store and the ATM allowed customers of a local, federally chartered savings and loan to obtain credits or implement debits in their accounts. Corresponding adjustments were made in the grocery store account to reflect the consumer's action. The Nebraska court concluded that this did not constitute unauthorized banking. Its analysis focused on the fact that accepting deposits was the essence of a banking operation and that this involved the creation of a creditor-debtor relationship between depositor and "bank." In the case of this ATM system, in contrast, the activity of the store was limited to "acting as an intermediary and assisting in the transfer of funds."[36] This result properly construes the relationship of the retail merchant to the transaction. The store acts through the funds transfer primarily as an agent for the bank or as a mere provider of a physical facility for the transaction. This analysis has been accepted in subsequent cases.[37] It should apply in any case in which the merchant does not itself provide the depository account for the consumer's funds.

The focus on the acceptance of deposits as the distinguishing criterion that requires chartering and examination as a depository institution also provides a line of demarcation concerning the types of activities that might be provided electronically by credit card and other, nondepository organizations. On-line debiting of a credit account through an electronic system does not constitute unlawful banking. Conversely, the creation of deposits against which charges can be debited is a banking operation.

---

[34] 12 USC § 378(a)(2) (1982).

[35] 228 NW2d 299 (Neb. 1975).

[36] Id. at 303.

[37] See Independent Banker's Ass'n of NY State v. Marine Midland Bank, NA, 583 F. Supp. 1042 (WDNY 1984); Bloomfield Fed. Sav. & Loan Ass'n v. American Community Stores Corp., 396 F. Supp. 384 (D. Neb. 1975).

¶ 10.05 ANTITRUST CONSIDERATIONS IN EFT SYSTEMS

In recent years, regional and national EFT systems have proliferated. In part, this is a result of increasing consumer familiarity with technology such as automated teller machine systems. In addition, retail merchants are increasingly involved with and receptive to computer-assisted inventory and accounting control systems, and advances in computer and communications technology permit geographically diverse systems to function as a closely related network.

In concept, EFT systems that extend beyond local markets could be developed by single, national organizations with sufficient financial resources and market access. This is especially likely to occur in the case of retail store systems or systems affiliated with national credit card organizations. In practice, however, and especially insofar as banks are concerned, regional and national EFT networks have been established based on cooperative action among several banks.[38] For banks participating in geographically diverse networks, resource sharing arrangements may be essential to avoid restrictions on interstate banking. Beyond this, joint operations spread risk and investment as well as enable deeper penetration of particular geographic markets than might be possible by a single organization. A decision to elect a joint venture format may be legally desirable and economically beneficial, but joint ventures involve potential antitrust liability that would not arise if the EFT system were established by a single organization. Antitrust restrictions on joint ventures among banks have had a large and ongoing role in defining the operative structure of the EFT payments for bank credit cards systems.[39]

Antitrust issues pertaining to joint ventures in a research environment are discussed in Chapter 4. The general purpose of antitrust law is to foster competition unaffected by limitations produced through monopolistic or cartel control of marketplaces. As applied to joint venture arrangements, a basic, potentially competing set of considerations is present. Joint operations among potential or actual competitors may reduce competition in relevant markets.[40] Conversely, since a joint venture does not entail a full merger of the participating companies, the venture commonly creates a new productive entity. This may contribute to an overall increase in competition, especially in the development of EFT systems,

---

[38] See Burchfield, Martin & Reed, "ATM Networks Go 'Live' Nationwide: Cirrus, Nationet, and Plus," Brandel & Hawke, *Electronic Financial Services* 121–150 (1984).

[39] See Worthen Bank & Trust Co. v. National BankAmericard, 485 F2d 119 (8th Cir. 1973); see ¶ 12.06[3].

[40] United States v. Penn-Olin Chem. Co., 379 US 158 (1964).

since cost and other factors might make independent bank action unfeasible.[41] As a result, analysis of the legality of joint ventures is complex and often uncertain where the participants are relatively strong economic entities. In general, three issues are involved:

1. Whether there is an unreasonable competitive restraint in the creation of the venture itself;

2. Whether restraints imposed on participants are ancillary to legitimate purposes of the venture and reasonable in scope; and

3. Whether access to the resources of the venture is unreasonably denied in cases in which the resources are essential to effective competition in the relevant market.[42]

[1] Market Effects and Reduced Competition

For any joint venture under antitrust law, there are conflicting considerations of size and access. On one hand, joint ventures that effectively include all current and potential participants in a relevant market may unreasonably dilute competition.[43] This creates an incentive to limit the scope of joint venture participation. On the other hand, joint agreement to exclude other participants may be viewed as a group boycott or, when joint resources are essential to competing in the market, as an unreasonable denial of access.[44]

As a result of these considerations, the definition of the appropriate or allowable scope of an EFT joint venture under antitrust laws is especially significant. The initial issue is a definition of the relevant market in which the effects of the EFT joint venture will be felt. Market definition involves consideration of both geographic area and type of service; the analysis should encompass services or geographic areas that consumers

---

[41] See Penny & Baker, *The Law of Electronic Fund Transfer Systems* ¶ 19.03 (1980).

[42] See generally Department of Justice, *Antitrust Guide to International Operations* 20 (1977); Pitofsky & Robert, "Joint Ventures Under the Antitrust Law: Some Reflections on the Significance of Penn-Olin," 82 Harv. L. Rev. 1007 (1969); Brodley, "Joint Ventures and Antitrust Policy," 95 Harv. L. Rev. 1523 (1982).

[43] Department of Justice, *Digest of Business Reviews: 1968–1982* 64 (1983) (letter disapproving of Nebraska proposal for statewide EFT system including essentially all institutions); see also Penny & Baker, *The Law of Electronic Fund Transfer Systems* ¶ 19.03[4][c] (1980).

[44] See Silver v. New York Stock Exch., 373 US 343 (1963); Associated Press v. United States, 326 US 1 (1945); United States v. Terminal RR Ass'n, 224 US 383 (1912); Worthen Bank & Trust Co. v. National BankAmericard, 485 F2d 119 (8th Cir. 1973).

would view as functionally interchangeable or in fact involving actual competition.[45] As a practical matter, the definition of the relevant market is an art, rather than a science, and reflects underlying beliefs about what should be the appropriate scope of allowable joint action. The definition of market must be sufficiently broad to incorporate the diverse electronic financial services that are currently available to consumers and that are in direct competition. It is inappropriate to define the relevant market solely in terms of bank services when other financial suppliers offer interchangeable services in a nonbanking context. In this regard, the Federal Reserve Board in approving two EFT joint ventures defined the "market" as "the provision to unaffiliated financial institutions of data processing services."[46] Similarly, the increasingly national basis of financial transactions should be considered. The relevant market for a joint ATM network is not necessarily the local area served by one of the banks involved.

Given a definition of market, the critical issues involve the effect of the joint venture concern on competition in that market. Competition can be adversely affected by including in the joint venture virtually all existing and potential competitors in the market. This is especially true where entry barriers effectively preclude competing systems. A policy statement issued by the Department of Justice in 1977 reflected this result. It indicated that the department would challenge ventures in EFT that were characterized by "the broad inclusion of more competitors than is necessary for efficient joint venture operation where the organization of rival joint ventures is a viable alternative."[47] Pursuant to this policy, the Department of Justice subsequently refused to give business review approval for a Nebraska EFT system that included two-thirds of all Nebraska banks at the time of review and was expected eventually to encompass all commercial banks in the state.[48]

The conclusion that a particular joint venture encompasses too many participants in the market entails both a close factual assessment of individual cases and clear value judgments. The general policy involved is clear, however, and has been relatively consistent for EFT systems. Antitrust policy is not against all joint ventures. Rather, as applied to EFT the emphasis is more accurately described as preserving the fact or potential

---

[45] See Pierce, "Competitive Implications of EFT," 2 Comp. LJ 133 (1980).

[46] See Federal Reserve Board, Order Approving Acquisition of Shares of Florida Interchange Group, July 12, 1983, Order Approving Acquisition of Monetary Transfer System, July 13, 1984.

[47] Department of Justice, Antitrust Div., *Policy Statement on Sharing, for National Commission on Electronic Fund Transfer* 3 (1977); see also Department of Justice, *Antitrust Guide to Research Joint Ventures* 4 (1980).

[48] Department of Justice, *Digest of Business Reviews: 1968–1982* 64 (1983).

of multiple, competing EFT systems. The concept is that a single, encompassing system is likely to stifle innovation and growth. Inclusive ventures that effectively foreclose the development or maintenance of competition are subject to challenge unless the market is such as would in fact support only a single system. In contrast, joint ventures that exploit economies of scale and other clear benefits of joint action should not be precluded.[49]

[2] Ancillary Restraints and EFT

In a joint venture, the participants agree to common actions toward particular objectives. In many cases, the agreement is carefully limited to actions essential to the purposes of the venture. If those purposes and the venture's market effect are allowable, no further issues arise. In other cases, however, restrictions agreed to by the parties relate to the joint activity, but are not necessarily central to and inherent in it. These situations give rise to antitrust issues, since the restrictions involve agreements among competitors. Antitrust case law examines such restrictions under the ancillary restraints doctrine. Restraints related to the joint venture are valid if they are reasonably essential to the legal purposes of the venture and are reasonably limited in scope to those purposes.[50] The policy judgment that joint ventures among actual or potential competitors are acceptable implies that related, agreed-to restraints are supportable. It does not, however, justify more expansive, unnecessarily restrictive agreements.

The analytical framework in the ancillary restraints doctrine involves significant policy decisions concerning the nature and scope of legitimate joint ventures. One application of the doctrine involves agreements to limit the size of a venture by excluding potential participants. Depending on the circumstances of the agreement and its relationship to the overall venture, such exclusions may be regarded as antitrust violations in the form of a group boycott.

This argument has had its most significant effect on joint ventures in the development of the Visa and Mastercharge credit card systems, which were created by agreements among a large number of participating banks. At the outset, each system maintained a restriction preventing members of one card system from joining the other. This so-called duality provision was challenged in *Worthen Bank & Trust v. National BankAmeri-*

---

[49] Penny & Baker, *The Law of Electronic Fund Transfer Systems* ¶ 18.03[4] (1980); Baxter, Cootner & Scott, *Retail Banking in the Electronic Age* (1977).

[50] See Louis, "Restraints Ancillary to Joint Ventures and Licensing Agreements," 66 Va. L. Rev. 879 (1980); Brodley, "Joint Ventures and Antitrust Policy," 95 Harv. L. Rev. 1523 (1982).

card[51] as a group boycott that violated Section 1 of the Sherman Act. Consistent with general law on ancillary restraints, the court concluded in *Worthen* that a rule of reason analysis should be applied to the duality provision. The restrictive agreement among potential competitors could be upheld if it had the effect and purpose of increasing or preserving competition. The court concluded that the information available concerning the effect of the agreement on competition was insufficient to reach a judgment. Prior to a decision on the merits, the parties settled the dispute. Subsequently, faced with continued antitrust uncertainty, the duality rule was abandoned and within a relatively short time dual membership in the two systems became commonplace. Now, the systems are generally not perceived as substantial competitors by consumers.[52] Participating banks offer essentially identical services in each system and there is little product differentiation or other basis for effective credit card competition.

Several current ATM networks have adopted provisions designed to maintain distinctions among the systems and between competitors. Under current market conditions, duality provisions in ATM joint ventures should, in virtually all cases, be enforceable under antitrust laws. The ATM network market is characterized by experimentation and a proliferation of competing systems. A decision that disallows discrete membership and identity would have adverse effects on competition and innovation in the EFT market.

Other restrictions in EFT joint venture agreements involve less clear analyses under antitrust law. One common restriction is a direct or indirect limitation on the charges for EFT services. In the absence of a necessary connection to the implementation of the joint venture and the offering of a new product, price fixing is a per se violation of antitrust law.[53] In an EFT environment, however, that necessary connection may exist; the setting of prices is then viewed under a rule of reason analysis in which the critical issue is the effect on competition.[54] It is not sufficient to examine only the effects on potential competition among joint venture participants, but consideration must also be given to competition between joint ventures.[55] In most cases, price fixing within an EFT system should be sustainable unless exercised in an anticompetitive manner.

---

[51] 485 F2d 119 (8th Cir. 1973).

[52] Penny & Baker, *The Law of Electronic Fund Transfer Systems* ¶ 20.02 (1980).

[53] See Monsanto Co. v. Spray-Rite Serv. Corp., 104 S. Ct. 1464 (1984).

[54] See NCAA v. Board of Regents of Univ. of Okla., 104 S. Ct. 2948 (1984) (restriction on television contracting and restraint of product available were illegal); Broadcast Music, Inc. v. Columbia Broadcast Sys., 441 US 1 (1979).

[55] See Continental TV, Inc. v. GTE Sylvania, 433 US 36 (1977).

Nevertheless, unless the agreements are essential to establishing the system, price-related agreements should be avoided because of the legal uncertainty they generate.

[3] Essential Facilities and Access

While the desired result in joint venture EFT systems is multiple, competing ventures, circumstances may arise in which failure to include certain participants may be an antitrust violation either as a group boycott or because competitors are denied access to essential facilities. The denial of essential facilities is an issue that arises in cases in which a joint venture controls a resource that is essential to competition in a particular market and that can not be replicated independently or in another venture. A doctrine of mandated access then applies: All potential competitors must be permitted access on a nondiscriminatory basis.[56] Compulsory access is not required merely because a joint venture enjoys a competitive advantage; it should be limited to cases in which a natural monopoly exists in that alternative options are not feasible.

Mandatory access concepts have been applied to exclusions from ACH systems. In two cases, ACH rules precluding access by savings and loans to ACH participation were dropped when court actions were filed by the Department of Justice.[57] In both cases, it was arguable that the market could not support competing systems and that the exclusions were based on anticompetitive purposes, rather than on legitimate purposes of the ACH ventures.

As applied to EFT systems, enforced access to full participation as a member in an EFT network should be required only where no feasible alternative is or can become available to the excluded entity. Under current market conditions, the availability of new network affiliations would preclude application of compelled access in most EFT cases. Stated simply, in a developmental stage of the EFT industry, too many current and future opportunities exist to allow a case for compelled access in the face of reasonable joint venture restrictions.[58]

---

[56] See Silver v. New York Stock Exch., 373 US 343 (1963); Associated Press v. United States, 326 US 1 (1945); United States v. Terminal RR Ass'n, 224 US 383 (1912); Worthen Bank & Trust Co. v. National BankAmericard, 485 F2d 119 (8th Cir. 1973).

[57] Penny & Baker, *The Law of Electronic Fund Transfer Systems* ¶ 19.03[4][c] (1980).

[58] A difficult question arises where state law requires that access be available to all institutions in a relevant market. Such a situation was present in a Nebraska system disapproved by the Department of Justice. Department of Justice, *Digest of Business Reviews: 1968–1982* 64 (1983) (letter disapproving of

PART B. TRANSACTION STRUCTURES

¶ 10.06 GENERAL MODELS AND PAYMENT SYSTEMS

Antitrust and regulatory issues affect the development of EFT and indirectly shape the type of transactions available in an electronic environment. For example, regulations requiring or encouraging joint ventures affect consumer access to EFT. Similarly, antitrust concerns may lead to a multiplicity of EFT service providers or, as with credit cards, a limited number of systems offering essentially similar services; either result affects EFT use in routine consumer purchases.

Beyond these indirect effects, significant policy issues must be faced in defining the legal impact and character of EFT transactions. These include resolving liability for unauthorized use, defining the buyer's right to rescind an electronic transaction without judicial involvement, and determining the extent to which EFT service providers will be subject to disputes that may arise in the underlying transaction in services or goods. The legal system has developed relatively stable patterns for the nonelectronic transactions that characterize the current economy. These patterns reflect not only the technology involved in the transaction, but also judgments about appropriate levels of risk and the character of the risk allocation. An electronic transaction environment introduces not only new technology in the transfer of funds and exchange of property, but also new transactional models. One salient question that must be addressed is the extent to which doctrine developed for the traditional models of consumer and other transactions should be applied to the electronic environment. Significant aspects of contemporary law are based on a cash transaction model that entails a face-to-face encounter involving an immediate transfer of value to the seller and the delivery of a product to the buyer. The traditionally predominant alternative model involves a delayed transfer of value through technology involving the movement of paper (checks, credit card receipts). In contrast, in an electronic environment more

---

Nebraska proposal for statewide EFT system including essentially all institutions); see also Penny & Baker, *The Law of Electronic Fund Transfer Systems* ¶ 19.03[4][c] (1980). The Department of Justice review applied to a situation in which state law mandated a sharing arrangement open to essentially all local institutions. Arguably, this mandatory situation is immunized from antitrust liability under Parker v. Brown, 317 US 341 (1943) (exempting action compelled by state law from antitrust provisions). Obviously, the Department of Justice disagreed. Asserting that Brown did not apply due to the fact that joining an EFT system was voluntary and not compelled. This position has been criticized. See Huber, *Bank Officer's Handbook of Government Regulation* 11-44 (1984). But see *National Commission on Electronic Fund Transfers, EFT and the Public Interest* 49–64 (1977).

appropriate models involve electronic transfer of value and transactions between parties, the representatives of which may never even meet. This change involves both opportunities and altered risks that require responsive legal structures.

[1] State Law and the Electronic Funds Transfer Act

Currently, the law relating to electronic transactions involves a blend of federal and state statutes and regulations. The predominant federal law is the Electronic Funds Transfer Act (EFTA) and regulations adopted pursuant to it by the Federal Reserve Board.[59] State law applies in areas not covered by the EFTA or other, preemptive federal legislation. Within the areas covered by the EFTA, state legislation or regulation is preempted only to the extent that it conflicts with the EFTA in a manner adverse to consumers. Legislation that enhances consumer protections beyond those provided by the EFTA is not preempted. Over 14 states have adopted legislation or administrative regulations relating to EFT.[60] The EFTA provides for a procedure of review by the Federal Reserve Board to determine if particular aspects of state law are preempted.[61]

The EFTA deals primarily with funds transfers, but has necessary implications for other aspects of electronic transactions. The EFTA applies to all electronic funds transfers involving accounts established primarily for personal, family, or household purposes.[62] "Electronic funds transfers" are defined as "[any transfer] initiated through an electronic terminal, telephonic instrument, or computer or magnetic tape, so as to order, instruct, or authorize a financial institution to debit or credit an account."[63] This definition of scope is intentionally broad. It encompasses all point of sale electronic transfer systems as well as all transfers that involve automated teller machines. It also encompasses preauthorized debits or credits in consumer accounts.

---

[59] 15 USC § 1693 (1983); Regulation E, 12 CFR § 226 (1983).

[60] See Leymaster, "Issues in Electronic Banking: State Consumer Protection Laws," Brandel & Hawke, *Electronic Financial Services* 9 (1984); Colo. Rev. Stat. § 11-6.5-109; Fla. Stat. Ann. § 659; Ill. Ann. Stat. ch. 17, § 1301 (Smith-Hurd); Iowa Code Ann. § 527 (West); Kan. Stat. Ann. § 9-1111; Md. Fin. Inst. Code Ann. § 10301; Mass. Gen. Laws Ann. § 167B (West); Mich. Comp. Laws Ann. § 488; Minn. Stat. Ann. § 47.63(3); Mont. Code Ann. § 32-6-303; NM Stat. Ann. § 58-16-13.

[61] For example, see the discussion of preemption of various portions of the Michigan EFT provisions. 46 Fed. Reg. 19,216 (1981).

[62] 15 USC § 1693(a)(2) (1983).

[63] 15 USC § 1693(a)(6) (1983).

Despite its intentionally expansive scope, the EFTA provides a number of express exclusions that are intended to enhance its focus on electronic transfer systems with a direct impact on consumers. The exclusions include:

1. Transfers initiated by check or the like;
2. Nontransfer systems such as check guarantee and authorization services;
3. Wire transfers through systems that are primarily business systems;
4. Transfers for the purchase of securities or commodities that are regulated by other pertinent agencies;
5. Transfers initiated by telephone, but not part of a prearranged plan of recurring transfers;
6. Transfers among a consumer's accounts or between the consumer and the institution holding the account.[64]

As is likely in any legislation related to the emerging communications and computer technologies, the scope provisions of the EFTA are strained as commercial activity and technology grow in directions that tend to blur existing categories. For example, the EFTA was drafted on the expectation that EFT systems would be based in financial institutions holding consumer accounts. This is built into the definitions of financial institution and transfer.[65] The EFTA is not applicable to electronic transactions in which an employer makes direct payments to an employee's creditors. Such direct payments are technically feasible, however, and involve the same issues presented by preauthorized debit systems involving a bank or other financial institution.

[2] EFT and Paper Systems

Framers of the EFTA intended to exclude paper-based payment systems, but the feasibility of this exclusion in the face of developing technologies is less than clear. Check payments are increasingly accomplished through electronically truncated procedures in which transmission of the actual check follows debit of the payor account based on electronically transmitted information. At this writing, the Federal Reserve Board has proposed to include POS transfers that involve EFT but are implemented by paper authorization, rather than at a computer terminal. These transfers would be covered where there will be "conversion of transaction

---

[64] 15 USC § 1693(a)(b); 12 CFR § 205.3 (1983).

[65] 12 CFR § 205.2(i) (1983).

information into an electronic form for transmission to the account-holding institution."[66]

Superficially, a transaction at the point of sale is different from that involving a personal check in that there is no expectation of subsequent transfer and presentation of the paper itself. This difference may not be significant, however, for issues such as forgery liability that are addressed in the EFTA and resolved differently for EFT transfers as contrasted to checks. Even if there is a significant difference now, the thrust of the technology is to blur the lines among traditionally dichotomous systems. This is true in the communications field; it will be equally true for EFT and other payment systems.

The implications of this blurring were addressed in the development of a Payments Code sponsored by the Permanent Editorial Board of the Uniform Commercial Code (UCC). Early drafts of the Payments Code encompassed all forms of payment, including both EFT and traditional systems such as checks. The various systems in large part were dealt with under similar liability rules pertinent to basic transaction risks. More recently however, virtually all consumer-related provisions have been deleted from the proposed Payments Code based on substantial political resistance to an amalgamation of all forms of payment into a cohesive liability scheme at the cost of relinquishing existing benefits specific to particular systems.[67]

This development is unfortunate. The similarities or variance in legal risk among payment systems should not be based primarily on tradition or vested interest, but on full assessment of the options that should be provided and the technology or other differences that should be treated as significant. Under current law, it is not clear whether the analysis has been done or whether it is reasonably implemented in current payment systems.

¶ 10.07 COMPULSORY USE OF EFT

In the absence of EFT systems, the options available for consumer funds transfer include payment by cash, check, and credit card. In most consumer settings, the parties are free to define the payment system used in the transaction. In concept, the choice is negotiated in particular transactions to reflect the differing legal and economic effects of the alternative systems. In practice, such negotiation may occur in commercial trans-

---

[66] 49 Fed. Reg. 2,204 (1984).

[67] Scott, "The Uniform New Payments Code: A Progress Report," Brandel & Hawke, *Electronic Financial Services* 57 (1984).

actions, but for consumer retail purchases the choice is predetermined by earlier judgments by the merchant and consumer as to whether to carry (accept) a credit card or to accept (establish) a checking account. Merchants are not required by law to accept checks or credit cards to accommodate consumers. Economic factors, however, provide incentive for most retailers to offer alternatives to cash payment. If alternatives are available, the choice among these options in a particular transaction is left to the consumer. Similar decision-making occurs for payroll disbursement and transactions involving payments to utilities and preexisting creditors.

Introduction of EFT systems into this preexisting set of transfer options may have either of two effects. The first, presumably most desirable for the consumer, would be that EFT systems simply are added to the prevailing options, creating a net increase in available choices. The alternative is that some or all existing options are replaced by EFT procedures that are not the functional or legal equivalent of the original options. For example, an EFT system involving POS electronic debits might replace personal checks at many or all retail establishments. An ACH system of preauthorized credits might replace payroll checks. While both EFT systems accomplish the same transfer of funds, they do so in a different manner and with a different speed that may or may not be desired by the individual, regardless of the benefit to the merchant.

One approach to these possibilities is to allow the marketplace to select among the various options. This is the general approach to personal checks and credit cards and is correct in relatively open marketplace conditions. This would include traditional retail environments in which POS terminals might compete with or replace personal checks. For the retail merchant, POS systems may be attractive in that they create the potential for a direct, instantaneous debit of the consumer's account and avoid the credit risk inherent in a check transaction. The retail options available to the consumer, however, are not determined only by convenience or cost to the retailer, but are part of the retailer's effort to obtain business. It is unlikely that a retailer would discard all alternatives for a system not favored by consumers. If other systems are discarded, it would be due to consumer acceptance of POS systems.

This market factor precludes the imposition of undesirable options on the general public, but arguably, the fact that POS might replace checks could have an adverse impact on lower income individuals. This possibility is even more pronounced if POS systems replace cash with the electronic equivalent. Lower income consumers may not have equal access to the accounts that are characteristically central to EFT systems. Retailer decisions to use EFT could result in effective exclusion of those with low incomes from particular retail markets. Partially in response to this possibility, at least one state (Massachusetts) has enacted rules that prohibit the conditioning of the "sale of goods or services to a consumer on such consumer's payment by means of an electronic fund transfer."[68] These regulations are not preempted by the federal EFTA since they expand protections afforded to the consumer.

The risk that EFT will supplant other funds transfers is more significant where the choice is not made in an open market environment. One such context involves payroll disbursement. ACH direct deposit systems provide cost savings to employers, especially those with large payrolls for whom an ACH system would eliminate substantial transfer and preparation costs associated with checks or cash. Arguably, direct deposit has substantial benefits for individuals in that it lessens the likelihood of robbery. The systems have become common in some governmental benefits disbursement procedures for this reason.

The EFTA makes no provision barring electronic distribution of payroll, even on a compulsory basis. It does, however, preclude actions that condition employment or the receipt of governmental benefits on acceptance of EFT to a particular financial institution.[69] Thus, the employer may require agreement to an electronic transfer to an account at an institution of the employee's choice or require that the employee select from a reasonable list of potential locations. The interest being protected is not refusal of ACH transactions. Rather, the statute seeks to preclude activity in the form of tying arrangements in which employees are directed to particular depository institutions.

The EFTA also limits the use of compulsory electronic transactions in the extension and repayment of credit. A financing institution is not prohibited from requiring use of an electronic payment system to repay a loan. It is prohibited, however, from conditioning the extension of credit on agreement to repayment through preauthorized debits to an account.[70] This provision applies only to credit transactions. Thus, one trial court has correctly held that the EFTA does not preclude conditioning a real estate lease on establishing a repayment system involving preauthorized transfers.[71] The benefit of such a requirement, of course, is greater speed and assurance of payment. Such transactions may be precluded by state laws, however.

---

[68] 209 CMR 31.07(3) (Mass. 1983).

[69] 15 USC § 1693k(2) (1983).

[70] 15 USC § 1693k(1) (1983).

[71] Lenox Manor, Inc. v. Gianni, 120 Misc. 2d 202 (NY Civ. Ct. 1983).

As this suggests, currently there are only minimal legal restraints on the right of the parties to elect electronic, rather than conventional payment systems. Whether this free market approach continues should depend on the direction that EFT implementation takes. In many environments, there are sufficient free market factors at work and legal intervention is not warranted. Tying and other clearly illicit activities involving funds transfer choices should be barred to avoid clear abuse, but otherwise the development of choices among available transfer systems should be left open.

¶ 10.08 PAPER DOCUMENTATION AND EFT ERROR

The primary advantage of EFT lies in the elimination of paper processing and the attendant costs and delays associated with paper-based systems. In concept, an EFT system associated with point of sale, automated teller machine, or direct preauthorized deposits through an automated clearinghouse can be totally electronic. All relevant information can be recorded and retained solely within the data processing system. Electronic records without "hard copy" tangible files are common in business and could easily be replicated in EFT systems.

While a totally electronic environment might achieve maximum efficiency, it has a number of drawbacks from the perspective of the user. These include the risks of fraud and forgery discussed later in this chapter.[72] A purely electronic transfer system, however, also produces significant reductions in information available to consumers. Arguably, this would lead to a corresponding loss of control by consumers over their own spending. Furthermore, electronic systems are more susceptible to untraceable error than are paper-based systems. By definition, in a paper system a paper trail exists to trace and describe pertinent transactions. This is absent in a purely electronic procedure. Additionally, a paper record of payment may be essential to resolve disputes pertaining to the underlying transaction itself. For these reasons, issues related to paper documentation and error resolution are major concerns in EFT. Both are expressly addressed by the EFTA.

[1] Documentation

In an EFT system, issues concerning information available to the consumer or business user arise at two distinct points. The most obvious is in the provision of information about the character of the system at the

---

[72] See infra ¶ 10.09.

time that the individual contracts to use it. Recognizing the significance of this preliminary information for consumer EFT users, the EFTA has established extensive disclosure requirements that must be communicated to the consumer in writing in "readily understandable language."[73] The disclosure must occur at the time of contract or before the first use of the service. It must include information about liability for unauthorized transfers, types of services available to the consumer, fees or charges associated with EFTs, stop order procedures, and information about documentation and error resolution.[74]

The second type of information required relates to particular transactions. In paper-based systems, the transaction itself requires a paper record such as a check or credit card form. The primary question concerning consumer information involves whether and under what conditions this paper record, or a copy of it, is transmitted to the consumer. In contrast, there is no step inherent in an EFT system that involves creation of a paper record. EFT systems thus can cause potential consumer problems that range from increased difficulty in identifying and correcting errors to disputes concerning the underlying transaction. The EFTA does require substantial paper documentation for particular transactions conducted within EFT systems. These requirements can be distinguished according to whether the transaction occurs at a computer terminal (POS and ATM transactions) or by preauthorized transaction (ACH systems or direct debit or deposit).

[a] Terminal-Based Transfers

For transactions implemented at an electronic terminal such as an ATM or a POS system, the EFTA requires contemporaneous documentation of the transfer and periodic statements concerning the account. For each transaction, the financial institution must make available to the consumer written documentation that includes the amount of the transfer, the date, the type of transfer, the type of account, identification linking the consumer to the transfer, the location of the terminal, and the name of any third party to or from whom the transfer occurred.[75] The form of documentation is not specified in the EFTA, but must be readily understandable to the consumer.

The obligation to provide documentation is imposed on the financial institution, but not on the retail merchant. Either through control of the

---

[73] 15 USC § 1693c(a) (1983). The Federal Reserve has promulgated a model disclosure format for optional use. 12 CFR § 205, app. A (1983).

[74] 12 CFR § 205.7 (1983).

[75] 15 USC § 1693d(a); 12 CFR § 205.9(a) (1983).

terminal or by contract with the merchant, however, the financial institution may fulfill its responsibility indirectly by documentation issued as part of a sale. This is consistent with the manner in which documentation of a transaction occurs in other systems. Since the receipts created in EFT systems are not essential to the transmission of the funds, the obligation is merely to make documentation available. The consumer can elect that it not be prepared in a specific transaction.

Beyond documenting specific transactions, the EFTA requires periodic statements for any account for which electronic access is available. The periodic statements must contain the same material provided on the receipts. In addition, the statement must indicate nontransactional information such as opening and closing balances, account number, and the number to which inquiries about the statement may be directed.[76]

One important aspect of documentation in a payment system is the extent to which it is usable in disputes about the payment or the underlying transaction. The EFTA specifies that periodic statements and the receipts created for individual transactions involving third parties are admissible evidence and constitute prima facie proof of the transfers in any subsequent litigation.[77] The prima facie effect of the documentation does not apply to deposit receipts from ATM systems, since there is no contemporaneous verification by another party of the consumer's alleged deposit.[78]

[b] Preauthorized Transfers

Preauthorized transfers include either direct deposits to the consumer's account or debits in the form of transfers to third-party payees. For either system, periodic statements are required.[79] In addition, each transfer may involve further documentation and notification procedures.

The consumer's primary interest in incoming funds is in receiving notification that the transfer has been made and the funds are available for use. Notice of the transfer may be provided by the transferor as part of a direct deposit system. In the absence of notification by the transferor, the financial institution must make confirmation of the transaction available to the consumer.[80] This can be provided by affirmative notice or by

---

[76] 15 USC § 1693d(c); 12 CFR § 205.9(b) (1983); see Huber, *Bank Officer's Handbook of Government Regulation* 20-22 (1984).

[77] 15 USC § 1693d(f) (1983); see also *National Commission on Electronic Fund Transfer, EFT and the Public Interest* 20,21 (1977).

[78] Official Staff Commentary to Regulation E, § 205.9-14.

[79] 12 CFR § 205.9(b) (1983).

[80] 12 CFR § 205.10(a) (1983).

establishing a telephone information system through which the consumer can determine whether the transfer was made.

Regardless of the notification procedure, funds received by preauthorized transfers are credited to the consumer's account when the ACH computer tape is received, subject to normal posting procedures. An exception is available to accommodate the right of the transferor to deliver funds early with instructions to make a delayed credit.[81]

Preauthorized debits from a consumer's account are subject to the EFTA periodic statement reporting requirements. The periodic statements adequately provide documentation about individual transactions. As a result, no further or contemporaneous documentation or notice to the consumer for preauthorized payments of a fixed amount is required under the EFTA. The financial institution is responsible for any failure to complete a preauthorized transaction as agreed. Presumably, the consumer can determine the current status of his account since he is aware of the fixed periodic amounts debited from the account. Greater information should exist where the preauthorized debits involve fluctuating amounts. While documentation of particular transfers is adequately provided in periodic statements, the fluctuating amounts raise an issue of communicating the current status of the accounts to the consumer. Additionally, depending on the nature and amount of fluctuation, situations may arise in which the consumer disputes or otherwise desires not to pay the particular bill.

The EFTA provides that where the preauthorized debit amount is subject to variation, either the payee or the financial institution involved in the preauthorized transactions must notify the consumer of the amount to be debited at least 10 days prior to the date on which the debit will occur.[82] This provides the pertinent information to the consumer for managing the account. It also permits the consumer to exercise his right to issue a stop order on the preauthorized transfer if he so desires. Stop orders under the EFTA must occur no later than three days prior to the scheduled debit date. The right to receive 10-days notice of the amount can be varied by agreement to provide for notification only if the variance in amount exceeds a specified range.

[2] Error Resolution

Documentation requirements bear on the resolution of alleged errors or other disputes within a funds transfer system. Beyond that, the EFTA

---

[81] 12 CFR § 205.10(a)(2) (1983).

[82] 15 USC § 1693e(b); 12 CFR § 205.10(d) (1983).

mandates error resolution procedures designed to ensure the consumer a reasonably prompt response to allegations of errors in recorded transfers.

The error resolution procedure applies to the range of issues that might arise concerning the accuracy of recorded transactions and also includes claims that a recorded transfer was not authorized.[83] It is discretionary for the consumer in the sense that a failure to comply with the statutory procedure by the consumer does not waive the error, but merely access to the error procedure. The procedures are initiated by a written consumer complaint that an error has occurred. To trigger application of the statutory procedure, the complaint must be made within 60 days after the financial institution transmitted a periodic statement that reflected the alleged error.[84] The complaint must merely be sufficient to provide information from which the financial institution can identify the allegedly erroneous transaction.

The consumer complaint triggers a statutory requirement that the financial institution promptly investigate the alleged error.[85] The EFTA provides for alternative times for response by the institution receiving the complaint. If the institution proceeds to investigate the matter, it must respond to the consumer within 10 business days acknowledging and correcting the error or explaining its reasons for concluding that no error is present. Alternatively, the financial institution may extend the time limits for investigation by provisionally recrediting the consumer's account in the disputed amount, allowing the consumer full use of the recredited funds.[86] This procedure extends the time for investigation to a total of 45 calendar days.

If an error is found during the investigation, the customer's account must be recredited within one business day.[87] If it is the opinion of the institution that there is no error in the consumer's account, the institution must send written notification to the consumer, explaining its conclusions.[88]

¶ 10.09 FORGERY AND FRAUD

Two types of forgery or fraud may occur in a payment system. The first consists of fraud in the underlying transaction, which only indirectly

---

[83] 15 USC § 1693f(f); 12 CFR § 205.11(a) (1983).

[84] 15 USC § 1693f(a) (1983).

[85] Id.

[86] 15 USC § 1693f(c); 12 CFR § 205.11(c) (1983).

[87] 15 USC § 1693f(b); 12 CFR § 205.11(e)(1) (1983).

[88] 15 USC § 1693f(d) (1983).

affects the payment procedure used by the parties. For example, an individual may be defrauded into purchasing a forged painting and paying for it by check. The issue is then the ability of the defrauded party to assert the fraud or take other protective action within the payment system.[89]

The more direct issue involves unauthorized use of a funds transfer or payment system itself. The risk of such conduct is inherent in any payment procedure in which funds are handled through third-party intermediaries, such as banks or credit card companies. The form of the fraud, however, differs among the various payment systems. For example, in both credit card and check payment systems, unauthorized use is most often associated with forgery and impersonation. Except with telephone use of credit cards, both systems are paper-based and commonly require a signature before the paper can be used to implement a funds transfer.

In contrast, most EFT systems have no provision for recording or verifying signatures. They do not require that a signature be entered for the fund transfer to occur. Instead, in EFT transfers funds are transferred based on presentation and use of a card accompanied by entry of a personal identification number. Thus, unauthorized use seldom entails forgery. In automated teller transactions, there is not even a need for impersonation. Future technology advances will enhance the security of EFT systems. At present, however, the systems convey significant potential for unauthorized use and lack traditional if often ineffectual safeguards based on personal contact between the user of the system and the person who dispenses value in response to the unauthorized use.

In any fraud or forgery, the optimal result is that the victim receive full restitution of loss from the party who committed the fraud. In most cases, however, this result is not realistically available. The thief has escaped or is judgment proof. As a result, the real issue in fraud cases involves allocating loss among parties who have not acted in a criminal manner. Depending on the manner in which the fraud occurred, loss must be allocated among two or three parties: the account holder, the financial institution at which the account existed, and when applicable, the party who dealt with the fraudulent party.

The primary consumer funds transfer systems allocate losses associated with fraud in three distinct ways. The differences are not necessarily justified by the risks in or the character of the three systems. With personal checks, Articles 3 and 4 of the UCC allocate loss based on a combination of considerations involving the type of fraud and the attributable fault of the parties. In general, the checking account owner is insulated

---

[89] See infra ¶ 10.10.

from liability unless the owner's negligence substantially contributed to the forgery or the owner was defrauded by an impostor or a padded payroll scheme.[90] Loss is allocated between the financial institution, the checking account, and the party that dealt with the thief. This allocation is based on complex statutory rules that in most cases place eventual loss on the party who dealt with the thief and was therefore in the best position to have avoided the loss.

In contrast, the credit card system applies a loss allocation procedure that is essentially independent of fault, at least as regards the liability of the card holder. Under federal law, the card holder's liability is limited to a maximum of $50, regardless of the holder's fault in losing the card or otherwise negligently failing to act to limit loss.[91] Loss allocation between the merchant and the card company is determined by contract.

For EFT transactions, the EFTA adopts a modified version of the liability structure established for the credit card system. The structure of consumer liability is based on a blend of fault in the form of failure to notify the financial institution of the loss of an access card, and no fault liability limitations that in most cases establish barriers to recovery above specific amounts. The consumer's liability for any losses occurring within two days after the theft or loss of an EFT card is limited to the lesser of $50 or the amount charged prior to notification of the loss being given to the financial institution.[92] This limitation applies whether or not the consumer was negligent in losing the card and/or in losing the PIN needed to allow access to the account. It represents an essential judgment that the financial institution and, through it, the system itself, rather than the individual consumer, should bear the burden of EFT fraud. As with credit cards, the $50 liability is intended to provide an incentive for consumers to police the use of their cards and to act to notify the financial institution to limit loss.

Unlike with credit cards, the EFTA provides circumstances in which the consumer's failure to report a loss of the access device may lead to liability in excess of $50. If no notice is given to the financial institution, the consumer is liable for up to a total of $500 for unauthorized use occurring during the period before 60 days after the institution transmitted a periodic statement that reflects an unauthorized transfer. If the consumer continues to fail to provide notice to the institution, the consumer has unlimited liability for losses subsequent to the expiration of 60 days

---

[90] UCC § 3-406.

[91] 15 USC § 1645; 12 CFR § 226.12(b) (1983).

[92] 15 USC § 1693g(a) (1983).

from the periodic statement.[93] Throughout all of these intervals, the consumer cuts off any liability for subsequent losses by notifying the financial institution.

The extended liability risk in EFT relates in part to the ability of the institutions to take protective actions limiting loss in the absence of notice from the consumer. In a credit card system, action by the card company may be induced as a result of exceeding credit limits or a failure to pay accumulated bills over a period of time. Neither of these indicates unauthorized use, but both may induce loss prevention activity. In contrast, in an EFT system the transfers are debited against existing balances. Recurrent, unauthorized debits would not induce reaction in the absence of notification of the fraud.

The EFTA liability structure may be modified by state law to the extent that the modifications enhance consumer protections. A number of states have acted to restrict consumer liability. For example, in several states, maximum liability is set at $50 regardless of notice or timing.[94] In other states, even the $50 limit requires proof of fault by the consumer leading to the loss.[95]

As these suggest, consumer EFT allocates loss for unauthorized use largely to the financial institution. By contract, the institution might reallocate some or all of the loss to merchants who use the EFT procedure or it might simply spread the risk as a cost of the service. The EFT loss allocation, however, only applies to consumer transactions covered by the EFTA. Thus, telephone transfers that are not part of a system of preauthorized transfer are not included.[96] Similarly, business use of EFT is not covered. As to transactions not covered by the EFTA, the appropriate source of law is unclear. The most likely option in the absence of contract allocation of fraud losses is adoption of UCC fault-based rules by analogy.

The nature of the loss allocation system for consumers creates a need to define an unauthorized transfer. In general, a transfer is unauthorized if it is made without actual authority and results in no benefit to the consumer whose account is accessed.[97] A transfer is not "unauthorized" within the meaning of the statute, however, if it is conducted by a person to whom the consumer "furnished" the access device voluntarily. This is true

---

[93] 15 USC § 1693g(a); 12 CFR § 205.6(b) (1983).

[94] See, e.g., Iowa Code Ann. § 527.8(1); Kan. Stat. Ann. § 9-1111(d); Minn. Stat. Ann. § 47.63(3).

[95] See, e.g., Colo. Rev. Stat. § 11-6.5-109; Mont. Ann. Code § 32-6-303(1)(2).

[96] Kashanchi v. Texas Commerce Medical Bank, 703 F2d 936 (5th Cir. 1983).

[97] 12 CFR § 205.2(1) (1983).

even if the party who received the device exceeded dollar limits that the consumer had imposed.[98] Consistent with loss allocation under the EFTA, the idea of furnishing the card to another should not be carried to the point of undermining the policy of insulating the consumer from loss regardless of fault.[99] Thus, an access device has not been furnished for use by another when the other party obtained the card by fraud or theft.[100]

¶ 10.10 LEVERAGE AND TRANSACTION DEFENSES

Beyond creating risks of error and fraud, noncash payment systems affect the relationship between the parties to the underlying transaction. The effects on this relationship differ substantially in existing payment systems. One pertinent issue in EFT systems used in a retail environment is defining the relative effect of the payment system in terms of the underlying transaction.[101]

The traditional model is a cash transaction. In this model, codified in the UCC, the seller has a right to insist on payment prior to delivery of the goods to the buyer.[102] The obligation to pay is preceded by a limited right to inspect the items. It is significant to note that in a cash transaction, payment itself alters the posture of the parties in relation to possible disputes about the delivered product. Once the cash has been transferred, if a defect materializes the buyer either must rely on the seller's good faith to correct the problem or sue to recover the money that has been delivered. The delivery of cash prior to receipt of the goods relinquishes any leverage that the buyer may have had by being able to refuse payment until performance by the seller.

This leverage is especially important in consumer transactions since it provides a vehicle to enforce contract terms without often unfeasible resort to the courts.[103] With the exception of EFT, all noncash forms of

---

[98] Official Staff Commentary to Regulation E, § 205.2-27.

[99] See Abrams v. Citibank, NA, 537 F. Supp. 1192 (SDNY 1982); Ognibene v. Citibank, NA, 537 Misc. 2d 219 (NY Civ. Ct. 1981); Official Staff Commentary to Regulation E, § 205.2-27.

[100] Official Staff Commentary to Regulation E, § 205.2-27. As to the analogous issue of unauthorized use of a credit card, see Martin v. American Express, Inc., 361 So. 2d 597 (Ala. Ct. App. 1978).

[101] See Scott, *New Payment Systems: A Report of the 3-4-8 Committee of the Permanent Editorial Board of the Uniform Commercial Code* (1978).

[102] UCC § 2-511(1): "Unless otherwise agreed tender of payment is a condition to the seller's duty to tender and complete any delivery."

[103] Nimmer, "Consumer Payment Systems: Leverage Effects Within an Electronic Funds Transfer System," 17 Hous. L. Rev. 487 (1980).

consumer payment alter the transaction in a way that extends the consumer's leverage. They do so in two distinct ways. In the personal check system, the extension occurs through the consumer's ability to stop payment on the check. In any check transaction, there is an inherent time lag between delivery of the check to the seller and payment by the buyer's bank. The length of time is determined by the actions of the seller and by the speed of the check collection process. During this "float" interval, there is a credit transaction and, more important, the consumer has a right to stop payment of the check under the UCC.[104] A stop payment does not relieve the buyer from an obligation to pay, but places the seller in a position of having to act affirmatively to obtain payment. This effectively retains consumer leverage to ensure performance of the contract. Of course, it also creates an opportunity for fraudulent nonpayment.

A similar retention of leverage exists in credit card purchases where the credit transaction is explicit. By contract with the card company, the retail merchant receives cash credit upon submitting the charge form to the card company. The card company assumes credit risks. For disputes about the underlying services or goods, however, federal law creates a procedure whereby the consumer can effectively return the retail merchant to a position of being forced to seek payment by solving disputes or suing. This is accomplished by obtaining a reversal of unpaid charges from the credit company based on an assertion that there is a dispute concerning receipt of the underlying goods or services.[105] By contract between merchant and card company, the recredit of the disputed charges typically results in a reversal of credits available to the merchant who must then obtain recovery from the consumer. The system provides a remedy for consumers in disputes about merchant performance, but also creates a risk of fraud for unsupported reversals of credits.

It is against this background that the introduction of POS systems must be considered. POS technology creates the possibility of an immediate transfer of value through direct electronic access to the consumer's account. There is a potential analogy to transfers present in a cash sale. The transaction itself, however, is implemented through the use of a card in much the same manner that a credit card purchase is implemented. The policy question involves whether the technology should be used to emulate a cash sale or whether restraints should be interposed to retain the leverage benefits available to consumers under other noncash systems. If leverage effects were retained in a POS system, they might parallel either the stop order power available under a checking system, or the substantively

---

[104] UCC § 4-403.
[105] 15 USC § 1666i(a) (1983).

restricted right to contest and reverse credit card charges. Under either format, if a POS system were functioning on-line with immediate access to the consumer account, it would be necessary by law either to require a deferred entry of debits for a particular period or to superimpose a concept of provisional debits and credits like that found in checking systems.

The desirability of a credit reversal right in EFT at the retail level has been widely discussed and is hotly contested by the industry.[106] This reversibility or leverage right was omitted from the EFTA. The arguments against it include the assertion that the risk of fraud is too great and that unlike in credit card systems the nexus between card company and merchant needed to effectuate a reversal of credit may not be present. A right to reverse EFT credits was incorporated in early drafts of the proposed New Payments Code, but was deleted because of industry resistance.[107]

---

[106] See *National Commission on Electronic Fund Transfer, EFT and the Public Interest* 15–24 (1977); Penny, "Questions Needing Answers: Effects of EFTs on the U.C.C.," 37 U. Pa. L. Rev. 661, 667 (1976); Nimmer, "Consumer Payment Systems: Leverage Effects Within an Electronic Funds Transfer System," 17 Hous. L. Rev. 487 (1980).

[107] Scott, "The Uniform New Payments Code: A Progress Report," Brandel & Hawke, *Electronic Financial Services* 57 (1984).

CHAPTER *11*

Electronic Publishing and Data Communications

¶ 11.01 INTRODUCTION

This chapter examines the legal issues pertaining to data communication and electronic publishing. Like other topics discussed in this book,
there is disagreement about the generic legal approach to be applied and
basic, unresolved social issues in defining the scope of telecommunications regulation. Telecommunications and related industries are major
and discrete subjects of study whose full consideration extends beyond
the scope of this book. The following is, accordingly, an introductory
review of selected issues.

PART A.   COMMUNICATIONS REGULATION

¶ 11.02 MERGING SYSTEMS AND REGULATION

Contemporary telecommunications and computer technologies produce a merging of traditional legal categories. Methods of communicating
information have historically been classified into three general groups:
print, broadcast, and common carrier. Each of these is distinct in the
extent of permissible intrusion into editorial, content, and associational
issues. In an electronic age, however, the categories are no longer clear,
and, as a result, the appropriate regulatory and judicial standards for
hybrid or new forms of communication are unclear.

Historically, the print medium has been subject to little or no direct
regulation. The substantive content and composition of such print communications as newspapers and books are generally protected from government control and are subject only to professional and marketplace
judgments. Some minimal restraints are imposed by libel and slander
laws, but even these are carefully constrained and limited.[1] The print
industry is the base on which many principles of free speech and free
association were built.

In contrast, broadcast media, including both radio and television, are
subject to relatively extensive regulation, although current trends are in the
direction of deregulation. The historical focus has been on federal and state
regulation of overall program patterns through allocation of prime time,
commercial showings, equal time, and fair access standards.[2] The justification for these intrusions on the broadcaster's control of its published content is related to the entry barriers and the relatively limited availability of

---

[1] See New York Times v. Sullivan, 376 US 254 (1964).

[2] See 47 USC §§ 154 et seq. (1976).

broadcast channels for commercial television or radio. In theory, content controls tend to ensure, rather than limit, basic free speech objectives.

The third method of communication is the telephone and telegraph wire systems. These have not been viewed as coextensive with or parallel to the broadcast and print media. The telephone has been associated with private transmissions among individuals and involves mass communication only because of the large number of individual calls handled. The aim of regulation does not focus on the content of conversations;[3] rather, a common carrier model applies. There is extensive rate and service regulation to ensure public access to service and, more recently in the AT&T breakup, competition that promotes technological and service improvements. Telephone companies are not traditionally involved in determining the content of communications, and the regulatory model assumes that they provide only a conduit for individual communicators.

These traditional categories overlap more and more as the development of new telecommunications technology accelerates. The new hybrid forms that result from the overlap require new regulatory models or, sometimes, no regulation at all. One early effort to classify the new forms arose when telephone lines began to be used for data communication and data processing in addition to voice transmission. As discussed in the following section, this technology led to an extensive, but largely futile, effort to distinguish communications services from data processing. A more recent example is the overlap between print and broadcast systems. Electronic media now transmit text previously associated with print. Furthermore, essentially similar transmissions are now made over broadcast systems, telephone lines, and within cable television systems. The effort to adjust regulatory and judicial response to the proliferation of communications options is a significant issue pertaining to the nature of information transmission in the information age.

¶ 11.03 DATA PROCESSING

The antitrust litigation that led to the AT&T divestiture has thrust the nation's telephone system into a period of massive change.[4] Even before that event, however, the increasingly widespread use of telephone lines for data processing and communications became an issue at the fed-

---

[3] As discussed in Chapter 12, there are significant issues concerning regulation of privacy rights in telephone communications. See ¶ 12.04; see also Title III of the Omnibus Crime Control and Safe Streets Act of 1968, 18 USC §§ 2510–2520.

[4] United States v. AT&T, 552 F. Supp. 131 (DDC 1982).

eral level, resulting in several major decisions by the Federal Communications Commission (FCC) that retain significance even after the AT&T breakup.

This regulatory involvement reflects the increasing flexibility of pertinent technology and, ultimately, the inability of regulations to keep pace with rapid changes in technology. The regulatory distinction between data processing and communications technology first became significant during the 1950s in a consent decree settling antitrust litigation concerning AT&T and Western Electric. This consent decree attempted to limit AT&T's use of monopoly power from the communications industry for advantage in other markets. It prohibited AT&T from selling equipment capable of performing data processing functions and, more generally, from entering any unregulated market.[5]

After this decree, various actions by the FCC and the courts resulted in the entry of service providers who used new technologies to enhance and alter the overall operation of telephone-like communications. The most significant decisions allowed the attachment of devices to the basic telephone lines that enhanced services[6] and permitted private and commercial microwave communications services to be created in competition with basic telephone carriers for long-distance services.[7]

This was a period of modification of telephone-related services. During this time, the FCC undertook a broad inquiry into data processing associated with telecommunications. Commonly known as Computer Inquiry I, the inquiry related expressly to the "problems presented by the interdependence of computer and communications services and facilities."[8] The investigation focused on the extent to which data processing, message-switching, and computer-based information systems should be subject to regulation.[9] The difficulty was that not only was computer technology using telephone systems to transmit information, but also telephone systems were making substantial use of computer technology to manage, transmit, and direct traditional messages.

---

[5] See Western Elec. Consent Decree, 1956 Trade Cas. ¶ 68,246 (CCH).

[6] See, e.g., Use of the Carterphone Device in Message Toll Tel. Serv., 13 FCC2d 420 (1968).

[7] See Allocation of Frequencies in the Bands Above 890 Mc, 27 FCC 359, reconsideration denied, 27 FCC 925 (1969); Microwave Communications, Inc., 18 FCC2d 953 (1969).

[8] See Regulatory and Policy Problems Presented by the Interdependence of Computer and Communications Services and Facilities, 7 FCC2d 11 (1966) (notice of inquiry).

[9] Id. at 17.

In 1970, the FCC ruled that it would exercise regulatory jurisdiction over *only* those aspects of the computer industry related to communication. To the extent that regulated communications carriers entered data processing fields, they would be required to do so through totally separate affiliates to prevent undue leveraging of economic and technical power across the two areas.[10] This decision required the FCC to distinguish data processing related to communications from data processing that merely used a communications system. It did so through a defined distinction between "data processing" and "message-switching" operations. Data processing included use of a computer for "the functions of storing, retrieving, sorting, merging and calculating data."[11] Message switching involved "computer-controlled transmission of messages ... wherein the content of the message remains unaltered."[12] The importance of this distinction was heightened when a federal court held that the FCC lacked authority to regulate data processing activities that merely used the communications systems.[13] Furthermore, under the early consent degree, AT&T was barred from the unregulated data processing market.

Whether or not it was initially defensible, developments in technology for computers and communications rapidly rendered the distinction between data processing and message switching impossible to apply. Disputes arose over various new devices and functions. For example, there was a significant dispute about the ability of AT&T to offer an "intelligent" terminal containing some data manipulation capability. The FCC eventually labeled this a communications device, regulated by the FCC and subject to FCC tariff.[14]

The net effect was the initiation of Computer Inquiry II in 1976.[15] As a result of this second inquiry, the FCC abandoned any attempt to distinguish data processing from message switching. Instead, after substantial experimentation, it adopted a distinction between regulated, "basic", services, which could be offered only by common carriers, and unregulated, "enhanced", services.

---

[10] Regulatory and Policy Problems Presented by the Interdependence of Computer and Communications Services and Facilities, 28 FCC2d 267 (1971).

[11] Computer Use of Communications Facilities, 28 FCC2d 267, 287 (1971).

[12] 47 CFR § 64.702(a)(2) (1979).

[13] GTE Serv. Corp. v. FCC, 474 F2d 724 (2d Cir. 1973).

[14] AT&T, 62 FCC2d 21 (1977), aff'd, IBM v. FCC, 570 F2d 452 (2d Cir. 1978).

[15] Amendment of Section 64.702 of the Commission's Rules and Regulations, 61 FCC2d 103 (1976) (notice of inquiry).

[Basic service involves] transmission capacity for the movement of information, whereas enhanced service combines basic service with computer processing applications that act on the format, content, code, protocol or similar aspects of the subscriber's transmitted information, or provide the subscriber additional, different, or restructured information, or involve subscriber interaction with stored information. [16]

In essence, basic service is the underlying "transmission pipeline" for information. [17]

The FCC decision in Inquiry II dealt with customer equipment sales and leasing, as well as with the structure required if a common carrier entered the deregulated, enhanced service market. The FCC acknowledged that any attempt to distinguish communications equipment from other equipment that might connect to telephone lines would be rendered artificial by the technology. All customer premises equipment was deregulated. Carriers were required to "unbundle" equipment and services for all on-site equipment. [18] For enhanced services offered by common carriers, the FCC restated the requirement that the services be offered only through totally separate affiliates.

The implications of these decisions are affected by the consent decree in the AT&T antitrust litigation. This decree resulted in a substantial restructuring of the AT&T system, characterized by substantial divestiture by AT&T and the establishment of local operating companies. [19] It also permitted AT&T to enter data processing and enhanced services, with the exception of a seven-year moratorium on entry into the electronic publishing industry.

¶ 11.04 ELECTRONIC PUBLISHING REGULATION

As with data processing and communication, the electronic publishing industry presents major policy issues regarding regulatory structure. One characteristic of this industry is that types of service and methods of

---

[16] Amendment of Section 64.702 of the Commission's Rules and Regulations, 77 FCC2d 384, 387 (1980), reconsideration denied, 84 FCC2d 50 (1980), aff'd, CCIA v. FCC, 693 F2d 198 (DC Cir. 1982), cert. denied, 103 S. Ct. 2109 (1983).

[17] Amendment of Section 64.702 of the Commission's Rules and Regulations, 84 FCC2d 50, 54 (1980), aff'd, CCIA v. FCC, 693 F2d 198 (DC Cir. 1982), cert. denied, 103 S. Ct. 2109 (1983).

[18] Amendment of Section 64.702 of the Commission's Rules and Regulations, 84 FCC2d 65 (1980).

[19] United States v. AT&T, 552 F. Supp. 131 (DDC 1982).

delivery vary widely; they are in the process of commercial definition. Nevertheless, it is helpful to organize this discussion around two basic types of publishing and the delivery systems with which they are associated.

These two publishing forms are teletext and videotext. Both involve the transmission of text and/or graphics for electronic reception by the user. Teletext is a one-way distribution system characterized by transmission of a continuing and repeating stream of pages or units of information.[20] The user, generally using a keyboard, a display unit (television or monitor), and a decoder allowing interception of the signals, intercepts selected pieces of information for display at the local terminal. In contrast, a videotext is an interactive two-way system. A database is accessed by the user through a communicating personal computer, terminal, or other device. The access is characterized by an inquiry system in which particular information is requested and retrieved from the database.[21]

Either form of publishing bears significant similarities to traditional print systems augmented by electronic technology. The extent to which this similarity should control doctrine is a regulatory and legal policy issue. Regulatory and other restrictions might be based on the method of delivery chosen for a particular system, and while this approach would produce consistency within technological delivery systems, it would ultimately lead to dissimilar regulation of identical products simply because they are transmitted by different technologies.

[1] Broadcast Teletext

While teletext can be delivered in a variety of ways, one commonly used form involves transmission by the so-called vertical blanking interval (VBI) of normal television broadcast signals. The FCC has authorized full service television stations to offer this service as long as it does not interfere with the signals of the originating or other broadcast stations.[22] However, if teletext is offered as part of a television broadcast signal, the extent to which the teletext is subject to content restrictions imposed on traditional forms of broadcast becomes a question. These content restrictions include the fairness doctrine and reasonable access[23] requirements that effectively force a dispersion of broadcast views on issues.

---

[20] See FCC, Teletext Transmission, 53 Rad. Reg. (P&F) 1309, 1310 (1983).

[21] See Shapiro, Kurland, Mercurio, *Cablespeech* 77–80 (1983).

[22] FCC, Teletext Transmission, 53 Rad. Reg. (P&F) 1309 (1983).

[23] See 47 USC § 312(a)(7) (1976).

While the form of transmission of traditional broadcast and teletext is similar, the nature of the systems differs. "Teletext" is defined by the FCC as "a data system for transmission of textual and graphic information included for display on viewing screens."[24] Teletext systems are more like traditional print media than any other form of electronic publishing. The content is determined, drafted, or selected by the publisher and made available to the reader who reads pertinent parts. The policy and constitutional issue is whether this similarity to traditional print controls substantive content and free speech questions.

In its original decision concerning teletext, the FCC determined that the service could be offered on either a broadcast model in which the broadcast station supported the system with subscriber or commercial income or, with FCC approval, on a common carrier in which the station merely provided the facility for another who supplied the content. If supplied as a broadcast service, the FCC ruled teletext ancillary to traditional broadcast systems and, thus not subject to the content restrictions commonly placed on broadcasters. The analogy to print media prevailed.

Despite the FCC ruling, the status of broadcast teletext is uncertain. The form has not yet attained widespread and commercially significant use, and no judicial challenges to the FCC position have occurred. However, broadcast teletext falls clearly within the statutory definition of broadcasting under the Communications Act and is at least presumptively subject to traditional broadcast regulation.[25] It is doubtful that the FCC may alter this through regulatory action. Furthermore, although the product is textual and similar to printed matter, the medium has the same use and access limitations that justify content regulation in traditional broadcasting environments.

Teletext services can also be offered through various other forms including cable television, discussed later in this chapter, or a private radio basis or common carrier system associated with direct broadcast satellites (DBS) and multipoint distribution service (MDS) systems. As to MDS and DBS systems, the FCC has taken a free-market approach to the developing technologies.[26] DBS is treated as a hybrid communications system and is not regulated. Teletext supplied through this system on either a private radio or a common carrier leased-space format, even though analogous to that delivered by broadcast, is currently unregulated.

Applying content regulations to teletext should not depend on the choice among forms of delivery for similar services. Rather, the decision

---

[24] FCC, Teletext Transmission, 53 Rad. Reg. (P&F) 1309 ¶ 44 (1983).

[25] 47 USC § 3(o) (1976).

[26] See In re DBS, 90 FCC2d 676 (1982).

should be based on the nature of the communication form involved. The connection between text transmitted electronically and text transmitted on paper should supply the reference for appropriate regulation. The FCC decision concerning broadcast teletext is consistent with the role of free expression in our society. However, the import of the decision can not be considered in isolation from other delivery options for electronic publishing: cable television and telephone lines.

[2] Cable Transmission

Both teletext and videotext can be delivered through cable systems. The commitment required to deliver each differs because of the differing roles of the user in defining the material supplied. The services can be delivered either in the VBI of a cable transmission or on a dedicated cable channel. This latter alternative is feasible even with the limited current market for electronic publishing, since most cable systems use far fewer than all available channels for other forms of entertainment.

State, local, and federal regulations apply to cable systems, but the degree of regulation is less than that applied to broadcast media. After more than three years of debate, Congress enacted the Cable Communications Policy Act of 1984 (Cable Act).[27] The Cable Act deals extensively with the permissible scope of federal, state, or local regulation of cable systems, but does not restrict the circumstances under which a cable system may elect to provide either videotext or teletext. Regulatory action similarly has not placed restrictions on cable operators at present.

Under current law, cable systems are not consistently treated as common carriers at the federal level with respect to making access available to secondary parties. The Cable Act does impose limited forms of required access to video programming, however. It authorizes franchising authorities to require designation or use of channels for public, educational, or government use.[28] In addition, the Cable Act requires the designation of part of the cable channel capacity for use by third parties not affiliated with the cable operator.[29]

These access or designation requirements represent exceptions to the general rule that treats the cable operator as essentially analogous to a publisher in control of the content of the various channels. Furthermore, the access requirements are expressly limited to video programming,

---

[27] Cable Communications Policy Act of 1984, 47 USC §§ 600 et seq. (1984 Supp.) (hereinafter cited as Cable Act).

[28] Cable Act § 611.

[29] Cable Act § 612.

which is defined in terms of services that are normally delivered by television stations. There was an express decision not to address the question of whether cable operators may provide nonvideo programming such as teletext or videotext.[30] Cable systems are not required to provide leased-channel or other access to videotext or teletext service providers.

Any tendency to treat cable systems in the form of common carriers with requirements of complete, equal accessibility at the state or local levels is preempted by the Cable Act. The arguable rationale for common-carrier-like treatment relates to the superficial technology similarity between cable systems and telephone systems. Both involve multipurpose wires connected physically to consumer locations. In fact, however, while cable lines provide convenient access to consuming publics, the telephone line exists as an alternative with broader coverage of the market. In any event, the types of services delivered in cable and telephone systems under traditional use are clearly distinct.

Content regulations relating to the fairness doctrine have not been applied to cable systems in which the operator serves merely as a conduit for the programs of others. In contrast, although there are no decisions pertaining specifically to videotext and teletext, content regulation is applied to cablecasting—that is, circumstances in which the cable system participates in defining content beyond merely providing a conduit.[31] This includes regulations relating to the transmission of indecent materials.[32] The Cable Act provides for criminal penalties for the transmission of obscene materials by cable,[33] and it expressly excludes any intention to preempt federal, state, or local laws pertaining to indecent-material transmission, invasions of privacy, or similar laws.[34]

All content regulations in cable transmission are the subject of ongoing uncertainty about restrictions on free speech in this medium, particularly restrictions on the transmission of indecent but not obscene materials. In a landmark decision, *FCC v. Pacifica Foundation*,[35] the Supreme Court upheld limitations on broadcast of indecent materials despite the infringement on free speech. The decision, however, was linked to the immediate impact and ubiquitous nature of broadcast radio and television. This is less clearly present in a multichannel system such as cable and, especially, in a relatively passive medium such as teletext. Because of

---

[30] 130 Cong. Rec. 14,285 (daily ed. Oct. 11, 1984).

[31] 47 CFR §§ 76.05, 76.209.

[32] 47 CFR § 76.215.

[33] Cable Act § 639.

[34] Cable Act § 638.

[35] 436 US 728 (1978).

the distinction, at least one state's law restricting transmission of indecent material by cable was held invalid on constitutional grounds by lower federal courts.[36]

[3] Telephone Videotext

A final method of transmitting electronic publications is transmission over telephone lines. This approach is often used for videotext or database systems. The widespread market penetration of telephones into consumer locations makes telephone line transmission of electronic publishing a preferred method. It is also the environment in which content and other regulation of publishing activity is likely to be the least intrusive.

As discussed previously,[37] the role of telephone systems in data communications has been the subject of intense regulatory action. Consistent with the traditional nature of the medium, however, this regulatory activity has involved tariffs and the ability of certain organizations to provide particular services, rather than content controls. The current regulatory distinction between enhanced services and basic services is readily applied to videotext. Electronic publishing falls within the non-common-carrier, unregulated, enhanced services. Historically, telephones have been treated as common carriers, and this remains true when they are used to transmit videotext. Telephone companies are bound to standards of access and rate regulation consistent with a common carrier. In contrast, the videotext provider, as a traditional publisher, is essentially unaffected by regulation of content.

One final point is relevant concerning telephone-based videotext. Under the consent decree pertaining to the restructuring of AT&T, the Bell local operating companies are prohibited from offering electronic publishing services of their own without consent of the court on a showing that there is no possibility of monopoly power abuse over the lines themselves. Similarly, AT&T is prohibited from entering electronic publishing over its own lines for at least a seven-year period.[38] Both exclusions intend to establish a barrier against exploitation of control over the common carrier service lines through which electronic publishing is likely to be channeled.

---

[36] Community Television of Utah v. Roy City, 555 F. Supp. 986 (D. Utah 1982).

[37] See supra ¶ 11.03.

[38] United States v. AT&T, 552 F. Supp. 131 (DDC 1982).

PART B. PRODUCT AND STRUCTURAL ISSUES

¶ 11.05 ANTITRUST AND OWNERSHIP

Neither videotext nor teletext oriented to general consumer markets has had sufficient market impact to generate the substantial disputes about competitive impact or ownership issues commonly associated with information providing systems.[39] In the absence of any current dispute or decided cases, discussion of these issues is speculative. However, some speculation is pertinent on the overall question of how electronic publishing can or will fit into existing information delivery systems.

An initial question involves the relationship between teletext and videotext media and existing rules concerning local ownership of multiple information services. Current FCC regulations prohibit one entity from owning a broadcast outlet *and* either a newspaper or cable television system in a single market.[40] In addition, Section 613 of the Cable Act codified the preexisting FCC prohibition on ownership of a cable and a television system in the same area.[41] These regulations are designed to prohibit or, at least, restrict monopolization of information sources and ideas by a single entity, their premise being that even in the absence of technological or regulatory barriers, economic constraints limit the number and variety of information sources available in any particular market. Within that limited field, it is important to avoid control by one entity.

In contrast, it is clear that for forms of videotext or teletext oriented to current events, entertainment schedules, and the like, a close relationship between the electronic media and print, broadcast, or cable might be economically efficient and editorially essential. Whether cross-ownership involving this electronic media should be permitted is contingent on both the nature of the publishing service and the scope of its impact. Significantly, the FCC historically has not banned all cross-ownership within the communications media. For example, existing regulations do not bar local cross-ownership of cable systems and newspapers. The rationale for this relates to the nature and impact of the media.

Similar rationales apply to the teletext and videotext systems. At least during their formative stages, these new forms of information delivery merit relatively wide latitude to insure growth. There is at present no a priori rationale for restrictions on any cross-ownership.

In addition to cross-ownership, a variety of antitrust questions may arise in the development of electronic publishing systems. Many of the

---

[39] See 9 CLT Rep. 6 (July 1983).

[40] 47 CFR §§ 73.636, 76.501.

[41] 47 USC § 613 (1984 Supp.); 47 CFR § 63.55.

initial service systems are joint ventures among relatively large, national companies already involved in some form of information services. As discussed in an earlier chapter,[42] joint ventures raise potential antitrust issues that are especially pertinent when the venture is horizontal and involves actual or potential competitors.[43] In electronic publishing, however, a permissive antitrust posture is warranted. Antitrust restraints apply to combinations that reduce competition. In many joint ventures in this area, a new competitive service is developed by parties who would be unlikely to commence the service on their own. There is a net competitive gain or, at least, a net service gain.[44]

Other antitrust issues may arise. For example, in most cases the publisher will desire exclusive or predominant access to the material from any particular source (e.g., newspaper, author). This is common practice in the publishing industry. The resulting exclusive dealing agreements may or may not have an impact on antitrust concerns depending on the nature of the agreement and the market in which it occurs.

A critical concern is the definition of the relevant market for analysis. For print and cable media, the tendency has been to define markets in terms of local regions such as the scope of the cable franchise or the range of the major metropolitan newspaper circulation.[45] A narrow market definition tends to impose greater restrictions on the activity of a major entity.[46] Local markets are relevant for many information services. However, it is important that the increasingly national nature of the information marketplace not be ignored in an analysis of electronic publishing. One consequence of both traditional and newer forms of electronic communication is that geographic limitations are less relevant when defining the competitive range of the service. A more important factor for electronic media may be the nature of the information provided. Thus, a news-oriented system that emphasizes national and international material is likely to be in a national market (e.g., The Wall Street Journal, The New York Times). In contrast, a system providing shoppers' news in a suburban area is clearly in a local market.

---

[42] See Chapter 4.

[43] See United States v. Penn-Olin Chem. Co., 378 US 158 (1964).

[44] See Brodley, "Joint Ventures and Antitrust Policy," 95 Harv. L. Rev. 1523 (1982).

[45] See, e.g., Home Placement Serv., Inc. v. Providence Journal Co., 682 F2d 274 (1st Cir. 1982), cert. denied, 75 L. Ed. 2d 500 (1983).

[46] See Berkey Photo, Inc. v. Eastman Kodak Co., 603 F2d 263 (2d Cir. 1979); Morning Pioneer, Inc. v. Bismarck Tribune Co., 493 F2d 383 (8th Cir. 1974), cert. denied, 419 US 836 (1974).

¶ 11.06 DEFINING THE PRODUCT

Teletext, videotext, or other potential forms of electronic publishing are characterized by the ability to make vast amounts of information electronically available in a readily accessible form. While much of the material provided resembles newsprint, video, or other products, aspects of the electronic publishing industry involving databases deal more directly with information as a primary commercial product. Unlike in other media, the product must be available over a relatively substantial period of time in order to serve as a commercially viable asset. As a result, there are critical issues concerning the extent to which vested rights in information can be established, retained, and enforced in an environment in which third-party access is an essential feature.

Electronic publishing involves a variety of product forms where significant and unanswered questions exist concerning the nature of protection available to the proprietor of the publishing enterprise against unauthorized use or reproduction of the information. To the extent that noncontractual protection is available, it will be grounded in copyright law. However, the information products typically offered by electronic publishers do not necessarily fit easily within traditional copyright law concepts and existing protections.

While it is possible to engage in electronic publishing by making available a single product analogous to a book or article, more commonly a publisher will make numerous items available to customers from a database. For purposes of this discussion, it is useful to distinguish distinct types of electronic information products that are commercially available. The first type consists of selected items of text or graphics characterized by substantial creativity in each item, as well as subjective judgment by the publisher in selecting the items. This group might include a database of articles, books, or video games that a subscriber can access and use either on a central computer or by copying to a local computer. Under copyright terminology, the publication of all of the items is a collective work consisting of copyrightable materials arranged or compiled into a collection that is potentially copyrightable in its own right.[47]

A second commercial product type consists of a collection of selected facts, public domain or noncopyrightable materials, where the individual items are chosen on the basis of subjective criteria applied by the publisher. This might entail, for example, a list of restaurants rated as excellent by the compiler of the information base. For reasons discussed in the following section, the names and addresses of the restaurants are

---

[47] 17 USC §§ 101, 103 (1982); see *Nimmer on Copyright* § 3.02.

not separately copyrightable, but the publisher may claim copyright protection in the collection itself. The collection would be described as a compilation, that is, a collected set of uncopyrighted material.[48]

The final product type includes comprehensive collections of individual items that contain essentially all of the possible entries selected on the basis of objective criteria for subject matter inclusion. The individual items may be either independently creative work or unprotected materials such as pure factual data. This form might involve an electronic telephone directory, a collection of all reported appellate decisions, or a collection of all works of a particular author.

These three types differ not only in form, but also in terms of what product is delivered to the potential user of the publishing system. For example, a comprehensive database is valuable to potential users because of its comprehensive nature and, presumably, because the electronic publication permits the user to conveniently access the material. In contrast, selective databases offer a product whose value is defined, at least in part, by the judgment of the author of the material. Thus, for example, in a selective database of restaurants described as excellent by the author, the subscriber typically seeks to obtain the benefit of the author's judgment and guidance.[49]

While the commercial product differs depending on whether the database is comprehensive or selective, it also differs based on whether the individual items in the collection are separately creative works or are mere statements of facts. The user of a video game benefits from the expression in the individual game and will be attracted to the product because of the perceived quality of this expression. However, the user of a database characterized by selected facts (e.g., current events) or comprehensive facts (e.g., population of all countries) is not concerned about the expressive character of the individual items, but is or is not attracted to the system because of a desire for the information that the materials convey.

These distinctions are commercially relevant and may be legally significant. The variations identify different items of value, but may not be equally protected under existing law. Nevertheless, each is potentially significant as a commercial product and involves potentially substantial creative and intellectual effort. The extent to which this effort and creativity are or should be protected is a major issue.

---

[48] 17 USC § 101 (1982).

[49] See Good Eating, Inc. v. Best Places To Eat, Inc., 131 F2d 809 (7th Cir. 1942).

¶ 11.07 INFORMATION AND PROPERTY

There are two levels of legal protection available to proprietors of electronic database systems. The first focuses on the individual items in the database. The second focuses more broadly on protection of the collection of materials as a whole.

To the extent that the publisher obtains protection in either of these elements, the protection will be grounded in federal copyright or contract law.[50] The Copyright Act (the Act) makes clear that both aspects of a database may be separately protectible. Indeed, copyright protection may vest in different persons based on different contributions. As to the individual items in a database, basic standards of authorship apply, restricted by the notion that copyright does not protect ideas, processes, or facts.[51] As to the collection of all of the items, separate authorship and, hence, protection may vest based on the selection, arrangement, and coordination of the database as a whole.

[1] Books and Articles

Otherwise copyrightable material retains its protected status when stored in a database. This result is clear, notwithstanding early concern about the protection of such works in a computer environment based on the doctrine of *White-Smith Publishing*.[52] As discussed in Chapter 1, this case held that a copy of a work must be directly perceivable by a human in order to receive copyright protection.

The *White-Smith* doctrine arose under old technology in an era prior to the development of new, mechanical methods of storage and reproduction. It is expressly overruled in the Act. Under current law, copyright protection extends to a work of authorship fixed in any medium from which it can be perceived "directly or indirectly" with the aid of a machine or other device.[53] Under the terms of this section of the Act, the capability to retrieve and print or display a work through the use of an appropriate program ensures that the work retains protection when stored or copied into a computer.

The extent to which preexisting licenses that convey rights in print and other media encompass electronic reproduction remains a question. For example, for creative works of authorship included within a database,

---

[50] See *Nimmer on Copyright* 2-157.

[51] See Denicola, "Copyright in Collections of Facts: A Theory for Protection of Nonfiction Literary Works," 91 Colum. L. Rev. 516 (1981).

[52] White-Smith Publishing v. Apollo, 209 US 1 (1908).

[53] 17 USC § 102 (1982).

significant issues may arise about the electronic publisher's right to reproduce the work in the data system.[54] In this case, the wording of the particular agreement is crucial. If the agreement is ambiguous, the appropriate presumption is that rights in a new medium are not conveyed unless the conveyance clearly extends to any and all future uses.

Rights under copyright law are divisible and may be separately conveyed. The overall objective of the system is to protect authors. In most cases, it can hardly be argued that an author intended to convey rights to a form of publication that did not even exist at the time of the original contract. It is equally implausible that the parties realistically evaluated these future rights in the original transaction. The valuation of teletext and videotext rights is properly done in an environment in which the existence of those forms of publishing is well-known and expressly acknowledged.

[2] Factual Items

Where a database consists of separately creative works, copyright protection precludes unauthorized reproduction of individual items. In many instances, however, the value of an electronic database lies not in the creative expression found in individual items, but in the factual information that the items convey. Databases consisting of compiled statistics, names, addresses, and the like, are especially common products in an electronic environment where the ease of storage and access provides a user with fingertip availability of information formerly available only with substantial research or storage capacity. The value of such compilations, however, rests in part on their comprehensive or selective nature, and in part on the particular information conveyed.

To the extent that the value of the database lies in the factual information in individual items, protection of the database owner is limited by the underlying premise that copyright protection does not extend to facts, but only to expression.[55] This restriction of copyright law is analogous to previously discussed limitations that preclude a copyright over an underlying idea or process.[56] It is based on presumptions about the balance

---

[54] See Bartsch v. Metro-Goldwyn-Mayer, Inc., 391 F2d 150 (2d Cir. 1968).

[55] See *Nimmer on Copyright* 2-157; see also Denicola, "Copyright in Collections of Facts: A Theory for Protection of Nonfiction Literary Works," 91 Colum. L. Rev. 516 (1981); Gorman, "Copyright Protection for the Collection and Representation of Facts," 76 Harv. L. Rev. 1569 (1963); Comment, "Copyrighted Compilations of Public Domain Facts: The Criterion of Infringement," 71 Nw. UL Rev. 833 (1977).

[56] See ¶¶ 1.02[3], 1.06.

between protecting an author and ensuring free and open discourse concerning ideas and data. While an author's unique expression can often be protected without inhibiting the free exchange and use of factual information and concepts, protection of the individual author gives way when necessary to ensure continued functioning of free expression and scholarly communication and use of data.

The exclusion of copyright protection for individual facts has several distinct applications. The first is copyright control over the information communicated in an otherwise expressive work. The cases quite clearly establish that copyright conveys no protection in communicated information and only potentially covers the form of communication. Thus, a book based on a scholarly conclusion that an air disaster was caused by sabotage grants the author no control over that theory or presumed fact, but only over the particular expression in the book.[57] Similarly, a factual story based on investigative research into a murder or kidnapping establishes copyright protection over the resulting writing, but not over the factual detail about the crime.[58]

In many databases this limitation denies the database owner protection over a significant aspect of what it offers that is of commercial value. Nevertheless, this result can be justified in terms of the conclusion that there is no authorship in factual data. Facts are created by events, the author merely reports them.[59] More correctly, exclusion of copyright protection for communicated information rests in a desire to avoid restricting the ability of subsequent scholars to use the information. Granting an author control over factual information as contrasted to the expression thereof would significantly impair development in the sciences and arts and this is too "high a price for increased incentive" for the author.[60]

Exclusion of copyright control over factual information may also extend to exclude protection even of the author's expression. This is most readily understood where the expression is primarily functional, austere, and severely limited. The expression "one white car" might theoretically contain both facts and expression. However, this has little practical significance. There is no difference between the factual information and the mode of expression used. In such cases, the predominant copyright principle is that there is no exclusive right in the factual information. The

---

[57] See Hoehling v. Universal City Studios, Inc., 618 F2d 972 (2d Cir. 1980).

[58] See Miller v. Universal City Studios, Inc., 650 F2d 1365 (5th Cir. 1981).

[59] Denicola, "Copyright in Collections of Facts: A Theory for Protection of Nonfiction Literary Works," 91 Colum. L. Rev. 516, 525 (1981).

[60] Id.

expression is not protected because to do so would indirectly protect the factual data.[61]

This fact-expression identity concept extends beyond the most austere cases and encompasses situations in which, while there may be several ways of expressing a particular set of facts, the alternatives are severely limited. In such situations, courts may undertake a broader reading of concepts of fair use[62] or may require virtually literal copying in order to establish substantial similarity.[63] Alternatively, there may simply be a conclusion that the particular expression is not protected under copyright law because of the limited, alternative modes of expressing a particular fact.[64] Under any of these guises, the basic copyright law theme is designed to guarantee the free exchange and use of information that is essential to ongoing scientific and intellectual growth among a community of scholars.

[3] Selection, Arrangement, and Effort

Beyond copyright protection for the individual items in the database, the database publisher may seek protection for the database itself. A database is either a compilation or a collective work depending on the nature of the material included.[65] Under either label, the publisher who selects material for inclusion is protected for the selection, arrangement, and coordination reflected in the database.[66] While compilations and collective works are clearly within the domain of copyright law, the scope and rationale for protection of these works is unclear and controversial.[67]

---

[61] See *Nimmer on Copyright* 2-157; Landsberg v. Scrabble Crossword Puzzle Game Players, Inc., 221 USPQ 1140 (9th Cir. 1984).

[62] See Dow Jones & Co. v. Board of Trade, 546 F. Supp. 113, 217 USPQ 901 (SDNY 1982).

[63] See Landsberg v. Scrabble Crossword Puzzle Game Players, Inc., 221 USPQ 1140 (9th Cir. 1984).

[64] Denicola, "Copyright in Collections of Facts: A Theory for Protection of Nonfiction Literary Works," 91 Colum. L. Rev. 516, 526 (1981).

[65] See *Nimmer on Copyright* § 3.02; see also Denicola, "Copyright in Collections of Facts: A Theory for Protection of Nonfiction Literary Works," 91 Colum. L. Rev. 516 (1981); Gorman, "Copyright Protection for the Collection and Representation of Facts," 76 Harv. L. Rev. 1569 (1963); Comment, "Copyrighted Compilations of Public Domain Facts: The Criterion of Infringement," 71 Nw. UL Rev. 833 (1977).

[66] 17 USC §§ 101, 103 (1982).

[67] See Dow Jones & Co. v. Board of Trade, 546 F. Supp. 113, 217 USPQ 901 (SDNY 1982); Rand McNally & Co. v. Fleet Management Sys., Inc., 221 USPQ 828 (ND Ill. 1983).

The statute refers to selection, arrangement, and coordination in the database. This establishes that a compilation of even public domain material or pure facts is copyrightable. However, one view is that this language requires a finding of at least minimum levels of creativity or originality for aspects of the work that may be subject to copyright protection.[68] This is essential to establish that the database is a "work of authorship" under the terms of the Act.

Under this view, selection and arrangement are the potentially copyrightable elements of a database. Thus, a compilation selecting all restaurants rated by the author as excellent is protected as to the selectivity and, hence, the essential content of the list. Similarly, the list of Dow Jones index companies is protected as to selectivity.[69] In contrast, a comprehensive list of all articles published in a magazine may reflect no creative selection. It may be protected only as to the arrangement of facts in the database in a manner that facilitates access and retrieval of particular items.[70]

As one basis for copyright protection, the emphasis on creative selection or arrangement is not controversial. Selection and arrangement not dictated solely by functional or obvious criteria satisfy all traditional aspects of copyright protection. The emphasis on these variables provides a means of protecting the author while not indirectly creating a monopoly on the facts in the database. A third party may copy or otherwise use particular items from the compilation, since this does not infringe selection or arrangement. However, wholesale appropriation is prevented, since such massive reproduction would be a taking of the expressive selection and arrangement.[71]

The difficulty of an emphasis on selection and arrangement arises if these are viewed as essential to establish a copyrightable work or an infringement of that work, rather than as merely sufficient, but not necessarily required for protection. The view that creativity in arrangement and selection are the sole protectible elements of a database creates difficulties in two situations. The first involves reproduction of all information from a comprehensive database, but with an original and distinct

---

[68] *Nimmer on Copyright* 2-41; Rand McNally & Co. v. Fleet Management Sys., Inc., 221 USPQ 828 (ND Ill. 1983).

[69] See Good Eating, Inc. v. Best Places to Eat, Inc., 131 F2d 809 (7th Cir. 1942) (restaurant list); Dow Jones & Co. v. Board of Trade of the City of Chicago, 546 F. Supp. 113, 217 USPQ 901 (SDNY 1982) (list of stocks); see also Schroeder v. William Morrow & Co., 566 F2d 1 (7th Cir. 1977) (list of garden suppliers).

[70] *Nimmer on Copyright* § 2.11D.

[71] Denicola, "Copyright in Collections of Facts: A Theory for Protection of Nonfiction Literary Works," 91 Colum. L. Rev. 516, 527 (1981).

organization. In such cases, the first author may have exercised no protectible selectivity (i.e., merely having collected all New York appellate cases), and the unauthorized work does not reproduce any protected arrangement of data. The second problem area involves situations in which selection and arrangement are dictated by functional, relatively obvious criteria such as an alphabetical listing of all persons in a city with a telephone. Under the foregoing, wholesale appropriation of both products is outside of the scope of copyright.

While these results might be conceptually justified, the reported cases do not consistently apply the creativity requirement in this manner. Instead, there is authority that protects authors of databases even where no appropriation of selection or arrangement occurs. [72] For example, telephone directories have long been protected from wholesale appropriation by copyright law. [73] Similarly, copyright protection attaches to some compilations against appropriation in a form that dramatically alters and, therefore, does not copy the arrangement of data of the original publication. [74]

As this implies, while there is support for the creativity concept as a limiting principle for copyright protection, other factors are often considered. One alternative emphasizes the amount of effort involved in creating the compilation for which protection is sought. One court described this as the "proposition that 'industrious collection' of information in the public domain may qualify for copyright protection." [75] Simply stated, some compilations or directories of factual data are "considered original works because of the labor expended in their preparation." [76]

---

[72] Id. at 529–531.

[73] See, e.g., Leon v. Pacific Tel. & Tel. Co., 91 F2d 484 (9th Cir. 1937); Northwestern Bell Tel. Co. v. Bedco, 501 F. Supp. 299 (D. Minn. 1980); Southwestern Bell Tel. Co. v. Nationwide Independent Directory Serv., Inc., 371 F. Supp. 900 (WD Ark. 1974).

[74] See Leon v. Pacific Tel. & Tel. Co., 91 F2d 484 (9th Cir. 1937) (altered alphabetical to numerical listing); National Business Lists v. Dunn & Bradstreet, 552 F. Supp. 89 (ND Ill. 1982); Triangle Publishing, Inc. v. New England Publishing Co., 46 F. Supp. 198 (D. Mass. 1942) (race forms); Rand McNally & Co. v. Fleet Management Sys., Inc., 221 USPQ 828 (ND Ill. 1983). But see Triangle Publishing, Inc. v. Sports Eye, Inc., 415 F. Supp. 682 (ED Pa. 1976). Compare New York Times Co. v. Roxbury Data Interface, Inc., 434 F. Supp. 217 (DNJ 1977) (altered directory data protected as fair use).

[75] Rand McNally & Co. v. Fleet Management Sys., Inc., 221 USPQ 828, 832 (ND Ill. 1983); see National Business Lists v. Dunn & Bradstreet, 552 F. Supp. 89 (ND Ill. 1982).

[76] Dow Jones & Co. v. Board of Trade, 546 F. Supp. 113, 217 USPQ 901, 903 (SDNY 1982). Compare Miller v. Universal City Studios, Inc., 650 F2d 1365 (5th Cir. 1981).

Reliance on underlying labor and effort fits within the statutory language. Selection can encompass effort in locating and listing particular items in a compilation, rather than solely sorting among available options. More telling, this interpretation responds to the view that wholesale appropriation of material collected with significant effort is unfair. To permit such appropriation would substantially reduce the original author's incentive to produce potentially valuable works. Equally important, standards applied elsewhere in copyright law are consistent with effort protection. An author's labor in producing a 1000-page novel is protected even though the actual expression is uninspired, pedestrian, and largely reports known facts.

Regardless of the criteria applied in judging the copyrightability of a database, minimal standards of effort, selectivity, or arrangement creativity must be present to establish protection. The required level of each of these has not been specified, but it is clear that obvious arrangements, such as chronological order for historical events and alphabetical listing for names, are not in themselves protectible.[77] Similarly, lists that are determined by functional criteria and are not substantial compilations are often not protectible.[78]

In an electronic database, the distinction among these bases for protection is important. In many cases, protection limited to the arrangement or selectivity of the database will not be meaningful in this environment. Electronic arrangement of data is fluid and has significantly different connotations than it would in a printed database. In a computer database, one advantage of the medium is the ease and flexibility of the search capacity that the electronic environment provides. This, however, is not determined by the arrangement of data in the computer in the traditional sense. Search capability and form are determined primarily by the access or search routines in the database program and the data storage form. The combined effects of these elements may constitute a protectible arrangement of data. However, the protection extends to the computer program, rather than the data itself, and appropriation of the program is seldom an issue that need be addressed in terms of compilations or collective works.

As is true in other publishing environments, some electronic databases may be characterized by substantial, subjective elements attributable to the author. Often, however, electronic databases are oriented less to selective recording of data than to comprehensive listing of mate-

---

[77] *Nimmer on Copyright* § 2.11D.

[78] See *Nimmer on Copyright* § 2.10; Dow Jones & Co. v. Board of Trade, 546 F. Supp. 113, 217 USPQ 901, 904 (SDNY 1982).

rial determined by objective criteria. To the extent that there are risks of large-scale appropriation of the database, protection would vest only by virtue of an emphasis on the effort to collect and maintain the database itself.

¶ 11.08 DATABASE INFRINGEMENTS

In most cases, computer databases are copyrightable compilations or collective works. Copyrightability, however, does not necessarily determine the scope of the resulting protection or whether that protection is adequate for the nature of the commercial product. These issues raise two general questions: (1) To what extent does actual reproduction or use of parts of the database constitute infringement? and (2) What types of electronic manipulation and remote access of the data are precluded under copyright?

[1] Downloading and Reproduction of Data

A third party does not infringe copyright protection unless it reproduces the copyrightable elements of the protected work.[79] Therefore, in any particular case it is essential not only to examine the conduct of the alleged infringer, but also to determine the basis on which copyright protection has been established for the appropriated material.

The clearest case involves database systems that contain sufficiently expressive material to make individual items copyrightable. The data in the system might consist of material such as articles and books compiled by the database proprietor. The copyright in each item may be held by the author or the owner of the database on license from the author. Reproduction of the copyrighted material is actionable under traditional standards of substantial similarity and fair use. Reproduction of any substantial segment of such a database will be an infringement of the copied items.

More complex issues arise when the items of data or text are not copyrightable. Under these circumstances, it is essential to delineate carefully the copyrightable elements of the database. The database copyright does not extend to or cover individual items. Instead, copyright protection extends only to the selection and arrangement of the data. As discussed previously, depending on the nature of the database and the doctrinal approach adopted by the court, this may refer to creative selectivity

---

[79] *Nimmer on Copyright* §§ 2.18A–2.18D; see Dow Jones & Co. v. Board of Trade, 546 F. Supp. 113, 217 USPQ 901 (SDNY 1982).

and arrangement or may encompass the effort expended in collecting the particular data.[80] The distinctions in analytical approach become central in identifying instances of infringement.

Regardless of the approach, downloading individual items of data into a local computer or reproducing them in printed form will not infringe the protected elements of the overall work unless or until the action rises to a level of wholesale reproduction of substantial portions of the database. The nature of the portions that must be reproduced before there is an infringement, however, will depend on the conceptual basis for protection accepted by the court. It is not an infringement to reproduce a database in full using a new arrangement of data unless copyright protection is based on industrious data collection or on selectivity in creating the database.[81] In contrast, if the copyright protection is premised on the author's selectivity in creating the database, substantial reproduction of items from the compilation is not an infringement if the items are selected based on different criteria chosen by the alleged infringer.

Reproduction of data from a public domain database is not infringement unless or until it rises to a level of copying substantially all of the data. Even then, however, it is important to distinguish between infringing an arrangement of data and infringing the author's selection. In a computer environment, arrangement or organization is controlled by and coextensive with the underlying data management system. Unlike in telephone directories or customer lists, it may not be productive to discuss arrangement of data in linear or one-dimensional form. Arguably, this implies that a database arrangement can not be infringed unless the copying includes the data management or search program. The alternative would be to conclude that the copyright protects any organizational structure that the program is capable of producing on command.

[2] Fair Use and Substantial Similarity

Infringement claims regarding primarily factual or public domain databases, like any other copyright infringement allegations, are based on the claim that a reproduced material is substantially similar to the origi-

---

[80] See supra ¶ 11.07[3]; see also 17 USC § 103 (1982).

[81] See Leon v. Pacific Tel. & Tel. Co., 91 F2d 484 (9th Cir. 1937) (altered alphabetical to numerical listing); National Business Lists v. Dunn & Bradstreet, 552 F. Supp. 89 (ND Ill. 1982); Triangle Publishing, Inc. v. New England Publishing Co., 46 F. Supp. 198 (D. Mass. 1942) (race forms); Rand McNally & Co. v. Fleet Management Sys., Inc., 221 USPQ 828 (ND Ill. 1983). But see Triangle Publishing, Inc. v. Sports Eye, Inc., 415 F. Supp. 682 (ED Pa. 1976). Compare New York Times Co. v. Roxbury Data Interface, Inc., 434 F. Supp. 217 (DNJ 1977) (altered directory data protected as fair use).

nal and that the reproduction does not involve "fair use."[82] An important limiting premise exists for both issues. The permitted scope of fair use and permissible reproduction is greater for works based on factual material or compilations than for more expressive works such as novels or short stories.[83]

The basis for this limitation on the author's rights rests in underlying philosophy regarding the balance between protecting an individual author and the need for preserving free use of factual material by a community of scholars. Due to the factual or objective nature of the original work, subsequent works independently based on similar criteria will necessarily have similar content. For example, the LEXIS database of federal decisions is substantially similar to that maintained by WESTLAW in selection and arrangement even though no copying occurs. Loose standards of infringing similarity in this environment might create an indirect monopolization of the underlying facts. Thus, in many instances, infringement is present only if there is literal or verbatim duplication of a factual work.[84]

Even beyond questions of sufficient similarity, standards of fair use for factual or compilation works are substantially more flexible than for other works. "Authors of compilations [are] held to grant broader licenses for subsequent use than persons whose work is truly creative."[85] In many cases, this will permit substantial reproduction of portions of a database as long as the reproduction and use of the information is for a purpose that does not directly compete with the purpose and market of the original compilation. Thus, in *New York Times v. Roxbury Data Interface, Inc.*,[86] fair use was found where the defendant used annual name indexes and the New York Times index to compile a work providing an integrated index based on names mentioned in New

---

[82] See ¶ 1.11[3].

[83] See Hoehling v. Universal City Studios, Inc., 618 F2d 972 (2d Cir. 1980); Landsberg v. Scrabble Crossword Puzzle Game Players, Inc., 221 USPQ 1140 (9th Cir. 1984); *Nimmer on Copyright* § 2.11. See Denicola, "Copyright in Collections of Facts: A Theory for Protection of Nonfiction Literary Works," 91 Colum. L. Rev. 516 (1981); Gorman, "Copyright Protection for the Collection and Representation of Facts," 76 Harv. L. Rev. 1569 (1963); Comment, "Copyrighted Compilations of Public Domain Facts: The Criterion of Infringement," 71 Nw. UL Rev. 833 (1977).

[84] See *Nimmer on Copyright* §§ 2.11A–2.11B; Landsberg v. Scrabble Crossword Puzzle Game Players, Inc., 221 USPQ 1140 (9th Cir. 1984); Dow Jones & Co. v. Board of Trade, 546 F. Supp. 113, 217 USPQ 901 (SDNY 1982).

[85] Dow Jones & Co. v. Board of Trade, 546 F. Supp. 113, 217 USPQ 901, 906 (SDNY 1982).

[86] 434 F. Supp. 217 (DNJ 1977).

York Times articles. Although the entire research for the defendant's work was based on the copyrighted compilation, the court found that the two works did not address similar markets and, more important, that the defendant's work did not impinge the commercial value of the first compilation.

Generally, reproduction of all of the data from the first compilation will not constitute fair use by a second author. This is true even where the arrangement of the reproduced work differs from that of the original, if the copyright protection of the first is recognized based on industrious collection rationales.[87] In some cases, however, even literal reproduction of a compilation may be treated as a fair use. This result occurred in *Dow Jones & Co. v. Board of Trade of Chicago.*[88] In *Dow Jones*, the compilation referred to was the list of stocks included within the Dow index. This list was reproduced by the defendant in connection with an offering of futures contracts based on Dow averages. The court noted that given the brevity of the list and the importance of the selected stocks, if any use was to be treated as fair use, it would have to entail literal and complete copying. In the particular case, although the use was commercial in nature, it did not detract from any realistic market for the Dow list.

[3] Remote Access

Beyond questions of what copying constitutes infringement, contemporary database systems raise more basic issues as to what acts constitute reproduction. These focus on systems of remote access to data stored in a host computer and are present whether or not the material accessed is included within a database in the traditional sense of the word. In general, the issue arises concerning three distinct types of material—audiovisual works, textual works, and computer programs. For purposes of this discussion, assume that the material has been copyrighted independently of any potential copyright in a database itself.

Regardless of the type of work involved, the basic rights of the copyright owner include the right to reproduce or distribute the work in cop-

---

[87] See Leon v. Pacific Tel. & Tel. Co., 91 F2d 484 (9th Cir. 1937) (altered alphabetical to numerical listing); National Business Lists v. Dunn & Bradstreet, 552 F. Supp. 89 (ND Ill. 1982); Triangle Publishing, Inc. v. New England Publishing Co., 46 F. Supp. 198 (D. Mass. 1942) (race forms); Rand McNally & Co. v. Fleet Management Sys., Inc., 221 USPQ 828 (ND Ill. 1983). But see Triangle Publishing, Inc v. Sports Eye, Inc., 415 F. Supp. 682 (ED Pa. 1976). Compare New York Times Co. v. Roxbury Data Interface, Inc., 434 F. Supp. 217 (DNJ 1977) (altered directory data protected as fair use).

[88] 546 F. Supp. 113, 217 USPQ 901 (SDNY 1982).

ies. The Act defines a "copy" as a material object in which the work is fixed and from which it can be directly or indirectly perceived.[89] Under these definitions, unauthorized remote access to computer-stored material is clearly an infringement only if the information accessed is stored in the accessing machine. Thus, access through a terminal with no independent storage would not constitute reproduction, since no new copy is made in the absence of fixing the work in a tangible object. However, if the accessed data is stored in a disk or other device, there has been a reproduction.

In cases of access without storage, the copyright infringement potentially involves other exclusive rights of the copyright holder. Specifically, these include the right to publicly perform and publicly display the work.[90] In the case of nonreproductive remote access, it is apparent that at least for textual works and audiovisual works, the essence of the access will be a display of the work. The Act defines "display" as "to show a copy of it, either directly or indirectly."[91] In this case, the copy being shown is the version stored in the host computer. However, the exclusive right does not encompass all displays of the work, but only actions that "display the work *publicly*." In the typical case, the public element may not be met, since an ordinary sequence of events involves access by a single user at a single terminal. Under traditional conceptions, public performance or display occurs "at a place open to the public or at any place where a substantial number of persons outside of a normal circle of a family and its social acquaintances is gathered; or to transmit . . . a performance or display . . . to the public."[92] Under this definition, the inclusion of a work in a public-accessible database is a display, but nonreproductive access by a remote user is not an infringement of copyright.

[4] Broadcast Teletext

Issues about the basic protection of a computer database will shape the growth of the electronic publishing industry. It is also apparent that the various methods of communicating the electronic publication may have an impact on copyright claims. This occurs with broadcast teletext.

Delivery of teletext materials in the VBI of a normal broadcast signal is one common form of delivery of teletext services. Under this form, the

---

[89] 17 USC § 101 (1982).

[90] 17 USC § 106(4)(5) (1982).

[91] 17 USC § 101 (1982).

[92] 17 USC § 101 (1982); see *Nimmer on Copyright* § 8.14[C].

otherwise unused portions of the broadcast signal become potentially valuable sites for teletext materials. Questions arise about the ability of various entities that receive, send, or retransmit the broadcast signal to alter or otherwise customize the material contained in the VBI. These questions involve relatively complex technology, but ultimately pertain to the extent that control over teletext is ancillary to control over primary broadcast signals.

One scenario that resulted in litigation involved a copyrighted, normal telecast that was broadcast with teletext included in the VBI of the signal. In *WGN v. United Video, Inc.,*[93] copyrighted broadcasts originated by WGN in Chicago were received by United Video (UV), a satellite operator functioning as a common carrier. UV retransmitted the signal to cable system operators for a fee. It did so without payment to or authorization from WGN under the so-called passive carrier exemption in the Act. This exemption permits retransmission of television broadcasts where the party making the second transmission "has no direct or indirect control over the content or selection of the primary transmission."[94] The intercepted and retransmitted programs were news broadcasts. UV deleted teletext signals included by WGN from the broadcast and inserted its own teletext. This was done in two newscasts. The first originally contained merely a teletext test pattern, while the second contained a WGN program guide and a news story.

The Seventh Circuit Court of Appeals held that the course of action followed by UV was not authorized under the passive carrier exemption. The court found that under the circumstances in this case the teletext and the broadcast program were one copyrighted work, even though a viewer would be forced to switch from one picture to another in order to view both. Thus, UV infringed the copyright by altering the content of the copyrighted work.

The resolution of rights in altering and controlling teletext signals is potentially central to the development of the industry. The court's decision allocates control over teletext signal content between the original broadcaster and a retransmitting passive carrier. Under the court's approach, the teletext and the broadcast program are one work and the retransmitting company must transmit the entirety if a three-part test is met. They are considered a single work if "[The] teletext is intended to be seen by the same viewers as are watching [the broadcast program] during the same interval of time ... and as an integral part of the ... pro-

---

[93] 693 F2d 622 (7th Cir. 1982).

[94] 17 USC § 111(a)(3) (1982).

gram." [95] The third part of the test is likely to be the most significant. It requires that the two elements are intended to be integral parts of the program. Presumably, this requires some substantive or creative integration and similarity of subject matter. However, the degree of similarity and the nature of the standard remain undefined at this time.

In the case of *WGN*, the right of a retransmitting entity to alter the VBI teletext of a broadcast is contingent solely on whether one or two copyrighted works are involved. If the two are intended as integral parts of a program, they must be retransmitted as is. If they are separable and intended as such, the retransmitting entity need not transmit the original teletext. In such cases, the second party in effect has control over the content of the teletext delivered in the broadcast signal.

¶ 11.09 CONTRACT ROYALTIES AND SERVICE

Among the issues presented by electronic publishing in videotext or teletext form is a basic decision as to the manner in which this form of publishing fits into the context of more traditional publishing activities. This issue arises most clearly with videotext or database-oriented systems in which materials are placed into electronic form and simply made available to subscribers to the system. The question is manifest in the context of determining appropriate methods of dealing with royalty computations and service charges for users.

In traditional book publishing, the relationship between author and publisher is relatively straightforward and stable. The publisher pays for publication rights in either a fee or a royalty based on the volume of sales (or a combination of these). The publisher is responsible for marketing the work. The contract may expressly or impliedly place obligations of good faith and best efforts on the publisher. [96] In general, the marketing is contingent on the individual product. For books, the author's royalties are not necessarily connected to the saleability of the publisher's entire line of books. In magazines, there is a direct connection, but the standard form of payment is in a lump sum not connected to sales volume. The author's relationship to the book's purchaser and to library systems is also relatively straightforward. The purchaser pays a single price for the volume and is able to use or not use it at leisure with no additional expense. Libraries provide free access and use of books. As long as additional copies are not made or purchased, the library payment is unchanged whether there

---

[95] WGN v. United Video, Inc., 693 F2d 622, 626 (7th Cir. 1982).

[96] See ¶ 5.13[4].

are one or 1000 users of a particular work. For both libraries and individuals, however, updates are available only at additional cost in the form of purchasing a second edition or of an explicit update charge.

These traditional models reflect a treatment of books as discrete products whose value may be defined by the information or textual content, but which can be sold independently of subsequent levels of use. This model might be applied to videotext databases. Thus, access to the database might be sold for a fee to the subscriber and delivered either in terms of permitted copying or, more likely, in terms of making the system available for access. Subsequent fees might be assessed for updates to or changes in the data or text. While this model might be workable, the nature of electronic systems has led to a different characterization of the system with attendant difficulties in implementing and monitoring contract performance.

In essence, rather than a product model, many if not most videotext publishers have opted for a use or service model. Under this model, an initial fee might be charged for access to the system, but the predominant billing system is calibrated to actual use of the data and text contained in the material. Thus, a typical WESTLAW license provides for a specified fee covering a minimum number of hours of use, followed by an hourly charge for further use. Similar forms are applied in most commercial systems.

This transforms the essence of the information transaction and has significant economic effects. Initially, it tends toward a system in which the author of works to be included in the data system is reimbursed based on the actual use of the materials. This would be analogous to paying royalties on the basis of the number of times that a novel is accessed by being taken off the shelf. In the case of data systems, however, the user has lost the ability to acquire the pertinent information or text in the database as it is able to do in a book. Instead, it has merely purchased a right to pay for actual use of the material.

It is as a result of this shifted characterization of the transaction that one-time copying of database contents by the user has become an important copyright issue. In essence, the user who makes a hard copy of some portion of a database (e.g., an article on open heart surgery) has replicated a magazine purchase in the context of a system that does not specifically provide for such transactions. The copyright holder presumably loses some income, since the "computer use" time to make a copy is probably less than the access time the user would have needed to read the work from the display screen. However, the loss is only in proportion to the extent to which there is a protectible interest in being able to charge and collect royalties based on use, rather than sale of a copy.

The information transaction is transformed in this manner largely by contract (license). However, an underlying policy issue is involved. It is most likely to arise in cases involving alleged fair use of an electronic work in the form of making a single hard copy or a disk copy for personal use. The standards in this context are not clear. Arguably, the copy has infringed the copyright proprietor's exclusive rights in the work unless there has been express authorization. Such argument supports the view that the proprietor can define electronic delivery of works in a manner unlike that accorded to more traditional deliveries. On the other hand, as long as there is no subsequent copying or commercial distribution of the copied work, it is arguable that no infringement occurs. This single copy falls within traditional boundaries of copyrighted work transactions. The copyright proprietor remains protected to the same degree as would have been the case for more traditional publishing forms.

This latter view is clearly preferable. It is supported by the recent Supreme Court decision in *Sony Corp. v. Universal City Studios*,[97] a case involving videotape recorders (VCRs). The Court held that VCR equipment sales were not contributory infringements of motion picture or television copyrights because VCR equipment has a significant, noninfringing use. That use consists of making copies of broadcast programs for personal use for delayed viewing. The analogy to database copying for personal use is obvious. The chief distinction in the two contexts is that television broadcasts are not transmitted subject to fees for use, while teletext commonly is subject to fees.

¶ 11.10 PRODUCT LIABILITY

Since the development of electronic publishing, concerns have lingered about the potential liability incurred for inaccurate information transmitted through the system. This concern encompasses the possibility that a form of product liability may be attached to information products delivered through electronic media.[98]

At one level, the concern seems clearly misplaced. At least in some of its manifestations, electronic publishing delivers a product that is not substantially dissimilar from that delivered through other forms of publishing, and there is no a priori rationale for the belief that the electronic form alters liability considerations. Clearly, delivery of fiction writing through electronic systems does not create liability for a poorly written work. Similarly, a publisher that serves essentially as a conduit for articles

---

[97] 104 S. Ct. 774 (1984).

[98] See ¶ 7.06[2].

is in a similar conduit position whether the articles are produced in electronic or paper form.

Historically, tort liability in the publishing industry concentrated almost entirely on issues of libel and slander. These are increasingly important issues in which personal privacy is balanced against constitutional policies relating to free speech. In a series of decisions, the Supreme Court constitutionalized substantial portions of libel law, imposing relatively stringent standards to establish liability.[99] These standards require proof of actual malice to find libel of public figures and are oriented toward protection of free speech interests even at the expense of some injury to individuals. While these standards are not necessarily ideal protections for the press, especially in clashes involving individual privacy interests, they establish a general perspective on balancing competing claims that is protective of speech.[100]

Issues of libel are relevant to electronic publishing, but are relatively remote, since the information currently provided in such systems seldom deals with personal matters of a sensitive nature. The more pertinent concern involves inaccuracy of information provided by the publishing service. For example, under what circumstances is the publisher liable for inaccurate information about stock prices that led to an inopportune sale of stock? Alternatively, is there liability in the publisher of LEXIS if an error in the search program or text entry resulted in a failure to locate a case that would have resolved a court case? Concerning these similar issues, there is virtually no case or statutory guidance available. Yet, as information electronically delivered becomes an increasingly valuable commercial product, the issue will necessarily arise.

In electronic or traditional publishing, assessing liability for inaccurate information requires consideration of several discrete issues. The first concerns the relationship between the information provider and the recipient of the inaccurate data. Liability for inaccurate information may arise from either of two aspects of this relationship. The first aspect is that in many cases there will be an express contract. It is with contracts that a significant difference exists between newspaper, book, or television distribution of information and electronic publishing. In the traditional forms, there is seldom an express agreement between the information provider and the recipient. Rather, the information provider merely places the information in an available form to be accessed by an interested party. As a consequence, liability can only be based on implicit representations or

[99] New York Times v. Sullivan, 376 US 254 (1964); Gertz v. Welch, 418 US 323 (1974).

[100] Bose Corp. v. Consumer Union of Am., 104 S. Ct. 1949 (1984).

duties. In contrast, in the electronic systems, an express agreement is common. The terms of the agreement provide an initial reference to define the provider's duties regarding data accuracy and completeness.

In the absence of express, contrary language, there are several ways in which the resulting contractual obligations might be characterized. Each results in the imposition of basic standards of accuracy unless the contract expressly disclaims them. For example, the terms of the agreement might be viewed as a service contract and the provider's obligation defined in terms of using reasonable efforts to provide accurate data. A higher, best efforts standard is inappropriate unless expressly agreed to by the parties. Alternatively, the transaction might be viewed as involving the delivery of a product and the Uniform Commercial Code (UCC) might suggest an implicit contractual obligation to provide that product (information) falling within reasonable standards of merchantability. In the context of information products, this would presumably include accuracy and completeness within normally acceptable standards of the industry. Of course, however, under either view, higher standards might be appropriate in particular cases. This might arise, for example, with databases expressly described as "comprehensive and complete."[101] Similarly, in the case of limited use database publishing, standards of fitness for the specific purpose might be imposed. Of course, since this is a situation involving contract liability, it would be feasible to disclaim representations, at least for nonconsumer transactions.

In the absence of contract, more difficult questions arise in defining the nature of the information product and the impact on the user. In general, there can be no liability for nonlibelous information in the absence of a clear reason to expect that a user will rely on the information to his detriment. If present, this reason to believe should establish at least a minimal duty to take *reasonable* steps to ensure the accuracy of data provided. The degree of duty, however, must be balanced against the fact that in this noncontractual environment restrictions on free expression are involved. Arguably, protecting the right to develop and disseminate information requires proof of more than mere negligence. A gross negligence standard may be appropriate.

Finally, especially for cases not based on express contract, issues arise as to whether a particular user did in fact reasonably rely on the inaccurate information. In many cases, this will defeat noncontractual liability.

----

[101] See Morris & Szabo, "Foreward: Removing Some Impediments to Development of America's Third and Fourth Generation Health Care Delivery Systems," 7 Am. J. L. & Med. v (1981).

CHAPTER *12*

Computer Privacy and Data Disclosure

¶ **12.01 INTRODUCTION**

The latter portion of the twentieth century has witnessed a significant and continuing increase in the importance of information and information services. This is partly reflected in the development of public database services. More generally, it is reflected in the routine and expanding reliance of decision-makers on data and data analysis systems in administering agencies and making policy decisions. There has been an expanding use of data-intensive activities such as standardized testing for schools or employment and opinion polls for political and commercial marketing. Similarly, various personal and business decisions relating to matters such as credit extension, welfare eligibility, insurance coverage, and the like are increasingly data-intensive.

The computer plays a vital role in this development, if only as a facilitating device. The power and data storage capacity of contemporary computer systems makes possible the accumulation and use of vast amounts of information. As analyses of these data become available, there is a tendency to demand more complete information about any particular decision. As social functions become increasingly dependent on information in computers, there is a need to protect the systems that provide these services. There is also a need to continually examine the effect of these systems on individual privacy. Inexorably, as the demand for more complete information increases, there is pressure against the ability of the individual to remain free from external scrutiny.

These developments require that society define protectible interests in particular types of information. There are clear rationales to support criminal law sanctions against various intrusions into information systems, and the result is that over 25 states have adopted computer crime legislation. This legislation, however, only partly touches on privacy as a protected interest. It is oriented more toward safeguarding property rights of commercial value and has only an indirect impact on privacy issues, such as where, for example, unauthorized access to a computer system is prohibited even for personal data. However, this legislation does not reflect mature consideration of privacy issues in computer systems, nor is it intended to do so. Coequal with the need to develop crime definitions pertaining to computers, there is a need to develop and articulate a cohesive understanding of privacy and the manner in which it should be protected in a computer and data-intensive environment.

¶ **12.02 DEFINING THE PRIVACY RIGHT**

Although individual privacy is a central value in our society, explicit protections for privacy are relatively recent. The contemporary network of statutory, judicial, and other protections around privacy interests is, at best, incomplete. This is not a result of disagreement with the general premise that U.S. law should protect individual privacy, but involves disagreement as to the constituent elements of protectible privacy and the manner in which these should be balanced against competing social interests. While virtually all responsible decision-makers accept the concept that individual privacy should be protected, there is widespread disagreement as to how to apply the general concept to particular situations.

In 1928, Justice Brandeis described the right to privacy as the right to be "let alone."[1] A more expansive and useable definition is that proposed by Westin in a landmark analysis of privacy interests written in 1967: "[Privacy is the] claim of individuals, groups, or institutions to determine for themselves when, how, and to what extent information about them is communicated to others."[2]

As Westin and most subsequent writers have recognized, the claim to privacy is not recognized in absolute, all-encompassing terms in any society. Privacy interests are balanced against various competing interests with the balance shifting in light of particular issues. The competing interests include the right of other persons as well as the government to have access to certain information pertinent to decision-making and, perhaps, to the enforcement of criminal and other social norms. The controversy involves defining the requisite information and the terms under which it is discoverable. Rather than an absolute principle, privacy interests are best conceptualized in terms of an ongoing tension and a process of adjustment. In essence, there is a balancing between the individual's interest in privacy and the society's right to know.[3]

The role of a legal system in a developing, information-intense environment is to establish pertinent rules of behavior and operational limits to preserve elements of self-determination concerning the disclosure of personal information.[4] These rules cannot ignore or reverse the data-

---

[1] Olmstead v. United States, 277 US 438, 478 (1928).

[2] Westin, *Privacy and Freedom* 7 (1967).

[3] See Miller, *The Assault on Privacy* (1971); Bazelon, "Probing Privacy," 12 Gonz. L. Rev. 587 (1977).

[4] See Ruggles, Pemberton & Miller, "Computer, Data Banks and Individual Privacy," 53 Minn. L. Rev. 211 (1968); Comment, "The Use and Abuse of Computerized Information: Striking a Balance Between Personal Privacy Interests and Organizational Information Needs," 44 Alb. L. Rev. 589 (1980).

intensive character of society, but should direct and channel it in a manner conducive to realistic conceptions of privacy. Defining those conceptions is a significant issue in the computer age.

[1] Recurring Issues

One frequently litigated privacy issue focuses on the right of the state or private entities to collect data about an individual.[5] Data collection occurs in a variety of settings and the context defines the nature of the issue. For example, there is a difference between the government's right to search a home for evidence of a crime and a prospective employer's right to inquire into the applicant's prior employment. In both cases, the individual's interest is the ability to control what information is disclosed and under what circumstances the data is obtained.

There is an element of protective response in many alleged privacy issues. Data not collected can not later be disclosed. In addition, there is a potential argument that some inquiries should not be made. The net effect is that the individual arguably should at least have the right to restrict information collection to matters relevant to a specific decision or inquiry validly undertaken. However, especially for private individuals, standards of relevance have not generally been imposed.

A related argument is that the individual should be required to respond only if the interest in obtaining information clearly outweighs the right to retain privacy and reasonable procedures have been invoked by the party seeking the information. This structure is present in the probable cause requirement of search and seizure law. However, search and seizure involves potential criminal proceedings involving severe sanctions and is characterized by direct involvement of government agents. These factors are not present in the private employment setting or in a wide variety of private data collections. Also, private contexts often have an element of voluntary submission by the subject of the inquiry.

These comparisons suggest a pattern that is relevant throughout the contemporary law of privacy. Through statute or judicial ruling, there is less reluctance to impose privacy restrictions on governmental data collection and use than on private actions.[6] However, even for governmental inquiries, substantial latitude is commonly allowed and, outside of criminal law, the interest in having complete data is most often superior to privacy interests.

---

[5] See Whalen v. Roe, 429 US 589 (1977); Buckley v. Valeo, 421 US 1 (1976).
[6] 20 USC § 1232(g) (1982).

A related privacy issue concerns the extent to which the individual can control or restrict the use of data that has been collected. The underlying view that individual privacy is a question of an individual's control over disclosure of data argues for a concept of restricted, rather than general, disclosure. For example, where data has been disclosed in a credit application, privacy concerns should prevent use of that information in connection with a job application without the consent of the applicant. This conception of privacy has not achieved substantial acceptance outside of governmental data banks and even in that context is only marginally implemented.[7] The basic competing premise involves efficiency and accuracy. Assuming that the original information is relevant to the second inquiry, requiring new data collection is wasteful and creates a risk of inaccuracy or misrepresentation.

A third privacy issue concerns the extent to which the individual has access to and can monitor the accuracy of the information collected about him. The interest in accuracy is the most well protected privacy right. In part, this is because maintaining accurate records is important to both the individual and the data user. In addition, the interest of the individual is relatively clear and understandable. The maintenance and use of inaccurate records may lead to immediate, tangible losses in the denial of credit, jobs, or other benefits. Conversely, the data user has no protectible interest in using inaccurate data.

[2] Computers and Privacy

Computer data systems affect each of these privacy issues in a manner adverse to the individual's interest. The computer alters the context in which privacy is defined and the competing interests balanced. Historically, privacy protection was augmented by cumbersome data collection and processing techniques that in themselves safeguarded individual interests and deterred governmental and private efforts to compile and use substantial amounts of information. As long as data about medical records, credit payments, marriages, children, and hotel bills were kept in hard copy file cabinets in unrelated business and governmental offices, there was little chance that they could be integrated into a large information pool about the individual. Even if that had been possible, hand processing and analysis would have been prohibitive. Now, these same data are accessible through powerful, communicating computer systems. Machine processing is not only feasible, but increasingly inexpensive. Thus, while the IRS might always have required reports on all interest paid on savings to all people in the country, it is only as a result of con-

---

[7] See infra ¶¶ 12.07, 12.10.

temporary computer systems that this information can be recorded and matched with tax returns for more than a few taxpayers.

Beyond the nascent ability to collect, store, and analyze vast sets of information about an individual, computer systems have also introduced a new factor into privacy issues. Previously, most privacy concerns have focused on the intrusion of large entities (e.g., government, business) into the privacy of the individual. Today, exposure to uncontrolled disclosure has greatly increased. The systems that store pertinent information about individuals are accessible through small machines located in homes and operated by novices through personal telephones. Common forms of communication among individuals are also subject to relatively easy interception. The personal computer, in connection with large computer systems accessible by telephone, has introduced the threat of individual voyeurism to an extent unimaginable in prior years.

PART A. DATA COMMUNICATIONS

¶ 12.03 COMMUNICATIONS PRIVACY

A convergence of expanding computer technology and rapid developments in telecommunications technology has dramatically changed the manner in which information is stored and transmitted, including the manner in which interpersonal communications are handled. These changes have outdistanced existing law pertaining to privacy safeguards against governmental or private intrusion into personal communications systems. The result is that under current law many of the communications that are engaged in electronically are exposed to interception or "eavesdropping" by unauthorized third parties without applicable legal restrictions.

The resulting privacy issues involve more than a need to correct outdated and incomplete statutes. They involve basic social issues that substantially affect not only the communications industry, but most of society. "The privacy questions raised by the new telecommunications age represent the single most important issue facing Congress today."[8] The issues include both defining the circumstances under which governmental agencies may intercept private electronic transmissions and delineating the sanctions against private parties who intercept transmissions without authority.

---

[8] Cong. Rec. 2954, March 21, 1984 (Burnham quoting Shattuck).

¶ 12.04 INTERCEPTED DATA TRANSMISSIONS

The clearest privacy issue pertaining to telecommunications concerns the extent to which governmental or private entities may intercept or "overhear" electronic transmissions. Two federal statutes currently place limited restrictions on such interceptions, whether conducted by the government or by private parties. The issue is whether these statutes provide adequate protection of privacy and other interests in the context of contemporary patterns of telecommunications.

In discussing this issue, the major changes in technology in telecommunications during the past two decades must be noted. Many users still regard the telephone as consisting primarily of voice transmission over wires when in fact significant aspects of the system no longer rely on wire transmissions. Virtually all transmissions of any distance involve microwave broadcasts, perhaps using satellites interspersed with traditional wires. Additionally, beyond voice transmission, a major use of telephones is electronic transmission of data including financial or written information. This use is especially relevant to privacy issues. Digital communication of computer data and nonverbal messages represents a form of telecommunications that was not present when current laws were originally enacted. Data communication may occur in the form of a transfer of raw or processed data between computer systems, such as when a microcomputer accesses WESTLAW or a local computer transmits inventory and sales information to a central processing facility. Alternatively, nonverbal communications are increasingly common as part of the so-called electronic mail industry.[9] In either form, the pertinent issue is whether nonverbal communications should receive the same or a lesser level of privacy protection as verbal communication.

[1] Federal Legislation

Two federal statutes currently provide limited rights of telecommunications privacy. The first is the Communications Act of 1935. This statute regulates the broadcast industry and prohibits any act to "intercept a radio communication and divulge" it.[10] The second, more directly relevant statute, is Title III of the Omnibus Crime Control and Safe Streets Act of 1968 (Title III). The relevant provisions apply to wiretapping and eavesdropping of voice communication. This statute was enacted amid significant controversy about the privacy and law enforcement implications of wiretapping. It prohibits private wiretapping and places substan-

---

[9] See infra ¶ 12.05.
[10] 18 USC § 605 (1982).

tial procedural and substantive restraints on the ability of governmental agencies to obtain warrants for wiretaps in criminal investigations.[11] The statutory provisions are more restrictive than required by constitutional norms.

These statutes reflect the era in which they were developed and may not resolve questions about privacy in current technology. Significant communications transmitted daily are not protected by either Title III or the Communications Act of 1935. This is because of the structure and focus of Title III, which was drafted in an environment where debate focused on voice communications and traditional forms of telephone transmission. Title III defines an "intercept" as the "aural acquisition of the contents of any wire or oral communication."[12] Under this definition, interceptions that do not involve wire or oral conversations and nonaural interceptions of data or other communications are not covered.[13]

Technology developments weaken the applicability of the wiretap provisions even for traditional voice telephone communications. Telephone systems rely on computer technology for switching and control operations and, more important in this context, an increasing number of all telephone transmissions are no longer handled entirely as voice or sound transmissions. Rather, the voice elements are reduced to digitized form for transmission and reassembly through computers. The resulting efficiencies are important to the telephone system, but while in digitized form interception of these transmissions is not covered by Title III. Any interception in that form would be a nonaural acquisition.

Equally important, for telephone communications of any significant distance transmission over wires is interspersed with microwave transmission, sometimes involving satellites. Broadcast of the signals increases exposure to unauthorized interception, but interception during this phase is arguably not covered by Title III since it does not involve a wire or oral communication. Furthermore, in hybrid transmissions involving both wire and radio transmission the Communications Act of 1935 is also inapplicable, as it is displaced by Title III.[14]

For transmissions over normal telephone systems, practical barriers currently provide some safeguard of privacy interests. The volume and diversity of information transmitted over public systems make intercep-

---

[11] 18 USC §§ 2510–2520 (1982).

[12] 18 USC § 2510(4) (1982).

[13] See United States v. New York Tel. Co., 434 US 159, 166 (1977); see also 130 Cong. Rec. S2952–2953 (March 21, 1984) (letter from S. Trott, Ass't Attorney Gen. to Hon. Patrick Leahy).

[14] United States v. Baxter, 492 F2d 150 (9th Cir. 1973).

tion of the radio aspects of the communication prohibitive and inefficient. Complex systems for routing digitized voice transmissions in which various aspects of the communications are routed in different paths make interception at that stage difficult. In both respects, wiretapping at the receiving or sending point is a more likely method of attempting an unauthorized interception. However, these practical barriers are not present for the increasingly numerous private networks established by large corporations.

As a matter of policy, the deficiencies in federal statutes present several distinct questions. For traditionally protected telephone conversations, preexisting policy should prevail despite changes in technology that may require redrafting of statutes. The fact that a telephone conversation is transmitted over microwave or reduced to digital form should not alter the underlying decision that the content of the conversation has privacy protections attached to it. Governmental interception should be subject to the same procedural and substantive restrictions that are present for wiretaps. Private interception should be prohibited.

For data or other nonverbal transmissions, an entirely new set of privacy issues must be considered. As discussed in the following section, governmental interceptions are subject to constitutional restrictions. The issue is whether telephonic data communication should receive the enhanced protections afforded against conversational wiretapping. As to this issue, it is arguable that communications between two machines involve a lesser expectation of privacy than verbal conversations between individuals. Similarly, especially for individuals, data communication is a less pervasive part of daily life than telephone conversation. As a result, it is arguable that the constitutional standard of protection is sufficient for data interception by government entities.[15]

The converse proposition reflects a more reasonable balancing of privacy and other interests. As data communication becomes increasingly significant to society, the enhanced protections afforded under wiretapping laws may become more appropriate. Establishing these protections as the norm from the outset will facilitate development of the communications system in a manner consistent with privacy expectations. As distinguishing between conversation and data communication interceptions may be impossible over the long term,[16] a consistent rule is desirable and it should be one that most clearly preserves existing privacy values. Fur-

---

[15] See Smith v. Maryland, 442 US 735 (1979); Katz v. United States, 389 US 347 (1967).

[16] See ¶ 11.02.

thermore, as seen in the following section,[17] constitutional standards allow government to acquire significant information about conversations and other transmissions even without a warrant. In an era in which computer data processing is increasingly sophisticated, accumulation of unprotected data such as the time, place, and recipient of a data or conversational transmission might breach the individual's right to control public knowledge about his lifestyle. Unless restraints are placed on data interceptions, such a result is likely.

Interceptions by private entities are not subject to constitutional restraints. In the absence of applicable federal legislation, private access to data transmissions of other parties may be covered by state legislation dealing with computer abuse.[18] However, not all states have enacted computer crime legislation and the interstate nature of telecommunications argues persuasively for federal action. An absolute bar to intentional interception of electronic transmissions is appropriate.

[2] Constitutional Limitations

For governmental interceptions, even absent statutory limitations, constitutional search and seizure rules apply to the interception of electronic communications. In the absence of consent by the people subject to the electronic interception, the Fourth Amendment requires probable cause and, in most cases, a warrant. Constitutional standards impose these requirements in any case in which the affected person has a reasonable expectation of privacy concerning the subject matter of the search.[19]

The existence of a reasonable expectation of privacy in the constitutional sense depends on the type of communication involved and the nature of the information sought. The content of normal telephone conversations is clearly protected by the Fourth Amendment. However, the Supreme Court has held that information about the numbers called and the number of calls made from a telephone was not subject to Fourth Amendment protection in a case that permitted local officials to use a pen register to record all numbers called from a particular phone.[20] The Court reasoned that an expectation of privacy could not attach to the numbers in light of the knowledge that the numbers called would or could be retained by the telephone company.

---

[17] See infra ¶ 12.04[2].

[18] See ¶ 9.07.

[19] Katz v. United States, 389 US 347 (1967).

[20] Smith v. Maryland, 442 US 735 (1979).

As applied to data transmissions over public telephone systems, a similar dichotomy is present in the absence of more restrictive statutes. While serving a different purpose than verbal conversations, use of a public telephone to transmit data involves an expectation of privacy between the sending and receiving point. Information about the content of the data transmission is subject to Fourth Amendment protection, while information about the time, the recipient of the transmission, or the number of transmissions made falls within the boundaries of the pen register decision discussed in the previous paragraph. These potentially significant details are committed to the control of the company providing the telephone service and may not be subject to an expectation of privacy.

As previously noted, this formulation may be inadequate to deal with the issues presented by contemporary data telecommunications. Arguably, heightened restrictions on governmental access are appropriate for data transmissions in the same manner that voice interceptions are subject to higher restraints under Title III.[21] Furthermore, even as to the recipient and other nonprivate data collected from an electronic system, the potential for mass data collection and analysis should lead to restrictions on government access. This is a matter of legislative, rather than constitutional, dimensions.

Transmissions made over proprietary, privately owned and operated systems within a company involve less uncertainty. In this situation, the electronic transmissions are, by hypothesis, not turned over to a third party. The analysis that there is no expectation of privacy because the third party retains noncontent data does not apply. For constitutional purposes, an expectation of privacy attaches to most proprietary systems for content, timing, and frequency of transmissions.

¶ 12.05 ELECTRONIC MAIL SYSTEMS

Beyond traditional voice communication and data transmission, current federal law is especially inadequate for communication of nonverbal messages. This form of communication involves the so-called electronic mail industry that is projected to become a major form of telecommunications in the near future.

In electronic mail systems, communicating computer systems are used to transmit nonverbal messages in lieu of traditional mail or interoffice delivery. In such systems, the sender might transmit a letter electronically to the computer of the recipient or to multiple recipients. This might

---

[21] 18 USC §§ 2510–2520 (1982).

involve use of a proprietary communications systems or use of telephones or other third-party systems. Alternatively, a transmitted message may be sent to and stored in a third computer from which the intended recipient can later retrieve it. These systems provide almost instantaneous transmission of messages, a relative certainty of delivery, and they eliminate the cost of paper reproduction and transmission. However, the privacy risks are manifold, especially where a third party is involved in providing the mail service.

Earlier discussion concerning protections for conversational and data communications applies to the transmission phase of electronic mail. Existing statutory law does not provide clear or consistent protections against governmental interception of transmissions. Title III proscriptions on wiretapping do not apply since there is no aural communication to intercept.[22] Constitutional standards focus on the existence of a reasonable expectation of privacy.[23] This expectation is present for the content of the messages in those systems in which the electronic mail is merely routed through a third-party common carrier or handled in a proprietary system. However, in systems involving third-party service providers, information as to time, recipient, and number of messages is potentially subject to governmental discovery without a warrant.

More important, there may be no constitutional protection of the content of messages in systems in which the message is stored in a third-party computer for later access by the intended recipient. This delayed access system is materially different from traditional telephone or mail systems, since the service provider is also the custodian of the message for at least a limited time. Arguably, submitting to this control by the third party relinquishes any right of privacy, since it explicitly risks disclosure by the custodian. An analogy to cases involving financial information held by banks is apt and indicates that constitutional protections are no longer present.[24] Absent statutory protection, governmental access to such stored information may violate no privacy interest of the sender or recipient.

If this analysis is accepted, there is a clear case for legislative action. As discussed in a further section,[25] significant privacy protections have been enacted for information held by cable television systems. Electronic mail is a potentially important industry. The communications that it han-

---

[22] See United States v. New York Tel. Co., 434 US 159, 167 (1977); United States v. Seidlitz, 589 F2d 152 (4th Cir. 1978).

[23] See supra ¶ 12.04[2].

[24] United States v. Miller, 425 US 435 (1976).

[25] See infra ¶ 12.13.

dles will contain substantial information about both the recipient and the sender, which includes but is not limited to the content of the message. The privacy issues in this context have a commercial connotation. Protection for data in the hands of a third party not only safeguards a privacy interest, but also encourages continued development of the industry.

The issues about governmental power to intercept transmissions are similarly present for governmental access to information stored in an electronic mail system. There is a seeming analogy betweeen electronic mail and the federal mail system operated by the U.S. Postal Service. This analogy, justified primarily by the name given to the services, might lead to the expectation that the third-party service company is merely a conduit for messages, receiving and transmitting them, but not able to access or disclose them to others. In fact, however, the computer-based system is not as simplistic as the analogy suggests. In electronic systems in which a message is deposited in the host computer for a period of time awaiting retrieval, that computer system has stored and retains the content information of the message. During that period, this information can be accessed by the owner of the system or other users who might break security codes. Furthermore, even after the recipient obtains the message, some information will be retained. This might be limited to billing information, but can also include the content of the message.

The privacy implications of third-party involvement are substantial. In the federal mail system, under federal law letters can not be opened without a search warrant and information concerning the destination of letters sent by a particular person is available only under restrictive standards.[26] A similar situation does not apply for electronic mail. The third party holding information about the sender may be free to deliver it to government officials without a warrant.[27] Of course, such actions would have serious business implications, but the absence of statutory restrictions represents a serious privacy law issue. Equally significant under present law, criminal justice agencies may access the information through a normal subpoena or warrant.

Is the third party free to voluntarily release the information for use by other private entities? The answer is not clear. No explicit statutory restraints exist. The only limits are in the form of practical business constraints or in the terms of the contract establishing the service.[28] The

---

[26] 39 CFR § 233.

[27] United States v. Miller, 425 US 435 (1976).

[28] Express contract provisions are common, especially for transmissions of clearly proprietary or trade secret information. See discussion in Chapter 3. Implied contract terms regarding nondisclosure have historically been found only for financial records held by a bank or similar depository. See infra ¶ 12.12.

choice between traditional mail and electronic mail substitutes is not made simply because of technology and speed. Use of electronic mail entails risks not present in the federal mail service. Arguably, this disparity should be eliminated by legislation protecting privacy rights in material submitted through electronic systems at least to the same extent that protections exist for normal mail systems.

PART B.   GOVERNMENTAL DATA AND DATABASES

¶ 12.06 DATA COLLECTION

A major perceived threat to privacy involves the accumulation and resulting use of data about individuals in various computer databases. To the extent that this entails governmental data collection, it relates in part to the pervasive regulatory role of government in current society. In order to regulate, pertinent information must be obtained and used. Additionally, as noted previously, there is an increased emphasis on data as a basis for policy-making and decision-making throughout both the government and the private sector. Federal and state governments and attendant agencies possess a large and increasing amount of data about individual citizens. Both the rationale for initially collecting this information and the potential that the data may be cross-matched into an integrated system entail individual privacy issues. However, neither risk has resulted in more than a limited reaction in the legislatures or the courts.

Governmental data collection creates concerns about individual privacy that are underscored by the belief that an individual should not be forced to relinquish personal information except to the extent that it is essential to governmental decision-making. In general, however, beyond search and seizure standards under the Fourth Amendment, few effective restrictions are imposed on data collection. Large amounts of information about individuals or groups are potentially relevant to agency decision-making. Furthermore, there is a belief that agency discretion is the best source for defining what information is needed in specific cases. Overall, a governmental right to know generally overrides an individual's interest in concealment.

Within the federal government, the Privacy Act of 1974 (Privacy Act) is the major legislation concerning individual privacy.[29] Portions of this act restrict data collection and retention by federal agencies to information "relevant" to agency activities. In practice, however, this restric-

---

[29] 5 USC § 522 (1982).

tion has little effect. The scope of most federal agency mandates is broad and the idea of relevance is often easily met.

In addition to the Privacy Act, the Paperwork Reduction Act of 1980 (Paperwork Reduction Act) provides that the federal Office of Management and Budget (OMB) may refuse to allow agency data collection if OMB concludes that another agency has already collected the information or it does not believe that the agency proposing to collect the information will in fact be able to use it. [30] This provision is seldom invoked. However, Paperwork Reduction Act requires that data collection forms used by the federal agencies inform the subject of the reason for requesting the data and whether compliance with the data request affects eligibility for benefits or other matters of consequence.

In the absence of comprehensive, enforceable legislative restraints, privacy interests affected by governmental data collection have intermittently been pursued in the federal and state courts. These cases are based on alleged infringements of constitutional rights to privacy. In general, however, courts faced with alleged privacy interests in this form have rejected the claim that data collection should be restrained. The overall result is that with the exception of certain areas closely aligned with criminal justice guarantees or personal decisions such as abortion and birth control little or no effective restraints exist against governmental data collection. If the data are relevant to an agency action, politically acceptable, and obtainable without a search and seizure, virtually any information can be collected.

[1] Constitutional Right of Privacy

A constitutional right of privacy was judicially recognized by the U.S. Supreme Court in 1965 in a landmark case involving birth control counseling. [31] The privacy right defined in that case and in subsequent Supreme Court decisions, however, is different from the informational privacy interest discussed here. According to the Supreme Court, the privacy right emanated from a coalescence of various amendments to the Constitution. [32] From the outset, however, it has been applied primarily to state and federal actions that tend to deny individuals the right to control personal decisions involving matters such as abortion, contraception, or marriage. It was, and remains, a substantive privacy right, defining

---

[30] 44 USC § 3501 (1982).

[31] Griswald v. Connecticut, 381 US 479 (1965).

[32] Roe v. Wade, 410 US 113 (1973).

various personal activities as so inherently a matter of personal choice that governmental intervention is precluded.

Efforts to apply this concept to mere governmental collection of data have been generally unsuccessful. A significant Supreme Court decision occurred in *Whalen v. Roe*.[33] In that case, the State of New York proposed a central computer data bank containing the names and addresses of all persons who obtained particular drugs pursuant to a doctor's prescription. The objective was to develop a capacity to monitor drug abuse where the abuser obtained multiple prescriptions of controlled drugs. The U.S. Supreme Court held that there were no constitutional barriers to the proposed system. The Court rejected not only the argument that the information was sufficiently personal for protection, but also the allegation that disclosure would deprive patients of the right to make personal decisions about medical treatment unencumbered by governmental intrusion or public disclosure. Central to this result was the fact that the act prohibited public disclosure of the collected data. Also, the Court noted that disclosure of medical information to third parties is common

> Disclosures of private medical information to doctors, to hospital personnel, to insurance companies, and to public health agencies are often an essential part of modern medical practice even when the disclosure may reflect unfavorably on the character of the patient. Requiring such disclosure to a representative of the State having responsibility for the health of the community does not automatically amount to an ... invasion of privacy.[34]

The Court in *Whalen* essentially required that the affected individual establish the harmful effects of data collection. This contrasts to an approach that might require the state to establish the need for intruding on privacy by collecting personal information. Indeed, outside of abortion, contraception, and the like, the Court has never held that a data collection system was invalid because the state could not demonstrate the necessity for the data.

One frequent argument about data collection focuses on the extent to which the data collection, *in itself*, adversely affects individual decisions about protected interests. For some people the mere knowledge that data is being collected may have an effect. In most cases this results from the belief that an effort to illicitly control personal behavior and decisions outside the appropriate scope of governmental regulation is being undertaken. The mere fact that personal decision-making may be affected, however, is generally inadequate to restrain governmental data collection.

---

[33] 429 US 589 (1977).

[34] Id. at 602.

In *Buckley v. Valeo*[35] the U.S. Supreme Court rejected a challenge to the Campaign Contributions Act based on the argument that reporting would deter some contributions to minority parties. Such effects are too remote to overcome the public interest served by the data collection. In contrast, in another case, the Court invalidated a requirement that the National Association for the Advancement of Colored People (NAACP) disclose membership rosters on free association and other grounds.[36] Similarly, while the Court has invalidated state actions that alter a woman's exercise of personal choice concerning an abortion, it upheld a data collection system concerning abortions where the system was directed merely to statistical purposes to aid the state's interest in public health.[37]

A factor closely related to potential effects on protected interests is the extent to which the collected data is kept confidential and subject to adequate safeguards against disclosure. In *Whalen*, the Court emphasized that prohibitions against public disclosure were present in the proposed drug reporting system and that there was no reason to suspect that they would not be enforced.[38] In most data collection privacy cases, the issue of safeguards is raised, but rejected by the court based on the facts of the case. In concept, however, data collection that leads inexorably to individualized public disclosure is a less acceptable intrusion on privacy than a system in which use and confidentiality of the data are maintained.

[2] Data Collection Accuracy

Both judicial decisions and legislative actions about data collection deal extensively with concerns about the accuracy of the data that is compiled. Although it is granted that state interests in data collection outweigh individual interests in privacy, the scope of the state interest cannot reasonably extend to the collection of unreliable or inaccurate information. In this regard, state and individual interests may merge. An individual has a clear interest in ensuring that collected data is accurate, and this interest is widely enforced since it is not inconsistent with state interests for data that is or may be used for law enforcement or other governmental purposes.

One aspect of a concern for accuracy is that governmental data collection procedures should reasonably ensure the accuracy of the collected

---

[35] 421 US 1 (1976).

[36] NAACP v. Alabama, 357 US 449 (1958).

[37] Planned Parenthood of Cent. Missouri v. Danforth, 428 US 52 (1976).

[38] See also Volkman v. Miller, 383 NYS2d 95 (App. Div. 1976).

data. The procedures required should be directly proportionate to the nature and potential effect of the collected information. For example, in cases that involved a reporting system concerning alleged child abusers, two federal district courts have held that data collection about child abuse can not be based on mere charges of abuse, but must only record court data about individuals following a final judicial determination that abuse occurred.[39] However, data on less volatile matters is not subject to the same level of restraint.

Consistent with a concern about assurances of accuracy, the Privacy Act expressly encourages data collection directly from the individual where possible. More important, the Privacy Act provides that subject to exceptions for sensitive data an individual may inspect the data collected. If there are inaccuracies, the individual may file a statement disagreeing with the record.[40] The agency must respond within 10 days and enter any appropriate correction. If there is a negative response, the individual may request a further review and ultimately, the individual has a right to judicial review. If a correction is agreed to or ordered, the agency must notify those people to whom the original file had been disclosed.[41]

These procedures provide a formal way to contest data records and correct errors. The weakness is that the individual must first have some cause to believe there is an error or at least some other incentive to review an agency file. Furthermore, unless an agency is cooperative, the procedures for review can be time-consuming and expensive.

¶ 12.07 DATA MATCHING AND THE COMPUTER STATE

While the collection of data intrudes on the sense of privacy, tangible harm to the individual does not arise until data is used by a governmental unit or entity. Use of collected data assumes a variety of forms. For example, in a welfare or medical benefits system, data concerning income, dependents, and expenses will be used for decisions about available benefits or coverage. In most cases, direct use of collected data for the purposes for which it was collected does not pose extended privacy risks.

A more difficult issue involves cross-matching information from multiple sources to draw inferences that could not be made from any one source. For example, it was recently reported that the Internal Revenue Service is attempting to access state data systems to correlate major asset

---

[39] See Brown v. Jones, 473 F. Supp. 439 (ND Tex. 1979); Sims v. Department of Public Welfare, 438 F. Supp. 1179 (SD Tex. 1977).

[40] 5 USC § 522(a) (1982).

[41] See generally 5 *Computer Law Service* § 5-2.

acquisitions with reported income.[42] Welfare officials in Massachusetts compare recipient lists for welfare, Medicaid, food stamps, and other benefits programs against private bank accounts in order to locate people with more assets than are permitted for particular programs.[43] Records of social security and the welfare agencies might be matched to determine eligibility for payments.

For all of these and a growing list of other examples, privacy interests are affected by a more efficient use of data by government agencies. Data matching is a unique computer age issue. Preexisting data systems contained practical safeguards against massive cross-referencing in that the effort was too time-consuming and costly. With contemporary computer databases and an increasing technological capacity to cross-reference from incompatible systems, the matching of records is feasible and efficient. This might involve intragovernmental matching or, indeed, cross-matching private records systems among, for example, credit card, telephone, and employee personnel records. The risk is the creation of an ability to substantially reconstruct an individual's life history for purposes of virtually any decision.

Reactions to data matching within government are polarized, reflecting widely divergent views of the role of government and the nature of privacy in a computer environment. At one extreme, data matching is viewed as a cost-efficient method of allocating resources and enforcing the limits and regulations associated with governmental programs. Routinely, when it is employed, matching identifies actual violators of applicable standards and produces a net increase in the level of law enforcement. At the other extreme, data matching is viewed as an integral step toward an environment in which governments are able to trace virtually all of the actions of an individual. Rather than an efficient enforcement device, this is seen as an unnecessary incursion into the privacy of a large number of people on a fishing expedition that can not be justified by the fact that some violators are found.[44] One aspect of this latter view is the implicit belief that preexisting inefficiencies in data analysis define a minimal level of privacy that should not be reduced through technological gains.

The relevant competing interests are captured relatively well within these positions, but it is clear that neither position should ultimately succeed in full. The privacy of an individual should not be sacrificed simply

---

[42] See Burnham, "Concern Growing About Legal, Ethical Misuse of Information by Computers," *Houston Chronicle* 18, § 1 (June 17, 1984).

[43] 130 Cong. Rec. S2957 (March 21, 1984).

[44] See Langan, "Computer Matching Programs: A Threat to Privacy?" 15 Colum. JL & Soc. Probs. 143 (1979).

because it is efficient and feasible to collect and cross-match data. Conversely, the use of technology can not be constrained by artificial reference to prior, inefficient manual systems. The need is to define a supportable balance avoiding central, comprehensive records that obliterate individual privacy, while accommodating an ability to accumulate and analyze data to enforce policies and ensure informed decision-making. There is a need to develop a new conception of privacy in an era of new technology, but existing statutory and case law have not even begun to effectively address this issue.

For the exchange and cross-matching of data among federal agencies, the primary statutory restrictions are in the Privacy Act. This statute generally prohibits the release of information about an individual without his written consent. This prohibition, however, is subject to eleven exceptions that include court orders, routine agency use, archival purposes, and similar events.[45] The result is a classic case of the exceptions that become the general rule. Especially under the "routine use" exception, data matching programs have been tacitly permitted under the Privacy Act. They have been forestalled, if at all, only by adverse publicity and political pressure.[46]

Reported cases concerning governmental actions taken in response to computer matching indicate a judicial willingness to accept matching as an appropriate procedure and to focus on substantive issues such as whether particular agency responses in reaction to matching data were appropriate. The earliest reported case, arising prior to the effective date of the Privacy Act, was *Jaffess v. HEW*.[47] *Jaffess* involved a match between social security and veterans' records that resulted in a reduction of the benefits paid to the plaintiff. The court concluded that

> [Despite] the recognition which courts have given to a constitutional right of privacy in other contexts, i.e., the most intimate phases of one's personal life, the present thrust of the decisional law does not include within its compass the right of an individual to prevent disclosure by one governmental agency to another of matter obtained in the course of the transmitting agency's regular functions.[48]

Similarly, in cases dealing with redeterminations of welfare eligibility, matching programs have been upheld and the pertinent question has

---

[45] 5 USC § 522(b)(1-11) (1982); see In re Grand Jury Subpoena, 535 F. Supp. 31 (ED Tenn. 1981) (grand jury subpoena equivalent to court order as an exception).

[46] 130 Cong. Rec. S2957 (March 21, 1984).

[47] 393 F. Supp. 626 (SDNY 1975).

[48] Id. at 629.

focused on whether the resulting data was sufficiently probative to warrant further action by the agency.[49]

¶ 12.08 DISCLOSURE OF COLLECTED DATA

There are relatively few direct restraints on governmental data collection where the data collection is relevant to agency activity. Furthermore, while there are significant concerns about excessively intrusive government, interagency data matching generally has not been prohibited.

One further area of concern consists of the circumstances under which personal data collected by the state about an individual can be disclosed to the public. The extent to which disclosure is permissible involves a balancing of distinct interests. As the data is more and more personal or controversial, there is an increasingly strong personal interest in avoiding disclosure without consent. In fact, as noted previously, failure to adequately assure the confidentiality of such information is, in concept at least, a potential basis for challenging a data collection program. Conversely, however, there is a competing concept that the public has a right to know about matters affecting or defining the operation of its agencies and programs. In some cases, at least, access to such information necessarily entails access to data collected about one or a group of individuals.

Within the federal system, these conflicting interests are reflected in the provisions of the Freedom of Information Act (FOIA).[50] The FOIA establishes procedures and substantive standards for the release of governmental information to private individuals. The purpose of the statute is to provide a forum to satisfy the public's right to know about the operations of government. However, the FOIA provides for a variety of exceptions to the obligation of disclosure. Among these is an exclusion of personnel, medical, and similar files that, if released, would constitute a "clearly unwarranted invasion of personal privacy."

While this standard remains largely undefined by case law, it clearly recognizes that the conflict between personal privacy and the public's right to information is a balanced, rather than an absolute, issue. The criterion for restricting the release of information about an individual is not merely that a privacy interest is infringed, but that disclosure would result in an unwarranted infringement of personal privacy. Thus, there is

---

[49] See 15,844 Welfare Recipients v. King, 474 F. Supp. 1374 (D. Mass. 1979); Greater Cleveland Welfare Rights Org. v. Bauer, 462 F. Supp. 1313 (ND Ohio 1978).

[50] 5 USC § 522 (1982).

a balance between the type of privacy interest compromised and the purpose or nature of the information requested. Presumably, in order to warrant any invasion of privacy, the request must pertain to a material inquiry about the operation of government or governmental programs. Requests merely to unearth personal information about an individual absent any connection to governmental activity are unwarranted invasions.

This privacy restriction pertains to personnel and other routinely collected data. Similar issues are raised, however, for proprietary or other sensitive information submitted to governmental investigations. In general, assuming that claims to secrecy are clearly asserted when the data are given over, the FOIA precludes disclosure to third parties without appropriate court orders. [51]

Beyond FOIA standards in the federal information environment, disclosure questions intermittently arise for state agency and law enforcement records. In general, judicial decisions support the right of state agencies to disclose information in their records in pursuing valid policy interests or in response to reasonable inquiries concerning governmental operations. This is most clearly the case where the information does not involve inherently confidential or sensitive subject matter. For example, in *Paul v. Davis* [52] the U.S. Supreme Court concluded that no privacy interest was infringed by the dissemination of a list of active shoplifters compiled based on arrest records. The Court's rationale encompassed both the justifiable policy interest in deterring shoplifting and the fact that arrest records were public information. Collection and distribution, therefore, did not disclose otherwise confidential data.

More controversial disclosure issues arise when the request for information relates in part to the operation of a governmental program and in part to identifying individual participants where public identification may have adverse professional effects. Several recent state court decisions have faced the question of whether state agencies are free to disclose data concerning the participation of doctors, hospitals, and clinics in reimbursement plans relating to abortions. Assuming that disclosure is not barred by state privacy legislation, the courts have concluded that disclosure does not infringe the privacy rights of the doctors. Given a professional decision to perform abortions, no substantial impact on their professional judgment and behavior was likely as a result of the disclosure. [53]

---

[51] 5 USC § 552(b)(4) (1982); see Davidson, "Protecting Computer Software: A Comprehensive Analysis," 1983 Ariz. St. LJ 611, 736 (1983).

[52] 424 US 693 (1976).

[53] Minnesota Medical Ass'n v. State, 274 NW2d 84 (Minn. 1978); see also State v. Harder, 641 P2d 366 (Kan. 1982).

In the abortion reimbursement cases, there was a connection between the requested disclosure and a reasonable concern in examining the cost and operations of a controversial public program. Absent such a connection, it is arguable that requests for data identifying individuals should be barred by basic rights of privacy. This is true at least where the information does not involve public record data in which no expectation of privacy attaches.

PART C.   PRIVATE DATA SYSTEMS

¶ 12.09 PRIVATE DATA SYSTEMS AND PRIVATE CONTROL

While privacy issues often focus on the acquisition and use of data by governmental agencies, potentially greater intrusions into individual privacy arise with the accumulation of data in the hands of private entities. Private acquisition of data may involve situations of unauthorized access to information for which there may be criminal penalties. In the following portion of this chapter, the focus is on private activities that involve at least initially authorized data acquisition.

[1] General Standards

Two initial premises define existing law in this field. The first is that absent special circumstances or legislation the parties to a voluntary transaction may define the nature and extent of information required for the transaction to proceed.[54] There is no a priori assumption that the requests of one private entity to another must be restricted to information that is externally or subsequently judged to be relevant or material to a particular transaction.

The second premise is less explicit, but equally significant. It concerns the right to control information collected voluntarily or incidental to particular transactions between the parties. In essence, absent a statute and unless there are special indicia of confidentiality (as between attorney and client) or contractual restraints, the third party in possession of information concerning another is free to control the dissemination and use of that information. That is, the mere fact that information pertains to or is

---

[54] This is, of course, subject to antitrust and other restrictions where the subject matter, relationship, or other circumstances of the transaction impose direct limitations. See Department of Justice, *Antitrust Guide Concerning Joint Venture Research* 3 (1980).

derived from someone gives that person no claim to control use of that information. For example, in *United States v. Miller*[55] the U.S. Supreme Court held that a bank customer had no reasonable expectation of privacy in cancelled checks and other transaction records held by his bank. Governmental acquisition of these records did not fall within the customer's Fourth Amendment protections.[56]

The basic premise about third-party control is valid for various databases, especially if the information in question is not of a highly personal character and there is a reasonably supportable purpose behind the disclosure.[57] For example, in *Reynauld v. Superior Court*[58] a California court upheld the informal delivery by the insurance company of Blue Shield insurance records to the state in connection with a medical fraud investigation. No prior hearing, notice, or warrant was required to protect the alleged privacy interests of the claimant. This does not, of course, imply that the third party will invariably disclose the data in response to requests, nor will he necessarily be required to do so, especially where personal data such as personnel records is involved.[59]

Some efforts have been made to place restrictions on the type of data that private entities may collect. Many of these restrictions relate less to privacy issues and more to overriding concerns about improper discrimination in credit or employment relationships. Thus, there have been restrictions on collection of racial, sexual, religious, and marital status data except for limited uses by creditors and employers.[60] Against this background of relatively minimal protections in the private sector, several areas of specific concern have attracted relatively extensive federal and state regulation. These include credit reporting services, educational records, and financial records.

---

[55] 425 US 435 (1976).

[56] The result in *Miller* was overruled for financial records by enactment of the Right to Financial Privacy Act, 12 USC § 340 (1982), pertaining to bank disclosures to federal agencies. In addition, at least nine states have enacted similar legislation or established restrictions by virtue of court decision. See, e.g., Okla. Stat. Ann. tit. 6, §§ 2201–2206; see also discussion infra at ¶ 12.12.

[57] As to personnel records, see Mironi, "Confidentiality of Personnel Records: A Legal and Ethical View," 25 Lab. LJ 270 (1974).

[58] 138 Cal. App. 3d 1, 187 Cal. Rptr. 360 (1982).

[59] See Detroit Edison Co. v. NLRB, 440 US 301 (1979) (refusal to disclose upheld).

[60] See Equal Credit Opportunity Act, 12 USC §§ 1691 et seq. (1982); 12 CFR § 202. Approximately 30 states have similar legislation. See, e.g., Ky. Rev. Stat. § 344.370; Wash. Rev. Code § 49.60.175. For employment data, over 25 states have legislative restrictions on collection and use. See, e.g., Colo. Rev. Stat. §§ 24-24-301 et seq.; Hawaii Rev. Stat. §§ 378-1 et seq.

[2] Tort Law

In addition, a limited body of common-law cases has developed establishing tort actions for invasion of privacy. The privacy torts have commonly been subdivided into four generic categories: (1) appropriation of the individual's name or likeness, (2) intrusion into the individual's private affairs, (3) public disclosure of embarrassing, private facts, and (4) publicly placing the individual in a false light.[61]

Of these, the potentially most significant for data compiled and manipulated through computer technology is that relating to intrusion into the private affairs of the individual. Historically, this form of tort has focused on physical intrusions and eavesdropping or clandestine surveillance. However, a recent federal appellate court decision suggested, in dicta, that the tort might apply to the collection of private information for no legitimate purpose.[62] This court, however, rejected a tort claim based on a private investigator's collection of information concerning a large number of prior insurance applications. This was deemed to have been made for a legitimate purpose in connection with an application for insurance.

¶ 12.10 FAIR CREDIT REPORTING

The most significant and frequently litigated privacy protection in the private sector is the Fair Credit Reporting (FCRA).[63] The FCRA is designed to regulate the extensive use of credit reporting agencies to obtain information concerning an individual's credit history. The FCRA applies to all reports made by consumer-reporting agencies about individuals. The FCRA focuses on the procedures by which the information is collected, the circumstances under which it is released, and the procedure by which a consumer affected by a credit report can ensure that the reported data is accurate.

The most visible aspects of the FCRA are its procedures for consumers to challenge and obtain corrections of inaccuracy and incompleteness in credit reports. Under the FCRA, users of consumer reports are required to notify the consumer of any adverse decision on a pertinent credit or other application. If the decision was based on a consumer report, the user must notify the consumer of the name of the reporting agency. The individual has a right to obtain information concerning the

---

[61] Restatement (Second) of Torts § 652A (1977).

[62] Tureen v. Equifax, Inc., 571 F2d 411 (8th Cir. 1978).

[63] 15 USC §§ 1681 et seq. (1982). The essential terms of the FCRA have been replicated in 11 states. See, e.g., Md. Com. Law Code Ann. § 14.1201; NH Rev. Stat. Ann. § 359-B.

content of the consumer report from that reporting agency. If the consumer disputes the accuracy or completeness of the report, the FCRA establishes procedures by which this dispute can be resolved. The reporting agency has a duty to investigate the accuracy of the report within a reasonable time.[64] If the data is inaccurate, the agency must correct it and, at the consumer's request, report the correction to recent users.[65] If the agency believes the data is correct, the consumer is permitted to include within the agency report an account of the nature of the dispute and alleged inaccuracy.

The FCRA also establishes limits on the preparation and distribution of credit information. A report may be issued only pursuant to the consumer's written instructions, a court order, or if the reporting agency has reason to believe that the report was being requested for a legitimate purpose in a transaction involving the individual. The FCRA enumerates permitted purposes limited to the extension of credit, review, or collection of an account, employment purposes, underwriting insurance, determining eligibility for certain government benefits, and a legitimate business need in connection with a transaction involving the consumer.[66] Beyond these purposes, disclosure of a report is prohibited. Anyone who knowingly provides credit data covered by the FCRA to an unauthorized recipient is subject to criminal penalties and civil damages.[67]

The FCRA also deals directly with the accuracy and relevance of the material in the report. The FCRA imposes limits on the age of material that can be used in the reports. Generally, adverse information can not be reported after seven years, but a 10-year period is allowed for bankruptcy information. More importantly, it requires that the agency maintain reasonable procedures to ensure the maximum possible accuracy of the data in its reports.[68]

The requirement that the reporting agency maintain reasonable procedures to ensure accuracy is enforceable by civil action by the affected consumer. This requirement has been the subject of frequent litigation and provides one of the few realistic checks on data collection in the private sector available to individuals. Under this provision, courts have focused on the extent to which collection and updating procedures followed by an agency reflect a reasonable effort to encompass current and accurate information. For example, in *Thompson v. San Antonio Retail*

---

[64] 15 USC § 1681(i)(a) (1982).

[65] 15 USC § 1681(i)(d) (1982).

[66] 15 USC § 1681(b) (1982).

[67] 15 USC § 1681(n)(r) (1982).

[68] 15 USC § 1681(e)(b) (1982).

Merchants Association[69] a computer-based data collection procedure was held to constitute a negligent failure to fulfill the duty to establish a reasonable updating procedure. The court noted that "[There was negligence] in [the] updating procedures. [The agency] failed to exercise reasonable care in programming its computer to automatically capture information into a file without requiring any minimum number of 'points of correspondence' between the consumer and the file [accepted as accurate by the client]."[70] In essence, to facilitate computer maintenance of records, the reporting agency relied almost exclusively on decisions by individual merchants to identify a match between a particular applicant and a file in the system. Once this decision was made, the computer was programmed to immediately accept all new data obtained by the merchant into the supposedly matching file. The thrust of the decision is that a minimum level of objective correspondence between an applicant and a file would have been a reasonable way of avoiding misidentification.[71]

¶ 12.11 EDUCATIONAL RECORDS

The Family Educational Rights and Privacy Act (Educational Rights Act)[72] imposes restrictions on the disclosure of educational files. The enforcement of this act is keyed to federal funding of educational institutions, which may be terminated in the event of noncompliance by the institution. No private cause of action is available to the affected individual.

The Educational Rights Act imposes both access requirements and restrictions on disclosure of records. Access to the institution's files is to be made available to parents, except for confidential letters of recommendation and personal financial statements of college students. On the other hand, the institution is prohibited from disclosing the content of a student's file except to school officials with a need to know, research organizations, governmental education officials, and people with enforceable subpoenas.[73]

¶ 12.12 FINANCIAL RECORDS

Among the most significant records held by third parties regarding an individual are those dealing with the individual's financial transac-

---

[69] 682 F2d 509 (5th Cir. 1982).

[70] Id. at 512.

[71] See also Lowry v. Credit Bureau, Inc., 444 F. Supp. 541 (ND Ga. 1978).

[72] 20 USC § 1232(g) (1982).

[73] 20 USC § 1232(g)(b) (1982).

tions. Such information may be in the possession of depository institutions, credit card companies, or other third parties. The existence of the data and the potential that it may be revealed to others is a significant privacy concern. The concern increases as private entities and governmental units are more able to cross-reference and analyze the large volume of data because of sophisticated computer systems, and it is further accentuated as society moves to an electronic, rather than cash, transaction environment. Electronic transactions create records about events that in a cash-based system would leave no retrievable record.

For financial information held by depository institutions, several sources of law establish at least minimal privacy protections. The initial question is the extent to which the depository institution can release information to third parties without a court order or other legally recognized compulsion. The primary source of law used to deal with this question is the depository contract. This contract can be drafted to expressly preclude disclosure of financial data and, except for cases of legal compulsion, it would be binding on the depository institution. In most cases, however, express terms about privacy and disclosure are not incorporated in the contract.

In the absence of express contract provisions, case law creates an implied contract that precludes disclosure of financial information by a bank or other depository institution except in the ordinary course of business or as the result of legal compulsion.[74] This even extends to disclosures for legitimate social purposes and forecloses random or arbitrary disclosure of data.[75] Secrecy (or privacy) is inherent in the bank-customer relationship.

Arguably, implied contract concepts could be extended to other third parties who are routinely involved with financial or other records concerning individuals. Such an approach could begin to build a common law of privacy in contract relationships that would enhance protections against the most extreme abuses in the private sector database situation. However, at least to date there has been relatively little extension of this contract analysis to environments where the close relationship that is characteristic of a bank and its customers is not present.[76] The norm

---

[74] See Peterson v. Idaho First Nat'l Bank, 367 P2d 284 (Idaho 1961); Annot., 92 ALR2d 900 (1963).

[75] See Suburban Trust Co. v. Waller, 408 A2d 758 (Md. Ct. Spec. App. 1979).

[76] Compare Reynauld v. Superior Court, 138 Cal. App. 3d 1, 187 Cal. Rptr. 360 (1982) (voluntary disclosure of medical insurance claims records not a violation of privacy expectations).

continues to be that third parties control disclosure of data in their hands in the absence of statutory or express contract restriction.

A second question is the extent to which financial data in a depository institution can be disclosed to the government. The basic contractual analysis discussed previously has been applied to preclude voluntary disclosure of financial data to law enforcement agencies.[77] Similarly, in several states search and seizure restraints have been applied under privacy concepts to invalidate use of data voluntarily disclosed to law enforcement agencies by a bank without legal compulsion.[78] In contrast, federal law expressly permits some voluntary disclosure to federal law enforcement agencies in the form of notification that the bank has information that "may be relevant to a possible violation of any statute or regulation."[79]

Federal law requires the collection of financial information and places limits on access to that information by federal governmental agencies.[80] The Bank Secrecy Act of 1970 requires depository institutions to maintain a variety of records pertaining to the financial dealings of customers. In addition, it authorizes the Secretary of the Treasury to require the creation, retention, and submission of records that it determines to have a "high degree of usefulness" in criminal, tax, or regulatory activities.[81] Based in part on these regulations and in part on normal business practices, depository institutions commonly create and retain substantial information concerning virtually all but very insignificant transactions in which they participate.[82]

The substantial information retained in depository institutions represents a potentially significant law enforcement resource. As a result, the procedures by which this information can be accessed for investigatory purposes are of significant interest. In 1976, the Supreme Court held in *United States v. Miller*[83] that the customer had no enforceable expectation of privacy for the records held by the bank. As a result, it validated the bank's handing over of the data to a grand jury based on a subpoena

---

[77] See Suburban Trust Co. v. Waller, 408 A2d 758 (Md. Ct. Spec. App. 1979).

[78] See Charnes v. DiGiacomo, 612 P2d 1117 (Colo. 1980); Commissioner v. DeJohn, 403 A2d 1283 (Pa. 1979); Burrows v. Superior Court, 529 P2d 590 (Cal. 1974).

[79] 12 USC § 3403 (c) (1982).

[80] Huber, *Bank Officer's Handbook of Governmental Regulation* 21-11–21-30 (1984).

[81] 12 USC § 1829(a)(1) (1982).

[82] Huber, *Bank Officer's Handbook of Governmental Regulation* 21-13 (1984).

[83] 425 US 435 (1976).

duces tecum issued and enforced without the customer's knowledge. The sole protection for the customer was thus limited to the implied terms of the deposit contract and these are overridden by proper legal process issued to the bank.

The decision in *Miller* has been overruled by federal legislation. The Right to Financial Privacy Act of 1978[84] enacted procedural restrictions on access to data in the possession of a depository institution by federal agencies. Disclosure to an agency is restricted to cases in which the customer authorizes it, there is a proper search warrant, administrative or judicial subpoena or summons, or pursuant to a formal written request where no subpoena or summons authority is available to the agency.[85]

With the exception of cases involving customer consent and cases involving search warrants, the federal agency must provide the customer with notice of the agency request prior to inspection of the financial records that are requested.[86] In cases involving a search warrant, customer protection is found in the probable cause standards common to the criminal justice system. For the other forms of process, the customer may challenge the data request by acting within 10 days after personal service of the notice or 14 days after mailing, if applicable. A challenge is limited to either contesting the procedural regularity of the process or challenging whether the requested data is relevant to the agency inquiry.[87]

¶ 12.13 CABLE PRIVACY

Cable television systems are increasingly significant sources of in-home entertainment. With the probable development of videotext and teletext systems as alternative methods of distributing information, the role of cable is likely to increase even further. While these developments reflect an expansion of options available to consumers within local entertainment and information systems, they also pose a significant threat to personal privacy. Inherent in the development of cable is the capacity to collect and retain substantial information about the behavior, information needs, and entertainment preferences of individuals for later assessment or retrieval by computer.

The potential significance of this threat to personal privacy has led to special legislative treatment of privacy issues in the cable environment.

---

[84] 12 USC §§ 3401 et seq. (1982).

[85] 12 USC § 3402 (1982).

[86] 12 USC § 3409 (1982).

[87] 12 USC § 3410 (1982).

One portion of the recently enacted Cable Communications Policy Act of 1984 (Cable Act)[88] has placed substantial restrictions on the collection, use, and dissemination of information by the operator of a cable system about its subscribers.

Section 631 of the Cable Act establishes several distinct restrictions relevant to privacy. Initially, it requires that the cable operator provide the subscriber with annual notification about the nature of any personally identifiable information that it collects about the individual, the intended use of the information, and the nature and frequency of any disclosure of the personally identifiable information that may occur. In addition, the operator must inform the subscriber of its right to enforce limitations on data collection and must provide the customer with access to information that has been collected.

Beyond disclosure provisions, the Cable Act places direct limitations on the extent to which personally identifiable information can be collected and the circumstances under which it may be disclosed. The collection restrictions limit the cable operator to collecting only such personally identifiable information as is necessary to render cable or other service to the customer and to detect unauthorized receptions of cable communications.[89] The operator's interest in maintaining information about the operation of its system is protected by the fact that data collection restrictions only apply to personally identifiable information. The operator may collect, use, and disseminate aggregate data that does not identify specific people.

Disclosure of personally identifiable information is restricted under the Cable Act. The operator is permitted to disclose this information only if necessary to render or conduct a legitimate business activity related to cable or other services provided or if disclosure is in response to a court order authorizing disclosure. The customer must receive notice of the court order.[90] In addition, the operator may disclose names and addresses of subscribers if the customer has had an opportunity to preclude this and the disclosure does not reveal viewing habits or transactions conducted by the customer. The privacy provisions of the Cable Act are enforceable by an aggrieved party. The court may order actual damages for any violation, but cannot award less than liquidated damages of $100 per each day of violation or $1000, whichever is higher.[91]

---

[88] 47 USC § 631 (1984 Supp.), Cong. Rec. S14294 (October 11, 1984); see Burnham, "Panel Use of Cable Information," *Houston Chronicle* 1, § 1 (July 5, 1984).

[89] 47 USC § 631(b)(2) (1984).

[90] 47 USC § 631(c)(2)(B) (1984).

[91] 47 USC § 631(f)(2) (1984).

Table of Cases

[References are to paragraphs (¶) and notes (n.).]

[References are to paragraphs (¶) and notes (n.).]

C

[References are to paragraphs (¶) and notes (n.).]

[References are to paragraphs (¶) and notes (n.).]

[References are to paragraphs (¶) and notes (n.).]

[*References are to paragraphs (¶) and notes (n.).*]

[References are to paragraphs (¶) and notes (n.).]

[References are to paragraphs (¶) and notes (n.).]

[References are to paragraphs (¶) and notes (n.).]

[References are to paragraphs (¶) and notes (n.).]

[References are to paragraphs (¶) and notes (n.).]

Index

[References are to paragraphs (¶).]

Independent contractors
confidentiality restraints, 3.08
development contracts, 6.19, 6.20
ownership of product, 4.05
works for hire, 4.05
Innovation in products
antitrust limitations
integrated systems, 4.09
single party and system
innovation, 4.08
obviousness, 2.15

J

Joint ownership
joint invention, 4.04[1][a]
software coauthorship, 4.04[1][b]
Joint ventures
antitrust standards
access by third parties,
4.10[4][c]
detrebling of damages, 4.10[2]
"research markets" defined,
4.10[4][a]
rule of reason standards,
4.10[1], 4.10[3]
secondary restraints, 4.10[4][d]
collateral research and
development, 4.04[2][b]
ownership of resulting product,
4.04[2]
preexisting works, 4.04[2][c]
R & D partnerships and taxation,
4.12

L

Leases
defining the transaction
contract law standards, 6.14[2]
federal tax standards, 6.14[3]
security interest, 6.14[1]
third-party lessors or sellers,
6.16[2]
warranty issues, 6.16
Leveraged transactions
antitrust generally, 5.03[1]
package licensing, 5.05
tying and antitrust, 5.04

Libel
inaccurate data, 11.10
Licensing
adaptation and derivation
restraints
custom software, 5.15[4]
mass-market software,
5.16[3][e]
owner of a copy, 1.11[1]
antitrust policy, 5.03[1]
assignment compared, 5.02[1]
disclosure restrictions
custom software, 5.15[1]
mass-market software,
5.16[3][d]
duration of the license, 5.07
end user restrictions
custom software, 5.15
mass-market software, 5.16
misuse law in general, 5.03[2]
most favored licensees, 5.09[3]
multiple licenses
package licensing, 5.05
royalty duration, 5.08[2]
tying arrangements, 5.04
new or derivative works, 5.06
antitrust and, 5.06[2]
contract provisions, 5.06[3]
grant-back agreements, 5.06[1]
reverse engineering
lessees, 3.07[2]
purchasers, 3.07[1]
royalties
computation, 5.09
differential rates, 5.09[2]
duration, 5.08
single system restrictions
custom software, 5.15[2]
mass-market software,
5.16[3][a]
trade secret licenses in general,
5.02[3]
transfer restrictions
custom software, 5.15[3]
mass-market software,
5.16[3][c]
tying arrangements
bundling, 5.04[2]
copyright and patent tying,
5.04[2][a]

[References are to paragraphs (¶).]

[References are to paragraphs (¶).]